ENCYCLOPEDIA
OF ISLAMIC LAW:
A COMPENDIUM OF THE VIEWS
OF THE MAJOR SCHOOLS

ADAPTED BY
LALEH BAKHTIAR

INTRODUCTION BY
KEVIN REINHART

ABC INTERNATIONAL GROUP, INC.

© 1996 Laleh Bakhtiar

Book Designer
Liaquat Ali

Library of Congress Cataloging in Publication Data

Bakhtiar, Laleh
    Encyclopedia of Islamic Law: A Compendium of the Views of the Major Schools

    Includes bibliographical references
    1. Islamic Jurisprudence

ISBN: 1-56744-498-9

Published by
ABC International Group, Inc.

Distributed by

KAZI Publications, Inc.
3023 West Belmont Avenue
Chicago IL 60618
312-267-7001

1-20-06
amazon.com
$26.37

TOWARDS UNITY

CONTENTS

PREFACE

The present work is based on two main Arabic sources: *al-Fiqh alal madhdhab al-arbaah* and *al-Fiqh alal madhdhab al-khamsa*. It offers a comparative study of the *Shariah* or Islamic Divine Law which according to authentic Islamic doctrines, embodies the Will of God in society. In the Islamic world view, God is the ultimate legislator. The major schools are: Hanafi, Hanbali, Shafii, Maliki and Jafari. The Hanafi school, the official school of the Ottoman Turks, is followed in Turkey, Pakistan and India. The Hanbali school is followed in Syria and Arabia while the Shafii school is followed in Egypt, Malaysia and Indonesia. The Malik school is followed in North and West Africa while the Jafari school is followed in Iran and by a large population of Iraq and Lebanon.

Based on *Hadith* literature and the *Sunnah* of the Prophet, it was through his deeds and sayings that the Will of God was made known to the Islamic *ummah*. The present work is divided into three parts: individual, economic and social issues. From the twenty-two pages of contents, it can be seen how detailed and encyclopedic in scope this work is. Individual issues include prescribed purity, prayer, fasting, and pilgrimage to Makkah while economic issues address the concerns of paying the poor-due, creating an endowment, inheritance, wills and bequests and legal disability. Finally, social issues include marriage and divorce.

With this work, the English speaking reader for the first time is able to make a comparison of the major schools. Their unity becomes apparent, but it is perhaps the differences which are of greater interest because it shows two important facts: first of all, how open the Law is to a variety of views and secondly, whereas the Hanafi, Hanbali, Shafii and Maliki schools have been separated from the Jafari for political reasons throughout Islamic history, the Jafari as often as not agrees with the Hanafi or Maliki school, for instance, while the Shafii and Hanbali as often as not differ. It is from this diversity of interpretations of the Law, interpretations which are based on the Quran and the *Sunnah*, that unity develops when each diverse group is willing to concede the possibility of the other's interpretation when it is based on the same two sources.

My deepest gratitude goes to my children for their patience, my teachers for their guidance, to KAZI Publications for its encouragement and to Professor Kevin Reinhart for his excellent introduction. Any success that may accrue from this work belongs to the Legislator.

INTRODUCTION

❝In difference is a mercy," the Prophet said, and unknown to most non-Muslims and many Muslims, this principle has guided the development and discovery of Islamic law from its beginnings.

The work presented here, an adaptation of al-Mughniyyah's *al-Fiqh ᶜalá l-madhāhib al-khamsah*, demonstrates the scope of Islamic law and the range of positions available within it. Many of the topics of Islamic law are collected and organized here, and within each section the author has systematically presented the opinions of the four Sunnī schools of law—Shāfiᶜī, Ḥanbalī, Mālikī, and Ḥanafī—together with the school of the so-called Twelver Shīᶜah, here called the Jaᶜfarī school after the most important of the latter Imāms, Jaᶜfar al-Ṣādiq. The editor/adapter's goal has been to point out the obvious, yet often-ignored fact of both the unity and diversity of Islamic legal thought, and specifically that the divergence between the Shīᶜī school—the Jaᶜfarī— and the four Sunnī *madhhabs* is no greater than that among the four Sunnī *madhhabs* themselves. Hence, only the school names are used in the translation, and not the divisive epithets Sunnī and Shīᶜī.

Shīᶜism and Sunnism are perhaps best understood as *denominations* of Islam. Though animosity between the two denominations has waxed and waned according to place and circumstances, at present Muslims are inclined to stress their unity in a world in which they are a minority. In accord with this emphasis, the trend recently has been to harmonize the two tendencies, and stress what is common between them. The most significant sign of this trend was the ruling of Maḥmūd Shaltūt, Rector of the Azhar Islamic University in Egypt, around 1383/1963, that the Shīᶜah were authentically Muslims, but of a different school (*madhhab*) rather than of a different sect (*firqah*). He embodied this ruling in the directive that the Azhar University, a center of Sunnism since the twelfth (c.e.) century, teach one kind of Shīᶜī law, the Jaᶜfarī (also called Twelver or Imāmī) school, alongside the four Sunnī schools. This ecumenical ruling was part of a larger movement to de-emphasize *madhhab* differences, a movement called *taqrīb* (bringing together) or *lā madhhabiyya* (no *madhhab*-ism).

To understand the work before the reader, it is useful first to consider some of the distinctive features of Islamic law, and then to consider the pluralism of Islam—the *madhhabs* or legal schools.

THE SCOPE OF THE SHARĪᶜAH

"The *sharīᶜah* is an ocean" is a sentiment often expressed, and Muslim scholars have sought to map and measure that ocean, partly by means of works such as the present one, which list in detail the differences and similarities among the schools. The purpose is informative—for the member of a particular school, he or she finds an easy source of guidance for normatively Islamic behavior. It is also just interesting to know the boundaries of acceptable Muslim conduct, which one finds by considering the acceptable variations on the rules of purity, or marriage, for example. In addition, since those qualified are invited always to reconsider and find anew the guidance of the *sharīᶜah* in the sources of Islamic knowledge, works such as this one are injunctions to consider and reconsider the rules of the schools. These works provide occasions to seek the most persuasive argument and the most firmly-grounded ruling on some particular issue. So this work can be considered by the reader as a kind of *Readers' Digest* of Islamic law, and also as a meditation on its rich variety.

This work offers something to non-Muslims as well. Islamic

law has formed the spine of Islam throughout its history. It has given Muslims a sense of unity and recognition in cultures as heterogeneous as the Chinese and the African, the Soviet and the American. Its results, particularly in the realm of day-to-day morality have impressed such diverse figures as Martin Luther and Edward Lane. If there is a possibility for such as thing as comparative ethics or comparative law, both the scope and content of Islamic law demand attention as a system that is theoretically rich and interesting, and as a system that, in part or in whole, has worked for more than a millennium. Attentive readers, both Muslim and non-Muslim have much to learn from this work, and indeed from all works of Islamic law.

ISLAMIC LAW AS LAW

Islamic law has a number of features that distinguish it from what one might ordinarily understand by the term "law." *Fiqh*, which we translate ordinarily as "Islamic law" really means "praxic understanding," that is, insight into how one ought to act and live as a Muslim. Consequently, the scope of Islamic law is much broader than one would ordinarily expect from the concept, "law." Islamic legists offer guidance about contracts, marriage and divorce, torts, crimes of property, and crimes of conduct, but also about ritual and ritual conditions, eating and drinking, table manners, government and state-craft, welfare taxes and wills. Not all of these subjects are covered in this present book, but in the vast volumes of Islamic law one can find extensive discussions of these topics and many more besides.

A concise handbook like the present one will surprise the reader with the extent of its reach, and the detail of its discussion. Yet even the largest work of *fiqh* does not comprehend the full range of Islamic law, because Muslims believe that for every conceivable human act in any possible circumstance there are correct ways to act, and very possibly, incorrect ways to act. This metaphysical concept of an underlying moral significance to all acts is expressed in the concept of *sharīᶜah*, often translated also as "Islamic law," but which means Law as the concept of "right action," in the abstract; *fiqh* is the human attempt to understand *sharī*ᶜah. And it is part of the sophistication of Islamic scholars that they recognized the limitations of humans in this enterprise, and sought, to the extent possible for human understanding, to ground life in objective, verifiable, sources of moral knowledge. For Muslims these sources are the *sunnah* of the Prophet, and the Qur'ān that Muḥammad brought.

The topics of Islamic law are as diverse as life itself. Usually the scope of Islamic law is summed up as "acts of ritual bondsmanship" (ᶜ*ibādāt*) and "acts of human interaction" (*mu*ᶜ*āmilāt*). These later are divided once more into the obligations of humans towards each other (*ḥuqūq al-insān*) and the obligations of humans towards God (*ḥuqūq allāh*). These latter correspond roughly to penal and criminal law, but it is noteworthy that it is only for the category of "obligations towards God" (*ḥuqūq allāh*) that sanctions are stipulated.

The acts of bondsmanship are for the most part the ritual acts of Islam. Purification (*ṭahārah*) addresses the question of how to place oneself in the state proper to the ritual worship of *ṣalāh*. Here are the discussions of how one loses that status, and how, through acts of ritual purification, one regains it. In general various acts perceived as losses of control (urination, defecation, menstruation, and according to some coughing, vomiting, or even laughing uproariously) take one out of the state of ritual capability. That state is restored through various washings with water, or, in its absence, various dry materials. In this section also the text discusses substances which, if present, invalidate the garments or place of worship. These include wine, pig-products, and other substances.[1] *Ṣalāh*, or ritual prayer, is a service of stipulated form and content through which the relation of humankind to God is represented. Included in this topic are the call to worship, the timings and places of worship etc. Fasting during the lunar month of Ramaḍān (*ṣawm*) is discussed in the next chapter. Ordinarily the welfare-tax (*zakāh*) would be discussed next but that section has been moved to a separate section on economic matters.

So the last of ritual chapters is the one on pilgrimage to Mecca (*ḥajj*). It is worth noting that most of the acts of the *ḥajj* ritual take place outside of Mecca in a course laid out between Mecca and Muzdalifah.

Following the ritual aspects of Islamic law, the reader will find the economic aspects discussed in chapters on the welfare-tax (*zakāh*)—what goods are taxable and at what rates, how the revenue may be spent etc.— and the conditions of establishing a pious endowment (*waqf*). The *waqf* is one of the distinctive features of pre-modern Islamic social institutions, and continues to be the means by which good deeds and religious institutions are supported in the Islamic world.

Finally, the author's last sections are on family law, the section seen by many Muslims as the core of Islamic public law (*muᶜāmilāt*). These topics include wills and inheritance in which the shares of each of the heritors is specified, as well as restrictions on will-making. Marriage is next, with specifications of contract, the woman's economic independence, the dowry, and impediments to marriage. Marriage is followed, as in life, with divorce: restrictions on its use, husband-initiated divorce, wife-initiated divorce, the period-of-waiting (*ᶜiddah*) and so on. This text is a very good survey of the school positions, but in its scope, and argumentation, it only scratches the surface of the very rich intellectual tradition of Islamic law.

One of the clichés about Islamic law is that in the view of the *sharīᶜah*, there is no distinction between church and state. This is a mistake, since it has never been argued that the state can determine morality, and until very recently it had never been argued that the religious scholars ought to rule. It has been argued that, to the contrary, the obligation of all Muslims but particularly Muslim scholars to 'commend the good and forbid the reprehensible' amounts to a tacit obligation to supervise the workings of society. It remains the case that only in Iran since the Revolution of 1979, have the scholars of law (*ᶜulamāʾ*) taken it upon themselves actually to govern.

The careful reader of this book will recognize that the real difference of *sharīᶜah* from the legal systems with which we are more familiar is that here there is no recognition of the difference between a crime and a sin. Eating pork, stealing, and concluding a sales contract improperly are all Proscribed (see below for the categorization of acts), even if the consequences of these acts (divine displeasure, cutting the hand, invalidation of the contract, respectively) are quite different.

DISCOVERING ISLAMIC LAW

Among the features of Islamic law several must be borne in mind by the reader. The first is that Islamic law is not legislated, but discovered by scholars. There is a right action in a given circumstance and the task of Muslims (indeed of all humankind) is to act in this right way. Through a complex and sophisticated combination of methods and sources whose study is called the "science of the principles of jurisprudence" (*ilm uṣūl al-fiqh)* one discovers how it is that God wishes humans to act. Those who are trained in this discipline are qualified to search for the correct action.

The first and foremost source of Islamic law is, of course, the Qurʾān, but making sense of the Qurʾān is not easily done. Muslim jurists were seldom naive literalists. Rather, a jurist begins his (or her) search for the moral stipulation by searching the Qurʾānic text for *all* relevant passages—those that pertain to the issue and also to the circumstances of the problem. The jurist then turns to the record of the Prophet Muḥammad's normative action (*sunnah*) as recorded in the manifold volumes of *ḥadīth*. These too are searched for all possibly relevant dicta. Only after having compiled this body of information, which is sorted and prioritized according to various rules of inclusiveness and chronology, can a jurist come to a decisions about the proper course of action in a particular circumstance.

Many Muslims and non-Muslims believe that since this law is discovered in unchanging sources, and not legislated, that Islamic law is, in a popular word, "immutable;" that it is necessarily inflexible and rigid, or at least, permanent. In the hands of conservative jurist, that certainly has been the case. Since, however, the finding of an act's assessment is grounded in a *complete* understanding of an act, *including its circumstances*, through the recognition of new and changing circumstances, Islamic law maintains considerable scope for flexibility and changes in norms of conduct.

THE ASSESSMENT OF ACTS

Another way in which Islamic law diverges from our ordinary expectations of the law, is in its assessments. Civil statutory law specifies conduct, and assesses a penalty for non-compliance. Thus, one is compliant or non-compliant, and the law is observed or not observed, an act is legal or illegal, and one is guilty or not-guilty of breaking the law. Not so with Islamic law, which is concerned not just with order, but with virtue; not merely with compliance but also with discipline and development. The result is a constellation of terms to assess an act. These are customarily understand to comprehend five categories.

Obligatory (traditionally defined as "that for the doing of which there is reward (from God) and for the neglect of which there is punishment")

Recommended (for the doing of which there is reward, but for the neglect of which there is no punishment)

Permitted (for neither doing nor neglecting is there punishment or reward)

Discouraged, or reprehensible (for the avoidance of which there is reward, but for the doing of which there is no punishment)

and Forbidden, or Proscribed, (for the avoidance of which there is reward, and for the doing of which there is punishment).

Therefore, the drinking of wine is assessed by jurists as "Proscribed"; eating horse is by most jurists Discouraged; drinking Coca Cola is Permitted; saying "In the Name of God" before eating is Recommended, and eating sufficiently to maintain health is Obligatory.

The reader of this work will also frequently find the phrase "it is *sunnah* to do such-and-such," which means it is

Recommended, and this recommendation is grounded particularly in the normative practice of the Prophet Muḥammad.

The consequence of this ranking system is that Islamic law is about not merely what one must and must not do, but what one ought and ought not to do. Its scope is not just legal performance, but ethics as well, and Muslims are strongly enjoined to do what is Recommended and avoid what is Discouraged. Law, then, is not just about compliance, and noncompliance, but about striving for virtue as well. It is not that law accords with or even is grounded in morality but that the two are intertwined to an extent that the separation of them, even for analysis, is in my view, untenable. This point must be borne in mind when we consider the call often heard among Islamists for a "return to Islamic law." Their perception is that civil, legislated law is capricious and legislated to preserve class or other temporal interests. To "return to Islamic law" is to assert the priority of morality and objectivity over expedience and interest.

MADHHABS

It is difficult to describe fully the rich concept of the *madhhab*, here translated as "school" of law, but from at least the third Islamic century it has been accepted that there is more than one way to be authentically Muslim. By the late fifth Islamic century the five schools as we know them—Shāfiᶜī, Ḥanbalī, Mālikī, Ḥanafī and Jaᶜfarī, and others besides— had been well-established.

The *madhhab* is best understood as a kind of discipline or method of evaluating and applying law. Shāfiᶜīs and Ḥanafīs, to take one example, differ in the categories with which they assess acts. The Shāfiᶜīs rank acts solely according to how incumbent upon the Muslim is the doing or not doing of that act. The Ḥanafīs rank acts according to how certain is the knowledge is that produces that ranking. Thus an Obligatory act for the Shāfiᶜīs is called *"wājib"*—incumbent, Obligatory. For the Ḥanafīs, however, incumbent acts can be *"farḍ"* —that is, an Obligatory act whose obligatory character is known with certainty and unambiguously from the texts of Qurʾān and ḥadīth. Or it can be a *"wājib"* act —which for the Ḥanafī means Obligatory, but known with a lesser degree of certainty from the sources of Islamic law. In short, for the Ḥanafī school, required acts are "obligatory and known to be so with certainty," and "obligatory and known to be so probabalistically." For the other schools, acts are only "required," or "not required," regardless of how unambiguous the means of moral knowledge.

Additionally, each *madhhab* is a kind of school-tradition. Given the complexity of Islamic law, and the variability of its understandings and methodologies, followers of a given *madhhab* rely for convenience's sake upon the insights of their founders and prominent early scholars within the school. The Jaʿfarī school traces its origin to Jaʿfar al-Ṣādiq (148/765), and Ḥanafīs cite the ʿIrāqīs Abū Ḥanīfah (150/767), Abū Yūsuf (182/798) and al-Shaybānī (189/805). Mālikīs are particularly informed by the tradition of the Medinan Mālik b. Anas (d. 179/796) and his tradition, including for instance Saḥnūn (d.240/854) compiler of the great work *al-Mudawwanah*. Shāfiʿīs value the insight and guidance of Aḥmad b. Idrīs al-Shāfiʿī (d. 204/820) who died in Egypt, together with that of his disciple al-Muzanī (d. 264/877). Ḥanbalīs likewise quote the Baghdādī Aḥmad b. Ḥanbal (241/855).

MADHHABS AND DIFFERENCES IN LAW

As a result of these varying methodological, and regional differences, the results of Shāfiʿī inquiries into the law differ in some particularities from the results of Ḥanafī inquiries. When *"madhhab"* refers to these ritual or practical differences, the term is often translated as "rite." Small though many of them are, cumulatively they add up to a substantial body of material with important consequences for Muslim life. This cumulative body of material is what we call the school of law. The result is often slight but a discerning viewer can tell Jaʿfarī *ṣalāh* from Mālikī version, or can hear regional and school differences in the *tashahhud* with which *ṣalāh* concludes. Likewise, Jaʿfarī rules of inheritance differ significantly from Sunnīs' and so do the rules of marriage. Yet, despite these manifest differences, Shaltūt's argument is persuasive: the range of opinion within the schools, and the principle of "difference being a mercy" as a Prophetic rationale allows one to see all these variations as permissible underneath the over-arching roof of Islam. Shīʿīs and Sunnīs are all Muslims, and their practices, differing slightly though they might be, are still the practices of Islam.

A. Kevin Reinhart
Dept. of Religion
Dartmouth College
Hanover New Hampshire

[1] I have discussed these matters in a preliminary form in "Impurity/No Danger," *History of Religions* v. 30/1 (August, 1990) pp. 1-24. A larger, monographic study, preliminarily titled *The Logic of Purity*, is currently underway.

PART ONE
INDIVIDUAL ISSUES

1
PRESCRIBED PURITY

1.1. INTRODUCTION

The leaders of all the schools of jurisprudence (*fiqh*) have considered prescribed purity (*taharah*) to be a basic condition for the validity of worship (*ibadah*). It is not an exaggeration to say no other religion has given such importance to prescribed purity as Islam.

Taharah literally means 'purity'. In the terminology of the jurisprudents it implies the removal of physical impurities like blood and excrement (*khabath*). Attaining a state of prescribed purity from a state which prohibits the performance of the prescribed prayer until it is removed (*hadath*) by either the ablution (*wudu*), the bath lustration (*ghusl*) or the dry ablution (*tayammum*) must be accompanied by the intention (*niyyah*) to seek nearness to God (*taqarrub*) and to obey His command regarding it.

On the other hand, prescribed purity of the hands, clothes, and utensils from impurity (*najasah*) requires no intention. For instance, if the wind carries an impure (*najis*) piece of clothing and it automatically falls into a 'large quantity' of water (*al-mal-kathir*, details follow), it attains prescribed purity.

Water brings about prescribed purity from both types of impurities: *khabath* which refers to such physical impurities as blood and excrement and *hadath*, minor impurity or a condition which occurs consequent to a person performing an act that prohibits them from performing the prescribed prayer. This accords with these statements of God, *"And He sends down upon you water from heaven to purify you thereby...."* (8:11). *"And We sent down from heaven pure water"* (25:48).

Tahur means that which is itself pure and capable of purifying other things as well. Considering that water is found either in a small (*qalil*) or a large quantity (*kathir*), and includes juicy extracts, solutions and water in its natural form, jurisprudents have divided water into two types: pure (*mutlaq*) and mixed (*mudaf*).

1.2. WATER

1.2.1. PURE WATER

Pure water (*mal-mutlaq*) is water that has retained its natural state—the state possessed when descending from the sky or welling up from the ground—so that it is correct to apply the word 'water' to it without the addition of any adjective which would alter its natural state. This includes rain water, sea water, river water, well water, spring water and water derived from hail and snow.

Water is considered to remain in its pure form if the change that occurs to it is due to factors usually unavoidable, e.g. mud, soil, stagnation, fallen leaves or collection of straw, etc., or the salt, sulfur, and other minerals that it contains at its source or picks up in its course. Pure water is considered pure and purifying from both types of impurity by absolute consensus of the major schools of Islamic Law. As to the statement that has been narrated from Abd Allah ibn Umar that he preferred dry ablution to sea water, it stands refuted by these words of the Prophet (ﷺ), "He whom the sea does not purify, will not be purified by God."

1.2.2. USED WATER

When the impurity is removed from a body, a piece of clothing or a utensil by pure water, the water separating from the object purified, either freely or by wringing, is called *ghusalah* (when it flows out freely) by the jurisprudents or *mustamal* (when the water is rung out). The water that is rung out is called used water (*mal-mustmal*) and impure because it is in a small quantity (*mal-qalil*) that has come into contact with an impurity and has consequently become impure, irrespective of whether it has itself undergone any change or not. Accordingly, it cannot remove either type of impurity.

A group of jurisprudents belonging to different schools observe that if this water, separating from the washed object, undergoes a change by the impurity, it is impure. Otherwise its state would be similar to the state of the washed object—if impure, then impure, and if pure, then pure.

This observation will not be correct unless we take into account the state of the object being washed before water has reached it, because the object containing an impurity is purified by the water poured over it. The water separating from it is impure due to its having come into contact with an impurity.

If water is used for removing impurity arising from a state which prohibits the performance of the prescribed prayer, it is considered pure but not purifying (*mutahhir*). This is the preponderant opinion of the Hanafi school and the apparent view of the Shafii and Hanbali. According to one of the two opinions narrated from Imam Malik, it is both pure and capable of purifying.[1]

The Jafari say that the water used for non-obligatory ablution and the non-obligatory bath lustration like the bath lustration, with the intention of repentance (*ghusl al-tawbah*), is pure as well as capable of purifying from both types of impurities. That is, it is valid to use it for the bath lustration, the ablution and for removing impurity. As to the water used for performing the obligatory bath lustration such as the bath lustration following sexual emission (*ghusl al-janabah*) and the bath lustration following menstruation (*ghusl al-hayd*), the Jafari jurisprudents concur that it can remove impurity, but they differ concerning its ability to purify from the state which prohibits the performance of the prescribed prayer. They also differ on the validity of a ablution and a second bath lustration with it.

1.2.3. A SUBSIDIARY ISSUE

In the case of a person in the state of major impurity following sexual emission (*janabah*) who dips himself or herself in a small amount of water after purifying the locale of impurity and makes the intention known for purification from the state which prohibits the performance of the prescribed prayer, the Hanbalis observe that the water will be considered used and that the impurity, also, will not be removed. The person will have to repeat the bath lustration. The Shafii, Jafari and Hanafi schools state that the water will be considered used, although the impurity will be removed and the person will not have to repeat the bath lustration.[2]

1.2.4. MIXED WATER

Mixed water (*mal-mudaf*) is either water extracted from fruit such as lime and grape juice or that which was pure initially before something was added to it that changed its character like rose-water and soda-water. It is pure, but does not remove impurities of blood and excrement as per the consensus of all schools except the Hanafi. The Hanafis consider valid the removal of blood or excrement with any non-oily liquid valid, except that which has been changed by cooking. Sayyid al-Murtada from among the Jafari concurring with them.

All the schools, except the Hanafi also agree that it is not valid to perform the ablution or the bath lustration with mixed water. According to Ibn Rushd,[3] Imam Abu Hanifah has considered the performance of the ablution with date-wine (*nabidh al-tamr*) valid during travel. Further, it has been mentioned by Ibn Qudamah[4] that according to Imam Abu Hanifah it is valid to perform the ablution with mixed water. Shaykh al-Saduq, a Jafari, held that it is valid to perform the ablution and the obligatory bath lustration following sexual emission with rose-water. In order to prove the validity of the ablution with mixed water, the Hanafis rely on the verse, "...*And when you can find no water, then have recourse to wholesome dust....*" (5:6).

They say that the verse means, "When you cannot find water, pure or mixed." Therefore, when pure water is available, it is not valid to resort to dry ablution. The same verse has been relied upon by the religious scholars of other schools to prove its invalidity. They observe that the word water in the verse brings to one's mind 'pure water' and not 'mixed water'. Hence the meaning of the verse is, "If you do not find pure water, then resort to dry ablution."

1.2.5. AL-KURR AND AL-QULLATAN

All the schools concur that if the color, taste or smell of water changes as a result of coming into contact with an impurity, it will become impure, irrespective of its being a small amount (*qalil*) or a large amount (*kathir*), flowing or stationary, mixed or pure. But if the smell of water is changed by the diffusion of the smell of impurity, without its coming into contact with it, such as where there is a carcass nearby and the air carries its smell to the water, the water will remain pure.

But in the case where impurity mixes with water without changing any of its qualities (color, taste and smell), Imam Malik, in one of the two opinions narrated from him, says that it is pure whether it is a small or a large amount. The other schools observe that it is impure if a small amount and pure if a large amount. But they differ in their definition of 'large'. The Shafiis and the Hanbalis state that a large amount is that which has reached two *qullah*s (literally meaning jar, pot or bucket) in accordance with the Tradition, "If water has reached two *qullah*s it is not affected by impurities of blood and excrement." Two *qullah*s equal 500 Iraqi ritl (1 ritl is approximately 330 grams). The Jafari observe that a large amount is that which is at least equal to a *kurr*, because of the Tradition, "If water has reached the extent of a *kurr* nothing makes it impure." A *kurr* is equal to 1200 Iraqi ritl. The Hanafis say that a large amount means a quantity of water whose other end remains motionless if one end of it is disturbed.[5]

From this discussion it becomes clear that the Malikis do

not take into consideration the measures *qullatan* or *kurr*, and there is no specific quantity for water in their opinion. Hence, large and small quantities are not determining in that when one of the qualities is changed, they become impure, not otherwise. Their opinion has been favored from among the Jafari by Ibn Abi Aqil who has acted on the general import of the Tradition, "Water is pure, and nothing makes it impure except that which affects its smell, taste or color," but this Tradition is a general one (*amm*) and the Tradition of large or small is particular (*khass*), and the particular enjoys precedence over the general. The Hanafis also do not take into account large and small amounts, relying instead on movement.

1.2.6. A SUBSIDIARY ISSUE

The Shafii and the Jafari schools observe that liquids other than water, for instance, vinegar and oil, become impure merely on coming into contact with an impurity, be its quantity small or large, and regardless of any change that may affect them. This opinion corresponds with the principles of the *Shariah* because that which is understood from the Prophet's Traditions is pure water. The Hanafis say that the rule applicable to other liquids is the same as that of pure water in relation to the water being a small or large amount. Hence only its small and not large quantity will become impure on contact. It has been mentioned in the margins of lbn Abidin, "The rule applicable to liquids, as per the most correct opinion, is the one applicable to water, and even if urine falls into a large quantity of juice, it will not be polluted, and if blood from someone's foot mixes with the juice it will not become impure."[6]

1.2.7. FLOWING AND STATIONARY WATER

The schools differ concerning flowing water. The Hanafis observe that every kind of flowing water—irrespective of its being a small or large amount and regardless of its connection to a source—will not become impure solely on contact. Rather, if there is impure water in one vessel and pure water in another and both of them are poured together from a height so that they mix in the air before coming down, all the water will be pure. Similar is the case if the two are made to flow on the ground.[7] Thus, the criterion is flow. Wherever and in whatever manner it is achieved, flowing water will enjoy the status of a large amount of water. But if it does not flow, then it is like a small amount even if it is connected to a source. On this basis, they have ruled that when rain water falls on impure ground and does not flow on it, the ground will remain impure.

Consequently, according to the Hanafis, water which does not become impure on coming into contact with impurity, is of two types: first, a body of stationary water whose other end remains motionless when one end of it is disturbed; second, flowing water, irrespective of its mode of flow. As to a small amount of water that becomes impure on coming into contact with impurity, it is a body of stationary water whose other end is set in motion if one end of it is disturbed.

The Shafiis neither differentiate between flowing and stationary water nor between one connected to a source and one not connected. The criterion is simply its quantity, small or large. Hence, large amounts of water, which is a body of water at least equal to a *qullatan*, will not become impure on contact, and that which is less than a *qullatan* will become impure, whether flowing or stationary, and whether welling from a source or not. They rely on the unqualified nature of the Tradition.

They say that when water is flowing and there is impurity in it, if the body of the flow containing the impurity has reached the quantity of a *qullatan* without there being a change in its qualities, all the water will be pure. If the quantity of the body is less than a *qullatan*, it will be impure, although the water above and beneath the flowing body of water will be pure. They interpret a flowing portion (*jiryah*) as the body of water between the two banks of a stream. Therefore, according to the Shafiis, the difference between flowing and stationary water is that stationary water is considered altogether as a single body of water, while flowing water, although its parts are connected with each other, is divided into flowing portions, each such portion having a separate status and becoming impure only if it is *qaril* and not otherwise.

Consequently, if one's hand is impure and one washes it in one of the portions of flowing water and this portion is less than a *qullatan*, it is not valid for one to drink from it or perform the ablution with it, because it is impure. One must wait for the next portion or move upstream or downstream.

A great difference can be noted between the opinions of the Shafii and the Hanafi schools concerning flowing water. The Hanafis consider flowing water—even if little—as capable of purifying. This is indicated by their example of two vessels of water, one pure and the other impure, where the water becomes pure if the two waters are mixed in a state of flow. The Shafiis, on the other hand, do not give credence to flow even if it is a big stream and consider each 'flowing portion' separately despite the portions being connected with each other.

The Hanbalis say that stationary water becomes impure solely on contact if it is less than a *qullatan*, irrespective of whether it is connected to a source or not. But flowing water does not become impure unless its qualities (color, smell and taste) change. Thus the rule applicable to it is the rule applicable to a large amount of water, even if it is not connected to a source. This opinion is close to the one held by the Hanafis.

As to the Maliki view, we have already mentioned that in their opinion a small amount of water does not become impure solely by contact. They also do not differentiate between stationary and flowing water. To sum up, they do not differentiate between small and large amounts, flowing and stationary, and water connected to a source and otherwise. The only criterion for them is the change of qualities due to impurity. Hence if an impurity changes any one of the qualities of water, it becomes impure. Otherwise, it remains pure irrespective of whether it is flowing or stationary, small or large.

The Jafari state that flow has no effect at all and the criterion is the existence of a source of flow or the presence of a large quantity of water. Hence, if water is connected to a source—even if through a trickle—it will fall under the rule applicable to a large amount. That is, it will not become impure solely on contact even if it is a small amount and stationary, because of the preservative power and abundance of the source. When water is not connected to a source, if it amounts to a *kurr*, nothing will make it impure except the change of one of its qualities. But if it is less than a *kurr*, it will become impure on contact irrespective of its being stationary or flowing, except where it flows downstream, where the upstream part will not become impure by an insignificant contact.

It follows that, according to the Jafari, the presence or absence of flow makes no difference. It is also observable that they stand apart from the other schools in considering the source of flow a criterion and in applying to the water connected to it the rule applicable to a large amount of water even though it may appear to be a small amount Allamah al-Hilli is an exception here because he does not attach any importance to source and considers water to become impure solely on contact if its quantity is less than a *kurr*. Rain water, during rain, is considered by the Jafari as equivalent to water connected to a source and a large amount of water. It does not become impure by contact and purifies the earth, clothes, vessels and other objects solely by raining upon them after the impurity itself is removed from them.

1.2.8. PURIFYING IMPURE WATER

Concerning a small amount of water that has become impure by contact without any of its qualities having undergone a change, the Shafiis observe that if water is added to this impure water so that they together add up to a *qullatan*, it will become both pure and purifying, irrespective of whether the water added is pure or impure. And if this water is later separated after its coming together, it will retain its prescribed purity. Therefore, if a person has two or more vessels, all containing impure water and all their water is collected in a single place so that their total volume reaches a *qullatan*, it will become both pure and purifying.[8]

The Hanbalis and most Jafari jurisprudents state that a

small amount of water is not purified after it is increased to a *kurr* or *qullatan* amount irrespective of whether the added water is impure or pure, because adding impure water to another of its kind does not make the whole pure. And similarly a small amount of water which is pure becomes impure by coming into contact with impure water. Hence, it is necessary for purifying it that it be connected to a *kurr* quantity or to water having a source of flow as per the Jafari view and to a *qullatan* as per the opinion of the Hanbalis.

If the qualities of a large amount of water have changed because of impurity, it will become pure if the change vanishes. It will not require anything else. This is the opinion of the Hanbali and the Shafii schools. The Jafaris say that if a large amount of water does not have a source of flow, it will not become pure on the vanishing of the change. Rather, it is necessary to add a *kurr* amount of pure water to it after the vanishing of the change, or to connect it with a source of flow, or it be rained on. If water has a source of flow, it becomes pure solely by the vanishing of the change even if it is *qalil*.

The Malikis observe that water which has become impure is purified by pouring pure water over it until the qualities of the impurity disappear. The Hanafis state that impure water becomes pure on flowing. Thus, if there is impure water in a tub and water is poured over it to make it overflow, it will become pure. Similarly, if there is impure water in a pool or a pit, and then another pit is dug beside it at a distance, even if small, and the water is made to flow in the channel between them so that it gathers in the other pit, it will become pure. Now if this water becomes impure a second time after becoming stationary in the second pit, a third pit will be dug to repeat the same process, and the water will again become pure. This process can go on infinitely.

Therefore, a body of water that could not be used while it was stationary, can validly be used for the ablution if caused to flow in any manner, even if it contains a carcass or people urinate in its downstream part without producing any noticeable effect in the flow. All this despite the knowledge that it is not connected to any source of flow.[9]

1.3. IMPURITIES

1.3.1. DOG

A dog is impure except in the opinion of Imam Malik, although he says that a vessel licked by a dog should be washed seven times not because it is impure, but because of obedience to the command of the Lawgiver (*taabbud*). The Shafii and the Hanbali schools observe that a vessel licked by a dog will be washed seven times, of these once with dust. The state that a vessel licked by a dog will be washed once with dust and then twice with water.

1.3.2. PIG

It is similar to a dog in the view of all the schools except the Jafari which considers it necessary to wash on contamination with it seven times with water only. Similar to it is a dead, large land rat.

1.3.3. CORPSE

The schools concur regarding the impurity of the carcass of a land animal—other than a human being—which possesses blood which flows out. As to the human corpse, the Maliki, Shafii and Hanbali schools consider it pure. The Hanafis consider it impure although it becomes pure after the bath lustration. The Jafari view is the same although they restrict it to the corpse of a Muslim. There is a consensus among all the schools concerning the prescribed purity of the musk derived from the musk-deer.

1.3.4. BLOOD

The Shafii, Hanbali, Hanafi and Maliki schools concur upon the impurity of blood. Among exceptions to this is the blood of a martyr as long as it is on his or her body, the blood retained in the body of a slaughtered animal, and the blood of fish, lice, flea and bugs. According to the Jafari, the blood of every animal whose blood flows out is impure irrespective of whether it is human blood or not, the blood of a martyr or a non-martyr. They consider the blood of an animal which does not flow out, whether it is a terrestrial or sea animal, as pure. Similarly, they consider the blood retained in a slaughtered animal as pure.

1.3.5. SEMEN

The Jafari, Maliki and Hanafi schools consider the semen of human beings and other animals as impure, although the Jafari exclude the animals whose blood does not flow out and regard their semen and blood as pure. The Shafiis regard the semen of human beings as well as other animals, except the dog and the pig, as pure. According to the Hanbalis, human semen and that of animals used for food is pure and that of other animals impure.

1.3.6. PUS

It is impure in the opinion of the Shafii, Hanbali, Hanafi and Maliki schools and pure according to the Jafaris.

1.3.7. HUMAN URINE AND EXCREMENT

This is considered impure by consensus.

1.3.8. ANIMAL EXCREMENT

Animals, other than the human being, are either birds or other animals. Among the two are those which are used for food and those which are not. Among the birds that are eaten is the pigeon and the hen, and of those which are not eaten are the eagle and the falcon (although Imam Malik permits all of them for food). Among animals other than birds, there are some which may be used for food such as the cow and the sheep, and others which are unlawful such as the wolf and the cat (although Imam Malik allows them).

The schools differ in their opinions regarding the prescribed purity of animal excrement. The Shafiis say that every kind of animal excrement is impure. The Jafaris state that the excrement of all birds is pure, so also that of every animal whose blood does not flow out. But the excrement of those animals whose blood flows out is pure, if permissible for food—such as the camel and the sheep. If not—such as the bear and other beasts of prey—their excrement is impure. The excrement of every animal whose lawfulness for eating is doubtful is pure.

The Hanafis observe that the excrement of animals other than birds is impure. The excrement of birds that excrete in mid-air like the pigeon and the sparrow is pure. The excrement of birds that excrete on the ground like hens and geese is impure.

According to the Hanbali and the Maliki schools, the excrement of animals permitted for food is pure, and that of animals forbidden for food whose blood flows on coming out, is impure, irrespective of its being a bird or any other animal. All the schools concur that the excrement of any animal that eats human excrement is impure.

1.3.9. LIQUID INTOXICANTS

All the schools consider them impure. The Jafari add a further qualification and that is that which is intrinsically liquid. By this condition they include an intoxicant that dries due to an external factor. Hence it continues to remain impure. A Jafari jurisprudent states that all the religious scholars of the major schools concur regarding the impurity of liquor, except a small group from among them and those whose opposition is not taken notice of by the major schools.

1.3.10. VOMIT

The Shafii, Hanafi, Hanbali and Maliki schools consider it impure while the Jafari regard it as pure.

1.3.11. GENITAL DISCHARGE

The Shafii, Maliki and Hanafi schools consider both the thin genital discharge emitted while caressing and the dense discharge emitted following urination, impure secretions, while the Jafari consider both pure. The Hanbalis differentiate between these secretions of animals that make lawful food and others which may not be used for food. They regard these secretions of the former as pure and of the latter as impure. The thin genital discharge emitted while caressing is called *madhy* and the dense discharge emitted following urination is called *wadhy*.

In the same manner as the Shafii, Hanafi, Hanbali and Maliki differ with the Jafari in considering vomit, thin genital discharge and dense discharge as impure, the Jafari differ with the other schools concerning the impurity of the sweat of a person who is in a state of impurity following sexual emission where the state arose from an unlawful sexual act. They say that the sweat of one who becomes impure because of fornication, sodomy, masturbation or copulation with an animal which perspires before performing the the bath lustration, is impure.

1.3.12. REMAINDERS

The Hanafi, Shafii and Hanbali schools state that the remainders of a dog and pig are impure. They also concur that the remainders of an ass and a donkey are pure, although not purifying. Rather, the Hanbalis observe that the ablution may not be performed by the water left-over by any animal whose meat is not eaten, except a cat and that which is smaller than it in size such as a rat or weasel. The Hanafis have added to the remainders of the dog and the pig, the remainders of a drunk person immediately after drinking, the remainders of a cat immediately after eating a mouse, and the remainders of a wolf, lion, panther, leopard, fox and hyena.[10] The Jafari state that the remainders of an impure animal such as that of a dog and pig are impure and that of a pure animal is pure, irrespective of its permissibility for food. That is, the remainders of every animal are subordinate to its own prescribed purity and impurity. The Malikis observe that the remaining water of a dog and a pig are pure and may be used for drinking and the ablution.[11]

1.4. RULES OF GOING TO THE TOILET

The Shafii, Maliki and Hanbali schools concur that it is not forbidden to face or keep one's back to the *qiblah* while relieving oneself in a toilet or in the open air provided there is a screen. However, they differ concerning relieving oneself out-doors without a screen. The Shafiis and the Hanbalis do not prohibit it while the Malikis do. The Hanafis say that it is re-prehensible to the extent of being forbidden, whether it be in closed or open space.[12] The Jafari observe that it is totally for-bidden to face or turn one's back to the *qiblah* while relieving oneself whether it be in a closed or open space, with or without a screen.

All the schools concur that pure water removes impurity from the urinary and anal outlets. The Shafii, Hanafi, Hanbali and Maliki concur that stones also suffice for purifying the two outlets. The Jafari say that the urinary outlet is not purified except with water. As to the anal outlet there is an option, either to use water or to wipe the opening three times with stones or a pure rag, provided the excrement has not spread around the outlet, in which case only water may be used.

According to the Jafari, Shafii and Hanbali schools, repeti-tion is necessary when stones and the like are used for wiping even if purification is achieved the first time. The Malikis and Hanafis do not consider repetition necessary and regard the purification of the outlet as sufficient. Similarly, the Hanafis allow the removal of an impurity from the two outlets with any pure liquid other than water.

1.5. THE PURIFIERS

1.5.1. PURE WATER
Pure water is pure and purifying by consensus.

1.5.2. OTHER LIQUIDS
Any pure liquid like vinegar and rose-water is a purifier only according to the Hanafis.

1.5.3. THE EARTH
The earth purifies the soles of the feet and the sole of shoes in the opinion of the Jafari and the Hanafi schools provided it is walked on or the feet are rubbed on it and the actual impuri-ty is thereby removed.

1.5.4. THE SUN

The Jafari observe that the sun purifies the earth and other fixed objects such as trees (including leaves and fruit), grass, buildings and poles. Similarly, it purifies straw mats among movable things, not carpets and sofas. The condition for its purifying is that these objects should dry solely as a result of the sun's heat without the aid of the wind.

The Hanafis state that drying purifies the ground and trees irrespective of its being achieved by the sun or the wind. The Shafii, Maliki and Hanbali schools concur that the ground is neither purified by the sun nor the wind. Rather it requires the pouring of water over it. They differ concerning the manner of its purification.

1.5.5. ALTERATION

Alteration (*istihalah*) is the changing of one substance to another (like the changing of deer's blood into musk). It results in purification by consensus.

1.5.6. FIRE

The Hanafis say that the burning of impurity by fire purifies provided the actual impurity disappears. They consider impure clay as pure when it is turned into fired clay and impure oil, pure when made into soap. The Shafii and Hanbali schools observe that fire is not among the purifiers. They hold an extreme position in this regard and consider even the ash and smoke of an impure object as impure. The Malikis regard the ash as pure and the smoke as impure.

According to the Jafari fire plays no part in purification and the criterion in it is a transformer. If impure wood is transformed into ash or impure water into steam, they become pure. But if wood becomes charcoal and clay becomes earthenware, the impurity will remain because transformation has not occurred.

1.5.7. TANNING

The Hanafis observe that tanning purifies the skin of a carcass and every other impure animal, except pigskin. As to the skin of a dog, it becomes pure by tanning.[13] The Shafiis say that tanning is a purifier, except for the skin of the dog and the pig. The Malikis, Hanbalis and Jafaris do not consider tanning as a purifier, although the Hanbalis allow the use of a impure, tanned skin where liquids are not involved, so that its use does not lead to the spread of impurity.

1.5.8. CARDING
The Hanafis say that cotton is purified on being carded.

1.5.9. DISPOSITION
According to the Hanafis, when a part of wheat and the like becomes impure, if a part of it equal to that which had become impure is disposed of by being eaten, gifted or sold, the remainder will be purified.[14]

1.5.10. RUBBING
The Hanafis say that semen, if removed by rubbing, does not require water, because prescribed purity is achieved by rubbing.

1.5.11. WIPING
The Hanafis observe that an object which has a polished surface like iron, copper and glass, becomes pure solely by wiping and does not require water. The Jafaris state that the removal of impurity from the body of an animal, achieved in any manner, is sufficient for purification, but vessels, clothes and the human body require to be purified by water after the removal of the impurity.

1.5.12. SALIVA
The Hanafis say that if the breast or a finger becomes impure, they become pure on being licked three times.[15]

1.5.13. BOILING
The Hanafis state that if impure oil or meat is boiled on a fire, they become pure. A group of Jafari jurisprudents observe that grape juice, on boiling, becomes impure and when two-thirds of it evaporates on boiling, it automatically becomes pure.

1.6. ABLUTION

1.6.1. CONDITIONS REQUIRING ABLUTION

1.6.1.1. DISCHARGE OF URINE, FECES AND BREAKING WIND

There is a consensus among Muslims that discharge of urine and excrement, as well as breaking wind, invalidate the ablution. The expulsion of worms, stones, blood and pus invalidate the ablution in the opinion of the Shafii, Hanafi and Hanbali schools but not in the opinion of the Malikis if these things have been produced in the stomach. But if they are not produced in the stomach (that is, as when someone has swallowed a pebble and it comes out) the ablution is invalidated. The Jafari observe that the ablution will not be invalidated unless these things, when discharged, are stained with excrement.

1.6.1.2. GENITAL DISCHARGE

According to the Shafii, Hanafi, Hanbali and Maliki schools, the thin discharge emitted while caressing and the dense discharge following urination invalidates the ablution, but does not according to the Jafari. The Malikis exempt a person who suffers with a chronic flow of thin discharge emitted while caressing.

1.6.1.3. LOSS OF CONSCIOUSNESS

If someone loses his senses due to intoxication, madness, fainting or epilepsy, the ablution is invalidated by consensus of all the schools. As to sleep, the Jafari say that sleep breaks the the ablution when it prevails over the mind, hearing and vision so that the person asleep neither hears nor understands the talk of those present nor sees anyone of them, irrespective of whether he or she is lying down, standing or sitting. The Hanbali view is nearly the same. The Hanafis observe that if a person who has performed the ablution, sleeps, lying down or reclining on one of his sides, his or her ablution is invalidated.

But if he or she dozes while sitting, standing, kneeling or prostrating, it will not be invalidated. Hence, if one sleeps while performing the prescribed prayers in any of its postures, his or her ablution remains intact even if he or she sleeps for a long period.[16]

1.6.1.4. EMISSION OF SEMEN
In the opinion of the Hanafis, Malikis and Hanbalis, emission of semen invalidates the ablution. It does not in the opinion of the Shafiis. The Jafari state that emission of semen requires the bath lustration and not the ablution.

1.6.1.5. TOUCH
The Shafiis observe that if a man in the state of the ablution touches the skin of a woman who is prohibited to him (that is, a woman who is not his wife or female relative within prohibited degrees of marriage) without there being any intervening medium (like clothing), his ablution will be invalidated. But if the woman is his wife or a female relative within the prohibited degrees of marriage such as one's mother or sister, the ablution will not be invalidated. The Hanafis say that the ablution is not invalidated except by touch accompanied with erection. The Jafari say that touch has absolutely no effect.

As to a person in the ablution touching his or her frontal or rear private parts without intervening medium, the Jafari and the Hanafi schools do not regard that as invalidating the ablution. The Shafiis and Hanbalis say that the ablution is invalidated by such a touch regardless of its being with the palm of one's hand or the back of the hand. The Malikis are said to differentiate between touching with the palm—in which case the ablution is invalidated—and touching with the back of the hand—in which case it remains intact.[17]

1.6.1.6. VOMITING
According to the Hanbali school, vomiting in general invalidates the ablution. In the opinion of the Hanafis it does so only when it fills the mouth. In the opinion of the Shafii, Jafari and Maliki schools, it does not invalidate the ablution.

1.6.1.7. BLOOD AND PUS

According to the Jafari, Maliki and Shafii schools, anything that comes out of the body from a place other than the two outlets—that is, blood and pus—does not invalidate the the ablution. The ablution is invalidated, the Hanafi schools says if it spreads from its source. The Hanbali school says that the ablution is broken if the quantity of blood or pus coming out is a large amount.

1.6.1.8. LAUGHTER

There is a consensus among all the Muslims jurists that laughter invalidates the prescribed prayer. It does not invalidate the ablution during the prescribed prayer except in the opinion of the Hanafis, who say that the ablution is invalidated if one laughs during the prescribed prayer, but not if laughter occurs while not performing the prescribed prayer.

1.6.1.9. MEAT OF A SLAUGHTERED ANIMAL

Only the Hanbalis consider the ablution to be invalidated if a person eats the meat of a slaughtered animal over which the Name of God has not been invoked at the time of slaughtering.

1.6.1.10. INTERMITTENT BLEEDING

Allamah al-Hilli, a Jafari jurisprudent, writes, "The discharge of intermittent bleeding, if its quantity is little, requires the ablution." Other Jafari jurisprudents, except Ibn Abi Aqil, have also adopted this view. Imam Malik observes that the ablution is not compulsory for a woman having intermittent bleeding.

1.6.2. ACTS REQUIRING ABLUTION

Jurisprudents consider impurity of *hadath* to be of two kinds: minor and major. Minor impurity requires only the ablution.[18] The major impurity is of two types: that which requires only the bath lustration and that which requires both the bath lustration and the ablution. The details will be given below. The presence of the minor impurity is a hindrance to the performance of the following acts:

1.6.2.1. PRESCRIBED AND RECOMMENDED PRAYERS

As per the consensus of all the schools. The Jafari have excepted the funeral prayer (*salat al-janazah*), observing that it is not necessary to be pure for the prescribed prayer for the dead, although it is recommended to be so, considering that it is a prayer and not a prescribed prayer in its real sense. This will be further discussed in its proper place.

1.6.2.2. CIRCUMAMBULATION AROUND THE KABAH

Like prescribed prayer, is not valid without prescribed purity according to the Maliki, Shafii, Jafari and Hanbali schools, in accordance with the Traditions.[19] The Hanafis say that one who performs the circumambulation of the Kabah in a state of impurity from blood or excrement performs it validly, though he or she sins thereby.

1.6.2.3. PROSTRATION REQUIRED
IN THE RECITATION OF SOME VERSES

According to the Shafii, Hanbali, Hanafi and Maliki schools, prescribed purity is obligatory for performing prostration made obligatory by the recitation of certain verses of the Quran and the prostration performed to express gratitude (*shukr*). The Jafari consider it recommended.

1.6.2.4. TOUCHING OF THE ARABIC SCRIPT OF THE QURAN

All the schools concur that it is prohibited to touch the script of the Quran without prescribed purity, but they differ regarding the permissibility of someone in a state of minor impurity of blood and excrement writing the Quran, reading it from a script or from memory, touching it through an intervening medium and wearing it as an amulet. The Malikis observe that it is not permissible for a person to write it or touch its binding even through an intervening medium, although that person may read it from a script or from memory. But the Malikis, differ among themselves regarding carrying it as an amulet.

The Hanbalis state that writing it and carrying it as an amulet with a cover is permissible. The Shafiis say that it is not permissible to touch its cover even if detached from it and its hanger while it is hanging from it, although it is permissible to write it, carry it as an amulet, and to touch a cloth embroidered with Quranic verses. The Hanafis observe that it is not permissible to write or touch the Quran even if it is written in a different language, but it is permissible to read it from memory.

According to the Jafari school, it is forbidden to touch the Arabic script of the Quran without an intervening medium, irrespective of whether the script is in the Quran itself or somewhere else. But it is not forbidden to recite or write it, or carry it as an amulet and to touch its non-Arabic transcription, excepting the glorious name, Allah, which it is forbidden for a person in a state of minor impurity to touch, regardless of the language in which it is written and irrespective of whether it occurs in the Quran or elsewhere.

1.6.3. THE ESSENTIALS OF ABLUTION

The essentials of the ablution (*faraid al-wudu*) include the following:

1.6.3.1. INTENTION

This means having the intention to perform an act with a motive of obedience and submission to the command of God Almighty. The schools concur that intention is essential for the ablution and its time is at the commencement of the ablution. The Hanafis say that the validity of the prescribed prayer does not depend upon the ablution performed with intention. Hence if a person washes to cool or cleanse himself and it includes those parts of the body which are washed in the ablution and then performs the prescribed prayer, that person's prescribed prayer is valid, because the purpose of the the ablution is to attain prescribed purity and it has been achieved. But they exclude water which is mixed with water left over by a donkey or mixed with date-wine, considering intention necessary in these cases.[20]

1.6.3.2. WASHING THE FACE

Washing the face means causing water to flow over it. It is obligatory to do it once. Its extent lengthwise is from the place where hair grows to the end of the chin. The Shafiis observe that it is also obligatory to wash the area under the chin. Its extent breadth-wise, in the opinion of the Jafaris and Malikis, is the area covered between the thumb and the middle finger (when the open hand with the thumb pushed back is stretched across the face), while in the opinion of the other schools it is the area between the two earlobes.

The Jafari consider it obligatory to start washing the face down from the top and invalid to do its reverse. The Shafii, Hanbali, Hanafi and Maliki schools say that it is obligatory to wash the face, irrespective of how it is done and from where it starts, although it is better to start from the top.

1.6.3.3. WASHING OF HANDS

The Muslims concur that it is obligatory to wash the hands along with the elbows once. The Jafari consider it obligatory to start from the elbows and consider its reverse invalid. Similarly, they consider it obligatory to wash the right hand before the left. The other schools observe that which is obligatory is to wash them, in any manner, although washing the right hand first and starting up from the fingers and washing towards the elbow is better.

1.6.3.4. WIPING THE HEAD

The Hanbalis observe that it is obligatory to wipe the whole head and the ears. In their opinion, washing suffices in place of wiping, provided the hand is passed over the head. The Malikis say that it is obligatory to wipe the whole head except the ears. The Hanafis regard as obligatory the wiping of one-fourth of the head. It also suffices if the head is dipped in water or water is poured over it. The Shafiis state that it is obligatory to wipe a part of the head, even if little. Washing and sprinkling also suffice in place of wiping. The Jafari observe that it is obligatory to wipe a part of the frontal part of the head and the wiping of a minimal area is sufficient. It is not valid to wash or sprinkle. They also consider it obligatory that the wiping should be with the wetness of the earlier act of the the ablution performed (that is, the washing of hands). Hence if hands are rinsed anew with water for wiping, the ablution will be invalidated. The Hanafi, Hanbali, Maliki and Jafari schools consider it obligatory that new water be used.[21]

As to wiping the turban, the Hanbalis permit it, provided an end of the turban hangs down in the manner termed *hanak*. The Hanafi, Shafii and Maliki schools say that it is valid in the presence of an excuse, not without it. The Jafari observe that it is in no manner valid to wipe the turban because of the words of the Quran (and wipe your heads), and the turban is not the head.

1.6.3.5. THE TWO FEET

The Shafii, Hanbali, Hanafi and Maliki schools state that it is obligatory to wash the two feet along with the ankles once. The Jafari observe that it is obligatory to wipe the two feet with the wetness of the earlier act of the ablution from the head of the toes to the ankles. By 'ankle' is implied the raised bone of the foot. It is valid to wipe the left foot before the right one in the opinion of all the schools, though it is against precaution (*khilaf al-ihtiyat*) in the view of the Jafari and against preference (*khilaf al- awla*) in the opinion of the other major schools.

The difference of opinion concerning the wiping or washing of the feet has its basis in the interpretation of the Quran, "*Oh believers, when you stand up to pray, wash your faces, and your hands up to the elbows, and wipe your heads, and your feet up to the ankles*" (5:6). Those interested in investigating the meaning of the verse should refer to al-Razi's exegesis of the Quran. The Hanafi, Shafii, Hanbali and Maliki schools allow the wiping of shoes and socks instead of washing the feet, while the Jafari consider it as invalid.

1.6.3.6. SEQUENCE

Sequence (*tartib*) is in accordance with what the verse mentions: First the face, then the hands, and then the head, followed by the feet. This sequence is obligatory and a condition for the validity of the ablution in the opinion of Jafari, Shafii and Hanbali schools. The Hanafi and Maliki schools say that the observance of the sequence is not obligatory and it is permissible to start with the feet and end with the face.

1.6.3.7. CONTINUITY

It is the observance of continuity (*muwalat*) in the washing of the different parts, i.e. to proceed immediately to the next act after having completed the earlier. The Jafari and Hanbali schools consider it obligatory, the former adding a further condition that the part washed earlier should not dry before beginning washing the next. Hence, if the whole of the part washed earlier dries, the ablution will be invalidated and it will be obligatory to start it anew. The Hanafi and Shafii schools say that continuity is not obligatory, although it is disapproved (*makruh*) to separate the washing of the different parts without a reason, and with a reason the sin disappears.

The Malikis observe that the observance of continuity is obligatory only when the person performing the ablution is conscious of it and when no unforeseen incident takes place (like the spilling of the water brought for performing the ablution). Hence if a person washes the face and forgets to wash the hands, or when he or she lacks the amount of water believed to be necessary for prescribed purity, he or she may complete the ablution from where he or she had left off, even if a period of time has passed.

1.6.4. CONDITIONS OF ABLUTION

Ablution has certain conditions. Among them are: The water used should be pure and must not have been used for removing the two types of impurity, as per the details given while discussing water. There should be no hindrance such as illness in the way of using water or any urgent need for it. Moreover, the parts of the body involved in the ablution should be pure and without a covering that might prevent water from reaching the skin. Also there should be sufficient time. The last condition will be dealt with in detail in the chapter on dry ablution. All or most of these conditions are accepted by all the schools.

The Jafari further consider it necessary that the water and the vessel used for ablution should not have been usurped, and the place where the ablution is performed and where its water falls should be legitimate and not encroached land. If either of these two conditions does not exist, the ablution will be invalid. In the view of the other schools the ablution will be valid although the performer of such an ablution will have sinned.[22]

1.6.5. RECOMMENDED ACTS OF ABLUTION

The number of acts recommended (*mustahabb*) in the ablution are numerous. They include starting by washing the hands, rinsing the mouth and drawing water into the nose. The Hanbalis consider the last two obligatory. Wiping the ears is also among them, though the Hanbalis consider it obligatory as well and the Jafaris, impermissible. Brushing the teeth and facing the *qiblah* while performing the ablution is recommended and so is the reciting of traditional prayers. It also includes, in the opinion of the Shafii, Hanbali, Hanafi and Maliki schools, the washing of the face and hands two and three times.

The Jafaris observe that washing once is obligatory, twice recommended, and thrice an innovation and the person doing so is a sinner if he or she performs it as a religious duty. But if he or she does not, there is no sin upon him or her, although the ablution will be invalidated on his or her wiping the head with this water. There are many other recommended acts which are mentioned in voluminous books.

1.7. UNCERTAINTY REGARDING PRESCRIBED PURITY

If a person who is certain of having been purified be uncertain as to whether an impurity has occurred or not, that person remains pure. But if a person, certain of an impurity having

occurred, doubts having achieved prescribed purity later, his or
her impurity shall remain. That is, he or she shall act in accordance with his or her earlier certainty and brush aside the
subsequent doubt. This is based on the following Tradition, "A
condition of certainty is never invalidated by a doubt, but it
can be invalidated by a certainty resembling it." This principle
has not been disregarded by anyone except the Malikis, who
say that if a person is certain of having been purified and
doubts later about the occurrence of an impurity, that person is
considered pure. But they do not differentiate between the two
situations.

If both prescribed purity and impurity in the form of
hadath have occurred and it is not known which of the two was
subsequent so as to be made the basis, the Hanafis consider
the person in such a situation pure while the authorities consider the impurity to prevail.

The Shafiis and Hanbalis observe that the opposite of the
earlier condition will be accepted. Hence if the person possessed prescribed purity earlier, that person will now be considered in the condition of impurity due to *hadath* and vice
versa.

There is a fourth view which takes the condition prior to
the occurrence of the prescribed purity and impurity because of
hadath by denying the effect of both, because both possibilities
being equal are nullified by the conflict, leaving the prior condition to be relied upon. That which is nearer to caution in this
matter of ritual is always to renew prescribed purity irrespective of whether the prior condition is known or unknown.

The Jafaris and Hanbalis say that when a person performing the ablution doubts whether he or she has washed a particular part or wiped his or her head, if the doubt occurs while
performing the ablution, he or she will repeat the doubtful part
and complete the rest of the ablution. But if the doubt occurs
after the completion of the ablution, it will not be heeded,
because it is a doubt which has occurred in a worship after its
completion.

Allamah al-Hilli has narrated from some Shafiis that they

do not differentiate between a doubt occurring during the ablution and one occurring after its completion. They consider it obligatory to restart from the place of doubt and to complete the ablution in both situations.[23]

The Hanafis observe that every part of the ablution will be viewed separately. Hence, if there occurs a doubt concerning a particular part before moving on to the next, it will be repeated and not otherwise. For example, if a person doubts having washed his or her face before starting to wash his or her hands, he or she will restart from the face, and if he or she has started washing the hands, he or she will carry on without heeding the doubt.

All the schools concur that the doubt of a chronically uncertain person (*kathir al-shakk*) is not a valid doubt. That is, his or her doubt has no value and it is obligatory for him or her to carry on without heeding it, whatever the circumstances.

1.8. BATH LUSTRATION AND DRY ABLUTION

A bath lustration (*ghusl*) is required after the following different states of major impurity caused by:
1. Sexual emission (*janabah*).
2. Menstruation (*hayd*).
3. Bleeding Following Childbirth (*nifas*).
4. Death (*mawt*).

These four states, where it becomes obligatory to perform the bath lustration, are recognized by all the schools. The Hanbalis add a fifth to this list: the bath lustration of a non-Muslim on his or her embracing Islam.

The Shafii and the Jafari schools observe that if a non-Muslim embraces Islam while being in a state of prescribed impurity caused by sexual emission, he or she will be required to perform the bath lustration of a person in this state, not for embracing Islam; but if he or she is not in this state, he or she will have no obligatory bath lustration to perform.

The Hanafis say that no bath lustration will be obligatory upon him or her on embracing Islam, irrespective of whether he or she is in a state of prescribed impurity or not.[24]

The Jafari add two more to the above four causes for the prescribed bath lustration: First, the bath lustration required of a woman at the end of her period when she has intermittent discharge of blood (*ghusl al-mustahadah*) and second, the prescribed bath lustration after touching a corpse. They consider it obligatory for a person who has touched a corpse after it has turned cold and before it has been given the prescribed bath lustration, to perform a bath lustration (more details will follow). From what has been mentioned it becomes clear that the number of obligatory baths are four in the opinion of the Hanafis and the Shafiis, five in the opinion of the Hanbalis and the Malikis, and six in the opinion of the Jafaris.

1.8.1. PRESCRIBED BATH ABLUTION FOLLOWING SEXUAL INTERCOURSE

This state of prescribed impurity which makes a bath lustration obligatory occurs in two situations: First, on the discharge of semen, whether in sleep or the waking state. The Jafari and the Shafii schools say that the discharge of semen makes the bath lustration obligatory regardless of whether one is sexually aroused or not. The Hanafis, Malikis and Hanbalis observe that this bath lustration is not obligatory unless the discharge is accompanied with pleasure. Hence if the discharge is due to a stroke or cold or disease, and without sexual arousal, no bath lustration it required. Second, if the seminal secretions are released internally without coming out of the body, the bath lustration is not obligatory except in the opinion of the Hanbalis.

1.8.1.1. A SUBSIDIARY ISSUE

If a person on waking up finds wetness in his clothes and is unable to ascertain whether it is semen or discharge, the Hanafis state that bath lustration is obligatory. The Shafii and Jafari schools say that it is not obligatory because of the pre-existence of prescribed purity is certain while the occurrence of impurity of *hadath* is doubtful. The Hanbalis observe that if he has seen something before sleeping which had excited him or thought about it, the bath lustration will not be obligatory. If the sleep was not preceded by any cause entailing such excitement, the bath lustration will become obligatory on the presence of any dubious wetness.

In regard to the insertion of the glans (the part of the male organ covered by foreskin prior to circumcision) into the vagina or anus (the latter of which is a forbidden act and will be discussed in its place), the schools concur that the mere insertion of the glans makes the bath lustration obligatory, even if no emission occurs, although they differ regarding the conditions, whether the sole insertion necessitates the bath lustration irrespective of its mode or if only a particular manner of insertion requires the bath lustration.

The Hanafis consider bath lustration obligatory on the fulfillment of the following conditions: First, puberty (*bulugh*). Hence if only one of the partners has attained puberty, the bath lustration will be obligatory only on the one who has attained puberty. If both of them have not attained puberty, bath lustration is not obligatory on either. Second, there should be no thick sheath preventing the warmth of the locale from being felt. Third, the person with the passive role should be a living human being. Hence if it is an animal or a corpse, bath lustration is not obligatory. (Note: these acts are forbidden and will be discussed as such in their place).

The Jafari and the Shafii schools say that the insertion of the glans suffices for making bath lustration obligatory, irrespective of whether the person has attained puberty or not, is the active or the passive partner, or if there exists a sheath or not, whether it is by choice or under duress, and whether the passive participant is alive or dead, a human being or an animal.

The Hanbalis and the Malikis observe that bath lustration is obligatory on both the partners if a sheath preventing the sensation of pleasure from being felt is not used, regardless of whether the passive participant is a human being or an animal and dead or alive.

As to puberty, the Malikis state that bath lustration is

obligatory upon the active partner if he has reached puberty and the passive participant is capable of having intercourse. It is obligatory upon the passive partner if the active partner is an adult. Hence, if a boy has intercourse with a woman, the bath lustration will not be obligatory upon her if she does not have an orgasm. The Hanbalis further stipulate that the male should not be less than ten years and the female not less than nine.

1.8.1.2. ACTS THE VALIDITY OF WHICH DEPEND UPON THE BATH LUSTRATION FOLLOWING SEXUAL EMISSION

All those acts which are dependent for their validity or permissibility upon the ablution are also dependent upon the bath lustration taking place following sexual emission, such as the prescribed prayers, circumambulation of the Kabah and touching the script of the Quran. To this is added halting in a mosque, with all the schools concurring that it is not permissible for a person in this state of prescribed impurity to remain in a mosque, although they differ regarding the permissibility of his or her passing through it, such as when he or she enters from one door and leaves through another. The Malikis and the Hanafis say that it is not permissible unless necessary. According to the Shafiis and the Hanbalis, on the other hand, passing is permissible though remaining is not. The Jafari observe that it is not permissible for a person in this state to either to remain or pass through al-Masjid al-Haram and al-Masjid al-Rasul, but he or she may pass through and not remain, in other mosques, in accordance with the verse, *"A person in the state of prescribed impurity resulting from sexual emission should not enter the place of worship in mosques except as passersby"* (4:93). The Jafaris exclude the above-mentioned two mosques on the basis of particular proofs.

As to the reciting of the Quran, the Malikis state that it is forbidden for a person in a state of prescribed impurity following sexual emission to recite anything from the Quran except a little for the sake of protection or citing it as a proof. What the Hanbalis observe is close to this view.

The Hanafis say that it is not valid except where the person is a teacher of the Quran and he or she instructs by pronouncing each word separately. The Shafiis consider it forbidden to even recite a single word except when it is with the intention of remembrance such as saying "In the Name of God" (*tasmiyah*), before meals.

The Jafari observe that it is not forbidden for a person in this state of prescribed impurity to recite the Quran except the four surahs, which are Surahs *Iqra, Najm, HaMim (Sajdah)* and *Alif Lam Mim Tanzil.* Reciting a part of them is also forbidden. Apart from these chapters, recital of the Quran is permissible although if it exceeds seven verses it is considered disapproved and the disapproval is aggravated if it exceeds seventy verses.

The Jafari have added to things dependent upon bath lustration for a person in this state of prescribed impurity, fasting during Ramadan and making up for missed fasts. They observe that the fast is not valid if a person remains in this state of prescribed impurity intentionally or forgetfully at dawn. But if he or she sleeps during the day or at night and wakes up in the morning to find that he or she had an emission during sleep, his or her fast remains valid. The Jafari are alone among the schools in holding this view.

1.8.1.3. THE ESSENTIALS OF BATH LUSTRATION FOLLOWING SEXUAL EMISSION

That which is obligatory in a ablution is also obligatory in the bath lustration following sexual emission—such as that the water used should be pure and unmixed, the prior purity of the body from a state of prescribed impurity called *kabath*, and the absence of anything on the body that may prevent water from reaching the skin, as already mentioned while discussing the ablution. Intention is also obligatory, except in the opinion of the Hanafis who do not consider it among the conditions for the validity of the bath lustration.

The Shafii, Hanbali, Hanafi and Maliki schools do not require any particular manner of performing the bath lustration. They consider it sufficient that it should include the whole body in any possible manner, irrespective of whether one begins from the top or the bottom. The Hanafis add that rinsing the mouth and drawing water into the nose is also obligatory. They also say that it is recommended to start with the head, washing next the right half of the body and then the left half. The Shafii and the Maliki schools observe that it is recommended to start with the upper parts of the body before moving to the lower parts, except the private parts, which it is recommended to wash first. According to the Hanbalis, washing the right half before the left is recommended. The Jafari recognize two forms of bath lustration following sexual emission: in sequence (*tartib*) and by immersion (*irtimas*). In the 'in sequence' form, one pours water on himself or herself. Here it is considered obligatory that the start should be made with the head, followed by the right half and then the left. If he or she breaks this order by washing first that which is to come later in the order, the bath lustration would be invalid. In the 'by immersion' form one submerges the whole body under water all at once, and if any part of the body remains unsubmerged it will not suffice. In the opinion of the Jafari bath lustration following sexual emission dispenses the need for ablution. They observe that every bath lustration requires the ablution, as well, except the bath lustration following sexual emission. The other schools do not differentiate between this bath lustration and other bath lustrations in that none of them suffices. The ablution is a requirement.

1.8.2. MENSTRUATION

Menstruation in Arabic (*hayd*) literally means 'flood' and in the terminology of the jurists it is the periodic blood discharge experienced by women during specific days. Its effect is abstention from prescribed worship and termination of the waiting period of a divorcee (if it is the third menses after the divorce). It is usually black or red, thick and warm, and comes out in spurts, although its qualities may differ from those mentioned depending upon constitution.

1.8.2.1. AGE OF MENSTRUATION

All the schools concur that any discharge that occurs before a girl reaches the age of nine years of age cannot possibly be menstrual. It is due to disease or injury. The same is true of the discharge of a woman who has reached the age of menopause. The schools differ concerning the age of menopause. The Hanbalis consider it to be fifty years, the Hanafis as fifty-five, and the Malikis as seventy. The Shafiis observe that as long as a woman is alive she can have menses, though generally it ceases at the age of sixty-two years. The Jafari say that the age of menopause for a non-Qurayshi woman and one whose being Quraysh is doubtful is fifty years and for a Quraysh woman, sixty years.

1.8.2.2. THE PERIOD OF MENSTRUATION

The Hanafis and the Jafaris state that the minimum period of menstruation is three days and the maximum, ten. Hence any discharge that does not last up to three days or exceeds ten days is not considered menstruation. The Hanbalis and the Shafiis observe that the minimum period is one day and night and the maximum fifteen days. According to the Malikis, its maximum period for a non-pregnant woman is fifteen days. They do not specify any minimum period. The Jafaris say that the minimum period between two menstruations is the maximum period of menstruation, that is, ten days.

1.8.2.3. A SUBSIDIARY ISSUE

The schools differ concerning menstruation during pregnancy, as to whether any discharge of blood during it can be considered menstruation or not. The Shafii, Maliki and most Jafari jurists observe that menstruation can accompany pregnancy. The Hanafis, Hanbalis and Shaykh al-Mufid from among the Jafari say that menstruation can never occur during pregnancy.

1.8.2.4. RULES APPLICABLE TO A MENSTRUATING WOMAN

All that is forbidden for a person who is in that state of prescribed impurity because of sexual emission is also forbidden for a menstruating woman, such as touching the script of the Quran, staying in a mosque and so forth. Prescribed prayer and prescribed fasting are not required of her during this period, although she will have to perform the missed days of the prescribed fast of the month of Ramadan. The missed prescribed prayers are not required of her in accordance with the Traditions and for saving her from the strain of performing the large number of daily prayers omitted.

It is forbidden to divorce a menstruating woman although in the opinion of the Shafii, Hanbali, Hanafi and Maliki schools, if given it is valid, although the divorcer will be considered as having sinned. Such a divorce is void in the opinion of the Jafari if the divorcer has consummated the marriage, or is not traveling, or if the divorcee is not pregnant. Thus the divorce of a menstruating woman who is pregnant, or whose marriage has not been consummated, or whose husband is away from home, is valid. This has been discussed in detail in the chapter on divorce.

All the schools concur that bath lustration following menstruation does not suffice for the ablution and the ablution of a menstruating woman prior to bath lustration does not remove her impurity as a result of the discharge of blood. There is also consensus regarding it being forbidden to have sexual intercourse with her during menstruation. As to any other kind of sexual contact with her between her navel and knees, the Jafaris and the Hanbalis say that it is permissible unconditionally, regardless of there being any covering in between or not.

The preponderant (*mashhur*) Maliki opinion is that it is not permissible even if there is a covering in between. The Hanafis and the Shafiis say that it is forbidden without a covering and permissible with it.

Most Jafari jurists observe that if a man, overcome by sexual desire, has intercourse with his menstruating wife, he must atone by giving a dinar in charity if the intercourse occurs during the initial days of the menstruation, a half dinar if in the middle of this period, and a quarter if in its last days.

The Shafii and the Malikis say that it is recommended and not obligatory to give charity. As to the woman, there is no atonement for her in the opinion of all the schools, although she will be considered a sinner if she is willing and co-operative.

1.8.2.5. THE MANNER OF BATH LUSTRATION

The bath lustration following menstruation is exactly like the bath lustration following sexual emission in that the water used should be pure and unmixed, the body should be pure, there should be nothing preventing the water from reaching the skin, the intention should have been made, and, according to the Jafari, the start should be made with the head, followed by the right and then the left half of the body. Also, according to the Jafari, it is sufficient to submerge the entire body under water. The Shafii, Hanbali, Hanafi and Maliki schools consider it sufficient to wash the whole body in any manner, as already mentioned while discussing the bath lustration following sexual emission.

1.8.2.6. INTERMITTENT DISCHARGE OF BLOOD

Intermittent discharge of blood (*istihadah*) is a term used by the jurists for the blood discharge which occurs outside the periods of menstruation and following childbirth and which cannot be considered menstruation (such as a discharge occurring after the maximum period of menstruation or within its minimum period). It is usually yellowish, cold, thin and flows out slowly as opposed to menstruation.

The Jafaris regard a woman having intermittent bleeding to be of three kinds: First, minor (*sughra*) flow when the blood stains the cotton without soaking it. Her duty is to perform the ablution for every prescribed prayer while changing the cotton. Thus she may not perform two prescribed prayers with a single ablution. Second, medium flow (*wusta*) when the blood soaks the cotton without flowing from it. Her duty is to perform one bath lustration every day before daybreak, change the cotton, and to perform the ablution before every prescribed prayer.

Third, major (*kubra*) flow when the blood flows after soaking the cotton. Her duty is to perform three bath lustrations daily, the first before the daybreak prayer, the second for the midday and afternoon prayers and the third for the sunset and night prayers. Most Jafari jurists observe that it is also obligatory in this situation to perform the ablution and change the cotton.

The Shafii, Hanbali, Hanafi and Maliki schools do not recognize these categories, as they do not consider it obligatory for a woman having intermittent bleeding to perform the bath lustration, saying, "She has no obligatory bath lustration to perform for any prescribed prayer or at anytime except a single bath lustration on the termination of menstruation. That is, the bath lustration is for menstruation and not for intermittent bleeding. This has been the opinion of the majority (*jumhur*) of scholars of the former and later generations."[25]

According to Shafii, Hanbali, Hanafi and Maliki schools, those things which are prohibited during menstruation, such as reading and touching the Quran, entering a mosque, retreating in a mosque, circumambulation of the Kabah, sexual intercourse, etc.—as already mentioned in detail while discussing the acts prohibited for one in the state of major impurity—are not prohibited during intermittent bleeding.[26]

The Jafari say that the 'minor' type of intermittent bleeding is considered as being in a state of minor prescribed impurity. Hence nothing that requires a ablution is permissible for her unless she performs the ablution. The 'medium' and 'major' types are regarded as being in a state of major impurity. Therefore, she is prohibited from everything requiring a bath lustration. She is like a menstruating woman as long as she has not performed what has been considered obligatory for her. Once she has performed this obligation, she is considered to be pure and it becomes valid for her to perform the prescribed prayer, enter a mosque, perform circumambulation of the Kabah and have sexual intercourse. The Jafaris regard the manner of performing the bath lustration following intermittent bleeding to be exactly similar to the mode of the bath lustration following menstruation.

1.8.2.7. BLEEDING FOLLOWING CHILDBIRTH

The Jafaris and Malikis state that bleeding following childbirth (*nifas*) is a uterine discharge that occurs during or after childbirth, not before it. The Hanbalis say that it is a discharge which occurs during or after childbirth or up to two or three days before it, along with signs of labor. According to the Shafiis, it occurs only after childbirth and not during or before it. The Hanafis observe that it is a postpartal discharge.

In the opinion of the Shafiis, Hanafis and Malikis, the bath lustration is obligatory upon a woman after giving birth, even if she has not had bleeding. The Jafari and Hanbalis do not consider it obligatory.

All the schools concur that there is no minimum period for bleeding following childbirth, although the maximum period is ten days as per the preponderant Jafari view, forty days in the opinion of the Hanbalis and the Hanafis, and sixty days in the opinion of the Shafiis and the Malikis.

Bleeding following childbirth is like menstruation in that prescribed prayer and prescribed fasting are not permissible, the missed days of fasting are obligatory, sexual intercourse, entering or making a halt in a mosque, and touching the script of the Quran is forbidden and so on. The manner and conditions for this bath lustration are exactly like those of the bath lustration following menstruation.

1.9. TOUCHING A CORPSE

The Shafii, Hanbali, Hanafi and Maliki schools observe that the touching a dead body does not result either in a minor or major impurity and that neither the ablution nor bath lustration is required. But it is recommended for a person who has given bath to a dead body and not just touched it, to perform the bath lustration.

Most Jafaris say that the bath lustration becomes obligatory on touching a corpse after it has turned cold and before it is given the bath provided in the *Shariah*. Hence if it is touched before turning cold and immediately after death or after it has been given the bath lustration for the dead, such a touch will not require anything.

The Jafaris do not differentiate between the corpse of a Muslim and a non-Muslim in relation to the bath lustration becoming obligatory on touch. Similarly they do not differentiate between the age of the dead body, whether it is of an adult, or a child or even a four-month old foetus. There is also no difference between a touch prompted by necessity or by choice. Further, the person touching may be sane or insane, an adult or a child. Hence the bath lustration will become obligatory on an insane person on attaining sanity and on a child on attaining puberty. The Jafaris even require a person who touches an amputated part of a dead or living person to perform the bath lustration if it contains a bone. Accordingly, if he touches an amputated finger of a living person, bath lustration will become obligatory. Also, if a tooth separated from a corpse is touched. But if a separated tooth of a living person is touched, bath lustration will be obligatory only if it has flesh attached to it and not otherwise.

Although the Jafaris require bath lustration on touching a corpse, they regard such a person as being in a state of a minor prescribed impurity, that is, he or she is prohibited from only those acts which require a ablution and not those which require the bath lustration. Therefore, it is valid for him or her to enter a mosque and remain in it, and to recite the Quran. The bath lustration required on touching a corpse is performed like the bath lustration following sexual emission.

1.9.1. THE RULES PERTAINING TO A DEAD BODY
These will be discussed in the following sections:

1.9.1.1. FACING A DYING PERSON TOWARDS THE QIBLAH
The schools differ in regard to how the placing of a dying person towards the *qiblah* (*ihtidar*) should be done. The Jafaris and the Shafiis observe that he or she will be made to lie on his or her back with the soles of his or her feet facing the

qiblah, so that if he or she sits up, he or she will be facing it.

The Malikis, Hanbalis and Hanafis state that the person should be made to recline on his or her right side with his or her face towards the *qiblah*, in the same manner as he or she would be buried.

As the schools differ in the manner of turning the dying person to face the *qiblah*, they also differ regarding its being obligatory. The Shafii, Hanbali, Hanafi and Maliki schools and a group from among the Jafaris consider it recommended and not obligatory, although the preponderant Jafari view is that it is obligatory until someone performs it and then others will be relieved of the duty of performing it (*wajib kifai*) like giving a bath lustration to the dead and their burial. But if no one performs it, they will all be responsible and liable for its neglect (*wajib aini*).

1.9.1.2. THE BATH LUSTRATION OF A CORPSE

The schools concur that a martyr in battle with infidels, will not be given the bath lustration. The schools, excepting the Shafiis, also concur that it is not permissible to give bath lustration for the dead to a non-Muslim. The Shafiis consider it permissible. There is also consensus that a foetus of less than four months does not require the bath lustration for the dead.

They differ where the foetus has completed four months. The Hanbalis and the Jafaris observe that it is obligatory to give it bath lustration for the dead. The Hanafis observe that if it is born alive and then dies or is still-born in a fully developed state, its bath lustration for the dead is obligatory. According to the Malikis, giving the bath lustration will not be obligatory unless a similar baby is considered by knowledgeable persons as capable of survival. The Shafiis state that if it is born after six months, bath lustration for the dead will be given, and even if born before six months, if all parts of its body have fully developed. But if it is not born fully developed but is known to have been alive, then the bath lustration for the dead will be given, but not otherwise.

1.9.1.3. SUBSIDIARY ISSUE

If a part of a corpse is destroyed by fire or disease or is eaten by an animal, will the bath lustration of the rest of the body be obligatory?

The Hanafis say that the bath lustration for the dead will not be obligatory unless most of the body or half of it with the head is present. The Malikis consider bath lustration for the dead to be obligatory if two-thirds of the body is present. The Hanbalis and the Shafiis observe that bath lustration for the dead will be given even if a small part of the body remains. The Jafaris state that if the part of the dead body found includes the chest or a part of it containing the heart, all the rules applicable to a complete corpse will apply to it and it will be given the bath lustration for the dead and shroud and prayer performed. But if the part found does not contain the chest or a part of it, it would be given bath lustration if it contains a bone and then buried by wrapping it in a piece of cloth. And if it does not contain a bone, it will be wrapped in a piece of cloth and buried without a bath lustration for the dead.

1.9.2. THE PERSON GIVING THE BATH LUSTRATION TO THE DEAD

It is obligatory that the person performing the bath lustration for the dead and the dead person being given the bath lustration belong to the same sex: men should give bath lustration for the dead to men and women to women.

The Jafari, Shafii, Maliki and Hanbali schools consider it permissible for either husband or wife to give the bath lustration for the dead to the other upon his or her death. The Hanafis say that it is not permissible for a husband to give the bath lustration for the dead to his wife because her death dissolves the marital bond. The wife, however, can give bath lustration for the dead to her dead husband because she is in her waiting period, that is, the marital bond exists in relation to her while it is nonexistent in relation to the husband.

If she dies after his divorcing her and the divorce is irrevocable, there is consensus that neither of them can give the bath

lustration for the dead to the other. But if it is a revocable
divorce, the Jafaris allow either of them to give the bath lustration for the dead to the other. The Hanafis and the Hanbalis
observe that such a wife can give the bath lustration for the
dead to the dead husband but not vice versa. The Malikis and
the Shafiis state that neither of them may give the bath lustration for the dead to the other. Moreover, they do not differentiate between a revocable and an irrevocable divorce. The
Jafaris allow a woman to give the bath lustration for the dead
to a boy of under three years and allow a man to give the bath
lustration for the dead to a girl of less than three years. The
Hanafis permit up to four years and the Hanbalis up to seven
years. The Malikis observe that a woman can give the bath
lustration to a boy up to the age of eight years and a man can
give a bath lustration to a girl of two years and eight months.

1.9.3. THE MANNER OF BATHING THE DEAD
The Jafaris say that it is obligatory that the dead body be
washed three times, first with water containing a little lotus,
then a second time with water containing a bit of camphor, and
a third time with plain water. The person performing the bath
lustration for the dead should start by first washing the head,
then the right half of the dead body and then the left.

The Shafii, Hanbali, Hanafi and Maliki schools observe
washing only once with plain water is obligatory, and the two
additional washings are recommended. There is no specific
manner of giving the bath lustration and it is valid in any
manner it takes place, just like the bath lustration following
sexual emission. The use of lotus and camphor is not obligatory
in their opinion. Rather, it is recommended if camphor or a
similar perfume is added to the water used for the last bath
wash.

Intention, the plainness and prescribed purity of the water
used, the removal of impurities from the dead body, and the
removal of anything preventing water from reaching the skin,
are indispensable for the validity of the bath lustration for the
dead.

The Jafaris state that it is disapproved to give the bath lustration to a dead body with hot water. The Hanafis say that hot water is better. The Hanbali, Maliki and Shafii schools observe that cold water is recommended.

All the schools concur that camphor is not to be added to water used for the bath lustration for the dead of a person who dies in the sacred state of the pilgrimage to Makkah. Similarly, they are of one opinion that in the sacred state, one must abstain from all kinds of perfumes.

If bath lustration for the dead is not possible due to the non-availability of water, or the body being burnt or affected by a disease in such a manner that it might cause the flesh to fall apart on being washed, there is a consensus that dry ablution would be resorted to in place of bath lustration for the dead. As to the method of the dry ablution, it is like the dry ablution performed by a living person. Details follow in the discussion on dry ablution. A group of Jafari jurists say it is obligatory to perform the dry ablution three times, the first in place of washing with water containing lotus, the second in place of water containing camphor, and the third in place of washing with plain water. But the authorities among them consider a single dry ablution as sufficient.

1.9.4. RUBBING SEVEN PARTS OF A DEAD BODY WITH CAMPHOR

The seven parts of a dead body which touch the ground while prostrating which are to be rubbed (*hunut*) with camphor after the bath lustration for the dead are the forehead, the two palms, the knees, and the heads of the big toes of the feet. The Jafaris alone among the schools consider this as obligatory in this manner and in this regard there is no difference between an adult and a child, even if an aborted foetus, nor between a male and a female, the only exception being a person in the sacred state of the pilgrimage. In addition to the seven locations, they regard the rubbing of the nose as recommended.

1.9.5. THE SHROUD

All the schools consider the providing of a shroud of a dead body as obligatory. The Shafii, Hanbali, Hanafi and Maliki schools observe that which is obligatory in providing a shroud is a single piece of cloth covering the whole body, though the use of three pieces is recommended.

The Jafaris state that the use of three pieces is obligatory, not recommended. The first is called *mizar* and resembles a loin-cloth extending from the navel to the knees; the second is the *qamis*, which covers the body from the shoulders to the shanks; and the third, called *izar*, covers the whole body.

The shroud should possess all the qualities necessary, irrespective of sex, for clothes worn while performing the prescribed prayer, such as their being pure, lawfully owned, their not being made of silk, gold or the skin or fur of an animal which is not eaten, and other qualities which will be mentioned in their appropriate place.

The Jafaris, the Shafiis and the Hanafis consider the husband responsible for the shroud of his wife if he is capable of providing it. The Malikis and the Hanbalis say that it is not compulsory for a husband to provide the shroud of his wife even if she is indigent. The amount necessary for the shroud and other expenses of burial is taken from the legacy of the deceased before the satisfaction of the claims of his or her debtors, the beneficiaries of his or her will, and his or her heirs, though not in preference over the share of the wife and the mortgage of a specific property.

1.9.6. THE DEATH OF AN INDIGENT PERSON

The Shafii, Hanbali, Hanafi and Maliki schools, and a group from among the Jafaris, observe that if the deceased does not leave behind any wealth, his or her shroud will have to be provided by the person who was supposed to maintain him or her when he or she was alive. But if he or she had no supporter, or had but he or she also is indigent, the shroud will be provided from the public treasury or from the poor-due if possible. Otherwise it will be the duty of all Muslims capable of providing it to do so.

A group of Jafari jurists say that if a person dies a pauper and there exists no one who maintained him or her while he or she was alive, it is not obligatory upon anyone to provide him or her with a shroud, because that which is obligatory is the performance of an act and not the spending of wealth. Therefore spending wealth is recommended on the basis of charity, and in the absence of a charitable person he or she will be buried without a shroud.

1.9.7. THE PRESCRIBED PRAYER PERFORMED FOR A MARTYR

The schools concur that it is obligatory to perform the prescribed prayer for Muslims and their children upon their death, irrespective of their school of Divine Law. They also concur that the prescribed prayer is not valid unless performed after the dead body has been given the bath lustration for the dead and shrouded, and that a martyr is not given bath lustration for the dead and shrouded, but is buried in his or her clothes. The Shafiis allow the option between burying him or her in his own or her own clothes and removing them and giving him or her a shroud. The schools differ regarding offering prescribed prayer over a martyr. The Shafiis, Malikis and Hanbalis observe that prescribed prayer will not be offered for him or her. The Jafaris and the Hanafis state that it is obligatory to offer the prescribed prayer for him or her in the same manner as for other dead.[27]

1.9.8. THE PRESCRIBED PRAYER OFFERED FOR CHILDREN

The schools differ regarding the prescribed prayer for a baby. The Shafiis and Malikis say that prescribed prayer will be performed for it if it had cried on being born, that is, the rule applicable to prescribed prayer is the one applied for establishing inheritance. The Hanbalis and Hanafis consider prescribed prayer obligatory for it if it has completed four months in the womb. The Jafari view is that prescribed prayer is not obligatory for the bodies of Muslim children unless they have reached the age of six years, though it is recommended to be performed for children under that age.

1.9.9. FUNERAL PRESCRIBED PRAYER IN ABSENTIA

The Jafari, Maliki and Hanafi schools observe that in no

situation is prescribed prayer *in absentia* valid. They argue that if it had been performed by the Prophet (﷽) and the Companions, it would have become widely known and a record would exist. Moreover, facing the *qiblah* with the dead body's face turned towards it and the presence of the person performing the prescribed prayer for the dead when the body is there are among its necessary conditions.

The Hanbalis and the Shafiis say that the prescribed prayer for the dead in absentia is valid. The basis of their argument is that the Prophet (﷽) performed it on hearing the news of Najashi's death. This argument has been countered by observing that this act was particular to the Prophet (﷽) or was particularly performed in the case of Najashi, and this explains why it was not repeated by the Prophet (﷽) when he heard of the death of prominent Companions who died away from where he was.

1.9.10. THE PARENTS OF THE DECEASED

The Jafaris state that the validity of the obligatory acts—whether bath lustration for the dead, shroud, rubbing seven parts of the body or prescribed prayer for the dead—for preparing the corpse for burial depends upon the permission of the guardians of the deceased. Any of these acts performed without the permission of the guardians are void and their repetition is obligatory. The parent may carry out these himself or herself or allow others to perform them. But where he nor she neither carries them out himself or herself nor permits others to perform them, his or her permission has is not needed.

The Jafaris give precedence to the husband in guardianship as regards the wife over all other relatives, and the parents besides the husband stand in the order applicable to inheritance. Hence the first category, which consists of her father and sons, has precedence over the second category, which includes her grandfather and brothers, which in turn has precedence over the third category to which paternal and maternal uncles belong. The father is given priority over all others in the first category and the grandfather over the brothers in the second. Where no male exists in a category, the right to guardianship will belong to the female relatives. Where there are several brothers or paternal and maternal uncles, the funeral rites will depend upon the permission of all of them. The Shafii, Hanbali, Hanafi and Maliki schools have made no mention of the parent while discussing the bath lustration for the dead and shroud, and this proves that his permission has no significance in their opinion for the performance of these rites. They do say who enjoys priority and has a better right to offer the prescribed prayer for the dead for the dead body. The Hanafis observe that those who have priority are the ruler, then his representative, then the judge, then the police chief, then the deceased person's imam in his life if he is higher in rank than the parent of the deceased, then the parent, and then as per the order applicable to authority with respect to marital affairs.

The Shafiis say that the father of the deceased will come first, followed by the son, then the full brother, then the brother on father's side, and so on in the order of inheritance. The Malikis state that foremost is the person whom the deceased has appointed in his or her will for performing the prescribed prayer for his or her body seeking the blessings of the former's righteousness. After him comes the caliph, then the son, the grandson, the father, the brother, the brother's son, the grandfather, the paternal uncle, etc., in the descending order. The Hanbalis give priority to the fair and just executor of the will, followed by the ruler, his representative, the father, the son, and so on in the order of inheritance.[28]

1.9.11. UNCERTAINTY CONCERNING A CORPSE

When a body is found and it is not known whether it belongs to a Muslim or a non-Muslim, if it is found in a Muslim locality it will be considered a Muslim's body; otherwise anyone who sees it has no obligation, for there is a doubt concerning the obligation itself.

Where the bodies of Muslims and non-Muslims are mixed and differentiating them is not possible, the Jafaris, Hanbalis and Shafiis observe that the prescribed prayer will be performed on all of them with a conditional intention of "if he is a

Muslim." The Hanafis say that the majority will be taken into consideration, and if the majority of bodies belong to Muslims, the prescribed prayer will be performed, not otherwise.

1.9.12. THE MANNER OF THE PRESCRIBED PRAYER

The dead body will be laid on its back and the persons offering the prayer will stand not far behind it[29] facing the *qiblah* with the head of the body to his or her right. There should be no intervening barrier in the form of a wall and the like and the persons performing the prayer should be standing unless they have a legitimate excuse. Then he or she will make the necessary intention and say, *"Allahu akbar"* (*takbir*, "God is Greater") four times.

The Malikis observe that a supplication (*dua*) is obligatory after each of the four *"Allahu akbars"* and the least that the persons performing the prayer must say is, "O God, pardon this deceased." If the deceased is a child, the supplication will be made for the parents. Greetings will be said after the fourth *"Allahu akbar"* and the persons performing the prescribed prayer for the dead will not raise their hands except in the first *"Allahu akbar."*

The Hanafis say that God will be praised after the first *"Allahu akbar,"* greetings and salutations (*salawat*) on the Prophet will be said after the second, the supplication (*dua*) after the third, and greetings and salutations after the fourth. The persons performing the prescribed prayer will not lift their hands except in the first *"Allah akbar."*

The Shafiis and the Hanbalis state that the first chapter of the Quran (*Surat al-Fatihah*) will be recited after the first *"Allah akbar,"* greetings and salutations to the Prophet after the second, supplication after the third, and greetings and salutations after the fourth. The person offering the prescribed prayer will lift his hands at every *"Allah akbar."*

According to the Jafaris, five recitations of *"Allahu akbar"* are obligatory in consonance with the number of daily prescribed prayers. The person offering the prescribed prayer will recite the two testaments (*shahadatayn*) after the first *Allahu akbar*; greetings and salutations for the Prophet after the second; supplication for the faithful, men and women, after the third; supplication for the deceased after the fourth; and end with the fifth without reciting anything after it. Lifting the hands at every *"Allahu akbar"* is recommended.

Our intention in mentioning these short forms was to show the minimum which is obligatory, otherwise all the schools have lengthy prescribed prayers which are mentioned in their appropriate place.

The Shafii, Hanbali, Hanafi and Maliki schools require prescribed purity and covering of the private parts while performing the prescribed prayer over the deceased, in the same manner as in the daily prescribed prayers. The Jafaris say that here prescribed purity and covering of the private parts are not conditions for its validity, though they are recommended. This is because the prescribed prayer for the dead said for the deceased is not the prescribed prayer in the real sense. Rather, it is a prayer or supplication, and hence, in their opinion, the leader (*imam*) in this prescribed prayer does not recite anything on behalf of the deceased.

1.9.13. THE PLACE OF THE PRESCRIBED PRAYER

The Shafiis observe that it is recommended to offer the prescribed prayer for the dead in a mosque. The Hanafis consider it disapproved to do so. The Jafaris and the Hanbalis consider it permissible provided there is no fear of contaminating the mosque.

1.9.14. TIME OF THE PRESCRIBED PRAYER

The Shafiis and the Jafaris state that the prescribed prayer for the dead can be performed at any time. The Maliki, Hanbali and Hanafi schools say that the prescribed prayer may not be performed at sunrise, midday and sunset.

1.9.15. THE BURIAL

The schools concur that it is not permissible, except where necessary, to place the body on the surface of the ground and to raise a tomb over it without digging, even if it it placed in a coffin. It is obligatory to place it in a pit, where it would be secure and which would keep its smell from spreading. They also concur that the body should be laid to rest on its right side with its face towards the qiblah and the head to the West and the feet to the East.[30] The Malikis say to lay the body to rest in this manner is recommended and not obligatory.

The Jafaris observe that a woman must be lowered into the grave by her husband or anyone from among her male relatives within prohibited degrees of marriage, or by other women. If none of these are present, then any righteous person may do it. The Hanbalis and the Hanafis state that the husband becomes a stranger after dissolution of the marital bond on death. Al-Ghazzali, a Shafii, observes, "Only a man may lower the body into the grave. Therefore, if the deceased is a woman, her husband or person related to her through kinship to whom marriage is forbidden may perform it, and in their absence her slaves, followed by two eunuchs, her relatives and then strangers."[31] This implies that a male stranger is preferred over a woman.

1.10. DISPOSING OF A CORPSE IN THE SEA

If a person dies on a ship far away from land, if it is possible to retain it for burial on land, retaining it will be obligatory. But if there is a fear of decay, it will be given the bath lustration for the dead and shrouded and the prescribed prayer for the dead recited and then it will be placed in a firm coffin or a barrel which can be capped and thrown into the sea. If this is not possible, a piece of iron or a stone will be tied to it. It is obvious that the jurists have dealt with this and similar issues because during those days there was no means of preserving the body from decay. But today, when it is possible to place it in cold storage or use other means which save the dead body from mutilation and harm, to retain the body becomes obligatory even if it is for a prolonged period of time.

1.11. MAKING THE GRAVE LEVEL WITH THE GROUND

All the schools concur that the *Sunnah* in respect of the grave is to make it at level with the ground, because the

Prophet did so while making the grave of his son, Ibrahim. This *Sunnah* is accepted by the Jafaris and the Shafiis.

1.12. REOPENING THE GRAVE

All the schools concur that it is forbidden to reopen the grave, irrespective of whether the deceased is an adult or a child, sane or insane, unless the body is known to have decomposed and turned into dust or there is cause to be concerned for the body, such as where the grave is in the way of a flood or at the bank of a river, or it has been buried in a usurped land either forcefully or due to ignorance or negligence and the owner refuses to give permission and take compensation, or if it has been wrapped in an impermissible kind of shroud, or when something of value belonging to the deceased or someone else has been buried along with the body.

The schools differ regarding reopening where the body has been buried without a bath lustration for the dead or after it which is not valid in the Divine Law. In this regard, the Hanafis and some Jafaris observe that it is not valid because it is irreverent and may cause mutilation of the corpse. The Hanbalis, Shafii, Malikis and most Jafari jurists observe that it may be reopened and bath lustration for the dead and prescribed prayer for the dead performed provided there is no fear of its having decayed. Some Jafaris further add that it may also be reopened where the establishment of a claim or right is dependent upon the examination of the body.

1.13. DRY ABLUTION

Performing dry ablution as a substitute for the ablution is justified under certain circumstances. It is performed in a particular manner and with specific substances and there are certain rules which are applicable to it.

1.13.1. CONDITIONS IN WHICH DRY ABLUTION IS PERFORMED

The schools differ concerning the permissibility of dry ablution by a healthy person who is not travelling, in the event of his or her not finding water for the ablution. The question is, does the absence of water justify the performance of dry ablution only in the state of journey or ill health, or is the permissibility general and includes the state of health and non-travel?

Imam Abu Hanifah observes that a healthy person who is not traveling will neither perform dry ablution nor prescribed prayer if he or she is unable to find water.[32] He cites a verse in the Quran as the basis of this opinion, *"If you are sick or on a journey, or if any of you comes from the privy, or you have touched women, and you can find no water, then perform dry ablution on wholesome dust"* (5: 6).

The Hanafis say that this verse is explicit and that the sole unavailability of water does not justify dry ablution unless the person is sick or on a journey. Therefore, if dry ablution is limited to a sick person and a traveler, a healthy person who is not traveling has no obligation to perform prescribed prayer in this situation because he or she cannot acquire prescribed purity.

The remaining schools concur that a person not possessing water will perform dry ablution and offer the prescribed prayer regardless of his or her being a traveler or not and irrespective of his or her being healthy or sick. This is in consonance with the following Tradition accepted by all the schools, "Wholesome dust is surely a purifier for a Muslim even if he does not find water for ten years." These schools omit the condition of travel mentioned in the verse since it also implies the usual non-availability of water during journeys in the past.

Apart from this, if the argument of Imam Abu Hanifah be accepted, the position of a traveler and a sick person would be more taxing than that of a non-traveling healthy person, because the prescribed prayer will be obligatory on the two and not on the latter.

The Shafiis and the Hanbalis say that if water available is not sufficient for performing complete prescribed purity, it is obligatory to perform as much of it as is possible with water and to do dry ablution for the remaining parts. Hence if he or she has water which is only sufficient for washing the face, he or she will wash the face and then resort to dry ablution. The other schools observe that the presence of insufficient water is equivalent to its absence, and nothing is obligatory in such a situation except dry ablution.

However, the issue of non-availability of water does not have that applicability in our times because water is available in sufficient quantity for all people and at all places, at home as well as during travel. The reason the jurists dealt in detail with the obligation of searching for water and the extent of effort to be made, and with the case when there is a danger to one's life, possessions or honor from robbers and wild animals and the case where he or she finds a well without a bucket, and the case where he or she has to pay more than the usual price for it, etc., was that travelers used to face great difficulty in obtaining water.

1.13.2. AVOIDING HARM TO HEALTH

The schools concur that among the reasons justifying dry ablution is the harm the use of water may do to one's health or the probability of such a harm. Anyone who fears falling ill, or fears that his illness would become more acute or prolonged or that its cure would become more difficult, can resort to dry ablution for prescribed purity instead of using water.

1.13.3. SUBSIDIARY ISSUE

Where there is no time for using water such as when a person wakes up in the morning and finds so little time left for the obligatory prescribed prayer that if he or she intends to procure water for prescribed purity, he or she would have to perform the prayer as a missed one after the appointed time while if he or she resorts to dry ablution, he or she would be able to perform it on time, is it obligatory for such a person to perform the dry ablution or must he or she perform the ablution with water?

The Malikis and the Jafaris observe that he or she should perform the prescribed prayer by dry ablution, but must repeat the prescribed prayer with ablution. The Shafiis say that in no situation is dry ablution permissible in the presence of water. The Hanbalis differentiate between the states of journey and stay, observing that if such a situation arises during a journey, he or she must perform the prescribed prayer with dry ablution without being required to repeat it. If it arises during a state of non-travel, there will be no justification for dry ablution.

The Hanafis state that dry ablution is permissible in such a situation for performing those supererogatory (*nafilah*) prescribed prayers which have a specific time of performance, like the *Sunnah* prayers after the noon and sunset prayer. But dry ablution is not permissible for a prescribed prayer if water is available, even if there is insufficient time; rather, he or she will perform the ablution and perform the missed prescribed prayer, and if he or she performs it with a dry ablution during the appointed time, he or she will have to repeat it after the time has passed.

1.13.4. THE SUBSTANCE WITH WHICH DRY ABLUTION IS PERFORMED

There is a consensus among the schools regarding the obligations of performing dry ablution on 'wholesome dust' (*al-said al-tahur*) in consonance with the verse and the Tradition, "The earth has been created a place for performing prostration and as a purifier." *Tayyib* means 'pure', and 'pure' means that which has not come into contact with impurities.

The schools differ concerning the interpretation of the word '*said*'. The Hanafis and a group of Jafaris understand it to mean the ground surface and therefore permit dry ablution on dust, sand and rocks and prohibit it on minerals such as quicklime, salt, arsenic, etc. The Shafiis interpret it as earth (*turab*) and sand and consider dry ablution obligatory on these two if they contain fine dust. They do not permit dry ablution on stones. The Hanbalis take it to mean only dust and hence dry ablution is not valid in their opinion if performed on sand and stones. This is also the opinion of most Jafari jurists, although they allow it on sand and rocks in case of necessity. The Malikis take the word *said* rather liberally and include in its meaning dust, sand, rocks, snow and minerals provided they have not been moved from their place. But they exclude gold, silver and precious stones and do not permit dry ablution on them under any condition.

1.13.5. THE MANNER OF PERFORMING DRY ABLUTION

The schools concur that dry ablution is not valid without intention. Even the Hanafis observe that it is required in dry ablution although not in the ablution. As they accept that dry ablution removes impurity (*hadath*) like the ablution and bath lustration, they allow the intention of removing impurity (*hadath*) to be made for its performance just like the intention of permissibility of the prescribed prayer (*istibahat al-salat*).

The other schools state that dry ablution only permits impurity (*hadath*) without removing it. Hence a person performing the dry ablution should make intention of permissibility of that which requires prescribed purity and not intention of the removal of the impurity (*hadath*). But a Jafari jurist says that the intention of removal of impurity (*hadath*) is valid with the knowledge that dry ablution does not remove it, because the intention of removal of impurity necessarily implies the intention of permissibility.

The best way of reconciling all these opinions for a person performing dry ablution is that he or she state the intention of seeking the nearness of God by obeying the command pertaining to dry ablution, irrespective of whether this command pertains to it as such or arises from the command of prescribed prayer or some other act which requires the performance of dry ablution.

The schools, in the same way as they differ in interpreting the word *said*, also differ in their interpretation of the words *wajh* (face) and *aydi* (hands) occurring in the verse. The Shafii, Hanbali, Hanafi and Maliki schools and Ibn Babawayh, a Jafari, say that by *wajh* is meant the whole face including the beard, and by *yadayn*, the hands and the wrists along with the elbows. Accordingly, the parts of the face and arms to be wiped in dry ablution are exactly the same as are washed in the ablution. Thus the hands will be struck twice on that with which dry ablution is valid. The first time the whole face will be wiped and the second time the two arms from the end of the fingers to the elbows. The Malikis and the Hanbalis say that the wiping of the hands is obligatory up to the wrist-bones, and recommended (*Sunnah*) up to the elbows. The Jafaris state that the word *wajh* is to be interpreted as 'part of the face' because '*ba*' in the verse connotes the meaning of a part when prefixed to an object (*maful*). And if the *ba* does not signify a part, it will have to be considered superfluous because the verb *amsahu* is transitive by itself. The part of the face that must be wiped in their opinion is from the upper part of the forehead where the hair grow, to the upper part of the nose including the eye-brows. They say, "By *yadayn* is meant only the hands (*kaffan*). Since the word *yad* in Arabic has various meanings and the most common of them in usage is *kaff*."[33]

Accordingly, the manner of performing the dry ablution in the Jafari school is by first striking on the earth with the palms and wiping the face from where the hair grows to the upper part of the nose, then striking a second time and wiping the entire back of the right hand with the left palm and then the entire back of the left hand with the right palm.

The Jafaris also consider sequence to be obligatory. Hence, if the hands are wiped before the face, the dry ablution becomes invalid. Similarly, it is necessary to start from the top and proceed downwards. Doing the opposite would invalidate it. Most of them consider striking on the earth as obligatory, so that if one only places his hands on it without striking, the dry ablution is invalidated. The Hanafis observe that if dust settles on his or her face and one places his or her hand on it and wipes it, he or she can do without striking the earth.

All the schools concur that the prescribed purity of the parts of the body involved in dry ablution is a necessary condition, irrespective of whether it is the wiping or the wiped part. The same applies to the substance on which dry ablution is being performed. They also concur that it is essential to remove one's ring while performing dry ablution and that just moving it, as in ablution is not sufficient.

They differ concerning continuity; the Jafaris and the Malikis require it between its different parts. Hence if there is a time gap between them which vitiates continuity the dry ablution becomes invalid.

The Hanbalis say that both continuity and sequence are obligatory if the dry ablution is for minor impurity (*hadath*), but none for major impurity (*hadath*). The Shafiis require sequence, not continuity. The Hanafis require neither sequence nor continuity.

1.13.6. THE RULES OF DRY ABLUTION

All the schools, except the Hanafi, concur that it is not valid to perform dry ablution for a prescribed prayer before its time has arrived. The Hanafis say that dry ablution is valid before the arrival of time.

The Jafaris observe that if one performs dry ablution before the time of prescribed prayer for any other purpose for which dry ablution is permissible and then the time of prescribed prayer arrives while his or her dry ablution is still intact, he or she may perform the prescribed prayer with that dry ablution. The Jafaris and the Hanafis allow the performance of two pre-scribed prayers with a single dry ablution. The Shafiis and the Malikis say that it is not permissible to offer two obligatory (*fard*) prescribed prayers with a single dry ablution. The Hanbalis allow them, both for the on time and missed pre-scribed prayers.

After one performs the dry ablution in accordance with the Shariah, he or she will be like one who has performed pre-scribed purity with water. Everything which is permissible for the latter will be permissible for him or her. The dry ablution is broken by all those kinds of major and minor impurities (*hadath*) which require renewal of the ablution or bath lustra-tion, as well as on the disappearance of the excuse of unavail-ability of water or disease.

If water becomes available after the performance of dry ablution but before beginning the prescribed prayer, the dry ablution becomes invalid in the opinion of all the schools. If it becomes available while he or she is performing the prescribed prayer, some Jafaris say that if that happens before his or her first bowing forward, both the dry ablution and prescribed prayer will be invalidated, and if after the first bowing forward, he or she will complete the prescribed prayer, which will be deemed valid.

The Shafiis, Malikis and Hanbalis, in one of the two opinions narrated by them, as well as some Jafaris state that after saying the first recitation of *"Allahu akbar"* which begins the sacred state (*takbir al-ihram*), he or she will continue the prescribed prayer without paying attention to the availability of water, and the prescribed prayer will be valid because God Almighty says, *"And do not invalidate your acts."* The Hanafis observe that such a prescribed prayer will be invalid. The schools concur that if the justification for performing dry ablution disappears after the performance of the prescribed prayer while there is still time, one is not obliged to repeat the prescribed prayer again.

If a person in state of a prescribed impurity following sexual emission performs dry ablution in place of bath lustration and then a minor impurity occurs and there is water enough for only performing the ablution, will the ablution be obligatory along with the repetition of dry ablution in place of the bath lustration?

The Malikis and most Jafaris observe that he or she will perform dry ablution in the place of the bath lustration. The Hanafis, Shafiis, Hanbalis and a group of Jafaris state that he or she will perform the ablution because the dry ablution was in place of the prescribed impurity following sexual emission and was broken by something other than sexual emission. Hence he or she will not be in the state of prescribed impurity following sexual emission again unless the sexual emission recurs, and he or she will be considered as being affected only by the minor impurity (*hadath*).

The Hanbalis differ from all the other schools in their acceptance of dry ablution for material impurities present on the body.[34]

If both the ways of acquiring prescribed purity (that is, with water and/or dry ablution) are not possible (such as in the case of a person who is imprisoned in a place where there is neither water nor any substance on which dry ablution is performed, or he or she is so ill that he or she can neither perform the ablution nor the dry ablution and there is no one to help him or her in performing them) will it be obligatory to perform the prescribed prayer without the prescribed purity? Further, presuming that the prescribed prayer is obligatory and he or she performs it, must he or she repeat it after prescribed purity becomes possible?

The Malikis say that he or she is not required to perform the prescribed prayer, neither on time or as missed. The Hanafis and Shafiis observe that it will remain obligatory, either as on time or missed. In the opinion of the Hanafis, the meaning of performing it on time is that he or she will simulate the movements of a person performing the prescribed prayer, while the Shafiis require him or her to perform the real prescribed prayer. After the excuse disappears, he or she will repeat this prescribed prayer as required by the *Shariah*. Most Jafaris state that he or she is not required to offer it on time, although it will remain obligatory as a missed prescribed prayer. The Hanbalis consider it obligatory as on time without it being so as missed.

1.13.7. THE SCHOOLS AND THE VERSE CONCERNING DRY ABLUTION

It is clear from the discussion on the topics of mixed water, the causes which invalidate the ablution, and dry ablution, that the difference of opinion among the schools of Islamic jurisprudence relate mostly to the interpretation of the words of the verse dealing with dry ablution. *"If you are sick or on a journey, or if any of you comes from the privy, or you have touched women and you can find no water, then perform dry ablution on wholesome dust and wipe your faces"* (5:6).

The jurists first differ concerning one for whom dry ablution is obligatory in the event of unavailability of water: is it one who is sick or on a journey, or does it also apply to a healthy non-traveler? Is the meaning of 'touching' women sexual intercourse or just touching them with the hand? Does the word 'water' mean only plain water (*mal-mutlaq*) or does it include mixed water as well? Does the word *said* mean just dust or does it signify the surface of the earth, irrespective of its being dusty, sandy or rocky? Does the word *wajh* mean the

complete face or just a part of it? Does the word *yad* imply only
the hand or does it include the hand and the forearm? Here we
will give a summary of the opinions discussed.

The Hanafi school observes that dry ablution is not valid in
the absence of water for a healthy person who is not traveling,
and thus the prescribed prayer is also not obligatory upon him
or her because the verse permits only a sick person and a traveler to perform dry ablution in the absence of water.

The Shafii, Hanbali, Hanafi and Maliki schools say that
touching a woman who is a 'stranger' with the hand has exactly the same effect as returning from the privy and breaks the
ablution. The Jafaris state that sexual intercourse breaks the
state of prescribed purity and not touching with the hand.

The Hanafis say that the meaning of it is water, pure or
mixed. The other schools say that the word 'water' occurring in
the verse is commonly understood to mean plain water and not
mixed water.

The Hanafis and a group of the Jafaris observe that the
word *said* means dust, sand and rock. The Shafiis say that it
means only dust and sand. According to the Hanbalis it means
only dust. The Malikis state that it includes dust, sand, rock,
snow and minerals. The Shafii, Hanbali, Hanafi and Maliki
schools say that by *wajh* in the verse is meant the whole face.
The Jafari say that it means only a part of it.

The Shafii, Hanbali, Hanafi and Maliki schools observe
that the word *aydi* should be interpreted as including the
hands, wrists and elbows. The Jafaris consider it to mean only
the hands.

This difference of opinion among the schools, if it proves
anything, proves that this divergence of views is superficial,
not substantial, and one of language and not of principle. It
resembles the difference between philologists concerning a particular word or between men of letters concerning the interpretation of a verse or couplet. This is the reason why we find that
jurists belonging to the same school differ among themselves
exactly like one school differing with another.

2

PRESCRIBED PRAYER

Prescribed prayer (*salat*) is either obligatory (*wajib*) or supererogatory (*mandub*). The most important of prayers are the prescribed prayers performed five times daily. There is consensus among Muslims that a person who denies or doubts their being obligatory is not a Muslim, even if he or she recites the two testimonies bearing witness to the oneness of God and the prophethood of Muhammad (☼) (*shahadah*), for these prescribed prayers are among the 'pillars' (*arkan*) of Islam. Their being obligatory is an established necessity of the faith (*al-din*) that does not need any strenuous endeavor to reason (*ijtihad*) or study, following the dictates of an expert (*taqlid*) or questioning.

The schools differ regarding a person who does not perform the prescribed prayers (*tark al-salat*) due to laziness and neglect although the person believes in its being obligatory. The Shafiis, Malikis and Hanbalis observe that he or she will be killed. The Hanafis state that he or she will receive perpetual imprisonment unless he or she starts performing the prescribed prayers. The Jafaris state that whoever neglects any obligatory duty such as the prescribed prayers, paying of alms (*zakat/khums*), going once in a lifetime on the prescribed pilgrimage to Makkah (*hajj*) and the prescribed fasting (*sawm*), will be chastened by the judge (*hakim*) in a manner deemed appropriate by him. [1]

2.1. THE DAILY SUPEREROGATORY PRAYERS

Supererogatory prayers (*rawatib*) are of various kinds, and among them are those which are performed along with the prescribed daily prayers. The schools differ regarding the number of their cycles (*rakahs*). The Shafiis consider them to be eleven cycles: two before the morning (*fajr*) prayer, two before the noon (*zuhr*) prayer and two after it, two after the sunset (*maghrib*) prayer, two after the night (*isha*) prayer and a single cycle called '*al-watirah*'.

The Hanbalis consider them to be ten cycles: two cycles before and after the noon prescribed prayer, two after the sunset and the night prescribed prayers, and two cycles before the morning prescribed prayer. According to the Malikis there is no fixed number for the supererogatory (*nawafil*) prayers performed with the prescribed prayer, although it is best to offer four cycles before the noon and six after the evening prescribed prayer. The Hanafis classify the supererogatory performed along with the obligatory into '*masnunah*' and '*mandubah*'.[2] The '*masnunah*' are five: two cycles before the morning prescribed prayer; four before the noon, and two after it, except on Friday; two after the evening and two after the night prescribed prayer. The '*mandubah*' are four: four or two cycles before the afternoon, six after the evening, and four before and after the night prescribed prayer. The Jafaris observe that the supererogatory are thirty-four cycles: eight before the noon prescribed prayer, eight before the afternoon, four after the evening, two after the night (recited while sitting and counted as a single cycle called '*al-watirah*'), eight cycles of the midnight prayer (*salat al-layl*), two cycles of *al-shaf*, a single of *al-watr*, [3] and two cycles before the morning prayer, called '*salat al-fajr*'.

2.1.1. THE TIME OF NOON AND AFTERNOON PRESCRIBED PRAYERS

The jurisprudents begin their discussions with the prescribed noon prayer, because it was the first prescribed prayer to be declared obligatory, followed by the afternoon, the evening, the night and the morning prescribed prayers, in that order. All the five prescribed prayers were made obligatory in Makkah on the night of Prophet's Nocturnal Journey (*isra*), nine years after the beginning of his mission. Those who hold this opinion cite as proof the Quranic verse which stipulates all the five prescribed prayers, "*Perform the prescribed prayer from the declining of the sun to the darkening of the night and the recital of the dawn; surely the recital of the dawn is witnessed*" (17:78).

The schools concur that the prescribed prayer is not valid if performed before its appointed time and that the time of the noon prescribed prayer sets in when the sun passes the meridian. They differ concerning its duration. The Jafaris say that the specific period of the noon prescribed prayer extends from the moment the sun crosses the meridian up to a period required to perform it, and the specific period of the afternoon prescribed prayer is the duration required to perform it just before sunset. The time between these two specific periods is the common period for the two prescribed prayers. That is the reason they consider it valid to perform both the prescribed prayers successively during their common period.[4] But if the time remaining for the end of the day is sufficient only for performing the noon prescribed prayer, the afternoon prescribed prayer will be offered first with the intention (*niyyah*) of being on time (*ada*) and later the noon prescribed prayer will be performed as delayed (*qada*).

The Hanafi, Hanbali, Shafii and Maliki schools observe that the time of the noon prescribed prayer begins when the sun crosses the meridian and continues until the shadow of an object becomes as long as its height. When the length of the shadow exceeds the height of the object, the time for the noon prescribed prayer comes to an end. Here the Shafiis and the Malikis add that these limits are for an unconstrained person (*mukhtar*), and for one who is constrained (*mudtarr*), the time for noon prescribed prayer extends even after an object's shadow equals its height. The Jafaris consider the time when an object's shadow equals its height as the best time for the noon prescribed prayer, and when it equals twice the height of the object as the best time for the afternoon prescribed prayer.

The Hanafis and the Shafiis state that the time of the afternoon prescribed prayer begins when the length of an object's shadow exceeds its height and continues up to sunset. The Malikis say that there are two times for the afternoon prescribed prayer, the first for ordinary circumstances and the second for exigencies. The former begins with an object's shadow exceeding its height and lasts until the sun turns pale. The latter begins from when the sun turns pale and continues until sunset.

The Hanbalis observe that one who delays offering the afternoon prescribed prayer until after an object's shadow exceeds twice its height, his or her prescribed prayer will be considered on time if performed before sunset, although he or she will have sinned because it is forbidden to delay it until this time. They are alone in all the schools in holding this opinion.

2.1.2. THE TIME OF EVENING AND NIGHT PRESCRIBED PRAYERS

The Shafii and the Hanbali schools state that the time for the evening prescribed prayer begins when the sun sets and ends when the reddish afterglow on the western horizon vanishes. The Malikis say that the duration for the evening prescribed prayer is narrow and confined to the time required after sunset to perform the evening prescribed prayer along with its preliminaries of prescribed purity and the call to prayer (*adhan*), and it is not permissible to delay it voluntarily. But in an emergency, the time for the evening prescribed prayer extends until dawn. The Malikis are alone in considering it impermissible to delay the evening prescribed prayer beyond its initial time. The Jafaris observe that the period specific to the evening prescribed prayer extends from sunset[5] for a duration required to perform it and the specific period of the night prescribed prayer is the duration required to finish it before midnight. The time between these two specific periods is the common time for both evening prescribed and night prescribed prayers. Hence they allow the joint performance of these two prescribed prayers during this common time.

That was with respect to someone who is in a position to act out of free choice, but as to a person constrained by sleep or forgetfulness, the time for these two prescribed prayers exceeds until dawn, which the period specific for the night prescribed prayer becoming the time required to perform it just before dawn and the specific period for the evening prescribed prayer becoming the time required to perform it just after midnight.

2.1.3. THE TIME OF MORNING PRESCRIBED PRAYER

There is consensus among the schools, with the exception of the Maliki, that the time for the morning prescribed prayer begins at daybreak (*al-fajr al-sadiq*) and lasts until sunrise. The Malikis say that the morning prescribed prayer has two times. For one in a position to act out of free choice it begins with daybreak and lasts until there is enough twilight for faces to be recognized and for one in constrained circumstances, it begins from the time when faces are recognizable and continues up to sunrise.

2.1.4. THE QIBLAH

The schools concur that the Kabah is the *qiblah* of one who is near it and is able to see it. They differ regarding the *qiblah* of one who is away from the Kabah and unable to see it. The Hanafis, Malikis, Hanbalis and a group of Jafari jurisprudents observe that the *qiblah* of one at a distance is the direction of the Kabah and not the Kabah itself.

The Shafiis and most Jafaris state that it is obligatory for one who is near the Kabah, as well as for one at a distance, to face the Kabah itself. Thus, if it is possible to ascertain that one is facing the Kabah itself, one must do so; otherwise the probability (*zann*) that one may be facing it is sufficient. It is obvious that one who is far away from the Kabah is in no way capable of ascertaining that he is facing the Kabah, considering that the earth is spherical. Consequently, the *qiblah* of one away from the Kabah will be the direction of the Kabah and not the Kabah itself.[6]

2.1.5 IGNORANCE OF THE DIRECTION OF THE QIBLAH

It is obligatory for a person ignorant of the direction of the *qiblah* to inquire and strive to determine its exact or approximate direction, and in case neither of the two is possible, the Hanafi, Hanbali, Maliki, and Shafii schools and a group from among the Jafaris say that a person may perform the prescribed prayer in any direction. His or her prescribed prayer will be valid and it will not be obligatory for him or her to repeat it except in the opinion of the Shafiis. Most Jafaris observe that the person will perform the prescribed prayer in four directions to comply with the command for the prescribed prayer and to ascertain its proper performance. But if there is not sufficient time for performing the prescribed prayer four times or if one is incapable of performing it in four directions, he or she will perform the prescribed prayer in the directions that he or she can.

2.1.6. A SUBSIDIARY ISSUE

If a person prays not facing the *qiblah* and comes to know about his or her mistake, the Jafaris state that if the error is known during the prescribed prayer and the correct *qiblah* lies between his or her two hands, the part of the prescribed prayer already performed will be valid and he or she will have to correct his or her direction for the remaining part of the prescribed prayer. But if it is known that he or she has been praying facing the East, or the West, or the North with his or her back towards the *qiblah* (this is with reference to Lebanon where the *qiblah* lies to the south), the prescribed prayer will be invalid and he or she will perform it anew. If the error is known after performing the prescribed prayer, it should be performed again if its time is still there, not otherwise. Some Jafaris say that the prescribed prayer will not be repeated if there is only a little deviation from the *qiblah*, irrespective of

whether its time is still there or not. But if it has been performed facing the East or the West, it should be repeated if
there is time, not otherwise. If the prescribed prayer is performed with one's back to the *qiblah*, it should be repeated
regardless of whether its time is still there or has passed.

The Hanafis and the Hanbalis observe that if after inquir-
ing and striving to find the *qiblah*, one is unable to ascertain
its approximate direction and performs the prescribed prayer
in a direction which turns out to be wrong, he or she must
change his or her direction accordingly if the mistake becomes
known during the prescribed prayer. However, if it is known
afterwards, his or her prescribed prayer is valid and the person
has no further obligation. The Shafiis say that if it becomes
certain that there has been a mistake in determining the
qiblah, it is obligatory to repeat the prescribed prayer, but if
there is only a likelihood of mistake, the prescribed prayer is
valid irrespective of whether the probability arises during the
prescribed prayer or after it.

As to one who neither makes an inquiry nor an effort to
determine the *qiblah*, but by chance performs the prescribed
prayer in the right direction, the Malikis and Hanbalis consider his or her prescribed prayer to be void (*batil*). The opinion of
the Jafaris and the Hanafis is that his or her prescribed prayer
is valid provided the person has no doubts while praying and
was sure about the direction of the *qiblah* at the time of starting the prescribed prayer, because, as pointed out by the
Jafaris, in such a situation it is correct for the person to make
the intention of acquiring nearness (*qurbah*) to God.

2.1.7. THE RULES OF MODESTY

This issue is one of those from which numerous bylaws are
derived, such as those specifying the parts of one's body that
must be covered (*awrah*) and the parts of another person's
body which it is forbidden to look at, those relating to the difference between relatives through marriage or lineage with
whom marriage is prohibited (*mahram*), the difference is due
to sameness or difference of sex, the difference between looking

and touching and similar rules which are discussed below.

2.1.7.1. Looking at One's Own Body

The schools differ concerning covering of one's private parts from one's own view and whether it is forbidden for one to uncover one's private parts in privacy. The Hanafis and the Hanbalis observe that in the same way that it is not permissible for a person to expose his or her private parts in the presence of anyone for whom it is not permissible to look at it, it is not permissible for him or her to expose them when alone without necessity, as arises at the time of bathing or answering the call of nature. The Malikis and Shafiis say that it is not unlawful, but disapproved (*makruh*) to be naked without necessity. The Jafaris, state that it is neither forbidden nor disapproved when no one is looking.[7]

2.1.7.2. A Woman, Her Husband and Near Relatives With Whom Marriage is Prohibited

The schools differ concerning the parts of the body a woman must cover in the presence of near relatives with whom marriage is prohibited—except her husband—and Muslim women.[8] In other words, what constitutes the private parts of a woman in the presence of Muslim women as well as people through relationship with whom marriage is prohibited?

The Hanafis and the Shafiis say that it is obligatory for her to cover the area between the navel and the knees in their presence. The Malikis and the Hanbalis observe that she must cover the area between the navel and the knees in the presence of women, and in the presence of near relatives with whom marriage is prohibited, her whole body except her head and arms. Most Jafaris state that it is obligatory for her to cover her rear and private parts in the presence of women and people with whom marriage is prohibited. To cover other parts as well is better though not obligatory, except where there is a fear of sin.

2.1.7.3. WOMEN AND STRANGERS

About the extent of the body to be covered by a woman in the presence of a 'stranger' (any male apart from those with whom marriage is forbidden), the schools concur that it is obligatory for her to cover her whole body except the face and hands (up to the wrists) in accordance with verse 24:31, "...*And reveal not their adornment save such as is outward; and let them cast their veils over their bosoms,*" considering that 'outward adornment' (*zahir al-zinah*) implies the face and hands. The word '*al-khimar*' (whose plural '*khumur*' occurs in the verse) means the veil which covers the head, not the face, and the word '*al-jayb*' (whose plural '*juyub*' occurs in the verse) means the chest. The women have been commanded to put a covering on their heads and to lower it over their chests. As to the verse, "*O Prophet, say to your wives and daughters and the believing women, that they draw their veils close to them...*" (33:59), the word '*al-jilbab*' (whose plural *jalabib* occurs in the verse) does not mean a veil covering the face; rather it is a shirt or garment.

2.1.7.4. MAN'S PRIVATE PARTS

The schools differ concerning the parts of a man's body which it is forbidden for others to see and for him to expose. The Hanafis and the Hanbalis state that it is obligatory for a male to cover the area between the navel and the knees before all except his wife. It is permissible for others, irrespective of their being men or women, people forbidden in marriage or strangers, to look at the rest of his body when there is no fear of sin.

The Malikis and the Shafiis say that there are two different situations for a male with respect to the extent he can expose his body: the first, in the presence of men or those women who are his wife or with whom marriage is forbidden; the second, in the presence of women to whom marriage is not forbidden. In the former instance, he is only supposed to cover the area between the navel and the knees, while in the latter it is forbidden for a woman stranger to look at any part of a man's body. Though the Malikis exclude the head and the arms if looked at without any sensual motive, the Shafiis do not permit any exception.[9]

The Jafaris differentiate between the parts of another person's body which can be looked at and those parts of one's own body which ought to be covered. They observe that it is obligatory for a male to cover only his rear and private parts, although it is obligatory for women who are prohibited in marriage to him, to abstain from looking at any part of his body except his head and hands (up to the wrist). To summarize the Jafari opinion—it is permissible for a male to view the body of other men, women whom through lineage are prohibited in marriage to him—except the rear and private parts—provided no sensual motive is involved. Similarly, a woman can view the body of other woman and men with whom her marriage is prohibited—excepting the rear and private parts—provided no sensual motive is involved.

2.1.7.5. CHILDREN

Concerning the body of a child, the Hanbalis say that it is not prohibited to touch or look at the body of a child below seven years. It is not permissible to look at the rear and private parts of a male child between the age of seven to nine years, and for 'strangers', the whole body of a female child above the age of seven. The Hanafis observe that no part of the body of a boy of four years and below is prohibited from being looked at. Above this age only his rear and private parts are prohibited from being looked at as long as sexual desire has not awakened in him. If he reaches the age of sexual desire, the rule applicable to adults will be applicable to him with respect to both the sexes.

The Malikis state that it is permissible for a woman to look at and touch the body of a boy below the age of eight years, and only look at it until the age of twelve. A boy above the age of twelve is considered similar to an adult. It is permissible for a man to look at and touch the body of a girl below two years and eight months, and to look at, although not touch, until she reaches the age of four years.

According to the Shafiis, the rules applicable to an adult apply to an adolescent male child. But if a child is below that age and is also incapable of describing what he sees, all parts of his body can be looked at. But if he can describe what he sees with a sexual interest, he will be considered similar to an adult. As to a girl below the age of adolescence, only if she has developed sexual appeal will she be considered similar to a full-grown woman, not otherwise, although it will be forbidden for anyone except someone who looks after her to look at her parts.

The Jafari observe that it is obligatory to cover one's private parts in front of a child of discriminating age who can describe what he or she sees, although not before one who is incapable of doing so, because in this respect he or she is similar to an animal. That was regarding the covering of the body in the presence of a child, but with respect to looking at a child's private parts, Shaykh Jafar states, "It is not obligatory to abstain from looking at the parts of a child below five years, although it is absolutely impermissible to look at them with a sexual interest."[10] From what research of the Jafari sources have shown, the age limit for the permissibility of looking at the child's private parts is six years, not five.

2.1.7.6. A WOMAN'S VOICE

All the schools concur that listening to the voice of a woman is not prohibited, except where pleasure is involved or where there is a fear of sin. The Jafari author of *al-Jawahir*, at the beginning of the chapter on marriage, has mentioned as his proof the continuing practice of Muslims belonging to different periods and regions, the sermons of Fatimah and her daughters, the innumerable instances of conversations of the wives of the Prophet, and the religious scholars (*ulama*)—which cannot possibly be considered as having taken place due to emergency—and the holding of mourning and wedding ceremonies by women in the presence of men from early times, the conversations between opposite sexes while conducting transactions, as well as the Quranic verse, *"Be not complaisant in your speech"* (33:32), in which not speech itself but its manner and complaisance have been prohibited.

2.1.7.7. THE COLOR, NOT THE SHAPE

The schools concur that it is obligatory to cover the body's color not its shape. This writer comments that if the color of the covering is similar to the color of the skin, so that it is not discernible from it, as in the case of skin-colored stockings, the presence or absence of the covering will be equal.

2.1.7.8. THE DIFFERENCE BETWEEN LOOKING AND TOUCHING

Every part that is permissible to touch may be looked at and every part that is forbidden to be looked at may not be touched. Here there is a general consensus among the schools because touching involves greater pleasure than looking, and no jurisprudent of any school claims concomitance between the permissibility of looking and the permissibility of touching. Hence, though it is permissible for a man to look at a female stranger's face and hands, it is not permissible for him to touch her except in an emergency, such as for medical treatment or for rescuing her from drowning.

The Hanafis exclude shaking hands with an older woman from the prohibition. It is stated, "It is not permissible to touch the hands or face of a young woman even with the assurance of absence of any sexual motive. As to an old woman who has no sex appeal, there is nothing wrong in shaking hands with her with the assurance of absence of a sexual motive."[11]

The Jafaris and the Hanafis allow touching the body of people with whom marriage is prohibited (*mahram*) provided no sexual motive or pleasure is involved. The Shafiis prohibit touching even those parts of a *mahram*'s body which it is permissible to look at. It is even not permissible in their opinion for a person to touch the belly or back of his mother, pinch her ankles or feet or kiss her face. Similarly, it is not permissible for a person to ask his daughter or sister to press his legs.[12]

2.1.7.9. THE DIFFERENCE BETWEEN EXPOSING AND LOOKING

The Jafari observe that there is no concomitance between the permissibility of exposing the body and the permissibility of looking at it. Hence it is permissible in their opinion for a man to expose the whole of his body except his rear and private parts, while it is not permissible for a non-*mahram* woman to look at it. Research has not turned up anyone expressing this opinion in the numerous books of the Shafii, Hanbali, Hanafi and Maliki schools reviewed.

2.1.7.10. OLDER WOMEN

God Almighty says in the Quran, "*And such women as are past child-bearing and have no hope of marriage, it is no sin for them if they put off their clothes, so be it that they flaunt no ornament; but to abstain is better for them, and God is All-hearing, All-knowing*" (24:60). This noble verse indicates that it is permissible for old women who have no desire for marriage due to their old age "to expose their face and a part of their hair and arms, and such other parts which aged women usually keep exposed." The Jafari scholars also point to the same, on condition that such exposure be not with the intent of display. Rather, it is to allow them to come out for fulfilling their needs, though it is better for them to keep themselves covered.[13] This permission is with the assumption that it is not permissible to expose any of the above-mentioned parts of the body if there is fear of its leading to something forbidden, because a woman, regardless of her age, remains an object of sexual interest. Hence the leniency in the case of an aged woman arises from her being similar to a young girl who is presumably not an object of sexual interest and pleasure. Therefore, if there is any likelihood of that kind, the rule applicable to her will be the rule applicable to young women.

Islam is lenient with respect to elderly women and strict

regarding young women. But in practice we observe the opposite of what the Quran has ordered. We see shamelessness and display of charms among young women, while elderly women keep themselves covered and are reserved. So where God is strict, they are lenient, and where He is lenient, they are strict.

2.1.8. *OBLIGATORY COVERING DURING PRESCRIBED PRAYER*

The schools concur that it is obligatory upon both men and women to cover those parts of their bodies during prescribed prayer which should ordinarily be kept covered before 'strangers'. Beyond that their positions differ. Is it obligatory for a woman to cover, fully or partly, her face and hands during prescribed prayer, although she is not required to do so outside prescribed prayer? Is it obligatory for a man to cover other parts of his body during prescribed prayer apart from the area between the navel and the knees, although it is not obligatory to do so outside prescribed prayer?

The Hanafis observe that it is obligatory upon a woman to cover the back of her hands and the soles of her feet as well, and upon a man to cover his knees, in addition to the area between the navel and the knees. The Shafiis and Malikis say that it is permissible for a woman to keep her face and both the palms and the back of her hands uncovered during prescribed prayer. The Hanbalis state that it is not permissible for her to expose any part except the face. The Jafaris observe that it is obligatory for both men and women to cover those parts of their body during prescribed prayer which they are supposed to cover ordinarily in the presence of a 'stranger'. Hence it is permissible for a woman to expose during prescribed prayer that part of her face which is washed during the shorter ablution, her hands up to the wrists, and her feet up to the ankles—both the back as well as the palms of hands and the soles of feet. For a man, it is obligatory to cover the rear and the private parts, although it is better to cover the entire area between the navel and the knees.

2 Prescribed Prayers 77

2.1.9.THE MATERIAL USED FOR COVERING DURING PRESCRIBED PRAYER

The covering should meet the following requirements where the ability and freedom to meet them exist:

2.1.9.1. PRESCRIBED PURITY

The prescribed purity of the covering and the body are necessary for the validity of prescribed prayer in the opinion of all the schools, although each of them concedes certain exceptions in accordance with the following details.

The Jafaris state that blood from wounds and sores, irrespective of its quantity, is considered excusable on the dress as well as the body if its removal entails difficulty and harm. A blood spot smaller than the size of a dirham coin, regardless of its being due to one's blood or that of someone else, is also excusable provided that it is in a single place and not in different places; it is not the blood of menstruation, bleeding following childbirth and intermittent bleeding; it is not the blood of anything intrinsically impure, such as dog and pig, or the blood of a dead person. Also excusable is the impurity of anything that does not constitute part of essential dress during prescribed prayer, like a sash, cap, socks, shoes, ring, anklet and that which one carries with oneself, like a knife or currency. The impurity of the dress of a woman rearing a child, irrespective of whether she is the mother or someone else, is exempted on condition that it be difficult for her to change it and that she washes it once every day. In other words, in their opinion every impurity on the dress or body is exempted in conditions of emergency.

The Malikis observe that cases of uncontrollable discharge of urine or excrement, as well as piles, are excusable as well as any impurity on the body or clothes of a woman suckling an infant that may be soiled by the infant's urine or feces, the body and clothes of a butcher, surgeon and scavenger and blood—even that of a pig—if it is less than the size of a dirham coin: the discharge from boils, the excrement of fleas, and other things which need not be mentioned because they occur rarely.

The Hanafis say that impurity, blood or anything else, if less than the size of a dirham coin is exempted. Also exempted in emergencies is the urine and excrement of a cat and mouse. Tiny splashes—as small as the point of a needle—of urine, the blood that unavoidably stains a butcher, and the mud on roads—even if it is usually mixed with impurity and provided the impurity itself is not visible—are exempted. Consequently, they consider impurity in a small quantity as exempted, such as the urine of an animal the eating of which is permissible, if it covers a fourth of the clothes and less than one-fourth of the body.

According to the Shafiis, every impurity which is in such a small quantity that the eye cannot see it, is exempted. So is the mud on roads which is mixed with a small quantity of impurity, worms present in fruits and cheese, impure liquids added in medicines and perfumes, excrement of birds, impure hair in small quantity if they do not belong to a dog or a pig, and other things as well which are mentioned in detailed works. The Hanbalis say that minute quantities of blood and pus are exempted, and so is the mud on roads whose impurity is certain, as well as the impurity that enters the eyes and washing which is harmful.

2.1.9.2. WEARING SILK

There is consensus among the schools that wearing silk and gold is forbidden for men both during and outside pre-scribed prayer, while it is permissible for women. This is in accordance with this statement of the Prophet, "Wearing silk and gold is unlawful for the men of my Community (*ummah*), while it is lawful for its women." Accordingly, the Jafaris observe that a man's prescribed prayer is not valid if he wears pure silk and any clothing embroidered with gold during it, regardless of whether it is a waistband, cap, socks, or even a gold ring. They allow wearing silk during prescribed prayer in times of illness and during war. The Shafiis state that if a man performs prescribed prayer while wearing silk or over something made of it, it will be considered a forbidden act, although his prescribed prayer will be valid.[14]

Research has not turned up an express statement in the books of the remaining schools concerning the validity or invalidity of prescribed prayer performed in silk, though the Hanafis as well as the Hanbalis (in accordance with one of two narrations) concur with the Shafiis regarding the general rule that if there is any command prohibiting something which is not directly connected with prescribed prayer—such as the command prohibiting usurpation—the prescribed prayer will be valid if it is not observed and the person will be considered as having performed an obligatory and forbidden act together. Accordingly, the prescribed prayer performed in a dress of silk is valid. The author of *al-Fiqh alal-madhahib al-arbaah* reports a consensus that it is valid for a man constrained to perform prescribed prayer while wearing silk, and it is not obligatory for him to repeat it.

2.1.9.3. LAWFULNESS OF CLOTHING

The Jafaris consider it necessary that the clothing worn be lawfully owned. Hence if a person performs prescribed prayer in usurped clothes with the knowledge of their being so, his or her prescribed prayer is invalid. This is also the opinion of Ibn Hanbal in one of the two statements narrated from him. The other schools regard prescribed prayer in usurped clothes as valid on the grounds that the prohibition does not directly relate to prescribed prayer so as to invalidate it. The Jafari are very strict concerning usurpation, and some of them even observe that if a person performs prescribed prayer in clothes in which a single thread is usurped, or carries with him or her an usurped knife, dirham, or any other thing, his or her prescribed prayer will not be valid. But they also say that if one performs prescribed prayer in usurped clothes out of ignorance or forgetfulness, his or her prescribed prayer is valid.

2.1.9.4. THE SKIN OF ANIMALS NOT USED FOR FOOD

The Jafaris are alone in holding that it is invalid to perform prescribed prayer while wearing the skin, even if tanned, of an animal whose flesh may not be eaten, as well as anything consisting its hair, wool, fur or feathers. The same is true of clothes bearing any secretion from its body—e.g. sweat and saliva—as long as it is wet. Hence, even if a single hair of a cat or any such animal happens to be present on the dress of a person performing prescribed prayer and he performs it with the knowledge of its presence, his or her prescribed prayer is invalidated. They exclude wax, honey, the blood of bugs; lice, fleas and other insects which have no flesh, as well as the hair, sweat and saliva of human beings. They also consider prescribed prayer invalid if any part of a dead animal happens to be on the clothes irrespective of whether the animal is one used for food or not, whether its blood flows when cut or not, and its skin is tanned or not.

2.1.9.5. SUBSIDIARY ISSUE

If there is only a single clothing to cover the body and that too is impure to an extent that is not excusable, what should one do if he or she has no alternative other than either performing prescribed prayer in the impure clothing or in the state of nature?

The Hanbalis say that the person should perform prescribed prayer in the impure clothing, but it is obligatory upon him or her to repeat it later. The Malikis and a large number of Jafaris observe that the person should perform the prescribed prayer in the impure clothing and its repetition is not obligatory upon him or her. The Hanafis and the Shafiis state that he should perform the prescribed prayer naked if necessary because it is not valid for him or to cover himself with the impure clothing.

2.1.10. THE PLACE OF PRESCRIBED PRAYER

2.1.10.1. AN USURPED PLACE

The Jafaris consider prescribed prayer performed in an

usurped place and usurped clothing as invalid provided it is done voluntarily and with the knowledge of the usurpation. The other schools observe that the prescribed prayer performed in an usurped place is valid, although the person performing it will have sinned, since the prohibition does not relate directly to prescribed prayer, rather, it relates to dispensations of property. Their position in this regard is the same as in the case of usurped clothing.

What a great distance between this opinion of the Shafii, Hanbali, Hanafi and Maliki schools that an usurper's prescribed prayer is valid in usurped property. The Jafaris also permit prescribed prayer in vast stretches of owned land which are either impossible or difficult for people to avoid, even if the permission of the owner has not been acquired.

2.1.10.2. PRESCRIBED PURITY OF THE PLACE

The Shafii, Hanbali, Hanafi and Maliki schools observe that the place should be free from both wet and dry impurities. The Shafiis observe that the prescribed purity of all that which touches and comes into contact with the body or clothes of the person performing the prescribed prayer is obligatory. Therefore, if he or she rubs himself or herself against an impure wall or cloth or holds an impure object or a rope lying over impurity, his or her prescribed prayer will be invalid. The Hanafis require only the location of the feet and the forehead to be ritually pure; the Jafaris restrict it to the location of the forehead, that is, the place of prostration. As to the impurity of other locations, the prescribed prayer will not be invalid unless the impurity is transmitted to the body or clothing of the person performing prescribed prayer.

2.1.10.3. PRESCRIBED PRAYER PERFORMED ON A MOUNT

The Hanafi and Jafaris require the place to be stationary; hence it is not valid in their opinion to perform prescribed prayer while riding an animal or something that swings back and forth, except out of necessity, because one who has no choice will perform prescribed prayer in accordance with his capacity.

The Shafiis, Malikis and Hanbalis observe that prescribed prayer performed on a mount is valid even during times of peace and despite the ability to perform it on the ground, provided it is performed completely and meets all the requirements.

2.1.10.4. PRESCRIBED PRAYER INSIDE THE KABAH

The Jafaris, Shafiis and Hanafis state that it is valid to perform prescribed prayer, obligatory or supererogative, inside the Kabah. The Malikis and the Hanbalis say that only supererogative, not obligatory, is valid therein.

2.1.10.5. A WOMAN'S PRAYER BESIDE A MAN

A group of Jafari jurisprudents observe that if a man and a woman perform prescribed prayer in a single place so that she is either in front of him or beside him, and there is neither any screen between them nor does the distance between the two exceed ten cubits, the prescribed prayer of the one who starts earlier will not be invalid, and if both start simultaneously, the prescribed prayer of both will be invalid.

The Hanafis say that if the woman is in front or beside a man, the prescribed prayer will be invalid if performed in a single place with no screen at least a cubit high between them, the woman has sex appeal, her shanks and ankles are adjacent to his, the prescribed prayer is not a prescribed prayer for the dead, and the prescribed prayer is being jointly performed, that is, either she is following him or both are following a single leader (*imam*). The Shafiis, Hanbalis and most Jafaris are of the view that the prescribed prayer is valid, though the manner of performance is disapproved (*makruh*).

2.1.10.6. THE LOCALE OF PROSTRATION

The schools concur that the place where the forehead is placed during prostration should be stationary and should not be inordinately higher than the location of the knees during prostration. They differ regarding that on which prostration is valid. The Jafaris state that it is not valid to perform prostration on anything except on earth and those things which grow on it and are not used for food or clothing. Therefore, a person cannot perform prostration on wool, cotton, minerals and that which grows on the surface of water, for water is not earth. They permit prostration on paper because it is made of a material which grows on earth. They argue their position by pointing out that prostration is a form of worship prescribed by the *Shariah* that depends for its particulars on textual evidence. The jurisprudents of all the schools concur regarding the validity of prostration on earth and that which grows on it, thus restricting it to that regarding which there is certainty. The Hanafi, Hanbali, Maliki, and Shafii schools observe that it is valid to perform prostration on anything, including even a part of one's turban, provided it is ritually pure. Rather, the Hanafis permit prostration on one's palm even without an emergency, though it is considered as disapproved.

2.1.11. THE CALL TO THE PRESCRIBED PRAYER

The call to the prescribed prayer (*adhan*) literally means 'announcement'. It means the announcement made in specific words at the time of prescribed prayer in the *Shariah*. It was introduced in the first year of the Hijrah at Madinah. The cause of its introduction, in the opinion of the Jafaris, was that Gabriel came down with the call to the prescribed prayer in a message from God to the Prophet (ﷺ). The Hanafi, Hanbali, Maliki and Shafii schools say that Abd Allah ibn Zayd saw a dream in which he was taught the call to prescribed prayer by someone. When he related his dream to the Prophet (ﷺ), the Prophet (ﷺ) approved it.

2.1.11.1. THE CALL TO THE PRESCRIBED PRAYER IS A *SUNNAH*

The Hanafis, Shafiis and Jafaris say that the call to the prescribed prayer is a *Sunnah* which has been emphatically recommended (*muakkadah*). The Hanbalis observe that it is the individual duty of non-traveling men in villages and towns to make the call to the prescribed prayer for the five daily prescribed prayers. The Malikis state that it is an obligatory duty in towns where the Friday prayer is held, and if the people of such a place abandon the call to the prescribed prayer, they should be fought on that account.

2.1.11.2. THE CALL TO THE PRESCRIBED PRAYER IS INVALID IN CERTAIN CASES

The Hanbalis observe that it is not valid to make the call to the prescribed prayer for the prescribed prayer for the dead or for a supererogatory prayer or for one performed to fulfill a vow (*al-salat al-mandhurah*). The Malikis say that it is not valid for a supererogatory or prescribed prayer for the dead or for an obligatory daily prayer performed after the lapsing of its time (*al-salat al-faitah*). The Hanafis state that it is valid for the prescribed prayers performed on the two festivals (*id*), for the prayer performed on the occurrence of an eclipse (*salat al-kusuf*), for prayers made for rain (*istisqa*), and for *tarawih* and *Sunnah* prayers. The Shafiis do not consider it valid for the prescribed prayer for the dead, *mandhurah* and supererogatory prayers. The Jafaris observe that the *Shariah* has introduced the call to the prescribed prayer only for the five daily prescribed prayer, and it is recommended for them, whether performed as 'on time' or 'missed', with a group or singly, during a journey or stay, both for men and women. It is not valid for any other prescribed prayer, recommended or obligatory, and the caller to the prescribed prayer will call out "*al-salat*" three times on occasions of *salat al-kusuf* and the festival prescribed prayers.

2.1.11.3. THE CONDITIONS FOR THE CALL TO THE PRESCRIBED PRAYER

The schools concur that the conditions for the validity of the call to the prescribed prayer are: maintaining continuity of its recital and the sequence of its different parts and that the caller to the prescribed prayer (*muadhdhin*) be a sane Muslim man.[15] The call to the prescribed prayer by a child of discerning age is valid. All the schools concur that prescribed purity is not required for the call to the prescribed prayer.

The schools differ regarding other aspects. The Hanafis and the Shafiis say that the call to the prescribed prayer is valid even without one's intention being make known. The other schools require one to make one's intention known.

The Hanbalis consider making the call to the prescribed prayer in any language other than Arabic as being unconditionally valid. The Malikis, Hanafis and Shafiis state that it is not valid for an Arab to make the call to the prescribed prayer in any other language, although it is valid for a non-Arab to make it in his own tongue, for himself and his colinguals.

The Jafaris observe that the call to the prescribed prayer is not valid before the arrival of the time of prescribed prayer except in the case of the morning prescribed prayer. The Shafiis, Malikis, Hanbalis and many Jafaris permit the making of the call to the prescribed prayer of announcement before the dawn. The Hanafis do not permit it, making no difference between the morning prescribed prayer and other prescribed prayers. This opinion is closer to caution.

2.1.11.4. THE FORM OF THE CALL TO THE PRESCRIBED PRAYER

The following is the form of the call to the prescribed prayer:

Allahu akbar—four times according to all the schools and twice according to the Malikis.

Ashhadu an la ilaha ill-Allah—twice according to all the schools.

Ashhadu anna Muhammadan Rasul Allah—twice according to all the schools.

Hayya alal-salat—twice according to all the schools.

Hayya alal-falah—twice according to all the schools.

Hayya ala khayr il-amal—twice according to the Jafaris only.

Allahu akbar—twice according to all the schools.

La ilaha ill-Allah—once according to the Hanafi, Hanbali, Maliki and Shafii schools and twice according to the Jafaris.

The Malikis and Shafiis permit repetition of the last line, considering it *Sunnah.* That is, the call to the prescribed prayer, according to them, is not invalid if it is recited only once, as the Jafaris hold. The author of *al-Fiqh alal-madhahib al-arbaah* mentions a consensus among the Hanafi, Hanbali, Maliki and Shafii schools regarding '*al-tathwib*' being recommended. *Al-tathwib* means reciting the words "*al-salatu khayrun min al-nawm,*" ('prescribed prayer is better than sleep') twice after "*hayya alal-falah.*" The Jafaris prohibit it.[16]

2.1.12. DECLARATION TO PERFORM THE PRESCRIBED PRAYER

For both men and women, it is recommended to recite the declaration to perform the prescribed prayer (*iqamah*) before every daily prescribed prayer with the prescribed prayer immediately following it. The rules applicable to the call to the prescribed prayer, such as continuity, sequence, its being in Arabic, etc., apply to the declaration to perform the prescribed prayer, as well. Its form is as follows:

Allahu akbar—twice according to all the schools except the Hanafis who require it four times.

Ashhadu an la ilaha ill-Allah—once according to the Shafiis, Malikis and Hanbalis and twice according to the Hanafis and Jafari.

Ashhadu anna Muhammadan Rasul Allah—once in the opinion of the Shafiis, Malikis and Hanbalis, and twice according to the Hanafis and Jafaris.

Hayya alas-salat—once in the opinion of the Shafiis, Malikis and Hanbalis, and twice according to the Hanafis and Jafaris.

Hayya alal-falah—once in the opinion of the Shafiis, Malikis and Hanbalis, and twice according to the Hanafis and Jafaris.

Hayya ala khayr il-amal—twice only according to the Jafaris.

Qad qamat is-salah—twice in the opinion of all schools, except the Malikis who recite it once.

Allahu akbar—twice in the opinion of all the schools.

La ilaha ill-Allah—once in the opinion of all the schools.

A group of Jafari jurisprudents observe that it is valid for a traveler and a person in a hurry to recite each sentence of both the call to the prescribed prayer and declaration to perform the prescribed prayer only once.

2.1.13. THE ESSENTIALS OF PRESCRIBED PRAYER

The validity of prescribed prayer is dependent upon having the prescribed purity—both from both types of impurity, *hadath* and *khabath*—setting in of its time, facing the *qiblah*, and wearing sufficient clothing. The fulfillment of these conditions before starting the prescribed prayer is necessary, and they have been discussed in detail in the preceding pages. Prescribed prayer also comprises certain essentials which are performed as parts of prescribed prayer. They are many, and among them are the following.

2.1.13.1. DECLARATION OF INTENTION

The jurisprudents of each school differ among themselves regarding the content of the intention required for prescribed prayer, that is, whether it is necessary to specify the prescribed prayer (such as its being noon or afternoon prescribed prayer), whether it is obligatory or supererogatory, complete or shortened, on time or missed, and so on.

The essence of the intention, as mentioned in the chapter on the prescribed ablution, is the intention to perform an act with the motive of obedience to a command of God Almighty. Specification of a particular prescribed prayer, whether it is obligatory or supererogatory, on time or missed, is dependent upon the intention of the person who is to perform the prayer. Thus if a person intends to perform a supererogatory prescribed prayer at the start and performs it with this intention, it will be supererogatory. If a person intends to perform an obligatory prescribed prayer, such as noon or afternoon prayer, it will be so. But if a person does not intend anything, it will be a waste of labor, although it is impossible for one not to intend anything because any act performed by a sane person cannot be without an intention regardless of whether it is expressed in specific words or not, and irrespective of whether the person is attentive to his or her intention or not. Therefore, all the schools concur that it is not necessary to express the intention in words. Similarly, it is also ordinarily impossible for one who knows the difference involved to intend noon while performing the afternoon or while performing a supererogatory prayer.

2.1.13.2. THE FIRST RECITATION OF *ALLAHU AKBAR* WHICH BEGINS THE SACRED STATE OF PRESCRIBED PRAYER

Prescribed prayer does not validly commence without the recitation of *"Allahu akbar"* which prohibits anything but the prescribed prayer (*takbirat al-ihram*). Its name derives from the Tradition of the Prophet, "Prescribed purity is the key to prescribed prayer; its consecration is the *takbirah*; and its termination is *taslim*." The Tradition means that with *takbirat al-ihram* it becomes forbidden to speak or perform any act incompatible with prescribed prayer, and by reciting *taslim*, those acts which were prohibited after reciting the *takbirah* become permissible again. Its formula is *"Allahu akbar."* According to the Jafaris, Malikis and Hanbalis no other form is permissible. The Shafiis observe that both *"Allahu akbar,"* and *"Allah al-akbar"* (with the addition of alif and lam to *"akbar"*) are permissible. The Hanafis state that any other synonymous words such as *'Allahu al-azam'* and *'Allahu al-ajall'* will do. All the schools, excepting the Hanafi, concur that it is obligatory to recite it in Arabic, even if the person performing the prescribed prayer is a non-Arab. It is obligatory for him or her to learn enough Arabic to recite it. If the person cannot learn, that person may translate it into his or her own tongue. The Hanafis observe that it is valid to recite it in any language even if one can recite it in Arabic.

There is consensus among the schools that at the time of reciting *takbirat al-ihram* all the conditions necessary for prescribed prayer (such as prescribed purity, facing the *qiblah*, covering the body, etc.) should be present, and that it should be recited—when one has the ability to do so—while standing stationary, and in a voice that the person can hear. The word '*Allah*' should precede '*akbar*', and the reverse, '*akbar Allah*', will not suffice for entry into standing in prescribed prayer.

2.1.13.3. STANDING UPRIGHT FACING THE *QIBLAH*

The schools concur that standing in the prescribed prayer (*qiyam*) is obligatory in the prescribed prayer from the beginning of *takbirat al-ihram* to the bending forward, and that standing upright, stationary and independently are its requisites. Hence it is not valid to recline on any support when one is able to stand without it. If one cannot stand, one may perform the prescribed prayer sitting. If this is not possible, while lying down on the right side facing the *qiblah* (in the same position that a dead body is placed in the grave). This is the opinion of all the schools except the Hanafis, who state that a person who cannot sit will perform the prescribed prayer lying down on his or her back with his or her feet pointing towards the *qiblah*, so that his or her gestures in place of the actual bending forward and prostration are made towards the *qiblah*.

If it is not possible to perform the prescribed prayer while lying on the right side, the Jafaris, Shafiis and Hanbalis permit the person to perform the prescribed prayer lying on his or her back by making gestures with his or her head. If gesturing with the head is not possible, he or she will gesture with the eyelids.

The Hanafis say that if his or her state is as bad as that, the duty of the prescribed prayer will no longer apply to him or her, although he or she will have to make up for the missed prescribed prayers when his or her condition improves and the hindrance is removed.

According to the Malikis, a sick person such as this is not required to perform the prescribed prayer and it is also not obligatory for him or her to make up for the missed prescribed prayers.

The Jafaris, Shafiis and Hanbalis state that the duty of the prescribed prayer does not disappear in any situation. If the person is unable to gesture by blinking his or her eyes, he or she will pass the prescribed prayer through his or her mind and move his or her tongue in reciting the recitation of the Quran (*qiraah*) and *dhikr*. If the person is unable to move the tongue, he or she will imagine it in his or her mind as long as his or her mind works.

To sum up, the prescribed prayer is obligatory upon those who are fully capable and those who are not so capable. It may not be neglected in any situation, and every person must perform it in accordance with his or her ability. Hence it is performed while standing, then sitting, then lying down on one's side, then lying down on one's back, then gesturing by blinking the eyes, and passing it through the mind, in that order. A fully capable person as well as one not capable will move from the previous state to the new situation which has come into existence. Hence if a fully capable person loses his or her ability during prescribed prayer or one not capable regains it, either of them will perform the remaining part in accordance with his or her ability. Therefore, if a person performs one cycle standing and is then unable to stand, that person will complete it sitting, and if the person performs the first cycle sitting and then regains the strength to stand, he or she will complete the remaining prescribed prayer standing.

2.1.13.4. RECITATION OF THE QURAN

The schools differ whether the recitation of the first chapter (*qiraah*) of the Quran, *Surat al-Fatihah*, is obligatory in every cycle, or in the first two cycles, or in all the cycles without there being any other alternative. They also give different answers to the following questions: Is the *basmalah* (recitation of "In the Name of God, the Merciful, the Compassionate") an essential part of *al-Fatihah* or is it valid to omit it? Is it obligatory or recommended to recite aloud or in a low voice? Is it obligatory to recite another chapter after the first chapter of the Quran in the first two cycles? Can the *tasbih* replace the chapter? Is the folding of arms during the prescribed prayer a *Sunnah* or is it forbidden? And so on.

The Hanafis observe that it is not obligatory to recite only the first chapter of the Quran, *Surat al-Fatihah*, in the daily prescribed prayer, and anything recited from the Quran may take its place, because God the Exalted, says, *"Therefore recite of the Quran so much as is feasible"* (73:20).[17] The recital from the Quran is obligatory in the first two cycles; but in the third cycle of the evening prescribed prayer and the last two cycles of afternoon and night prescribed prayers there is an option between reciting from the Quran or saying the *tasbih* or keeping quiet.[18]

Moreover, the Hanafis say that it is valid to forego the *basmalah* because it is not a part of any chapter. Neither reciting aloud nor in a low voice are recommended, and a person performing the prayer, praying alone, is free to recite in a voice that he or she alone can hear or in a voice audible to others. There is no raising of the hands, palms up (*qunut*) while standing (*qiyam*) and offering a prayer in the prescribed prayer with the exception of the single cycle recommended prayer (*salat al-watr*). As to folding the arms during prayer (*takattuf*), it is part of the *Sunnah* (*masnun*) and not obligatory. Its preferable form is for a person to place the palm of his right hand on the back of his left hand below the navel, and for a woman to place her hands on her chest.

The Shafiis state that the first chapter of the Quran, *Surat al-Fatihah*, is obligatory in every cycle, without there being any difference in this regard between the first two cycles and the other cycles and between obligatory and recommended prescribed prayer. The *basmalah* is a part of the chapter and cannot be omitted under any circumstance. The recitation should be aloud in the morning prayer and the first two cycles of evening and night prescribed prayers; the remaining recitals are to be in a low voice. The raising of the hands palms up while standing (*qunut*) is recommended only in the morning prayer, and is to be performed after rising from the bending forward of the second cycle. Similarly, it is recommended to recite another chapter after the first chapter of the Quran only in the first two cycles. The folding of the arms is not obligatory, but a *Sunnah* for both the sexes. Its preferable form is to place the right hand palm on the back of the left hand between the chest and the navel and towards the left side.

According to the Malikis, reciting the first chapter of the Quran, *Surat al-Fatihah*, is necessary in every cycle, without there being any difference in this regard between the earlier and later cycles and between the prescribed and recommended prayer, as observed earlier by the Shafiis. It is recommended to recite another chapter after first chapter of the Quran in the first two cycles. The *basmalah* is not a part of the chapter and it is recommended to omit it altogether. Reciting aloud is recommended in the morning prescribed prayer and the first two cycles of evening and night prescribed prayers. *Qunut* is to be recited only in the morning prayer. The folding of the arms is valid in their opinion, although it is recommended to keep the hands hanging freely in the obligatory prayers.

The Hanbalis consider the first chapter of the Quran, *Surat al-Fatihah*, to be obligatory in every cycle, and to recite a chapter after it in the first two cycles as recommended. The morning prayer and the first two cycles of evening and night prayers are to be recited aloud. The *basmalah* is a part of the chapters although it will be recited in a low voice and not aloud. *Qunut* is to be recited in *salat al-watr* only. The folding of the arms is a *Sunnah* for both men and women and its preferable form is to place the right hand palm on the back of the left hand below the navel.

It is evident that the folding of the arms, which the Hanafi, Hanbali, Maliki and Shafii jurisprudents call '*qabd*' and the Jafari jurisprudents '*takfir*' i.e. to conceal—is not obligatory in the opinion of the Hanafi, Hanbali, Maliki and Shafii schools.

The Jafaris state that reciting the first chapter of the Quran, *Surat al-Fatihah*, is necessary in the first two cycles of every prescribed prayer and no other chapter can suffice in its place but it is not obligatory in the third cycle of evening and the last two cycles of four cycle prescribed prayers. Rather, one has an option between it and *tasbih*. '*Tasbih*' means the recitation of *subha Allah wal hamdullillah wa la ilah ill-Allah wa Allah akbar* three times, although even once is sufficient. It is obligatory to recite another complete chapter in the first two cycles, and the *basmalah* is a part of the chapters which cannot be omitted under any circumstance. It is obligatory to recite aloud only the chapters and not the other recitations in the morning prayer and the first two cycles of the evening and night prescribed prayers. The recitation of the Quran in the noon and afternoon prescribed prayers is to be done, except for the *basmalah*, in a low voice in their first two cycles and also in the third cycle of the evening and the last two cycles of night prescribed prayers.

Qunut is recommended in the five daily prescribed prayers and its place is the second cycle after the recital of the chapter and before bending forward. The minimum level of voice considered loud is that a person nearby be able to hear it, and the minimum for low voice is that the person himself be able to hear it. The schools concur that reciting aloud is not prescribed for women, nor is reciting in a voice lower than what can be heard by herself. If a person performing the prescribed prayer voluntarily recite loudly something which is to be recited in a low voice and vice versa, his prescribed prayer will be invalid, if this is not done due to ignorance or forgetfulness.

The Jafaris also consider saying "*amin*" during prescribed prayer to be forbidden and a cause for invalidating the prescribed prayer, irrespective of whether one is praying individually or as a leader or as performing the prescribed prayer behind a leader, because it is something adopted by the people, and nothing adopted by them is capable of being included in the prescribed prayer. The Hanafi, Hanbali, Maliki and Shafii schools concur that it is recommended in accordance with the narration of Abu Hurayrah that the Prophet (ﷺ) said, "When the *imam* says, '*ghayr il maghdubi alaymhim wa la-dd allin*' then say, '*Amin* '."

The Jafaris negate the authenticity of this Tradition. Most

Jafaris consider folding the arms (*takattuf*) in prescribed prayer to render it invalid because there is no explicit statement in support of it. Some of them say that folding of the arms is forbidden and one who does it sins, although his or her prescribed prayer is not invalidated. A third group from among them observes that it is disapproved and not forbidden.

2.1.13.5. BENDING FORWARD

There is consensus among the schools that bending forward, hands upon the knees (*ruku*) is obligatory in prescribed prayer, but they differ regarding the extent to which it is obligatory and the necessity of staying motionless in that position.

The Hanafis observe that it is obligatory to bend down in any possible manner and staying motionless is not obligatory. The remaining schools consider it obligatory to kneel down until the palms of the person performing the prescribed prayer reach his or her knees and to stay motionless during the bending forward.

The Shafiis, Hanafis and Malikis state that it is not obligatory to recite anything during the bending forward, although it is *Sunnah* that the person say, "*Subhana rabbi al azim.*"

The Jafaris and the Hanbalis consider *tasbih* to be obligatory during the bending forward and its formula in the opinion of the Hanbalis is "*Subhana rabbi al-azim,*" and according to the Jafaris "*Subhana rabbi al-azim wa bi hamdih*" or just "*Subhan allah*" three times. It is recommended in the opinion of the Jafaris to add after the *tasbih* a benediction for Muhammad and his Family, "*allah humma salli ala Muhammadin wa ali Muhammad.*"

The Hanafis say that it is not obligatory to return to the standing position after bending forward. It is sufficient, although disapproved, to perform the prostration straightaway.

The other schools consider it obligatory to return to the standing position and recommended to recite the *tasmi*, which is to say, "*samiallahu li man hamidah*" (God hears one who praises Him). According to the Jafaris, it is obligatory to stay motionless in this standing up.

2.1.13.6. PROSTRATION

There is consensus among the schools that prostration (*sujud*) is obligatory to be performed twice in each cycle. They differ regarding its details, as to whether it is obligatory to prostrate with all the seven parts of the body touching the ground while performing it or if it is sufficient to lay on the ground only some of them. These seven parts are: the forehead, the palms, the knees and the big toes.

The Malikis, Shafiis and Hanafis state that it is obligatory to place only the forehead on the ground in prostration, and placing the other parts is recommended.

The Jafaris and the Hanbalis observe that it is obligatory to place all the seven parts on the ground while performing prostration. It has been narrated from the Hanbalis that they add the nose to these seven, thus making them eight.

The difference of opinion regarding reciting *tasbih* and being motionless during prostration is similar to the difference mentioned concerning bending forward. Those who consider them obligatory there, consider them obligatory here, as well. The Hanafis do not consider it obligatory to sit between the two prostration. The remaining schools consider it obligatory.

2.1.13.7. SITTING WITH FOLDED KNEES AND BEARING WITNESS

Sitting with knees folded and bearing witness (*tashahhud*) is done twice in prescribed prayer. The first, after the second cycle of noon, afternoon, evening and night prescribed prayers, which is not followed by greetings and salutations (*taslim*) and the second in the last cycle of the two, three, and four cycle prescribed prayers, which is followed by *taslim*.

The Jafaris and the Hanbalis state that the first *tashahhud* is obligatory. The remaining schools consider it recommended and not obligatory. The second *tashahhud* is considered obligatory by the Shafiis, Jafaris and Hanbalis, and recommended by the Malikis and Hanafis.[19]

2.1.13.8. SENDING GREETINGS

The Shafiis, Malikis and Hanbalis observe that *taslim* is

obligatory. The Hanafis do not consider it obligatory.[20] The Jafaris differ among themselves, a group considers it obligatory, while others, including al-Mufid, Shaykh al-Tusi and Allamah al-Hilli, regard it as recommended. It has only one form in the opinion of the Hanafi, Hanbali, Maliki and Shafii schools and it is:

> *as-salamu alaykum wa rahmatullah*
> *as-salamu alaykum wa rahmatullah*

The Hanbalis say that it is obligatory to recite it twice. The others consider reciting once as sufficient. The Jafaris state that *taslim* consists of two formulas:

> *as-salamu alayna wa ala ibadi-l-lahi-s-salihin*
> *as-salumu alaykum wa rahmatu l-lahi wa barakatuhu*

One of them is obligatory. Hence, if a person recites the former, the latter will be recommended, and if he or she recites the latter, he or she will stop at it. As to:

> *as-salamu alayka ayyahan-nabiyyu wa rahmatu-l-lahi wa*
> *barakatuhu*

it is not a part of *taslim*, and is a recommended addition to the *tashahhud*.

2.1.13.9. SEQUENCE

Proper sequence (*tartib*) is obligatory between the different parts of prescribed prayer. Hence the first recitation of *Allahu akbar* which begins the sacred state of the prescribed prayer (*takbirat al-ihram*) must precede the recitation of the Quran, the recitation of the Quran must precede the bending forward, hands upon the knees, the bending forward, hands upon the knee must come before the prostration, and so on.

2.1.13.10. CONTINUITY

Continuity (that is, to occur one after another) is obligatory between the parts of prescribed prayer and between the different portions of a part. Therefore, the recitation of the Quran must begin immediately after the *takbirah al-ihram* and bending foreword, hands upon the knees, must similarly follow the recitation of the Quran, and so on. The verses, words and letters must not be recited in a manner breaking continuity.

2.1.14. ERROR AND DOUBT DURING PRESCRIBED PRAYER

The schools concur that a willful violation of any obligatory act in prescribed prayer renders it invalid and that a flaw by mistake (*sahw*) can be atoned for by performing the prostration for mistakes (*sujud al-sahw*) as described below.

The Hanafis state that the form of *sujud al-sahw* is that the person performing the prayer should perform two prostrations followed by sitting with folded knees and bearing witness (*tashhahud*) and offering greetings (*taslim*) and benediction for the Prophet (صلى الله عليه وسلم). This prostration should be performed after *taslim*, provided there is sufficient time for that prescribed prayer. Hence if, for instance, someone makes an involuntary error in the prescribed prayer for dawn and finds that the sun has risen before his or her performing *sujud al-sahw*, the person is not required to perform it any more. The cause necessitating *sujud al-sahw* is the person performing the prescribed prayer omitting an obligatory part or adding an extra essential part—such as bending forward or prostration. If numerous lapses occur in a single prescribed prayer, the two prostrations will suffice for them all, because their repetition is not valid in their opinion. And if there occurs a lapse in the *sujud al-sahw* it requires no rectification.[21]

The Malikis observe that in its form, *sujud al-sahw* consists of two prostrations followed by *tashahhud* without any supplication and benediction for the Prophet. As to the place of this prostration, in the event that it is on account of an omission or due to both an omission and an addition, it will be performed before the *taslim*. If the cause is only an addition, then after the *taslim*. Moreover, *sujud al-sahw* atones for an involuntary omission of a recommended part of the prescribed prayer. Therefore, if the omitted part is an obligatory part of prescribed prayer, it cannot be atoned by *sujud al-sahw* and must be performed. However, if the mistake is one of involuntary addition—such as an extra bending forward or two, or one or two additional cycles—it is atonable by *sujud al-sahw*.

The Hanbalis say that it is valid to perform *sujud al-sahw* before or after the *taslim*. It consists of two prostrations followed by *tashahhud* and *taslim*. Its causes are involuntary addition or omission as well as doubt. An example of addition is to perform an additional standing or sitting. One who sits where he is supposed to stand or vice versa will perform *sujud al-sahw.*

Where there is an omission, the following procedure is to be followed in their opinion. If the person remembers the omission before starting the recitation of the Quran of the next cycle, it is obligatory for that person to perform the part omitted as well as *sujud al-sahw.* If that person comes to remember it only after starting the *qiraah* of the next cycle, the former cycle will be annulled and the latter will take its place and *sujud al-sahw* will also be performed. To illustrate the same, if a person forgets the bending forward in the first cycle and becomes aware of it after performing the prostration of the same cycle, that person will perform the bending forward and then repeat the prostration, and if the person becomes aware of it only after starting the *qiraah* of the second cycle, the former cycle will be considered null and void and the second cycle will take its place.

An example of doubt necessitating *sujud al-sahw* is the case when a person doubts whether the bending forward has been performed or not, or has a doubt regarding the number of cycles performed. Here the person will consider that portion of the prescribed prayer he or she is sure of having performed as the basis and will perform the remaining prescribed prayer, and carry out *sujud al-sahw* on finishing it. Two prostrations suffice for several mistakes, even if their causes differ, and a lapse committed by someone prone to making mistakes will not be considered a lapse.

According to the Shafiis, the place of *sujud al-sahw* is after the *tashahhud* and benediction of the Prophet and before the *taslim.* Its mode of performance is like the one prescribed by the above-mentioned schools. The reasons for its performance are: omission of an emphasized (*muakkadah*) Sunnah, a little additional recital, the recital of the first chapter of the Quran (*Surah al-Fatihah*) by mistake, the following of a leader (*imam*) whose prescribed prayer is faulty, a doubt in the number of cycles, and the omission of a specific part.

The Jafaris differentiate between the rules applicable to cases of doubt and those applicable to errors. They state that no attention will be paid to a doubt arising concerning any act of prescribed prayer after its completion, or the doubt of a person performing the prescribed prayer behind a leader regarding the number of cycles if the leader has ascertained their number and vice versa, with each of them referring to the memory of the other. No significance is attached to the doubts of a person who doubts excessively, and similarly to a doubt repeating any act of a prescribed prayer arising after entry into its subsequent act. Hence if a doubt occurs regarding the recitation of the first chapter of the Quran after starting the recitation of the Quran of the subsequent chapter, or regarding the chapter after having gone into the bending forward, or with respect to the bending forward after having entered the prostration, the prescribed prayer will be continued without heeding the doubt. But if the doubt occurs before starting the performance of the subsequent act it is obligatory to rectify it. Hence a person who has doubt regarding the recital of the first chapter of the Quran before starting the subsequent chapter, will recite it, and similarly the chapter if he or she has a doubt concerning its recital before entering the bending forward.

As to *sujud al-sahw*, it is ordained for every omission and addition, except for reciting aloud instead of in a low voice and vice versa—as it does not entail anything—and except for any omission or addition that does not pertain to the pillars of the prescribed prayer, because their omission or addition invalidates the prescribed prayer irrespective of its being willful or by mistake. The pillars in their opinion are the following five: intention, *takbirat al-ihram*, standing, bending forward with hands upon the knees and the two prostrations of one cycle. It is not obligatory to perform any part omitted by mistake after the prescribed prayer except prostration and *tashahhud*, which are alone required to be performed among the forgotten parts. These will be performed after the completion of the prescribed prayer, followed by *sujud al-sahw*, which consists of making two prostrations and reciting:

basmillah wa billah, allah humma
salli ala muhammadin wa ali muhammad

in the state of prostration, followed by *tashahhud* and *taslim*. The number of *sujud al-sahw* required is equal to the number of the causes entailing it. They consider the mistake of a person committing excessive mistakes and a mistake committed while rectifying one as no mistake.

The Shafiis, Malikis and Hanbalis observe that if the person performing the prescribed prayer has a doubt regarding the number of cycles performed, he or she will consider the number of cycles he or she is certain of having performed as the base and will complete the prescribed prayer by performing the rest.

The Hanafis state that if the doubt of a person performing the prescribed prayer is for the first time in his or her life, he or she will repeat it from the beginning. But if it occurs to that person that he or she has doubts in the prescribed prayer earlier as well, he or she will think for quite a while and will act in accordance with what seems more probable to him or her. But if the doubt remains even after thinking, he or she will consider the number of cycles he or she is certain of having performed as the base.

The Jafaris say that if the doubt concerning the number of cycles performed occurs in a two-cycle prescribed prayer (such as the dawn prescribed prayer, the prescribed prayer of a traveller, the Friday congregational prescribed prayer; the prescribed prayer of the Festival; the prescribed prayer when an eclipse occurs) or in the evening prescribed prayer or in the first two cycles of night, noon and afternoon prescribed prayers, that prescribed prayer will be invalidated and it will be obligatory to begin it again from the beginning. But if the doubt occurs in the cycles subsequent to the first two cycles of the four-cycle prescribed prayers, the person will, because of caution, perform prescribed prayer after completing the prescribed prayer and before performing any act incompatible with prescribed prayer. For example, if a doubt arises after the completion of the two prostrations of the second cycle as to whether it is the second or the third cycle, the person will take the greater number of cycles as the basis and complete the prescribed prayer. He or she will then perform as caution (*ihtiyat*) two cycles while sitting or a single cycle standing. If the doubt concerns his or her being in third or fourth cycle, that person will consider it the fourth cycle and complete the prescribed prayer and follow it up with a single cycle standing or two cycles sitting by way of caution. If the doubt concerns his or her being in second or fourth cycle, he or she will consider it the fourth cycle. He or she will then offer two cycles standing. If there is a doubt regarding its being second, third or fourth cycle, he or she will assume it to be the fourth cycle, and offer following it two cycles standing and two cycles sitting.

According to them, the reason for performing these cycles is to preserve the prescribed form of prescribed prayer and avoid additions and omissions. Their point is illustrated by the example of a person who has a doubt between its being third or fourth cycle. He will consider it to be the fourth cycle and perform a single cycle separately after completing the prescribed prayer. If the prescribed prayer has been complete, the additional cycle performed separately will be considered as supererogatory, and if the prescribed prayer had been incomplete, the separate cycle will complement it. However, this manner of performing the cautionary prayer (*salat al-ihtiyat*) is particular to the Jafaris.

They limit this procedure to the obligatory prescribed prayer and among them to noon, afternoon and night prescribed prayers only. As to the supererogatory prayers, the person performing the prescribed prayer is free to consider the minimum or maximum cycles probably performed as the basis, provided such supposition does not invalidate the prescribed prayer (such as where he or she doubts his or her being in second or third cycle with the knowledge that the supererogatory comprises only two cycles. Here he or she will consider the minimum number of cycles probably performed as the basis. It is better in all recommended prayers to consider the minimum ascertainable number of cycles as the basis. If a doubt concerning cycles arises in the prescribed prayer for caution, the maximum number of the prescribed prayers probably performed will be made the basis, except where doing so invalidates the prescribed prayer, in which case the minimum number of prescribed prayers will be the basis. Some Jafaris observe that one is free to choose as basis either the minimum or the maximum prescribed prayers probably performed.

2.2. THE FRIDAY PRESCRIBED CONGREGATIONAL PRAYER

2.2.1. ITS OBLIGATORY ACTS

There is consensus among all the Muslims regarding the Friday prescribed prayer (*salat al-jumuah*) being obligatory in accordance with the words of God, the Exalted, "*O believers, when proclamation is made for prayer on the Day of Congregation hasten to God's remembrance and leave trading aside*" (62:9) as well as the *mutawatir* Traditions narrated by all the major schools of Divine Law. They differ as to whether its obligatory acts are conditional to the presence of the ruler or his deputy or if it is obligatory unconditionally.

The Hanafis and the Jafaris state that the presence of the ruler or his deputy is necessary. The Friday prayer is not obligatory if neither of them is present. The Jafaris require the ruler to be just. Otherwise his presence is equal to his absence. To the Hanafis, his presence is sufficient even if he is not just.

The Shafiis, Malikis and Hanbalis attach no significance to the presence of the ruler. A large number of Jafaris observe that in the absence of a ruler or his representative and the presence of a just jurist, there exists an option between performing either the Friday or the noon prescribed prayer, although preference lies with the performance of the Friday prayer.[22]

2.2.2. CONDITIONS OF THE FRIDAY PRESCRIBED PRAYER

The schools concur that the requirements for other prescribed prayers (such as covering the body, and facing the *qiblah*) also apply to the Friday prescribed prayer, that its time is from when the sun crosses the meridian up to when the shadow of an object equals its height, and that it can be performed in a mosque as well any other place, except in the opinion of the Malikis who do not consider it valid except in a mosque.

There is also consensus that it is obligatory for men, not for women, that one who performs it is not required to perform the noon prayer, that it is not obligatory for the blind, and that it is not valid except when performed in congregation. They differ regarding the minimum number of persons required to form a congregation. The Malikis state that its minimum is twelve, excluding the leader. The Jafaris consider it to be four, excluding the leader. In the opinion of the Shafiis and Hanbalis, it is forty, including the leader; according to the Hanafis it is five, although some of them say it is seven.

The schools, excepting the Hanafi, concur in its being prohibited for someone upon whom the Friday prescribed prayer has become obligatory and its conditions fulfilled, to travel after the sun has crossed the meridian before performing it. The Hanafis allow it.

2.2.3. THE FRIDAY SERMONS
There is consensus that the two sermons are a requirement for convening the Friday prescribed prayer and that they are to be delivered before the prescribed prayer part begins, although after the setting in of its time and not earlier. They differ regarding the obligatory acts of standing while delivering them. The Jafaris, Shafiis and Malikis require it, but not the Hanafis and Hanbalis.

As to their content, the Hanafis say that the sermon will be considered delivered even by a minimal *dhikr*, such as uttering "*al-hamdullah*" or "*astaghfirullah*," although such brevity is disapproved. The Shafiis observe that it is necessary in both the sermons to praise God, invoke blessings on the Prophet, to exhort to piety, to recite a verse in at least one of the sermons, although reciting it in the first is better, and to supplicate for the faithful in the second sermon. According to the Malikis, anything considered by custom as a sermon suffices, provided it includes exhortation and announcement of good news. The Hanbalis consider it essential to praise God, invoke blessings on the Prophet (☺), recite a verse and counsel piety. The Jafaris state that it is obligatory in each of the sermons to praise and extol God, invoke blessings on the Prophet and his family, preach, and recite something from the Quran, and in the second sermon, to implore God's forgiveness and to pray for the faithful. The Shafiis and Jafaris observe that it is obligatory for the preacher to separate the two sermons by sitting down for a short while between them. The Malikis and Hanafis consider it recommended.

According to the Hanbalis, the sermon should be delivered in Arabic, if possible. The Shafiis consider Arabic necessary if the people are Arabs, and if they are non-Arabs, the preacher should preach in their language even if he is well-versed in Arabic. The Malikis say that it is obligatory to preach in Arabic even if the people are non-Arabs and do not understand a word of Arabic. If there is no one among them who knows Arabic, there is no obligation to perform the Friday prescribed prayer. The Hanafis and the Jafaris do not consider Arabic a condition for delivering the sermons.

2.2.4. *ITS MODE OF PERFORMANCE*

The Friday prescribed prayer comprises two cycles, just like the morning prescribed prayer. The Jafaris and the Shafiis observe that after the recitation of the first chapter of the Quran in each cycle, it is recommended to recite *Surat al-Jumuah* in the first cycle and *Surat al-Munafiqun* in the second. The Malikis state that *Surat al-Jumuah* will be recited in the first cycle and *Surat al-Ghashiyah* in the second. According to the Hanafis it is disapproved to confine to a particular chapter.

2.3. THE FESTIVAL PRESCRIBED PRAYER

The schools differ concerning the prayers performed on the two festivals (*al-fitr* and *al-adha*), as to whether they are obligatory or recommended. The Jafaris and the Hanafis observe that it is obligatory for every individual if the conditions mentioned for the Friday prescribed prayer are fulfilled. If some or all of these conditions do not exist, there is no obligatory acts in the opinion of the two schools, except that the Jafaris add that in the absence of conditions necessary for its obligatory acts, one can perform it as recommended either singly or in congregation (*jamaah*), both during a journey and stay. According to the Hanbalis it is *fard kifai*. The Shafiis and the Malikis consider it a recommended *Sunnah*.

In the opinion of the Jafaris and the Shafiis its time is from sunrise until the sun crosses the meridian. According to the Hanbalis, its time is from when the sun rises to the height of a spear until it crosses the meridian.

The Jafaris say that delivering of two sermons is obligatory here as in the Friday prescribed prayer. The other schools consider it as recommended. All the schools concur that the sermons are to be delivered after the prayer part, as against the Friday prescribed prayer, in which they are delivered before.

According to the Jafaris and the Shafiis, it can be validly performed individually as well as in congregation. The other schools consider congregation necessary for the festival prescribed prayer (*salat al-id*).

As to the mode of its performance, it comprises two cycles, performed differently by the various schools in the following manner. The Hanafis say that *takbirat al-ihram* should be said after making the intention, followed by the praise of God. Then will follow three more *takbirah*s, with an interval of silence equaling three *takbirah*s, and it is also correct to say:

subhan Allah wa alhamdullilah
wa la ilaha ill-Allah wa Allahu akbar

Then will follow recital of the first chapter of the Quran, another chapter, then bending forward and prostration, in that order. The second cycle will begin by reciting the first chapter of the Quran, which will be followed by another chapter, three *takbirah*s, bending forward and prostration. After this the prescribed prayer will be completed.

The Shafiis say that after saying the *takbirat al-ihram*, the *dua al-istiftah*²³ will be recited, followed by seven *takbirah*s, reciting after every two of them in a low voice.

subhan Allah wa alhamdullilah
wa la ilaha ill-Allah wa Allahu akbar

Then after *taawwudh*: the first chapter of the Quran and *Surat al-Qaf* will be recited, followed by bending forward and prostration. After standing up for the second cycle and saying a single *takbirah* for it, five more *takbirah*s will be added, reciting after every two of them :

subhan Allah wa alhamdullilah
wa la ilaha ill-Ahhal wa Allahu akbar

This will be followed by the first chapter of the Quran and *Surat al-Iqtarabat*, and then the prescribed prayer will be completed

The Hanbalis say that the *dua al-istiftah* will be recited followed by six *takbirah*s reciting after every two of them in a low voice:

wal hamdullilah kathiran wa suban Allah bukrat
wa asilen wa salli Allah ali muhammad wa alihi wa sallam
tasliman

This will be followed by *ta'awwudh, basmalah, al-Fatihah* and *Surat Sabbihisma Rabbik*. The cycle will be then completed. Upon standing up for the second cycle, five *takbirah* as, apart from the *takbirah* for the standing, will be said, reciting after every two of them what was mentioned concerning the first cycle. Then the *basmalah*, will be followed by *Surat al-Ghashiyah* and bending forward and the prescribed prayer will then be completed.

The Malikis say that after the *takbirat al-ihram*, six more *takbirah*s will be said, followed by al-*Fatihah, Surat al-Ala*, bending forward and prostration. Then standing up for the second cycle and saying the *takbirah* for it, five more *takbirah*s will be said, followed by *al-Fatihah, Surat al-Shams* or a similar *Surah*. The prescribed prayer will then be completed.

The Jafaris say that the *takbirat al-ihram* will be followed by *al-Fatihah* and another *Surah*. Then five *takbirah*s will be said with the raising of the hands, palms up while standing and offering a supplication after each of them, then bending forward and prostration will follow. After standing up for the second cycle, *al-Fatihah* and another chapter will be recited, followed by four *takbirah*s, each of them followed by *qunut*. Then the bending forward will be performed and the prescribed prayer completed.

2.4. THE PRAYER OF THE ECLIPSES

The Hanafi, Hanbali, Maliki and Shafii schools observe that the solar and lunar eclipse prescribed prayer is an emphasized *Sunnah* and not obligatory. The Jafaris state that it is obligatory for every *mukallaf*. It does not have a special form in the opinion of the Hanafis. Rather it is to be performed in two cycles like a supererogatory prayer, each cycle comprising a single standing and bending forward. The person performing the prayer is free to perform it in two, four, or more cycles.

According to the Hanbalis, Shafiis and Malikis, it has two cycles, with each cycle consisting of standing twice and bending forward twice. After the *takbirat al-ihram, al-Fatihah* and another chapter will be recited, followed by bending forward. After rising from the bending forward, hands upon the knees, *al-Fatihah* and another chapter will be recited, followed by bending forward and prostration. Then standing up for the second cycle, it will be performed like the first, and the prescribed prayer completed. It is also valid to perform it in the manner of a supererogatory prayer.

There is consensus that it can be performed singly as well as in congregation, except that the Hanafis observe regarding the lunar eclipse prescribed prayer that it has not been enacted for congregation, and has to be performed singly, at home. As to its time, all the schools excepting the Malikis concur that it begins and ends with the eclipse. The Malikis say that its time begins when the sun is at a spear's height above the horizon and continues until noon. The Hanafis and the Malikis say that a two-cycle prescribed prayer is recommended at the time of any fearsome incident, such as an earthquake, thunderbolt, unusual darkness, epidemic, etc. According to the Hanbalis, it is recommended only for earthquakes.

The schools concur that this prescribed prayer does not have a call to prescribed prayer and declaration to perform the prescribed prayer, although an announcer will call out "*al-salat*" three times according to the Jafaris, and "*al-salat jamaah*" according to the other schools.

The Jafaris observe that the prescribed prayer is obligatory upon every individual during solar and lunar eclipses, earthquakes, and on the occurrence of all unsettling celestial phenomena such as the sky's darkening or becoming extraordinarily red, strong winds, big sounds, etc.

If performed in congregation, the leader will recite only the chapters on behalf of those following him, just as in the daily prayers. The time for performing the prescribed prayer for solar and lunar eclipses is the period of their occurrence one who does not perform them at that time will perform them later as missed. There is no specific time for prescribed prayer to be performed consequent to earthquakes and similar fearsome incidents. Rather, it is obligatory to perform these cycles as soon as their causes occur, although in the event of delay they can be performed as 'on time" as long as one is alive.

Its mode of performance is that after *takbirat al-ihram*, recitation of the first chapter of the Quran followed by another chapter are recited, then bending forward. Upon rising up from the bending forward, again the recitation of the first chapter of the Quran and another chapter will be recited, followed again by bending forward. This will continue until five bending forward are performed, and they will be followed by two prostrations. On standing up for the second cycle, the first chapter of the Quran will be recited and another chapter will follow, followed by a bending forward. This will be repeated until five bending forward are performed in the second cycle as well. Then will follow two prostrations, *tashahhud* and *taslim*. Thus altogether there are ten bending forward and every five of them is followed by two prostrations, both in the first and the second cycles.

2.5. PRESCRIBED PRAYER FOR RAIN

Prayer for rain (*salat al-istisqa*) has been expressly mentioned in the Quran and the *Sunnah*, and there is consensus concerning it. God Almighty says, "*When Moses prayed for water for his people....*" (2:60) and "*I said, 'Ask forgiveness of your Lord; surely He is ever All-forgiving, and He will lose heaven upon you in torrents'*" (71:10-11).

A Tradition reports that once when the people of Madinah were facing drought and the Prophet (ﷺ) was delivering a sermon, a man stood up and said, "Horses and women have perished. Pray to God to give us rain." The Prophet (ﷺ) extended his hands and prayed. Anas narrates, "The sky was clear like a piece of glass. Then the wind began to blow. The clouds emerged and gathered and the sky poured forth its blessings. We went forth wading through the pools until we reached our homes. It continued to rain until the next Friday, and the same person stood up again and said, 'O Prophet of God, houses have fallen and the caravans have been detained. So pray to God to stop it.' The Prophet (ﷺ) smiled and then said, 'O God, make rain around us, not upon us.' Then I looked at the sky and saw it that the clouds had split and formed a garland around Madinah."

The occasion for this prescribed prayer is drought, scanty rainfall, and drying up of springs. The schools concur that if rain is delayed even after performing the prescribed prayer, it is recommended to repeat it. If it is preceded by three days of fasting and the people go forth on foot, in a humble and supplicating manner, accompanied by their women and children, their elderly, men and women, and cattle, it will be more conducive for invoking Divine Mercy.

There is consensus that it is valid to perform it individually as well as in congregation, and that it does not have a call to the prescribed prayer and declaration to perform the prescribed prayer. It is recommended for the leader to deliver a sermon after the prescribed prayer. As to its mode, the schools concur that it comprises two cycles, to be performed like the two cycles of the prescribed prayer for festivals in accordance with what each school specifies in that regard. The Malikis and the Hanafis say that it is like the prescribed prayer for festivals although without the additional *takbirah*. The Jafaris observe that it is recommended after every *takbirah* to recite a prayer, hands in front, palms up imploring the mercy and blessing of God and seeking rainfall. The Hanafi, Hanbali, Maliki and Shafii schools state that this kind of supplication will be mentioned by the preacher after the prescribed prayer during the sermon, not in the prescribed prayer itself.

2.6. MISSED PRESCRIBED PRAYER

2.6.1. INTRODUCTION

There is consensus among the schools that it is obligatory to perform missed prescribed prayer (*salat al-qada*) of every obligatory prescribed prayer omitted either intentionally, or on account of forgetfulness, ignorance or sleep, and that there is no missed prescribed prayer for a woman for the prayers left during her monthly period and bleeding following childbirth, because prescribed prayer is not obligatory during these periods. The schools differ regarding one who is insane, unconscious or intoxicated.

The Hanafis state that missed prescribed prayers are obligatory upon one who loses one's senses by consuming an unlawful intoxicant, such as wine or something of its kind. As to someone insane or fainting, that person is not required to perform the prescribed prayer in the following two situations: firstly, if the state of fainting or insanity continues for a period exceeding five cycles (hence if it lasts for less than that period the person should perform its missed time); secondly, if the recovery from insanity or fainting does not occur at the time of prescribed prayer (hence if he or she recovers and does not perform the prescribed prayer), its missed time will be obligatory upon him or her.

The Malikis are of the opinion that an unconscious or insane person has to perform missed prescribed prayers. An intoxicated person will perform missed prescribed prayers if the cause of intoxication is the drinking of something forbidden, but if it is something lawful such as sour milk there is no missed prescribed prayer for it. According to the Hanbalis, an unconscious person and one intoxicated by something forbidden will perform missed prescribed prayer, although an insane person is not required to do so.

The Shafiis state that an insane person whose state of insanity extends over the entire period of a prescribed prayer will not perform its missed time. The same applies to one in a swoon or one intoxicated, provided he or she is not responsible for his or her state.

The Jafaris consider it obligatory for anyone who has consumed an intoxicant to perform missed prescribed prayer, irrespective of whether the person drinks it knowingly or unknowingly, voluntarily or out of an exigency or under duress. As to an insane person and one has fainting spells, that person has no missed prescribed prayer to perform.

2.6.2. THE MODE OF PERFORMING MISSED PRESCRIBED PRAYER

The Hanafis and Jafaris observe that a person who has omitted an obligatory prescribed prayer will perform the missed prescribed prayer exactly in the manner he or she would have performed it at the right time. Hence if a person with an outstanding complete prescribed prayer intends to perform it during journey, he or she should perform it completely, and one performing a shortened prayer (*qasr*) as missed prescribed prayer at home will perform it shortened. Similar is the rule respecting recital in a high or low voice. Hence if evening and night prescribed prayers are performed, missed prescribed prayer during daytime, their recital will be loud, and in the missed prescribed prayer of noon and afternoon prescribed prayers during night, the recital will be in a low voice.

The Hanbalis and the Shafiis state that the one who intends to perform the missed prescribed prayer of a *qasr* prayer during a journey will perform it shortened in accordance with the prescribed prayer missed by that person. But if the person happens to be staying, it is obligatory upon him or her to perform it complete as missed prescribed prayer. This was with respect to the number of cycles.

As to its recital in a high or low voice, the Shafiis say that the one who performs the missed prescribed prayer of noon at night will recite in a loud voice and one performing the missed prescribed prayer of evening during daytime will do so in a low voice. The Hanbalis require all missed prescribed prayer to be recited in a low voice, irrespective of their being those that are recited in a high voice or low, and regardless of whether the missed prescribed prayer is performed during daytime or at night, except where the person performing it is a leader and the prescribed prayer is one which is recited in a high voice and it happens to be nighttime.

The schools, excepting the Shafii, concur that sequence should be maintained in the performance of the prescribed prayers missed. Thus the missed prescribed prayer of one missed earlier will be performed before the missed prescribed prayer of one missed later. Hence if evening and night prescribed prayers are missed, the former will be offered before the latter, as is the case while performing them on time.

According to the Shafiis, the maintaining of sequence in prayers missed is *Sunnah* and not obligatory. Hence the prescribed prayer of a person who performs the night (*isha*) prayer before the evening (*maghrib*) prayer is valid.

2.7. PROXY FOR ACTS OF WORSHIP

There is a general consensus that appointing a proxy for carrying out prescribed prayers and fasts for a living person is not valid in any situation irrespective of whether he or she is capable or incapable of performing them himself or herself. The Jafaris state that it is valid to appoint a proxy for carrying out prescribed fasts and prayers on behalf of a dead person. The Hanafi, Hanbali, Maliki and Shafii schools observe that it is not valid in the case of a dead person, in the same manner as it is not valid for a living one.

The schools concur that appointing a proxy for the longer pilgrimage is valid in the case of a living person provided he or she is incapable of performing it himself or herself, and with greater reason in the case of a dead person. An exception are the Malikis who say that the appointing of a proxy, both for a living or a dead person, is of no consequence.

The Jafaris are alone in observing that it is obligatory for a child to perform the missed prescribed prayer of the prescribed fasts and prayers left unperformed by his or her father or mother. But they differ among themselves and some of them state that it is obligatory to perform all that which has been missed by them, even if intentionally. Others say that it is necessary to perform the missed prescribed prayers of only those acts which they has been unable to perform due to illness or some similar cause. There are others who observe that nothing except that which has been missed by them during death-illness is to be performed as missed prescribed prayer by the child.

2.8. CONGREGATIONAL PRESCRIBED PRAYER

The Muslims are one voice regarding congregational prescribed prayer (*salat al-jamaah*) being a ceremony and symbol of Islam. It was performed perpetually by the Prophet (صلى الله عليه وسلم) and by the rightly-guided caliphs after him. The schools differ as to whether it is obligatory or recommended.

The Hanbalis state that it is obligatory upon every person capable of it. But if he or she forsakes the congregation and prays individually, his or her prescribed prayer will be valid, though he or she will have sinned.

The Jafaris, Hanafis, Malikis and most Shafiis observe that it is neither obligatory individually (*ayni*) nor collectively (*kifai*) but is emphatically recommended.

According to the Jafaris, the *Shariah* has ordained congregation only for obligatory, not for recommended prayers, except for prescribed prayer for rain and the Festival prescribed prayer despite the absence of its conditions. The Shafii, Hanbali, Hanafi and Maliki schools consider it ordained for both obligatory and recommended prayers.

2.8.1. CONDITIONS FOR CONGREGATION
PRESCRIBED PRAYER

The following conditions have been laid down for the validity of congregation:

1. Being a Muslim. There is a consensus about it.

2. Sanity. They concur regarding it.

3. According to the Jafaris, the Malikis, and the Hanbalis in one of the two opinions narrated from Imam Ahmad, justice of the leader is necessary. The Jafaris site as their evidence the Prophet's statement, "A woman will not act as a leader for a man, nor a libertine (*fajir*) for a believer," the consensus of the Jafari, as well as the reason that the leader in prescribed prayer be suggestive of leadership, and a *fasiq* is not competent to assume it under any circumstance. But they also observe that if a person were to trust someone and pray behind him, later coming to know that he is a *fasiq* person, it is not obligatory upon him to repeat the prayer.

4. Being a male is necessary, and a woman cannot act as an leader for men, although other women can follow her as their leader according to all the schools except the Malikis who say that a woman cannot act as an leader even for women.

5. The Malikis, Hanafis and Hanbalis consider maturity as a requirement for the leader. The Shafiis are of the opinion that it is valid to follow a child of discriminating age. The Jafaris have two opinions. In accordance with the first, maturity is necessary, and according to the second the leader of an adolescent is valid.

6. As per consensus, the minimum number of persons required for congregation is two, one of them being the leader. This does not include the Friday prescribed prayer.

7. The person performing the prescribed prayer behind a leader should not stand ahead of the leader, in the opinion of all the schools except the Malikis, who observe that the prescribed prayer of the person performing the prescribed prayer behind a leader will not be invalid even if he stands ahead of the leader.

8. The congregation should be conducted in a single place

and there should be no partitions. The Jafaris state that here should not be an unusual distance between the person standing in prayer behind a leader and the leader without there being a connection through the continuity of the rows. The performance of the prescribed prayer in congregation is not valid if there exists between the leader and a male person standing in prayer behind a leader an obstacle which prevents the latter from seeing the leader or seeing those ahead of him who see the leader. Women are excepted and they can follow a male leader despite the presence of a partition provided the acts of the leader are not uncertain for them.

The Shafiis observe that a distance of more than 300 cubits between the leader and the person standing in prayer behind a leader is not objectionable provided there exists no obstacle. The Hanafis are of the opinion that if a person whose house adjoins a mosque follows the leader from that person's house with only a wall separating them, the prescribed prayer will be valid, provided the actions of the leader are known to that person. But if the house and the mosque are separated by a road or stream, following the leader is not valid. The Malikis state that the difference of place does not preclude the validity of following the leader; hence if the leader and the person standing in prayer behind a leader are separated by a road, stream or wall, the prescribed prayer will be valid as long as the person standing in prayer behind a leader is capable of ascertaining the acts of the leader.

9. There is consensus that it is necessary for the person standing in prayer behind a leader to make the intention of following the leader (*niyyat al-iqtida*).

10. The identity of the prescribed prayer of the person standing in prayer behind a leader and the leader. The schools concur that following the leader is not valid if the two cycles differ in their pillars and acts (such as the daily prescribed prayers as compared to the prescribed prayer for the dead or the festival prescribed prayer). They differ regarding the remaining matters. The Hanafis and the Malikis observe that it is not valid for a person offering the noon prescribed prayer

to follow one offering the afternoon prescribed prayer, and for one offering a missed prescribed prayer to follow someone offering the prescribed prayer on time, and vice versa.

The Jafaris and the Shafiis consider all these as valid. The Hanbalis consider it invalid to offer the noon prescribed prayer behind someone offering the afternoon prescribed prayer and vice versa, but they consider valid the offering of noon prescribed prayer as missed prescribed prayer behind someone performing it on time.

11. The recitation of the Quran by the leader should be perfect. Hence the schools concur that it is not valid for a person knowing the correct recitation to follow one who does not know it, and if he or she does so, his or her prescribed prayer will be invalid. According to the Hanafis, the prescribed prayer of both the leader and the person standing in prayer behind a leader will be invalid. They have a sound ground for holding the opinion that an illiterate person should follow, as far as it is possible, someone whose recital is correct, and it is not valid for him or her to pray singly where he or she can pray with a correct recitation by attending a congregation.

2.8.2. FOLLOWING THE LEADER

There is consensus that one praying with the prescribed ablution can follow a leader who prays with dry ablution and that it is obligatory for the person standing in prayer behind a leader to follow the leader in the recital of the *adhkar*:

> *sami Allah liman hamidah*
> *subhana rabbiya-l-azimi wa bi hamdi*
> *subhana rabbiya-l-ala wa bihamdhi*

They differ concerning following him in the recitation of the Quran.

The Shafiis observe that the person standing in prayer behind a leader should follow the leader in the prescribed prayers that are recited silently and not in those that are recited loudly, and it is obligatory for him or her to recite the first chapter of the Quran in all the cycles.

The Hanafis state that the person should not imitate the

leader either in the prescribed prayer where the recitation is silent nor in that where it is loud. Rather, it has been narrated from Imam Abu Hanifah that the recitation of a person standing in prayer behind a leader is a sin.[24]

According to the Malikis, the person standing in prayer behind a leader should perform the recitation in the prescribed prayer where it is silent, not in the prescribed prayer where it is loud.

The Jafaris do not consider it obligatory for the person standing in prayer behind a leader to perform the recitation in the first two cycles, but consider it obligatory in the third cycle of evening prescribed prayer and the last two cycles of the four-cycle prescribed prayers.

All the schools concur concerning the obligatory acts of following the leader actions by the person standing in prayer behind a leader, but differ in their interpretation of the term 'following' (*mustabaah*).

The Jafaris state that the meaning of 'following' is that every act of the person standing in prayer behind a leader should neither precede the corresponding act of the leader nor follow it after an inordinate delay; rather it should be either simultaneous or follow it with a small lag.

In the opinion of the Hanafis, 'following' is achieved by performing simultaneously or immediately afterwards or with some lag the acts performed by the leader. Hence if the person standing in prayer behind a leader performs bending forward after the leader raised his head from the bending forward but before his going down for prostration, he or she will be considered as having 'followed' the leader in the bending forward.

The Malikis say that the meaning of 'following' is that every act of the person standing in prayer behind a leader should take place after the corresponding act of the leader without preceding it or occurring simultaneously with it or following it after excessive delay so that the person standing in prayer behind a leader will perform bending forward before but before the leader has raised his head from it.

The Hanbalis are of the opinion that 'following' implies that the person standing in prayer behind a leader should neither precede the leader in any of the acts of prescribed prayer nor delay any act after the leader has performed it. Hence the leader should not enter the bending forward after the leader has finished it and the leader should not have ended the bending forward before the person standing in prayer has entered it.

2.8.3. JOINING THE CONGREGATION IN THE MIDDLE OF THE PRESCRIBED PRAYER

If a person joins the congregation after the leader has finished one or more cycles, the schools concur that he or she will make the intention for congregation and continue to perform it with the leader. But the question is whether that person will consider the cycles being performed along with the leader as the initial part of his prescribed prayer or the end part of it. For example, if that person performs only the last cycle of the evening prescribed prayer with the leader, there remain two more cycle which have to be performed: now will the third cycle which that person has performed with the leader be considered his third cycle as well with the first two cycles remaining to be performed or will it be considered the first cycle with the second and the third cycle remaining to be performed?

The Hanafis, Malikis and Hanbalis observe that the part of the prescribed prayer which the person standing in prayer behind a leader performs with the leader will be considered the end part of the former's prescribed prayer. Therefore if that person performs only the last cycle of evening prescribed prayer in congregation, it will be considered the last cycle as well and that person will perform after it a cycle in which he or she will recite the first chapter of the Quran and another chapter, followed by *tashahhud* and in the next cycle, the first chapter of the Quran and another chapter. To put it briefly, in such a situation he or she will offer the third cycle before the first two cycles by considering the part of his or her prescribed prayer performed with the leader as the end part, and the part performed without the leader as the initial part.

The Shafiis and the Jafaris state that the part of the prescribed prayer which the person standing in prayer behind a
leader performs with the leader will be considered the initial
part of his or her prescribed prayer, not the end part of it.
Hence if he or she performs the last cycle of evening prescribed
prayer with the leader, he or she will count it as his or her
first cycle and will stand up for performing the second cycle
which will include sitting back on knees and bearing witness
and will follow it up with the third cycle that will be the end
part of his or her prescribed prayer.

2.8.4. PREFERENCE FOR THE LEADER
The Hanafis say that if equally qualified men gather for
the prescribed prayer, the person most learned in its rules will
be preferred for leading it, followed by one with the best recitation, then the most pious, then the one whose acceptance of
Islam was earlier, then the eldest, then the one superior in
character, then the most handsome, then the noblest in respect
of lineage, and then the most cleanly dressed, in that order. If
they are all equal in respect of these qualities, the selection
will be by casting lots among them.

The Malikis are of the opinion that the ruler or his deputy
will lead the prayers, followed by the leader of the mosque,
then the master of the house, then the one most learned in the
Traditions, then the most just, then the one having the best
recitation, then the most devout, then the one preceding others
in his acceptance of Islam, then the one having the best lineage, then the one with the best character, and then the one
who is best dressed, in that order. If they are equal in these
respects, lots will be cast among them.

The Hanbalis observe that the most learned in jurisprudence and having the best recitation will be preferred, followed
by one who excels only in recitation. Then comes the one who
excels in the rules of prescribed prayer, followed by the one
who excels in recitation but does not know the law of prescribed prayer, then the most aged, then the person with the
best lineage, then the one who has migrated earliest, then the

most God-fearing, and then the most pious, in that order. If
they are equal in these qualities, lots will be cast.

The Shafiis prefer the ruler, then the leader of the mosque,
then the one most learned in jurisprudence, then the one having the best recitation, then the most ascetic, then the most
pious, then the one who has migrated earliest, then the most
eloquent, then the best in terms of lineage, then the best in
character, then the cleanest in matters of dress, body and craft,
then the one with the best voice, then the most handsome, and
then a married person, in that order. In the event of their
being equal in respect of these qualities, lots will be cast.

The Jafaris state that if a number of persons are eager to
lead the prayers for the sake of the spiritual reward (*thawab*)
and not for any worldly purpose, the one whom the persons
standing in prescribed prayer behind a leader prefer on the
basis of the preferential qualities mentioned in the *Shariah*
with a religious intent in mind and not with mundane intentions, will be the leader. But if they differ, it is better that a
jurisprudent be preferred, followed by one who has the best
recitation, then the most eloquent, and then one who enjoys a
preference in accordance with the *Shariah*.

2.9. PRESCRIBED PRAYER DURING TRAVEL

The schools concur that the shortening (*qasr*) of prayers
during travel is limited to the obligatory four-cycle prayers.
Hence noon, afternoon and night prescribed prayers will be
performed in two cycles, like the morning prayer. The schools
differ as to whether the prescribed prayer of the traveler (*salat
al-musafir*) is obligatory during travel or if there is an option
between it and complete prescribed prayer? The Hanafis and
the Jafaris observe that it is obligatory and has to be performed. The other schools state that there is an option and a
person may either perform it as if a traveler or complete.

2.9.1. CONDITIONS FOR THE PRESCRIBED PRAYER OF A TRAVELER

Shortened prescribed prayer of a traveler requires the following conditions:

1. There is consensus that traveling over a certain distance is a condition. The distance, in the opinion of the Hanafis, is twenty-four parasangs in the direction of journey; less than this is not permissible for the shortened form of the prescribed prayer. The Jafaris consider it to be eight parasangs in the direction of journey or to and from together.[25] The Hanbalis, Malikis and Shafiis regard it as sixteen parasangs, only in the direction of journey, though it does not matter if the distance traveled is less than this distance by two miles (eight miles, in the opinion of the Malikis). A parasang is equal to 5.04 km.[26] Hence the minimum distance to be traveled in the opinion of the Hanafis, the three other schools, and the Jafaris is 120.96 kms, 80.64 kms and 40.32 kms respectively.

2. The schools concur that the intention to travel the complete distance should be present at the start of the journey, and that the intention of a 'follower'—such as wife, servant, captive or soldier—is subject to the intention of the 'commander' whom he follows, provided that the one under command knows the intention of that commander or leader. In the event of ignorance he or she will perform the prescribed prayer complete.

3. Shortened prescribed prayer (*qasr*) is not valid in the opinion of the Shafii, Hanbali, Hanafi and Maliki schools except after leaving behind the buildings of a town. The Jafaris observe that leaving the constructed areas is not sufficient. Rather, it is necessary that either the walls of the town should disappear from sight or its call to the prescribed prayer should not be heard. The limit they have set for the beginning of the journey is also the limit for terminating it. That is, if a person is returning back home, he or she is supposed to pray the shortened form of prescribed prayer until he or she sees the walls of his town or is able to hear its call to prescribed prayer.

4. The journey should be for a legitimate purpose. Hence if it is for an illegitimate purpose, such as a journey for the sake

of committing theft, etc., he or she may not pray the shortened form of the prescribed prayer in the opinion of all the schools, except the Hanafis, who observe that he or she will pray the shortened form of the prescribed prayer in all journeys even if the journey is an illegitimate one. At the most he or she will be sinning by performing an unlawful act.

5. In the opinion of the Hanafi, Hanbali, Maliki and Shafii schools, the traveler may not pray in a congregation being led by a local leader or another traveler whose prescribed prayer is complete. If he or she does so, it is obligatory for him or her to perform the complete prescribed prayer. The Jafaris do not accept this condition and consider it valid for a person whose prescribed prayer is complete to pray behind a person praying the shortened prescribed prayer and vice versa, provided each performs his or her own duty. Therefore, if a traveler prays the noon, afternoon and night prescribed prayers behind a local resident, he or she will perform two cycles and sitting back on your knees and bearing witness (*tashahhud*) along with the leader and say the greetings to the Prophet (ﷺ) individually, while the leader continues with his prescribed prayer until its end. And if a local person prays behind a traveler, he will perform two cycles in congregation and complete the remaining part of his prescribed prayer individually.

6. The intention of the shortened prescribed prayer is essential for the prescribed prayer being so performed. Hence if a person prays without making the intention of the shortened prescribed prayer, he or she will perform that prescribed prayer complete in the opinion of the Hanbalis and the Shafiis. The Malikis state that it is sufficient to make the intention of the shortened prescribed prayer in the first shortened prescribed prayer of the journey, and it is not necessary to repeat it in every prescribed prayer.

The Hanafis and the Jafaris observe that the intention of performing the shortened prescribed prayer is not a condition for it becoming obligatory, so that if one does not make it, he or she will have to perform it complete, because the actual status of a duty is not altered by intentions. Moreover, such a person has intended the journey from the very beginning. However, the Jafaris say that if a traveler intends to stay at a particular place and later changes his or her mind, he or she will offer the shortened prescribed prayer as long as he or she has not performed any complete prescribed prayer. Hence if that person performs even one complete prescribed prayer and then changes his or her plan of staying there, he or she will continue to perform prescribed prayer completely.

7. The intention should not be to stay continuously at one place for: fifteen days in the opinion of the Hanafis, ten days in the opinion of the Jafaris, and four days in the opinion of he Malikis and the Shafiis, and a period during which more than twenty prescribed prayer become obligatory in the opinion of the Hanbalis. The Jafaris further add that if he or she is unable to decide for how long he or she will stay at a particular place, he or she will continue to perform the shortened prescribed prayer for thirty days, and after this period it will be obligatory for him or her to perform complete prescribed prayer even if it happens to be a single one.

8. The traveler's nature of work should not require continuous travel—that is, one who hires out his or her beasts of burden or a tradesman whose trade requires continuous traveling so that he or she is unable to stay at home for the stipulated period of days. This condition has been upheld only by the Hanbalis and the Jafaris.

9. The traveler should not be a nomad who has no fixed house and keeps moving from place to place. Only the Jafaris have expressly stated this condition.

10. The Hanafis, Hanbalis and Malikis observe that if a traveler changes his or her mind and intends to return to the place from where he or she began his or her journey, in the event of his or her not having traveled the distance required for performing the shortened prescribed prayer, that person's journey will be considered concluded and that person will perform his or her prescribed prayer complete. But if he or she has

traveled the distance stipulated by the *Shariah*, he or she will pray the shortened prescribed prayer until returning back to his or her native place.

The Shafiis say that whenever a person decides to turn back in the course of his or her journey, that person will perform his or her prescribed prayer complete.[27] This implies that he or she will start performing the prescribed prayer complete on his or her way back despite having traveled the stipulated distance, because the absence of the mention of any conditions proves inclusiveness and generality.

The Jafaris state that if one desists from his or her journey or becomes hesitant before covering the stipulated distance, it is obligatory for that person to offer the prescribed prayers completely. If the stipulated distance has been covered, that person will pray the shortened prescribed prayer. The continuous presence of the intent of journey is a condition as long as the stipulated distance has not been traveled, but after it has been covered, the subject is, of necessity, realized and its existence no longer depends upon intention.

2.9.2. Conditions Entailing Shortened Prescribed Prayer Entail the Breaking of the Fast

There is consensus among the schools that every condition that entails the shortened prescribed prayer is also a condition for the validity of breaking one's fast during a journey, although some schools have added other conditions for the validity of breaking the fast which will be mentioned in the chapter on fasting. The Jafaris add no further conditions. They observe that one who breaks the fast (consequent to traveling) will perform the prescribed prayer as shortened prescribed prayers, and he or she who performs the prescribed prayer as shortened prescribed prayer will break his or her fast.

2.10. Successive Performance of Two Prescribed Prayers

The Maliki, Shafii and Hanbali schools consider it permissible while traveling to perform noon and afternoon prescribed prayers, as well as evening and night prescribed prayers, successively by either advancing the performance of one of them or delaying the performance of the other. The Hanafi school observes that it is not valid to perform two prescribed prayers successively because of the excuse of being on a journey under any circumstance. The meaning of 'advancing' their successive performance is to perform the noon and afternoon prescribed prayers in the time meant for noon prescribed prayer, and by 'delaying' is meant their successive performance in the time specified for the afternoon prescribed prayer.

2.11. IGNORANCE AND FORGETFULNESS

The Jafaris observe that the prescribed prayer of one who intentionally performs complete prescribed prayer while traveling is invalid, and he or she is supposed to repeat it on time if its time has not elapsed, and as missed if it has lapsed. But if a person who is ignorant about the shortened prescribed prayer being obligatory does so, that person will not repeat the prescribed prayer, irrespective of whether its time has lapsed or not. If a person performs it complete out of forgetfulness and then remembers while its time has not lapsed, that person will repeat the prescribed prayer, and if he or she remembers it after its time has lapsed, he or she will not repeat it.

The Jafaris further state that if the time of a prescribed prayer sets in while a person is at home and capable of performing it and that person sets out on a journey before performing it, he or she will perform it in shortened form. But if the time of a prescribed prayer comes while a person is traveling and the traveler does not perform it until he or she has reached his or her native place or a place where he or she intends to remain for ten days, he or she will perform the prescribed prayer complete. Hence the criterion is the time when the prescribed prayer is performed and not the time when it becomes obligatory.

2.12. THE INVALIDATING CAUSES OF PRESCRIBED PRAYER

The following causes render prescribed prayer invalid (*mubtilat*):

1. Speech. Its minimum is anything composed of two letters, even if they are meaningless, and of a single letter if it makes sense (such as the word *qaf*, which is a verb in the imperative case of the root *waqa*). The prescribed prayer will not be invalidated by uttering a single letter which has no meaning and by an involuntary sound comprising many letters. The Hanafis and the Hanbalis do not differentiate between intentional speech and anything spoken by mistake in respect of its being a cause that invalidates prescribed prayer. The Jafaris, Shafiis and Malikis observe that prescribed prayer is not invalidated by anything spoken by mistake provided it is short and does not vitiate the form of the prescribed prayer.

The Jafaris and the Malikis are of the opinion that prescribed prayer is not invalidated by clearing the throat, irrespective of whether it is done due to necessity or not. The other schools consider it a cause that invalidates prescribed prayer if done needlessly but not otherwise, such as for clearing one's voice for better phonation or for signaling the leader to correct himself or herself.

The schools concur that it is valid to supplicate during prescribed prayer, seeking blessing and forgiveness from God except that the Hanafis and the Hanbalis restrict this supplication to what has been mentioned in the Quran and the *Sunnah*, or that which is sought only from God, such as provision (*rizq*) and blessings (*barakah*).

To recite the glorification of God (*tasbih, subhan Allah*) to indicate that one is performing prescribed prayer, or to guide the leader, or to correct his mistake, is not considered as a speech that invalidates prescribed prayer.

The Hanafi, Hanbali, Maliki and Shafii schools state that included in speech that invalidates prescribed prayer is the returning of *salam*. Hence if someone says *salam* to a person who is praying and he or she returns the salam verbally, the prescribed prayer becomes invalid. However, there is no harm if the salutations is returned by a gesture.

The Jafaris observe that it is obligatory for the person performing the prayer to return a salutation which contains the word '*salam*' with a similar salutation, though not any other salutation such as 'good morning', etc. They also specify that the form of the salutation being returned should be exactly like the initial salutation without any difference. Hence the reply of '*salam alaykum*' will be the same without alif and lam, and the reply of '*as-salam alaykum*' will be with the *alif* and *lam*.

2. Every action which destroys the form of the prescribed prayer invalidates it. The schools concur that the form is destroyed by any act which gives an onlooker the impression that the person performing that act is not praying.

3. There is a consensus regarding eating and drinking though they differ regarding the quantity that invalidates prescribed prayer. The Jafaris observe that eating and drinking invalidate prescribed prayer if they distort the form of prescribed prayer or violate any of its conditions, such as continuity, etc. The Hanafis observe that every form of eating and drinking invalidates prescribed prayer, irrespective of the quantity consumed, even if it is one sesame seed or a drop of water and regardless of whether it is done intentionally or otherwise. The Shafiis state that any food or drink which reaches the stomach of a *musalli*, irrespective of its being a small or a large quantity, invalidates prescribed prayer if the person performing the prescribed prayer does so intentionally and with the knowledge of its being forbidden. But if done out of ignorance or forgetfulness, a small quantity will not invalidate prescribed prayer, though a large quantity will. According to the Hanbalis, a large quantity will invalidate prescribed prayer, whether consumed intentionally or by mistake, and a small quantity only if consumed intentionally, not otherwise.

4. The occurrence of any minor or major impurity which invalidates the prescribed shorter ablution or bath ablution, will also invalidate prescribed prayer in the opinion of all the

schools except the Hanafis, who observe that it will invalidate prescribed prayer if it occurs before the last sitting by a duration equal to *tashahhud*, and if it occurs after it and before *taslim*, the prescribed prayer will not become invalid.

5. The schools concur that laughter invalidates prescribed prayer, though the Hanafis apply to it the same rule that they apply to *hadath*, as mentioned above.

* * *

Considering the importance of the causes that invalidate prescribed prayer and their number and diversity, and considering that each school has its own opinion, which at times concurs or differs with the opinions of other schools, it would be appropriate to give a summary of these causes in accordance with the opinion of each school separately.

The Shafiis observe that the causes invalidating prescribed prayer are: *hadath*, which necessitates the performance of the prescribed shorter ablution or bath ablution (*ghusl*); speech; crying; groaning, in certain situations; inordinate movement (s); a doubt concerning intention; indecision concerning discontinuing the prescribed prayer while continuing to perform it; shifting one's intention from one prescribed prayer to another, except where it is an obligatory prescribed prayer, for it is valid to change one's intention to that of a supererogatory prescribed prayer in order to perform the obligatory prescribed prayer with congregation; exposure of one's private parts when one is capable of covering them; nakedness, as soon as a covering becoming available; the presence of prescribed impurity to an inexcusable extent, when one does not speedily remove it from oneself; the repetition of *takbirat al-ihram*; intentional omission of a pillar of the prescribed prayers; praying in congregation behind a leader who is not fit for leadership due to his disbelief, etc.; performing an additional pillar intentionally; the reaching of any food or drink to the stomach; turning away with the chest from the *qiblah*; and wrongly performing a pillar involving a movement out of sequence.

The Malikis say that prescribed prayer is invalidated by omitting a pillar, intentionally or by mistake, if the person performing the prescribed prayer, thinking that his prescribed prayer is correct, does not remember having omitted it until after taslim and the passage of an inordinate duration; intentionally performing an additional pillar, such as bending forward or prostration; performing *tashahhud* out of place while sitting; laughter, both intentional and otherwise; eating and drinking intentionally; speaking intentionally and not for correcting the leader; vomiting, if intentional; puffing intentionally with the mouth; occurrence of anything that invalidates the shorter ablution; exposure of the private parts or any part of them; impurity falling on the person performing the prescribed prayer (*musalli*); inordinate movement; performing four additional cycles in a four-cycle prescribed prayer knowingly or by mistake; doing prostration before *taslim*; inadvertent omission of three *masnun* acts which the Prophet (ﷺ) and the rightly-guided caliphs performed regularly from among the *Sunnah* of prescribed prayer and then failing to perform the prostration for a mistake (*sujud al-sahw*).

The Hanbalis state that the causes that invalidate prescribed prayer are: any inordinate movement; the presence of impurity to an inexcusable extent; turning one's back to the *qiblah*; incidence of any impurity (*hadath*) invalidating the shorter ablution; intentional exposure of the private parts; reclining heavily on a support without any excuse; returning to perform the first *tashahhud* after starting the recitation, provided the person performing the prescribed prayer is aware and conscious of it; performing an additional pillar intentionally; intentionally changing the sequence of the pillars; mispronunciation that results in a change of meaning despite being capable of proper pronunciation; intending to disrupt the prescribed prayer or indecision regarding it; a doubt regarding *takbirat al-ihram*; laughter, speech, both intentional or otherwise; saying *taslim* intentionally before the leader; eating and drinking, even if due to forgetfulness or ignorance; needlessly clearing the throat; any puffing that may be construed as phonation of two letters; and weeping if not out of the fear of God.

According to the Hanafis, the causes that invalidate prescribed prayer are: speech, whether intentional, by mistake, or
due to ignorance; any supplication not out of the Quran or
Sunnah; any inordinate movement; turning the chest away
from the *qiblah*; eating and drinking; clearing the throat without reason; saying "uff" (i.e. 'fie' or 'ugh'; an expression of anger
or displeasure); groaning; saying 'Ah! (*taawuuh*); weeping loudly; saying "*al-hamdullah*" on sneezing; saying "*Inna lillah...*"
on hearing some bad news and "*al-hamdullah*" on hearing
some pleasing news; saying "*subhan Allah*" or "*la ilaha illa
lah*" as an expression of surprise; availability of water for one
praying with dry ablution; the rising of the sun for one offering
the morning prayer or its crossing the meridian for one performing *salat al-id*; the falling off of a bandage from one who
attains recovery; willful occurrence of *hadath*, but if the
hadath is involuntary it will not invalidate the prescribed
prayer, though one will have to perform the shorter ablution
again and recommence the prescribed prayer from where he
had left it.[28]

The Jafaris observe that the causes that render prescribed
prayer invalid are: ostentation (*riya*); uncertainty in intention;
performing any act of prescribed prayer while having made up
one's mind to discontinue it; changing one's intent from a preceding prescribed prayer to a subsequent prescribed prayer,
such as from noon to afternoon prescribed prayer. However, the
transition from afternoon to noon prescribed prayer is permissible. Hence if a person makes the intention of performing
afternoon prescribed prayer with the idea that he or she has
performed the noon prescribed prayer and remembers during
it that he or she has not performed the noon prescribed prayer,
it is valid for that person to shift the intention to offering the
noon prescribed prayer. Similarly, it is permissible to shift from
the intention of congregation to intention of performing it individually; but the opposite is not valid.

It is valid, however, for a person performing an obligatory
prescribed prayer individually to change his or her intention

to that of a supererogatory prescribed prayer in order to perform the obligatory prescribed prayer with congregation. Prescribed prayer is also invalidated by an additional *takbirat al-ihram*. Hence if one says *takbirah* for a prescribed prayer and then repeats it, the prescribed prayer becomes invalid and a third *takbirah* will be necessary. Again if he says *takbirah* for the fourth time, the prescribed prayer will become invalid and a fifth *takbirah* will be necessary; thus every even *takbirah* results in the prescribed prayer becoming invalid due to the addition of a pillar, and becomes valid again by every odd *takbirah*. Among the causes that invalidate prescribed prayer is the incidence of impurity (*najasah*) to an extent not excusable, when the person performing the prescribed prayer is unable to remove it without any inordinate movement that may vitiate the form of the prescribed prayer. The availability of water during prescribed prayer for a person praying with dry ablution invalidates both the dry ablution and the prescribed prayer, provided it becomes available before performing the bending forward of the first cycle; if later, he or she will complete the prescribed prayer which will be valid. A prescribed prayer will also be invalidated by: the absence of certain conditions, such as the covering and the lawfulness of a particular location; the occurrence of a *hadath*; intentional deviation with the whole body from the *qiblah* either to the right or the left or any other direction in between; speaking voluntarily and weeping on account of one's worldly woes; laughter; any act that destroys the form of prescribed prayer; eating and drinking; the intentional addition or omission of a part; and the omission, intentional or otherwise, of a pillar from among the five pillars. The five pillars are: intention, *takbirat al-ihram*, standing (*qiyam*), bending forward and the two prostrations for every cycle.

2.13. CROSSING IN FRONT OF THE PERSON PERFORMING THE PRESCRIBED PRAYER

The schools concur that someone's passing in front of a person performing the prescribed prayer does not invalidate the prescribed prayer, but they differ regarding its impermissibility.

The Jafaris state that it is neither impermissible for a person to pass in front of a person performing the prescribed prayer for the latter to pray in such a place. But it is recommended for the person performing the prescribed prayer to place before him or her an 'obstruction' if there is no barrier before him or her to prevent anyone passing by. The 'obstruction' can be a stick, a rope, a pile of earth, etc. which the person performing the prescribed prayer may place before him or her as a mark of veneration for prescribed prayer, which signifies detachment from the creation and attention towards the Creator.

The Malikis, Hanafis and Hanbalis observe that it is unlawful to cross over in front of a person performing the prescribed prayer in any circumstance, irrespective of whether he has placed an obstruction or not. Rather, the Hanafis and the Malikis add that it is unlawful for the person performing the prescribed prayer to create interference for passers by if he or she can keep out of their way. According to the Shafiis, it is forbidden to cross over in front of the person performing the prescribed prayer if he or she has not placed an obstruction, and if he or she has done so, it is neither forbidden nor disapproved.

3
PRESCRIBED FASTING
3.1. INTRODUCTION

Prescribed fasting in the month of Ramadan is one of the 'pillars' of the Islamic faith. No proof is required to establish its being obligatory and one denying it goes out of the fold of Islam, because it is obvious like the prescribed prayer, and in respect of anything so evidently established both the learned and the unlettered, the elderly and the young, all stand on an equal footing. It was declared an obligatory duty (*fard*) in the second year of the Hijrah upon each and every one capable of carrying out religious duties, i.e. a sane adult (*mukallaf*) and breaking it is not permissible except for any of the following reasons:

3.1.1. MENSTRUATION AND BLEEDING FOLLOWING CHILDBIRTH
The schools concur that fasting is not valid for women during menstruation and bleeding following childbirth.

3.1.2. ILLNESS
The schools differ here. The Jafaris observe that fasting is not valid if it would cause illness or aggravate it, or intensify the pain, or delay recovery, because illness entails harm (*darar*) and causing harm is unlawful. Moreover, a prohibition concerning an a rite of worship invalidates it. Hence if a person

fasts in such a condition, his or her fast is not valid (*sahih*). A predominant likelihood of its resulting in illness or its aggravation is sufficient for refraining from fasting. As to excessive weakness, it is not a justification for not undertaking the fast as long as it is generally bearable. Hence the extenuating cause is illness, not weakness, emaciation or strain, because every duty involves hardship and discomfort.

The Hanafi, Hanbali, Shafii and Maliki schools state that if one who is fasting (*saim*) falls ill, or fears the aggravation of his illness, or delay in recovery, he or she has the option to fast or refrain. Fasting is not incumbent upon that person. It is a relaxation and not an obligation in this situation. But where there is likelihood of death or loss of any of the senses, it is obligatory for the person not to fast and his fasting is not valid.

3.1.3. A WOMAN IN THE FINAL STAGE OF PREGNANCY AND NURSING MOTHERS

The Hanafi, Hanbali, Shafii and Maliki schools say that if a pregnant or nursing woman fears harm for her own health or that of her child, her fasting is valid though it is permissible for her to refrain from fasting. If she opts for not fasting, the schools concur that she is bound to perform its missed days later. They differ regarding its substitute (*fidyah*) and atonement (*kaffarah*). In this regard the Hanafis observe that it is not at all obligatory. The Malikis are of the opinion that it is obligatory for a nursing woman, not for a pregnant one.

The Hanbalis and the Shafiis say that giving the substitute is obligatory upon a pregnant and a nursing woman only if they fear danger for the child, but if they fear harm for their own health as well as that of the child, they are bound to perform the fasts missed only without being required to give a substitute. The substitute for each day is the feeding of one needy person (one mudd), which amounts to feeding one destitute person (*miskin*).[1]

The Jafaris state that if a pregnant woman nearing childbirth or the child of a nursing mother may suffer harm, both of them ought to break their fast and it is not valid for them to continue fasting due to the impermissibility of harm. They concur that both are to perform the missed fasts as well as give the substitute, equaling the feeding of one needy person, if the harm is feared for the child. But if the harm is feared only for her own person, some among them observe that she is bound to perform the missed fasts but not to give the substitute. Others say that she is bound to perform the missed fasts and give the substitute as well.

3.1.4. Travel

The Hanafi, Hanbali, Shafii and Maliki schools add a further condition to these, which is that the journey should commence before dawn and the traveler should have reached the point from where the prescribed prayer becomes overdue before dawn. Hence if he or she commences the journey after the setting in of dawn, it is unlawful for him or her to break the fast, and if he or she breaks it, its making up for will be obligatory upon him or her without an atonement (*kaffarah*).

The Shafiis add another condition, which is that the traveler should not be one who generally travels continuously, such as a driver. Thus if he travels habitually, he is not entitled to break the fast. In the opinion of the Hanafi, Hanbali, Shafii and Maliki schools, breaking the fast is optional and not compulsory. Therefore, a traveler who fulfills all the conditions has the option of fasting or not fasting. This is despite the observation of the Hanafis that performing the prescribed prayer as the shortened form during journey is compulsory and not optional.

The Jafaris say that if the conditions required for praying the shortened form of the prescribed prayer are fulfilled for a traveler, his or her fast is not acceptable. Therefore, if that person fasts, he or she will have to perform the missed fasts without being liable to atonement. This is if the person starts his or her journey before midday, but if he or she starts it at midday or later, that person will keep the prescribed fast and in the event of his or her breaking it, will be liable for the atonement of one who deliberately breaks the prescribed fast. And if a traveler reaches his or her hometown, or a place where he or she intends to stay for at least ten days, before midday without performing any act that breaks the fast, it is obligatory upon that person to continue fasting. In the event of the breaking of the prescribed fast, he or she will be like one who deliberately breaks the prescribed fast.

3.1.5. ACUTE THIRST

There is consensus among all the schools that one suffering from a malady of acute thirst can break his fast, and if that person can carry out the missed fasts later, it will be obligatory upon him or her without any atonement, in the opinion of the Hanafi, Hanbali, Shafii and Maliki schools.

In the opinion of the Jafaris, that person should feed a needy person by way of atonement. The schools differ in regard to acute hunger, as to whether it is one of the causes permitting breaking the fast, like thirst. The Hanafi, Hanbali, Shafii and Maliki schools say that hunger and thirst are similar and both make breaking the fast permissible. The Jafaris state that hunger is not a cause permitting breaking the prescribed fast except where it is expected to cause illness.

3.1.6. ELDERLY

Old people, men and women, in late years of life for whom fasting is harmful and difficult, can break the prescribed fast, but are required to give a substitute by feeding a needy person for each prescribed fast day omitted.

The same is true of a sick person who does not hope to recover during the whole year. The schools concur upon this rule excepting the Hanbalis, who say that giving a substitute is recommended and not obligatory.

3.1.7. FAINTING

The Jafaris state that fasting is not obligatory upon one has fainted, even if it occurs only for a part of the day, unless where he or she has formed the intention of fasting before it and recovers subsequently, whereat he or she will continue the prescribed fast.

3.1.8. EXCUSE NOT TO FAST NO LONGER PRESENT

If the reason permitting not fasting no longer exists such as the recovery of a sick person, maturing of a child, homecoming of a traveler, or termination of the menses, it is recommended in the view of the Jafaris and the Shafiis, to refrain (*imsak*) from things that break the fast (*muftirat*) as a token of respect. The Hanbalis and the Hanafis consider refraining as obligatory, but Malikis consider it neither obligatory nor recommended.

3.2. CONDITIONS OF PRESCRIBED FASTING

As mentioned earlier, fasting in the month of Ramadan is obligatory for each and every sane adult. Hence, fasting is neither obligatory upon an insane person in the state of insanity nor is it valid if he or she observes it. As to a child, it is not obligatory upon him or her, although valid if observed by a person at the age of discretion (*mumayyiz*). Also essential for the validity of the fast are Islam and intention. Therefore, as per consensus, neither the fast of a non-Muslim nor the fast of one who has not formed the intention is acceptable. This is apart from the aforementioned conditions of freedom from menses, bleeding following childbirth, illness and travel.

As to a person in an intoxicated or unconscious state, the Shafiis observe that his or her prescribed fast is not valid if he or she is not in his or her senses for the whole period of the prescribed fast. But if that person is in his or her senses for a part of this period, the prescribed fast is valid, although the unconscious person is liable for the missed fasts, whatever the circumstances, irrespective of whether his or her unconsciousness is self-induced or forced upon him or her. But the missed fasts is not obligatory upon an intoxicated person unless he or she is personally responsible for his or her state.

The Malikis state that the fast is not valid if the state of unconsciousness or intoxication persists for the whole or most of the day from dawn to sunset. But if it covers a half of the day or less and he or she was in possession of his or her senses at the time of making the intention and did make it, becoming unconscious or intoxicated later, making up for the prescribed fasts is not obligatory upon him or her. The time of making the intention known for the fast in their opinion extends from sunset to dawn.

According to the Hanafis, an unconscious person is exactly like an insane one in this respect, and their opinion regarding the latter is that if the insanity lasts through the whole month of Ramadan, it is not obligatory to make up for the missed fasts. If it covers half of the month, he or she will fast for the remaining half and make up for the prescribed fasts missed due to insanity.

The Hanbalis observe that it is obligatory for a person in a state of intoxication, irrespective of whether these states are self-induced or forced upon the person, to make up for missed prescribed fasts. In the opinion of the Jafaris, making up for missed fasts is only obligatory upon a person in an intoxicated state, irrespective of its being self-induced or otherwise; it is not obligatory upon an unconscious person even if his or her loss of consciousness is brief.

3.3. THINGS OBLIGATORY TO REFRAIN FROM DURING THE PRESCRIBED FAST

Those things from which it is obligatory to refrain during the fast (*muftirat*), from dawn to sunset, are:

3.3.1. EATING AND DRINKING DELIBERATELY

Both eating and drinking (*shurb*) deliberately invalidate the prescribed fast and necessitate making up for the fasts missed in the opinion of all the schools, although they differ as to whether atonement is also obligatory. The Hanafis and the Jafaris require it, but not the Shafiis and the Hanbalis.

A person who eats and drinks by an oversight is neither liable to make up for missed fasts nor atonement, except in the opinion of the Malikis, who only require its being made up. Included in drinking is inhaling tobacco smoke.

3.3.2. SEXUAL INTERCOURSE

Sexual intercourse when deliberate, invalidates the prescribed fast and makes one liable to make up for missed fasts and atonement, in the opinion of all the schools. The atonement is the freeing of a slave, and if that is not possible, fasting for two consecutive months; if even that is not possible, feeding sixty poor persons. The Jafaris and the Malikis allow an option between any one of these. That is, a sane adult may choose between freeing a slave, fasting or feeding the poor. The Shafiis, Hanbalis and Hanafis impose atonement in the abovementioned order. That is, releasing a slave is specifically obligatory, and in the event of incapacity fasting, becomes obligatory. If that, too, is not possible, giving food to the poor becomes obligatory. The Jafari state that all the three atonements become obligatory together if the act breaking the fast (*muftir*) is itself forbidden, such as eating anything usurped (*mahsub*), drinking wine, or fornicating. As to sexual intercourse by oversight, it does not invalidate the prescribed fast in the opinion of the Hanafis, Shafiis and Jafaris, but does according to the Hanbalis and the Malikis.

3.3.3. SEMINAL EMISSION

There is consensus that it invalidates the prescribed fast if caused deliberately. The Hanbalis say that if the thin genital discharge emitted while caressing (*madhy*) is discharged due to repeated sensual glances and the like, the prescribed fast will become invalid. The Hanafi, Hanbali, Shafii and Maliki say that seminal emission will necessitate making up for the prescribed fast without atonement. The Jafaris observe that it requires both making up for it and atonement.

3.3.4. VOMITING

It invalidates the fast if deliberate, and in the opinion of the Jafaris, Shafiis and Malikis, also necessitates making up for the fast. The Hanafis state that deliberate vomiting does not break the prescribed fast unless the quantity vomited fills the mouth. Two views have been narrated from Imam Ahmad Hanbal. The schools concur that involuntary vomiting does not invalidate the prescribed fast.

3.3.5. CUPPING
Cupping breaks the fast only in the opinion of the
Hanbalis, who observe that the cupper and the patient both
break the fast.

3.3.6. INJECTION
Injection invalidates the prescribed fast and requires the
fast to be made up in the opinion of all the schools. A group of
Jafari jurisprudents observe that it also requires atonement if
taken without an emergency.

3.3.7. INHALING A DENSE CLOUD OF SUSPENDED DUST
Inhaling a dense cloud of suspended dust invalidates the
fast only in the opinion of the Jafaris. They say that if a dense
suspended dust, such as flour or something of the kind, enters
the body, the fast is rendered invalid, because it is something
more substantial than an injection or tobacco smoke.

3.3.8. APPLICATION OF COLLYRIUM
Application of collyrium (*kohl*) invalidates the fast only in
the opinion of the Malikis, provided it is applied during the day
and its taste is felt in the throat.

3.3.9. THE INTENTION TO DISCONTINUE THE PRESCRIBED FAST
If a person intends to discontinue his or her fast and then
refrains from doing so, his or her prescribed fast is considered
invalid in the opinion of the Jafari and Hanbalis; not so in the
opinion of the other schools.

3.3.10. SUBMERGING HEAD OR BODY UNDER WATER
Most Jafaris state that fully submerging the head, alone or
together with other parts of the body, under water invalidates
the prescribed fast and necessitates both making up for the
fast and atonement. The other schools consider it inconsequential.

3.3.11. STATE OF IMPURITY FOLLOWING SEXUAL EMISSION
The Jafari observe that a person who deliberately remains

in the state of impurity following sexual emission after the dawn during the month of Ramadan, his or her fast will be invalid and it is obligatory for the fast be made up as well as atoned for. The remaining schools state that the person's fast remains valid and he or she is not liable to anything.

3.3.12. DELIBERATELY ASCRIBING SOMETHING FALSELY TO GOD OR THE MESSENGER

The Jafaris observe that a person who deliberately ascribes something falsely to God or the Messenger (i.e. if he or she speaks or writes that God or the Messenger said so and so or ordered such and such a thing while he or she is aware that it is not true), his or her fast will be invalid and that person will be liable for making it up as well as for an atonement. A group of Jafari jurisprudents go further by requiring of such a fabricator the atonement of freeing a slave, fasting for two months, and feeding sixty poor persons.

3.4. THE VARIOUS KINDS OF FASTS

The jurisprudents of various schools classify fasts into four categories: obligatory, supererogatory, unlawful and disapproved.

3.4.1. PRESCRIBED FAST

All the schools concur that the obligatory prescribed fasts are those of the month of Ramadan, their being made up, the expiatory fasts performed as atonement, and those performed for fulfilling a vow. The Jafaris add further two, related to the pilgrimage to Makkah and retreating to the mosque during the last ten days of Ramadan (*itikaf*).

We have already dealt in some detail with the fast of Ramadan, its conditions and the things that invalidate it. Here we intend to discuss its making up for and the atonement to which one who breaks it becomes liable. Other types of obligatory fasts have been discussed under the related chapters.

3.4.1.1. MAKING UP FOR THE PRESCRIBED FASTS

The schools concur that a person liable for the missed prescribed fasts of Ramadan fasts is bound to perform it during the same year in which the fasts were missed by that person, that is, the period between the past and the forthcoming Ramadan. The person is free to choose the days he or she intends to fast, excepting those days on which fasting is prohibited (their discussion will soon follow). However it is obligatory upon him or her to immediately begin making up for them if the days remaining for the next Ramadan are equal to the number of fasts missed in the earlier Ramadan.

If one capable of performing the fasts missed during the year neglects it until the next Ramadan, he or she should fast during the current Ramadan and then perform the missed fasts of the past year and also give an atonement of feeding a needy person for each day in the opinion of all the schools except the Hanafi which requires the person to perform only the missed fasts without any atonement. And if the person is unable to perform the missed fasts such as when his or her illness continues throughout the period between the first and the second Ramadan, he or she is neither required to make up for them nor required to give atonement in the opinion of the Hanafi, Hanbali, Shafii and Maliki schools, while the Jafaris say that he or she will not be liable to make up for the fasts missed but is bound to give food to a needy person as atonement for each fast day missed.

If one is capable of performing the missed fasts during the year but delays it with the intention of performing it just before the second Ramadan so that the missed fasts are immediately followed by the next Ramadan, and then a legitimate excuse prevents him or her from performing the missed prescribed fasts before the arrival of Ramadan, in such a situation he or she will be liable only to make up for the missed fasts not for atonement.

The Jafaris observe that one who breaks a Ramadan fast due to an excuse, and is capable of later for making it up but fails to do so during his lifetime it is obligatory upon his or her eldest child to perform the fasts missed on his or her behalf.

The Hanafis, Shafiis and Hanbalis state that charity (*sadaqah*) of feeding one need person for each prescribed fast missed will be given on his or her behalf.

According to the Malikis, the legal guardian (*wali*) will give to charity (*sadaqah*) on the person's behalf if he or she has so provided in the will. In the absence of a will it is not obligatory.

In the opinion of the Hanafi, Hanbali, Shafii and Maliki schools, a person performing the prescribed fasts of Ramadan that were missed can change his or her intention and break the fast both before and after midday without being liable to any atonement provided there is time for him or her to perform the missed fasts later.

The Jafaris observe that it is permissible for him or her to break this fast before midday and not later, because continuation of the fast becomes compulsory after the passing of the major part of its duration and the time of altering the intention also expires. Hence if he or she acts contrarily and breaks the fast after midday, he or she is liable to atonement by giving food to ten poor persons. If he or she is incapable of doing that, he or she will fast for three days.

3.4.1.2. FASTS OF ATONEMENT

The fasts of atonement are of various kinds. Among them are atonement fasts for involuntary homicide, fasts for atonement of a broken oath or vow, and atonement fasts for saying to one's wife, "You are as my mother's back," (*zihar*). These atonement fasts have their own rules which are discussed in the related chapters. Here we shall discuss the rules applicable to a person fasting by way of atonement for not having observed the prescribed fast of Ramadan.

The Shafiis, Malikis and Hanafis say that it is not permissible for a person, upon whom fasting for two consecutive months has become obligatory consequent to deliberately breaking a prescribed fast, to miss even a single fast during these two months, because that would break their continuity. Hence, on the missing of a fast, with or without an excuse, the person should fast anew for two months. The Hanbalis observe that if a person misses a fast due to a legitimate excuse, the continuity is not broken.

The Jafaris state that it is sufficient for the materialization of continuity that the person fast for a full month and then a day of the next month. After that he or she can skip days and then continue from where he or she had left off. But if he or she misses a fast during the first month without any excuse, he or she is bound to start anew. If, however, it is due to a lawful excuse, such as illness or menstruation, the continuity is not broken and he or she will wait until the excuse is removed and then resume the fasts. The Jafaris further observe that one who is unable to fast for two months, or release a slave or feed sixty poor persons, has the option either to fast for eighteen days or give whatever he or she can as charity. If even this is not possible, he or she may give alms or fast to any extent possible. If none of these are possible, he or she should seek forgiveness from God Almighty.

The Shafiis, Malikis and Hanafis state that if a person is unable to offer any form of atonement, he or she will remain liable for it until he or she comes to possess the capacity to offer it, and this is what the rules of the *Shariah* require.

The Hanbalis are of the opinion that if he or she is unable to give atonement, his or her liability for the same disappears, and even in the event of that person's becoming capable of it later, he or she will not be liable to anything.

The schools concur that the number of atonements will be equal to the number of causes entailing it. Hence a person who breaks two fasts will have to give two atonements. But if he or she eats, drinks or has sexual intercourse several times in a single day, the Hanafis, Malikis and Shafiis observe that the number of atonements will not increase if the fast has been broken several times, irrespective of its manner.

The Hanbalis state that if in a single day there occur several violations entailing atonement, if the person gives atonement for the first violation of the fast before the perpetration of the second, he or she should offer an atonement for the latter

3 Prescribed Fasting 145

violation as well, but if he or she has not given atonement for
the first violation before committing the second, a single atonement suffices.

According to the Jafaris, if sexual intercourse is repeated a
number of times in a single day, the number of atonements will
also increase proportionately, but if a person eats or drinks a
number of times, a single atonement suffices.

3.4.2. PROHIBITED FASTS

All the schools except the Hanafi concur that fasting on the
days of the day marking the end of the month of Ramadan (*id
al-fitr*) and the 10th of Dhil Hijjah (*id al-adha*) is forbidden.
The Hanafis observe that fasting on these two days is disapproved to the extent of being forbidden. The Jafaris say that
fasting on the days of the 11th, 12th and 13th of Dhil Hijjah
(*tashriq*) is prohibited only for those who are at Mina. The
Shafiis are of the opinion that fasting is not valid on these days
both for those performing the pilgrimage to Makkah as well as
others. According to the Hanbalis, it is forbidden to fast on
these days for those not performing the pilgrimage to Makkah,
not for those performing it. The Hanafis observe that fasting
on these days is disapproved to the extent of being forbidden.
The Malikis state that it is forbidden to fast on the eleventh
and the twelfth of Dhil Hijjah for those not performing the pilgrimage to Makkah, not for those performing it.

All the schools except the Hanafi concur that it is not valid
for a woman to observe a supererogatory fast without her husband's consent if her fast interferes with the fulfillment of any
of his rights. The Hanafis observe that a woman's fasting without the permission of her husband is disapproved not forbidden.

There is consensus among the schools that refraining
(*imsak*) is obligatory upon one who does not fast on a "doubtful
day" (*yawm al-shakk*) that later turns out to be a day of
Ramadan, and he or she is liable to make up for it later. Where
one fasts on a doubtful day that is later known to have been a
day of Ramadan, they differ as to whether it suffices without

requiring that it be made up. The Shafii, Maliki and Hanbali schools observe that this fast will not suffice and it is not obligatory to be made up. In the opinion of the Hanafis, it suffices and does not require to be made up. Most Jafaris state that its being made up is not obligatory upon him, except when he had fasted with the intention of Ramadan.

3.4.3. SUPEREROGATORY FASTS

Fasting is considered recommended on all the days of the year except those on which it has been prohibited. But there are days whose fast has been specifically stressed and they include three days of each month, preferably the 'moonlit' days (*al-ayyam al-bid*), which are the thirteenth, fourteenth and fifteenth of each lunar month. Among them is the day of Arafah (9th of Dhil Hijjah). Also emphasized are the fasts of the months of Rajab and Shaban. Fasting on Mondays and Thursdays has also been emphasized. There are other days as well which have been mentioned in elaborate works. There is consensus among all the schools that fasting on these days is recommended.

3.4.4. DISAPPROVED FASTS

It is mentioned in *al-Fiqh alal-madhahib al-arbaah* that it is disapproved to single out Fridays and Saturdays for fasting. So is fasting on the day of *Now Ruz* (21st March) in the opinion of all the schools except the Shafii, and fasting on the day or the two days just before the month of Ramadan.

It has been stated in Jafari books on jurisprudence that it is disapproved for a guest to fast without the permission of his host, for a child to fast without the permission of its father, and when there is doubt regarding the new moon of Dhil-Hijjah and the consequent possibility of the day being that of the festival.

3.5. EVIDENCE OF THE NEW MOON

There is a general consensus among Muslims that a person who has seen the new moon is himself or herself bound to act in accordance with this knowledge, whether it is the new moon of Ramadan or Shawwal. Hence it is obligatory upon one who has seen the former to fast even if all other people do not,[2] and to refrain from fasting on seeing the latter even if everyone else on the earth is fasting, irrespective of whether the observer is just (*adil*) or not, man or woman. The schools differ regarding the following issues:

3.5.1. SIGHTING OF THE NEW MOON
The Hanbalis, Malikis and Hanafis state that if the sighting (*ruyah*) of the new moon has been confirmed in a particular region, the people of all other regions are bound by it, regardless of the distance between them. The difference of the horizon of the new moon is of no consequence. The Jafaris and the Shafiis observe that if the people of a particular place see the new moon while those at another place do not, in the event of these two places being close by with respect to the horizon, the latter's duty will be the same; but not if their horizons differ.

3.5.2. DAY NEW MOON OBSERVED
If the new moon is seen the during day, either before or after midday, on the 30th of Shaban, will it be reckoned the last day of Shaban (in which case, fasting that day will not be obligatory) or the first of Ramadan (in which case fasting is obligatory)? Similarly, if the new moon is seen during the day on the 30th of Ramadan, will it be reckoned a day of Ramadan or that of Shawwal? In other words, will the day on which the new moon is observed be reckoned as belonging to the past or to the forthcoming month?

The Jafaris, Shafiis, Malikis and Hanafis observe the at it belongs to the past month and not to the forthcoming one. Accordingly, it is obligatory to fast on the next day if the new moon is seen at the end of Shaban, and to refrain from fasting the next day if it is seen at the end of Ramadan.

3.5.3. NEW MOON OF RAMADAN
The schools concur that the new moon is confirmed if sighted, as observed in this Tradition of the Prophet ( ), "Fast on

seeing the new moon and stop fasting on seeing it." They differ regarding the other methods of confirming it.

The Jafaris observe that it is confirmed for both Ramadan and Shawwal by the testimony of a sufficiently large number of people whose conspiring over a false claim is impossible (*tawatur*), and by the testimony of two just (*adil*) men, irrespective of whether the sky is clear or cloudy and regardless of whether they belong to the same or two different nearby towns, provided their descriptions of the new moon are not contradictory. The evidence of women, children, *fasiq* men and those of unknown character is not acceptable.

The Hanafis differentiate between the new moons of Ramadan and Shawwal. They state that the new moon of Ramadan is confirmed by the testimony of a single man and a single woman, provided they are Muslim, sane and just (*adil*). The Shawwal new moon is not confirmed except by the testimony of two men or a man and two women. This is when the sky is not clear. But if the sky is clear—and there is no difference in this respect between the new moon of Ramadan and Shawwal—it is not confirmed except by the testimony of a considerable number of persons whose reports result in certainty.

In the opinion of the Shafiis, the new moon of Ramadan and Shawwal is confirmed by the testimony of a single witness, provided he is Muslim, sane and just. The sky's being clear or cloudy makes no difference in this regard. According to the Malikis, the new moon of Ramadan and Shawwal are not confirmed except by the testimony of two just men, irrespective of the sky's being cloudy or cloudless. The Hanbalis say that the new moon of Ramadan is confirmed by the testimony of a just man or woman, while that of Shawwal is only confirmed by the testimony of two just men.

There is consensus among the schools, excepting the Hanafi, that if no one claims to have seen the new moon of Ramadan, fasting will be obligatory after the thirtieth day, allowing thirty days for Shaban. According to the Hanafis, fasting becomes obligatory after the 29th day of Shaban.

This was with respect to the new moon of Ramadan. As to

the new moon of Shawwal, the Hanafis and the Malikis observe that if the sky is cloudy, thirty days of Ramadan will be completed and breaking the fast will be obligatory on the following day. But if the sky is clear, it is obligatory to fast on the day following the 30th day by rejecting the earlier testimony of witnesses confirming the first of Ramadan regardless of their number. The Shafiis consider ending the fast obligatory after thirty days even if the setting in of Ramadan was confirmed by the evidence of a single witness, irrespective of the sky's having been cloudy or clear. According to the Hanbalis, if the setting in of Ramadan was confirmed by the testimony of two just men, breaking the prescribed fast (*iftar*) following the thirtieth day is obligatory, and if it was confirmed by the evidence of a single just witness, it is obligatory to fast on the thirty-first day as well. In the opinion of the Jafaris, both Ramadan and Shawwal are confirmed after the completion of thirty days regardless of the sky's being cloudy or clear, provided their beginning was confirmed in a manner approved by the *Shariah*.

3.6. THE NEW MOON AND ASTRONOMY

This year (1960) the governments of Pakistan and Tunisia have decided to rely upon the opinion of astronomers for the confirmation of the new moon with a view of putting an end to confusion[3] and the general inconvenience resulting from not knowing in advance the day of the festival (*id al-fitr*), which at times comes as a surprise, and at other times is delayed despite all the preparations. This decision of the two governments has become an issue of heated controversy in religious circles. The protagonists of the move observe that there is nothing in the religion that disapproves of reliance on the opinion of astronomers; rather it is supported by this verse, "...*And waymarks; and by the stars they are guided*" (16:16). The opponents state that the decision contradicts the above-mentioned prophetic Tradition, "Fast on seeing the new moon and stop fasting on seeing it."

This is because the word sighting (*ruyah*) implies sighting the moon with the eyes, which was common among the people during the time of the Prophet. As to using a telescope or relying on astronomical calculations, they are inconsistent with the literal import of the Tradition, they point out.

In fact, none of the sides has advanced sound reasons, because 'guidance by the stars' implies determination of land and sea routes with the help of the stars, and not determination of days of months and new moons. As to the Tradition, it does not contradict sound scientific knowledge, because 'seeing' is a means for acquiring knowledge and not an end in itself, as is the case with any means that helps confirm facts. However, some scholars believe that the judgments of astronomers do not lead to certain knowledge, nor do they remove all doubts as removed by vision, because their judgments are based on probability not on certainty. This is evident from their divergent judgments about the night of the new moon as well as the time of its occurrence and the period that it remains (above the horizon).

If a time comes when the astronomers attain accurate and sufficient knowledge, so that there is consensus among them and they continue prove to be right to the extent that their forecasts become a certainty like the days of the week, then it will be possible to rely upon them. Rather, then it will be obligatory to follow their judgments and to reject everything that goes against them.[4]

4

THE PRESCRIBED PILGRIMAGE

4.1. THE ACTS OF THE PRESCRIBED PILGRIMAGE

At the beginning, in order to make it easier for the reader to follow the opinions of the major schools of jurisprudence about various aspects of the prescribed pilgrimage to Makkah, we shall briefly outline their sequence as ordained by the *Shariah*.

The pilgrim coming from a place distant from Makkah assumes the sacred state (*ihram*)[1] from the place 'at the appointed time' (*miqat*)[2] on his or her way, or from a point parallel to the closest 'place at the appointed time' (*miqat*), and starts reciting 'Here I am, my Lord...' (*talbiyah*).[3] In this there is no difference between one performing the minor pilgrimage (*umrah mufradah*) or any of the three types of prescribed pilgrimages to Makkah (i.e. *tamattu, ifrad, qiran*). However, those who live within the sacred area (*haram*)[4] of Makkah assume the sacred state (*ihram*) from their houses. [5]

On sighting the Kabah, the pilgrim recites, *"Allahu akbar,"* "God is greater" (*takbir*) and *"la ilaha ill-Allah,"* "There is no god except God," (*tahlil*) which is recommended (*mustahabb*).[6] On entering Makkah, the pilgrim takes a bath lustration, which is again recommended. After entering the Masjid al-Haram, first the pilgrim greets the Black Stone (*al-hajar al-aswad*)—if possible kisses it, otherwise makes a gesture with his or her hand—then makes the sevenfold circumambulation of the Kabah of the first entry, which is recommended for pilgrims performing the *hajj al-ifrad* or *hajj al-qiran* pilgrimage. Then the pilgrim offers the two cycles (*rakat*) of prescribed prayer of the circumambulation (*tawaf*), again greets the Black Stone, if possible, and leaves al-Masjid al-Haram. After this, the pilgrim remains in the sacred state in Makkah. On the 8th day of the month of Dhil Hijjah (*tarwiyah*) or a day earlier, the pilgrim goes to Arafat.

If the pilgrim has come for either the minor pilgrimage (*umrah mufradah*) or prescribed pilgrimage (*hajj al-tamattu*), he or she performs the circumambulation (*tawaf*) of the entry, which is obligatory, and prays the two cycles of the prescribed prayer of circumambulation. Then the pilgrim performs the running (*say*) between Safa and Marwah, and, following it, the complete shaving of the head (*halq*)[7] or partial cutting of the hair of the head (*taqsir*). Then the pilgrim is relieved of the sacred state and its related restrictions. Things prohibited while in the sacred state become permissible for the pilgrim, including sexual intercourse.[8] Then the pilgrim proceeds from Makkah, after assuming the sacred state for a second time, early enough to be present at the halting (*wuquf*) at Arafat referred to as "the place of halting" (*mawqif*) by noontime on the 9th of Dhil Hijjah. Assumption of the sacred state (*ihram*) on the 8th day (*tarwiyah*) of Dhil Hijjah is preferable.

The pilgrim, irrespective of the type of prescribed pilgrimage to be performed, turns towards Arafat, passing through Mina. The period of the halting at Arafat for the Hanafi, Shafii and Maliki schools is from noon of the 9th until the daybreak of the 10th. For the Hanbali school, it is from the daybreak of the 9th until the daybreak of the 10th. For the Jafari, it is from noon until sunset on the 9th and in exigency until the daybreak of the 10th.[9] The pilgrim offers supplications (*dua*) at Arafat, preferably (*istihbaban*) in an imploring manner.

Then the pilgrim turns towards Mudalifah (also called al-Mashar al-Haram), where he or she offers the evening (*maghrib*) and night (*isha*) prescribed prayers on the night of the festival (*id al-adha*, the 10th of Dhil Hijjah). Offering the two prayers immediately after one another is recommended by all the major schools. According to the Hanafi, Shafii and Hanbali schools, it is obligatory to spend the night before the the festival at Mudalifah. For the Jafari, it is not obligatory but preferable. After the daybreak, the pilgrim makes the halt at al-Mudalifah (Mashar al-Haram) which is obligatory for the Jafari and recommended for the other schools. And at Mudalifah, preferably, the pilgrim picks up seven pebbles to be thrown at Mina.

After this, the pilgrim turns towards Mina before sunrise on the day of the festival. There the pilgrim performs the ritual throwing of stones, called *ramy* at Jamarat al-Aqabah, no matter which of the three kinds of prescribed pilgrimage the pilgrim is performing. The stoning is performed between sunrise and sunset, preferably (*istihbaban*) accompanied by the recitation of "*Allah Akbar*" ("God is Greater," *takbir*) and "*subhan Allah*" ("Glory be to God," *tasbih*).

Then if the pilgrim is a non-Makkan on the prescribed pilgrimage (*hajj al-tamattu*), he or she should slaughter the sacrificial animal (a camel, cow, or a sheep), by agreement of all the major schools. However, it is not obligatory for one on *hajj al-ifrad*, again by consensus of all the major schools. For one on *hajj al-qiran*, the sacrifice is obligatory from the viewpoint of the Hanafi, Hanbali, Shafii and Maliki schools, and for the Jafari, it is not obligatory except when the pilgrim brings the sacrificial animal (*al-hady*) along with him or her at the time of assuming the sacred state. For a Makkan performing the prescribed pilgrimage (*hajj al-tamattu*), the sacrifice is obligatory from the viewpoint of the Jafari school, but not according to the Hanafi, Hanbali, Shafii and Maliki schools.

After this, the pilgrim, if a male, performs the shaving of the head (*halq*) or, if male or female, cutting of the hair (*taqsir*), irrespective of the kind of prescribed pilgrimage he or

154 Part One: Individual Issues

she is performing. After the shaving of the head (*halq*) or cutting of the hair or cutting of a nail (*taqsir*), everything except sexual intercourse becomes permissible for him or her according to the Hanbali, Shafii and Hanafi schools, and according to the Maliki and Jafari schools, everything except intercourse and perfume.

Then the pilgrim returns to Makkah on the same day, that is, the day of the festival, performs the circumambulation for the prescribed pilgrimage (*tawaf al-ziyarah*), prays its related two cycles of prescribed prayers regardless of which kind of prescribed pilgrimage he or she is performing. After this, according to the Hanafi, Hanbali, Shafii and Maliki schools, the pilgrim is free from all restrictions including that of sexual intercourse. Then the pilgrim performs the search (*say*) between Safa and Marwah if on the prescribed pilgrimage (*hajj al-tamattu*), by agreement of all the major schools. For the Jafari school, the running (*say*) after circumambulation of the prescribed pilgrimage (*tawaf al-ziyarah*) is also obligatory for one performing hajj al-qiran and hajj al-ifrad. But for other schools, it is not obligatory if the pilgrim had performed the running (*say*) after the circumambulation (*tawaf*) of first entry, otherwise it is. For the Jafari, it is obligatory for all the types of prescribed pilgrimage to perform another circumambulation after this search. Without this circumambulation, called *tawaf al-nisa*, one is not relieved of the interdiction of abstinence from intercourse.

Then the pilgrim returns to Mina on the same day, that is, the 10th, where the pilgrim sleeps on the night of the 11th, performs the threefold throwing of stones (*ramy al-jamarat*) during the interval from the noon until the sunset of the 11th—by consensus of all the major schools. For the Jafari, the throwing of stones (*ramy*) is permissible after sunrise and before noon. After this, on the day of the 12th, the pilgrim does what he or she had done the day before. All the legal schools agree that he or she may now depart from Mina before sunset. And if he or she stays there until sunset, the pilgrim is obliged to spend the night of the 13th there and to perform the threefold throwing of stones on the day of 13th.

After the throwing of stones, the pilgrim returns to Makkah, before or after noon. On entering Makkah, the pilgrim performs another circumambulation, called the farewell circumambulation (*tawaf al-wada*), which is recommended for the Jafari and Maliki schools and obligatory for the non-Makkans from the viewpoint of the remaining three. Here the acts of the the prescribed pilgrimage to Makkah come to conclusion.

4.2. THE CONDITIONS FOR THE PRESCRIBED PILGRIMAGE

The conditions (*shurut*) which make the prescribed pilgrimage obligatory for a Muslim are: maturity (*bulugh*), sanity (*aql*), and ability (*istitaah*).

4.2.1. MATURITY

The prescribed pilgrimage to Makkah is not obligatory for children, regardless of whether a child is of the age of discretion (*mumayyiz*) or not (*ghayr mumayyiz*). For a child the age of discretion, the prescribed pilgrimage to Makkah is voluntary and valid. However, it does not relieve him or her of the obligation to perform the obligatory pilgrimage to Makkah (called *hijjat al-islam*) later as an adult possessing the ability. On this all the major schools of jurisprudence are in agreement.

It is permissible for the guardian (*wali*) of a child who has not reached the age of discretion to take him or her along on the pilgrimage. The child in the sacred state is instructed to say the *talbiyah* ("*Allahuma labayyk*," "Here I am my Lord") if the child can say it well, or otherwise says it himself or herself on the child's behalf. It is done with caution in case the child commits some forbidden act for the pilgrims (*hujjaj*). The accompanying guardian also tells the child to perform every act that the child can perform himself or herself, and what he or she cannot, the guardian performs it on the child's behalf.

The schools of Islamic Divine Law differ on two questions relating to the pilgrimage of a child who has attained discretion: firstly, whether his or her pilgrimage is valid, irrespective of the permission of the guardian; secondly, whether he or she is relieved of the obligation of the pilgrimage if he or she attains adulthood before the halting in Arafat (*mawqif*). According to the Jafari, Hanbali, and Shafii schools, the guardian's permission is a condition for the wearing of the sacred dress to be valid. According to the Hanafi school, the idea of validity is inapplicable to the child's pilgrimage, even if he or she has attained discernment, and regardless of whether he or she obtains the permission of the guardian or not because, according to this school, there is nothing to a child's pilgrimage except its significance as an exercise.[10]

According to the Jafari, Hanbali and Shafii schools, if the child attains adulthood before halting in Arafat (*mawqif*), his or her obligatory duty of performing the pilgrimage (*hijjat al-islam*) is thereby fulfilled. And according to the Jafari and Maliki schools, the duty is fulfilled if the child renews the sacred dress as an adult, otherwise not which means that the child should start the pilgrimage all over again from the beginning.[11]

4.2.2. SANITY

Basically the condition of insanity relieves a person of all duties. Even if he or she were to perform the prescribed pilgrimage, and presumably in the way expected of a sane person, it would not fulfill his or her obligatory duty were he or she to return to sanity. If the insanity is periodic, when regained for a sufficiently long interval it is obligatory for him or her to perform the prescribed pilgrimage with all its conditions and in all its details. However, if the interval of sanity is not sufficient to perform all the acts of the prescribed pilgrimage, he or she has done his or her obligation.

4.2.3. ABILITY

All the major schools of Islamic Law agree that ability is a requirement for the prescribed pilgrimage to become obligatory, as mentioned by the Quranic verse: "... *if he is able to make his way there..*" (3:97). However, there is disagreement about the meaning of ability. In the Traditions, it has been defined as consisting of "*al-zad wa al-rahilah.*" '*Al-rahilah*' implies the expenses of the journey to Makkah and back and '*al-zad*' stands for the expenses required for transport, food, lodging, passport fees, and the like. Moreover, the funds needed to meet such expenses must come out of the surplus after paying one's debts, after arranging for one's family's livelihood, meeting the requirements of one's source of income (such as land for a farmer, tools for a craftsman, capital for a tradesman, and so on), and without compromising the security of his life, property and honor. All schools agree about it except the Malikis, who say that the duty of pilgrim is obligatory for anyone who can walk. The Malikis also do not consider the necessity of providing for the living expenses of the family. Rather, they consider it compulsory for one to sell off his essential means of life, such as land, livestock, tools, and even books and unessential clothes.[12]

If a person upon whom the pilgrimage duty is not obligatory due to absence of ability, takes upon himself or herself the burden and performs the pilgrimage, in case he or she attains the ability afterwards, is his or her first pilgrimage sufficient or should he or she perform the pilgrimage once again? According to the Maliki and Hanafi schools, yes, repetition is not compulsory. According to the Hanbali school, yes, but a duty left unattended, such as an unpaid debt, must be discharged. According to the Jafari school, it does not suffice the obligation of pilgrimage if he or she attains ability afterwards. The pilgrimage performed before the attainment of ability is considered supererogatory. Later, with its realization, repetition of the pilgrimage becomes obligatory.

4.2.4. DISPATCH WITHOUT DELAY

The Jafari, the Maliki and the Hanbali schools consider the obligation of the pilgrimage to be immediately applicable (*fawri*), that is, it is not permissible to delay it from the moment of its possibility. It is sinful to delay, although the prescribed pilgrimage performed with delay is correct and fulfills the obligation. The author of *al-Jawahir* says, "The immediacy of the obligation of the prescribed pilgrimage means that it is necessary to take initiative to perform the prescribed pilgrimage in the first year of attaining ability, and failing that at one's next earliest opportunity...." Thereafter, there is no doubt about the sinfulness of the delay if one were to forgo the first opportunity in the case of absence of another.

According to the Shafii school, the obligation of the prescribed pilgrimage is not immediate (upon attainment of ability). Rather one may delay it and perform it when he wishes.[13] According to Abu Yusuf, the prescribed pilgrimage is an immediate obligation. Muhammad ibn al-Hasan considers delay (*tarakhi*) permissible. Imam Abu Hanifah has no explicit text on the matter, although some of his contemporaries state that he implicitly believes in the immediacy of the obligation.

4.2.5. WOMEN AND THE PRESCRIBED PILGRIMAGE

Are there any additional conditions for women with regard to performance of the pilgrimage? All the major schools agree that it is not required that a woman should obtain the husband's permission for the prescribed pilgrimage duty, nor may he prevent her from undertaking it. However, there is a difference of opinion about whether the prescribed pilgrimage is obligatory upon her or not if she does not find a husband or a person with whom marriage is prohibited (*mahram*) to accompany her on the journey. According to the Jafari, Maliki and Shafii schools, the company of a person with whom marriage is prohibited or that of the husband is not at all a condition, regardless of whether she is young or old, married or unmarried. The company of such a person is a means of her safety, not an end in itself. Accordingly, we have two cases: either she feels confident of her security on the journey, or she does not. In the first case, the prescribed pilgrimage is obligatory upon her and the presence of a legal companion is irrelevant. In the second case, she lacks the requirement of ability, in spite of the presence of a legal companion. There is, then, no essential difference between a man and a woman in this respect. According to the Hanbali and Hanafi schools, the company of the husband or legally approved companion is a provision for the woman's pilgrimage, even if she is elderly. It is not permissible for her to perform the pilgrimage without his company. The Hanafi school further stipulates the condition that her location should be at a distance of three days' journey from Makkah.

4.3. BEQUEST

Al-Mughni, a text of Hanbali jurisprudence, states, "If a person bequeaths money to another, it is not binding upon that person to accept it, and it does not make the recipient 'able' (*mustati*), irrespective of whether the bequeather is a relative or a stranger, regardless of whether the bequest suffices for the expenses of the journey and food. According to Imam Shafi, if the bequest is made by one's son, enough to enable him to undertake the journey, the prescribed pilgrimage becomes obligatory. This, because it enables him to perform the prescribed pilgrimage without having to bear a stranger's favor or without any accompanying encumbrance or harm.

According to the Jafari school, if the bequest is an unconditional gift made without the provision of performing the pilgrimage by the recipient, the pilgrimage is not binding, irrespective of who makes the bequest. But if the bequest is made with the condition that one perform the pilgrimage, the acceptance of the bequest is binding and may not be rejected, even if the bequest is made by a stranger since it makes the pilgrim able to undertake the pilgrimage.

4.4. MARRIAGE

What if one has only enough money either to get married or to perform the pilgrimage? Which of them is prior? The Hanafi text[14] mentions this question being put to Imam Abu Hanifah, who, in his reply, considered that priority lies with the pilgrimage. The generality of this answer in which he gives priority to the pilgrimage, taking into consideration that marriage is obligatory under certain conditions, allows us to conclude that for Imam Abu Hanifah delay in pilgrimage is not permissible. According to the Shafii, Hanbali and Jafari scholars, marriage has priority if there is likelihood of distress (*haraj*) or difficulty (*mashaqqah*) in refraining from marriage. In that case priority does not lie with the pilgrimage.[15]

4.5. POOR-DUE AND TWENTY-PERCENT TAX

Payment of the the poor-due (*zakat*) and the twenty-percent tax (*khums*) has priority over the pilgrimage. The condition of ability is not realized until both are paid off, like other kinds of debts.

4.6. ABILITY BY CHANCE

If someone travels to a place in the vicinity of the holy city of Makkah, on business or for some other purpose, and his stay continues until the pilgrimage season, and if it is possible for him or her to reach the Kabah, he or she thereby becomes able (*mustati*). And if he or she were to return home without performing the pilgrimage, by consensus of all the schools, that person is not relieved of the obligation.

4.7. DEPUTATION

Muslim acts of worship are divisible into three categories, depending on a duty's nature whether it mainly involves physical acts, financial expenditure, or both.

4.7.1. PHYSICAL ACTS OF WORSHIP

Physical acts of worship are those which, like the prescribed fast and prayer, do not involve any financial aspect. According to the Hanafi, Hanbali, Shafii and Maliki schools, such duties cannot in any circumstance be delegated to a proxy (*naib*), either on behalf of a living or a dead person. But according to the Jafari school, taking a proxy is permissible on behalf of a dead person, although not for a living person, to perform

the prescribed fast and prayer for him or her, and under all circumstances.

4.7.2. FINANCIAL DUTIES

The purely financial duties or acts of worship are those
which do not involve physical acts, such as paying the poor-due
and twenty percent tax. All legal schools agree in regard to
such duties that it is permissible to take a proxy. It is permissible for one to depute another to take out the poor-due and pay
other kind of charity (*sadaqat*) from his or her assets.

4.7.3. PHYSICAL AND FINANCIAL DUTIES

Some duties have both physical and financial aspects, such
as the pilgrimage, which requires such physical acts as circumambulation of the Kabah, the search between Marwah and
Safa, the throwing of stones, and financial expenditures such
as for the journey and its accompanying requirements. All the
major legal schools agree that one who is capable of undertaking the pilgrimage in person and fulfills all the conditions
thereof, should do so himself or herself in person. It is not permissible for a person to depute another to undertake it, and if
someone does so it would not relieve that person of the obligation to perform it himself or herself. If a person does not do it
in his or her life, according to the Shafii, Hanbali and Jafari
schools, he or she is not relieved of the duty because of the preponderance of the financial aspect, and it is obligatory to hire
someone to perform the pilgrimage with a similar expenditure.
In case he does not make a will for the pilgrimage, the amount
should be taken out from his undivided heritage.[16] According
to the Hanafi and Maliki schools, the person is relieved of the
obligation due to the physical aspect but if mentioned it in his
or her will, the expense is taken out from the one-third of the
legacy, like all other bequests, and if he or she does not have
sufficient funds, deputation is not obligatory.

4.8. THE PHYSICALLY INCAPABLE

One who meets all the financial conditions for the pilgrim-

age, but is incapable of undertaking it (*al-qadir al-ajiz*) personally due to old age or some incurable disease, all the legal
schools agree, is relieved of the obligation of performing the
pilgrimage in person, for God says , "*...and He has laid no
impediment in your religion...*" (22:78). However, it is obligatory upon him or her to hire someone to perform the pilgrimage
for him or her. But if a person does not, is it a negligence of a
duty whose fulfillment continues to remain upon that person?
All the legal schools, with the exception of the Maliki, agree
that it is obligatory upon him or her to hire someone to perform the pilgrimage for him or her. The Maliki says that the
pilgrimage is not obligatory upon one who is incapable of
undertaking it in person.[17]

Furthermore, if a sick person recovers after deputing someone to perform his or her pilgrimage, is it obligatory upon him
or her, upon recovery, to perform the pilgrimage in person?
According to the Hanbali school, another pilgrimage is not
obligatory. But according to the Jafari, Shafii and Hanafi
schools it is obligatory, because what was fulfilled was the
financial obligation, and the physical obligation has remained
unfulfilled.

4.9. DEPUTATION IN THE RECOMMENDED PRESCRIBED PILGRIMAGE

According to the Jafari and Hanafi legal schools, if one who
has performed the prescribed pilgrimage to Makkah at least
once wants to depute another for a voluntary, recommended
pilgrimage, he or she may do so, even if incapable of undertaking it in person. But according to the Shafii school, it is not
permissible. There are two narrations from Imam Ahmad ibn
Hanbal, one indicating prohibition and the other permission.
According to the Maliki school, it is permissible for an incurable sick person and for one who has performed the prescribed
pilgrimage to hire another for the pilgrimage. The pilgrimage
so performed is valid, though disapproved. It is not considered
as the pilgrimage of the hirer (*mustajir*) and is counted as the
recommended pilgrimage of the hired (*ajir*). The hirer gets the

reward for providing assistance in the performance of the pilgrimage and shares the blessings of the prayers offered. When the pilgrimage is performed for the benefit of a dead person, irrespective of whether he or she has asked for it in his or her will or not, it is counted neither as fulfillment of the duty nor as a supererogatory act, nor does it relieve that person of the duty of the obligatory pilgrimage.[18]

4.9.1. THE CONDITIONS FOR THE DEPUTY

The deputy should fulfill the conditions of adulthood, sanity, belief in Islam, exemption from the duty of the prescribed pilgrimage, and ability to perform the pilgrimage properly. A man may represent a woman and a woman may represent a man, even if both the deputy and the one whom he represents have not performed the prescribed pilgrimage before.[19]

Should the deputy commence the journey from his or her own place or that of the deceased whom he or she represents, or from one of the places of the appointed time? According to the Hanafi and Maliki schools, the deputy should commence the pilgrimage journey from the place of the deceased, if he or she has not specified the starting point. Otherwise according to his or her wish. According to the Shafii school, the pilgrimage commences from one of the places of the appointed time if the deceased person has specified one, then the deputy must act accordingly, otherwise the deputy is free to choose one of the places of the appointed time. According to the Hanbali school, the deputy must start from the place that the deceased was obliged to begin from if he or she had performed the pilgrimage himself or herself, and not from the place of death. If the deceased person had attained ability at a place to which he or she had migrated, later returning to his or her own place, the deputy should start from the place of migration, not from the deceased person's home, except when the distance between the deputy's home-town and the place of migration is less than what is required for shortened prescribed prayers performed by a traveler.[20]

According to the Jafari school, the pilgrimage is divided

into two types depending upon where one starts. The first is one which starts from one of the places of the appointed time (*miqati*) and the second is one which starts from the town of the deceased (*baladi*). If the deceased has specified one of these two kinds, then the one specified is done. If the deceased has not specified, any one of the two may be performed. Otherwise the pilgrimage is *miqati* and, if possible, starts from the *miqat* nearest to Makkah, or else the miqat nearest to the town of the deceased. The cost of *al-hijjat al-miqatiyyah* is taken out from the undivided legacy in the case of obligatory pilgrimage, and the expense exceeding the cost of *al-hijjat al-miqatiyyah* is taken from the one third of the legacy.[21]

4.9.2. DELAY BY THE DEPUTY

Once the deputy is hired, it is obligatory for him or her to act without delay. The deputy may not postpone the pilgrimage beyond the first year. Also, it is not permissible for the deputy to depute another, since the duty is his or her own. If we do not know that the deputy actually went on the pilgrimage and performed all its essential acts, or if we doubt whether the deputy performed them correctly and properly or not, or whether the deputy failed to fulfill any of its obligatory essentials, then we assume that the deputy acted correctly and properly, unless there is proof to the contrary.

4.9.3. CHANGE OF PURPOSE BY THE DEPUTY

According to the Hanafi and Jafari schools, if one specifies to the deputy a particular kind of pilgrimage, such as the prescribed pilgrimage *hajj al-tamattu*, *hajj al-ifrad*, or *hajj al-qiran*, then it is not permissible for the deputy to make any change of purpose. However, if a particular town was specified as the starting point and the deputy starts from another town, the purpose of the one who hires the deputy is considered as fulfilled if the said specification was not really intended by the hirer if by mentioning the route he or she meant the pilgrimage itself and not specifically the route.[22]

4.10. THE MINOR PILGRIMAGE

4.10.1. THE MEANING OF THE MINOR PILGRIMAGE

The word *umrah* in common speech means "visit," and in the *Shariah* it means paying a visit to the the Sacred House of God, the Kabah, in a specific form.

4.10.2. THE KINDS OF MINOR PILGRIMAGES

The minor pilgrimage is of two kinds, the first which is performed independently of the prescribed pilgrimage (called *al-umrat al-mufradah al-mustaqillahan al-hajj*), and the second kind which is performed in conjunction with the prescribed pilgrimage (*al-umrat al-mundammah ila al-hajj*). All the major legal schools of Law agree that the *al-umrat al-mufradah*, the independent *umrah*, can be performed at all times of the year, although it is meritorious to perform it during the month of Rajab according to the Jafari, and in Ramadan according to the Hanafi, Hanbali, Shafii and Maliki schools. The time of the conjugate *umrah*, which is performed before the prescribed pilgrimage and in the course of the same journey by the pilgrim coming to Makkah from distant countries, by consensus of all major schools, extends from Shawwal to Dhil Hijjah. However, there is disagreement among jurists about the month of Dhil Hijjah, whether the entire month or only the first ten days belong to the pilgrimage season. Anyone who performs the conjugate *umrah* is considered relieved of the obligation to perform the *umrut al-mufradah* by those who believe in its being obligatory.

4.10.3. DIFFERENCE BETWEEN THE TWO KINDS OF MINOR PILGRIMAGES

The Jafari scholars make a distinction between the *umrat al-mufradah* and *umrat al-tamattu*, citing the following reasons:

1. The *tawaf al-nisa* (to be explained later) is obligatory in the *umrat al-mufradah*, not in the *umrat al-tamattu* and, according to some jurists, is forbidden.

2. The time of *umrat al-tamattu* extends from the 1st of the

month of Shawwal to the 9th of Dhil Hijjah whereas *umrat al-mufradah* can be performed at all times of the year.

3. The pilgrim (*mutamir*) performing the *umrat al-tamattu* is required to shorten his hair (*taqsir*), whereas the pilgrim (*mutamir*) of *umrat al-mufradah* can choose between shortening his hair or completely shaving his head (*halq*), as shall be explained later.

4. The *umrat al-tamattu* and the pilgrimage occur in the same year, which is not the case with *al-umrat al-mufradah*.

According to the Maliki and Shafii schools, for the pilgrim (*mutamir*) of *umrat al-mufradah* all things are permissible, even sexual intercourse, after the shortening of hair (*taqsir*) or the head shave (*halq*), irrespective of whether he brings along with him the sacrificial offering (*hady*) or not.[23] But according to the Hanbali and Hanafi schools, the pilgrim (*mutamir*) all things are permissible after *taqsir* or *halq* if he does not bring the sacrificial offering; otherwise he remains in the state of the sacred dress (*ihram*) until he gets through the prescribed pilgrimage and the 'umrah on the day of sacrifice (*yawm al-nahr*).

4.10.4. THE CONDITIONS FOR THE MINOR PILGRIMAGE

The conditions for the visit are essentially the same as mentioned in the case of the prescribed pilgrimage.

4.10.4.1. THE STATUS OF THE MINOR PILGRIMAGE

According to the Hanafi and Maliki schools, the minor pilgrimage is not obligatory but a highly recommended *Sunnah* (*sunnah muakkadah*). But according to the Shafii and Hanbali schools and the majority of Jafari jurists, it is obligatory for one who is able, and recommended for one who is not able. In support, they cite the Quranic verse, *"Perform the prescribed pilgrimage and the minor pilgrimage for God"* (2:196).[24]

4.10.4.2. THE ACTS OF THE MINOR PILGRIMAGE

According to Shafii, Hanbali, Hanafi and Maliki schools, whatever is obligatory or *Sunnah* for the pilgrimage is also obligatory and *Sunnah* for the minor pilgrimage. But the minor pilgrimage does differ from the pilgrimage in certain respects: there is no specific time for performing the minor pilgrimage; it does not involve the halt in the plain of Arafat; neither the departure thenceforth to Mudalifah, nor the throwing of stones.[25] The Jafari school mentions, "The obligatory acts (*afal* or *amal*) of the pilgrimage are twelve: the sacred dress; the halting at Arafat; the halting at al-Mashar al-Haram; the entry into Mina; the throwing of stones; the sacrifice; its related shaving of the head or cutting of the hair; the the sevenfold circumambulation of the Kabah, and its relevant cycles of the prescribed prayers; the search; the *tawaf al-nis*a and its related prayer cycles. The obligatory acts of *umrat al-mufradah* are eight: intention; the sacred dress; the circumambulation; its related prayers; the search; the *taqsir*; the *tawaf al-nisa*; and its related prayer cycles.[26]

This indicates that all the legal schools agree that the acts of the pilgrimage exceed those of the minor pilgrimage (*umrah*) by the acts associated with the halting. Moreover, the Jafari school considers it obligatory for the performer of the *umrat al-mufradah* to perform a second circumambulation, the *tawaf al-nisa*. Similarly the Maliki school differs from others in considering *halq* or *taqsir* as non-obligatory for *umrat al-mufradah*.

4.10.4.3. TWO SUBSIDIARY ISSUES

1. The obligation of *umrat al-mufradah* is not connected with the ability for the prescribed pilgrimage. If, supposedly, it is possible for a person to go to Makkah at a time other than that of the prescribed pilgrimage and not possible at the time of the prescribed pilgrimage, then the minor pilgrimage (*umrah*) instead of the prescribed pilgrimage becomes obligatory for that person. If the person dies without performing it, its expense is taken out from his or her legacy.[27]

Similarly, if one has ability for *hajj al-ifrad* instead of the minor pilgrimage, it becomes obligatory upon him or her because each of them is independent of the other. This applies to *umrat al-mufradah*. As to *umrat al-tamattu*, which shall be explained later, its obligation depends upon that of the pilgrimage, since it is a part of it.

2. According to the Jafari, it is not permissible for one intending to enter Makkah to cross the 'place at the appointed time' or enter its sacred area without getting into the state of the sacred dress, even if he or she has performed the pilgrimage and the minor pilgrimage many times before. Only when the exit and entry recur several times during a month, or when after entering the city as a pilgrim (*muhrim*) he goes out and re-enters for a second time in less than thirty days, it is not obligatory. Therefore, the sacred state with respect to entry into Makkah is comparable to the ablution before touching the Quran.

According to Imam Abu Hanifah, it is not permissible to go beyond the place at the appointed time and enter the sacred area without being in the sacred state, but entry into the remaining area is permissible without it. Imam Malik does not agree with this, and two opinions are ascribed to Imam Shafi on the matter. This much of discussion about the minor pilgrimage is sufficient for throwing light upon it, so that the reader may grasp its difference with the pilgrimage, though only in some aspects. What we shall say later will offer further clarification.

4.11. THE FORMS OF THE PRESCRIBED PILGRIMAGE

All the major legal schools agree that there are three kinds of prescribed pilgrimage: *tamattu, qiran,* and *ifrad.* They also agree that by *hajj al-tamattu* is meant performance of the acts of the minor pilgrimage (*umrah*) during the months of the pilgrimage. The acts of the pilgrimage itself are performed completing the minor pilgrimage. They also agree that by *hajj al-ifrad* is meant performing the pilgrimage first and then, after performing the acts of the pilgrimage, assuming the sacred state for performing the minor pilgrimage and its related acts. The Hanafi, Hanbali, Shafii and Maliki schools agree that the meaning of the *hajj al-qiran* is to be in the sacred state for the pilgrimage and minor pilgrimage together. Then the *talbiyah* uttered by the pilgrim is: *"labayyk, allahumma, bi hajj wa umrah."*

According to the Jafari school, the *hajj al-qiran* and *hajj al-ifrad* are one and the same. There is no difference between them except when the pilgrim performing the *hajj al-qiran* brings the sacrifice at the time of assuming the sacred state. Then it is obligatory upon him or her to offer what he or she has brought. But one who performs the *hajj al-ifrad* has essentially no obligation to offer the sacrifice. In brief, the Jafari do not consider it permissible to interchange two different sacred states[28] or to perform the prescribed pilgrimage and minor pilgrimage with a single intention under any condition. The other legal schools permit it in *hajj al-qiran*. They say that it has been named *'qiran'* because it involves union between the pilgrimage and the minor pilgrimage. But the Jafari say that it is because of the additional feature of the sacrifice accompanying the pilgrim at the time of assuming the sacred state.[29]

According to the Hanafi, Hanbali, Shafii and Maliki legal schools, it is permissible for the pilgrim, Makkan or non-Makkan, to choose from any of the three forms of the prescribed pilgrimage: *al-tamattu, al-qiran* or *al-ifrad*, without involving any reprehensibility. Only Imam Abu Hanifah considers *hajj al-tamattu* and *hajj al-qiran* as disapproved for the Makkan. The Hanafi, Hanbali, Shafii and Maliki schools also differ as to which of the three kinds of pilgrimage is superior to the others. The best according to the Shafii school is *al-ifrad*, and *al-tamattu* is superior to *al-qiran*. According to the Hanafi school, *al-qiran* has greater merit than the other two. The best according to the Maliki school is *al-ifrad*, and according to the Hanbali and Jafari schools is *al-tamattu*.

According to the Jafari school, the pilgrimage (*hajj al-tamattu*) is obligatory upon one living at a distance of over forty-eight miles from Makkah and he or she may not choose any other kind except in emergency. The *hajj al-qiran* and *hajj al-ifrad* can be performed by the people of Makkah and those living around it within a distance of forty-eight miles and it is not permissible for them to perform except one of these two kinds. This view is based on the verse, *"And complete the pre-scribed pilgrimage and minor pilgrimage in the service of God, but if you are prevented (from completing it), send an offering for sacrifice such as you may find and do not shave your head until the offering reaches the place of sacrifice..."* (2:196).

Moreover, according to the Jafari school, it is not permissible for one obliged to perform the prescribed pilgrimage (*hajj al-tamattu*) to change over to something else, except for the problem of shortage of time available or, in the case of women, due to impending menses. In those cases, it is permissible to change either to *al-qiran* or *al-ifrad* on condition that the minor pilgrimage (*umrah*) is performed after the prescribed pilgrimage. The limit of the shortage of time is failure to be present at the halt in Arafat until noon. For one whose duty is *al-qiran* or *al-ifrad*, such as the natives of Makkah or those from its surrounding region, it is not permissible to change to the pilgrimage except in exigency such as the fear of impending menses. All major schools agree that the sacrifice is not compulsory for one performing the *hajj al-ifrad* although better if performed voluntarily.

4.12. THE SACRED STATE

4.12.1. PLACES OF THE APPOINTED TIME OF THE SACRED STATE

The sacred state is compulsory for all the various kinds of prescribed pilgrimage as well as minor pilgrimages and is regarded as their basic element by the Jafari, and as obligatory by other schools. All the major schools agree that the place of the appointed time of the people of Madinah from where they assume the sacred state is Masjid al-Shajarah, also known as Dhul Hulayfah[30] for the pilgrims of al-Sham (which includes the Syrians, the Lebanese, the Palestinians and the Jordanians, noting further that the routes have changed from what they used to be in the past), Morocco and Egypt, the place at the appointed time is al-Juhfah.[31] For the pilgrims of Iraq, it is al-Aqiq.[32] For those from Yemen and others who take the same route, it is Yalamlam.[33]

According to the Jafari, Qarn al-Manazil[34] is the place at the appointed time for the people of al-Taif and those who take their route towards Makkah. But according to the Hanafi, Hanbali, Shafii and Maliki schools, it is the place at the appointed time of the people of Najd. The place at the appointed time for those from Najd and Iraq according to the Jafari is al-Aqiq. All the legal schools agree that these places of the appointed time also apply to those who in their journey take similar routes, even though they may not be natives of those regions. For instance, if a Syrian starts on the prescribed pilgrimage from Madinah, it is permissible for him to assume the sacred dress from Dhul Hulayfah. If a pilgrim starts on the pilgrimage from Yemen, the place at the appointed time is Yalamlam. If from Iraq, then al-Aqiq, and so on. If one does not pass the mentioned places of the appointed time on one's route, the place for that place is the place parallel to any one of them.

If someone lives at a place nearer to Makkah than any of the prescribed places at the appointed time, then that person assumes the sacred state from the place of his residence. For someone who resides in Makkah itself, the place at the appointed time is Makkah. For one performing the *umrat al-mufradah*, the places at the appointed time, according to the Jafari, are the same as·for the pilgrimage.

4.12.2. THE SACRED STATE BEFORE THE PLACE AT THE APPOINTED TIME

The Hanafi, Hanbali, Shafii and Maliki schools agree on the permissibility of assuming the sacred state before the point of the place at the appointed time, but disagree as to which has greater merit. According to Imam Malik and Imam Abu Hanbal, the sacred state before the place at the appointed time is more meritorious. According to Imam Abu Hanifah, the merit lies in assuming the sacred state while starting the pilgrimage journey from one's town. Two opinions are ascribed to Imam Shafi in this regard. However, according to the Imam Jafar, assuming the sacred state before the place of the appointed time is not permissible except for one who intends to perform the minor pilgrimage in the month of Rajab and is afraid of missing it if assuming the sacred state is delayed until the place at the appointed time is reached, and for one who makes a vow to assume the sacred state before the place at the appointed time.[35]

4.12.3. ASSUMING THE SACRED STATE AT THE PLACE AT THE APPOINTED TIME

There is consensus among all the schools that it is not permissible to cross the place at the appointed time without being in the sacred state. One who does so must return to the place at the appointed time for assuming the sacred state. If he or she does not return, according to the Hanafi, Hanbali, Shafii and Maliki schools, his or her prescribed pilgrimage is correct although he or she should offer a sacrifice in atonement. But if there be any impediment, such as fear of insecurity on the way or shortage of time, there is no sin. This, regardless of whether there are other places at the appointed time before him or her on his or her path or not.

According to the Jafari, if he or she has deliberately neglected to assume the sacred state at the appointed time while intending to perform the prescribed or minor pilgrimage, if he or she does not turn back to the place at the appointed time, there being no other place before him from which he or she can assume the sacred state, his or her assuming of the sacred state and pilgrimage are invalid, whether he or she had a valid pretext for not returning or not. But if his or her failure to assume the sacred state at the appointed time was on account of forgetfulness or ignorance, if it is possible to return, he or she must do so. If it is not possible, then it should be done from the next place at the appointed time before him or her. Otherwise he ought to assume the sacred state as far as possible outside the sacred area of Makkah, or within it, although the former is preferable.[36]

4.12.4. THE SACRED STATE BEFORE THE MONTHS OF THE PILGRIMAGE

According to the Jafari and Shafii schools, assuming the sacred state before the months of the prescribed pilgrimage is invalid if assumed with the purpose of the pilgrimage, although it is valid when assumed for the purpose of the minor pilgrimage (*umrah*). They cite in this regard the Quranic verse (2:197). But according to the Hanafi, Maliki and Hanbali schools, it is permissible but disapproved.[37]

4.12.5. The Sacred State: Its Obligations and Recommendations
4.12.5.1. Recommended for the Sacred State

There is no disagreement among the legal schools with respect to the sacred state being an essential pillar of the minor pilgrimage and all the three forms of the prescribed pilgrimage, namely, *tamattu, qiran* and *ifrad*. Also, there is no difference of opinion that preparing oneself for the sacred state is the first act of the pilgrim, irrespective of whether his or her purpose is the minor pilgrimage (*umrah al-mufradah*), or any of the three forms of the prescribed pilgrimage. There are certain obligations (*wajibat*) and recommended acts related to the sacred state.

The legal schools agree that it is recommended for anyone intending to get into the sacred state to cleanse his or her body, clip his or her fingernails, shorten his moustache, and to take a bath (even for women undergoing menstruation or bleeding following childbirth, for the aim is a state of purity). It is also recommended for one intending the prescribed pilgrimage to abstain from cutting the hair of his head from the beginning of the month of Dhul Qadah, to remove the hair from his body and armpits, and to enter the sacred state after the noon or any other prescribed prayers. It is also recommended to pray six, four or at least two cycles of prescribed prayer. However, freedom from the state of prescribed impurity is not a condition for the sacred state to be valid.

According to the Hanafi and Maliki schools, if water is not available, one is relieved of the duty to take the bath ablution, and dry ablution as an alternative is not permissible. According to the Hanbali and Shafii schools, dry ablution substitutes for bath lustration. The Jafari jurists differ on this matter, some consider it permissible, others not. According to the Jafari school, it is recommended to leave the hair of the head uncut, but according to the Shafii, Hanafi and Hanbali schools, it is recommended to shave the head.[38]

According to the Hanafi school, it is *Sunnah* for one who wants to assume the sacred state to scent his or her body and clothes with a perfume whose trace does not remain after the sacred state has been assumed except the smell. According to the Shafii school, it is *Sunnah*, except when one is fasting, to apply perfume to the body after the bath. Also, perfuming the clothes does not matter. According to the Hanbali school, one may perfume the body and the clothes but this is disapproved.[39]

According to the Hanafi, Maliki and Shafii schools, it is recommended for the pilgrim to pray two cycles of the prescribed prayer before assuming the sacred state. According to the Jafari school, it is best to assume the sacred state after the noon prescribed prayer or any other prescribed prayer. If the pilgrim has no obligatory prayer to make at the time of getting into the sacred state, he or she should offer six, or four or at least two cycles for the the sacred state.[40]

4.12.5.2. MAKING A COVENANT WITH GOD

The Jafari say that for one intending the sacred state it is recommended to make a covenant with God at the time of assuming the sacred state by saying, "O God, indeed I wish to fulfill Your command, but if any impediment keeps me from completing it or a barrier obstructs me from it, exonerate me." Imam Abu Hanifah, Imam Shafi and Imam Ahmad ibn Hanbal also consider it recommended. However, this covenant (*ishtirat*) does not help in relieving one of the obligation of the prescribed pilgrimage if one were to encounter an impediment which keeps him or her from getting through it.

4.12.5.3. THE OBLIGATORY ASPECTS OF THE SACRED STATE

The obligatory aspects of the sacred state, with some difference between the legal schools on some points are three:

declaring one's intention, the recitation of "Here I am," (*tal-biyah*), and putting on of the clothes of the sacred state.

4.12.5.3.1. DECLARATION OF INTENTION

Obviously declaring one's intention known is essential to every voluntary act for every such act is motivated by conscious intent. Therefore, some scholars have pointed out that had we been assigned a duty to be performed without making our intention known, it would have been impossible to be carried out. However, when the question of intention is raised in relation to the pilgrim (of the prescribed or recommended pilgrimage), what is meant is whether he or she becomes pilgrim solely on account of the making his or her intention known or if something else is required in addition, acknowledging that the sacred state is void if assumed frivolously or absent-mindedly.

According to the Hanafi school, the sacred state is not considered to commence solely by declaring one's intention unless it is accompanied by the utterance of the recitation of, "Here I am..." (*talbiyah.*).[41] According to the Shafii, Jafari and Hanbali schools, the sacred state is assumed merely by declaring one's intention (*niyyah*).[42] The Jafari add that it is obligatory for the declaring of one's intention to coincide with the commencement of the sacred state, and it is not sufficient for the act of declaring one's intention to occur in the course of assuming the sacred state. Also while declaring one's intention, it is essential to specify the purpose of the sacred state, whether it is the prescribed or minor pilgrimage, and if the prescribed pilgrimage, whether it is *hajj al-tamattu*, *hajj al-qiran* or *hajj al-ifrad*, whether he or she is performing the prescribed pilgrimage for himself or herself or as a deputy of someone else, whether for the prescribed pilgrimage (*hijjat al-islam*) or for something else. If one assumes the sacred state without specifying these particulars, postponing their determination to future, the sacred state (*ihram*) is invalid.[43]

According to the Hanafi text, *al-Mughni*, "It is recommended to specify the purpose of assuming the sacred state." Imam Malik is of the same opinion. Two opinions are ascribed to the Hanafi. According to one of them, it is adequate if one assumes the sacred state with a general, non-specific purpose of pilgrimage—without determining the exact purpose, whether the prescribed or minor pilgrimage. The sacred state thus assumed is valid and makes one a pilgrim. Afterwards, he or she may select any of the kinds of pilgrimage." All the major schools agree that if one assumes the sacred state with the intention to follow another person's intention, his or her sacred state is valid if the other person's purpose is specific.[44]

4.12.5.3.2. THE RECITATION OF "HERE I AM..."

The legitimacy of the recitation of "Here I am..." (*talbiyah*) in assuming the sacred state is acknowledged by all the major schools, but they disagree as to its being obligatory or recommended, and also about its timing. According to the Shafii and Hanbali schools, it is *Sunnah*, preferably performed concurrently with assuming the sacred state. However, if the intention to assume the sacred state is not accompanied by *talbiyah,* the sacred state is correct.

According to the Jafari, Hanafi[45] and Maliki schools, the *talbiyah* is obligatory, although they differ about its details. According to the Hanafi school, pronouncement of *talbiyah* or its substitute such as *tasbih,* or bringing along of the sacrificial animal (*al-hady*) is a provision for the sacred state to be valid. According to the Maliki school, the sacred state (*ihram*) neither becomes invalid if *talbiyah* is recited after a long gap of time, nor if it is not pronounced altogether. However, one who fails to pronounce it must offer a blood sacrifice.

According to the Jafari, neither the sacred state for *hajj al-tamattu* nor *hajj al-ifrad* nor their conjugate *umrah*'s nor for *al-umrat al-mufradah* is valid without *talbiyah*. However, one who intends to perform *hajj al-qiran* may choose between *talbiyah, ishar*[46] or *taqlid. Ishar* for this school is exclusively restricted to a camel, although hanging an old horseshoe around the neck of the sacrificial animal (*taqlid*) may apply to a camel or the other forms of sacrificial animals.

4.12.5.3.3. THE FORMULA OF THE RECITATION "HERE I AM"

All the legal schools agree that prescribed purity is not a proviso for pronouncing *talbiyah*.[47] As to its occasion, the pilgrim (*muhrim*) starts reciting it from the moment of assuming the sacred state (*ihram*), being recommended for him or her to continue it—all the major schools agree—until the throwing of stones of *jamarat al-aqabah*. To utter it loudly is recommended for men and not for women, except in mosques where prescribed prayers are offered in congregation, particularly in the Mosque of Arafat. According to the Jafari school, it is recommended to discontinue reciting the *talbiyah* on sighting the houses of Makkah. A woman may recite the *talbiyah* just loud enough to be heard by herself or someone near her. It is also recommended to proclaim blessings on the Prophet and his family.[48]

4.12.5.3.4. THE PILGRIM'S DRESS

All the major schools agree that it is not permissible for a male pilgrim to wear stitched clothing, shirts or trousers, nor may he cover his face. Also, it is not permissible for him to wear shoes (*khuffan*) except when he cannot find a pair of sandals (*nalan*),[49] and that after removing the covering on the back of the heels from the base. A woman, however, should cover her head, keep her face exposed, except when she fears that men may stare at her. It is not permissible for her to wear gloves, but she may put on silk and wear shoes. According to Imam Abu Hanifah, it is permissible for a woman to wear gloves.[50]

The book *al-Fiqh alal-madhahib al-arbaah*, under the heading, "That which is required of one intending the sacred state before a male starts to assume it," states, "According to the Hanafi school...among other things he wears a loin-cloth (*izar*) and cloak (*rida*). The loin-cloth covers the lower part of the body from the navel to the knees. The cloak covers the back, the chest and the shoulders, and its wearing is recommended."

According to the Maliki school, it is recommended to wear the loin-cloth, cloak, and sandals (*nalan*) but there is no restriction on wearing something else that is not stitched and does not encircle any of the parts of the body. According to the Hanbali school, it is *Sunnah* to put on a new, white, and clean cloak and loin-cloth together with a pair of sandals before assuming the sacred state. According to the Shafii school, the cloak and loin-cloth should be white, new or washed ones.

According to the Jafari school, the cloak and the loin-cloth are obligatory, preferably of white cotton. The male pilgrim may put on more than these two pieces of clothing on condition that they are not stitched. Also it is permissible to change the clothes in which one commenced the sacred state, although it is better to perform the circumambulation in the same cloak and loin-cloth as worn at the beginning. All the requirements of the dress for the prescribed prayers apply to the dress of the sacred state, such as the prescribed purity, its being non-silken for men, not made of the skin of an animal eating whose flesh is not permissible. According to some Jafari jurists, clothing made of skin is not permissible in the performance of the prescribed prayers and assuming the sacred state . In any case, the disagreement between the legal schools about the pilgrim's dress is very limited. This is well indicated by the fact that whatever is regarded as permissible by the Jafari is also considered permissible by the remaining schools.

4.12.6. RESTRICTIONS OF THE SACRED STATE
There are certain restrictions for the pilgrim, most of which are discussed below.

4.12.6.1. MARRIAGE
According to the Jafari, Shafii, Maliki and Hanbali schools, it is not permissible for the pilgrim to contract marriage for himself or herself or on behalf of another. Also he or she may not act as another's agent for concluding a marriage contract, and if he or she does, the contract is invalid. Furthermore,

according to the Jafari school, he or she may not act as a witness to such a contract.

According to Imam Abu Hanifah, marriage contract is permissible and the contract concluded is valid. According to the Hanafi, Maliki, Shafii and Jafari schools, it is permissible for the pilgrim to revoke divorce of his former wife during her waiting period. According to the Hanbali school, it is not permissible. From the viewpoint of the Jafari, if one enters a marriage contract with the knowledge of its prohibition, the woman becomes unlawful for him for life merely by the act of concluding the contract, even if the marriage is not consummated. But if done in ignorance of the interdiction, she is not prohibited to him, even if consummation has been affected.[51]

4.12.6.2. INTERCOURSE

All the major legal schools agree that it is not permissible for the pilgrim to have sexual intercourse with his or her spouse or to derive any kind of sexual pleasure from one's spouse. If the pilgrim performs intercourse before leaving the sacred state[52] the pilgrim's prescribed pilgrimage becomes void, although he or she must perform all its acts to the conclusion. Thereafter, he or she must repeat the prescribed pilgrimage the next year, performing it 'separately' from his or her spouse.[53] The seclusion is obligatory according to the Jafari, Maliki and Hanbali schools, and voluntary from the viewpoint of the Shafii and Hanafi schools.[54] Moreover, according to the Jafari, Shafii, and Maliki schools, besides the fact that his or her prescribed fast becomes invalid, he or she must sacrifice a camel in atonement, and according to the Hanafi school, a sheep.

All the major legal schools agree that if he or she has intercourse with his or her spouse after the first time after leaving the sacred state—after the *halq* or *taqsir* in Mina, after which everything except intercourse and also perfume according to the Jafari school— become permissible for the pilgrim, the prescribed pilgrimage is not void, nor is the pilgrim called upon to repeat it. Nevertheless, the pilgrim must offer a camel, according to the Jafari and Hanafi schools and according to one of the two opinions ascribed to Imam Shafi. But according to the Maliki school, the pilgrim is obliged to offer a sheep only.[55]

If the wife yields willingly to intercourse, her prescribed pilgrimage is also void and she must sacrifice a camel in expiation and repeat the prescribed pilgrimage the year after. But if she was forced, then nothing is required of her, but the husband is obliged to offer two camels: one on his own behalf, and the second on hers. If the wife was not in the sacred state of *ihram*, but the husband was, nothing is required of her, nor is she obliged to offer anything in atonement, nor is anything required of the husband on her account.[56]

If the husband kisses his wife, his prescribed pilgrimage is not void if it does not result in ejaculation. On this all schools are in agreement. But according to the Hanafi, Hanbali, Shafii, and Maliki schools, the pilgrim is obliged to make a sacrificial offering in atonement even if it be a sheep. The Jafari author of *al-Tadhkirah* says that the sacrifice of a camel is obligatory only if the kiss is taken with sexual desire, otherwise he should sacrifice only a sheep. If he ejaculates, the prescribed fast is void according to the Maliki school, but remains valid according to the other schools, although he should make an offering in atonement, which is a camel according to the Hanbali school and a group of Jafari jurists, and a sheep according to the Shafii and Hanafi schools.[57]

4.12.6.3. USE OF PERFUME

All the legal schools agree that the pilgrim, man or woman, may not make use of any perfume, either for smelling, or for applying on himself or herself, or for scenting edibles. Indeed it is not permissible to wash the dead body of a pilgrim, nor to perform *hunut* upon it by applying camphor or any other kind of perfumery. If the pilgrim uses perfume forgetfully or on account of ignorance, he or she needs not make any offering in atonement according to the Jafari and Shafii schools. But according to the Hanafi and Maliki schools, he or she must make a sacrificial offering. In this relation two different opinions are ascribed to Imam Ahmad ibn Hanbal.

However, when one is forced to use perfume on account of disease, it is permissible and no sacrificial offering is required. According to the Jafari school, if one uses perfume intentionally, he or she must offer a sheep, irrespective of the use, whether applied to the body or eaten. However, there is nothing wrong with perfuming the Kabah even if it contains saffron, and the same applies to fruits and aromatic plants.[58]

4.12.6.4. USE OF COLLYRIUM

The author of *al-Tadhkirah* states, "There is consensus among the Jafari jurists on the point that darkening the eyelids with collyrium (*kohl*) or applying it when it contains perfume is not permissible for the pilgrim, man or woman. Apart from that (i.e. *ihram*) it is permissible." According to the author of *al-Mughni*, "Collyrium containing antimony is disapproved, and does not require any sacrificial animal." There is no disapproval of the use of collyrium without antimony, as long as it does not contain any perfume.

4.12.6.5. SHORTENING OF NAILS AND HAIR AND CUTTING OF TREES

All the major legal schools agree about impermissability of shortening the nails and shaving or shortening of the hair of the head or the body in the sacred state, a sacrificial animal being required of the offender.[59] As to cutting of trees and plants within the sacred area, all the legal schools agree that it is impermissible to cut or uproot anything grown naturally without human mediation. Imam Shafi states that there is no difference between the two with regard to the prohibition and a sacrificial animal is required for both. The cutting of a large tree requires the sacrifice of a cow and the cutting of other plants, a sheep. According to Imam Malik, cutting of a tree is a sin, although nothing is required of the offender, regardless of whether it has grown with or without human mediation.

According to the Jafari, Hanafi and Hanbali schools, cutting of something planted by human hands is permissible and does not require a sacrifice but anything grown by nature requires one. The sacrifice of a cow is obligatory according to the Jafari school for cutting a big tree and a sheep for cutting smaller plants. According to the Hanafi school, the owner of the tree is entitled to a payment equivalent to the cost of the sacrificial animal.[60]

All the major schools agree that there is no restriction for cutting a dry tree or for pulling out withered grass.

4.12.6.6. LOOKING INTO A MIRROR

It is not permissible for a pilgrim to look into a mirror and all the major schools agree that there is no sacrifice of an animal required for doing so. However, there is no restriction on looking into water.

4.12.6.7. USE OF HENNA

According to the Hanafi school, it is permissible for the pilgrim, man or woman, to dye with henna any part of his or her body, except the head. According to the Shafii school, it is permissible, with the exception of hands and feet. According to the Hanafi school, dyeing is not permissible for the pilgrim, man or woman.[61] The predominant view among the Jafari jurists is that dyeing is disapproved not unlawful.[62]

4.12.6.8. USE OF SHADE AND COVERING THE HEAD

All the major schools agree that it is not permissible for the male pilgrim to cover his head voluntarily. According to the Maliki and Jafari schools, it is not permissible for him to immerse himself under water until the head is completely submerged, although it is permissible for him, all the major schools except the Shafii agree, to wash his head or pour water over it. The Malikis say that with the exception of the hands it is not permissible to remove dirt by washing. If he covers the head forgetfully, nothing is required of him according to the Jafari and Shafii schools, but a sacrificial animal is required according to the Hanafi school.

All the schools, with the exception of the Shafii, agree that it is impermissible for the pilgrim to shade himself while moving. Neither it is permissible for him to ride an automobile, an airplane or the like, which are covered by a roof. But it is permissible while walking to pass under a shadow. [63] If one needs shadow in case of exigency, such as illness or intense heat or cold, it is permissible, but an atonement is required according to the Jafari school. All the major schools agree that it is permissible for the pilgrim when stationary in a place to be under the shade of a roof, wall, tree, tent, etc. According to the Jafari school, it is permissible for a woman to use shadow while moving about.[64]

4.12.6.9. STITCHED CLOTHING AND RING

All the major schools agree that it is forbidden for the male pilgrim to wear stitched clothes and clothes which encircle body members, e.g. turban, hat and the like. These are permissible for women, with the exception of gloves and clothes which have come into contact with perfume. According to the Jafari school, if the pilgrim wears stitched clothes forgetfully or in ignorance of the restriction, nothing is required of him. But if one wears them intentionally to protect himself from heat or cold, he should offer a sheep. Also according to them it is not permissible to wear a ring for adornment, but it is permissible for other purposes. Also, it is not permissible for woman to wear jewelry for the sake of adornment.

4.12.6.10. LYING AND ARGUING

God, the most Exalted, says in the Quran, "...*There should be no obscenity, neither impiety, nor disputing in the pilgrimage*" (2:197). In this verse, the meaning of '*rafath*' is taken to be sexual intercourse, to which reference has been made earlier. *Fusuq* is taken to mean lying, cursing, or commission of sins. In any case, all of them are forbidden for the pilgrims of the prescribed pilgrimage and the non-pilgrims as well. The stress here is meant to emphasize abstention from them in the sacred state. The meaning of *'jidal'* is arguing. According to an Jafari school, "It (i. e. *'jidal'* in the above-mentioned verse) means using such expressions as 'Yes, by God!' or 'No, by God!' in conversation. This is the lowest degree of *jidal*." According to the Jafari school, if the pilgrim tells a lie once, he or she must offer a sheep; if twice, a cow; if three times, a camel. And if he or she swears once taking a veritable oath, there is nothing obligatory upon him or her, but if he or she repeats it three times, he or she is obliged to sacrifice a sheep.

4.12.6.11. CUPPING

All the major schools agree on permissibility of cupping (*hijamah*) in case of necessity, and the Hanafi, Hanbali, Shafii and Maliki schools permit it even when not necessary as long as it does not require removal of hair. The Jafari jurists disagree on this issue. Some of them permit it and others not.[65]

4.12.6.12. HUNTING

All the major schools are in agreement about the prohibition on hunting (*al-sayd*) of land animals, either through killing or through sacrifice and also on guiding the hunter or pointing out the game to him in the sacred state. Also prohibited is meddling with their eggs and their young ones. However, the hunting of water animals is permitted and requires no sacrificial animal. This, in accordance with the Quranic verse, *"Permitted to you is the game of the sea and the food of it, as a provision for you and for the travelers; but forbidden to you is the game of the land, so long as you remain in the sacred state and fear God, unto whom you shall be returned"* (5:96).

The prohibition on hunting within the precincts of the sacred area apply to the pilgrim and the non-pilgrim (*muhill*) equally. However, outside the sacred area the prohibition applies only to the pilgrim. If the pilgrim (*muhrim*) slaughters a game, it is considered a dead animal not slaughtered in accordance with ritual requirements and its flesh is unlawful for all human beings. The major legal schools agree that the pilgrim may kill a predatory bird called *hadah*, crows, mice and scorpions. Others include wild dogs and anything harmful.

According to the Jafari and Shafii schools, if the game hunted on land resembles some domestic beast in shape and form (such as the onyx which resembles the cow), he or she has the choice between: (1) giving the meat of one of similar beasts of his livestock in charity after slaughtering it; (2) estimating its price and buying food of the amount to be given in expiation and charity to the needy, distributing it by giving two dry measures equal to 800 grams (*mudd*) to every individual; (3) fasting, a day for every two dry measures equal to 800 grams (*mudd*).

The Malikis hold the same viewpoint, except that, they add that the price of the hunted animal itself should be estimated, not that of its domestic equivalent. The Hanafis say that one who hunts in the sacred state should arrange for the estimated price of the hunted animal, whether there is a domestic animal similar to it or not. When the price has been estimated, he is free to choose between: (1) purchasing livestock of the money and giving its meat away in charity; (2) giving it from his own livestock; (3) purchasing food of the amount to be given away in charity; (4) fasting, a day for every dry measure equal to 800 grams (*mudd*) of food to be given away.[66]

In this connection all the legal schools base their position on the Quranic verse, *"O believers, slay not the game while you are in the sacred state. Whosoever of you slays it wilfully, there shall be reparation—the like of what he has slain, in livestock, as shall be judged by two men of equity among you, an offering on reaching the Kabah or atonement—food for poor persons or the equivalent of that in fasting, so that he may taste the mischief of his action. God has pardoned what is past; but whoever offends again, God will take vengeance on him; God is All-Mighty, Vengeful"* (5:95).

The meaning of the phrase *"two men of equity"* in the above verse is that two equitable witnesses should judge whether a certain domestic animal is similar to the hunted wild beast. He or she should slaughter the equivalent livestock and give its meat in charity on arrival in Mecca. According to the Jafari work al-Sharai, "Every pilgrim who wears or eats anything forbidden for him should slaughter a sheep, regardless of whether his or her action was intentional, forgetful, or on account of ignorance." The Jafari and Shafii schools agree that no atonement is required of someone who commits an unlawful act forgetfully or in ignorance, except in the case of hunting, in which case even killing by mistake requires atonement.

4.12.6.13. THE LIMITS OF THE SACRED AREAS OF MAKKAH AND MADINAH

The prohibition of hunting and cutting of trees applies both to the sacred areas of Makkah and that of Madinah. According to *Fiqh as-sunnah*, the limits of the sacred area of Makkah are indicated by signs in major directions, which are one-meter-high stones fixed on both sides of the roads. The limits of the sacred area of Makkah are as follows: (1) the northern limit is marked by al-Tanim, which is a place at a distance of six kms. from Makkah; (2) the southern limit is marked by Idah, twelve kms. from Makkah; (3) the eastern limit is al-Jaranah, sixteen kms. from Makkah; (4) the western limit is al-Shumaysi, fifteen kms. from Makkah.

The limits of the sacred area of the Prophet's shrine in Madinah extend from Ir to Thawr, a distance of twelve kms. Ir is a hill near the *miqat* and Thawr is a hill at Uhud.

Hilli states in his work *al-Tadhkirah*, "The sacred area of Makkah extends over an area of twelve miles (one *barid*) by twelve miles (one barid) and the sacred area of Madinah extends from Ayir to Ir.[67]

4.13. CIRCUMAMBULATION

Circumambulation is an essential part of the minor pilgrimage (*umrah*) and the *tawaf al-ziyarah* (also called *tawaf al-ifadah*) is a pillar of the prescribed pilgrimage (*hajj al-tamattu*), *hajj al-ifrad* and *hajj al-qiran*. As said earlier, the assumption of the sacred state is the first act of the pilgrim regardless of whether he or she comes for the minor pilgrimage (*umrah al-mufradah*) or for any of the three types of prescribed pilgrimage.

Now, after the assuming of sacred state, what is the next step for the pilgrim? Is it the seven-fold circumambulation of the Kabah or the halting or something else? The answer is that it depends on the intention with which the pilgrim assumes the sacred state. If it is for the minor pilgrimage, then the next step is the seven-fold circumambulation of the Kabah, regardless of whether it is for the prescribed or minor pilgrimage. Thus circumambulation is the second step for the pilgrim intending the minor pilgrimage by agreement of all the major schools.

However, if the purpose of the sacred state is the prescribed pilgrimage only such as in the case of pilgrim on *hajj al-ifrad* or one intending to perform the prescribed pilgrimage after getting through the acts of the minor pilgrimage—the second step is (as shall be explained later) halting in Arafat. In other words, one who enters Makkah with the sole purpose of the shorter or prescribed pilgrimage, performs the seven-fold circumambulation of the Kabah before everything else, then the search between Safa and Marwah and then cutting or shortening the hair. After this, if on the prescribed pilgrimage, the pilgrim assumes the sacred state for a second time but the pilgrim is not required to perform another seven-fold circumambulation after this assumption of the sacred state. The seven-fold circumambulation of the Kabah (pertaining to the acts of the prescribed pilgrimage, as we shall explain) comes after getting through the halt at Arafat and passage through Mina.

4.13.1. KINDS OF CIRCUMAMBULATION

The imams of the Hanafi, Hanbali, Shafii and Maliki schools distinguish between three kinds of circumambulation (*tawaf*):

4.13.1.1. THE CIRCUMAMBULATION OF ARRIVAL

The circumambulation of arrival (*tawaf al-qudum*) is the circumambulation performed by those coming from outside

Makkah and from beyond its outskirts within a radius of eighty-eight kms on entry into Makkah. It is similar to the two cycles of prescribed prayer performed as 'greeting of the mosque' (*tahiyyat al-masjid*). These schools agree on its being recommended and no penalty is required for default according to all except the Maliki's who require a blood sacrifice.

4.13.1.2. THE CIRCUMAMBULATION OF THE MINOR PILGRIMAGE

This circumambulation (*tawaf al-ziyarah*, also called '*tawaf al-ifaidah*') is performed by pilgrims after completing the acts of Mina, the throwing of the stones of *jamarat al-aqabah*, the sacrifice, and the *halq* or the *taqsir*. The pilgrim performs this circumambulation on returning to Makkah. It is called *tawaf al-ziyarah* because it is performed on the minor pilgrimage to the Kabah after leaving Mina. It is called *tawaf al-ifadah* 'because the pilgrims pour forth into Makkah from Mina. It is also called *tawaf al-hajj* because by consensus of all the schools it is a pillar of the prescribed pilgrimage.

After performing this circumambulation, all things become permissible for the pilgrim who follows any of these schools, even sexual intimacy with women. The Jafari, who disagree, say that sex is not permitted before performing the search between Safa and Marwah followed by a second circumambulation, which they call *tawaf al-nisa*. This shall be further explained below.

4.13.1.3. THE CIRCUMAMBULATION OF FAREWELL

It is the last circumambulation, the circumambulation of farewell (*tawaf al-wada*) performed by the pilgrim before departing from Makkah. The Hanafi and Hanbali schools consider it obligatory, although all that is required of the defaulter is a sacrifice. The Malikis consider it recommended and do not require any penalty for the default. Imam Shafi has two opinions on this matter.[68]

The Jafari agree with the Hanafi, Hanbali, Shafii and Maliki schools about the legitimacy of the above three kinds of circumambulation and regard the second circumambulation, that is, *tawaf al-ziyarah,* as a pillar of the prescribed pilgrimage whose omission makes the prescribed pilgrimage invalid.[69]

However, the first kind, that is, *tawaf al-qudum,* is considered recommended (*mustahabb*) and may be omitted. Regarding the third, i.e. *tawaf al-wada,* they agree with the Maliki school in its being recommended, there being nothing on the defaulter. However, the Jafari add another kind of circumambulation to the above three, the *tawaf al-nisa* which they consider obligatory, its omission being impermissible in the minor pilgrimage as well as in all the three kinds of prescribed pilgrimage (i.e. *tamattu, qiran* and *ifrad*). They do not permit its omission except in case of *umrat al-tamattu,* considering the *tawaf al-nisa* performed during the course of *hajj al-tamattu* as sufficient. The Hanafi, Hanbali, Shafii and Maliki schools state that there is no obligatory circumambulation after the *tawaf al-ziyarah,* after which sexual intimacy is permissible. The Jafari say that it is obligatory upon the pilgrim, after performing *tawaf al-ziyarah* and the running (*say*), to perform another circumambulation, the *tawaf al-nisa,* which derives its name precisely because of the sanction of permissibility of relations with women (*nisa*) following it. They say that if the pilgrim defaults in regard to this circumambulation, sexual relations are forbidden for man and woman (for men even the conclusion of marriage contract), unless he or she performs it in person or deputes another to perform it on his/her behalf; and if he or she dies without performing it or without deputing someone to do it for him or her, it is incumbent upon the heir to have it performed on the behalf of the dead person. According to them, even in case of a child who has attained discernment who fails to perform the *tawaf al-nisa* while performing the prescribed pilgrimage, even if he or she omits it by mistake or on account of ignorance, sexual relations are forbidden after adulthood nor he or she may conclude a marriage contract (*aql*) unless he or she performs it himself or herself or deputes another for the job.

To summarize, the Jafari consider three circumambulations to be obligatory for the pilgrim on the prescribed pilgrimage: (1) the circumambulation of the conjugate minor pilgrimage, of which it is a pillar; (2) the *tawaf al-ziyarah* (or *tawaf al-hajj*), which is a pillar (*rukn*) of the prescribed pilgrimage; and (3) the *tawaf al-nisa*, which is also an obligatory part of it, although not a pillar similar to the *Surat al-Fatihah* in relation to the prescribed prayers. The Hanafi, Hanbali, Shafii and Maliki agree with the Jafari in all except *tawaf al-nisa*, which they do not recognize. However, of a pilgrim on the *hajj al-ifrad* or *hajj al-qiran*, only two circumambulations are required by the Jafari.[70]

4.13.2. ENTRY INTO MAKKAH

All the schools agree that it is recommended for one entering Makkah to perform the bath lustration, pass through its heights during the approach towards the city, enter through gate Bani Shaybah, raise his hands on sighting the Kabah (al-Bayt al-Haram), pronounce *takbir* and *tahlil*, and to recite whatever he or she can of certain prayers prescribed by tradition. The Maliki's, however, disagree about the practice of raising the hands for the supplication. Thereafter, he or she approaches the Black Stone. If possible kisses it or caresses it with his or her hand or else just makes a gesture with his or her hand, and prays.

According to the Jafari, it is recommended while entering the sacred area of Makkah to be barefooted, to chew the leaves of a plant called '*adhkhir*' used for refreshing the mouth, or to clean the mouth to purge its odor.

4.13.3. THE CONDITIONS OF CIRCUMAMBULATION

According to the Shafii, Maliki and Hanbali schools, prescribed purity (*taharah*, i.e. freedom from *hadath* and *khabath*) is required. Thus the circumambulation of one who is *junub* or a woman undergoing *hayd* or *nifas*, is not valid. Also, it is necessary to cover one's private parts completely as in the prescribed prayers.[71]

The author of the *Fiqh as-sunnah* says, "In the opinion of the Hanafi's, freedom from *hadath* is not an essential requirement. However, it is an obligation whose omission may be compensated through a blood sacrifice. So, if one performs the circumambulation in the state of minor impurity (*hadath asghar*) his or her circumambulation is valid, though one is required to sacrifice a sheep. If the circumambulation is performed in the state of *janabah* or *hayd*, the circumambulation is valid, although the sacrifice of a camel is required during the pilgrim's stay in Makkah."[72]

According to *al-Fiqh alal-madhahib al-arbaah*,[73] "The prescribed purity of the clothes, the body, and the location of prescribed prayer is only a highly recommended *Sunnah* (*sunnah muakkadah*) from the Hanafi viewpoint. This is true even of circumambulation, there being no penalty even if all the clothes are completely impure."

According to the Jafari, the prescribed purity from *hadath* and *khabath* is a condition for validity of an obligatory circumambulation. In the same way, covering the private parts (*satr al-awrah*) with a ritually clean cloth legitimately owned (*ghayr maghsub*) is also a requirement. Moreover, it should not be made of silk or the skin of an animal whose flesh may not be eaten, nor made of golden fabric requirements which are the same as for the prescribed prayers. It may be said that the Jafari are even more stringent with regard to circumambulation than the prescribed prayers. They consider a blood spot of the size of a dirham as pardonable for one performing the prescribed prayer, but not for one performing the circumambulation. Further, they consider wearing of silk and gold as impermissible even for women during the circumambulation which is permissible for women in performing the prescribed prayer. According to the Jafari, circumcision is a requirement for circumambulation, without which it is invalid, both for an adult man and a child.[74]

4.13.4. THE MANNER OF PERFORMING THE CIRCUMAMBULATION

According to the Jafari and Hanbali schools, one's intention must be specified in every circumambulation. According to the Maliki, Shafii and Hanbali schools, a general declaration of intention for the prescribed pilgrimage is sufficient and no separate making of one's intention for the circumambulation is required.[75] As pointed out earlier, declaring one's intention as a motive behind all voluntary actions is an inevitable and necessary matter.

Ibn Rushd, in his *Bidayat al-mujtahid*, writes, "The Hanafi, Hanbali, Shafii and Jafari jurisprudents are in consensus on the opinion that every circumambulation, whether obligatory or not, begins from the Black Stone (and according to the *Fiqh as-sunnah* ends thereat). The pilgrim, if he or she can, kisses it, otherwise touches it with his or her hand. Then, with the Kabah on his or her left, starts moving towards the right to make the seven circumambulations, walking with a moderately fast pace (*ramal*) during the first three rounds and with an ordinary pace during the last four rounds. The fast pace (*ramal*)[76] applies to the *tawaf al-qudum* performed on entry into Makkah by the pilgrim for the shorter and prescribed pilgrimage, not one on *hajj al-tamattu*. Also no fast pace is required of women pilgrims. Then the pilgrim kisses *al-rukn al-Yamani* (the south-western corner or *rukn* of the Kabah) which falls before the one with the Black Stone mounted in it during the counter-clockwise rounds made during the circumambulation.

According to the Jafari, there are certain things obligatory in circumambulation:

1. The declaration of one's intention, to which reference has already been made.

2. The circumambulation should be made on foot, and in case of inability on a mount. Many Jafari jurists do not recognize this requirement and a group of them explicitly permit circumambulation on a mount. They cite the precedent of the Prophet who performed circumambulation on camel back, according to traditions in *al-Kafi* and *Man la yahduruhu al-faqih*.

3. The circumambulation should begin and end at the Black Stone. This is stated in many books on the Divine Law. "The circumambulation should be begun at the Black Stone so

that the first part of one's body is in front of the first part of
the Black Stone. then the pilgrim begins moving with the
Black Stone on his left, ending the last circumambulation
exactly in line with the point where he commenced his first,
thus ensuring that the seven rounds are completed without
advancing or falling behind a single step or more. The danger
of advancing or falling behind necessitates that the first circumambulation should commence at the beginning of the
Black Stone because if begun in front of its middle, one cannot
be sure of having advanced or fallen behind some steps. If one
began from its end, then the beginning may not be said to have
commenced from the Black Stone..." and so on.

The author of the *Jawahir al-kalam* criticizes this kind of
meticulousness reflecting a balanced and moderate taste and
temperament. He says, "The difficulty and the exasperating
impediment inherent in realizing such a requirement is not
concealed...To give it consideration is to fall into silly scruples."
The debate is similar to the depraved and unseemly musings of
madmen.[77] And it has been narrated of the Prophet ( ) that
he performed circumambulation on camelback and attaining
this kind of precision is infeasible when on a mount."

That which can be understood from the remarks of the
author of *al-Jawahir* is that he agrees with the author of *al-
Sharai* who confines himself to this statement without adding
another word—"It is obligatory to begin and end the circumambulation at the Stone." This means, as is also apparent from
his above mentioned remarks—that in the opinion of the
author of *al-Jawahir*, it is sufficient to fulfill this condition in
the commonly understood sense. Sayyid al-Hakim, in *al-
Munsik*, holds a similar position when he says, "The pilgrim
performing the circumambulation should begin a little before
the Stone with the intention of performing what is really obligatory. When he performs in this fashion he knows that he
began at the Stone and finished thereat."

4. The Kabah must be on the left during circumambulation.

5. The *hijr* of Ismail must be included in the circumambulation. That is, the circumambulation should be made around it

and without entering it[78] and it should be kept to the left while making the circumambulation. Thus if one passes between it and the Kabah during the circumambulation, making it fall to his right, the circumambulation becomes invalid.

6. The body should be completely out of the Kabah (because God says that the circumambulation should be made around and so outside the Kabah, not inside it). Also if one were to walk on its walls or on the protruding part of its walls' foundations, the circumambulation would be invalid.

7. The circumambulation should be performed between the Kabah and the rock called the Station of Abraham (*maqam al-Ibrahim*), which is a stone on which Abraham stood during the building of the Kabah.

8. The circumambulation should consist of seven rounds, no more no less. Obviously, recognition of these points requires an informed guide to indicate them to the pilgrims.

After finishing the circumambulation, it is obligatory to offer the two cycle prescribed prayer behind the Station of Abraham regardless of the crowd. If it is not possible, one may offer the prescribed prayer in front of it, and if that, too, is not possible, anywhere in al-Masjid al-Haram. It is not permissible to begin a second seven-fold circumambulation without performing the two-cycle prescribed prayer. If one forgets performing them, it is obligatory on him or her to return and perform them. But if returning were not feasible, he or she can offer them wherever he or she can. This is true of the obligatory circumambulation. But if the circumambulation were a recommended one, the pilgrim can offer the two cycles wherever he or she can.[79]

This shows that the jurists of all the legal schools are in agreement over certain points: the circumambulation starts and ends at the Black Stone; the Kabah should be on the left during the circumambulation; the circumambulation should be made outside the Kabah; seven rounds should be made; kissing the Black Stone and the corner is recommended. However, they disagree with respect to the permissibility of break between successive rounds of the circumambulation. According to the

Maliki, Jafari and Hanbali schools, continuity without break (*muwalat*) is obligatory. According to the Shafii and Hanafi schools, it is *Sunnah* (that is, recommended, *mustahabb*) to observe a break, so if there is a substantial break between the rounds without any excuse, the circumambulation is not invalidated.[80] Similarly according to Imam Abu Hanifah, if one leaves off after the fourth round, one must complete one's circumambulation if one is in Makkah. However, if one leaves Makkah, one must compensate it with a blood sacrifice.[81]

The schools disagree with respect to the necessity of the circumambulation being undertaken on foot. The Hanafi, Hanbali and Maliki schools consider it obligatory. According to the Shafii school and a group of Jafari scholars it is not obligatory and one may perform the circumambulation on a mount. Also, they disagree with respect to the two cycle prescribed prayer after the circumambulation. According to the Maliki, Hanafi and Jafari schools, the two cycle prescribed prayer (*rakatayn*)—which is exactly like the dawn prescribed prayer— are obligatory. The Shafii and Hanbali schools regard it as recommended.

4.13.5. ACTS RECOMMENDED DURING THE CIRCUMAMBULATION

The book, *Fiqh as-sunnah*, discussing the topic under the heading "*Sunan al-tawaf*," states, "Of things which are *Sunnah* in circumambulation are: kissing the Black-Stone while beginning the seven fold circumambulation, accompanied with *tahlil* and *takbir*, to raise the two hands as in the prescribed prayer, to greet the Stone by drawing one's hands upon it (*istilam*), to kiss it soundlessly, to lay one's cheek on it if possible, otherwise to touch it only." Other recommended are: *idtiba'*[82] for men, *ramal*, and *istilam* of al-Rukn al-Yamani.

According to *al-Lumat al-Dimashqiyyah*, a Jafari work, of things recommended in circumambulation are: to halt in front of the Black Stone, to make the prayer later offered with the hands raised, to recite the *Surat al-Qadr*, to remember God, to walk peacefully, to draw one's hand on the Black Stone, to kiss it if possible otherwise to make a gesture towards it, to draw one's hand on every corner of the Kabah every time one passes by or to kiss it, to draw one's hand on *al-mustajar* which is in front of the door and before al-Rukn al-Yamani—during the seventh round, and to keep oneself as near as possible to the Kabah. It is disapproved to speak during the circumambulation, apart from the remembrance of God and recitation of the Quran.

4.13.6. THE DUTIES OF THE CIRCUMAMBULATION

According to the Jafari, if a woman begins her monthly cycle during the circumambulation, she discontinues the circumambulation and performs the search between Safa and Marwah, if it happens after the fourth round. Then, once she is freed of her monthly period, she completes the circumambulation after attaining the prescribed purity, and she is not required to repeat the search. But if her monthly period occurs before completing the fourth round, she waits until the day of Arafah. If by that time she can attain the prescribed purity and is in a position to complete the remaining acts, she does so. Otherwise her prescribed pilgrimage is converted to *hajj al-ifrad*.

As mentioned earlier, the Hanafis permit the circumambulation for a woman in the state of her monthly period, and do not require the prescribed purity. According to the Hanafi work, *Fath al-qadir,* one who leaves three or fewer rounds of the *tawaf al-ziyarah* should sacrifice a sheep; if four, he remains in the sacred state as long as the pilgrim does not complete the rounds of circumambulation. But if the pilgrim leaves off more than four rounds, it is as if that pilgrim had not started the circumambulation at all.

According to the Jafari, if after completing the rounds of the seven fold circumambulation, one doubts whether one has performed them correctly as required by the *Shariah* or whether one performed the exact number of rounds, one's doubt is of no consequence. One's circumambulation is considered valid and complete. But if the doubt occurs before finishing the circumambulation, the pilgrim should consider whether he or she has performed at least seven rounds, such as when he or she doubts whether he or she made seven or eight rounds. If he or she is certain of having performed seven rounds, then the circumambulation is considered valid. However, if one is not certain of having performed seven rounds—as in the case when one doubts whether one is in one's sixth or seventh round, or in his fifth or sixth—in that case one's circumambulation is invalid and one should start afresh. It is preferable in such a case to complete the present circumambulation before starting afresh. This is true of an obligatory circumambulation. In case of a recommended circumambulation, the basis is the least number of rounds under seven one is certain of having performed, regardless of whether the doubt occurs during or after the last round. For the non-Jafari schools, the rule is the least number of rounds one is certain of having performed—a rule which is similar to the one they apply to the doubt in the number of cycles of the prescribed prayer.

These are the duties the recommended acts and the obligatory acts of circumambulation, which, like the bending forward and prostration in the prescribed prayers, is always the same in all cases, whether as a part of the minor pilgrimage (*umrah al-mufradah*), the prescribed pilgrimage (*umrat al-tamattu*), *hajj al-qiran*, or *hajj al-ifrad*, and regardless of whether it is *tawaf al-ziyarah*, *tawaf al-nisa*, *tawaf al-qudum*, or *tawaf al-wada*.

As mentioned above, the circumambulation is the next act after attaining the sacred state in the prescribed pilgrimage (*umrat al-tamattu*), but in the prescribed pilgrimage, its turn comes after the pilgrim has gone through the rituals of Mina—on the day of the festival—as shall be explained later.

4.14. RUNNING BETWEEN SAFA AND MARWAH AND THE CUTTING OF HAIR

4.14.1. RUNNING BETWEEN SAFA AND MARWAH

The major schools agree that the search follows the seven fold circumambulation or the two-cycle prescribed prayer for those who consider this obligatory. They also agree that one who performs the running before the circumambulation should revert and perform his circumambulation first and then the search. Research has not shown any opinion holding that the search must immediately follow the circumambulation.[83]

4.14.1.1. THE RECOMMENDED ACTS OF THE RUNNING

According to *Fiqh as-sunnah*, it is recommended to ascend the hills of Safa and Marwah, and, facing the Kabah, to pray to God for some religious or secular matter. It is well known that the Prophet, going out from Bab al-Safa, ascended Safa until he could see the Kabah. Facing it, he three times declared the Unity of God and magnified Him. Then praising God he said, "There is no god except God. He is One, and has no partner. To Him belongs the Kingdom and the Praise. He gives life and makes to die and He is powerful over everything. There is no god except God. He is One. He has fulfilled His promise and granted victory to His slave, vanquishing all the parties (those who practice infidelity to the One God). He is One."

The recommended acts of the running according to the Jafari book *al-Jawahir* are the following: to draw one's hand on the Black Stone; to drink from the water of Zamzam and to sprinkle it on oneself; to leave al-Masjid al-Haram through the door facing the Black Stone; to ascend the Safa hill; to face the Iraqi corner; to praise God and magnify Him; to prolong one's stay at Safa; and, after seven *takbirs*, to say three times: *la ilaha ill-Allah wahdahu la sharika lahu, lahu al-mulk wa lahu al-hamd yuhii wa yumit wa huwa hayy la yumutu biyadi al-kaayr wa huwa ala kull shay qadir*. After this the pilgrim recites the prayer recommended by Tradition (*al-dua al-mathur*).

As can be seen from the above, there is no divergence in this matter between the Jafari, Hanafi, Hanbali, Shafii and Maliki schools, except for some difference of expressions used. Research has not shown any jurist who regards the prescribed purity from *hadath* and *khabath* as obligatory for the search. Most of the schools have expressly stated its being only recommended and the same is true (except for the Shafii) of the drawing of the hand on the Black Stone before leaving for the search.

Also, all the schools are explicit about the of covering the distance between 'the *Milayn*' (an expression used by the Hanafis and Malikis) or 'the intervening distance' (*wasat al-masafah*, an expression used by Shafiis) or 'between the Minaret and the Alley of the Pharmacists' (as Jafari say) with a fast pace (*harwalah*).[84] Without doubt, an informed guide is necessary to enable the pilgrims to recognize the points designated as *'milayn'* or 'the Alley of the Pharmacists' (*Zuqaq al-Attarin*), or 'the Minaret'.

4.14.1.2. The Way of Performing the Running

Although there is agreement between the schools about the necessity of the search, they disagree about its being an essential part of the rites of the prescribed pilgrimage. According to the Jafari, Shafii, and Maliki schools, it is a pillar. According to Imam Abu Hanifah, it is not a pillar, although it is obligatory. Two different traditions are narrated from Imam Ahmad ibn Hanbal.[85]

All are agreed on the number of laps being seven, and that the performer of the running should begin at the Safa hill going towards the Marwah hill, and return again to Safa,[86] covering this distance seven times. Thus the pilgrim makes four laps going from Safa to Marwah and three laps while returning from Marwah to Safa, beginning his or her first lap from Safa and finishing the seventh at Marwah.

The schools disagree as to the permissibility of running on a mount in spite of the ability to walk, and all of them, with the exception of the Hanbalis, permit it regardless of whether one can walk or not. The Hanbalis say that it is permissible only for one who cannot walk.

Research has not found any opinion regarding continuity (*muwalat*) between the laps as obligatory,[87] with the exception of the Hanbalis, who, as also mentioned by the author of *al-Fiqh alal-madhahib al-arbaah*, consider it obligatory. Also, it is said of Malikis that according to them if the gap between the laps were to become inordinate, one should begin the running again. However, if the gap were not prolonged, such as when one discontinues for selling or purchasing something, it is forgivable.

The Jafari also say that it is obligatory, while going and returning, to keep one's face turned towards one's destination. Therefore, if someone were to turn his face away from it or were to walk backwards, or in a lateral way, it is not correct. However, there is nothing wrong in turning the face this way and that way while continuing to face the destination in the course of movement. Therefore, it is obligatory that the body should face Marwah while going and should be toward Safa while returning, and it is not permissible to make the approach with only a shoulder facing the direction of the destination—as may happen due to overcrowding of the pilgrims; also, while moving, the face in particular should remain in the right direction.

4.14.1.3. THE DUTIES OF THE RUNNING

One who cannot perform the running, either on foot or on a mount, may deputize another to perform it on his or her behalf, and the prescribed pilgrimage would be correct. There is nothing wrong in looking to the right or the left or turning back to look during the coming and the going. If someone makes more than seven laps intentionally, his or her running is invalid, but not if the lapse was unintentional. If one were to have doubts about the number of the laps performed after finishing one's running, it is assumed to have been correct and nothing is required of one. The author of *al-Jawahir* bases this ruling about the doubt after finishing on the principle of negation of *haraj*, as well as on Tradition.

However, if the doubt were to occur before finishing the running, the author of *al-Jawahir* says that there is no difference of opinion about, nor any objection against, the invalidity of the running in case of any doubt about the number of the laps performed, whether of having exceeded or fallen short of the required number. In both cases the running at hand is invalid. If one suspects one's having begun from Safa, one's running is correct. But if one thinks that one might have started from some other place, it is invalid. Also if one suspects the number of laps already performed, and does not know how many one has completed, one's running is invalid.

If one has recorded the number of laps performed, but doubts whether one started the first one from Safa or Marwah, one should consider the number of one's present lap and the direction one is facing. If, for instance, the number is an even one (2, 4, or 6) and the pilgrim is at Safa or facing it, one's running is correct because this shows that one had begun at Safa. Similarly, if the number is odd (3, 5, or 7) and one is at Marwah or facing it. But if the case is reverse, that is in an even lap one is facing Marwah or in an odd one facing towards Safa, one's running is invalid and should be begun again.[88] According to the other schools, the rule is to take the minimum one is certain of having performed, as in the case of the prescribed prayer.[89] According to Imam Abu Hanifah the prescribed pilgrimage is not invalid even if the running is omitted altogether, because it is not a pillar and can be made good by a sacrifice.[90]

4.14.2. *Cutting of the Hair*

According to Imam Ahmad ibn Hanbal and Imam Malik, it is necessary to shave (*halq*) or shorten the hair (*taqsir*) of the entire head. According to Imam Abu Hanifah the same of a one-fourth portion of the head is sufficient. According to the Shafii, cutting of three hair suffices.[91] According to the Jafari, at this stage of *taqsir* one has the free choice of performing it by shortening either the hair of the head, the beard, or the mustaches or the fingernails.

All the major schools agree that *taqsir* is an obligatory rite, though not a rule. According to Sayyid al-Hakim, its relationship to the prescribed pilgrimage is the same as that of the greetings and salutations with respect to the prescribed prayer, because after this, the pilgrim can leave the sacred state in the same way as one performing the prescribed prayer is after the *salam*. The *taqsir* or the *halq*, whatever be the divergence of opinion about them, is to be performed once during the minor pilgrimage (*umrah al-mufradah*) and twice during the prescribed pilgrimage (*hajj al-tamattu*).

4.14.2.1. CUTTING THE HAIR
IN THE MINOR PILGRIMAGE

According to the Jafari, one performing the prescribed pilgrimage (*umrat al-tamattu*) has to perform the shortening of the hair (*taqsir*) after the running. It is not permissible for that pilgrim to perform the shaving of the head. After it everything forbidden to the pilgrim in the sacred state becomes permissible. But if the pilgrim performs the shaving of the head, he should sacrifice a sheep. However, if on minor pilgrimage (*umrah al-mufradah*), he may choose between shaving the head and *taqsir*, regardless of whether he brings along with him the sacrificial animal or not.

If the shortening of the hair is omitted intentionally and the pilgrim had planned to perform the prescribed pilgrimage (*hajj al-tamattu*) and had assumed the sacred state before performing the shortening of the hair, the minor pilgrimage is invalid and it is then obligatory upon that pilgrim to perform *hajj al-ifrad*— that is, the rites of prescribed pilgrimage followed by *umrah al-mufradah*, and it is better for the pilgrim to repeat the prescribed pilgrimage again the next year.[92]

According to the Hanafi, Hanbali, Shafii and Maliki schools, one has a choice between shortening the hair and shaving the head after finishing the running. As to relief from the sacred state, if one were performing a non-*tamattu umrah*, one can leave the sacred state after the shaving of the head or cutting hair, regardless of whether the animal sacrifice accompanies the pilgrim or not. But if one is performing *umrat al-tamattu*, one can leave the sacred state if not accompanied by the sacrificial animal but if accompanied he remains in the sacred state.[93]

4.14.2.2. CUTTING OF THE HAIR
IN THE PRESCRIBED PILGRIMAGE

The second type of *taqsir* is a part of the rites of all the various kinds of prescribed pilgrimages— *al-tamattu, qiran,* or *ifrad*—to be performed by the pilgrim after the animal sacrifice in Mina. All the schools agree that here one has a choice between *taqsir* and *halq, halq* being more meritorious. They disagree, however, in regard to one with matted hair, whether he must shave his head or if, like others, he also has a choice between *halq* and *taqsir*. The Hanbali, Shafii and Maliki schools prescribe only *halq* for him, but the Jafari and the Hanafi give him the same choice as others. All the legal schools agree that women do not have to perform the shaving of the head. Rather, they may perform only the cutting.

Imam Abu Hanifah and a group of Jafari jurisprudents say that one who is bald, completely or partially, as when only the frontal portion of the head is hairless, must nevertheless draw the razor over the hairless portion of the head. The rest only consider it recommended.[94]

According to the Jafari, the *halq* or the *taqsir* is obligatory in Mina. Therefore, one who departs without *halq* or *taqsir* should return to perform either of the two, regardless of whether his lapse was intentional or not, and despite the knowledge or out of ignorance. However, if it is difficult or not feasible for the pilgrim to return, that pilgrim may perform it wherever possible. As to the rest, they say that it should be performed within the sacred area.[95]

All agree that sex is not permitted after the *halq* or the *taqsir*. The Malikis include perfume as also being impermissible. The Jafari include with the above two hunting (*sayd*), which is forbidden because of the respect for the sanctity of the sacred area. Apart from these three things, the rest are permissible by the consensus of all the major schools. For the Hanafi, Hanbali, Shafii and Maliki schools, everything, including sex, becomes permissible after the *tawaf al-ziyarah*. As for the Jafari, sex and perfume are not allowed until after the *tawaf al-nisa*.

4.15. HALTING IN ARAFAT

The pilgrim performing the minor pilgrimage (*umrah al-mufradah*) or *hajj al-tamattu* first assumes the sacred state, then performs the circumambulation, offers the two cycles of the prescribed prayer, then performs the search, then cutting. This order is obligatory, and in it while the sacred state precedes all the other steps, the circumambulation precedes the prescribed prayer, the prescribed prayer is prior to the search, and at the end is cutting the hair. [96]

4.15.1. THE SECOND RITE
OF THE PRESCRIBED PILGRIMAGE

The rites of the prescribed pilgrimage, as in the case of the minor pilgrimage, start with the sacred state. However, the rite which, along with assuming the sacred state in the case of the prescribed pilgrimage and considered one of the pillars of the prescribed pilgrimage by consensus, is the halting in Arafat, there being no difference whether one is on *hajj al-ifrad* or *hajj al-tamattu*, although it is permissible for those on *hajj al-ifrad* or *hajj al-qiran* to enter Makkah to perform a circumambulation after assuming the sacred state and before proceeding to Arafat. This circumambulation—called *tawaf al-qudum*—resembles the two cycles of the prescribed prayer called *tahiyyat al-masjid*, recommended as a mark of respect to a mosque. Sayyid al-Hakim, in his book on the rites of the prescribed pilgrimage, says, "It is permissible for one intending *hajj al-qiran* or *al-ifrad* to perform the recommended circumambulation on entering Makkah and before proceeding to the halt (*wuquf*) in Arafat." Ibn Hajar, in *Fath al-bari bi sharh al-Bukhari*, writes, "The Hanafi, Hanbali, Shafii and Maliki schools agree that there is no harm if one who has assumed the sacred state for *hajj al-ifrad* performs a circumambulation of the Holy House," that is, before proceeding to Arafat. One on the prescribed pilgrimage (*hajj al-tamattu*), as said, should perform the circumambulation of *umrat al-tamattu* instead of the *tawaf al-qudum*.

4.15.2. BEFORE THE HALT IN ARAFAT

There is consensus among the legal schools that it is recommended for the pilgrim to go out from Makkah in the sacred state on the 8th of Dhil Hijjah (the day of *tarwiyah*) passing towards Mina on the way to Arafat.

According to the Jafari books *al-Tadhkirah* and *al-Jawahir*, it is recommended for one intending to proceed towards Arafat not to leave Makkah before offering the noon and afternoon prescribed prayers. The Hanafi, Hanbali, Shafii and Maliki schools say that it is recommended to offer them at Mina.⁹⁷

In any case, it is permissible to proceed to Arafat a day or two before the 8th of Dhil Hijjah (*tarwiyah*), in particular for the ill, the aged, women, and those who are claustrophobic. Also it is permissible to delay until the morning of the 9th so as to arrive at Arafat when the sun crosses the meridian (*zawal*).

Research has not found any jurist who considers it obligatory to spend the night before the day of the halt at Arafat in Mina or to perform some rite there. Allamah al-Hilli, in his *Tadhkirah*, writes, "To spend the night of Arafat at Mina for resting is recommended but it is not a rite, nor is there anything against one who does not do it." *Fath al-bari* and *Fath al-qadir* say something similar.

4.15.3. THE PERIOD OF THE HALT IN ARAFAT

There is consensus among the legal schools that the day of the halt in Arafat is the 9th of Dhil Hijjah, but they disagree as to the hour of its beginning and end on that day. According to the Hanafi, the Shafii, and the Maliki schools, it begins at midday on the 9th and lasts until the daybreak on the 10th. According to the Hanbali school, from daybreak on the 9th until daybreak on the 10th. According to the Jafari, from midday on the 9th until sunset on the same day, for one who is free to plan and, in case of one in an exigency, until the following daybreak.

It is recommended to take a bath before the halt in Arafat, to be performed like the Friday bath. There is no rite to be performed in Arafat except one's presence there. One may sleep or stay awake, sit, stand, walk around or ride a mount.

4.15.4. THE BOUNDARIES OF ARAFAT

The boundaries of Arafat are Arnah, Thawbah, and from Nimrah to Dhul Majaz, which are the names of places around Arafat. One may not make the halt in any of those places nor in Taht al-Arak because they are outside the limits of Arafat. If one were to make the halt in any of those places, one's pilgrimage is invalid by consensus of all the schools, with the exception of the Maliki, according to which one may halt at Arafat although he will have to make a sacrifice.

The entire area of Arafat is permissible for the halt and one may make the halt at any spot within it by consensus of all schools. It is related by Imam Jafar Sadiq that when the Prophet made the halt at Arafat, the people crowded around him, rushing along on the hoof prints of his camel. Whenever the camel moved, they moved along with it. When he saw this, the Prophet said, "O people, the area permissible for the halt is not confined to where my camel stands, rather this entire Arafat is the area permissible for the halt," and pointed to the plains of Arafat. "If the area permissible for the halt were limited to where my camel stands, the place would be too small to hold the people."[98]

4.15.5. THE CONDITIONS APPLICABLE TO THE HALT

Prescribed purity is not a condition for the halt at Arafat by consensus of all the schools. According to the Jafari and the Maliki schools, the halt at Arafat must be made with prior intention and with the implied knowledge that the place where he is halting is indeed Arafat. Thus if he or she were to pass on without knowing or know without intending the halt, it is not considered the halt as such.

According to the Shafii and the Maliki schools, neither intent nor knowledge is a condition. All that is required is freedom from insanity, intoxication, and loss of consciousness. According to the Hanafis, neither intent, nor knowledge, nor sanity is a condition. Whosoever is present in Arafat during the specific period, the pilgrim's prescribed pilgrimage is correct, intent or no intent, whether he knows the place or not, whether sane or insane.[99]

Is it necessary to make the halt in Arafat for the full specified period or is it sufficient to be present there for some time, even if it is for a single moment? According to the Jafari, there are two kinds of periods for the halt, depending on whether one arrives at a time of one's own choice (*ikhtiyari*) or the time is forced upon one by circumstances beyond one's control (*idtirari*). In the case of the former, the period of halt for that pilgrim is from midday on the 9th until sunset on the same day; in the case of the latter, the period lasts until the daybreak of the 10th. So one who can make the halt from noon until sunset for the entire period, it is obligatory upon the pilgrim; although it is not a pillar to halt for the entire period, but to halt for a part of it. That is, without it, the prescribed pilgrimage would not be valid, the rest being obligatory. This means that if someone omits the halt, his or her prescribed pilgrimage is invalid because he or she has not performed one of its pillars. But if one makes a short halt, one has omitted only an obligatory act which is not a pillar, and so one's prescribed pilgrimage does not lose its validity on this account. Moreover, if someone cannot make the halt for the entire period at his or her disposal, due to some legitimate excuse, it is sufficient for him or her to make the halt for a part of the night of the festival. According to the Shafii, the Maliki and the Hanbali schools, mere presence even if for a single moment, is sufficient.[100]

According to the Jafari, if one leaves Arafat intentionally before the midday, one must return. But if one does not, one must sacrifice a camel, and if that is beyond one's means, fast for eighteen days in succession. But if the lapse were by oversight and one does not discover it until the time is past, it is alright upon condition that the pilgrim is present at the halt in

Mashar al-Haram on time. But if the pilgrim remembers before the period expires, he or she must return as far as possible, and if he or she does not, he or she must sacrifice a camel. The Malikis say that one who makes the halt in Arafat after midday and leaves Arafat before sunset must repeat the prescribed pilgrimage the following year if he or she does not return to Arafat before daybreak on the 9th. But all other jurisprudents say that his prescribed pilgrimage is complete.[101]

According to *al-Fiqh al-musawwar ala madhhab al-Shafi,* "If one forgets and omits the halt, it is obligatory upon him to change his or her prescribed pilgrimage into *umrah,* and then complete the remaining rites of the prescribed pilgrimage after performing its rites. Also he must repeat the prescribed pilgrimage in the immediate following year."

It is recommended for one performing the halt in Arafat to: observe prescribed purity, face the Kabah, recite supplications and seek God's forgiveness *(istighfar),* with due surrender, humility, and with a heart-felt presence before God.

4.16. THE HALT IN MUDALIFAH

The halt in Mudalifah is the next rite after the halt in Arafat, by consensus of all the schools. They also agree that when the pilgrim turns to Mudalifah (where Mashar al-Haram is situated) after the halt in Arafat, he or she is acting in accordance with the following Divine verse of the Quran, *"When you pour forth from Arafat, then remember God in al-Mashar al-Haram, remembering Him in the way you have been shown"* (2:198).

Also, there is agreement that it is recommended to delay the evening prescribed prayer on the night preceding the festival until Mudalifah is reached. The author of *al-Tadhkirah* writes that when sun sets in Arafat, then one should go forth before the evening prescribed prayer towards al-Mashar al-Haram and recite there the supplication prescribed by tradition. The author of *al-Mughni* says, "It is *Sunnah* (i.e. recommended) for one leaving Arafat not to offer the evening prescribed prayer until Mudalifah is reached, whereat the evening prescribed prayer and the night prescribed prayer should be offered together. There is no difference regarding this, as Ibn al-Mundhir also points out when he says, "'There is consensus among the religious scholars, and no divergence of opinion, that it is *Sunnah* for the pilgrim to offer the evening and the night prescribed prayers together. The basis for this is that the Prophet offered them together."[102]

All the legal schools, with the exception of the Hanafi, agree that if one were to offer the evening prayer before reaching Mudalifah and not offer the two prayers together, one's prescribed prayer is nevertheless valid despite its being contrary to what is recommended. Imam Abu Hanifah does not consider it valid.

4.16.1. THE BOUNDARIES OF MUDALIFAH

According to *al-Tadhkirah* and *al-Mughni*, Mudalifah has three names: Mudalifah, Jam, and Mashar al-Haram. Its limits are from Mazamayn to Hiyad, towards the valley of Muhassir. The entire Mudalifah is permissible for the halt, like Arafat, and it is legitimate to make the halt at any spot inside it. According to *al-Madarik*, it is a settled and definite matter among the Jafari jurisprudents that it is permissible, in case of overcrowding, to ascend the heights towards the hill, which is one of the limits of Mudalifah.

4.16.2. THE NIGHT AT MUDALIFAH

Is it obligatory to spend the entire night before the festival at Mudalifah, or is it sufficient to halt in Mashar al-Haram even for a moment after the daybreak? It is assumed, of course, that the meaning of halting is mere presence. One may be walking around, sitting or riding a mount, as in the case of the halt at Arafat. According to the Hanafi, Shafii and Hanbali schools, it is obligatory to spend the entire night at Mudalifah and the defaulter is required to make a sacrifice.[103] According to the Jafari and the Maliki, it is not obligatory, though meritorious. This is what Shihab al-Din al-Baghdadi, the Maliki, in his *Irshad al-salik*, and al-Hakim and al-Khui have confirmed. However, no one has considered it a pillar.

As to halting in Mashar al-Haram after the daybreak, Ibn Rushd, in *al-Bidayah wa al-nihayah*, cites the consensus of the Hanafi, Hanbali, Shafii and Maliki jurists to the effect that it is one of the *Sunan* (sing. *Sunnah*) of the prescribed purity, not one of its duties (*furud*; sing. *fard*).

According to *al-Tadhkirah*, "It is obligatory to halt in Mashar al-Haram after the daybreak and if someone were to leave intentionally before the daybreak after halting there for the night, the pilgrim must sacrifice a sheep." Imam Abu Hanifah also says that it is obligatory to halt after daybreak. The rest of the schools permit departure after midnight. Therefore, with the exception of the Jafari and the Hanafi schools, others permit departure from Mudalifah before daybreak.

The Jafari say that the time of halt in Mashar al-Haram is of two kinds: the first (*ikhtiyari*) is for one who has no reason for delaying and that is the entire period between the daybreak and the sunrise on the day of the festival. Whoever leaves knowingly from Mashar before daybreak and after being there for the whole or part of the night, his prescribed pilgrimage is not invalidated if he had halted at Arafat, although he must sacrifice a sheep. If he had left Mashar on account of ignorance, there is nothing upon him, as made explicit in the above quotation.

The second (*idtirari*) is for women and those who have an excuse for not halting between daybreak and sunrise. Their time extends to midday on the day of the festival. The author of *al-Jawahir* says that there is both textual evidence from the Traditions as well as consensus to support the above prescription, and the edicts (*fatawa*) of Sayyid al-Hakim and Sayyid al-Khui are also in accordance with it. The latter has not stated midday as the *idtirari* time limit, but says that it is sufficient to make the halt after sunrise.

The Jafari also say that the halt in the two specified periods of time is a pillar of the prescribed pilgrimage. Therefore, if someone does not perform it altogether either in the *ikhtiyari* period for the night or in the *idtirari* period, that pilgrim's prescribed pilgrimage is invalid if he or she had not spent the night there but not if the default was on account of a legitimate excuse, on condition that he or she had performed the halt at Arafat. So one who fails to make the halts at Arafat and the Mashar, neither in the *ikhtiyari* nor in the *idtirari* period, his or her prescribed pilgrimage is invalid even if the failure was on account of a legitimate reason. It is obligatory upon him or her to perform the prescribed pilgrimage the year after if the prescribed pilgrimage intended was an obligatory one and if it was a recommended pilgrimage, it is recommended for him or her to perform it the next year.[104] The halt in Mashar al-Haram is held in greater importance by the Jafari than the one in Arafat. That is why they say that one who loses the chance to be present at the halt in Arafat but participates in the halt at the Mashar before the sunrise, his or her prescribed pilgrimage is complete.[105]

4.17. RECOMMENDED ACTS IN MASHAR

According to the Jafari it is recommended for one performing the prescribed pilgrimage for the first time to put his or her feet on the ground of the Mashar.[106] According to the Jafari, the Shafii and the Maliki schools, it is recommended while leaving for Mina to gather seventy pebbles at Mudalifah for the throwing of the stones (*ramy al-jamarat*). The reason for this, according to the author of *al-Tadhkirah*, is that when the pilgrim arrives in Mina he or she should not be detained by anything from the rite of the throwing of stones. Imam Ibn Hanbal is narrated to have said that the pebbles may be gathered from any place. There is no disagreement that it suffices to gather them from whatever place one wishes.

The maintenance of the prescribed purity, the pronouncing of *"la ilaha ill-Allah"* ("there is no god but God," *tahlil*), *Allahu akbar* ("God is Greater," *takbir*), and supplication (the prescribed one or something else) is also recommended.

4.18. AT MINA

All the schools are in agreement that the rites after the halt at Mashar al-Haram are those of Mina, that departure from Mudalifah is after the sunrise, and that one who leaves before sunrise, passing beyond its limits, according to al-Khui, must sacrifice a sheep as atonement.

At Mina one performs several rites which continue from the Day of Sacrifice (*yawm al-nahr*)— the day of the festival—until the morning of the 13th or the night of the 12th. The obligatory acts of the prescribed pilgrimage are completed in Mina. The three days following the day of the festival (the 11th, 12th, and the 13th) are called *ayyam al-tashriq*.[107]

Three rites are obligatory at Mina on the day of the festival: (1) throwing of stones at the Jamrat al-Aqabah; (2) slaughtering of the sacrificial animal; (3) *halq* or *taqsir*. Agreeing that the Prophet performed first the throwing of stones, then the sacrifice and then the *taqsir*, the schools disagree whether this order is obligatory and if it is impermissible to change that order, or if the order is only recommended and may be altered.

According to Imam Shafi and Imam Hanbal, there is nothing upon one who changes the order. Imam Malik says that if someone performs the shaving of the head before the sacrifice or the throwing of stones, he or she must make a sacrifice. If he or she was performing *hajj al-qiran* then two sacrifices.[108] According to the Jafari, it is a sin to change the order knowingly and intentionally, although repetition is not required. The author of *al-Jawahir* says, "I have not found any difference of opinion on this point," and *al-Madarik* states that the jurists are definite on this point.

4.18.1. JAMRAT AL-AQABAH

4.18.1.1. THE NUMBER OF JIMAR

The throwing of stones (*ramy al-jimar*) in Mina is obligatory upon all pilgrims, whether *tamattu, qiran* or *ifrad*. This rite is performed ten times during the four days. The first throwing of stones, in which only one point, called *Jamrat al-Aqabah*, is stoned, is performed on the day of the festival. On the second day, that is, the 11th of Dhil Hijjah, the three *jimar* are stoned, and again every three on the third and the fourth day. This applies to the pilgrim who spends the night of the 12th in Mina. Otherwise there is no throwing of stones for the pilgrim on that day.

4.18.1.2. *JAMRAH* OF THE 10TH OF DHIL HIJJAH

The legal schools agree that it suffices to perform the throwing of stones of the *jamrat al-aqabah* any time from sunrise until sunset on the 10th of Dhil Hijjah, but disagree as to its performance before or after that period. According to the Maliki, Hanafi, Hanbali and Jafari schools, it is not permissible to perform the throwing of stones of the *jamrat al-aqabah* before the daybreak and, if performed without an excuse, must be repeated. They permit it for an excuse like sickness, weakness, or insecurity (fear). According to the Shafii school, performing the rite earlier is unobjectionable, for the specified period is recommended not obligatory.[109] However, if delayed until after sunset on the day of the festival, according to Imam Malik, the defaulter must make a sacrifice if he or she performs the rite during the night or the next day. According to the Shafii, nothing further is required if he or she performs the rite of the throwing of stones in the night or the next day.[110]

According to the Jafari, the time of this throwing of stones extends from sunrise until sunset on that day. If forgotten, the rite must be performed the next day. If again forgotten, on the 12th, and if one fails again, it can be performed on the 13th. But if one forgets until one has left Makkah, one may carry it out the following year, either himself or herself or through a deputy who carries it out on his or her behalf.[111]

4.18.1.3. THE CONDITIONS OF THE THROWING OF STONES

There are certain conditions for the validity of throwing of stones:

1. Intention: stated by the Jafari explicitly.
2. Each stoning must be carried out with seven pebbles. There is agreement on this point.

3. The pebbles must be thrown one at a time, not more. Again there is consensus on this point.

4. The pebbles must strike the known target. There is also consensus on this point.

5. The pebbles must reach their target through being thrown. Thus if they are tossed in some other manner, it does not suffice according to the Jafari and Shafii schools, and is not permissible according to the Hanbali and Hanafi schools.[112]

6. The pebbles must be of stone, not of other material, like salt, iron, copper, wood or porcelain, etc. This is accepted unanimously by all the schools except that of Imam Abu Hanifah, who says that it is all right if pebbles are made of some earthen material, such as porcelain, clay or stone.[113]

7. The pebbles must be 'new', that is, not used for stoning before. The Hanbalis state this condition expressly.

8. Prescribed purity is not a condition in the throwing of stones, although recommended.

The Jafari say that it is recommended that the pebbles be about the size of a finger tip and rough, neither black, nor white, nor red. The other schools say that their size must be about that of the seed of a broad bean (*baqila*).

The Jafari also say that it is recommended for the pilgrim to perform all the rites facing the qiblah, with the exception of the throwing of stones of the *jamrat al-aqabah* on the day of the festival, which is recommended to perform with one's back towards the *qiblah* since the Prophet had performed this rite in that way. The other schools say that facing the *qiblah* is recommended even in this rite.

Also, it is recommended to perform the throwing of stones on foot although riding a mount is permissible, not to be farther from the *jamrah* than ten cubits, to perform it with the right hand, to recite the prayers prescribed by tradition and other prayers. The following is one of the prayers prescribed by Tradition, "O God, make my prescribed pilgrimage a blessing, a forgiving of my sins. O God, these pebbles of mine, reckon them and place them high in my actions. God is Great. God, repel Satan from me."

4.18.1.4. UNCERTAINTY

What if one doubts whether the pebble thrown has struck its target or not? It is assumed not to have hit. If one doubts the number thrown, he or she may count from the least number of which he or she is sure he or she has thrown. *jamrat al-aqabah* is the first rite performed by the pilgrim in Mina on the day of the festival, which is followed by the slaughter (*dhabh*) then shaving of the head or cutting hair. After that he proceeds to Makkah for the circumambulation the same day. On this day, there is no other rite of throwing stones for him.

4.19. THE SACRIFICE

The second obligatory rite in Mina is the animal sacrifice. The issues related to it are: (1) its kinds, obligatory and recommended, and the various kinds of obligatory sacrifice; (2) regarding those for whom the sacrifice (*hady*) is obligatory; (3) the requirements of the animal to be sacrificed; (4) its time and place; (5) the legal rules about its flesh; (6) the substitute duty of one who can neither find the animal to sacrifice nor possess the means to purchase one.

4.19.1. THE KINDS OF ANIMALS TO BE SACRIFICED

The animal to be sacrificed is of two kinds: obligatory and recommended. The recommended sacrifice is the one mentioned in the following verse of the Quran, "*So pray unto thy Lord and sacrifice,*" (108:2), which is interpreted as a commandment to the Prophet to sacrifice after the festival prescribed prayer. A tradition relates that the Prophet sacrificed two rams, one white and the other black.

According to the Malikis and the Hanafis, the sacrifice is obligatory for every family once every year. It is, they say, similar to the *zakat al-fitr*. The Jafari and the Shafii schools say that the recommended sacrifice can be carried out in Mina on any of the four days, the day of the festival and the three days following it (called *ayyam al-tashriq*). But at places other than Mina the sacrifice may be carried out only during three days: the day of the festival, and the 11th and the 12th. According to the Hanbalis, Malikis, and Hanafis, its time is three days whether in Mina or elsewhere. In any case, the best time for the sacrifice is after sunrise on the day of the festival during a period sufficient for holding the festival prescribed prayer and delivering its two sermons .

The obligatory sacrifices, in accordance with the Quranic text, are four: (1) The sacrifice related to *hajj al-tamattu* in accordance with the verse: *"... if in peacetime anyone of you combines the shorter with the prescribed pilgrimage, he must offer such sacrifice as he can .... "* (2:196).

(2) The sacrifice followed by the shaving of the head, which is an obligation open to choice, in accordance with the verse, *"But if any of you is ill or suffers from an ailment of the head, he must offer a sacrifice (fidyah) either by fasting or by alms-giving or by offering a sacrifice"* (2:196).

(3) The sacrifice related to the penalty *(jaza)* for hunting, in accordance with the verse, *"He that kills game by design, shall present, as an offering near the Kabah, a domestic beast equivalent to that which he has killed, to be determined by two honest men among you...."* (5:95).

(4) The sacrifice related some hindrance which keeps one from completing the rites of the prescribed pilgrimage such as illness or interruption due to an enemy *(ihsar)*,[114] in accordance with the following verse, *"If you cannot, offer such sacrifice as you can afford ..."* (2:196).

Besides the above four, there are also the obligatory sacrifices related to any of the following: a pledge *(ahd)*, a vow *(nadhr)*, or an oath *(yamin)*.

4.19.2. FOR WHOM IS THE ANIMAL SACRIFICE OBLIGATORY?

The animal sacrifice is not obligatory by consensus of all the schools, upon one performing the minor pilgrimage *(umrah al-mufradah)* nor on one performing *hajj al-ifrad*. Similarly, there is consensus regarding its being obligatory upon the non-Makkan pilgrim on *hajj al-tamattu*. The Hanafi, Hanbali, Shafii and Maliki schools add that it is also obligatory upon the pilgrim on *hajj al-qiran*. According to the Jafari, it is not obligatory on one on *hajj al-qiran* except with a vow (*nadhr*) or when he or she brings along with him or her the sacrificial animal at the time of assuming the sacred state.

There is disagreement regarding whether the Makkan performing *hajj al-tamattu* must offer a sacrifice or not. According to the Hanafi, Hanbali, Shafii and Maliki schools, the animal sacrifices not obligatory upon the pilgrim. It is stated in *al-Mughni*, "There is no disagreement among scholars that the sacrifice of *tamattu* is not obligatory for those living in the neighborhood of Masjid al-Haram." The Jafari say that if the Makkan performs *hajj al-tamattu* the animal sacrifice is obligatory for him or her.[115] The major legal schools, however, agree that the obligatory animal sacrifice is not one of the pillars of the prescribed pilgrimage.

4.19.3. REQUIREMENTS OF THE ANIMAL TO BE SACRIFICED

The animal to be sacrificed must meet the following requirements:

1. It must be a type of cattle, such as camel, cow, sheep, or goat, by consensus of all the major schools. As stated in *al-Mughni*, according to the Hanafi, Maliki, Shafii and Hanbali schools: if a sheep, it must be at least six months old; if a goat, one year old; if a cow, two years old; and if a camel, five years old. This agrees with the Jafari view as stated in *al-Jawahir*, with the difference that the camel must have entered its sixth and the goat its second year. Sayyid al-Hakim and Sayyid al-Khui have said that it suffices if the camel has entered its sixth year and the cow or the goat its third. As to the sheep, they add, to be cautious, the sheep must have entered its second year.

2. The sacrificial animal must be free of any defect, and, by consensus, must not be one-eyed, lame, sick or old and decrepit. There is disagreement, however, regarding its acceptability in case of castration, being without horns or with broken ones, missing or mutilated ears or tail. Such are not acceptable according to Sayyid al-Hakim and Sayyid al-Khui, but acceptable according to the author of *al-Mughni*..

Allamah al-Hilli, in *al-Tadhkirah*, says that the female camel and cow and male sheep and goats are to be preferred, although the permissibility of the converse in the two cases is not disputed by any school. The author of *al-Mughni* says that the sex of the sacrificial animal is irrelevant.

4.19.4. TIME AND PLACE OF THE SACRIFICE

As to the occasion of the sacrifice, it is, according to the Maliki, Hanafi, and Hanbali schools, the day of the festival and the two days following it. Imam Abu Hanifah adds that this time is specific for the sacrificial rite of *hajj al-qiran* and tamattu' but for the others he sets no such time limit. The Malikis do not recognize any difference between various kinds of animal to be sacrificed.

The Hanbalis say that if the sacrifice is made before its time, it must be made again. If after its time: in case of the recommended, the lapse of time cancels it and in case of the obligatory, it must be fulfilled. According to the Hanafis, slaughtering the sacrificial animal before the three days of the festival is not sufficient, but is if done later although an atonement is required for the delay. According to the Shafiis, the time of the obligatory sacrifice for *hajj al-tamattu* starts with assuming the sacred state. Therefore, performing it earlier than the day of the festival is permissible and there is no time limit for delaying, although it is best performed on the festival day.[116]

The Jafari regard making one's intention known as being obligatory in slaughtering, and say that its time is on the day of the festival although it is acceptable until the third day following it, or even until the end of Dhul Hijjah, although the delay is a sin. The author of *al-Jawahir* reports that there is no divergence among Jafari jurisprudents on this point, even if the delay is without a legitimate excuse. It is not permissible, according to the Jafari, to make the sacrifice before the 10th of Dhil Hijjah.

As to the place, it is the sacred area according to the Hanbali, Shafii, and Hanafi schools, which includes Mina[117] and other places, as mentioned above while discussing the sacred state and the limits of the sacred areas of Makkah and Madinah.

According to the Jafari, there are three conditions for slaughtering the animal in Mina: (1) that the animal to be sacrificed must have been brought while the pilgrim was in the sacred state assumed for the prescribed pilgrimage, not in the sacred state assumed for the minor pilgrimage; (2) the pilgrim should have halted for some time of the night with the animal in Arafat; (3) he should have made the resolve to make the sacrifice on the day of the festival or the following day. Also the Jafari say that the pilgrim of *hajj al-tamattu* may make the sacrifice nowhere but in Mina, even if his or her pilgrimage is supererogatory. But the animal to be sacrificed brought along in the sacred state of the minor pilgrimage (*umrah*) is to be slaughtered in Makkah.[118]

In any case, for all the schools offering of the sacrifice is legitimate and preferable at Mina. Ibn Rushd says that the consensus of the religious scholars is in favor of slaughtering the animal at Mina. Secondly, the difference between the Jafari and the other schools is that the Jafari specify Mina, while others allow an open choice between Mina and other places inside the sacred area of Makkah.

4.19.5. THE FLESH OF THE SACRIFICIAL ANIMAL

The Hanbalis and the Shafiis say that the flesh of the sacrificial animal whose slaughtering inside the sacred area is obligatory is to be distributed among the poor inside it. The Hanafis and Malikis say it is permissible to distribute it inside or outside the sacred area. The Shafiis say one may not oneself eat the flesh of an obligatory sacrificial animal but that of a voluntary or recommended sacrificial animals permissible. The Malikis say that with the exception of the sacrifice made as a substitute for hurting someone, hunting, or sacrifice vowed specifically for the poor, and the voluntary sacrificial animal which dies before reaching its destination, the flesh of the animal may be eaten in all cases.[119]

The Jafari say that a third of the flesh should be given to

the poor believers; another third to other believers, even the well off and the remaining third may be consumed by the pilgrim.[120]

4.19.6. THE SUBSTITUTE DUTY

All the legal schools agree that when the pilgrim cannot find the sacrificial animal nor possesses means to acquire one, its substitute is to keep fasts for ten days, three of which, for successive days, are to be kept during the days of the prescribed pilgrimage and the remaining seven on returning home. This is in accordance with the Divine verse,[121] "*...if he lacks the means let him fast three days during the pilgrimage and seven when he has returned; that is ten days in all*" (2:196).

The criterion of capacity to offer the sacrificial animal is ability to arrange one in the place, and when it cannot be done, the duty of sacrifice is changed into that of the fasts. This holds even if the pilgrim should be a man of means in his own homeland. This is because the obligation is specific to the occasion and so is the capacity to fulfill it. A similar case is that of availability of water for the prescribed purity.

4.19.7. ANIMAL SACRIFICE BY A DEPUTY

It is preferable that the pilgrim should slaughter the animal himself, though it is permissible to ask someone else to do it, because it is one of the rites in which delegation is possible. The deputy makes the intention known of slaughtering on behalf of the one who deputizes and it is better that both of them should make the intention together. According to the Jafari it is recommended for the pilgrim to put his hand on that of him who slaughters or at least be present at the time of slaughtering.

4.19.8. THE POOR AND THE NEEDY

In regard to the verse, "*...and eat of their flesh and feed with it the poor and the needy...* " (22:36), Imam Jafar Sadiq said, "The poor is the person who is content with what you give him or her and does not show his or her displeasure and does not frown or twitch his or her mouth in irritation. The needy is one who comes to you for charity and presents himself or herself."

4.19.9. THE SUBSTITUTE FOR CAMEL SACRIFICE

If the sacrifice of a camel is obligatory upon someone, whether as atonement (*kaffarah*) or as a vow, and the pilgrim cannot arrange it, that pilgrim must sacrifice seven sheep one after another, and if that is not possible fast for eighteen days.[122]

4.19.10. TAQLID AND ISHAR

Taqlid in this context, means putting a shoe or the like in the neck of the sacrificial animal. *Ishar* means making an incision in the right side of the hump of a camel or cow and letting it be stained by blood. The Hanbali, Shafii and Maliki jurists regard *ishar* and *taqlid* as recommended. Imam Abu Hanifah says that the *taqlid* of the sheep and the camel is *Sunnah*, but *ishar* is by no means permissible due to the pain it causes to the animal.[123]

4.19.11. CHARITY TO NON-MUSLIMS

In general the Jafari permit the giving of non-obligatory charity or making of endowment in favor of a Muslim or a non-Muslim. Sayyid Abu al-Hasan al-Isfahani, in his *Wasilat al-najat*, says, "In giving of recommended charity, poverty or possession of faith in Islam is not a condition for the recipient. He may be a well-to-do man, a non-Muslim living under the protection of an Islamic state (*dhimmi*), and a total stranger (not a blood relation of the giver of charity)."

4.19.12. THE BURNING OR BURYING OF SLAUGHTERED ANIMALS

It is a custom among pilgrims nowadays to offer money to whoever would accept the sacrificial animal,[124] which on receiving either buries or throws away because the number of the slaughtered animals is great and nobody is around to make use of their meat. Research has not turned up any objection to this practice. In 1949 a group of Egyptian pilgrims asked al-Azhar jurists for an edict (*fatwa*), asking the permission for giving the price of the sacrificial animal as help to the needy. In reply, al-Shaykh Mahmud Shaltut, in Vol. 1, No. 4 of the journal *Risalat al-Islam* which was issued by the Dar al-Taqrib at Cairo, considered it obligatory to make the slaughter even if it should require burning or burial of the bodies of the slaughtered beasts.

4.20. BETWEEN MAKKAH AND MINA

As mentioned, the first rite in Mina on the 10th is the throwing of stones (*ramy* of *jamrat al-aqabah*), after that the offering of the sacrificial animal, and thirdly, shaving of the head or cutting hair. We have already discussed the third under the head "*halq* or *taqsir.*" We have referred to the rule about doing the halq or taqsir before the animal sacrifice when discussing the order of the rites under the head "In Mina," where the reader will find these details.

When the pilgrim completes his rites in Mina on the day of the festival (such as *ramy* and *dhabh*), he returns to Makkah to perform the *tawaf al-ziyarah*. Then he offers its related two cycle (*rakatayn*) prescribed prayer and performs the search between Safa and Marwah. According to the Hanafi, Hanbali, Shafii, and Maliki schools, he returns to Mina after that circumambulation and everything becomes permissible to him thereupon, even sex. According to the Jafari, he has to perform another circumambulation, the *tawaf al-nisa*, and offer its related two cycle prescribed prayer. Sex does not become permissible to the pilgrim, from the Jafari viewpoint, without this circumambulation, which we have already discussed in detail above.

4.20.1. THE NIGHT AT MINA

After completing the circumambulation, the pilgrim must return to Mina during what are called *layali al-tashriq*, which are the nights of the 11th, 12th, and 13th—with the exception of one who, being in a hurry, departs after midday and before sunset on the 12th. The person who leaves under these circumstances on the third day, is in accordance with the verse, *"He that departs on the second day incurs no sin."* (2:203).

According to Imam Abu Hanifah, to stay overnight in Mina is *Sunnah* not obligatory. Those who consider it obligatory agree that it is a rite and not a pillar. They disagree, however, regarding the necessity of atonement for the defaulter. According to Imam Ahmad ibn Hanbal, there is none. According to Imam Shafi, a dry measure of 800 grams (*mudd*);[125] and according to Malikis, a sacrifice.[126] The Jafari say that if one spends the night at a place other than Mina, there is nothing else required of him or her if he or she spends it at Makkah praying all the night until morning. But if the night is spent there without prayer, or somewhere else, in prayer or otherwise, he or she must sacrifice a sheep, even if the default was on account of oversight or ignorance."[127] There is no obligatory rite for the nights in Mina, although spending them in prayer and worship is recommended.

4.20.2. STONING DURING THE AYYAM AL-TASHRIQ

The schools agree that there is no rite except stoning of the three *jimar* everyday during the three days called *ayyam al-tashriq,* regardless of whether the pilgrim is performing *hajj al-tamattu, al-ifrad* or *al-qiran.* As to the number of pebbles and other things they have been mentioned under *"jamrat al-aqabah."*

According to the Jafari, the time of stoning on each of the three days extends from sunrise until sunset, midday being the preferable hour. The other schools say that it extends from midday until sunset, and if done earlier should be repeated. Imam Abu Hanifah permits ramy before midday only on the third day. Throwing of stones after sunset is permissible only for those with a valid excuse. All the major schools are in consensus about the number of times of throwing stones and the way of performing the throwing of stones on the three days.

Below is the way of its performance as described by *al-Tadhkirah* and *al-Mughni.*

The pilgrim performs the throwing of stones on each of the three days by throwing twenty-one pebbles, seven in each of the three times. He begins at the first *jamrah, al-jamrat al-ula,* which is the farthest of them from Makkah and nearer to Masjid al-Khayf. It is recommended to toss the pebble in a fashion called *hadhf,*[128] from the left side standing at Batn al-Masil, and to say *takbir* with every pebble that is thrown and to pray. After that, he proceeds to the second *jamrah,* called *al-jamrat al-wusta,* halts at the left side of the way, and, facing the *qiblah,* praises God and prays for blessings upon the Prophet, then moving ahead a little prays, and then throws the pebbles in the same way as above, then pauses and prays after the last pebble. Then he moves on to the third point called *jamrat al-aqabah,* and performs the rite of throwing of stones (*ramy*) as before, without any pause after finishing. With this the rites of throwing stones (*ramy*) for the day are complete.[129]

The total number of pebbles thrown on the three days is sixty-three (that is, if one spends the night of the 13th in Mina), twenty-one each day. With the seven thrown on the day of the festival the total number is seventy.

The author of *al-Tadhkirah,* after the above description, says that there is no difference of opinion about it. The author of *al-Mughni* makes a similar remark, adding that Malik has opposed the raising of hands. The description of the rites of throwing of stones given by the author of *al-Mughni* is similar if not exactly the same as the one given above by the author of *al-Tadhkirah.* All schools, except Imam Abu Hanifah, agree about the order of the throwing of stones of the *jimar,* and that if one of them is stoned out of turn, then it is obligatory to repeat the rite in the correct order. Imam Abu Hanifah says that the order is not binding.[130]

The throwing of stones may be performed on foot or from a mount, though the former is better. It is permissible for one who has an excuse that someone else may perform it for him, and there is nothing upon one if he omits the *takbir*, the prayer or the pause after the second *jamrah*.

If the throwing of stones is delayed by a day intentionally or on account of ignorance or oversight or is put over completely until the last day of *tashriq* and is performed on a single day, the pilgrim does not incur an atonement according to the Shafiis and the Malikis. Imam Abu Hanifah says that if one, two, or three pebbles are delayed by a day, for every pebble delayed a poor man must be fed; if four are delayed by a day, a sacrifice becomes essential. The Hanafi, Hanbali, Shafii and Maliki schools are in consensus that if one does not perform the throwing of stones at all until the days of *tashriq* are past, he is not obliged to perform the rite later any time. But they disagree as to the related atonement, which, according to the Malikis is sacrifice regardless of some—even one—or all of the pebbles being omitted. According to the Hanafis, the sacrifice is required for omitting all, and for fewer one must feed a poor man for every pebble omitted. The atonement according to Shafiis is a *mudd* of food for every pebble if two are omitted; for three a sacrifice becomes obligatory.[131]

The Jafari say if the throwing of stones at one or more *jimar* is forgotten, the rite must be performed during the days of *tashriq*, but if forgotten altogether until one reaches Makkah, the pilgrim is obliged to return to Mina to perform them if the days of *tashriq* are not past. Otherwise he must perform the rite himself the following year or depute another to perform it. In any case there is no atonement.[132] This agrees with the edict of al-Sayyid al-Hakim and al-Sayyid al-Khui, with the difference that the former regards the legal grounds in favor of the obligation of completion of the rite as stronger, whereas the latter considers it as dictated by caution, and both agree that intentional omission of throwing of stones does not invalidate the prescribed pilgrimage.

We referred earlier to the consensus of all the schools that it is sufficient for the pilgrim to remain for only two days of *tashriq* in Mina and that he or she may depart before the sunset on 12th. If the pilgrim remains until sunset, it is obligatory upon him or her to stay overnight and perform the rite of the throwing of stones on the 13th. The Jafari, however, say that the permissibility of leaving on the 12th is only for one who has not violated the prohibition on hunting and sex in the sacred state. Otherwise the pilgrim is obliged to remain in Mina on the night of the 13th. Offering the prescribed prayer in the Masjid al-Khayf at Mina is recommended, so also on the hill called Khayf.[133]

On returning to Makkah after the rites of Mina, it is, according to Jafaris and Malikis, recommended to perform the *tawaf al-wada*, which, according to Hanafis and Hanbalis, is obligatory for non-Makkans and those who do not wish to stay on in Makkah after returning from Mina. There is no *tawaf al-wada*, nor any substitute, for women who enter their periods before the departure, even from the viewpoint of those who consider the circumambulations obligatory. However, it is recommended for her to bid farewell to the House from the door nearest to it and without entering al-Masjid al-Haram.

4.21. VISITING MADINAH

The pilgrimage to Madinah is a highly recommended duty. The Prophet is reported to have said, "Whoever visits my grave after my death is like one who has migrated with me in my life." He also said, "A prescribed prayer in my mosque is like a thousand ones offered elsewhere with the exception of al-Masjid al-Haram, as to which a prescribed prayer there is equal to a thousand in my mosque." It is emphasized that the recommended prescribed prayer in the Prophet's Mosque should be offered between his tomb and the *minbar*, where, a Tradition says, is a 'garden of the gardens of Paradise'. To visit all other mosques of Madinah, like Masjid al-Quba, Mashrabah Umm Ibrahim, Masjid al-Ahzab, etc. and also the graves of the martyrs, in particular that of Hamzah at Uhud, is also recommended.

PART TWO
ECONOMIC ISSUES

5

PRESCRIBED POOR-DUE AND TWENTY-PERCENT TAX

Poor-due (*zakat*) is of two kinds: on property and on individuals. The schools concur that payment of poor-due is not valid without making one's intention known. Its obligation depends on the following conditions.

5.1. CONDITIONS FOR POOR-DUE ON PROPERTY

5.1.1. SANITY AND ADULTHOOD

The Hanafis and the Jafaris observe that sanity and adulthood are necessary for liability to poor-due; hence the property of a child or an insane person is not liable to it.[1] The Malikis, Hanbalis and Shafiis state: that neither sanity nor adulthood is required. It is obligatory on the property of a minor as well as an insane person and the guardian is responsible for its payment from his ward's property.

5.1.2. NON-MUSLIMS

The Hanafis, Shafiis and Hanbalis say that poor-due is not obligatory upon a non-Muslim.[2] According to the Jafaris and the Malikis, a non-Muslim is as liable to it as a Muslim, without there being any difference.

5.1.3. COMPLETE OWNERSHIP

Complete ownership is necessary for the incidence of poor-due. Every school has elaborate discussions concerning the definition of 'complete ownership'. What is common in their observations is that the owner should have complete control over the property and must be able to dispense it at his will. Hence lost property or property usurped from its owner although he will retain its ownership—will not be liable to poor-due. As to debt, it will be liable to poor-due only after the creditor has recovered it (for example, the wife's dower owed by the husband), for a debt is not possessed unless collected. The rule applicable to the debtor will be discussed later.

5.1.4. POSSESSION

A lunar year of uninterrupted possession for property other than grain, fruits and minerals. Details are given below.

5.1.5. MINIMUM

The possession of a certain minimum (*nisab*) which differs with the kind of property liable to poor-due, as will be explained later.

5.1.6. DEBT

Is a debtor who possesses property to the extent of the minimum liable to poor-due? In other words, does debt prevent liability to poor-due? The Jafaris and the Shafiis state that the property's freedom from debt is not a condition; hence a debtor will be liable to poor-due even if the debt covers his entire property equaling the minimum. Rather, the Jafaris say that if one borrows something on which poor-due is payable, in a quantity equaling its minimum and it remains in his possession for a year, the borrower shall be liable to poor-due. According to the Hanbalis, debt prevents liability to poor-due. Hence a debtor who possesses property should first meet the debt; he or she will pay poor-due if the remainder reaches the minimum limit, not otherwise.

The Malikis are of the opinion that debt prevents the incidence of poor-due on gold and silver, not on grain, livestock and minerals. Therefore a debtor possessing gold and silver in the quantity of minimum is supposed to meet the debt, and poor-due is not obligatory upon him or her. But if the debtor possesses something other than gold and silver in the quantity of the minimum, he or she is liable to poor-due. The Hanafis observe that if the debt is a duty owed to God, such as the obligation of the longer pilgrimage and atonement, and persons have no claims against him or her, such a debt does not prevent liability to poor-due. But if the debt is owed to persons or to God when there is such a claim against him or her as outstanding poor-due whose payment is demanded by the ruler (imam), such a debt prevents liability to poor-due on all kinds of property except crops of the field and fruits. All the schools concur that ornaments, jewelry, one's dwelling, clothes, household articles, mount, weapons and other things of personal use such as instruments, books and tools are not liable to poor-due. The Jafaris also exclude gold and silver ingots. Related details are given below.

5.2. KINDS OF PROPERTY LIABLE TO POOR-DUE

The Quran considers the needy as real sharers in the wealth of the rich. It says, *"And in their possessions is a share for the beggar and the deprived"* (51:19). The verse does not differentiate between wealth acquired through agriculture, industry or trade in respect of this right, and hence the jurisprudents of all the schools acknowledge it as obligatory in livestock, grain, fruits, currency and minerals. However, they differ in delimiting some of these categories, in specifying the minimum applicable to some of them, and the size of the share of the needy in some others. Thus the Jafaris consider it obligatory to pay one-fifth (*khums*) from the profits of trade, while the other schools prescribe one-fortieth (2 1/2%) on merchandise. The same applies to minerals, of which the Hanafis, Jafaris and Hanbalis prescribe payment of 20% while the remaining two schools that of 2 1/2%. The following description gives the details of the points of agreement and difference in the schools.

5.2.1. POOR-DUE ON LIVESTOCK

There is a consensus that poor-due is obligatory upon three kinds of livestock: camels, cattle, sheep and goats. They concur that poor-due is not obligatory upon horses, mules and donkeys, except when they form a part of merchandise. The Hanafi consider horses to be liable to poor-due only when these include mares.

5.2.1.1. THE CONDITIONS

There are four conditions for the incidence of poor-due on livestock:

5.2.1.1.1. THE MINIMUM OF CAMELS

The minimum of camels is as follows: If the number of camels is five, one sheep; if it reaches ten, two sheep; for fifteen, three sheep; and for twenty, four. All the schools agree on this prescription. But if the number of camels reaches twenty-five, the poor-due, according to the Jafaris, is five sheep, and a camel in its second year according to the other schools. However, the Jafaris consider that as poor-due of twenty-six camels; thus if the number of camels reaches this limit they form a single minimum. The schools concur that the poor-due of thirty-six camels, is a camel in its third year; of forty-six camels, a camel in its fourth year; of sixty-one camels, a camel in its fifth year; of seventy-six camels, two camels in their third year; of ninety-one camels, two camels in their fourth year.

The schools also concur that there is no additional poor-due for camels if their number be over ninety-one and below. For this number the different opinions of the schools and their details can be found in elaborate works. There is consensus that there is no poor-due on less than five camels, as well as on the number above a particular minimum and below the next minimum.

5.2.1.1.2. THE MINIMUM OF CATTLE

The poor-due for every thirty cattle is a cow or ox in its second year (*tabi* or *tabiah*); for every forty, a cow in its third year (*musinnah*). Thus for sixty, the poor-due is two cows or oxen in their second year; for seventy, one cow or ox in its second year and one cow in its third year; for eighty, two cows in their third year; for ninety, three cows or oxen in their second year; for 100, two cows or oxen in their second year and one in its third year; for 110, two cows in their third year and one cow or ox in its second year; for 120, three cows in their third year, or four cows or oxen in their second year, and so on. No poor-due is levied on a number which exceeds a certain limit but falls short of the next higher limit. All the schools concur regarding the above-mentioned minimum.[3] The Malikis define *tabi* as one which has completed two years and entered the third, and *musinnah* as one which has completed three years and entered the fourth.

5.2.1.1.3. THE MINIMUM OF SHEEP

The schools concur that the poor-due for forty sheep is one sheep; for 121, two; for 201, three. The Jafaris state that if their number reaches 301, the poor-due is four sheep up to 400; from then on for each extra 100 the poor-due is one sheep. The Hanafi, Hanbali, Maliki, and Shafii schools observe that the poor-due for 301, like that for 201, is three sheep up to 400, on which four sheep become due; thereafter for each extra 100 the poor-due is one sheep. There is consensus among the schools that a number between any two limits is exempt from poor-due.

5.2.1.2. GRAZING

'Grazing livestock' is livestock which grazes freely on public pastures for most of the year and whose owner does not bear the cost of providing it with grass except rarely. This is a condition on which all the schools excepting the Maliki concur. The Malikis levy poor-due on both 'grazing' and 'non-grazing' livestock.

5.2.1.3. ONE YEAR OF OWNERSHIP

All the livestock in the minimum should be owned by its owner for a complete lunar year. Thus if its number falls short of the minimum, even by one during the year, it will not be liable to poor-due even if the minimum materializes at the end of the year (that is, if a person owns forty sheep at the beginning of the year and after a few months their number is reduced by one for some reason, such as sale, gift or death, and later becomes forty again, poor-due will not be levied at the end of the year). The Jafaris, Shafiis and Hanbalis concur regarding this condition, while the Hanafis observe that if the number falls below the minimum during the year but is resumed at the end of it, poor-due will be levied as if the minimum had existed throughout the year.

5.2.1.6. WORK ANIMALS

The animals should not be those intended for work, such as an ox used for tilling or a camel for transport. Hence there is consensus among the schools, excepting the Maliki, that poor-due is not levied on animals used for work, irrespective of their number. According to the Malikis, poor-due is levied on both working as well as other animals without any difference. The schools concur that if a person possesses many kinds of livestock of which no single kind reaches the number required for minimum, it is not obligatory upon him or her to consider them jointly (thus if he has less than thirty cattle and less than forty sheep, it is not obligatory to make up the minimum of the cattle with the sheep or vice versa).

The schools differ where two persons jointly own a single minimum. The Jafaris, Hanafis and Malikis state that they are not liable to poor-due, together or singly, unless the share of each one of them separately reaches the minimum limit. The Shafiis and the Hanbalis observe that wealth owned jointly is liable to poor-due if it reaches the minimum limit, even if each share falls short of it.

5.2.2. POOR-DUE ON GOLD AND SILVER

The jurisprudents prescribe poor-due on gold and silver if

their respective minimum are reached. According to them the minimum of gold is twenty mithqal (4.8 grams) and that of silver 200 dirhams (2.52 grams). They further require that the minimum be owned for one complete year. The rate of poor-due on these two is 2 1/2%. The Jafari observe that poor-due is obligatory on gold and silver coins used as money, not on ingots or jewelry. The Hanafi, Hanbali, Maliki and Shafii schools concur that poor-due is obligatory on gold and silver ingots in the same manner as on money coined from them. They differ regarding poor-due on jewelry made of them; some consider it obligatory, others do not.

The above remarks concerning poor-due on gold and silver coins will suffice, for they have practically no role in our times. As to bank-notes, the Jafaris prescribe the payment of one-fifth (*khums*) of the surplus left after a year's expenses. Details are given below. The Shafiis, Malikis and Hanafis state that poor-due is not obligatory on bank notes unless all the conditions including minimum and the completion of a year are fulfilled. The Hanbalis say that poor-due is not obligatory on bank-notes except when converted into gold or silver.

5.2.3. *POOR-DUE ON CROPS AND FRUIT*

The schools concur that the rate of poor-due on crops of the field and fruits is ten-seventy if irrigated by rain or river water, and five percent if irrigated by Artesian wells and the like. There is also consensus among the schools, excepting the Hanafi, that the minimum for crops and fruits is approx. 910 kg. There is no poor-due under this limit. The Hanafis prescribe poor-due irrespective of the quantity of the produce.

The schools differ regarding the kinds of crops and fruits on which poor-due is obligatory. The Hanafis prescribe poor-due on all fruits and crops and all agricultural produce except wood, hay, and Persian cane. The Malikis and the Shafiis prescribe poor-due on everything that is stored as a provision, such as wheat, barley, rice, dates and raisins. The Hanbalis require poor-due on everything that is weighed and stored from among fruits and grains. The Jafaris do not levy poor-due on anything except wheat and barley among grains, and dates and raisins from among fruits. Apart from these, it is recommended, not obligatory.

5.2.4. POOR-DUE ON MERCHANDISE

'Merchandise' (*mal al-tijarah*) consists of property whose ownership is acquired through commercial transactions made for profit. It is necessary here that the ownership be acquired through the owner's own activity; hence, if acquired through inheritance, there is consensus that it will not be considered merchandise. According to the Hanafi, Hanbali, Maliki, and Shafii schools, poor-due is obligatory on merchandise. The Jafari consider it recommended. The poor-due is paid from the price of the commodities of trade at the rate of 2 1/2%. The schools concur that a year's passage is necessary for the incidence of poor-due. It is considered to begin from the time commercial transactions commence. When a year passes and profit is made, poor-due becomes payable. The Jafaris observe that the capital should remain undiminished throughout the year. Thus if it is reduced during the year, poor-due will not be levied. When restored, the new year will be reckoned from the date of recovery.

According to the Shafiis and the Hanbalis, the criterion for liability to poor-due is only the position at the end of year. Thus if the minimum is not reached at the beginning of the year or during it but only at its end, poor-due becomes obligatory.

The Hanafis state that the criterion is the position at the beginning and the end of the year not what happens in its middle. Thus if at the beginning of the year a person owns merchandise fulfilling the minimum and its value falls below this limit during the year recovering to reach the limit at the end of the year, he will be liable to poor-due. But if the minimum is not reached either at the year's beginning or end, poor-due will not be levied.

Also, the value of merchandise should reach the minimum. On evaluation its total value will be compared with the minimum of gold and silver; poor-due will be levied if it equals or exceeds any of them, not if it is less than the minimum of silver. The authors of *al-Fiqh alal-madhahib al-arbaah* calculate this minimum as 529.2/3 Egyptian piasters.

5.3. THE CHARACTER OF LIABILITY
The schools differ as to whether poor-due pertains to the property itself that is liable to poor-due so that one entitled to receive it has a share in it together with the owner (like all property owned jointly by partners), or if it is a personal liability like other debts, though it pertains to a specific property, like the debt pertaining to the legacy of a deceased person.

The Shafiis, Jafaris and Malikis state that poor-due is obligatory upon the poor-due able property itself and its recipient is a real co-sharer in it with the owner in accordance with the statement of God, the Most High, "*And in their wealth is a share for the beggar and the deprived*" (61:19). They point out that there is also a *tawatur* of Traditions stating that God has made the rich and the poor partners in wealth. However, the *Shariah* has out of lenience permitted the owner to pay poor-due out of his other assets not subject to poor-due. The Hanafis observe: The incidence of poor-due pertains to the property subject to poor-due itself. It is like the claim of a mortgagor over mortgaged property and is not met except by being handed over to the recipient. Two views have been narrated from Imam Ahmad, one of which agrees with the Hanafi position.

5.4. CLASSES ENTITLED TO RECEIVE POOR-DUE
The schools concur that there are eight different classes of those who deserve to receive poor-due as mentioned in the following verse of *Surat al-Tawbah*, "*Charity (sadaqat) is for the poor and the needy, their collectors, those whose hearts are to be conciliated, the ransoming of slaves , debtors, in God's way, and the traveler..*" (9:60).

The views of the schools in determining these classes are as follows:

5.4.1. THE NEEDY

According to the Hanafis, *'faqir'* is someone who owns less than the minimum even if he is physically fit and earning. As to one who owns any property equal to the minimum of its category after providing for his basic needs such as house, articles, clothes, and etc. it is not valid to spend poor-due on him or her. The proof they offer is that poor-due becomes obligatory upon one who owns assets equal to the minimum of anything and one who is himself liable to poor-due cannot receive it. According to the other schools, the criterion is need, not ownership. Poor-due is unlawful for one who is not in need even if he owns nothing, and lawful for a needy person although he may own one or several minimums, because the word *'faqr'* means need. God, the Exalted, says, *"O men, you are the ones that have need of God"* (35:15). The Shafiis and the Hanbalis say that one who possesses half of what suffices him or her will not be considered a needy person; consequently it is not permissible for him or her to receive poor-due.

According to the Jafaris and the Malikis, *'faqir'* in the context of the *Shariah* is one who does not possess a year's provision for himself and his family. Thus one who owns property or livestock not sufficient to provide his family for a whole year can be given poor-due. The Jafaris, Shafiis and Hanbalis further observe that it is not permissible for one capable of earning to receive poor-due. The Hanafis and the Malikis permit him or her to receive poor-due and it may be given to him or her. The Jafaris state that one's claim to be needy will be accepted without requiring a witness or an oath, provided the person has no visible wealth and the falsehood of his or her claim is not known. This is because once two men came to the Prophet while he was distributing charity and asked him to give them something from it. The Prophet lifted his eyes and fixing his glance on them said, "If you like I will give it to you, for there is no share in it for one who is well provided or one who makes an earning." Thus he left it to them to benefit from poor-due without requiring witness or oath.

5.4.2. THE DESTITUTE

The Jafaris, Hanafis and Malikis consider a destitute person (*miskin*) to be one who is worse off than a needy person. The Hanbalis and the Shafiis, however, define needy as someone worse off than a destitute person because, they say a needy person is one who has nothing or lacks even half of what he or she needs, while a destitute person is one who possesses more than half of what he or she needs, and he or she is provided the other half from poor-due. Whatever be the case, there is no essential difference between the schools in their interpretation of the terms *'faqir'* and *'miskin,'* for the objective is that poor-due be used to fulfill the urgent need for housing, food, clothing, medical care, education, and such other needs.

The schools, excepting the Maliki, also concur that it is not permissible for one liable to poor-due to give it to his parents, grandparents, children, grandchildren or wife. The Malikis allow its payment to grandparents and grandchildren because their maintenance is not one's obligation in their opinion.

There is also consensus that it is valid to give poor-due to brothers, uncles and aunts. However, the prohibition on giving of poor-due to one's father and children pertains only to the share meant for the two classes of the needy (needy and destitute). Hence if they belong to a class other than these two, they are permitted to receive it, that is, if the father or the son is a warrior fighting in the way of God, or one of 'those whose hearts are to be conciliated,' or a debtor whose debt arises out of a legitimate act, or one involved in a case of peacemaking, or a collector of poor-due, because these classes of recipients are entitled to receive poor-due even if they are well off.[4] However, it is preferable to give poor-due to a relative whose maintenance is not obligatory upon the giver.

The schools differ regarding the transfer of poor-due from one town to another. The Hanafis and the Jafaris observe that it is preferable and more meritorious to spend the poor-due on the residents of the town except where some urgent need necessitates its transfer to another place. The Shafiis and the Malikis do not permit the transfer of poor-due from one town to another. The Hanbalis allow its transfer to a place at a distance where prescribed prayer does not become delayed for one making the journey, and forbid its transfer beyond that distance.

5.4.3. COLLECTORS OF POOR-DUE

As per consensus, by in the verse is meant the collectors of poor-due.

5.4.4. THOSE WHOSE HEARTS ARE TO BE CONCILIATED

They are those who are won over by paying a part of poor-due in the interest of Islam. The schools differ as to whether this category still holds or if it has been abrogated, and if not abrogated whether this winning over is restricted to non-Muslims or includes Muslims of weak conviction as well.

The Hanafis observe that this principle was introduced in the *Shariah* at the advent of Islam when the Muslims were weak. But now, when Islam has become firmly established, this provision has no applicability due to the absence of its cause. The other schools have elaborately discussed the different kinds of 'those whose hearts are to be conciliated'. Their observations may be summarized as follows: the regulation holds and has not been abrogated; the share poor-due of pertaining to person who is won over to paying the poor-due in the interest of Islam can be given to a Muslim as well as a non-Muslim, on condition that this bestowal secures the advantage of Islam and Muslims. The Prophet gave poor-due to Safwan ibn Umayyah, who was an idolater, and to Abu Sufyan and his like, after they embraced Islam, as a measure of precaution to safeguard Islam and Muslims from their malice.

5.4.5. FREEING OF SLAVES WITH POOR-DUE MONEY

It implies the buying of slaves with poor-due funds to set them free. This provision clearly shows that Islam devised numerous ways to end slavery. in any case, this provision has no practical application in our times.

5.4.6. DEBTORS WHO HAVE FALLEN INTO DEBT FOR SOME NON-SINFUL CAUSES

The schools concur that they may be given poor-due to help them repay their debts.

5.4.7. SABIL ALLAH

The Hanafi, Hanbali, Maliki, and Shafii schools consider it to imply those warriors who have volunteered to fight for the defense of Islam. The Jafaris observe that apart from warriors, this category includes building of mosques, hospitals, schools and other public works.

5.4.8. IBN AL-SABIL

This refers to a traveler who is cut off from his or her hometown and means. Hence it is valid to give him or her poor-due to an extent that will enable him or her to reach his or her hometown.

5.5. SUBSIDIARY ISSUES

The schools concur that it is unlawful for one belonging to the Banu Hashim to receive poor-due from someone who is not a Hashimite himself. But he may receive poor-due from a Hashimite.

Is it permissible to give one's entire poor-due to a single miskin? The Jafaris permit it even if it makes the recipient well off by being given all at once. The Hanafis and the Hanbalis state: It may be given to a single person if this does not make him sufficiently provided. The Malikis permit giving of one's entire poor-due to a single recipient provided he is not a collector of poor-due, because he may not take more than the remuneration of his work. The Shafiis are of the opinion that it is obligatory to so spread out the poor-due as to include all the eight categories, if they exist in the absence of some of them it should be distributed among the categories present. A minimum of three persons from each category should receive it.

The property liable to poor-due is of two types. First, that which is possessed for a year, such as livestock and merchandise. In this case, poor-due does not become obligatory before the completion of a year. A 'year' in the opinion of the Jafaris means eleven months of possession of the property liable to poor-due and the setting in of the twelfth month.

The second type does not require the passage of a year like fruits and grains. Poor-due becomes obligatory upon them at the time of harvest. As to the time of payment, there is consensus that it is when the fruits are gathered and dried in the sun, and when the crop is harvested and the straw and husk removed. One who delays taking out the poor-due after its time has arrived and its payment has become possible is a sinner (though he or she remains liable to it), because he or she has delayed the carrying out of a time-bound obligation and been negligent.

5.6. POOR-DUE PAID AT THE END OF THE MONTH OF FASTING

The poor-due which is due at the end of the month of fasting (*zakat al-fitr*) is also called *zakat al-abdan* (the *zakat* of the bodies). Its pertinent issues include the following questions: by whom it is to be paid? for whom? what is its quantity, its time of payment, and who are its eligible recipients.

The Hanafi, Hanbali, Maliki and Shafii schools state that *zakat al-fitr* is obligatory upon every financially capable Muslim, major or minor. Thus it is obligatory for a guardian to pay it out from the property of his ward to the needy. A financially capable person in the opinion of the Hanafis is one who owns property equal to a minimum of poor-due or something equal in value after meeting all his needs. According to the Shafiis, Malikis and Hanbalis, it is one who possesses anything in excess of his and his family's food on the day and night of the festival (*id*), apart from such essential needs as house, clothes and other necessities. The Malikis add that one who is capable of borrowing will be considered capable if he or she hopes to repay it. According to the Jafaris, poor-due at the end of the month of the prescribed fast is obligatory only upon a

capable sane adult. Therefore it is not obligatory on a child's
property or that of an insane person based on the Tradition.
"The Lawgiver's Pen has absolved these three obligations: a
child until he (or she) reaches the age of puberty; an insane
person, until he (or she) regains sanity; and a person in sleep
until he (or she) wakes up." A financially capable person in
their opinion is one who possesses either actually or potential-
ly, a year's provision for himself and his family—such as when
he possesses an asset that he can utilize or a skill by which he
can earn.

The Hanafis observe that it is obligatory for a capable person to pay the poor-due at the end of the prescribed fast for
himself, his minor children, his servant, and his major child if
he happens to be insane. But if the major child is sane, his
poor-due is not obligatory upon the father. Also the wife's poor-
due is not obligatory upon the husband. The Hanbalis and the
Shafiis consider it obligatory to pay the poor-due at the end of
the prescribed fast for oneself as well as those whose maintenance is obligatory upon one; such as wife, father and son. The
Malikis say that it is obligatory for oneself and for those one is
maintaining; they include: one's indigent parents; sons, who
have no means of their own, provided they are still young and
incapable of earning themselves; indigent daughters who have
not yet been married; and wife. The Jafaris state that it is
obligatory to pay the poor-due at the end of the prescribed fast
for oneself and for all those whom one feeds on the night of the
festival, irrespective of whether their maintenance is obligatory upon one or not, and regardless of their being children or
adults, Muslims or non-Muslims, relatives or strangers. Hence
if a guest comes to his house moments before the new moon for
the month of Shawwal is sighted and joins the family, it
becomes obligatory to pay the poor-rate at the end of the prescribed prayer for him as well. Similarly, if a child is born to
him or he marries before or at the time of sunset preceding the
night of *id al-fitr*. But if the child is born, or he marries, or a
guest arrives, after sunset, it will not be obligatory to pay the

poor-due for them. Anyone whose poor-due is obligatory upon another is not required to pay his own poor-due even if he or she is wealthy.

5.7. ITS QUANTITY

The schools, excepting the Hanafi, concur that the obligatory quantity of the poor-due following the prescribed fast per head is approx. 3 kg or wheat, barley, dates, raisins, rice, maize or any other staple crop. The Hanafis consider half a *sa* of wheat per head as sufficient.

5.8. TIME OF OBLIGATORY PAYMENT

The Hanafis observe that its obligation commences from the dawn of the day of the festival marking the end of the prescribed prayer and continues until the end of life, because the poor-due marking is among those obligations which do not have a time limit and it is valid to pay it early or late. The Hanbalis say that it is forbidden to delay its payment beyond the day of the festival and it may be paid two days before it, although not earlier. The Shafiis state that the time it becomes obligatory extends from the last part of Ramadan (that is, from a little before sunset on the last day of Ramadan) up to the first part of Shawwal. It is *Sunnah* to set it aside during the early part of the day of festival and forbidden to delay it beyond the sunset of that day without an excuse.

There are two narrations from Imam Malik, and in accordance with one of them its obligation commences from sunset on the last day of Ramadan. The Jafaris observe that the poor-due following the prescribed fast becomes obligatory with the falling of the night of the festival, and its payment is obligatory from sunset up to noon on the day of the festival; it is meritorious to pay it before the festival prescribed prayer. But if no deserving person (*mustahaqq*) is found at that time, it should be set aside with the intent of giving it at the first opportunity. If the payment is delayed beyond this time despite the presence of a deserving recipient, it remains obligatory to pay it later, because this obligation is not annulled in any situation.

5.9. DESERVING PERSONS

The schools concur that those entitled to receive ordinary poor-due, as per the Quranic verse, *"Charity (sadaqat) is for the poor and needy..."* (9:60), are also entitled to receive the poor-due following the prescribed fast. In the place of paying in kind, it suffices to pay the price of the cereals, and it is recommended to give it to one's needy relative, and then to the neighbors, as there is a Tradition which says, "The neighbor of someone paying charity is more entitled to receive it."

5.10. TWENTY-PERCENT TAX

The Jafari assign a separate chapter to twenty-percent tax in their books on jurisprudence, after the chapter on the poor-due, and its basis is, *"Know that whatever booty you take, the fifth of it is God's and the Messenger's, and the near kinsman's and the orphans and for the needy and the traveler"* (8:41). They do not confine the scope of the term *'ghanimah'* to the spoils of war acquired by Muslims, but consider it to include seven categories, mentioned below along with what information we could gather about the views of other schools regarding each category:

5.10.1. BOOTY ACQUIRED IN WAR
All the schools concur that it is liable to twenty percent tax.

5.10.2. MINERALS
It includes everything that is of value extracted from the earth—apart from soil—e.g. gold, silver, lead, copper, mercury, petroleum, sulfur, etc.

The Jafaris observe that it is obligatory to pay the twenty - percent tax on minerals if their value reaches the minimum of gold, which is twenty dinars, or the minimum of silver, which is 200 dirhams. There is no twenty percent tax below this limit. The Hanafis state that there is no minimum for minerals, and their twenty percent tax is obligatory irrespective of value. The Malikis, Shafiis and Hanbalis are of the opinion that there is no levy if the mineral extracted is lesser in value than the minimum, but if it reaches that limit it is liable to poor-due at the rate of 2 1/2%.

5.10.3. BURIED PROPERTY

It consists of articles of value buried at a place whose inhabitants have perished and there is no sign left of them, such as sites which the archeologists excavate for this purpose. The Hanafi, Hanbali, Maliki and Shafii schools state that twenty percent tax is obligatory on buried property, and it has no minimum and therefore entails twenty-percent tax irrespective of its worth. The Jafaris observe that buried property is like minerals with respect to minimum and liability to twenty-percent tax.

5.10.4. RETRIEVED FROM THE SEA

The Jafaris say that which is retrieved from the sea through diving, that is, pearls and corals, is liable to twenty-percent tax if its value is one dinar or more after deducting the cost of retrieval. In the opinion of the Hanafi, Hanbali, Maliki, and Shafii schools, there is no levy on such things, whatever their value.

5.10.5. SURPLUS AFTER NEEDS MET

The Jafaris observe that twenty-percent tax is obligatory upon the surplus remaining after a person has made provision for himself and his family for a period of one year, irrespective of his profession and the mode of income—trade or industry, agriculture or office work, or work on daily wages, or real state, gift or something else. Hence if there remains a single piaster or anything of that value after a year's expenditure, it is liable to twenty percent tax.

5.10.6. ILLEGITIMATE WEALTH MIXED WITH LEGITIMATE

The Jafaris state that if a person comes to acquire some illegitimate wealth which gets mixed with his legitimate wealth and neither the quantity of the illegitimate wealth nor its owner is known, he or she is obliged to pay twenty percent tax from his or her whole wealth in the way of God. If he or she does so, his or her remaining wealth will become permissible irrespective of whether the unlawful portion was lesser or greater than a fifth. But if the illegitimate wealth is identifiable, it is obligatory to return it itself; and if it is not identifiable but its quantity is known, he or she will return that quantity fully even if it equals all his wealth. If he or she knows the people from whom he or she has embezzled it without knowing the quantity of the portion due to them, he or she is bound to seek their satisfaction by reaching a settlement or seeking their pardon. In short, the payment of twenty-percent tax from adulterated wealth is correct only when both the quantity and the owner of its illegitimate portion are not known.

5.10.7. Non-Muslim Purchase of Land

According to the Jafaris, if a non-Muslim (*dhimmi*) purchases land from a Muslim, the non-Muslim is personally liable to pay its twenty percent tax.

5.11. Uses of Twenty percent Tax

The Shafiis and the Hanbalis observe that the twenty-percent tax will be divided into five parts, of which one part will be the share of the Prophet and used for the benefit of Muslims. Another part will be the share of those who have descended from Hashim through their fathers (*dhawi al-qubra*), irrespective of any distinction between the rich or the poor among them. The three other parts will be spent on orphans, the poor and the travelers, whether they belong to the Banu Hashim or not. The Hanafis consider the share of the Prophet as annulled after his demise. As to the those belonging to Banu Hashim, they are like other poor in receiving twenty percent tax, they say that they will be entitled to it on account of their need, not by virtue of their kinship with the Prophet. The Malikis state that the ruler has complete authority over twenty percent tax funds and he may use it for any purpose that he deems fit. According to the Jafaris, the shares of God, the Prophet and the descendants from Hashim through their fathers will be paid to a representative of the leader, to be spent for the benefit of the Muslim community. The other three parts are to be given to the orphans, the needy and travelers belonging exclusively to Banu Hashim.

6

ENDOWMENT

Wuquf and *awqaf* are the plurals of *waqf* and its verb is 'waqafa', though 'awqafa' is also rarely used, as in *al-Tadhkirah* of Allamah al-Hilli. The word 'waqf' literally means 'to detain' and 'to prevent', as in *wuqiftu 'an sayri*, i.e. 'I was prevented from making my journey.'

In the context of the *Shariah* it implies a form of gift in which the corpus is detained and the usufruct is set free. The meaning of 'detention' of the corpus is its prevention from being inherited, sold, gifted, mortgaged, rented, lent, etc. As to dedication of the usufruct, it means its devotion to the purpose mentioned by the founder, doner (*waqif*) without any pecuniary return.

Some jurisprudents consider endowment (*waqf*) to be illegal in the Islamic *Shariah* and regard it as contradictory to its basic principles except where it concerns a mosque. But this view has been abandoned by all the schools of jurisprudence.

6.1. PERPETUITY AND CONTINUITY

All schools, excepting the Maliki, concur that a endowment is valid only when the founder intends the endowment to be perpetual and continuous, and therefore it is considered a lasting charity. Hence if the endower limits its period of operation (such as when he makes endowment for ten years or until an unspecified time when he would revoke it at his or her own pleasure, or for as long as he or his children or she and her children are not in need of it, and so forth) it will not be considered a endowment in its true sense.

Many Jafari jurisprudents hold that such a condition nullifies the endowment, although it will be considered as valid detention[1] if the owner of the property intends detention. But if he or she intends it to be a endowment, it will be void both as endowment as well as detention. By a valid detention is meant that the usufruct donated by the owner for a particular object will be so applied during the period mentioned and return to him after the expiration of that period.

The Malikis say that perpetuity is not necessary in endowment and it is valid and binding even if its duration is fixed, and after the expiration of the stipulated period the property will return to the owner. Similarly, if the founder makes a provision entitling himself or the beneficiary to sell the endowment property, the endowment is valid and the provision will be acted upon.[2]

If a endowment is made for an object which is liable to expiration (such as a endowment made for one's living children, or others who are bound to cease existing) will it be valid? Moreover, presuming its validity, upon whom will it devolve after the expiration of its object?

The Hanafis observe that such an endowment is valid and it will be applied after the expiration of its original object to the benefit of the poor. The Hanbalis say that it is valid and will thereafter be spent for the benefit of the nearest relation of the founder. This is also one of two opinions of the Shafiis. The Malikis are of the opinion that it is valid and will devolve on the nearest poor relation of the founder (*waqif*), and if all of them are wealthy, then on their poor relatives.[3] The Jafari state that the endowment is valid and will devolve on the heirs of the founder.[4]

6.2. DELIVERY OF POSSESSION

Delivery of possession implies the owner's relinquishment of his authority over the property and its transfer to the purpose for which it has been donated. According to the Jafari, delivery is a necessary condition for the deed of endowment to become binding, though not for its validity. Therefore, if a founder dedicates his property by way of endowment without delivering possession, he is entitled to revoke it.

If a founder makes a endowment for public benefit (like a mosque or a shrine or for the poor), the endowment will not become binding until the custodian (*mutawalli*) or the judge (*hakim al-shar*) takes possession of the donated property, or until someone is buried in the donated plot of land, in the case of a graveyard, or prayers are offered in it, if it is a mosque, or until a poor person uses it with the permission of the founder, in a endowment for the benefit of the poor. If delivery is not effected in any of the above-mentioned forms it is valid for a *waqif* to revoke the endowment.

If a endowment is made for a private purpose, such as for the benefit of the founder's children, if the children have attained majority, it will not become binding unless they take possession of it with his permission, and if they are minors the need for giving permission does not arise because the founder's possession of it as their guardian amounts to their having taken possession.

If the founder dies before possession has been taken, the endowment becomes void and the property assigned for endowment will be considered his heritage. For example, if he makes the charitable endowment of a shop and dies while it is still in his use, it will return to the heirs.

The Malikis say that the sole taking possession does not suffice and it is necessary that the donated property remain in the possession of the beneficiary or the custodian for one complete year. Only after the completion of one year will the endowment become binding and incapable of annulled in any manner.

The Shafiis, and Ibn Hanbal in one of his opinions, state that an endowment is completed even without delivering possession. Rather, the ownership of the endowment will cease on the pronouncement of endowment.[5]

6.3. OWNERSHIP OF THE ENDOWMENT PROPERTY

There is no doubt that prior to donation the endowment property is owned by the doner, because a person cannot make endowment of a property that he does not own. The question is whether, after the completion of the endowment, the ownership of the property remains with the founder, with the difference that his control over its usufruct will cease, or if is it transferred to the beneficiaries. Or does the property becomes ownerless, being released from ownership? The jurisprudents hold different opinions in this regard. The Malikis consider it to remain in the ownership of the doner, although he or she is prohibited from using it.

The Hanafis observe that an endowment property has no owner at all, and this is the more reliable opinion according to the Shafii school.[6] The Hanbalis say that the ownership of the endowment property will be transferred to the beneficiaries.

Shaykh Abu Zuhrah has ascribed to the Jafari the view that the ownership of the endowment property remains with the founder. He then observes[7] that this is the preponderant view of the Jafari. He does not mention the source relied upon by him for ascribing this view, and I do not know from where he has extracted it, for it has been mentioned in *al-Jawahir*, which is the most important and authentic source of Jafari jurisprudence. According to most jurisprudents, when a endowment is completed, the ownership of the doner ceases; rather, it is the preponderant view and the authors of *al-Ghunyah* and *al-Sarair* have even reported an consensus (*ijma*) on this view.[8]

Although all or most Jafari jurisprudents concur that the ownership of the founder ceases, they differ as to whether the endowment property totally loses the characteristic of being owned (in a manner that it is neither the property of the founder, nor of the beneficiaries, and, as the jurisprudents would say, is released from ownership) or if it is transferred from the founder to the beneficiaries.

A group among them differentiate between a public endowment (that is, mosques, schools, sanitariums, etc.) and a private endowment (that is, an endowment for the benefit of one's descendants). The former is considered as involving a release from ownership and the latter a transfer of ownership from the founder to the beneficiary.

The difference of opinion regarding the ownership of endowment property has practical significance in determining whether the sale of such property is valid or not, and in the case where a endowment is made for a limited period or for a terminable purpose. According to the Maliki view that the endowment remains the founder's property, its sale is valid and the corpus will return to the waqif on expiration of the period of endowment or when the object for which the endowment was made terminates. But according to the view which totally negates the ownership of endowment property, its sale will not be valid, because only owned property can be sold, and a endowment for a limited period will also be invalid. According to the view which considers the ownership of endowment property as transferred to the beneficiaries, the property will not return to the doner. The consequences of this difference will be more obvious from the issues to be discussed below. It is necessary to understand this divergence of viewpoints because it affects many issues of endowment.

6.3.1. THE ESSENTIALS OF ENDOWMENT

There are four pillars or essentials of endowment: (1) the declaration (*al-sighah*); (2) the founder (*waqif*); (3) the property given as endowment (*al-mawqufah*); (4) the beneficiary (*al-mawquf alayh*).

6.3.1.1. THE DECLARATION

There is a consensus among all the schools that a endowment is created by using the word '*waqaftu*' (I have made a endowment), because it explicitly signifies the intention of endowment without needing any further clarification. They differ regarding the creation of endowment by the use of such words as '*habastu* ' (I have detained), *sabbaltu* (I have donated as charity), *abbadtu* (I have perpetually settled), etc., and go into needless details.

254 Part Two: Economic Issues

The correct view is that an endowment is created and completed by using any word which is capable of proving the intention of creating a endowment, even if it belongs to another language, because here words are means of expressing one's intention, not an end in themselves.[9]

6.3.1.2. THE CREATION OF AN ENDOWMENT WITHOUT THE DECLARATION

Is a endowment completed by an act (such as when someone builds a mosque and calls the people to pray in it, or allows burials to take place in a piece of land with an intention of making it a endowment for a graveyard) without one uttering 'waqaftu' or 'habastu' or similar words, or is it necessary that the declaration take place, the act by itself being insufficient?

The Hanafi, Maliki and Hanbali schools say that an act by itself is sufficient and the property becomes, consequent to the act, a endowment.[10] The Shafiis observe that an endowment is completed only by the recital of the declaration.[11]

6.3.1.3. ACCEPTANCE

Does endowment require acceptance or is its declaration as endowment (by the founder) sufficient? In other words, is endowment created by a single decision, or is it necessary that there be two concurrent decisions?

In this context the jurisprudents have divided endowments into public (in which the doner has no specific beneficiary in his mind, that is, endowments made for the poor and endowments of mosques and shrines) and private endowments (that is, an endowment made for the benefit of one's children).

The Shafii, Hanbali, Hanafi and Maliki schools concur that a public endowment requires no acceptance, and according to the Malikis and most Hanafi jurisprudents a private endowment, like a public one, requires no acceptance. The Shafiis incline towards the necessity of acceptance.[12] The Jafari jurisprudents differ among themselves, holding one of the following three opinions.

1. Necessity of acceptance in both public and private endowments.

2. Absence of such necessity in both kinds of endowments.

3. A distinction is made between a public and private endowments, and acceptance is necessary only in the latter. This is the same view which the Shafiis have favored, and is also the correct one.[13]

6.3.2. *UNCONDITIONALLY OPERATIONAL*

The Malikis observe that it is valid for an endowment to depend upon a contingency. Therefore, if the owner says, "When such and such a time comes, my house will become a endowment," it is valid and the endowment is completed.[14] The Hanafi and the Shafii schools state that it is not valid to make a endowment contingent on the occurrence of an event; rather, it is obligatory that endowment be unconditional, and if it is made to depend upon a contingency, as in the above-mentioned example, it will remain the property of the owner.[15]

It should be pointed out that these two schools allow divorce to depend upon a contingency, while they disallow similar dependence in other spheres of jurisprudence, despite the fact that caution and stringency are more necessary in marital issues when compared to other issues.

The Hanbalis say that an endowment can be made contingent on the occurrence of death. Apart from this, dependence on any other contingency is invalid.[16]

Most Jafari jurisprudents consider its being unconditionally operational (*tanjiz*) as obligatory and do not permit its being made contingent on a future event.[17] Therefore, if a person says, "When I die, this property will become an endowment," it will not become a endowment after his or her death. But if he or she says, "After my death make this property an endowment," it will be considered a will for creating a endowment and the executor of the will will be responsible for creating the endowment.

6.3.3. THE FOUNDER

The schools concur that sanity is a necessary condition for the creation of a endowment. Therefore, an endowment created by an insane person is not valid, because the *Shariah* does not burden him with any duty and does not attach any significance to his decisions, words or deeds.

The schools also concur upon maturity as a necessary condition. This implies that a endowment created by a child, irrespective of his or her being discerning or not, is invalid, and neither is the guardian is entitled to create a endowment on his or her behalf, nor is the judge empowered to act as a guardian in this regard or to allow the creation of such an endowment. Some Jafari jurisprudents consider a endowment created by a child over ten years as valid, but most of them oppose this view.

An idiot is also incapable of creating a endowment, for it is a disposition of property and an idiot is not authorized to carry out acts of such a nature.[18] The Hanafis say that it is valid for an idiot to bequeath one-third of his wealth provided that the bequest is for charitable purposes, irrespective of whether it is in the form of a endowment or otherwise.[19]

6.3.4. THE INTENTION TO SEEK GOD'S GOOD-PLEASURE

There is no doubt that the intention to seek God's good pleasure (*niyyat al-qurbah*) for creating an endowment is necessary for its creation. Hence if a declaration signifying the creation of endowment is made by a person who is intoxicated, unconscious, or asleep, or is made in jest, the recital will be void, because of the principle of unchanged status of the ownership of the property.

The schools differ on the question as to whether the intention to seek God's good-pleasure is a necessary condition like sanity and puberty (so that if a founder makes an endowment for a worldly motive it would fail to be operative) or if it becomes operative without it.

The Hanafis say that intending God's good pleasure is a necessary condition and requires to be fulfilled, either presently or ultimately. That is, the property donated should necessarily be used for charitable purposes, either from the time of creation of the endowment or at a later date. In other words, when one makes a endowment for the benefit of some wealthy people presently alive, and after them, for the benefit of their destitute descendants.[20]

The Maliki and Shafiis observe that the intention to seek God's good-pleasure (*niyyat al-qurbah)* is not necessary in a endowment.[21] The Hanbalis state that it is necessary that endowment be made for a pious, spiritual purpose (for example, for the poor or for mosques, bridges, books, for relatives, etc.,) because the *Shariah* has created the institution of endowment for acquiring spiritual reward, otherwise the purpose for which it was incorporated in the *Shariah* is not achieved.[22]

From among the Jafari, the authors of *al-Jawahir* and *Mulhaqat al-urwah* observe that the intention of seeking God's good-pleasure is not a condition for the validity of endowment or for taking its possession. Rather it is essential for acquiring its spiritual reward. Therefore a endowment is completed without the presence of a spiritual motive.

6.4. FINAL ILLNESS RESULTING IN DEATH

An illness resulting in death or generally capable of causing it is called final illness (*marad al-mawt*).

All the schools concur that if a person in such an illness makes a endowment of his or her property, it will be valid and will be created from the bequeathable third, and if it exceeds this limit the consent of the heirs is necessary regarding the excess.

Summarily, all those conditions required of a seller, that is, sanity, puberty, maturity, ownership, absence of a legal disability, such as insolvency or idiocy, are also necessary for a founder.

6.5. ENDOWED PROPERTY

The schools concur that endowed property should fulfill all the conditions required of a saleable commodity that it should be a determinate article owned by the founder. Therefore the endowment of a receivable debt or an unspecified property (such as when the owner says 'a field from my property' or 'a part of it') or that which cannot be owned by a Muslim (for instance, swine) is not valid. The schools also concur that the endowed property should have a usufruct and must not be perishable. Hence that which cannot be utilized except by consuming it (that is, eatables) will not be valid as a endowment. To this class also belongs the endowment of usufruct. Therefore, if a tenant makes a endowment of the usufruct of a house or land which he has rented for a specific period, it will not be valid, because the notion of endowment as something in which the property is detained and its usufruct dedicated for a charitable purpose is not fulfilled here.

There is consensus as well regarding the validity of endowment of immovable property, that is, land, building, orchard, and so forth. All the schools, except the Hanafis, concur on the validity of endowment of movable property, such as animals, implements and utensils, for they can be utilized without being consumed. According to Imam Abu Hanifah, the endowment of movable property is not valid. But of his two pupils, Abu Yusuf and Muhammad, the former accepts the endowment of movable property provided it is attached to an immovable property (for instance, cattle and implements attached to an agricultural land) and the latter limits its validity to the weapons and horses used in war.[23]

The schools further concur that it is valid to make endowment of an inseparate share (*musha*) in a property (that is. an undivided half or one-fourth or one-third) except where it is a mosque[24] or graveyard, because these two are incapable of being jointly owned.[25]

According to the author of *Mulhaqat al-urwah*, a work on Jafari jurisprudence, the endowment of the following forms of property is not valid:

1. Mortgaged property
2. Property whose possession cannot be delivered (for instance, a bird in the sky and a fish in water, even if they are owned by the founder)
3. A stray animal

4. Usurped property which the founder or the beneficiary are unable to recover. However, if this property is made an endowment for the benefit of the usurper, the endowment is valid.

6.6. THE BENEFICIARY

The beneficiary (*al-mawquf alayh*) is the person entitled to the proceeds of the endowment property and its usufruct. The following requirements must be fulfilled by the beneficiary:

1. The beneficiary should exist at the time of the creation of the endowment. If the beneficiary is not living, the Jafari, Shafii and Hanbali schools consider the endowment as invalid, while the Maliki school regards it as valid. It is stated in *Sharh al-zarqani ala mukhtasar Abi Diya*, "An endowment in favor of a child to be born in the near future is valid, although it will become binding only on its birth. Therefore, if it is not conceived or miscarries, the endowment will become void."

According to all the schools, when the beneficiary ceases to exist, after having existed at the time of the creation of endowment, the endowment is valid (as when a person creates a endowment for his existing children and their future descendants). Regarding a endowment in favor of a fetus, the Shafii, Jafari and Hanbali schools consider it invalid, because a fetus is incapable of owning property until it is born alive. This principle is not negated by the allocation of a share in inheritance for an unborn child in anticipation of its birth and by the validity of a bequest in its favor, because these two instances have specific proofs for their validity. Furthermore, the allocation of a share in inheritance for an unborn child is meant to safeguard its right and to avoid the complications which would arise as a result of redistribution.

2. He should be capable of owning property. Hence it is neither valid to create a endowment nor to make a bequest in favor of an animal, as done by Westerners, especially women, who bequeath part of their wealth to dogs. Regarding the endowment of mosques, schools, sanatoriums etc., it is actually a endowment in favor of the people who benefit from them.

3. The purpose of the endowment should not be sinful (as it would be when made for a brothel, or a gambling club, pub, or for highwaymen). As to a endowment made in favor of a non-Muslim, there is consensus about its validity, in accordance with this declaration of God Almighty, "*God does not forbid you respecting those who have not waged war against you on account of your religion and have not driven you forth from your homes, that you show them kindness and deal with them justly. Verily, Allah loves the doers of justice*" (60:8).

The Jafari jurisprudent al-Sayyid Kazim al-Yazdi observes in the chapter on endowment of his book *Mulhaqat al-urwah*, "...Rather, it is also valid to create a endowment in favor of a *harbi* and to show kindness to him in order to encourage him to righteous conduct."

Al-Shahid al-Thani states, "A endowment in favor of non-Muslims is valid, because it is not sin and also because they are creatures of God and a part of humanity which has been honored by Him."[26]

4. The beneficiary should be specifically known. Thus a endowment created in favor of an unidentified man or woman will be void.

The Malikis say, "An endowment is valid even if the founder does not mention the purpose of the endowment. Hence if he says: "I dedicate this house of mine as endowment," without adding anything else, the endowment will be valid and its usufruct will be spent for charitable purposes.[27]

5. The Jafari, Shafii and Maliki schools observe that it is not valid for a founder to create a endowment for the benefit of his own person or to include himself among its beneficiaries, because there is no sense in a person transferring his property to himself. But if, for instance, he makes a endowment in favor of the poor and later becomes poor himself, he will be considered one of them, and similarly if he creates a endowment in favor of students and later becomes a student himself. The Hanafi and Hanbali schools, however, permit such a endowment.[28]

6.7. AN ENDOWMENT FOR THE PRESCRIBED PRAYERS

The invalidity of a endowment created for the founder's benefit reveals the invalidity of a large number of such endowments in the villages of Jabal (Lebanon) which have been created by their founders to meet the expenses of the prescribed prayers (*al-waqf alal-salat*) to be offered posthumously on their behalf. This is so even if we accept the validity of a proxy reciting recommended prescribed prayers (*mustahabb salat*) on behalf of the dead—aside from its validity with respect to the obligatory prescribed prayers (*wajib al-salat*)—because it is in fact a endowment in one's own favor.

6.8. DOUBT CONCERNING ENDOWMENT

The Jafari author of *al-Mulhaqat* observes that if a doubt arises as to which among two persons is the beneficiary, or which among two purposes is the intended object of the endowment, the solution is effected by drawing lots or by effecting a compulsory compromise (*al-sulh al-qahri*). Compulsory compromise means distribution of the usufruct among the two parties or purposes. If the purpose of the endowment is unknown and we do not know whether it is for a mosque or for the poor or for some other purpose, the endowment will be applied to charitable purposes. If a doubt arises as to which of two properties is subject of a endowment (such as where we know the existence of a endowment, but are not certain whether it relates to the founder's house or shop) resort will be made to drawing lots or to a compulsory compromise; i.e. a half of both the house and the shop will be treated as endowment.

6.9. CONDITIONS OF A FOUNDER AND HIS PRONOUNCEMENT

6.9.1. THE FOUNDER'S INTENTION

If an endowment is a gift and a charity, the founder is the giver of that gift and charity. It is obvious that any sane and mature adult free of financial disability is free to grant from his property whatever he wishes to anyone in any manner he chooses. It is stated in the Traditions, "People have been given full authority over their properties." Accordingly, the jurisprudents say, "The conditions laid down by the founder are like the words of the Lawgiver, and his pronouncements are like His pronouncements as regards the obligation of following them. Similar is the case of one who makes a vow (*nadhir*), one who swears an oath (*halif*), one who makes a will (*wasiyyah*) and one who makes a confession (*muqirr*)."29

Consequently, if the intention of the founder is known (that he or she had a specific intention and none else), it will be followed even if it is against the commonly understood meaning of his words. For instance, if we know that the founder intends by the words 'my brother' a particular friend of his or hers, the endowment will be given to the friend, not to his or her brother. This is because usage is valid as a means of determining one's intention, and where we already know the intention, the usage loses its significance. But if we are unaware of the intention, the usage is followed, and if there is no particular usage concerning it and nothing special is understood from the words of the founder, the literal meaning will be resorted to, exactly as in the procedure applied regarding the words of the Quran and the *Sunnah*.

6.9.2. THE PERMISSIBLE CONDITIONS

We had observed that a founder meeting all the conditions is entitled to lay down conditions of his choice. Here we mention the following exceptions.

1. A condition is binding and enforceable when it is contiguous to the creation of endowment and occurs along with it. Thus, if the founder mentions it after completing the deed, it will be null and void, because the founder has no authority over the endowment property after its ownership has passed on from him or her.

2. He or she may not lay down a condition which contradicts the nature of the contract (for instance, the condition that the ownership of the endowment property will be retained by him or her, so that he or she could pass it on as inheritance to his or

her heirs, or sell it, or gift it or rent it or lend it if he so intends). The presence of such a condition implies that it is and is not a endowment at the same time. Because the presence of such a condition abrogates the deed creating the endowment, the endowment will be left without a deed, while the presumption is that it is not executed without a deed. In other words, such a founder is similar to the seller who declares, "I sell this to you on the condition that its ownership will not be transferred to you and that its consideration will not be transferred to me." This is the reason why the jurists have concurred that every condition contrary to the contract, apart from being void, also nullifies the contract.

But the famous legist al-Sinhuri mentions in his compilation of select laws from Islamic jurisprudence that the Hanafis exclude mosques from the above rule. Hence a void condition does not nullify its endowment, while in endowments other than for mosques such a condition is void and also nullifies the endowment.[30]

3. The condition should not oppose any rule of the Islamic *Shariah*. For instance, it should not require the performance of a prohibited or the omission of an obligatory act. It is mentioned in the Traditions, "He who lays down a condition contradicting the Book of God Almighty, it will neither be valid for him nor against him."

Excepting the above-mentioned kind, all other conditions mentioned at the time of the deed that neither contradict its spirit nor any rule of the Book and the *Sunnah* are valid and their fulfillment is obligatory by consensus (for instance if the founder lays down the condition that a home is to be built for the poor from the agricultural produce of the endowment or if it is to be spent on the scholars, and so forth). Summarily, the founder, like anyone else, is required to base all his dispensations on the principles of logic and the *Shariah*, irrespective of whether they pertain to endowment or matters of diet, travel, and so forth. Therefore, if his act is in accordance with the *Shariah* and reason, it is obligatory to respect it, not otherwise.

6.9.3. THE CONTRACT AND THIS CONDITION

There is no doubt that a void condition, whatever its form, does not require to be fulfilled. It is also evident that a void condition which is contrary to the spirit of a contract nullifies the contract itself. Hence there is consensus regarding its being void in itself and its nullifying effect extending beyond itself, without there being any difference between endowment and other forms of contract in this regard.

The schools differ regarding a condition which is contrary to the Quran and the *Sunnah* without going against the spirit of the contract (for instance, when a person makes his house a endowment in favor of Zayd on condition that he perform forbidden acts in it or abstain from performing obligatory duties), as to whether the invalidity of this condition necessitates the annulment of the contract as well (so that the carrying out of the contract is not necessary, in the same way as fulfillment of the condition is not necessary), or if the invalidity would be limited to the condition.

According to the Hanafis,[31] the conditions which contradict the regulations of the Shariah are void, while the endowment is valid. It does not become void due to their invalidity, because an endowment is a charity and charities are not invalidated by void conditions.

The Jafari differ among themselves. Some among them observe that the presence of a void condition does not necessitate the annulment of the contract while others consider that necessary. A third group abstains from expressing any view.[32]

Our view here is that the invalidity of a condition which contradicts the precepts of the Quran and the *Sunnah* does in no manner entail the invalidity of the contract. The reason is that a contract possesses certain essentials and conditions, such as, the offer, its acceptance, the contracting party's sanity, maturity, and ownership of the subject of transaction, and its transferability. When these aspects of the contract are fulfilled, the contract is undoubtedly valid. As to the presence of void conditions, which have no bearing, immediate or remote, on the essentials and conditions of the contract but exist only marginally, their invalidity does not extend to the contract. Even if it is presumed that the invalidity of a condition creates a discrepancy in the contract—such as an uncertainty resulting in risk in a transaction of sale—the contract will be void in such a situation as a result of the uncertainty, not because the condition is void.

It has been mentioned that the jurisprudents divide the conditions into valid and invalid ones, and regard the fulfillment of the former as obligatory. They have also divided invalid conditions into those which contradict the spirit of the contract and those which do not, yet contradict the rules of the *Shariah*. They concur that the first kind is both invalid and invalidating, and differ concerning the second, some considering it as invalid without being invalidating, while others consider it both invalid and invalidating.

The jurisprudents then differ regarding many particular cases and issues as to whether they belong to the class of invalid conditions, and supposing that they do, as to whether they are invalidating as well. Here we shall mention a few of such cases.

6.9.4. THE OPTION TO REVOKE

According to the Shafii, Jafari and Hanbali schools, if a founder lays down a condition giving himself or herself the option for a known period to either confirm the endowment or revoke it, the condition is void along with the endowment, because this condition is contrary to the spirit of the contract. According to the Hanafis both are valid.[33]

6.9.5. INCLUSION AND EXCLUSION

According to the Hanbalis and the preponderant Shafii opinion, if a founder lays down a condition entitling him to exclude from the beneficiaries of the endowment whomever he or she wishes and to include others as beneficiaries, the condition is not valid and the endowment is void, because the condition is contrary to the spirit of the contract and invalidates it.[34] The Hanafis and the Malikis consider the condition valid.[35] The Jafari make a distinction between the right to include and the right to exclude. They state that if he or she lays down a condition stipulating an option to exclude whomever he or she wishes from the beneficiaries, the endowment is void, and if the condition is that he or she may include those who would be born in the future among the beneficiaries, it is valid, irrespective of whether the endowment is in the favor of his own children or those of someone else.[36]

6.9.6. FOUNDER'S MAINTENANCE AND THE PAYMENT OF DEBTS

The Jafari and the Shafii schools say that if one creates a endowment in favor of someone and includes a condition requiring the payment of his or her debts and the provision of the maintenance from the proceeds of the endowment, the endowment and the condition are both void.[37]

6.9.7. SONS AND DAUGHTERS

If an endowment is created in favor of sons, it will not include daughters, and vice versa. If it is created in favor of children, both are included and will equally share the benefit. If the founder states, "The male will receive twice the female's share," or "they will both share equally" or "the female will receive twice the male's share," or states, "the women that I have married will not have a share in it," all these provisions are valid, considering that they are conditions laid down by the founder. Research has not turned up any view which differs from what has been mentioned, excepting the one which Abu Zuhrah narrates from the Malikis.[38] There it is stated, "Consensus prevails among the Malikis that it is a sin to create a endowment in favor of sons to the exclusion of daughters, and to entitle someone to its benefit on condition of his or her abstinence from marriage; and some of them consider its sinful character the cause of its invalidity."

The Malikis also state, "The words of the founder will be understood according to the common usage and they are like the words of the Lawgiver with respect to the obligation of their observance. Indeed, it has been narrated from Umar ibn Abd al-Aziz that he made an effort to include daughters in endowments made in favor of sons, but he was not a Maliki. Apart from this, if his effort proves anything, it proves his compassionate and humanitarian disposition."

6.9.8. THE GRANDCHILDREN

In the same way as the jurisprudents differ concerning the validity of some conditions, as to whether the invalid ones are just void or are void as well as invalidating, they also differ concerning the meaning of certain words, and among such instances is the case where the founder says, "This endowment is in favor of my children," without making any further clarification. Here the question arises as to whether the words 'my children' includes grandchildren as well, and if they do, whether they include both the sons' and the daughters' children or the sons' children only.

The preponderant (*mashhur*) Jafari view is that the words 'my children' do not include grandchildren, although Sayyid al-Isfahani states, "The word 'children' includes both male and female grandchildren," and this is the correct view because that is what it means in customary usage, which is the criterion in this regard.

The author of *al-Mughni* has narrated from Ibn Hanbal that the word 'child' (*walad*) applies to one's sons and daughters and to the son's children, not to the daughter's children.

The Shafiis observe that the word 'child' includes both sons and daughters, but it does not generally include grandchildren. But the words *walad al-walad* (grandchild), according to them as well as the Hanafis, include both the sexes.[39]

The Malikis say that females are covered by the word *awlad*, but not by the phrase *awlad al-awlad* (children's children).[40] This view of the Malikis is self-contradictory, because both the word *awlad* and the phrase *awlad al-awlad* are derived from the same root, *w.l.d.* How can it include both the sexes when used singly and only males when used in a construct phrase?

6.9.9. THE MANAGEMENT OF AN ENDOWMENT

The guardian (*wilayah*) over endowment (*al-wilayah al-waqf*) is the authority granted to someone for managing, developing and utilizing the endowment and for applying its yield for its specified purpose. This guardianship is of two kinds: general and particular. The general guardianship is enjoyed by the *wa al-'amr*, and the particular one by any person appointed by the founder at the time of the creation of endowment or by *hakim al-shar'*.

The schools concur that the trustee (*mutawalfi*) should be an adult, sane, mature and trustworthy person. Rather, the Shafii and some Jafari jurisprudents include the condition of being just as well. In fact, trustworthiness and reliability (*wathaiqah*), along with the ability to fully administer the endowment, suffice.

The schools concur that the trustee is a trustee and is not liable except in the event of breach of trust and misfeasance. The schools, except the Maliki also concur that the founder is entitled to grant himself the authority of administering the endowment, either alone or along with another person, for life or for a fixed period. He or she is also entitled to give this authority to someone else.

According to *Fath al-bari*, Imam Malik has stated, "It is not valid for a founder to grant himself or herself the guardianship, for then it may become a endowment in one's own favor, or the passage of time may lead to the fact of its being a endowment being forgotten, or the founder may become insolvent and apply it for his or her own benefit, or he or she may die and his or her heirs may apply it for their own benefit. But if there is no fear of any of these conditions arising, it does not matter if he or she keeps its administration in his or her own hands.

The schools differ where the founder does not grant anyone this authority, to himself or someone else. The Hanbalis and the Malikis observe that the authority of managing the endowment will rest with the beneficiaries provided they are known and limited, otherwise the judge will exercise it.[41]

The Hanafis state that the guardian will remain with the founder even if he or she does not explicitly mention it.[42] The Shafiis differ among themselves, holding three opinions. The first opinion is that the guardian will rest with the founder, the second that it will rest with the beneficiaries, and the third that it will be exercised by the judge.[43] The preponderant view among the Jafari is that when the founder does not name the trustee the guardianship belongs to the judge, which he may exercise personally or appoint someone to it. Al-Sayyid Kazim,[44] and Sayyid al-Isfahani, observe, "This is correct in respect of public endowments, but as to private endowments it is for the beneficiaries to safeguard, improve, rent the endowment and realize its income without the judge's permission," and this has been the practice.

The Jafari say that if the founder retains the guardianship over the endowment for himself or herself and is not trustworthy, or gives it to a person of known impiety, the judge is not empowered to annul the guardianship of either the founder or the person appointed by him. This is mentioned by Allamah al-Hilli. Rather, the author of *al-Mulhaqat* observes that if the founder provides that the judge should have no say in the affairs of his or her endowment, it is valid, and if the person appointed by the judge to administer the endowment dies, this power will rest with the beneficiaries or just individuals from among Muslims.

The Hanafi author of *Fath al-qadir*[45] states, "If the founder retains the guardianship himself or herself, in the event of his or her being untrustworthy, the judge is bound to abrogate his or her authority. Similarly, if he or she provides that the ruler and the judge are not empowered to abrogate his authority and hand it over to another, the condition is void because it opposes the rule of the *Shariah.*"

It is difficult to reconcile this view with that of Abu Zuhrah[46] has narrated from *al-Bahr*, that a judge is not to be removed on grounds of impiety for in such a circumstance the trustee is better entitled to remain, because the administration of justice is a more elevated and sensitive job.

When the founder or judge has appointed a trustee, no one has any authority over him as long as he is fulfilling his obligatory duty. But if he falls short of his duty or breaches the trust reposed in him, so that his remaining would be harmful, the judge is empowered to replace him, though it is better that he appoint, as observed by the Hanbalis, a trustworthy and energetic person alongside the former.

If the person appointed by the founder dies, or becomes insane, or is affected by any other disability which renders him incapable, the guardianship will not return to the founder unless he or she had so stipulated at the time of executing the endowment contract. The Malikis permit its return to the founder, and he or she is also empowered to remove the trustee at his or her pleasure.

The Jafari and the Hanbalis state that if the guardianship is granted to two persons, they will act independently if so stipulated by the founder, and if one of them dies or becomes incapable of performing his or her duty, the other will singly perform the task. But if the founder provides that they act jointly and not individually, it is not valid for any one of them to act individually. Where there is no explicit provision in this regard, the founder will be understood to have meant that they should not act individually, and hence the judge will appoint another person and make him join the existing one.[47]

It has been narrated in *Fath al-qadir* from Qadi Khan al-Hanafi that where the founder grants the guardianship to two persons, if one of them provides in his or her will that his or her companion is entitled to exercise guardianship over the endowment, after he or she dies it becomes valid for the person alive to exercise guardianship over the whole endowment.

The author of *al-Mulhaqat* observes that if the founder provides a part of the benefits of the endowment for the trustee, the same will hold good irrespective of whether it is a large or a small amount, and if nothing is provided, he or she will be entitled to the compensation for a comparable job (*ujrat al-mithl*). This is in concurrence with what Madkur narrates in *Kitab al-waqf* regarding the Egyptian law.

The schools concur that the trustee appointed by the founder or the judge is entitled to appoint an agent for the achievement of any purpose of the endowment, irrespective of whether the appointing authority explicitly provides for it or not, except where it insists on his or her performing it personally.

The schools also concur that the trustee is not empowered to transfer the guardianship after him or her to another person where the original guardian prohibits it. Similarly, they concur upon the validity of his or her delegating the guardianship to someone else where he or she has been authorized to do so. But where the guardian has made no mention of this issue, either affirmatively or negatively, the Hanafis hold that he or she is entitled to do so, while the Jafari, Hanbali, Shafii and Maliki schools consider that he or she is not so entitled, and if he or she does delegate it, his or her act is null and void.

6.9.10. THE CHILDREN OF RELIGIOUS SCHOLARS

There exist in our times religious scholars who give the guardianship over endowments in their hands to their children and then to their grandchildren and so on until the day of resurrection. They hide their intention by using the words "...the most capable in order of capability from this lineage."

Questions have been raised in this regard. Is the intention of such an religious scholar, while transferring this authority to his progeny, the betterment of the endowment and society, or is it only for securing the private advantage of his descendants? Does the motivation of this idea come from moral sense, continence, piety and self-denial for the cause of the faith, or is it motivated by a wish to provide some booty for his descendants by selling and exploiting one's religion? Does such a person have knowledge of the future through which he knows that the most capable among his descendants would be better for the cause of Islam and Muslims than the most capable individual from someone else's descent?

Consequently, the question is asked, "Why does this religious scholar not take a lesson from the rift he has observed and witnessed between the children of the religious scholars and the people of the place where the endowment exists, as well as between the children themselves in determining 'the most capable' and their eventually concurring over the distribution of endowment as if it were inherited property?"

6.9.11. THE SALE OF AN ENDOWMENT

Are there actually causes which justify the sale of endowment property? What are these causes if they exist? And if such a sale is valid and takes place, what is the rule concerning the proceeds? May we replace it (the original endowment property) with something capable of fulfilling the objectives of the endowment, so that a new property takes the place of the old one and is governed by the rules applicable to it? We will discuss the opinions of the different schools in detail and this discussion will make clear the replies to these as well as some other questions.

Numerous views have been expressed in this regard and the clash of opinions visible here is not to be seen in any other issue of jurisprudence, or at least in the chapter on endowment. The author of *al-Jawahir* has dealt with the medley of conflicting opinions and we mention here a collection of his observations that the jurisprudents differ regarding the sale of endowment in a manner the like of which we do not generally encounter in any other issue of endowment. Some of them absolutely prohibit the sale of endowment, some others allow it under certain circumstances, while a group among them refrains from giving any opinion. Rather, the number of opinions expressed is so large that each jurisprudent has his own specific view, and there are instances where a single jurisprudent has expressed contradictory views in the same book; for example, the view expressed by him in the chapter on sale contradicts his opinion in the chapter on endowment. Sometimes contradictory ideas have been expressed in a single argument, so that that which is observed in the beginning differs from the observations at the time of conclusion. The author of *al-Jawahir* has recorded twelve different opinions and the reader will learn about the most important among them from the issues discussed below.

6.9.11.1. MOSQUES

The rule applicable to a mosque, in all the schools of Islamic law, differs from the rules applicable to other forms of endowment in a number of ways. Hence all the schools, except the

Hanbali, concur that it is not permissible to sell a mosque irrespective of what the circumstances may be, even if it lies in ruins or the people of the village or locality where it is located have migrated and the road to it is cut in such a manner that it is certain that not a single person will pray in it. Despite all this, it is obligatory that it remain in the same state without any change. The reason given for this is that the endowment of a mosque severs all links between it and the founder as well as everyone else except God Almighty, and, therefore, it is at times termed release from ownership (*fakk al-milk*) and at times liberation from ownership (*tahrir al-milk*). That is, earlier it was confined, while now it has become free from all constraints. Now when it is not the property of anyone, how can its sale be valid when it is known that sale cannot take place without ownership? Consequently, if a usurper utilizes a mosque by residing in it or cultivating it when it is a piece of land, although he be considered a sinner, he is not liable for any damages, because it is not owned by anyone.

It is noteworthy that its ceasing to be anyone's property precludes its ownership through sale or purchase, but this prohibition does not apply if its ownership is acquired through acquisition (*al-hiyazah*), like all other forms of natural bounties (*al-mubahat al-ammah*).

The Hanbalis say that if the residents of a village migrate from the locale of the mosque and it stands in a place where no one prays in it, or if it is too small for the number of people praying in it and its extension or building a part of it is also not feasible without selling a part of it, its sale is valid, and if it is not possible to draw any benefit from it except through sale, it may be sold.[48]

The opinion of the Hanbalis is similar in some aspects to the view expressed by the Jafari jurisprudent al-Sayyid Kazim, who observes in *Mulhaqat al-urwah* that there is no difference between the endowment of a mosque and its other forms.

Thus dilapidation, which justifies the sale of other forms of endowment property, will also justify the sale of a mosque. As to the 'release from ownership', it does not hinder its sale in his view so long as the property has value. The correct view, in our opinion, is that it is not valid to own a mosque through a contract of sale, though it is valid to do so through acquisition.

That which gives strength to the view expressed by this great jurisprudent, that there is no difference (between the various kinds of endowment), is that those who permit the sale of a endowment which is not a mosque if it is in a dilapidated condition, do so because in a dilapidated state the structure is either unable to fulfill the purpose for which it was endowed or loses the quality made by the founder as the subject of the endowment (such as where he endows an orchard because it is an orchard and not because it is a piece of land). This logic applies exactly in the case of a mosque as well, because the condition that it should be used as a place of prayer was what caused it to be made a endowment. Now when this condition is not being fulfilled, the property ceases in its use as a mosque. In such a situation, the rule applicable to a non-mosque endowment will also be applied here, in that it can be owned through any of the forms of acquisition of ownership, even if it be through acquisition.

6.9.11.2. PROPERTIES BELONGING TO MOSQUES

Generally mosques have assets in the form of endowments of shops, houses, trees or land, whose profits are utilized for the repairs and carpeting of mosques and for paying its attendants. Obviously, these forms of property do not enjoy the sanctity of a mosque and its merit as a place of worship, because there is a difference between a thing and the properties subject to it.

The two also differ with respect to the rules applicable to their sale. Therefore those who prohibit the sale of a mosque allow the sale of a mosque's assets because there is no causal connection according to the Divine Law considering that a mosque is used for worship, a purely spiritual activity, while the endowment of a shop (owned by a mosque) is destined for material benefit. Hence a mosque belongs to the category of public endowments—or rather it is one of the most prominent of its forms—while the properties owned by it are private endowments belonging specifically to it. Consequently, it is doubtlessly valid to sell endowment properties belonging to mosques, cemeteries, and schools, even if we accept the invalidity of the sale of a school or a graveyard.

But is it valid to sell the properties subject to a endowment unconditionally, even if there is no justifying cause such as its being in a dilapidated condition or dwindling returns—or is it necessary that there exist a justifying cause so as to be treated exactly like an endowment in favor of one's descendants and other forms of private endowment?

These properties are of two types. The first type is one where the trustee buys the property from the proceeds of the endowment, such as where a mosque has an orchard which the trustee rents out, or buys or builds a shop from its proceeds for the benefit of the endowment, or obtains a shop from charitable donations received. In such a situation, both sale and exchange are valid if beneficial, irrespective of whether there exists any justifying cause mentioned by the jurisprudents, because these properties are not endowment but only the proceeds or assets belonging to the endowment. Hence the trustee is free to deal with them in the interest of the endowment, exactly as he deals with the fruits of an orchard endowed for the benefit of a mosque.[49] An exception is where the religious judge supervises the creation of the endowment of a real estate bought by the trustee, in which case the real estate will not be sold unless there exists a cause justifying its sale. But where the trustee creates a endowment, it has no effect without the judge's permission, because the trustee is appointed for managing the endowment and its utilization, not for creating endowments.

The second type of property is one where the benefactors endow it as a endowment for the benefit of a mosque or school (as when a person provides in his will that his house, shop or land be made a endowment for the benefit of a mosque or school, or he himself makes a endowment of it). This kind of property is considered a private endowment and its sale is valid if the justifying causes, such as dilapidation or dwindling returns amounting to almost nothing, exist. But if they do not exist, it is not valid. While discussing the rule applicable to a mosque's mat, Shaykh al-Ansari says, "A difference has been made between what is 'free' property (e.g. a mat purchased from the income of a mosque; in this case it is valid for a trustee to sell it if it is beneficial, if it has fallen into disuse or even if it is still new and unused) and between what is part of a endowment in favor of the mosque (that is, a mat which a person buys and puts in the mosque, or the cloth used to cover the Kabah; the like of these are the public property of Muslims and it is not valid for them to alter their condition except in cases where the sale of endowments is valid)."[50]

Thus when it is valid for a trustee to sell a new mat of the mosque which he has purchased from its funds, it is without doubt valid for him to sell other such items, and that which indicates an absence of difference (between a mat and something else) is the Shaykh's own observation soon after the above quotation. There he states, "The rule applicable to baths and shops which have been built for income through letting them and the like, is different from the rule applicable to mosques, cemeteries and shrines."

Exactly similar is the following view of al-Naini, "Where a mosque is ruined or forsaken, in a manner that it is no longer in need of the income from its endowment and other sources, the income from endowments pertaining to it will be spent in worthy causes, though it is better that it be spent on another mosque."[51] Similarly, if the endowment is in favor of a certain school or hospital which lies in ruins, its income will be used for charitable purposes or for another institution of its kind.

6.9.12. ENDOWMENTS WHICH ARE NOT MOSQUES

We have referred to the opinions held by the different schools concerning mosques, and pointed out that the Jafari, Shafii, Hanafi and Maliki schools are opposed therein to the Hanbalis. But concerning endowments other than mosques, the Jafari have their own specific stand regarding their sale. We will first mention the views of the Hanafi, Hanbali, Maliki and Shafii schools and then deal separately with the opinion of the Jafari. Since the Hanbalis have allowed the sale of a mosque on the existence of a justifying cause, it is more in order for them to allow the sale and exchange of a endowment which is not a mosque, provided a justifying cause exists.

As to the Shafiis, they absolutely prohibit its sale and exchange even if it is a private endowment (that is, in favor of one's progeny) and even if a thousand and one causes exist, though they allow the beneficiaries to use up the private endowment themselves in case of necessity (that is, using a dried fruit tree as fuel, though its sale or replacement is not valid for them).

The Malikis[52] permit the sale of a endowment in the following three situations. First, where the founder stipulates its sale at the time of creation of endowment; here his condition will be followed. Second, where the endowment is a movable property and is considered unfit for its prescribed purpose; here it will be sold and the amount realized will be used to replace it. Third, an immovable property will be sold for the expansion of a mosque, road or cemetery. Apart from these its sale is not valid, even if it lies in ruins and is not being utilized for any purpose.

As to the Hanafis, according to Abu Zuhrah,[53] they allow the replacement of public and private endowments of all kinds except mosques. They have mentioned the following three situations in this regard:

1. That the founder should have specified it at the time of creation of endowment.

2. The endowment should fall in a condition of disuse.

3. Where replacement is more profitable and there is an increase in its returns, and there exists no condition set by the founder prohibiting its sale.

This was a brief account of the views of the Shafii, Hanbali, Hanafi and Maliki schools regarding a endowment which is not a mosque, and, as noticed, they, as against the Jafari, do not differentiate between private and public endowments—excepting mosques—from the point of view of their sale.

6.9.13. PUBLIC AND PRIVATE ENDOWMENTS

The Jafari divide endowments into two categories and specify the rules applicable to each one of them as well as their consequences.

Private Endowment: It is an endowment which is the property of the beneficiaries, i.e. those who are entitled to utilize it and its profits. To this category belong endowments in favor of one's progeny, religious scholars, or the needy, the endowments of immovable property for the benefit of mosques, cemeteries, schools, etc. It is regarding this category that there is a difference of opinion between the jurisprudents as to whether its sale is valid when the justifying causes are present or if it is totally invalid even if a thousand and one causes exist.

Public Endowment: It is a endowment for the common benefit of people in general, not for a specific group or class among them. To this category belong schools, hospitals, mosques, shrines, cemeteries, bridges, carvanserais of the past, springs and trees dedicated for the use of passers-by, because they are not meant for any specific Muslim individual or group to the exclusion of other individuals or groups.

The Jafari concur that these public endowments cannot be sold or replaced in any situation even if they are in ruins or about to be destroyed and fall into disuse, because, according to them, or most of them, they are released from ownership, i.e. gone out of the ownership of the earlier owner without becoming anyone's property. Thus on becoming endowment such a property becomes exactly like the free gifts of nature, and it is obvious that there can be no sale except where there is ownership. This is in contrast to private endowments which involve the transfer of ownership of the founder to the beneficiaries in some particular manner. Hence (in the case of public endowments), if the purpose of a endowment becomes totally impossible to achieve (such as a school which has no students and consequently no lessons can be held in it) it is valid to transform it into a public library or a conference hall.

We have already pointed out in the discussion on mosques that though they are precluded from being owned through sale, it is valid to own them through acquisition. We also said that the author of *Mulhaqat al-urwah* has criticized the jurisprudents on the basis that there is no difference between public and private endowments and that the reason justifying the sale of a private endowment also justifies the sale of a public endowment. He does not concede that a public endowment involves release and freedom from ownership, and there is no impediment to sale in his opinion even if it is accepted to be such, because, according to him, the factor justifying a thing's sale is that it should possess value.

However, we have some remarks to make about the opinion of the jurisprudents as well as that of the author of *al-Mulhaqat*. We reject the position of the jurisprudents on the ground that though the absence of ownership prevents ownership of a endowment through a contract of sale, it does not prevent its ownership through acquisition. Similarly, ownership by itself does not validate sale, because mortgaged property, which is certainly owned (by the mortgagor), cannot validly be sold without the consent of the mortgagee.

We reject the position of the author of *al-Mulhaqat* because possession of value by itself is not sufficient, for the un-owned gifts of nature, (such as fish in the water or the birds in the sky), though they possess value, cannot be sold (in that state). Therefore, as observed earlier, the only way of ownership is through acquisition.

6.9.14. CEMETERIES

We have already mentioned that cemeteries are public endowments like mosques and that the Jafari do not consider their sale valid in any situation, even if they are in ruins and their signs have been wiped out. I consider it useful to specifically discuss cemeteries in this chapter for the following two reasons.

1. The necessity of mentioning the rules in this regard, because there are numerous Muslim cemeteries which have been forsaken and are used for other purposes.

2. Usually there is a difference between cemeteries and other forms of endowments. This difference will become clear in the following discussion.

If we know about a cemetery that a person had donated his land for that purpose and it was used for burial, the rule applicable to public endowments will apply to it, and it will be reckoned among endowments whose sale is invalid, even if its signs have disappeared and the bones of the buried have decayed.

But if we know that the cemetery was previously an unused land not owned by anyone and the people of the village used it as a cemetery as is usually the case then it is not a endowment *ab initio*, neither public nor private; rather it will remain the common property of all and its acquisition is valid for anyone who takes the initiative. But if a corpse is buried in a part of it, both the opening of the grave and using it in a desecrating manner is not valid. But anyone can personally utilize any part of this land by either cultivating it or building upon it if it is without graves or there are old graves whose occupants' bones have decayed.

Using this land is valid for him, exactly like it is valid for him to use abandoned land or land whose original user has migrated and it has reverted to its previous state.

Where we are unaware of the history of a piece of land which is being used as a cemetery—i.e. as to whether it was an owned land which was endowed by the owner, so that it would be considered a endowment and governed by its rules, or if it was an ownerless land which the villagers later used for burying their dead—it will not be considered a endowment because the presumption is the absence of A endowment unless its existence is proved according to the *Shariah*.

Here one might say, "An endowment is proved if it is popularly known to be such. Therefore why cannot the endowment of a cemetery be similarly proved?" The reply is that if it is popularly known that a certain cemetery is a endowment and it has been narrated generation after generation that a particular person had endowed it for a cemetery, it would definitely be confirmed as a endowment. But if all that is widely held is that it is a cemetery, the sole knowledge of its being a cemetery is not sufficient to prove that it is an endowment. It could have been common land.

6.9.15. *A Subsidiary Issue*

If a person digs a grave for himself to be buried in it at the time of his death, it is void for others to bury in it another corpse even if there is extra space in the cemetery. But it is better to leave it for him, refraining from troubling a believer.

6.9.16. *Causes Justifying the Sale of Endowment Property*

We have already mentioned that Jafari jurisprudents concur that the sale of public endowments, such as mosques and cemeteries, and so forth, is not valid. But regarding private endowments (for example, the endowments made in favor of one's progeny, scholars, or the needy) there is a difference of opinion between them where there exists a cause justifying their sale. The following causes justifying the sale of private endowments have been mentioned by these jurisprudents.

1. Where there remains no benefit of any kind in the property from the viewpoint of the purpose for which it was endowed (e.g. a dried branch not yielding fruit, a torn mat fit only for being burnt, a slaughtered animal which can only be eaten), there is no doubt that this cause justifies sale.

2. Sayyid Abu al-Hasan al-Isfahani observes, "The articles, carpets, cloth coverings of tombs, and similar items cannot be sold if they can be utilized in their present state. But if they are not required in the location any longer, and their being there would only damage and destroy them, they should be utilized in a similar alternative place, and if such a place does not exist or exists but does not need them, they will be used for public benefit. But where no benefit can be derived from them except by selling them and their retention amounts to their damage and destruction, they will be sold and the proceeds used for the same place if it is in need of it. Otherwise, it will be used in any other similar place if possible or for public benefit."[54]

3. If a endowment is in ruins (such as a dilapidated house or an orchard which is not productive) or its benefit is so little as to be reckoned nonexistent, if its repair is possible it will be repaired, even if it entails its being rented out for years.

Otherwise, its sale will become permissible, provided its proceeds are applied for replacing the former property as mentioned below.

4. If the founder provides for the sale of endowment property in case of dispute between the beneficiaries, or dwindling profits, or any other reason which does not make an unlawful act, lawful and vice versa, his desire will be carried out.

5. Where dispute occurs between the beneficiaries of a endowment threatening loss of life and property and there is no way of ending it except through its sale, the sale is permissible and the amount realized will be distributed among the beneficiaries.

This is what the jurisprudents say using the argument of countering of a greater by a lesser harm. But it is obvious that it is not valid to remove harm from one person by shifting it to another, and the sale of the endowment entails loss to the succeeding generations of beneficiaries.

6. If it is possible to sell part of a dilapidated endowment property and repair the remaining part with the proceeds of the sale, such a sale is permissible.

7. If a mosque is ruined, its stones, beams, doors, and so forth will neither be treated in accordance with the rules applicable to the mosque itself, nor the rules applicable to fixed property endowed for the benefit of a mosque which forbid its sale except on the presence of a justifying cause. Rather, the rules applicable to them will be those which apply to the income of the mosque and its endowments such as the rent of a shop belonging to or endowed in favor of the mosque. In this regard the trustee is free to utilize it in any manner beneficial for the mosque.

6.9.17. THE SALE PROCEEDS OF AN ENDOWMENT

Where a endowment is sold on the presence of a justifying cause, how will the sale proceeds be used? Will they be distributed among the beneficiaries exactly like the income generated by the endowment, or is it necessary, if possible, to buy with these sale proceeds a similar property to replace the one sold?

Shaykh al-Ansari as well as many other religious scholars

observe that the rule applicable to the sale proceeds is the rule applicable to the endowment sold, in that it is the property of the succeeding generations. Therefore, if the sale proceeds are in the form of immovable property, it will take the place of the endowment sold. If it is cash, we will buy with it the most suitable replacement. The replacement does not require the reciting of a declaration for making it a endowment, because the fact that it is a replacement naturally implies that the latter is exactly like the former. Hence al-Shahid states, "The replacement is owned on the basis of the ownership of the replaced property, and it is impossible that it be owned separately."

Then Ansari observes at the conclusion of the discussion on the first cause validating the sale of a endowment, "If it is not possible to buy immovable property from the sale proceeds the money will be kept in the custody of a trustworthy person awaiting a future opportunity. If deemed beneficial, it is also permissible to do business with it, though the profits will not be distributed among the beneficiaries, as is done in the case of the income generated from the endowment. Rather the rule applicable here will be the rule applicable to the endowment itself because it is part of the property sold and not a true increase."

This is what Ansari has said. It is difficult to see the difference between the profits of the sale proceeds[55] of a endowment and the income generated from the endowment itself. Therefore, as the income of the endowment is distributed among the beneficiaries, it is appropriate that the profits from the sale proceeds invested be similarly distributed, although it may be said that the income from the endowment's immovable property does not belong to the class of the endowment property itself but is separate from it, whereas the profits from business are in the form of money which does not differ from it, and where there is a difference, the rule applicable will also differ. Whatever the case, if the mind is set to work, it finds a solution for every difficulty and doubt from a theoretical point of view. But, obviously, practice should be the criterion, and the tangible reality is that usage does not distinguish between the two situations, and therefore it should be resorted to.

Shaykh Naini observes, "If another property is purchased from the sale proceeds of the first property, the latter will neither take the place of the former nor will it be considered a endowment similar to the former. Rather it is exactly like the income generated from a endowment, and it is permissible to sell it without any justifying cause if the trustee considers its sale to be beneficial."[56]

6.9.18. SOME CURIOUS ENDOWMENTS

There are some curious and interesting historical endowments from the eras of the Mamluks and earlier Uthmanis such as the following:

An immovable property was endowed for providing grass for the mule ridden by the Shaykh of al-Azhar at that time.

A woman created a endowment of 3000 feddans (1 Egyptian feddan = 4200.833 sq. metre) for the benefit of the 'ulama' who followed Imam Abu Hanifah.

Some pasha endowed 10,000 feddans for covering the graves of his relatives with branches of palm and myrtle.

A person endowed parts of his wealth for the water-carriers of the city mosque.

Another created a endowment for the reciter of the Friday sermon.

A lady created a endowment for providing ropes for pails used for supplying water to a mosque.

An endowment for providing caftans and outer garments for old persons.

An endowment for incensing study sessions.

An endowment in Egypt whose income is to be used to buy young male servants to save them from the censure of their mistresses.[57]

In Homs there is a endowment for those who sight the new moon of the end of Ramadan. For this reason there is a multitude of claims of having sighted it in that region. There are also present endowments in some villages of Jabal Amil for providing shrouds for the dead.

7

INHERITANCE

7.1. RULES CONCERNING ESTATES

7.1.1. AN ESTATE

An estate (*al-tarikah*) comprises the following things: First of all, that which the deceased owned before his death in the form of:

a. tangible property,

b. debts,

c. any pecuniary right, that is, the right consequent to demarcation of ownerless vacant land with an intention of cultivating it, where he or she intends to cultivate ownerless vacant land and demarcates it by constructing a wall or something of the kind, thus acquiring a right to cultivate it in preference to others; or an option (*haqq al-khayar*) in a contract of sale; or the right of pre-emption; or the right of retaliation (*qisas*) for murder or injury, where he is a guardian of the victim (that is, if a person kills his son and then dies before retaliation, causing the right of retaliation to change into a pecuniary right payable from the murderer's estate, exactly like a debt).

Second, that which the decedent comes to own at his death, that is, compensation for unintentional homicide (*al-qatl al-khata*) where the heirs opt for compensation instead of retaliation. The rule applicable to this compensation is the one applicable to all other properties, and all those entitled to inherit, including husband and wife, will inherit from it.[1]

Third, that which the decedent comes to own after his death, like, for example, an animal caught in a net that he had placed during his lifetime and similarly where he is a debtor and his creditor relinquishes the debt after his death or someone volunteers to pay it for him. Also, if an offender mutilates his body after his death and amputates his hand or leg, compensation will be taken from him. All these will be included in the estate.[2]

7.1.2. DEDUCTIONS FROM AN ESTATE

Different types of deductions are made from an estate. Some of them are deducted from only a third of an estate and discussion regarding them has preceded in the chapter on wills. Some deductions are made from the whole estate and they too are of different types. Hence, if the estate suffices, they will be completely met and what remains of it after these deductions and the execution of the last will and testament will be for the heirs. All the schools concur on this. If an estate falls short of meeting these deductions, the more important among them will be given precedence over those of lesser importance. If anything remains after the preferred deductions are made, the next in order will follow. Otherwise only the deductions of higher preference will be covered. The schools differ regarding the order of preference of these deductions.

The Jafari state that the first deduction, before any other thing, is to meet the obligatory funeral expenses, such as expenses of bath ablution for the dead, shrouding, carrying the body and digging the grave, if required, irrespective of whether the decedent has made a will to this effect or not. Therefore, funeral expenses, according to them, are prior to debts, irrespective of the debts being related to the fulfillment of religious duties (*haqq Allah*) or to creditors (*haqq al-nas*). They bring proof in the words of Imam Jafar Sadiq, "The first thing which is deducted from the decedent's estate is the shroud (funeral expenses), then debt, then the will, and then the inheritance."

The Jafari jurists differ among themselves regarding the case where a creditor has a right over the estate itself, such as where the decedent dies after mortgaging his property with a pledgee, the property being all that he owned. Here, a group of jurists give the funeral expenses preference over the right of the pledgee, because of the general nature of the traditions which include the words of Imam Jafar Sadiq in which no difference has been made between pledged and unpledged properties. Other jurists give precedence to the right of the pledgee because the owner of the pledged property is forbidden by the *Shariah* to exercise his rights of ownership, and that which is forbidden by the *Shariah* is like that which is forbidden by reason.[3]

After meeting the funeral expenses, the repayment of debts will start, irrespective of their being *haqq Allah* or *haqq al-nas*, such as unpaid poor-due or the twenty percent tax (*khums*), pecuniary atonements, the returning of the *mazalim*,[4] the unperformed prescribed pilgrimage, and other similar religious and non-religious liabilities. All these debts are in a single category. Therefore, if all of them cannot be completely met from the estate, they will be covered pro rata as are the liabilities of an insolvent person,[5] allowing no exception to this except the poor-due or twenty-percent tax, provided these relate to the actual items of their incidence present, in which case the two will be preferred over other debts. But if these two are due (without the items of incidence being present), they will be treated as all other debts.

The major schools of Islamic Divine Law concur that funeral expenses are preferred over the debts payable from the estate before death. The Hanafi, Hanbali, Shafii and Maliki then differ among themselves in giving precedence to funeral expenses over debts relating to the estate, such as an article which the owner pledged before his death. The Hanafi, Shafii and Maliki schools say that those claims which are related to specific parts of the estate will be given precedence over funeral expenses.[6] The Hanbalis observe that funeral expenses will be preferred over all other claims and debts including a pledge, penal damages, etc.[7]

In short, according to all the schools, the funeral expenses have precedence over debts unrelated to specific items of the estate, and the Hanafi, Shafii and Maliki schools give priority to debts related to specific items of the estate over funeral expenses, while the Hanbali school gives priority to funeral expenses in this case. Some Jafari jurists favor the view of the first three schools, and others concur with the Hanbalis.

7.1.3. HEIRS AND THE DECEDENT'S ESTATE

The schools concur that the estate devolves on the heirs immediately after the death if there is no debt or will involved. They also concur that the remainder of the estate exceeding debts and bequests stands transferred to the heirs. The schools differ whether that part of the estate covered by debts and bequests will be considered transferred to the heirs or not.

The Hanafis state that the part which equals the value of debt will not be included in the property of the heirs. Consequently, if the complete estate is covered by debt, the heirs will not own anything from it. But they have a right to free the estate from the creditors by paying them their claim on the estate. If the estate is not totally covered by debt, the heirs will own the remainder.

The Shafiis and the majority of Hanbali jurists say that the heirs will come to own the indebted part of the estate, irrespective of whether the debt covers the whole estate or only a part of it. However, the debt will relate to the whole estate and the estate will be liable for it.[8]

The Jafari differ among themselves on the issue. The majority of them hold the opinion that the estate will be transferred to the heirs whether totally covered by debts or not. The debts will be linked to it in one of the various ways, like a claim of pledge, or like the claim of damages resulting from the crime of a slave, or linked directly in a way not resembling any of these two ways. In any case, a debt will not hinder the actual act of inheritance, although it hinders the right of disposal in regard to that which is covered by the debt. This opinion is close to the Shafii view.[9]

The result of the difference of opinion appears in the increase in the estate which takes place between the time of death and the time of repayment of the debt. According to the opinion of the Shafiis, the Hanbalis and most of the Jafari jurists, the increase belongs to the heirs and they will dispose it without any hindrance from the creditors and others. But according to the Hanafi view, the increase will be subject to the estate being linked to the debts payable from it.

7.2. CAUSE OF INHERITANCE AND IMPEDIMENTS TO INHERITANCE

7.2.1. THREE CATEGORIES OF INHERITANCE

    a. blood relationship (*al-qarabah*),

    b. marriage concluded by a valid contract, and

    c. *al-wila*

We can bring these three causes under two headings: consanguinity (*nasab*) and affinity (*sabab*). By *nasab* is meant blood relationship and sabab includes both marriage and *al-wila*. *Al-wila* is a bond existing between two persons which creates between them a relationship similar to *nasab*. Hence a person manumitting a slave becomes his *mawla* and inherits from the latter if he or she has no other heir. *Al-wila* with its different meanings and forms will not be discussed because it has no practical application today.

Blood relationship (*al-qarabah*) is established between two persons through legitimate birth when one of them is a direct descendant of the other (such as fathers how soever high, and sons how soever low), or when both of them are descendants of a third person (such as brothers and maternal and paternal uncles). Legitimate birth materializes through a valid marriage as well as through 'intercourse by mistake'. But the marital bond will not materialize except through a valid marriage between man and woman. There is no difference of opinion regarding mutual inheritance between husband and wife. The schools, however, differ concerning the right of inheritance of certain relatives. The Shafii and the Maliki schools deny them such a right and consider them exactly like strangers. These relatives are: daughter's children, sister's children, daughters of brothers, children of uterine brothers, all kinds of paternal aunts, uterine paternal uncle, maternal uncles and aunts, daughters of paternal uncles and the maternal grandfather. Therefore, if a person dies and has no relatives except one of those mentioned, the estate goes to the public treasury (*bayt al-mal*) and they will not receive anything, according to the Shafii and Maliki schools, because they are neither among the sharers (*dhawa al-furad*) nor among the residuaries (*asabat*).[10] The Hanafi and the Hanbali schools consider them capable of inheriting in the particular situation where there are no sharers and residuaries. The Jafari consider them capable of inheriting without this condition. Details will follow.

7.2.2. IMPEDIMENTS TO INHERITANCE

The schools concur that there are three obstacles to inheritance:

a. difference of religion

b. murder

c. slavery (not discussed because not applicable today)

7.2.3. DIFFERENCE OF RELIGION

There is consensus that a non-Muslim will not inherit from a Muslim.[11] The schools differ regarding a Muslim inheriting from a non-Muslim. 'He or she inherits,' say the Jafari; 'He or she does not,' say the Hanafi, Hanbali, Shafii and Maliki schools.

If one of the decedent's sons or relatives who is a non-Muslim becomes a Muslim after his or her death and after the distribution of the heritage between the heirs, he or she is not entitled to inherit by consensus. The schools differ as to whether he or she inherits if he or she becomes a Muslim after the death but before the distribution of the estate. He or she inherits according to the Jafari and the Hanbalis, and not, according to the Shafii, the Maliki and the Hanafi schools. The Jafari state that if there is a single Muslim heir, he or she will take the whose heritage and the conversion of another to Islam will not entitle him or her to inheritance.

7.3. AN APOSTATE

An apostate (*murtadd*) from Islam does not inherit in the opinion of the Hanafi, Hanbali, Shafii, and Maliki schools, irrespective of his apostasy being *an fitrah* or *an millah*[12] except if he or she returns and repents before the distribution of the estate. The Jafari observe that an apostate '*an fitrah*', if a male, will be sentenced to death without being asked to repent, and his wife will observe the waiting period of death from the time of his apostasy. His estate will be distributed even if he is not executed. His repentance will also not be accepted concerning the dissolution of his marriage or the distribution of his estate or the obligatory acts of his execution, although it will be accepted in fact and by God, as well as in regard to other issues such as the ritual cleanliness of his body and the validity of his acts of worship. Similarly, he may own after his repentance new properties acquired through work, trade, or inheritance.

An apostate '*an millah*' will be asked to repent. If he does so, he will have all the rights and obligations of Muslims. If he does not repent, he will be executed and his wife will observe the waiting period of divorce from the time of his apostasy. Then if he repents while she is undergoing the waiting period, she will return to him and his property will not be distributed unless he dies or is killed.[13]

A woman will not be sentenced to death irrespective of her apostasy being '*an fitrah*' or '*an millah*'. But she will be imprisoned and beaten at the times of the prescribed prayer until she repents or dies. Her estate will be distributed only after her death.[14]

7.3.1. INHERITANCE OF FOLLOWERS OF OTHER RELIGIONS

The Maliki and the Hanbali schools say that followers of different religions will not inherit from each other. Hence a Jew will not inherit from a Christian and vice versa, and similarly the followers of other religions.

The Jafari, Hanafi and Shafii schools state that they will inherit from one another because they are a single religious group, considering that all of them are non-Muslims. But the Jafari lay down a condition in the case of a non-Muslim inheriting from another of his kind, that there be no existing Muslim heir. Therefore, if such an heir is present, even though distant, his presence will prevent a non-Muslim heir, even if he is closely related, from inheriting. This condition is not relevant to the Hanafi, Hanbali, Shafii, and Maliki schools, because according to them, as mentioned earlier, a Muslim does not inherit from a non-Muslim.[15]

7.3.2. THE GHULAT

Muslims are unanimous in holding that the *ghulat* are polytheists (*mushrikun*) and do not belong to Islam and Muslims in any manner. The Jafari have been specially severe concerning the issue of the *ghulat* because a large number of their Hanafi, Hanbali, Shafii, and Maliki brothers have unjustly attributed to them the deviations of the *ghulat*. The Jafari jurists have unequivocally mentioned in their books on doctrine and law that the *ghulat* are *kafir*. Accordingly, Shaykh al-Mufid says, "The *ghulat* pretend to follow Islam. They are those who attribute divinity and prophethood to Ali ibn Abi Talib and his descendants through Fatimah bint Muhammad,[16] and exceed all limits and deviate from the mean concerning their excellence in the religion and the world. They are misguided unbelievers, whom Ali ibn Abi Talib ordered to be killed and burnt his descendants judged them as unbelievers and apostates from Islam."[17]

The Jafari jurists mention them in their legal works in the chapter on prescribed purification and consider them ritually impure. Their mention also occurs in the chapter on marriage, where it is observed that the marriage of Muslim women with them, as well as marrying their women, is unlawful, although the jurists permit marriage with women of the People of the Book. The mention of *ghulat* is also made in the chapter on *jihad* where they are considered polytheists in a state of war. In the chapter on inheritance, the jurists prohibit their inheriting from Muslims.[18]

7.3.3. ONE WHO DENIES AN ESSENTIAL OF THE FAITH

There is consensus among the schools that a person who denies any of the established and known doctrines of the faith and considers an unlawful as lawful or vice versa, making that his or her creed, leaves Islam and becomes an infidel. To this category also belongs one who attributes infidelity to the One God to a Muslim.[19]

7.3.4. HOMICIDE

The schools concur that homicide when intentional and without legal authority impedes inheritance. This is based on the Tradition, "There is no share in inheritance for a murderer." Moreover, since the murderer's act expedites inheritance, his intention will be frustrated. Apart from this, the schools differ. The Jafari observe that he or she who kills his or her relative as retaliation or in self-defense or on the orders of a just judge, or for similar other reasons justified by the *Shariah*, in these instances homicide is no obstacle to inheriting. Also, unintentional homicide (*al-qatl khata*) is no hindrance.[20]

The author of *al-Jawahir* states that the intentional act of a child and a lunatic is considered a mistake (*khata*). Similarly, a mistake includes a quasi-intentional act (*shibh al-amd*). An instance of a quasi intentional act is where a father beats his or her child with an intention of correcting him or her and the child dies as a result of the beating. Al-Sayyid Abu al-Hasan al-Isfahani writes, "Some of the causes which lead to death—like digging a well on a road, if a relative falls in it—the person having dug the well will inherit from him, although he will be liable to pay the compensation." Accordingly, there is no hindrance to the concurrence of the liability to compensation and inheritance.

Each one of the Hanafi, Hanbali, Shafii and Maliki imams has a separate opinion in this case. The opinion of Imam Malik concurs with the Jafari. The opinion of Imam Shafi is that unintentional homicide is an obstacle to inheritance, just like intentional murder. The same is the case where the murderer

is a child or a lunatic. The opinion of Imam Ahmad is that a
homicide that calls for punishment, even if of a monetary kind,
impedes inheritance. This excludes lawful killing, such as
killing for retaliation, or in self-defense, or in war, the killing of
a rebel at the hands of a just person—in all these cases he will
inherit. The opinion of Imam Abu Hanifah is that a homicide
which hinders inheritance is one which necessitates retaliation
or compensation or atonement. This includes *al-qatl al-khata*
but not *al-qatl bi al-tasbib* (where the accused is an indirect
cause of homicide) or homicide by a lunatic or a minor.[21]

7.4. DISTRIBUTION OF THE ESTATE

As pointed out earlier, inheritance results due to marriage
or consanguinity, and there is no difference of opinion that the
husband or wife has a share with all other heirs, the husband
being entitled to one-fourth when there are descendants and
one-half in their absence, and the wife to one-eighth in the
presence of descendants and one-fourth in their absence. The
schools differ concerning a daughter's offspring, whether
he/she is in the category of descendants whose presence is
capable of lowering the share of the spouse from its higher to
its lower limit or if his/her presence and absence has no effect.
Details of this will come while discussing the inheritance of
spouses.

There is again no difference of opinion that the distribution
of the heritage begins with the 'shares,' whose shares have
been determined by the Quran and that there are six kinds of
these shares. But the schools differ regarding the number of
shares entitled to these shares and regarding the residuaries
(those entitled to the remainder after the sharers have
received their shares).

The schools also differ about the capacity to inherit of a
daughter's children, uterine paternal uncles and aunts, and
maternal uncles, aunts and grandfather. We mentioned earlier
that these heirs fall in the category of distant kindred in the
classification adopted by the Hanafi, Hanbali, Shafii, and
Maliki schools, and the rules applicable to them differ from
those applicable to the sharers and residuaries.

7.4.1. THE SHARES AND SHARERS

A 'share' is a fixed portion of the heritage determined by the Quran. According to consensus there are six such shares: 1/2, 1/4, 1/8, 1/3, 2/3 and 1/6. Some have summarized it by saying, "1/3 and 1/4, and the double and half of each."

Half is the share of the only daughter if there is no son sharing with her. According to the Hanafi, Hanbali, Shafii and Maliki schools the son's daughter is like the daughter, while according to the Jafari she takes the place of her father. Half is also given to the only sister, either full or half on the father's side, if there is no brother sharing with her. A husband gets half if the wife has no offspring to inherit from her. One-fourth is the husband's share if the wife has a descendant and the wife's if the husband has no descendant. One-eighth is the share of a wife if the husband has a descendant. Two-thirds is the combined share of two or more daughters in the absence of male children, and of two or more sisters, full or consanguine, if there is no brother sharing with them. One-third is the share of the mother if the decedent has no male child, or brothers whose presence, as per the forthcoming details, prevents her from inheriting more than one-sixth. Two or more uterine brothers and sisters also inherit one-third. One-sixth is the share of the father and the mother in the presence of a child. The mother also gets one-sixth if the decedent has brothers. The same is the share of a single uterine brother or sister. The inheriting of one-sixth as sharers by the above three enjoys concurrence.

The Hanafi, Hanbali, Shafii and Maliki schools add to these sharers entitled to one-sixth, one or more son's daughters along with the daughter of the decedent. Hence if the decedent has a daughter and a son's daughter, the former will take half and the latter one-sixth. But if the decedent has two or more daughters and a son's daughter, the latter will be prevented from inheriting unless she has a male counterpart of her class, such as when she has a brother or, lower in order, her brother's son, i.e. the great grandson of the deceased. One-sixth is also given to the paternal grandfather in the absence of the father.

A grandmother, just like a mother, inherits a sixth if she is a paternal or maternal grandmother or mother of the paternal grandfather. Thus if she is the mother of the decedent's mother's father, she will not inherit. If two parallel grandmothers, such as the mother's mother and the father's mother are present together, the share of one-sixth will be equally divided between them.[22]

Some of the six different shares coexist with some others. Hence, a half can exist with a half (e.g. husband and sister, each receiving a half), with one-fourth (e.g. husband and daughter, she receiving a half and he one-fourth), with one-eighth (e.g. wife and daughter, the former getting an eighth and the latter a half), with one-third (e.g. husband and mother, where her share is not reduced by a brother, he receiving a half and she a third), and with one-sixth, (e.g. husband and the only uterine brother or sister, the former receiving a half and the latter one-sixth).

One-fourth can coexist with two-thirds (e.g. husband and two daughters, he receiving a fourth and they two-thirds), with one-third (e.g. wife and two or more uterine brothers or sisters, she receiving one-fourth and they one-third) and also with one-sixth, (e.g. wife and a single uterine brother or sister, the former receiving one-fourth and the latter one-sixth).

One-eighth can coexist with two-thirds (e.g. wife and two daughters, she receiving one-eighth and they two-thirds) and with one-sixth (e.g. wife and either parent in the presence of a child). Two-thirds can coexist with one-third (e.g. two or more consanguine sisters along with uterine brothers) and with one-sixth (e.g. two daughters and either parent). One-sixth can coexist with itself (e.g. parents in the presence of a child). Those shares which do not coexist are: one-fourth and one-eighth, one-eighth and one-third, and one-third and one-sixth.

7.4.2. THE RESIDUARIES

According to the Hanafi, Hanbali, Shafii, and Maliki schools, there are three types of consantinguous residuaries (*al-asabat*):[23] a residuary by himself (*asabah bi nafsiha*), a residuary through another (*asabah bi ghayriha*), and a residuary along with another (*asabah maa ghayriha*).

A 'residuary by himself' includes all males between whom and the decedent there is no intervening woman. The meaning of being such a residuary is that he is independent of others (in his right to inherit as a residuary) and that he is a residuary in all cases and situations. A 'residuary through another' and 'residuary along with another,' are residuaries in certain cases without being so in others, as will become clear later.

The 'residuaries by themselves' are the closest of residuaries and inherit in the following order:
the son,
then the son's son, howsoever low; he takes the place of his
    father,
then the father,
then the paternal grandfather, howsoever high;
then the full brother;
then the half brother by father;
then the son of the full brother;
then the son of the half brother by father;
then the full paternal uncle,
then the consanguine paternal uncle (who is father's half
    brother by grandfather),
then the son of the full paternal uncle,
then the son of the consanguine paternal uncle.

If some of them exist along with others, the son will supersede the father, in the sense that the father will take his share—which is one-sixth and the son will take the remainder as a residuary.

According to the Hanafi, Hanbali, Shafii and Maliki schools, the son's son will similarly supersede the father, and the father will supersede the paternal grandfather. They differ regarding the paternal grandfather as to whether he will supersede the brothers in inheritance or if they inherit jointly with him, so that all of them are considered as belonging to the same class. Imam Abu Hanifah observes that the grandfather will supersede the brothers and they will not inherit anything

along with him. The Jafari, Shafii and Maliki schools state
that they will inherit with him because they belong to his
class.

Among the residuaries, those related from both sides will
supersede those related from only one side. Hence a full brother will supersede a consanguine brother and the full brother's
son will supersede a consanguine brother's son. Similarly, in
the case of paternal uncles, the degree of their nearness (to the
decedent) is taken into consideration, and the nearest is preferred. Therefore, the decedent's paternal uncle supersedes his
father's paternal uncle, and he in turn will supersede the
grandfather's paternal uncle.

The following four female relatives are considered 'residuaries through another':
1. daughter or daughters,
2. son's daughter or daughters,
3. full sister or sisters,
4. consanguine sister or sisters.

It is known that all the above-mentioned inherit as sharers
in the absence of a brother.[24] One of them is entitled to a half,
and if more, to two-thirds, and if they have a brother they
inherit as residuaries—according to the Hanafi, Hanbali,
Shafii, and Maliki schools but not if they are alone, and will
share the heritage with him, the male receiving twice the
share of females.

As regards 'residuaries along with another,' they are full or
consanguine sister or sisters that inherit along with a daughter or son's daughter. Therefore, a sister or sisters inherit as
'sharers' if there is no daughter or son's daughter inheriting
along with them, and inherit as residuaries with a daughter or
son's daughter. Hence the daughter or the son's daughter will
take her share and the full or consanguine sister or sisters will
take the remainder, thereby becoming residuaries along with
the daughter.

After this explanation it becomes clear that a full or consanguine sister inherits in three different ways. She is a sharer
if she has no brother and the decedent no daughter, a 'resid-

uary through another' if she has a brother, and a 'residuary along with another' if the decedent has a daughter. The same applies in the case of two or more sisters. It also becomes clear that full and consanguine paternal uncles will not share in the heritage along with the daughter except in the absence of full or consanguine brothers and sisters.

The Hanafi, Hanbali, Shafii and Maliki schools concur that if there is a single residuary without any sharers, he will inherit the whole heritage, and in the presence of a sharer he will take the remainder after the sharer has taken his share. If there is no residuary, according to the Maliki and the Shafii schools, the excess will go to the *bayt al-mal*, and according to the Hanafi and the Hanbali schools it goes to the sharers by way of 'return' (*radd*), and the estate will not go to the *bayt al-mal* in the absence of sharers, residuaria and distant kindred.

The Jafari do not recognize these three different kinds of residuaria and limit the heirs to 'sharers' and 'residuaries' without differentiating between male and female residuaries. Hence, a single son is entitled to the whole estate. A single daughter and a single sister too are similarly entitled. They classify the heirs, both males and females, into three categories:

1. Parents and children, howsoever low.
2. Brothers and sisters (and their children), howsoever high, and grandparents, both paternal and maternal, howsoever high.
3. Paternal and maternal uncles and aunts and their children.[25]

Whenever there exists a male or a female heir in the higher category, it will prevent all others belonging to the lower category from inheriting, whereas in the opinion of all the other schools these different categories may combine and inherit together, and at times all the three categories may inherit together, such as a mother along with a uterine sister and a full paternal uncle, in which case the mother receives one-third, the sister one-sixth, and the uncle the remainder.

7.5. SHARING OF INHERITANCE

The six kinds of shares determined in the Quran at times equal the whole estate, such as two daughters along with parents (2/3 + 1/6 + 1/6). Here the question of *awl* and *tasib* does not arise, because the two daughters will take two-thirds and the parents one-third.

At times the total of the shares does not exhaust the whole estate, such as a single daughter, whose share is half, or two daughters, whose share is two-thirds. This in Hanafi, Hanbali, Shafii and Maliki schools results in *tasib*.

When the total shares exceed unity—such as when the husband, the parents and the daughter inherit together, the share of the husband, the daughter and the parents being one-fourth, one-half and one-third respectively—the estate cannot cover all the three shares together. This results in *awl. Awl* will be discussed below. As to *tasib*, it has been defined here as the sharing of inheritance by the residuaries along with the closely-related sharers (such as where the decedent has two or more daughters and no son, or where he does not have any children, but has one or more sisters, no brother, and a paternal uncle). Here, the Hanafi, Hanbali, Shafii and Maliki schools regard the brother of the decedent as an heir along with the daughter or daughters, and he receives one-half with the one daughter, and one-third if there are two or more daughters. Similarly, they regard the paternal uncle to be an heir along with a sister or sisters.

The Jafari state that *tasib* is void, and it is obligatory that that which remains after the sharers have received their shares be returned to the closely-related sharers. Hence, (in the above example) the whole estate, according to them, will be inherited by the daughter or daughters and the brother will receive nothing, and if the deceased has no child at all, but has a sister or sisters, they will inherit the whole estate to the exclusion of the paternal uncle, because a sister is nearer to the decedent than he and the 'nearer excludes the remote'.

This difference between the Hanafi, Hanbali, Shafii and Maliki schools and the Jafari originates from the tradition from Tawus. The Hanafi, Hanbali, Shafii and Maliki schools accept this Tradition while the Jafari reject it. The Tradition states, "Give the sharers their respective shares, and of what remains, the first in order is a male relative." It has also been narrated in another form, "And what remains is for the male relative."

Hence, the daughter being a sharer is entitled to half the estate. The brothers being the nearest male relatives of the decedent after her will be given the remaining half. Similarly, if the decedent has no children at all, and has a sister without any brother, the sister will take half as a sharer and the other half will be inherited by the decedent's paternal uncle, because he is the decedent's nearest male relative after his sister.

The Jafari do not endorse the veracity of the Tawus Tradition and reject its attribution to the Prophet because, according to them, Tawus is an unreliable (*daif*) narrator. Had they endorsed this Tradition they would have concurred with the Hanafi, Hanbali, Shafii and Maliki schools, in the same manner as the Hanafi, Hanbali, Shafii, and Maliki schools would have concurred with them if they had rejected this Tradition. After rejecting this Tradition's attribution to the Prophet, the Jafari negate *tasib*[26] on the basis of the Quranic verse, *"Men are entitled to a share of what the parents and near relatives leave, and women are entitled to a share of what the parent and near relative leave, whether it is little or more, a determined share"* (4:7).

Similarly, the inheriting of the whole estate by a single sister contradicts the explicit verse, *"If a childless man dies and he has a sister, her share is half of what he has left, and he shall be her heir if she have no child; then if there be two sisters, their share is two-thirds"* (4:176).

The Jafari give the following reply in regard to the first verse (4:11).

The Quran has determined the share of two or more daughters to be two-thirds and that of a single daughter as half; but it is necessary that there be another person so that the remainder after the deduction of the share could revert to him. The Quran does not specifically mention this person, and had it done that, there would have been no difference of opinion. The *Sunnah* also makes no mention of it, neither explicitly nor implicitly. Hence nothing remains to prove specifically to whom the remainder goes, except the following verse of the Quran, *"Some relatives are preferred over some others in the ordinance of God"* (33:6). It proves that the nearer relative is to be preferred to the more distant, and there is no doubt that one's daughter is more closely related to one than one's brother, because she is related to him directly while his brother is related to him through either parent or both of them. Therefore, in such a case, the remainder will revert to the daughter or daughters, to the exclusion of the brother.

The Hanafi and the Hanbali schools observe that if the deceased leaves behind a daughter or daughters and there exists none else from among the sharers and the residuaries,[27] the whole estate will devolve on the daughter, half as a share and the other half by 'return', and similarly on the two daughters, two-thirds as their share and the remaining by way of 'return'. If the verse does not prove the negation of the 'return' devolving on the sharers in this case, it will similarly not negate it in other cases, because a single proof is incapable of being broken into parts.

Furthermore, the Hanafi and Hanbali schools say that if the decedent leaves behind a mother and there are no other sharers and residuaries, she will take a third as a sharer and the remaining two-thirds by way of 'return'. If a mother can take the whole estate, it is similarly obligatory that the daughter be also entitled to it, because both of them belong to the class of sharers.

The Hanafi, Hanbali, Shafii and Maliki schools concur that if the decedent leaves behind his father and a daughter, the father will take one sixth as a sharer and the daughter will similarly take half as a sharer, and the remainder will revert to the father, despite the Quranic verse. Hence as the share determined by this verse does not negate the father's right to receive more than one-sixth, similarly the share determined in the verse will not negate the daughters' right to receive more than two-thirds nor a single daughter's right to the excess over half, especially after the shares of both the daughters and the father have been mentioned in the same verse and the same context.

The Quran says, "*And call two witnesses from among your men, but if there are not two men, then one man and two women*" (2:282). This verse explicitly states that a debt is proved by two male witnesses and also by the evidence of a male and two female witnesses. Some of the Hanafi, Hanbali, Shafii and Maliki schools consider it provable by a single male witness and an oath; rather, Imam Malik says that it is proved by the evidence of two women and an oath. Hence, as this verse does not prove that a debt is not provable by a single male witness along with an oath, similarly the verse relating to inheritance does not prove the invalidity of reverting the remainder to a daughter or daughters, and to a sister or sisters.

The Jafari reply in regard to the second verse (4:176), that the word *walad* is applicable to both a male and a female child, because it is derived from birth (*wiladah*), which includes son and daughter, and also because the common denominator between a person and his relatives is kinship, which is inclusive of males and females. The Quran has used the word *awlad* for children of both sexes. God charges you concerning your children,"...*to the male the like of the portion of two females....*" (4:11) "...*and it behooves not the All-merciful to take a child.*" (19:92).

As these verses show, the word walad, stands for 'child', irrespective of sex. "*O mankind, we have created you from a male and a female....*" (49:13) Accordingly, since a son prevents the brother from inheriting, a daughter will also prevent him. What has been said about the daughter's inheritance applies in the case of the sister as well. Apart from this, the Jafari have raised a number of objections against the Hanafi, Hanbali, Shafii and Maliki schools, bringing to their notice certain conclusions that follow logically from their thesis, which are as unnatural as they are opposed to analogical reasoning

(*qiyas*), which is practiced by these schools. Among these criti-
cisms is the one mentioned in *al-Jawahir*, that if the decedent
has ten daughters and a son, the son, in this case, will take one
sixth and the daughters the remaining five sixths. If in the
place of the son the decedent has a paternal uncle's son (i.e. if
he leaves behind ten daughters and a paternal uncle's son),
according to the rule of *tasib* the uncle's son will receive one-
third and the daughters two-thirds, and consequently the son's
position here is worse than that of the uncle's son!

   This is despite the fact that man has greater affection for
his children when compared to his brothers, and he sees in his
children, sons and daughters, an extension of his own existence. It is for this reason that we see individuals belonging to
the Lebanese families having only daughters changing their
school of jurisprudence from Hanafi, Hanbali, Shafii, and
Maliki to Jafari solely because they fear that their brothers
and uncles will become coheirs with their children.

   Presently, there are many Hanafi, Hanbali, Shafii, and
Maliki scholars thinking of forsaking the principle of *tasib* and
accepting the Jafari view concerning the inheritance of a
daughter, exactly as they have abandoned the view invalidating bequest in favor of an heir and have accepted the Jafari
view despite the consensus of the Hanafi, Hanbali, Shafii, and
Maliki schools regarding its invalidity.

7.6. SHARES EXCEED THE ESTATE

   Where the shares exceed the estate, *awl* is applied such as
where the decedent leaves behind a wife, parents and two
daughters (the shares being, the wife's one-eighth, the parents'
one third, the two daughters' two-thirds; here the estate falls
short of the sum of one-eighth, one-third and two-thirds
(27/24). Similarly, if a woman dies and leaves behind her husband and two agnate sisters, the share of the husband is one
half, and that of the sisters two-thirds. Here the estate falls
short of the sum of half and two-thirds (7/6). *Awl* occurs only if
the husband or the wife is present.

   The schools differ regarding the issue. Will the deficit, in
such a case, be diminished proportionately from the shares of

all the sharers, or will it be diminished from the shares of only some of them?

The Hanafi, Hanbali, Shafii and Maliki schools accept the doctrine of *awl*, the rule that all the shares will be diminished proportionately, exactly as the creditors' claims when the assets fall short of meeting them. Hence if the heirs are wife, parents and two daughters, according to these schools it will be an instance of *awl*. The obligation is met by dividing the estate into 27 parts, though it earlier comprised 24 parts. The wife will take 3/27 (i.e. her share becomes 1/9 instead of 1/8), the parents take 8/27 and the daughter 16/27. The Jafari do not accept the doctrine of *awl* and keep the corpus (in the previous example) fixed at 24 parts by diminishing the share of the two daughters. Hence the wife takes her complete share of 1/8 (which is 3/24), the parents take 1/3 (which is 8/24), and the remainder goes to the two daughters.

The Jafari always diminish the share of the daughters or sisters, and the shares of the husband, the wife and the parents remain unaltered because the daughters and the sisters have been assigned a single share and do not face a reduction from a higher to a lower share. They, therefore, inherit as sharers in the absence of a male heir and as residuaries in his presence. At times they are entitled along with him to less than what they are entitled to when alone. However, the share of the husband is reduced from a half to one-fourth, the wife's from one-fourth to one-eighth, the mother's from one-third to one-sixth, and in certain cases the father inherits one-sixth as a sharer. The share of none of them further diminishes from its determined minimum and nothing is reduced from it. Hence, when the shares exceed the corpus, a start will be made from this minimum limit and the remainder will go to the daughters or sisters.

Shaykh Abu Zuhra quotes Ibn Shihab al-Zuhri[28] as having said, "If it were not for the preference given to the *fatwa* of the just leader Umar ibn al-Khattab over the edict of Ibn Abbas, the observation of Ibn Abbas is worthy of being followed by every scholar and worthy of consensus over it." The Jafari have adopted the opinion of Ibn Abbas—may God be pleased with both of them—which is a good rule as pointed out by Ibn Shihab al-Zuhri who was an ocean of knowledge.

7.7. EXCLUSION

By exclusion (*hujb*) is meant the exclusion of some relatives from inheritance. *Hujb* is either exclusion from the actual inheritance itself (such as the exclusion of the grandfather by the father, which is called '*hujb al-hirman*' or prevention from a part of the inheritance (such as the reduction of the husband's share by a child from a half to one-fourth, which is called *hujb al-nuqsan*').

The schools concur that parents, children, husband and wife are not excluded by *hujb al-hirman*, and whenever present they will take their share from the inheritance and no impediment prevents them from it, because they are the nearest to the decedent, being related to him without any intermediary, while all others are related through an intermediary.

The schools concur that the son excludes brothers and sisters from inheritance, and, with greater cause, the paternal and maternal uncles. The son does not prevent the paternal grandfather and the maternal grandmother, in the opinion of the Hanafi, Hanbali, Shafii and Maliki schools, and the son's son in the absence of the son, is exactly like the son, inheriting as his father would have inherited and excluding in the same manner.

There is consensus among the schools that the father excludes the brothers and sisters from inheritance, as well as the paternal grandfather. But the maternal grandmother, according to the Hanafi, Hanbali, Shafii, and Maliki schools, inherits along with the father and takes one-sixth in the absence of the mother, and in the opinion of the Hanbalis the paternal grandmother inherits along with the father, i.e. her son. The Shafii, the Hanafi and the Maliki schools say that she will not inherit with him, because she is excluded by him.[29]

The Jafari state that the father is similar to the son and none of the grandparents inherit along with him, because they belong to the second category while he belongs to the first of the categories of heirs.

The Hanafi, Hanbali, Shafii and Maliki say that the mother excludes all kinds of grandmothers,[30] but does not exclude grandfathers, brothers or sisters, nor the full and agnate paternal uncles and aunts, and all of them share the inheritance with her.

The Jafari observe that the mother, like the father, excludes all kinds of grandparents, brothers and sisters. The Hanafi, Hanbali, Shafii and Maliki schools state that the daughter does not exclude the son's son, and two or more daughters exclude the son's daughters, except when they have a male counterpart. But a single daughter does not exclude the son's daughters. A single daughter or daughters exclude cognate brothers.

The Jafari say that a daughter is like a son and excludes the children's children, both male and female, and, with greater jurisdiction, the brothers and sisters.

The schools concur that a grandfather and brother exclude paternal uncles and aunts, and a child, male or female, brings down the husband's share from a half to one-fourth and the wife's share from one-fourth to one-eighth. The schools differ regarding the minimum number of brothers or sisters required to diminish the mother's share from one-third to one-sixth. The Malikis say that the minimum required to diminish her share is two brothers. The Hanafi, the Shafii and the Hanbali schools observe that two brothers or two sisters suffice.

The Jafari state that brothers do not diminish the share of the mother unless the following conditions are fulfilled.

1. There should be two brothers, or a brother and two sisters, or four sisters. Hermaphrodites will be considered sisters.

2. The absence of impediments to inheritance, such as homicide and difference of religion.

3. That the father be present.

4. The brothers should be either full or agnate.

5. They should have been born. Hence, unborn brothers do not exclude.

6. They should be alive. Hence, if one of them is dead, he will not exclude.

On the whole, the difference between the Hanafi, Hanbali,

Shafii and Maliki schools and the Jafari school is that the
Jafari prefer the nearer relative to the more distant, irrespective of his or her belonging to the same category (e.g. the son
supersedes the son's son, and the father supersedes the grandfather) or another category (e.g. the son's son supersedes the
brothers). They say that one who is related through both parents excludes his consanguine (agnate) counterpart on the
same side. Hence a full sister excludes a consanguine brother,
and a full paternal aunt excludes a consanguine paternal
uncle; but a full paternal uncle does not exclude a consanguine
maternal uncle, because they are not from the same side. The
Jafari do not discriminate between male and female heirs
regarding their right to inheritance. Therefore, in the same
way as the children's children represent the children in their
absence, the children of brothers and sisters represent their
parents in their absence.

The Hanafi, Hanbali, Shafii and Maliki schools do accept
the doctrine of preferring the nearer relatives to the more distant ones, though not totally. Rather, they lay down the condition of unity of class, i.e. the nearer one excludes another who
is related through him or her, except the uterine (cognate)
brothers, who are not excluded by the mother though they are
related through her, and similarly the great grandmother, who
inherits with the grandmother, i.e. with her daughter. But if
he/she is not related through another, he/she is not excluded;
e.g. the father, though he excludes the paternal grandfather,
does not exclude the mother's mother, and similarly the mother, though she excludes the maternal grandmother, does not
exclude the paternal grandfather. The uncles and aunts of the
decedent are preferred over the uncles and aunts of the decedent's father. Similarly, the grandparents of the decedent are
preferred over his/her father's grandparents. The nearer
grandmother excludes the more distant grandmother. All this
is due to the doctrine of the nearer being preferred.[31] These
schools also differentiate between male and female heirs.
Hence, the brothers of the decedent inherit with his daughters,
though they do not inherit with his sons. The brothers' chil-

dren do not inherit with the grandparents in the opinion of
these schools, as opposed to the Jafari.

7.8. THE RETURN

The question of 'return' (*al-radd*) arises only in the case of
the sharers, because their shares are fixed and determined. At
times they exhaust the whole estate (e.g. parents and two
daughters, the parents receiving one-third, and two-thirds
going to the two daughters), and on other occasions they do not
exhaust it (e.g. a daughter and the mother, the former receiving half and the latter one sixth). In the latter case, the question arises as to what is to be done with the remaining one-
third and to whom should we return it. In the event of there
being no specific shares for the heirs (such as brothers and
uncles, who do not inherit as sharers) the question of return
does not arise.

The Hanafi, Hanbali, Shafii, and Maliki schools say that
the excess of the sharer's shares is given to the residuaries.
Hence if the deceased has a single daughter she will take half
and the remainder goes to the father. In his absence, it goes to
the full or consanguine sisters because they are residuaries
with a daughter; and in their absence to the full brother's son;
and in his absence to the consanguine brother's son; and then,
in this order: the paternal uncle, the consanguine uncle and
the paternal uncle's son. In the absence of all of them, the
excess will be returned to the sharers in the proportion of their
shares, except the husband and the wife, as they are not entitled to the return. For example, if a decedent leaves behind
mother and a daughter, the mother will take one sixth and the
daughter half as their respective shares, and the remainder
will be given to them as 'return' by division into four parts, the
mother receiving one-fourth and the daughter three-fourths.
Similarly, if he leaves behind a consanguine and a uterine sister, the former will take the daughter's share and the latter
the mother's share.

The Shafii and the Maliki schools say that if there is no
residuary, the remainder, after the assignment of the sharers'

shares, will go to the *bayt al-mal*. The Jafari observe that the sharers are entitled to the remainder in proportion to their shares by way of 'return' if there exists no relative in their category. If such a relative exists, after the sharer takes his share the remainder will go to that relative (e.g. when the mother and the father are heirs, after the mother takes her determined share, the remainder shall go to the father). If there exists with a sharer a relative who does not belong to his category, the sharer will take his share and then also the remainder by way of 'return' (e.g. when the decedent is survived by his mother and a brother, she, after taking one-third as a sharer, will take the remainder by way of 'return,' the brother receiving nothing because he belongs to the second category, while she belongs to the first category). Similarly, if there exists a consanguine sister with a paternal uncle, she will inherit the first half as a share and the second half by way of 'return,' to the exclusion of the uncle, because he belongs to the third category while she belongs to the second category.

The Jafari do not give the 'return' to a uterine brother or sister in the presence of a consanguine brother or sister. Hence if the decedent is survived by a uterine and a consanguine sister, the former is entitled to one-sixth and the latter to a half (as sharer) as well as the remainder by way of 'return,' to the exclusion of the uterine sister. Yes, a uterine brother or sister is entitled to the 'return' if there is none belonging to their category, such as if the decedent is survived by a uterine sister and a consanguine paternal uncle, the whole estate will devolve on her to his exclusion, because he belongs to the third category, while she belongs to the second category.

The Jafari also do not entitle the mother to the 'return' in the presence of those who prevent her from inheriting in excess of one sixth. Hence if the deceased has a daughter and parents, and also brothers—who exclude the mother from inheriting one-third—the remainder will go only to the father and the daughter. But if there are no brothers to exclude the mother, the 'return' will be shared by the father, the daughter, and the mother in proportion to their shares.

It will be seen while discussing the inheritance of husband

and wife, that the Jafari entitle the husband and not the wife
to inherit by way of 'return' in the absence of all other heirs
apart from them.

7.9. THE INHERITANCE OF A FETUS, DISOWNED
AND ILLEGITIMATE CHILDREN

7.9.1. THE INHERITANCE OF A FETUS

If a person dies while his wife is pregnant, the distribution
will be postponed, if possible, until childbirth. Otherwise, a
share will be withheld for the child. The schools differ regarding the share to be withheld. The Hanafis observe that the
share of a single son will be withheld for the child in the womb,
because it is generally so and it is improbable that it should
fall short.[32]

Muawwad Muhammad Mustafa in *al-Mirath fi al-Shariah
al-Islamiyyah* and Muhammad Muhammad Safan, quoting
from *al-Sirajiyyah*, state that Imam Malik and Imam Shafii
have said that a share of four sons and four daughters will be
withheld.[33]

A child in the womb will inherit on condition of its being
born alive[34] and its mother giving birth to it in less than six
months—or even in six months, if her husband copulates and
dies immediately afterwards.[35] It is also necessary for the maximum gestation period not to expire after the death, in accordance with the difference among the schools regarding this
period, as already mentioned in the chapters on marriage and
divorce. Therefore, as per consensus, if the child is born after
the expiry of the maximum gestation period, he will not inherit.

7.9.2. THE CHILD DISOWNED BY THE FATHER

The schools concur that there will be no mutual inheritance
between the couple if the husband accuses the wife of adultery,
and between the child born thereafter and its father and paternal relatives. However, the child, its mother and maternal relatives will inherit mutually. While inheriting from the child, its
relatives through both parents and relatives through the mother enjoy the same status. Hence his full and uterine brothers

are considered equal in status. The Jafari observe that if the father takes back his accusation and accepts the child, the child will inherit from the father (*walad al-mulaanah*), but the father will not inherit from the child.

7.9.3. THE ILLEGITIMATE CHILD

The Hanafi, Hanbali, Shafii and Maliki schools concur that an illegitimate child (*walad al-zina*) is similar to a child disowned by the father, in all that which has been mentioned concerning the absence of mutual inheritance between the child and the father and the presence of such inheritance between the child and its mother.[35] The Jafari say that there is no mutual inheritance between an illegitimate child and its fornicatrix mother, in the same manner as there is no such inheritance between the child and its fornicator father, because there is a common impeding cause between the two, i.e. fornication.

7.10. THE MARRIAGE AND DIVORCE OF AN ILL PERSON

The Hanafi, the Shafii and the Hanbali schools say that marriage during illness is similar to marriage during health in respect of each spouse inheriting from the other, irrespective of whether the marriage is consummated or not. In this context an 'ill person' means one in his death-illness. The Malikis observe that if a marriage contract is concluded during the illness of either spouse, the marriage will be considered invalid except where it has been consummated.[36]

The Jafari state that if a person marries during death-illness and dies before consummation, the wife will neither be entitled to *mahr* nor inheritance from him. Further, he will not be entitled to inherit her if she dies before him, prior to consummation, and then he dies after her as a result of that illness. If a woman marries during death-illness, the rule applicable to a healthy woman applies to her concerning the right of the husband to inherit from her.[37]

The schools concur that if an ill person divorces his wife and dies before the completion of the waiting period, the wife will inherit from him irrespective of the revocability or irrevocability of the divorce.[38] They also concur that she will not inherit if he dies after the completion of her waiting period and before her marriage with another. The Malikis and the Hanbalis observe that she will inherit regardless of the length of time. The Hanafi and the Shafii schools state that after the completion of her waiting period she becomes a stranger and is not entitled to any share in the inheritance.[39]

This opinion is in accordance with the Islamic jurisprudential principles, because the marital bond snaps on the completion of the waiting period, making her marriage with others permissible, and every woman whose marriage with others becomes permissible does not inherit from her former husband. This principle cannot be departed from except on the presence of a Quranic verse or a confirmed tradition.

The Jafari say that if a husband divorces his wife during his death-illness in a revocable or irrevocable manner (as in the case of a triple, menopausal divorcee with whom marriage has not been consummated), and then dies before the completion of one year from the date of divorce, she will inherit from him if the following three conditions are fulfilled:

1. that his death be the result of the illness during which he divorced her;

2. that she should not have remarried;

3. that the divorce should not have been given on her demand.

7.11. THE FATHER'S SHARE IN INHERITANCE

Following are the different situations relating to the father's share in inheritance:

1. The schools concur that the father, in the absence of the mother, children, children's children, grandmothers and spouse, is entitled to the whole estate, though by relationship (*qarabah*) according to the Jafari, and through *tasib* according to the rest, i.e. the difference lies in naming the cause leading to inheritance, not in the actual inheritance and his share in it.

2. If a spouse exists with the father, he or she will take the

maximum share to which he or she is entitled and the remainder, as per consensus, will go to the father.

3. If there are with the father a son, or sons, or sons and daughters, or the son's son howsoever low, the father will take one-sixth and the remainder, as per consensus, will go to the others.

4. If there is a single daughter with the father, they will be entitled to a half and one-sixth respectively as sharers. The remaining one-third will return to him by way of *tasib* according to the Hanafi, Hanbali, Shafii and Maliki schools. Hence the daughter receives half as share, and the father the other half as share and 'return'. The father excludes the grandfathers, brothers and sisters, both paternal and maternal, irrespective of their being full, consanguine or uterine.

The Jafari observe that the remainder will return to the father and the daughter together, and not solely to the father. The remainder will be divided into four parts, the father receiving one part and the daughter three parts, because in every instance of 'return' in which two shares are involved, the remainder will be divided into four parts, and if three sharers are involved, it will be divided into five parts.[40]

5. If there are two or more daughters with the father, according to the Hanafi, Hanbali, Shafii and Maliki schools the daughters will take two-thirds and the father one-third.

The Jafari say that the father receives one-fifth and the daughters four-fifths, because the one-sixth which remains after they have taken their shares returns to all of them and not solely to the father, as mentioned in the preceding example.

6. If a maternal grandmother is present with him, she will take one-sixth and he the remainder, because in the opinion of the Hanafi, Hanbali, Shafii and Maliki schools a maternal grandmother is not excluded by the father.[41]

The Jafari observe that the father will receive the whole estate and the grandmother is not entitled to anything in any manner, because she belongs to the second category and he to the first.

7. If there are the father and mother together, she will take

one-third if not prevented from it according to the Hanafi, Hanbali, Shafii and Maliki schools, by two brothers or sisters, and by two brothers or one brother and two sisters or four sisters according to the Jafari, as mentioned while explaining *hujb*; the father will take the remainder. But if she is partially excluded by the brothers, her share will be reduced to one-sixth and the father will take the rest. A consensus prevails here.

A question might be appropriately raised here: Why do the Jafari not return the remainder to both parents, as is done by them if a daughter inherits with the father?

The reply is that both the father and the daughter are sharers when they inherit together, and when sharers inherit together each takes his determined share and the remainder 'returns' to all of them in proportion to their shares. In the present case, the father while inheriting with the mother inherits as a residuary and not as a sharer because there is no child present, whereas the mother inherits as a sharer, and whenever a sharer inherits together with a residuary the latter takes the remainder.[42]

8. If a daughter's son is present with the father, the father will take the whole estate and the daughter's son, according to the Hanafi, Hanbali, Shafii and Maliki schools, will get nothing because he is among the distant kindred.

The Jafari say that the father will receive one-sixth as his share and the daughter's son will take half as his mother's share. The remainder will return to both exactly in the manner mentioned in the fourth illustration pertaining to his inheriting with the daughter.

7.12. THE MOTHER'S SHARE IN INHERITANCE

Following are the different situations relating to the mother's inheritance:

The Jafari observe that the mother is entitled to the whole estate in the absence of the father, children, children's children and spouse. The other schools say that the mother will not receive the whole estate except in the absence of all sharers and residuaries, i.e. in the absence of the father, the paternal

316 Part Two: Economic Issues

grandfather, children, children's children, brothers, sisters, their children, grandfathers howsoever high, paternal uncles and their children. As to the presence of grandmothers, they do not prevent her from inheriting the whole estate, because all of them are excluded by her in the same manner as the grandfathers are excluded by the father. Similarly, maternal uncles and aunts do not prevent her from inheriting the whole estate, because they are related to the decedent through her and one who is related through another person is excluded by that person.[43]

If the situation mentioned in the first mode prevails along with the presence of a spouse, the spouse will take his/her maximum share and the remainder will go to the mother.

If with the mother are present a son, or sons, or sons and daughters, or son's son howsoever low, according to consensus she will take one-sixth and the remainder will be taken by the others.[44]

If a single daughter inherits with the mother and there are no other residuaries, such as the paternal grandfather, brothers, and paternal uncles, and no sharers, such as sisters and spouse, the mother will receive one-sixth and the daughter half as sharers, and the remainder, according to the Jafari, the Hanafi and the Hanbali schools, will be shared by both after dividing it into four parts, the mother receiving one part and the daughter, three parts.

The Shafii and Maliki schools state that the remainder will go to the bayt al-mal. It has been mentioned in al-Iqna fi hall alfaz Abi Shuja'[45] that if an orderly system of bayt al-mal does not exist, as when the ruler is unjust, the remainder will return to the sharers in proportion of their shares.

If there are two daughters inheriting with the mother in the absence of all other sharers and residuaries, as in the preceding illustration, the views expressed there apply here as well, except that the remainder here will be divided into five parts, one part going to the mother and the other four to the two daughters.

The case where she inherits with the father has been discussed in the preceding section regarding the father's share in inheritance.

Where she inherits with the paternal grandfather in the absence of the father, the Hanafi, Hanbali, Shafii and Maliki schools observe that the paternal grandfather will represent the father, and the rule is the same in both cases.

The Jafari say that the mother is entitled to the whole estate, to the exclusion of the grandfather, because he belongs to the second category and she to the first. As per consensus, the grandmothers, paternal as well as maternal, do not inherit with the mother and, similarly, the maternal grandfather too does not inherit with her. According to the Hanafi, Hanbali, Shafii and Maliki schools, none of the grandparents except the paternal grandfather inherit with the mother, and none of them inherit with the father except the maternal grandmother. But the Jafari do not consider grandparents capable of inheriting with either parent.

If a full or consanguine brother is present with the mother, she will, according to the Hanafi, Hanbali, Shafii and Maliki schools, take one-third as sharer and the remainder will go to the brother on account of *tasib*, and if there are with her two full or consanguine or uterine brothers or sisters,[46] she will take one-sixth and the remainder will be taken by the brothers, because she is excluded by them from inheriting more than one-sixth. According to the Jafari, she will take the whole estate by share and 'return', to the exclusion of the brothers.

If along with her are present a full or consanguine sister or two such sisters, the rule is like the case where a daughter or two daughters are present with her, as mentioned in the fourth and fifth case.

If a single uterine brother or sister is present with her and there exists no other sharer or residuary, he/she will take one-sixth and the mother, one-third, as sharers, and the remainder will return to them in proportion to their shares. If there are with her two or more uterine brothers or sisters, they and the mother will each take one-third as sharers and the remainder will be proportionately shared by them together, because that which remains after the sharers have been assigned their shares returns to them proportionately in the opinion of the Hanafi and Hanbali schools and escheats to the *bayt al-mal* according to the Shafiis and the Malikis. The Jafaris give the whole estate to the mother.

If a full sister and a consanguine sister are present with her, the mother will take one-third, the full sister half, and the consanguine sister one-sixth to complete the two-thirds (for her one-sixth and the full sister's half add up to two-thirds, the maximum which two or more sisters can inherit). The Jafaris entitle the mother to the whole estate.

According to the Maliki, Hanafi, Hanbali and Shafii schools, the presence with her of full or consanguine paternal uncles and aunts is like that of full or consanguine brothers with respect to inheritance and their respective shares.

Where there are with her a paternal uncle and a uterine sister, the mother will take one-third, the sister one-sixth, and the remainder will go to the uncle. Hence the uncle who, according to the Jafaris, belongs to the third category, inherits together with the sister who belongs to the second category and the mother who belongs to the first category. The Jafaris entitle the mother to the entire estate.

The Hanafi and the Hanbali schools observe that the husband will take half, the mother one-sixth, and the uterine brother one-third. The full brothers will receive nothing as they are residuaries and the inheritance is exhausted by the sharers alone. That is, every sharer takes his share and nothing remains for the residuaries.

The Maliki and the Shafii schools say that one-third will be distributed among the full and uterine brothers, a male receiving the share of two females.[47] The Jafari state that the whole estate goes to the mother.

If only a daughter's daughter is present with the mother, according to the Hanafi, Hanbali, Shafii and Maliki schools, the mother will take one-third as sharer and the rest as 'return' and the daughter's daughter will receive nothing. The Jafari say that the position of the mother with the daughter's daughter is similar to her position with the daughter, as mentioned in the fourth case.

The Hanafi, Hanbali, Shafii and Maliki schools observe that if the father and a spouse are present with the mother, the mother will take one-third of what remains after the spouse has taken his or her share, not a third of the undivided estate. The stated reason, as mentioned in *al-Mughni*, is that if she takes one-third of the original estate, her share will exceed the father's share. Al-Shaykh Abu Zuhrah says in *al-Mirathinda al-Jafariyyah*, "The father's taking half the mother's share appears far-fetched from the viewpoint of the intent of the Quranic verse." He means that on the basis of the mother's taking one-third from the original estate and not from the remainder, her share will be 8/24ths, the husband's share 12/24ths and the father's 4/24ths, which is half the mother's share. It is improbable for the verse to have intended such a result. But if she takes one-third of the remainder, her share will be 4/24ths and the father's will be 8/24ths, which is twice her share; this is more probable and possibly what might have been intended by the verse.

The author of *Kashf al-haqaiq* says that if the paternal grandfather is present instead of the father, he will not cause the mother to take one-third of the remainder; rather, she will take one-third of the original estate. Accordingly, this situation arises only when the father and a spouse are present with the mother, and other instances are not covered by it. The Jafari say that the mother is entitled to one-third of the original estate and not to a third of the remainder, irrespective of the presence of a spouse because the literal sense of the Quranic verse: "....*for his mother is one-third....*" proves that it is one-third of what the decedent has left, and this statement has not been restricted to a situation where a spouse is not present. Further, the rules of the *Shariah* are not derived by reasoning or by applying the criterion of improbability.

7.13. THE INHERITANCE OF CHILDREN AND GRANDCHILDREN

7.13.1. THE SONS

In the absence of the decedent's parents and spouse, a son is entitled to the whole estate, and similarly two and more sons. When the sons and daughters inherit together, a male receives twice a female's share. A son, as per consensus, excludes grandchildren, brothers, sisters and grandparents. There is consensus that a son's son is like a son in the son's absence.

7.13.2. THE DAUGHTERS

The Jafari observe that a daughter of two or more daughters, in the absence of the parents and spouse, will inherit the whole estate. A single daughter takes half as her 'share' and the other half as 'return', and similarly two or more daughters take two-thirds as their 'share' and the remainder as 'return', without anything going to the residuaries. The Hanafi, Hanbali, Shafii and Maliki schools say that full and agnate sisters are residuaries with daughter or daughters. This implies that a single daughter will inherit half of the estate as her share in the absence of a son or another daughter and that two or more daughters will inherit two-thirds as their share in the absence of a son. Hence if the decedent has a daughter, daughters, or a son's daughter, and also has a full or an agnate sister or sisters, if the decedent has no brother the sister or sisters will inherit the remainder as residuaries after the daughter or daughters have taken their share. A full sister is like a full brother in the application of *tasib* and in excluding an agnate brother's son and those who come after him in the order of residuaries, and an agnate sister is a residuary like an agnate brother and excludes a full brother's son and those residuaries who come after him.[48]

The Jafari state that none of the brothers or sisters inherit along with a daughter or daughters, nor with a son's daughter or a daughter's daughter, because a 'daughter', howsoever low, belongs to the first category of heirs, whereas brothers and sisters belong to the second. The Hanbali and the Hanafi schools state that if there is no sharer, residuary, or any other heir except daughters, they will be entitled to the whole estate, partly as a share and partly by the way of 'return'. But if the father is present with them, he will take the remainder after their share is given. If the father is not present, the remainder will go to the grandfather, and in his absence to the full brother, then to the agnate brother, then to the full brother's son, then to the agnate brother's son, then to the full paternal uncle, then to the agnate paternal uncle's son. When none of these residuaries and sharers (such as sisters) is present, the daughters take the entire estate even if the decedent has daughters' children, sisters' children, brothers' daughters, uterine brothers' children, paternal aunts of all kinds, uterine paternal uncles, maternal uncles and aunts, and maternal grandmother. The Maliki and the Shafii schools say: If the above-mentioned situation arises, a daughter or daughters will take their prescribed share and the remainder will go to the *bayt al-mal*.[49]

7.13.3. *CHILDREN'S CHILDREN*
The schools differ where the decedent is survived by children and grandchildren. The Hanafi, Hanbali, Shafii and Maliki schools concur that a son excludes both grandsons and granddaughters from inheritance. That is, the children's children do not inherit anything in the presence of a son. But, if the decedent leaves behind a daughter and son's children, if the son's children are all males or some males and some females, the daughter will take a half and the other half will go to the son's children, who divide it among themselves in the proportion of the male taking twice a female's share. If there are son's daughters along with a daughter, the daughter will be entitled to a half and the son's daughter or daughters to one-sixth and the remainder will go to the sister.[50]

If the decedent has two daughters and son's children, and there is no male among the son's children, the latter will not be entitled to anything. But if there is a male among them, the two or more daughters will take two-thirds and the remainder will go to the son's children, who divide it among themselves in the proportion of the male taking the share of two females.[51] A daughter excludes the children of another daughter in a manner similar to the exclusion of a son's son by a son.

The Jafari say that none of the grandchildren inherit in the presence of a single child, male or female, of the decedent. Hence if he leaves behind a daughter and a son's son, the entire estate will go to the daughter to the exclusion of the son's son.

If the decedent has no surviving children, male or female, though has children's children, the Hanafi, Hanbali, Shafii and Maliki schools concur that a son's son is like a son and represents him in excluding others from inheritance, in the application of tasib, etc. And if there are sisters inheriting with the son's son, the estate will be divided in the proportion of a male receiving twice a female's share. The Hanafi, Hanbali, Shafii and Maliki also concur that son's daughters are like daughters in the absence of daughters, in that a single son's daughter is entitled to half the estate, and if they are two or more they are entitled to two-thirds. Like daughters, they exclude uterine brothers from inheritance, and share the estate with the son's son, a male receiving twice a female's share, irrespective of whether the son's son is their own brother or their paternal uncle's son. To sum up, a son's daughter is similar to a daughter. In other words, the children of the decedent's son are exactly like his own children.[52]

According to the Shafii and the Maliki schools, daughters' children do not inherit anything irrespective of their sex, because they are considered as distant kindred. Hence if none among the sharers and residuaries exist, the daughters' children will be excluded from inheritance and the estate will go to the public treasury. The same applies to the son's daughters' children. The Hanafi and the Hanbali schools state that the son's daughters' children will inherit in the absence of sharers and residuaries.[53] The Jafari observe that the children's children represent the children in their absence and each among them takes the share of the child through whom he is related. Therefore, the daughter's children, even if several and males, are entitled to one-third, and the son's children, even if a single daughter, are entitled to two-thirds. They distribute their share among themselves equally if of the same sex, and if they differ then a male is entitled to twice a female's share, irrespective of their being son's children or daughter's children, and the nearer descendants exclude the remote ones. They inherit jointly with the decedent's parents and the 'return' reverts to the daughter's children, males or females, in the same manner as it does to the daughter. If the husband or the wife inherits with them, they are entitled to their minimum share.[54]

7.14. THE INHERITANCE OF BROTHERS AND SISTERS

7.14.1. BROTHERS AND SISTERS

In the opinion of the Hanafi, Hanbali, Shafii, and Maliki schools, brothers and sisters inherit in the absence of the son and the father,[55] and inherit jointly with the mother and daughters. According to the Jafari, they do not inherit except in the absence of parents, children and the children's children, male or female. Brothers and sisters are of three kinds:

1. full,
2. agnate (consanguine),
3. cognate (uterine).

7.14.2. FULL BROTHERS AND SISTERS

The following situations pertain to the inheritance of full brothers and sisters:

Where males and females inherit together and there does not exist along with them any sharer or residuary (i.e. in the absence of the father, mother, daughter, grandmother, son and son's son), they are entitled to the whole estate and distribute it in accordance with the rule that a male receives twice a female's share.

Where they consist of males, or males and females, and

there is along with them a uterine brother or sister, the uterine brother or sister will take one-sixth and the remainder will go to the full brothers and sisters, a male taking the share of two females. If there are two or more uterine brothers or sisters, they are entitled to one-third irrespective of their sex, with the remainder going to the full brothers and sisters.

Where the decedent has a full sister, she is entitled to a half as her share; if more than one, their share is two-thirds. If there does not exist along with a full sister or sisters a daughter or any uterine brothers and sisters, or *sahih* grandfathers[56] and *sahih* grandmothers, the remainder, according to the Jafari, will return to the sister or sisters.

The Hanafi, Hanbali, Shafii and Maliki schools say that the remainder will return to the residuaries who are: the full paternal uncle, and in his absence the agnate paternal uncle, in his absence the full paternal uncle's son, and then the agnate paternal uncle's son, and in his absence the remainder will return, according to the Hanafi and the Hanbali schools, to the sister or sisters because only the sharers are entitled to the return conditional on the absence of residuaries; but according to the Shafii and the Maliki schools the remainder will go to the public treasury.

To sum up, the position of full sisters is like that of daughters. A single sister takes a half, and two or more two-thirds, and if they inherit jointly with full brothers they divide the estate, with a male taking twice a female's share.

The Hanafi, Hanbali, Shafii and Maliki schools say that if the decedent has a full and an agnate brother, the former will inherit to the exclusion of the latter, and the agnate brother will take the full brother's place in his absence.

If the decedent has a full sister and one or more agnate sisters the full sister takes a half and the agnate sister or sisters one-sixth, except when there is also an agnate brother, in which case they are entitled along with their brother to a half, which they distribute in the proportion of a male taking twice a female's share.

If the decedent has full and agnate sisters, the full sisters are entitled to two-thirds and the agnate sisters receive nothing unless accompanied by an agnate brother, in which case they, along with their brother, are entitled to the remainder, which they distribute in the proportion of a male receiving twice a female's share. To sum up, a full brother excludes an agnate brother. A single full sister does not exclude agnate sisters. Full sisters exclude the agnate sisters from inheritance when not accompanied by a male counterpart. The Jafari state that full siblings exclude agnate siblings irrespective of their number and sex. Therefore, if the decedent leaves behind a full sister and ten agnate brothers, she will inherit to their exclusion.

If there is with a sister or sisters a daughter or two daughters of the deceased, the daughter or daughters will take their respective Quranic share of half or two-thirds, and the remainder, according to the Hanafi, Hanbali, Shafii and Maliki schools, will go to the sister or sisters. A son's daughter is exactly like a daughter in this respect. The Jafari observe that the whole estate will go to the daughter or daughters and the sisters will receive nothing.

7.14.3. AGNATE BROTHERS AND SISTERS

Agnate brothers and sisters take the place of full brothers and sisters in their absence, and the same rule applies to both. A single sister will receive a half and two or more sisters two-thirds; the principle of 'return' is similarly applicable to both in the manner mentioned earlier.

7.14.4. UTERINE BROTHERS AND SISTERS

Uterine brothers and sisters do not inherit in the presence of the father, the mother, the paternal grandfather, children, sons' daughters (i.e. the uterine brothers and sister are excluded by the mother, the daughter and the son's daughter). We have mentioned earlier while discussing the inheritance of the mother and the daughter that according to the Hanafi, Hanbali, Shafii and Maliki schools full and agnate brothers and sisters inherit with the mother and the daughter. Rather, if they are present along with daughters' children, it is only they, according to the Hanafi, Hanbali, Shafii and Maliki schools, who inherit by excluding the daughters' children, even if they are males. The uterine brothers and sisters are not excluded by the presence of full or agnate brothers and sisters, and a single uterine brother or sister inherits one-sixth. If more than one, they inherit one-third, irrespective of their sex, and, according to consensus, they share the inheritance equally, with a female receiving a share equal to that of a male.[57]

7.14.5. A SUBSIDIARY ISSUE

The author of *al-Mughni* observes that if there exists a full, an agnate and a cognate sister, the first will take a half, and the second and the third one-sixth, with the remainder returning to them in the proportion of their shares. This implies that the corpus be divided into five parts, the full sister taking three of them and the other two sisters one each. The Jafari say that the full sister will take a half and the uterine sister one-sixth, without the agnate sister receiving anything because of her exclusion by the full sister; the remainder will return solely to the full sister.[58] Here the corpus will be divided into six parts, five of them going to the full sister and one to the uterine sister.

7.14.6. CHILDREN OF BROTHERS AND SISTERS

The Hanafi, Hanbali, Shafii and Maliki schools say that an agnate brother excludes from inheritance a full brother's son, and the full brother's sons exclude the agnate brother's sons. As to the children of sisters of all kinds (full, agnate and uterine), the uterine brothers' children and the full and agnate brothers' daughters, all of them belong to the group of distant kindred who do not inherit anything in the presence of full or agnate paternal uncles and their children. In the absence of full or agnate uncles and their children, they are entitled to inherit in the opinion of the Hanafi and Hanbali schools, while according to the Shafii and Maliki schools they are not so entitled and are considered essentially incapable of inheriting and the estate escheats to the *bayt al-mal*.[59]

The Jafari state that the children of brothers and sisters of all kinds do not inherit in the presence of even a single brother or sister of any kind, and when no brother or sister is present, their children take their place, each taking the share of the person through whom he is related to the decedent. Hence, one-sixth is the share of the son of a uterine brother or sister, and one-third is the share of the children of uterine brothers when the number of the brothers is more than one. The remainder goes to the children of a full or agnate brother, the full brother's children excluding the agnate brother's children. Hence an agnate brother's son does not inherit with a full brother's son. The children of uterine brothers and sisters share the inheritance equally among themselves like their parents, while the children of agnate brothers and sisters share their inheritance with disparity, a male taking twice a female's share, like their parents. The higher in generation among the brothers' and sisters' descendants exclude those of the lower generation; hence a brother's grandson is excluded in the presence of a sister's daughter, in accordance with the rule that the nearer excludes the remote. The children of brothers, like their parents, inherit jointly with the grandparents in the absence of their parents. Hence a brother's or sister's son will inherit with the paternal grandfather, and similarly the great grandfather will inherit with the brother in the absence of the grandfather.

7.15. THE MATERNAL GRANDFATHER

The Hanafi, Hanbali, Shafii and Maliki schools observe that the maternal grandfather is included in the category of distant kindred who do not inherit in the presence of a sharer or residuary. Accordingly, the maternal grandfather does not inherit with the paternal grandfather, the brothers and sisters, the children of full or agnate brothers, the paternal uncles or their sons. When all of them are absent and there is no sharer present, according to the Hanafi and the Hanbali schools, the maternal grandfather is entitled to inherit. According to the Shafii and the Maliki schools, he is never entitled to any inheritance. The Jafari say that the maternal grandfather inherits with the paternal grandfather and with brothers and sisters of all kinds, and, likewise, he excludes paternal and maternal uncles and aunts of all kinds from inheritance, because he belongs to the second category of heirs, whereas they belong to the third. Hence if a maternal grandfather is present with a full paternal uncle, he takes the whole estate to the exclusion of the paternal uncle.

7.16. GRANDMOTHERS

There is consensus that the mother excludes from inheritance all kinds of grandmothers. The Hanafi, Hanbali, Shafii and Maliki jurists state that in the absence of the mother, her mother represents her and inherits jointly with the father and the paternal grandfather, taking one-sixth in their presence. Similarly, there is no difference of opinion concerning the maternal and paternal grandmothers inheriting jointly. According to the Hanafi, Hanbali, Shafii and Maliki schools, they are entitled to one-sixth, which they share equally among themselves.

The nearer grandmother excludes the more distant grandmother on her side. Hence the mother's mother excludes the latter's mother. The father's mother also excludes similarly. The nearer maternal grandmother (e.g. the mother's mother, prevents a remote paternal grandmother (e.g. the paternal grandfather's mother). The Hanafi, Hanbali, Shafii, and Maliki schools differ among themselves as to whether or not a nearer paternal grandmother, such as the father's mother, excludes a remote maternal grandmother, such as the maternal grandfather's mother.[60] According to the Hanbalis, the father's mother inherits with her son. Hence when they inherit together, she takes one-sixth and he the remainder. The Jafari say that if the maternal grandmother is present along with the paternal grandmother, the former takes one-third and the latter two-thirds, because the maternal grandfathers and grandmothers take one-third irrespective of whether they are one or more, dividing their share of the estate equally, and the paternal grandparents take two-thirds, whether one or more, and divide their share with disparity (a male taking twice a female's share).

7.17. THE PATERNAL GRANDFATHER

The Hanafi, Hanbali, Shafii and Maliki schools concur that the father's father represents the mother in her absence and inherits jointly with the son, like the father, although differing from the father in respect of his wife, the father's mother, because she does not inherit with the father, except in the opinion of the Hanbalis, but inherits jointly with the paternal grandfather, i.e. with her husband. The father also differs from the paternal grandfather in the case of both parents jointly inheriting with a spouse. Here, the mother inheriting jointly with the father and spouse receives one-third of the remainder after deducting the share of the spouse, and while inheriting jointly with the paternal grandfather and spouse she receives one-third of the original estate and not one-third of the remainder.

The Hanafi, Hanbali, Shafii and Maliki also concur that the paternal grandfather excludes from inheritance uterine brothers and sisters as well as the children of full and agnate brothers. These schools differ among themselves concerning whether the paternal grandfather excludes full and agnate brothers and sisters or if he inherits jointly with them.

Abu Hanifah observes that the paternal grandfather excludes all kinds of brothers and sisters from inheritance, exactly in the manner that they are excluded by the father. This is despite the fact that according to the Hanafi, Hanbali, Shafii and Maliki schools the maternal grandfather excludes none of the different kinds of brothers and sisters, because he is included, as mentioned earlier, among distant kindred.

The Maliki, Shafii and Hanbali schools and the two disciples of Abu Hanifah, Abu Yusuf and Muhammad ibn al-Hasan, state that full and agnate brothers and sisters inherit jointly with the paternal grandfather. The manner of their inheriting with him is that he will be given the greater of these two: one-third of the whole estate or a brother's share. Accordingly, if there exist a brother and a sister, he will receive equal to a brother's share and take two-fifths of the estate, and if there exist three brothers, he will take one-third because a brother's share will be one-fourth.[61]

The Jafari observe that the grandparents, brothers and sisters inherit together and belong to the same category. Hence if they exist together and are related to the decedent from the father's side, the grandfather and the grandmother will take the share of a brother and a sister respectively and the estate will be distributed with each male receiving twice a female's share. And if they are all related through the mother, they will distribute the estate with a male receiving twice the share of a female.

And if they exist together and are related to the deceased from either side—such as if there are with the maternal grandparents full or agnate brothers and sisters the grandfather or the grandmother or both together will inherit one-third and the brothers and sisters two-thirds.

And if the paternal grandparents exist along with uterine brothers and sisters, a sole uterine brother or sister will receive one-sixth; if they are more than one, they will be entitled to one-third, distributed equally among males and females, with the remainder going to the grandparents who distribute it with the grandfather receiving twice the share of the grandmother.

'Children' howsoever low, of brothers and sisters of all kinds, represent their parents in their absence while inheriting along with all kinds of grandparents, each one of them inheriting the share of the person through whom he or she is related.

7.18. THE INHERITANCE OF PATERNAL AND MATERNAL UNCLES AND AUNTS

The Hanafi, Hanbali, Shafii and Maliki say that aunts, both paternal and maternal, uterine paternal uncles and all kinds of maternal uncles and aunts do not inherit with full or agnate paternal uncles and their sons.[62] Hence if there exists a full or agnate paternal uncle or his son, all the above mentioned will be excluded from inheritance because they belong to the class of distant kindred, whereas he belongs to the class of residuaries, and according to them the residuaries supersede the distant kindred. Rather, the Shafii and the Maliki schools do not consider them capable of inheriting at all, as mentioned repeatedly above. A full paternal uncle inherits in the absence of full or agnate brothers and their sons, and not with full and agnate sisters, because though residuaries, they (the sisters) supersede the paternal uncle in the application of the doctrine of *tasib*. A full paternal uncle inherits jointly with the daughter and the mother, because the two inherit as sharers and he as a result of *tasib*, and when a residuary inherits jointly with a sharer, the sharer takes his share and what remains of the estate goes to the residuary. And if there is no sharer at all, the residuary receives the whole estate. Accordingly, if there are daughter's children or daughter's son's children with full or agnate paternal uncle or their sons, according to the Hanafi, Hanbali, Shafii and Maliki the whole estate will go to the uncle or his son to the exclusion of the daughter's children, even if there happen to be males among them. According to the Jafari the opposite applies and the whole estate is inherited by the daughter's children to the exclusion of the paternal uncle.

In the absence of a full paternal uncle, the agnate paternal uncle takes his place, and in his absence the full paternal uncle's son becomes entitled, and in his absence the agnate paternal uncle's son. As to the mode of inheritance of a full paternal uncle and those who take his place, he takes, as pointed out earlier, the whole estate in the absence of all sharers, and in their presence he takes the remainder. To sum up, a full or an agnate paternal uncle is exactly like a full brother, or an agnate brother in the absence of a full brother.

The nearer 'paternal uncle' will supersede the distant one. Hence the decedent's paternal uncle supersedes his father's paternal uncle, and the father's paternal uncle supersedes the grandfather's paternal uncle. Similarly, the full paternal uncle supersedes the agnate paternal uncle. In the absence of full and agnate paternal uncles and their sons, according to the Hanafi and the Hanbali schools, uterine paternal uncles, paternal aunts of all kinds, maternal uncles and maternal aunts become entitled to inherit. If one of them exists solely, he will receive the whole estate, and if they exist together, the agnates will receive two-thirds and the cognates one-third. Hence if the decedent is survived by a maternal uncle and a paternal aunt, the uncle will receive one-third and the aunt two-thirds. The uterine maternal uncles and aunts distribute the estate in the proportion of a male receiving twice the share of a female, despite the fact that the uterine brother's children distribute the estate by allocating equal shares to males and females.[63] The Jafari state that in the absence of the parents, children, children's children, brothers, sisters, brothers' and sisters' children and the grandparents, the uncles and aunts, both maternal and paternal and of different kinds, become entitled to the estate. Some among them inherit to the exclusion of some others, while others among them inherit jointly.

If there exist paternal uncles and aunts and there are no maternal uncles and aunts with them, then a single paternal uncle or aunt is entitled to the entire estate irrespective of whether he or she is a full, an agnate or a uterine uncle or aunt. If there exist two or more paternal uncles and aunts related similarly to the decedent, and they are all full or agnate, they will distribute the estate with the male taking twice the female's share. If they are all uterine, they will distribute it without any difference between males and females. But if the paternal uncles and aunts differ in the manner of their relationship with the deceased (some being full, some agnate and others uterine) then only the agnates among them will be excluded from inheritance by the full paternal uncles, for they inherit only in the latter's absence. The agnate paternal uncle and aunt will take the same share which the full paternal uncle and aunt would take if present. If full or agnate paternal uncles and aunts exist together with uterine paternal uncles and aunts, a sole uterine uncle or aunt will be entitled to one-sixth, and if more than one, they together will be entitled to one-third, sharing it equally without differentiating between the sexes.

If there exist maternal uncles and aunts but no paternal uncle or aunt, a sole maternal uncle will take the whole estate irrespective of his being full, agnate or uterine. If there are two or more maternal uncles or aunts who are similarly related to the deceased (i.e. they are all either full or agnate or uterine), they will distribute the estate equally among themselves, a male receiving an equal share with a female.

But if they differ in the manner of their relation with the deceased (i.e. some are full, some agnate and others uterine) only the agnates among them will be excluded by their full counterparts. Where the full or agnate maternal uncles or aunts inherit with their uterine counterparts, a sole uterine uncle or aunt will take one-sixth, and if more than one, they together will be entitled to one-third, sharing it equally without differentiating between the sexes, with the remainder going to the full or agnate maternal uncles and aunts who also share it equally without differentiating between the sexes.

If a paternal and a maternal uncle or aunt inherit together, the maternal uncle or aunt will take one-third irrespective of their being one or more, and the paternal uncle or aunt two-thirds irrespective of their being one or more. The maternal uncles and aunts will distribute their share of one-third as they distributed it while they were the sole heirs in the absence of paternal uncles and aunts, and the paternal uncles and aunts will also similarly distribute their share of two-thirds.

In the absence of all paternal and maternal uncles and aunts their children take their place, each of them taking the share of the person through whom he or she is related, irrespective of their being one or more. Hence if one paternal uncle has a number of children and another paternal uncle only one daughter, the single daughter will be entitled to a half and the children of the other uncle to the other half. The nearer from among the paternal or maternal side excludes the remote from its own side as well as from the opposite side. Hence a paternal uncle's son does not inherit in the presence of a paternal or a maternal uncle, except in the particular instance where a full paternal uncle's son is present with an agnate paternal uncle, when the whole estate goes to the paternal uncle's son. A maternal uncle's son does not inherit in the presence of a maternal or a paternal uncle. Hence if a paternal uncle's son is present with a maternal uncle, the entire estate goes to the maternal uncle, and if a maternal uncle's son is present with a paternal uncle, the whole estate goes to the paternal uncle.

Paternal and maternal uncles and aunts of the decedent and their children supersede in inheritance the paternal and maternal uncles and aunts of his father. Every child born to a nearer relative supersedes the remoter relative. Hence if a paternal uncle's son exists with the father's paternal uncle, the former is entitled to the estate, and similarly a maternal uncle's son when present with the father's maternal uncle, following the rule of the supersedence of the nearer relative.

If the husband, or wife, is present with paternal and maternal uncles or aunts, the husband or the wife will be entitled to his or her maximum share, the maternal uncles or aunts to one-third, irrespective of their number, and the remainder will go to the paternal uncles or aunts irrespective of their number. Hence the reduction of share is borne by the paternal uncle in all cases where the spouse is present along with the paternal and maternal uncles. Therefore, if the husband is present with a maternal uncle or aunt and a paternal uncle or aunt, the husband will take three-sixths, the maternal uncle or aunt two-sixths, and the paternal uncle or aunt one-sixth. If there is a wife, she will take three-twelfths, the maternal uncle or aunt four-twelfths, and the remainder of five-twelfths will go to the paternal uncle or aunt.

7.19. THE INHERITANCE OF THE SPOUSES

The schools concur that the husband and the wife inherit jointly with all other inheritors without any exception, and that the husband is entitled to half the wife's estate if she does not have any child, neither from him nor from another husband, and to one-fourth if she has a child, either from him or from another husband. They also concur that a wife is entitled to one-fourth if the husband has no child, neither from her nor from another wife, and to one-eighth if he has a child from her or from another wife.

The Hanafi, Hanbali, Shafii and Maliki schools observe

that here, by 'child' is meant only the decedent's own offspring or the son's child, irrespective of its sex. A daughter's child, on the contrary, does not prevent a spouse from taking his or her maximum share. Rather, the Shafii and the Maliki schools say that the daughter's child neither inherits nor excludes others because it belongs to the category of distant kindred.

The Jafari state that by 'child' is meant one's offspring as well as the children's children, irrespective of their being sons or daughters. Hence a daughter's daughter, exactly like a son, reduces the share of either spouse from the higher to the lower value.

If there are many wives, they will distribute their share of one-fourth or one-eighth equally among themselves. The schools concur that if a person divorces his wife revocably and then one of them dies during the waiting period of the divorcee, they will inherit from each other as if the divorce had not occurred.

The schools differ regarding the situation where there is no other heir except the spouse as to whether the remainder will return to the spouse or escheat to the *bayt al-mal*. The Hanafi, Hanbali, Shafii, and Maliki say that it will return neither to the husband nor to the wife.[64] The Jafari are divided on this issue into three groups, each having a different opinion.

The first view is that it will return to the husband and not to the wife. This is the preponderant opinion and the jurists have acted accordingly. The second view is that it returns to both the husband and the wife in all situations. The third view is that it returns to both in the absence of accessibility to a just imam, as is the case at the present, and it returns to the husband and not the wife in the presence of a just imam. This is the opinion of al-Saduq, Najib al-Din ibn Said, al-Allamah al-Hilli and al-Shahid al-Awwal, and their argument is that some Traditions say that it returns to the wife while some other Traditions say that it does not return to her; hence we consider the first group of Traditions to be applicable in the absence of a just imam and the second group of Traditions to be applicable in the event of his presence.

7.20. A MISSING PERSON'S PROPERTY

A missing person is one who has disappeared with no news of his whereabouts and it is not known whether he is alive or dead. We have discussed in the chapters on marriage and divorce about the rules applicable to his wife and her divorce after four years, and here we intend to discuss the distribution of his property as well as his right to inheritance if any relative of his dies during the period of his disappearance. It is obvious that the divorce of the wife after four years neither entails that his estate be distributed after this period nor that it shouldn't; rather, it is possible that the wife be divorced but the estate be not distributed because there is no causal relationship between divorce and death.

The schools concur that it is obligatory to delay the distribution of his estate so that a period of time passes after which he is not expected to be alive,[65] and the specification of this period is the prerogative of the judge and differs with circumstances. When the judge gives a ruling announcing his death, the surviving relative nearest to him as regards inheritance at the time of this announcement will inherit him, but not any of his relatives who has died during the period of his disappearance. If a relative of the missing person dies during the period of his disappearance in which there is no news of him, it is obligatory to set aside his share, which will be considered like the rest of his property until his actual condition is known or until the judge rules announcing his death after the period of waiting.

7.21. INHERITANCE OF PERSONS KILLED BY DROWNING, FIRE AND DEBRIS

Jurists of the major schools have discussed the issue of the inheritance of persons killed by drowning, fire, building collapse and the like. They differ regarding the inheriting of one of them from another in an obscure situation in which it is not known whose death among them took place earlier.

The Imams of the Hanafi, Hanbali, Shafii and Maliki schools have observed that none among them inherits from the other and the estate of each one of them will be transferred to the living heirs, excluding the heirs of the other decedent, irrespective of whether the cause of death, and the resultant ambiguity, is drowning, building collapse, murder, fire or plague.[66]

The Jafari jurists have done extensive work on this issue, and those of the last generation have sufficiently elucidated it by going into minute details which have not crossed the minds of the jurists of early and latter eras. Before going into the specifics of the inheritance of victims of drowning, building collapse, etc., they take up the more general issue of two incidents of known occurrence but of unknown sequence, in which the precedence of each to the other leads to different legal consequences. The latter day Jafari jurists view the issue of the inheritance of victims of drowning and the like as a particular case of a more general problem that is not limited to any single chapter or issue of jurisprudence, but relates to any two events of known occurrence but of obscure precedence and subsequence, irrespective of whether the two events relate to contracts, inheritance, crime, etc. Hence the problem includes two contracts of sale, one concluded by the owner himself with A regarding a particular article, and the second by his agent concerning the same article with B, it being unknown which of the two preceded the other so that the validity of the former and the invalidity of the latter contract could be ascertained. The problem thus concerns any two events in which the consequences of one event are dependent on the precedence of the other over it, where there is nothing to prove that the two events took place simultaneously or successively. Therefore, the issue of drowned persons or the like is not an independent issue. Rather, it is one of the many particular issues that come in the purview of a general rule. Thus we see that the Jafari religious scholars initially concentrate on elucidating the rule itself and then discuss. The issue of inheritance of victims of drowning and the like to see whether the general rule is applicable to them or if they are excluded from its application. There is no doubt that this manner of presenting the argument is more beneficial.

As the understanding of this rule depends upon the comprehension of two other closely-related principles, they will be explained to the extent necessary so as to grasp the said rule, although a discussion of these two principles is not less beneficial than that of the rule itself. These two principles are as follows: (a) The presumption of non-occurrence of an event whose occurrence is doubtful. (b) The presumption of delayed occurrence of an event known to have occurred.

7.22. THE PRESUMPTION OF NON-OCCURRENCE

Suppose you had a relative living abroad with whom you used to correspond. At one point he stopped writing to you and you did the same. After a long period of time it came to your mind that you should write to him. You wrote to him at his earlier address without the doubt troubling your mind that he might have died or moved to another place. What led you to pay no attention to the possibility of his death or change of his address? Similarly, we believe in the honesty and integrity of a person, and rely upon him by depositing with him our valuables. Then he acts in a manner which raises a doubt in our minds that he might have changed, yet, we, despite this doubt, continue to treat him in the past manner. The same rule applies to all correspondence, transactions and communications.

The secret here is that man is led by his nature to accept the continuity of an earlier situation until the contrary is proved. Hence if A is known to be alive and later a doubt arises about his death, the presumption accepted by human nature is to consider him alive until his death is known in some manner. This is what is meant by 'the presumption of non-occurrence of an event' whose occurrence has not been proved.

Hence, when we know that someone owes a debt for a particular sum and later claims having repaid it, the presumption is that he owes the debt until its repayment is proved. That is, we ought to know the payment of debt in the way that we know the fact of indebtedness, because knowledge is not annulled by anything except knowledge and a doubt arising after knowledge has no effect. Therefore, one who makes a claim which contradicts the earlier condition of something, the burden of proof rests on him to prove his claim, and he whose claim is in accordance with the earlier condition is only liable to take an oath. The gist of the above discussion is that the principle of presumption of non-occurrence of an event means the acceptance of an earlier existing situation until the contrary is proved.

7.23. THE PRESUMPTION OF THE DELAYED OCCURRENCE OF AN EVENT

If a judge has knowledge of A's being alive on Wednesday and of his being among the dead on Friday, without knowing whether he died on Thursday or on Friday and has no clue to determine the time of his death, how should he decide the issue? Should he rule that A died on Friday, or that he died on Thursday?

Three different periods are involved in this case: the period in which he was known to be living, i.e. Wednesday; the time at which he is known to be dead, i.e. Friday; the period between the two times, i.e. Thursday, in which he is neither known to be alive nor dead. The above principle requires that this intermediate period be considered similar to the period preceding it, not to the period subsequent to it. That is, the period of ignorance about his life will be regarded similar to the preceding period in which he was known to be alive. Hence we will remain on our knowledge of his being alive until the time of the knowledge of his death. The result is that his death will be presumed to have taken place on Friday. The same rule is applicable to every event of known occurrence in which a doubt arises regarding the time of its occurrence, provided that it is a single event and not a chain of events.

7.24. THE KNOWLEDGE OF OCCURRENCE OF TWO EVENTS WITH IGNORANCE OF THEIR ORDER OF SUCCESSION

Having explained the two principles concerning the pre-

sumption of non-occurrence of an event and the delayed occurrence of a single event, let us examine the general rule which
is the end of this discussion. The general rule concerns two
events known to have occurred in which the consequences of
each are dependent on its preceding the other, while there
exists total ignorance about the precedence of any one of them.
Among the instances when this problem arises are: the conclusion of two contracts, one concluded by the owner and the other
by his agent; the occurrence of a birth and the making of a gift
of property; the deaths of two mutual heirs none of whom is
known to have died before the other.

The application of this rule depends upon the judge's
knowledge of the time of occurrence of each one of the two
events or his ignorance about the time of occurrence of both
events or one of them. Hence three different situations arise:

Where the judge comes to know the time of occurrence of
both the events by examining the statements made by the parties to the suit or through circumstantial evidence. Here he
will rule in accordance with his knowledge.

Where the judge is ignorant of the precedence of one event
over the other, though he comes to know the time of occurrence
of one of them (such as, his knowing that a horse was sold on
June 2, without knowing whether or not it was defective on
June 1, to justify its return, or became such on June 3, to make
it unreturnable). Here the event whose time of occurrence is
known will be given precedence over the event whose time of
occurrence is unknown, because the presumption of delayed
occurrence of an event will not be applicable to an event whose
time of occurrence is known; this knowledge prevents the
application of the presumption to it. As to the event whose
time of occurrence is unknown, the presumption of delayed
occurrence is applicable to it because this principle is relied
upon in instances of ignorance.

To sum up, if two events take place one whose time is
known and the other whose time is unknown, the one whose
time is known will be considered as having occurred earlier
irrespective of whether the two events are of the same kind

(e.g. the death of two persons, or the conclusion of two contracts) or of different kinds.

Where the judge is ignorant of the time of occurrence of both the events, there is no rule capable of determining the precedence or subsequence of either event, because there are no grounds for applying the principle of presumption to one of them as opposed to the other. Therefore, the presumption of delayed occurrence of an event is applicable only where a single event has taken place, or where two events occur and the time of occurrence of one of them is known. But where both the events have no known time of occurrence and there is nothing to differentiate between the time of occurrence of the two, reliance on the principle of presumption becomes impossible.[67]

7.25. VICTIMS OF DROWNING AND BURIAL UNDER DEBRIS

At times, there are two close relatives who do not inherit from each other, for example, two brothers who have children—such a case does not come in the purview of our present discussion, for the inheritance of each is received by his own children, irrespective of his and his brother's death occurring simultaneously or successively.

At times, only one of the two decedents is entitled to inherit from the other (e.g. two brothers of whom only one has children). This situation is also outside our ambit of discussion (because the estate of the brother having children will be transferred to his children, and the estate of the childless brother will be transferred to his relatives, excluding the brother who has died along with him by drowning, fire, etc.). This is because a condition of inheritance is that the heir be known to live at the time of death of the person being inherited (while in the above case we have no knowledge of the brother having children being alive at the time of the childless brother's death).[68]

There are other cases where both are entitled to inherit from each other (e.g. a son and a father; two brothers who do not have surviving parents and are childless; a couple, where the heirs of some of them are not those of the other). This situation is the focus of our discussion, and the Jafari jurists lay down two conditions for the mutual inheritance of each from the other.

The deaths of both should be the result of a single cause, and should result specifically either by drowning or by being buried under fallen debris (such as where they are in a building which collapses upon them or in a boat which sinks with them). Hence if one of them dies by drowning and the other due to fire or the collapse of a building, or both die together in a plague or battle, they will not inherit mutually. Reportedly, the French law requires the unity of cause for mutual inheritance, but does not limit the causes to drowning and burial under debris, as observed by the Jafari; rather, in that law, mutual inheritance also takes place if the cause of death is fire.

The time of death of both should be unknown. Hence if the time of death of just one of them is known, only the one whose time of death is unknown will inherit.

To give an example, suppose a building collapses on a couple or a boat sinks with both aboard and during the rescue operations the husband is found taking his last breath at five o'clock. Two hours later the wife is found dead, and no one knows whether she died before, after or simultaneously with the husband. The time of death of the husband is known, while that of the wife is unknown. The principle of presumption of delayed occurrence of an event requires that the wife, whose time of death is unknown, inherit the husband whose time of death is known, while he is not entitled to inherit anything from her. Where the situation is reversed, the time of death of the wife being known and that of the husband remaining unknown, the husband will inherit not the wife. In other words, where the time of death of only one of them is known, the person whose time of death is unknown inherits from the one whose time of death is known, without the latter inheriting from the former. As the right to inherit is limited to the person whose time of death is unknown, there is no difference made in this situation by the cause of death, and the result is the same irrespective of whether the cause of death is drowning, fire, burial under fallen debris, epidemic or war.

But if the time of death of both is unknown, such as where the couple is found dead without the time of death of any of them being known, both are entitled to inherit mutually; that is, each inherits from the other. This difference between a situation where the time of death of one of two decedents is known and where the time of death of neither is known, has neither been reported from any foreign law, nor have I found it in the books of the early and latter Hanafi, Hanbali, Shafii and Maliki jurists nor the early Jafari jurists. This difference is only mentioned in the works of principles of jurisprudence of recent Jafari jurists.

To sum up, the Jafari limit the scope of mutual inheritance to the situations where the cause of death is either drowning or falling debris and where the time of death of both the decedents is unknown. Accordingly, if both die natural deaths, or by fire or are killed in battle, or as a result of a plague, etc., mutual inheritance will not take place, and the estate of each decedent will be transferred to his own living heirs without any of the two decedents inheriting from the other.

And where the time of death of only one of them is known, the decedent whose time of death is not known will inherit from the one whose time of death is known, without the latter inheriting from the former .

7.26. THE MODE OF MUTUAL INHERITANCE

The method applied in mutual inheritance is that it is first assumed, in the example given above, that the husband died before the wife. Consequently, her share of his estate is separated and her heirs inherit her property which existed while she was alive, along with her share of her husband's estate that was added to it. Then it is assumed that the husband died after the wife. Consequently, his share of her estate is separated and his heirs inherit his property which existed prior to his death, along with his share of the wife's estate which was added to it. None of the two will inherit from the property which each of them has inherited from the other. Hence, if the wife possessed 100 liras and the husband 1000 liras, the wife inherits from his 1000 and the husband from her 100 only, because if one of them inherits from the property which the other has inherited from him, it will lead to a person inheriting a part of his own property after his death! And it is impossible for a person to inherit a thing which he has left to be inherited by another. To sum up, if two mutual heirs die by drowning or being buried under falling debris, when neither the sequence of their deaths is known nor the time of death of one of them, according to the Jafari, each of them will inherit from the other from the property each owned prior to death.

7.27. ILLUSTRATIONS

A study of the above discussion will show that in many cases the Hanafi, Hanbali, Shafii and Maliki schools exclude women and those related through them from inheritance. The daughter's children, paternal aunts, uterine paternal uncles, the maternal grandfather, maternal uncles and maternal aunts are not entitled to inheritance in the presence of any of the residuaries who are relatives of the deceased through the father. A full, or agnate, brother's daughter does not inherit with her own brother, and similarly a paternal uncle's daughter does not inherit with her own brother. Had there not been an explicit mention in the Quran of the inheritance of daughter, agnate sister, or sisters, and uterine brothers and sisters, their situation would have been similar to that of other female relatives and those related through them.

According to the Hanafi, Hanbali, Shafii and Maliki system of inheritance, a woman inherits only where her share has been specifically mentioned in the Quran or where analogical reasoning leads to her being considered equal to a female sharer—such as where a son's daughter is considered equivalent to a daughter. Apart from this, women are deprived from inheritance. The Jafari have considered both males and females as equally entitled to inherit, and the following examples illustrate this.

Where the decedent has left behind a daughter and a full or an agnate brother: The Hanafi, Hanbali, Shafii and Maliki schools: Daughter: 1/2 Brother: 1/2. The Jafari: The whole estate goes to the daughter to the exclusion of the brother.

Where the heirs are a daughter and the mother: The Hanafi, Hanbali, Shafii and Maliki schools: Mother: 1/6 Daughter: 3/6. The remaining 2/6 will be taken by the paternal grandfather if present, otherwise by the full brother, in their absence by the agnate brothers, and so on in the descending order of residuaries. The Jafari: Mother: 1/4 Daughter: 3/4. The residuaries receive nothing.

Where the deceased is survived by the parents and daughter's children: The Hanafi, Hanbali, Shafii and Maliki schools: Mother (in the absence of a *hajib*): 2/6 Father: 4/6 The daughter's children receive nothing. The Jafari: Mother: 1/6 Father: 2/6 Daughter's children: 3/6.

Where a woman is survived by her parents and husband. The Hanafi, Hanbali, Shafii and Maliki schools: Husband: 6/12 Mother: 2/12 Father: 4/12. The Jafari: Husband: 3/6 Mother: 2/6 Father: 1/6.

Where the heirs are the parents and a wife: The Hanafi, Hanbali, Shafii, and Maliki schools: Wife: 3/12 Mother: 3/12. Father: 6/12. The Jafari: Wife: 3/12 Mother: 4/12 Father: 5/12.

Where the father and daughter inherit: The Hanafi, Hanbali, Shafii and Maliki schools: Father: 1/ 2 Daughter: 1/2. The Jafari: Father: 1/4 Daughter: 3/4.

Where the daughter and the paternal grandfather are present: The Hanafi, Hanbali, Shafii and Maliki schools: Daughter: 1/2 Grandfather: 1/2. The Jafari say that the daughter inherits the whole estate to the exclusion of the grandfather.

Where the decedent is survived by a wife, the mother, and the paternal grandfather that the Hanafi, Hanbali, Shafii and Maliki schools: Wife: 3/12 Mother: 4/12 Grandfather: 5/12. The Jafari: Wife: 1/4 Mother: 3/4 The grandfather receives nothing.

Where the decedent is survived by the paternal and maternal grandfathers: The Hanafi, Hanbali, Shafii and Maliki schools that the whole estate is inherited by the paternal grandfather with the maternal grandfather receiving nothing. The Jafari: Paternal grandfather: 2/3 Maternal grandfather: 1/3.

Where the decedent is survived by the maternal grandmother and the maternal grandfather that the Hanafi, Hanbali, Shafii, and Maliki schools: The whole estate is inherited by the maternal grandmother to the exclusion of the maternal grandfather. The Jafari: Maternal grandmother: 1/2 Maternal grandfather: 1/2.

Where the decedent is survived by the maternal and paternal grandmothers: The Hanafi, Hanbali, Shafii and Maliki schools: They will together inherit 1/6 which they will distribute equally, and the remainder will go to the highest in the order of residuaries, and in their absence it will revert to the grandmothers in the opinion of the Hanafi and Hanbali school and escheat to the *bayt al-mal* in the opinion of the Maliki and the Shafii schools. The Jafari: Maternal grandmother: 1/3 Paternal grandmother: 2/3.

Where the decedent leaves behind a son's daughter and a daughter's daughter. The Hanafi, Hanbali, Shafii and Maliki schools: The son's daughter is entitled to a half and the remainder is given to the residuary without anything being given to the daughter's daughter. The Jafari: Each one of them will take the share of the person through whom they are related. Son's daughter: 2/3 Daughter's daughter: 1/3.

Where the decedent leaves behind a daughter's son and a son's daughter: The Hanafi, Hanbali, Shafii and Maliki schools: The son's daughter gets a half and the remaining half goes to the residuary, without the daughter's son receiving anything. The Jafari: Daughter's son: 1/3 Son's daughter: 2/3.

Where the decedent leaves behind a daughter and a son's daughter: The Hanafi, Hanbali, Shafii and Maliki schools: Daughter: 3/6 Son's daughter: 1/6 The remainder goes to the residuary. The Jafari: The daughter takes the whole estate to the exclusion of the son's daughter.

Where the decedent is survived by two daughters and a

son's daughter: The Hanafi, Hanbali, Shafii and Maliki schools: Two or more daughters receive two-thirds and the remainder goes to the residuary, with the son's daughter receiving nothing. The Jafari: The whole estate goes to the daughters.

Where the decedent leaves behind two daughters, son's daughters and a son's son: The Hanafi, Hanbali, Shafii and Maliki schools: The two daughters receive two-thirds and the remaining one-third goes to the son's daughters and son's son who distribute it with a male receiving twice the share of a female. The Jafari: The whole estate goes to the two daughters without the son's children receiving anything.

Where the decedent is survived by a daughter and a full or agnate sister: The Hanafi, Hanbali, Shafii and Maliki schools: Daughter 1/2 Sister 1/2. The Jafari: The whole estate goes to the daughter and the sister receives nothing.

Where the decedent leaves behind 10 daughters and a full or agnate sister: The Hanafi, Hanbali, Shafii and Maliki schools: Sister: 1/2 10 daughters: 1/2. The Jafari: The 10 daughters are entitled to the whole estate without the sister receiving anything.

Where the decedent is survived by a daughter and a uterine brother: The Hanafi, Hanbali, Shafii and Maliki schools: The daughter receives a half as the sharer and the remainder goes to the residuaries. The uterine brother receives nothing. The Jafari: The whole estate goes to the daughter.

Where the decedent leaves behind a daughter, a full or an agnate sister, and a full or an agnate paternal uncle: The Hanafi, Hanbali, Shafii and Maliki schools: Daughter 1/2 Sister 1/2 The paternal uncle receives nothing. The Jafari: The daughter receives the whole estate.

Where the decedent is survived by a full or an agnate paternal uncle and a similar aunt: The Hanafi, Hanbali, Shafii and Maliki schools: The uncle receives the whole estate to the exclusion of the aunt. The Jafari: Uncle: 2/3 Aunt: 1/3.

Where the decedent leaves behind a daughter and a full or an agnate paternal uncle: The Hanafi, Hanbali, Shafii and

Maliki schools: Daughter: 1/2 Uncle: 1/2. The Jafari: The whole estate goes to the daughter.

Where the decedent is survived by a daughter, a full or an agnate paternal uncle's son and a uterine paternal uncle: The Hanafi, Hanbali, Shafii, and Maliki schools: Daughter 1/2 Uncle's son 1/2. The uncle receives nothing. The Jafari: The whole estate goes to the daughter.

Where the decedent leaves behind maternal uncles and aunts and a full or an agnate paternal uncle's son: The Hanafi, Hanbali, Shafii and Maliki schools: The paternal uncle's son receives the whole estate without the maternal uncles and aunts receiving anything. The Jafari: The maternal uncles and aunts will take the whole estate without the paternal uncle's son receiving anything. The method of distributing the estate between the maternal uncles and the maternal aunts has been mentioned earlier while discussing their inheritance.

Where the decedent is survived by a paternal uncle's daughter and a full or an agnate paternal uncle's son: The Hanafi, Hanbali, Shafii and Maliki schools: The whole estate goes to the paternal uncle's son without the paternal uncle's daughter receiving anything, even where she is the full sister of the paternal uncle's son. The Jafari: Uncle's daughter: 1/3 Uncle's son: 2/3.

Where the decedent leaves behind a maternal grandfather and a full or an agnate paternal uncle: The Hanafi, Hanbali, Shafii and Maliki schools: The paternal uncle takes the whole estate to the exclusion of the maternal grandfather. The Jafari: The whole estate is inherited by the grandfather to the exclusion of the paternal uncle.

Where the decedent is survived by a full or an agnate brother's son and five sons of another full or agnate brother. The Hanafi, Hanbali, Shafii and Maliki schools: The estate will be divided according to the number of sons and not as per the number of fathers. Hence the estate will be divided into six parts with each receiving one part. The Jafari: The estate will be divided into as many parts as there are fathers and not into as many parts as there are heirs; each will receive the share of the person through whom he is related to the deceased. Hence one brother's son will receive five-tenths and the other brother's five sons will together receive five-tenths, each getting one-tenth.

Where the decedent leaves behind a brother's son and a full or an agnate brother's daughter: The Hanafi, Hanbali, Shafii and Maliki schools: The male will inherit not the female, even though she is his full sister. The Jafari: They inherit jointly, the male receiving twice a female's share.

These examples are enough to give a complete picture of the intrinsic difference between the rules of inheritance of the Jafari and the rules of inheritance of the Hanafi, Hanbali, Shafii and Maliki schools.

8

WILL AND BEQUEST

The major schools concur regarding the legality of making a will and its permissibility in the Islamic *Shariah*. A will is a gift of property or its benefit subject to the death of the testator. A will is valid irrespective of its being made in a state of health or during the last illness, and in both cases the rules applicable are the same according to all the schools. A will requires a testator (*musi*), a legatee (*musalahu*), the bequeathed property (*musa bihi*), and the declaration (*sighah*) of bequest.

8.1. THE DECLARATION

No specific wording is essential for making a will. Hence any statement conveying the intention of gratuitous transfer of property or its benefit after the death of the testator is valid. Thus if a testator says, "I make a will in favor of so and so," the words indicate testamentary intention, without needing the condition 'after death' to be specified. But if he says, addressing the executor: "Give it," or "Hand it over to so and so," or when he says, "I make so and so the owner of such and such a thing" it is necessary to specify the condition, 'after death', because without this consideration his words do not prove the intention of making a will.

The Jafari, Shafii and Maliki schools observe that it is valid for a sick person who cannot speak to make a will by comprehensible gestures. Al-Shirani, in *al-Mizan*, narrates from Imam Abu Hanifah and Imam Ahmad Hanbal, the invalidity of making a will in this condition. In *al-Fiqh alal-madhdhib al-arbaah*[1] this opinion is ascribed to Hanafis and Hanbalis that if a person suffers loss of speech due to illness, it is not valid for him or her to make a will by gestures, unless it continues for a long period of time and he or she becomes dumb, settling down to communicating in familiar gestures. In that case, his or her gestures and writing will be considered equivalent to his or her speech.

Al-Shirani ascribes this opinion to Imam Abu Hanifah, Imam Shafi and Imam Malik that if a person writes his or her own will and it is known that it is in his or her handwriting, it will not be acted upon unless he or she has it attested. This implies that if a will written in his or her handwriting is found which he or she neither got attested nor made known its contents to people, the will will not be probated even if it is known to have been made by him or her.

Imam Ahmad Hanbal says that it will be acted upon, unless he or she is known to have revoked it. Researchers among the Jafari jurisprudents observe that writing proves a will, because the apparent import of a person's acts is similar to the import of his or her spoken statements, and writing is the sister of speech in the sense that both make known his or her intent; rather, writing is the superior of the two in this regard, and is preferable to all other evidence that proves intent.[2]

8.2. THE TESTATOR

There is consensus among all the schools that the will of a lunatic in the state of insanity and the will of an undiscerning child are not valid. The schools differ regarding the will of a discerning child. The Malikis, the Hanbalis, and Shafii, in one of his two opinions, observes that the will of a child of ten complete years is valid because the Caliph Umar probated it. The Hanafis say that it is not valid except where the will concerns his funeral arrangements and burial. And it is well-known that these things do not require a will. The Jafari are of the opinion that the will of a discerning child is valid if it is for a good and benevolent cause and not otherwise, because Imam Jafar Sadiq considered it executable only in such cases.[3]

According to the Hanafis, if a sane adult makes a will and then turns insane, his or her will is void if his or her insanity is complete and continues for six months; otherwise, it is valid. If he or she makes a will in sound mind and then develops a condition of delusion leading to mental derangement lasting until death, his or her will will be void.[4] The Jafari, Maliki and Hanbali schools are of the opinion that subsequent insanity does not nullify a will even if it continues until death, because subsequent factors do not nullify preceding decisions. The Hanafis, the Shafiis and the Malikis consider the will of an idiot as valid. The Hanbalis observe that it is valid in regard to property and invalid regarding children. Therefore, if he or she appoints an executor over them, his or her will will not be acted upon.[5] The Jafari state that the will of an idiot is not valid concerning his or her property and valid in other matters. Thus if he or she appoints an executor over his or her children, his or her will is valid, but if he or she wills the bequest of something from his or her property, it is void.

The Jafari are unique in their opinion that if a person inflicts injury upon himself or herself with an intention of suicide and then makes a will and dies, his or her will is void. But if he or she first makes a will and then commits suicide, his or her will is valid. The Maliki and the Hanbali schools regard the will of an intoxicated person as invalid. The Shafiis say that the will of a person in a swoon is not valid. But the will of a person who has intoxicated himself or herself voluntarily is valid. The Hanafi school is of the opinion that a will made in jest or by mistake or under coercion is not valid.[6] The Jafari observe that a will is not valid if made in a state of intoxication or stupor, in jest, by mistake, or under coercion.

8.3. THE LEGATEE

The Hanafi, Hanbali, Maliki and Shafii schools concur that a will in favor of an heir is not valid unless permitted by other heirs. The Jafari observe that it is valid in favor of an heir as well as a non-heir, and its validity does not depend upon the permission of the heirs as long as it does not exceed a third of the estate. The courts in Egypt earlier used to apply the opinion of the Hanafi, Hanbali, Maliki, and Shafii schools, but then switched over to the Jafari view. The Lebanese Hanafi, Hanbali, Maliki and Shafii *Shariah* courts continue to consider a will in favor of an heir as invalid. But since some years their judges have inclined towards the other view and have brought a bill to the government authorizing wills in favor of heirs.

All the schools concur that it is valid for a non-Muslim living under the protection of an Islamic State (*dhimmi*) to make a will in favor of another dhimmi or a Muslim, and for a Muslim to make a will in favor of a *dhimmi* or another Muslim, in consonance with the verse, *"God does not forbid you respecting those who have not made war against you on account of your religion, and have not expelled you from your homes, that you show kindness to them and deal with them justly; surely God loves the just. God only forbids you respecting those who made war with you on account of your religion, and expelled you from your homes and assisted in your expulsion, that you befriend them. And whosoever takes them for friends—they are the evildoers"* (60:8-9).

The schools differ regarding the validity of a will made by a Muslim in favor of a *harbi*.[7] The Malikis, Hanbalis and most of the Shafiis consider it valid. According to the Hanafi and most Jafari jurisprudents, it is not valid. The schools concur regarding the validity of a will made in favor of a fetus, provided it is born alive. Bequest is similar to inheritance, and there is consensus that afterborn children inherit; hence their capacity to own bequests as well.

The schools differ as to whether it is necessary for the fetus to exist at the time of making the will. The Jafari, Hanafi and

Hanbali schools, as well as Imam Shafi in the more authentic of his two opinions, say that it is necessary, and a fetus will not inherit unless it is known to exist at the time of making the will. The knowledge of its existence is acquired if its mother has a husband capable of intercourse with her and it is born alive within a period of less than six months from the date of the bequest. But if it is born after six months or more, it will not receive anything from the legacy, because of the possibility of its being conceived after the time of the bequest. This opinion is based on the invalidity of a bequest in favor of one not in existence. The Malikis state that bequest in favor of existing fetus as well as one to be conceived in the future is valid, for that they regard a bequest in favor of someone non-existent as valid.[8]

If a person makes a will in favor of a fetus and then twins, a boy and a girl, are born, the legacy will be distributed among them equally because a bequest is a gift, not an inheritance; thus it resembles his or her giving them a gift after their birth. The schools concur that it is valid to make a will for public benefit, such as for the poor and destitute, for students, for mosques and schools. Imam Abu Hanifah excludes bequest in favor of a mosque or something of the kind, because a mosque does not have the capacity to transfer ownership. Muhammad ibn al-Hasan, his pupil, considers it valid, the income of the legacy being spent for the mosque. This has been the custom among the Muslims in the East and the West, in the past and at the present.[9]

The schools differ where the legatee is a specific person, as to whether his acceptance is necessary or if the absence of rejection on his or her part is sufficient. The Jafari and the Hanafi schools observe that his or her not rejecting the bequest is sufficient. Therefore, if the legatee is silent and does not decline the bequest, he or she will become the owner of the legacy after the testator's death. The Jafari are of the opinion that if a legatee accepts the bequest during the life of the testator, he or she is entitled to decline it after his or her death; also if he or she refuses the bequest during the testator's life, he or she is entitled to accept it after his or her death, because his or her acceptance and refusal have no effect during the life of the testator, for ownership does not materialize during such time. According to the Hanafi school, if he or she refuses during the testator's life, he or she is entitled to accept after his or her death; but if he or she accepts during his or her life, he or she cannot reject it thereafter. The Shafii and the Maliki schools state that it is necessary that the legatee accept the bequest after the death of the testator, and his or her silence and non-refusal do not suffice.[10]

The Hanafi, Hanbali, Maliki and Shafii schools observe that if the legatee dies before the testator, the will becomes void because the bequest then becomes a gift to a dead person, and this causes it to become void.[11] The Jafari say that if the legatee dies before the testator and the testator does not revoke the will, the heirs of the legatee will take his or her place and play his or her role in accepting or rejecting the bequest. Thus if they do not reject the bequest, the legacy will be solely their property, which they will distribute between themselves in the form of an inheritance, without it being incumbent upon them to pay from this bequest the debts of the decedent or to comply with his or her will in regard to the bequest. They argue that acceptance of the bequest was the decedent's right, which is transferred to his or her heirs, like the option to reject.[12]

According to Imam Malik and Imam Shafi in one of his two opinions, a bequest in favor of the murderer of the testator is valid regardless of its being an intentional or unintentional homicide. The Hanafis validate the bequest if permitted by the testator's heirs. The Hanbalis observe that the bequest is valid if it is made after the injury causing death, and is void if murder takes place after the bequest.[13] The Jafari say that a bequest is valid in favor of a murderer, because the proofs regarding the validity of a will are general. The verse includes a murderer as well as others, and to limit it to a non-murderer requires proof.

8.4. THE LEGACY

The schools concur that it is necessary that the bequest be

capable of being owned, such as property, house and the benefits ensuing from them. Therefore, the bequest of a thing which
cannot be owned customarily (that is, insects) or legally (that is,
wine, where the testator is a Muslim) is not valid, because
transfer of ownership is implicit in the concept of bequest and
when it is not present there remains no subject for the bequest.

There is consensus among the schools regarding the validity of the bequest of the produce of a garden, perpetually or for
a specific number of years. The Jafari extend the meaning of
bequest to its utmost limit, permitting therein that which they
do not permit in a sale and other transactions. They consider as
valid a bequest of something non-existent with a probability of
future existence, or something which the testator is incapable of
delivering (that is, a bird in the sky or a straying animal), or
something which is indeterminate (that is, the bequest of a
dress or animal without mentioning what dress and which animal). They further observe that it is valid for the testator to be
vague to the utmost extent, he may say, 'I promise to give something', 'a little', or 'a large quantity', 'a part', or 'a share', or 'a
portion', [14] to a certain person.

None of these forms is valid in a transaction of sale, though
valid in a bequest. The author of *al-Jawahir* says, "Perhaps the
validity of all these forms is due to the general nature of the
proofs validating wills, which include all these forms and all
interests that are capable of being transferred.... Perhaps the
rule in bequests is that all things can be bequeathed except
those that are known to be non-bequeathable," i.e. those which
have been excluded by a canonical proof (that is, wine, swine,
endowment, the right to *qisas,* the punishment for *qadaf,* etc.).
Some of them have stated that it is not valid to sell an elephant,
though it can be validly bequeathed.

Abu Zuhrah says that the religious jurisprudents have
extended the scope of the rules of bequest and have permitted
in it that which they do not permit in other forms of transfer,
e.g. the bequest of something indeterminate. Thus if you make
a will using the words, 'a share', 'a piece', 'something', 'a little',
etc, the will will be valid.... and the heirs will have to give any

quantity they desire from among the probable quantities understood from that word. This observation is in concurrence with
the view of the Jafari, and, accordingly, there is an agreement
concerning this issue.

8.5. THE EXTENT OF TESTAMENTARY RIGHTS

A gratuitous bequest is operative only up to one-third of the
testator's estate in the event of having heir, irrespective of the
bequest being made in illness or good health. As per consensus,
any excess over one-third requires the permission of the heirs.
Therefore, if all of them permit it, the will is valid, and if they
refuse permission, it becomes void. If some heirs give permission and others refuse, the will will be executed by disposition
of the excess over one-third from the share of the willing heirs.
The permission of an heir will not be effective unless he be a
sane and mature adult. The Jafari observe that once the heirs
give permission, they are not entitled to withdraw it, regardless
of whether the permission was given during the life of the testator or later. The Hanafi, the Shafii and the Hanbali schools
say that the permission given by the heirs or their refusal to do
so will have no consequences except after the testator's death.
Thus if they give permission during his or her lifetime and then
change their minds and decline permission after his or her
death, it is valid, irrespective of the permission having been
given during the health of the testator or during his illness.[15]
The Malikis are of the opinion that if the heirs give permission
during the illness of the testator, they are entitled to withdraw
it, and if they permit while he or she is healthy, the will will be
executed from their share of the legacy, without their having a
right to revoke the permission.

The Jafari, the Hanafi and the Maliki schools state that
when permission is granted by the heir for that which exceeds
one-third of the legacy, it is considered approval of the testator's
act and the operationality of the bequest, not as a gift from the
heir to the legatee. Accordingly, it neither requires possession,
nor other rules applicable to a gift apply to it.

The schools differ concerning a testator who has bequeathed

all his or her wealth and does not have any specific heir. Imam Malik observes that the bequest is only valid up to one-third of the legacy. Imam Abu Hanifah states that it is permissible for the whole legacy. Imam Shafi and Imam Ahmad have two opinions, and so do the Jafari, the more reliable of them being the one declaring its validity.[16]

There is consensus among the schools that inheritance and bequest are operational only after the payment of the debt of the decedent or his or her release from it. Therefore, the one-third from which the will is executed is a third of what remains after the payment of debt. They differ concerning the time at which the one-third will be determined: Is it a third at the time of death or at the time of the distribution of the estate? The Hanafis say that the one-third will be determined at the time of distributing the estate. Any increase or decrease in the estate will be shared by the heirs and the legatees. Some Hanbali and Maliki jurisprudents concur with this opinion. The Shafiis observe that the one-third will be determined at the time of the testator's death.[17]

The Jafari state that that which the decedent comes to own after his death will be included in his estate (for example, the reparation for unintentional homicide and for intentional murder, where the heirs compromise over reparation, and as when the decedent had during his life set up a net and birds or fish are trapped in it after his death; all these will be included in the estate and from it a third will be excluded). This observation of the Jafari is close to the Hanafi view.

The Jafari, Shafii and Hanbali schools state that if the decedent is liable for payment of the poor-due or any obligatory expiation or to perform the prescribed pilgrimage or other obligatory duties of monetary nature, these will be taken from his or her whole estate, not from a third of it, irrespective of his or her having willed to this effect or not, because these duties are related directly to God (*haqq Allah*), and as mentioned in the Traditions have a greater right to be fulfilled. If the decedent has made a provision for their fulfillment in his will and has determined their expenses from a third of his estate, his word will be acted upon, in consideration of the heirs. The Hanafis and the Malikis observe that if he or she has provided for his or her unfulfilled duties in the will, their expenses will be taken from a third of his or her estate and not the whole, and if he or she makes no provision for them in his or her will, they will annul on his death.[18] The schools concur that a will for performing recommended acts of worship will be executed from a third of the estate.

8.5.1. CLASHING WILLS

If the bequeathable third is insufficient for meeting all the provisions of a will (such as where the testator has made a bequest of one thousand for Zayd, two thousand for the poor, and three thousand for a mosque, while his bequeathable third is five thousand, and the heirs do not permit the excess to be met from their share), what is the rule here? The Maliki, Hanbali and Shafii schools say that the bequeathable third will be distributed among them in proportion to their amounts; i.e. the deficit will affect every legatee in proportion to his share in the will.[19] The Jafari state that if the testator makes many wills exceeding his bequeathable third, and the heirs do not permit the excess, on the wills being conflicting to one another (such as when he says, "One-third of my estate is for Zayd," and says later, "One-third is for Khalid,") the later will will be acted upon, and the former ignored. And if the wills include obligatory and non-obligatory provisions, the obligatory provisions will be given precedence. If the wills are of equal weight, then if the testator has included them in a single statement and said, "Give Jamal and Ahmad 1000," while his. or her bequeathable third is 500, this amount will be distributed among the two, each receiving 250. But if the testator gives precedence to one of them and says, "Give Jamal 500, and Ahmad 500," the whole amount will be given to the first and the second will will be considered void because the first will has completely exhausted the bequeathable third and no subject remains for the second.

The Hanafi, Hanbali, Maliki and Shafii schools observe that if a testator bequeaths a specific thing in favor of a person, and then bequeaths the same thing in favor of another, that thing will be equally distributed between them. Thus, if he or she says, "Give this car to Zayd after my death," and says later, "Give it to Khalid," it will become the joint property of both). The Jafari say that it belongs to the second, because the second will implies abandonment of the earlier one.

According to the Jafari, if a testator bequeaths a specific thing to every heir equal to each heir's share of the legacy, the will is valid. If he or she says, "The garden is for my son Ibrahim, and the house is for his brother, Hasan," and the will will be executed if there is no favoritism involved, because there is no clash of interests of the heirs. Some Shafii jurisprudents and some Hanbalis concur with this view.

There is consensus among the schools that the thing bequeathed, regardless of its being an undifferentiated part (e.g. one-third or one-fourth of the whole estate) or something specific, the legatee will become its owner on the testator's death, regardless of the legacy's presence. Thus he or she takes his or her share along with the heirs if the subject of legacy is present, and similarly when the subject of legacy, not present earlier, appears.

When the subject of legacy is something distinct, independent and determinate, the Jafari and the Hanafi schools say that the legatee will not become its owner unless the heirs possess twice its value (as their share of the testator's estate). But if the testator has assets not present or debts (receivable), and the subject of bequest is more than one-third in value of what the heirs possess, the heirs are entitled to resist the legatee and stop him or her from taking more than a third of the total estate into possession, especially where the assets not present are in danger of perishing or when it is unfeasible to reclaim them. When the thing not present earlier turns up, the legatee is entitled to the remaining part of the bequest to the extent of a third of the entire present assets. But if nothing turns up, the rest of the legacy is for the heirs.

8.5.2. REVOCATION OF WILL

There is consensus among the schools that a will is not binding on the testator or the legatee. Thus it is valid for the former to revoke it, regardless of its being the bequest of an asset, or benefit or guardianship. Discussion regarding the second point will follow shortly.

A revocation by the testator may take place by word or deed (that is, his or her bequeathing an article and then consuming, gifting or selling it). The Hanafis are said to hold that selling is not considered a revocation, and the legatee is entitled to receive its price.

8.5.3. BEQUEST OF BENEFITS

The schools concur regarding the validity of a bequest of benefit (e.g. the lease of a house, the right to reside in it, an orchard's produce, a goat's milk, and other such benefits which accrue in course of time) irrespective of the testator's restricting the benefit to a specific period or his or her bequeathing it perpetually.

The schools differ concerning the method of deriving the benefit from the bequeathable third. The Hanafis observe that the value of the bequeathed benefit will be estimated from the subject of the benefit, irrespective of whether the bequest of the benefit is temporary or perpetual. Thus, if a testator bequeaths the right to reside in a house for a year or more, the value of the whole house will be estimated, and if its value covers a third of the legacy, the will will be operational; otherwise it will be inoperational and void.

The Shafii and Hanbali schools say that the value of the benefits will be estimated in separation from the property. If a third of the property covers the value of the benefit, the bequest will be fully operational, if not, to the extent covered by a third of the property.[20]

Researchers among the Jafari state that if the bequest of the benefit is not perpetual, the calculation of its value is easy because the article or property will retain its own value after subtracting the value of the benefit. Therefore, if a testator bequeaths the benefit of an orchard for a period of five years, the value of the whole orchard will be initially estimated. Supposing its estimate is 10,000, it will be re-estimated after deducting from it the benefit of five years. Supposing the re-estimated value is 5000, the difference of 5000 will be deducted from a third of the estate if it can bear it. Otherwise, the legatee will be entitled to the benefit to the extent of a third of the legacy, be it the benefit of a year or more. But if the bequest of the benefit is perpetual, the value of the orchard along with its benefit will be estimated initially, and then the procedure followed in a temporary bequest will follow. If one asks, "How and in what way can we estimate the value of a property devoid of benefit, for that which has no benefit has no value?" The reply is that there are some benefits that have value even if little. Thus, in an orchard, the broken branches and dry wood can be utilized by the heir. If a tree dries up due to some reason, the land it covered can be of use. If a house falls into ruins and the legatee undertakes no repairs, the heirs may benefit from its stones and land. The meat and hide of a goat can be used after it is slaughtered. In all situations a property is not devoid of benefits apart from the bequeathed benefit.

8.6. THE DISPOSITIONAL RIGHTS OF AN AILING PERSON

Here, by an 'ailing person' is meant one whose death follows his illness, in a manner that the illness creates apprehensions in the minds of people that his or her life is at an end. Therefore, a toothache, eye pain, a slight headache, and the like are not considered alarming forms of illness. Thus, gifts made by a person suffering from an alarming sickness, who may recover from it and die after his or her recovery, will be considered valid.

8.6.1. POWERS OF DISPOSITION OF A HEALTHY PERSON

There is no doubt nor disagreement between the schools that when a healthy person disposes of his wealth, completely and unconditionally—i.e. without making it contingent upon his death—his disposition is operative from his property, irrespective of the disposition being obligatory (e.g. the payment of a debt) or an act of favor (e.g. giving a gift, or creating an endowment).

But if a healthy person makes the disposition of his or her property contingent upon his or her death, it becomes a bequest, as mentioned. Therefore, if it is a non-monetary obligatory (for example, prescribed prayer, prescribed pilgrimage, and so forth), it will be executed from a third of his or her legacy, and if it is a debt, it will be paid from the undivided estate, according to the Jafari, Shafii and Hanbali schools, and from a third, according to the Hanafi and Maliki schools.

8.6.2. THE POWERS OF DISPOSITION OF AN ILL PERSON

Those dispositions of an ill person that are contingent upon his or her death are bequests, and the rules applicable to them are those mentioned above concerning valid will,[21] because there is no difference between a will made during a state of health or illness, provided the ill person is mentally sound and completely conscious and aware.

If an ill person disposes his or her wealth without making it contingent upon his or her death, it will be seen whether his or her disposition is for his or her own use, such as his or her buying an expensive dress, enjoying food and drink, spending on medicine and for improving his or her health, traveling for comfort and enjoyment, and so forth. All these dispositions are valid and no one, including heirs, may object.

And if he or she disposes it impartially, such as when he or she sells, rents or exchanges his or her possessions for a real consideration, these transactions of his or hers are enforceable from his or her estate and the heirs are not entitled to dispute it, because they do not lose anything as its consequence.

If he or she disposes in a complete form without making it contingent upon his or her death, and his or her dispositions include acts of favor (such as when he or she gives a gift or alms, or relinquishes a debt, or pardons a crime entailing damages, or sells for less than its actual price or buys at a higher price, or makes other such dispositions which entail a financial loss for the heirs), such dispositions will be operational from a third of his or her estate.[22] The meaning of its being from a third of his or her estate is that its enforcement is delayed until his or her death. Thus if he or she dies in his or her illness and a third of his or her estate covers his or her completed gratuitous acts, it is clear that they are enforceable from the very beginning, and if the third falls short of them, such dispositions in excess of the third are invalid without the heirs' permission.

8.6.3. WILLS AND COMPLETED DISPOSITIONS DURING ILLNESS

The difference between a will and dispositions (*munjazat*) during illness is that the will is made contingent upon death, whereas dispositions during illness are not made contingent upon death, irrespective of their being incontingent perpetually or being contingent upon some event capable of conditionality (such as when he or she makes a vow during illness to sacrifice a particular ram if he or she is granted a son and then a son is born to him posthumously or to her and then she dies; such an act will be considered among dispositions during disease). According to *al-Mughni* (a Hanbali legal text) and *al-Tadhkirah* (a book on Jafari jurisprudence), there are five similarities and six differences between dispositions during illness and a will, and the similar wording of the two texts shows that al-Allamah al-Hilli, the author of *al-Tadhkirah* (d.726/1326), has taken it from Ibn Qudamah, the author of *al-Mughni* (d.620/1223).[23] It is useful to give a summary here of their views.

The five similarities between dispositions during illness and a will are the following:

1. Both depend for their execution on a third of the estate, or the consent of the heirs.

2. Dispositions during illness are valid in favor of an heir, exactly like a will, according to the Jafari; according to the other four schools, they are not valid in favor of an heir, as in the case of a will.

3. Both of them have a lesser reward with God compared to charity given during health.

4. Dispositions contest with wills, within the one-third of the

estate (from which both are to be enforced).

5. Both will be enforced from the one-third of the estate only at the time of death, neither before nor after it.

The six differences between a will and dispositions during illness are:

1. It is valid for a testator to revoke his will, while it is not valid for a donor during ailment to revoke his gift after its acceptance by the recipient and his taking its possession. The secret here is that a will is a bequest conditional to death, and, consequently, as long as the condition is not fulfilled, it is valid to recant it, whereas a gift during illness is unrestricted and unconditional.

2. Dispositions are required to be accepted or rejected immediately and during the life of the donor, whereas a will is not required to be accepted or rejected until the death of the testator.

3. Dispositions require the fulfillment of certain conditions, such as knowledge of the gift and absence of harm; a will is not bound by these conditions.

4. Dispositions enjoy precedence over a will if one-third of the estate falls short of meeting both of them together, except when the will involves the setting free of a slave, in which case a will takes precedence over completed gifts. This is the view of the Jafari, Hanafi and Shafii schools.[24]

5. If one-third of the estate is not sufficient to enforce all the dispositions, then, according to the Shafiis and Hanbalis, the first among them will be enforced first, and so on. But if the one-third is not sufficient to fulfill several wills, the deficit will affect all of them, as pointed out while discussing clashing wills. The Jafari enforce both wills and dispositions on a first-come-fist basis.

6. If a donor during his or her last illness dies before the recipient has taken possession of the gift, the option lies with the heirs; if they desire they may grant it. But a will has to be compulsorily accepted after the death of the testator, without requiring the consent of the heirs.

The sixth difference has been mentioned by the author of *al-*

Mughni, while the author of *al-Tadhkirah* does not mention it. It is better not to mention this difference, as done by al-Allamah al-Hilli, because dispositions during sickness have many forms, such as gift, the relinquishing of a debt, favoritism in sale or purchase, etc. Hence, when dispositions are not limited to gifts, it is not appropriate,

Firstly, to say, "If a donor during his or her last illness dies before the recipient has taken possession...." Secondly, if a donor during his or her last illness makes a gift and dies before the recipient has taken its possession, according to the Hanbali, Shafii, Jafari and Hanafi schools, the gift is void because taking possession is a condition for its completion, and if the recipient takes possession before the death of the donor the gift is concluded and will be accounted for in the third of the estate, like a will, and will not depend for its execution on the consent of the heirs, provided it does not exceed a third of the estate. Hence it is not in fact a disposition without taking possession and after the death of the donor, for it to be said that it differs from or is similar to a will. After taking possession, the rules concerning wills will apply to it. From this it is clear that the mention of the sixth difference is out of place.

8.6.4. ACKNOWLEDGMENT DURING SICKNESS

The Hanafi, Hanbali, Maliki and Shafii schools concur that if during the last illness a person acknowledges the debt of a non-heir, his or her acknowledgment is enforceable from the undivided estate, exactly like his or her acknowledgment during health. They differ where he or she acknowledges the debt of an heir. The Hanafi and Hanbali schools observe that the other heirs are not bound by this acknowledgment and it will be considered void unless that heir brings a valid proof to establish his or her claim. The Malikis say that the acknowledgment is valid if the decedent is not accused of partiality, and is void if so accused (that is, when a person having a daughter and a cousin brother acknowledges a debt of his or her daughter, it will not be accepted, and if he or she acknowledges in favor of his or her cousin, it will be accepted, because he or she cannot be accused here of depriving his or her daughter and transferring the wealth to his or her cousin). The reason for rejecting the acknowledgment is accusation and therefore it is limited to those instances where there is an accusation.[25] The Jafari state that if he makes an acknowledgment during last illness for an heir or a stranger, concerning a property or a debt claim, it will be seen. If there are any indications raising the suspicion that he or she is not sincere in his or her acknowledgment, so that it seems, going by ordinary factors, farfetched that the thing acknowledged should belong to the person to whom it has been acknowledged to belong and that the sick person intends to impress this on others for some reason, the rule applicable to such an acknowledgment is the one applicable to a will: it will be executed from a third. But if the ill person is secure from suspicion in his or her acknowledgment, so that there is no indication to prove that he or she has lied (such as when there has been between him or her and the person in whose favor he or she has made the acknowledgment, earlier dealings which ordinarily explain such an acknowledgment, the acknowledgment will be enforced from the original estate, whatever its value.

This is when the condition of the person acknowledging is known; what if it is not known? If the heir says that the decedent was not honest in his or her acknowledgment, then the burden of proof rests on the person in whose favor the acknowledgment has been made, to prove that he or she owns the thing which the decedent acknowledged as his or hers during his or hers last illness. If he or she proves this by bringing two just witnesses (*al-bayyinah*), the acknowledgment will be enforced from the original estate; otherwise, the heir will take an oath that he or she does not know that the thing acknowledged by the decedent belongs to that person; then the acknowledgment will be enforced from a third of the estate.[26]

8.7. APPOINTMENT OF THE EXECUTOR

Wisayah is an undertaking by a person to execute the will of another after his or her death, such as clearing his or her debts, pursuing his or her debtors, the care and maintenance of his or her children, and other such functions. Responsibility for these functions is called *al-wilayah* or *al-wasiyyat al-ahdiyyah*, and the person charged with performing it called an authorized executor (*al-wasi al-mukhtar*).

8.7.1. REQUIREMENTS FOR AN AUTHORIZED EXECUTOR

1. He or she should be a *mukallaf*, i.e. a sane adult, because a lunatic and a minor do not have authority over themselves so there is no question of their exercising authority over the affairs of others. However, the Jafari observe in this regard that it is not valid for a child to act as an executor individually, though valid if he or she acts together with an adult. Then the adult will execute the will individually until the minor attains majority, and then he or she will join him or her in its execution. The Hanafis state that if a minor is appointed as executor, the judge will replace him or her with another, and if the minor has executed the will before being removed by the judge, his or her acts of execution of the will are valid and enforceable. Similarly, if he or she attains majority before being removed, he or she will continue with the execution of the will.[27]

2. The executor's nomination must be determinate. Thus if the testator appoints one of two persons without determining which one of them is to be the executor, the appointment of both is void.

3. The specification of the subject of will. Thus if the testator makes a will without specifying it (as when he or she says, "So and so is my executor," and does not mention the thing over which he or she is to exercise this authority), the appointment is void according to the Jafari, Hanafi, Shafii and Hanbali schools. It has been narrated from Imam Malik that such an executor will have authority over the whole estate.

4. That the executor be a Muslim. Thus it is not valid, as per consensus, for a Muslim to appoint a non-Muslim executor. But the Hanafis state, "If a Muslim appoints a non-Muslim, it is for the judge to replace him or her with a Muslim, though the appointment itself will be considered valid." Hence if the non-Muslim executor executes the will before his or her removal by

the judge, or becomes a Muslim, he or she will remain an executor, as in the case of a minor.

5. The Shafii school observes that it is obligatory that the executor be a just person. The Maliki, Hanafi and researchers among the Jafari state that it is sufficient that he or she be trustworthy and truthful, because being just is a means here and not an end, and when the executor strives to fulfill the provisions of the will—as is obligatory for him or her—the purpose is achieved.[28] The Hanbalis say that if the executor is dishonest, the judge will appoint a trustworthy person as a co-executor. This opinion is in consonance with the opinion of al-Sayyid al-Hakim in *Minhaj al-salihin* where he observes that if a dishonest act is committed by the executor, a trustworthy person will be appointed alongside him or her to stop him or her from doing so. If this is not possible, he or she will be replaced by another.

6. As reported in *al-Fiqh alal-madhahib al-arbaah, bab al-wasiyyah*, the Hanafi, Maliki and Shafii schools require the executor to be capable of executing the provisions of the will. Al-Allamah al-Hilli has stated in *al-Tadhkirah* that apparently, the view taken by the Jafari, is that it is valid to appoint an executor incapable of executing the will, and his incapacity will be compensated by the supervision of the judge. That is, the judge himself will supervise the dispositions, or appoint a capable, trustworthy person to cooperate with the executor.

8.7.2. REFUSAL TO ACT AS EXECUTOR

The testator is entitled to revoke the appointment of an executor, and the executor is entitled to reject his appointment by announcing his or her refusal, because *al-wasiyyat al-ahdiyyah* in this situation is not binding, as per consensus. The schools differ regarding the validity of a rejection to act as executor by an executor without informing the testator. The Jafari and Hanafi schools say that it is not valid in any situation for an executor to reject his or her appointment after the death of the testator, and it is not valid during his or her life without informing him or her. The Shafii and Hanbali schools observe that it is valid for an executor to reject his or her appointment at the beginning as well as during its course, without any restraint or condition. Therefore, he or she can reject before acceptance and after it, during the testator's life, by announcing it or without doing so, as well as after his death.[29]

8.7.3. APPOINTMENT OF TWO EXECUTORS

There is consensus among the schools that a testator is entitled to appoint two or more executors. If he or she categorically mentions that each one of them is independent in his or her dispositions, his or her word will be acted upon. Similarly, if he or she categorically mentions that both should act together, then neither of them will have independence of individual action. The schools differ where the testator does not specify anything concerning their acting individually or jointly. The Jafari, Shafii, Maliki, and Hanbali schools observe that both have no power to act individually. So if they quarrel and disagree, the judge will compel them to agreement. If he or she is unable to do so, he or she will replace both of them.

The Hanafis say that each of the two executors is free to act individually concerning seven things: shrouding of the deceased, payment of his or her debt, recovering of his or her will, returning of articles held in trust by the decedent, buying necessary food and clothing for the minor heirs, acceptance of a gift on their behalf, and perusal of legal proceedings initiated for or against the decedent. This is because agreement in such things is difficult and delays are harmful. Therefore, to act individually is valid in them.[30]

Al-Sayyid Abu al-Hasan has remarked in *al-Wasilah*, "If one of the two executors dies or turns insane or anything occurs to him which annuls his appointment as an executor, the second will become independent in the execution of the will, and there is no need to appoint a new co-executor.'"

Ibn Qudamah states in *al-Mughni* that the judge will appoint a trustworthy person as his counterpart, because the testator was not satisfied with the individual supervision of the surviving executor, and no difference of opinion has been narrated in this issue except from the Shafiis. If both the executors die or their condition changes in a manner annulling their appointment, should the judge appoint two new executors or one will suffice? Here the schools differ. The correct view is that the judge will pay attention to expediency. Consequently, if it is expedient to appoint two executors, he will do so. Otherwise it will be adequate to appoint one, because what is important is the will's execution. The reason for the multiplicity of executors is usually the concern and affection of the executor for the legally disable heir or his friendship with the testator. In any case, there is no doubt that when one or more executors (as the case may be) die, it is as if there was no executor from the very beginning.

The Jafari, Shafiis and Hanbalis in the more preponderant of the two narrations from Imam Ahmad Hanbal, state that an executor is not entitled to hand over the job of executing the will to another without the prior permission of the testator. The Hanafi and Maliki schools observe that it is valid for an executor to appoint by will another person to fulfill the duties for which he was appointed executor.

8.7.4. APPOINTING AN EXECUTOR FOR MARRIAGE

The schools differ as to whether anyone having authority concerning marriage of a ward is entitled to transfer it to another through a will (for instance, when a father authorizes the executor of his will concerning the marriage of his daughter or son). Imam Malik considers it valid. Imam Ahmad observes that if the father mentions the name of the specific person to whom his child should be married, it is valid to appoint an executor for marriage, not otherwise. Al-Shaykh Abu Zuhrah, in *al-Ahwal al-shakhsiyyah, bab al-wilayah*, narrates from a multitude of religious jurisprudents that it is not valid to appoint an executor for marriage. The Jafari hold the same opinion.

8.7.5. AN EXECUTOR ACKNOWLEDGMENT

If an executor makes an acknowledgment of the decedent's liability regarding some property or debt, his acknowledgment is not executable against the heirs, minor or major, because it is an acknowledgment regarding another's dues. If the issue is raised in the court, the executor will be considered a witness, required to fulfill all the qualifications for a competent witness. provided he is not himself a party to the case.

If an executor gives evidence in favor of minor heirs or the decedent, his testimony will not be accepted, because his testimony affirms his own right of disposal in regard to the subject of his evidence.

8.7.6. *LIABILITY OF AN EXECUTOR*

If anything suffers damage at the hands of the executor, he or she is not liable for it unless he or she has violated or neglected his or her duty. If a minor heir on attaining majority accuses the executor of breach of trust or negligence, the burden of proof will rest on the heir, and the executor shall take an oath, because the executor is a trustee, and in accordance with the Tradition, "A trustee is liable for nothing except an oath." Anyone accusing an executor of breach of trust or negligence is entitled to proceed against him or her legally, provided that he or she is sincere in his or her intent and by doing so seeks the pleasure of God. But if it is known that he or she has no aim except harassment and defamation of the executor, due to some enmity between them, his or her plea will not be heard.

If a person dies intestate, and it is not possible to refer to a judge, a reliable and trustworthy person from among Muslims may take charge of the affairs of his or her estate, taking care to do what is good and beneficial, especially in matters which may not be delayed. It is the judge's duty to later on endorse these dispositions, and he may not invalidate them.

8.7.7. *PROBATING A WILL*

The schools concur that a will concerning property or its benefit is proved by the testimony of two males or a male along with two female, witnesses from among just Muslims, in accordance with the verse, "*And call in two witnesses from among your men, or if they are not two men, then one man and two women, such witnesses as you approve of...."* (2:282).

The schools differ concerning the acceptability of the testimony of just witness from the People of the Book in the particular case of proving a will. The Jafari and Hanbalis observe that the testimony of the People of the Book is valid in the case of a will only during a journey when none else is available in accordance with the verse, *"O believers, the testimony between you when any of you is visited by death, at the time of making a will, shall be two just (adil) men from among you, or two others from another folk, if you are journeying in the land and the affliction of death befalls you"* (5:106).

The Hanafi, Shafii and Maliki schools observe that the testimony of a non-Muslim will not be accepted under any condition, neither in case of a will nor in anything else. They add that the meaning of the words in the verse is, 'from among those who are not your relatives', and not, *"...from those who do not belong to your religion..."*

The Jafari, Hanbali and Shafii schools say that ownership of a property is proved by the evidence of one witness along with an oath. The Hanafis observe that a judgment will not be given on the basis of a single witness and an oath.[30] The Jafari state that the right to one-fourth of a bequeathed property is proved by the evidence of a single woman; to a half by the evidence of two women; to three-fourths by the evidence of three women, and to the whole property by four women witnesses, being just being essential in all the cases. This opinion is particular to the Jafari.

This was as regards the bequest of property or its benefit. Concerning the nomination of an executor, it is not proved except by the evidence of two male just Muslims. Hence, as per consensus, the evidence of the People of the Book or women, both individually and jointly with men, or a single male witness along with an oath, will not be accepted.

9
LEGAL DISABILITY

L
egal disability literally means to prohibit, refuse, prevent, deprive, detain. This meaning is also evident from the Quranic verse, *"Upon the day that they see the angels, no good tidings that day for sinners. they (the angels) shall say, 'A ban forbidden"* (25:22). Legally it implies prohibiting the dispositions of a person with respect to all or some of his property. The causes of disability, which we will discuss here, are four: (1) insanity (*al-junun*); (2) minority (*al-sighar*); (3)mental retardation (*al-safah*); (4) insolvency (*al-iflas*).[1]

9.1. INSANITY
In accordance with explicit traditions as well as consensus, an insane person is prohibited from all dispositions, irrespective of whether his insanity is permanent or recurring. But if a person suffering from recurring insanity manages his or her property during the period he or she is free from it, his or her dispositions are binding. Further, where it is uncertain whether a particular disposition belongs to the period of sanity, it will not become binding. As sanity is a condition for the validity of an agreement and an uncertainty regarding it amounts to an uncertainty concerning the existence of the contract itself, not its validity, consequently its very basis is negated. In other words, where there is uncertainty about the validity of a contract due to uncertainty concerning the presence of sanity at the

time of its conclusion, we will presume that the situation before the contract continues to exist and will leave it at that. The rule applicable to an insane person is also applied to a person in a state of unconsciousness and intoxication. If an insane person cohabits with a woman and she becomes pregnant, the child will be considered his, exactly as in the case of 'intercourse by mistake'.

9.2. MINORITY

A minor is considered legally incapable by consensus and there is a difference of opinion regarding some dispositions of a child of discerning age, as will be mentioned later. When a minor matures mentally and attains puberty he or she becomes an adult and all his or her dispositions become enforceable. The Jafari and the Shafii schools observe that when a child reaches the age of ten, his or her will shall be considered valid in regard to matters of charity and benevolence. More than one Jafari jurist, relying on some traditions, has said that his or her divorce is also valid.

9.3. LIABILITY

If an insane person or a child destroys another person's property without his or her permission, they are considered liable, because liability pertains to the laws of obligations in which mental maturity and puberty are not considered as conditions.[2] Therefore, if they have any property that is being administered by their guardian, compensation will be claimed from this property. Otherwise, the person entitled to the compensation will wait until the insane person regains sanity and the child attains puberty and then claim from them his or her dues.

9.4. A DISCERNING CHILD

A discerning child is one who can in general distinguish between that which is harmful and beneficial and who understands the difference between contracts of sale and rent and between a profitable bargain and one entailing loss. The

Hanafis say that the dispositions of a discerning child without his or her guardian's permission are valid provided they involve sheer benefit, that is, the acceptance of gifts, bequests and endowments without giving anything in return. But the dispositions in which the possibility of profit and loss exists such as transactions of sale, mortgage, rent and bailment—are not valid except by the permission of the guardian. As to a non-discerning child, none of his or her dispositions are valid, irrespective of the permission of the guardian, and regardless of the thing involved being of petty or considerable worth.

The Hanbalis observe that a discerning child's dispositions are valid with the permission of the guardian. So are those of a non-discerning child, even without the guardian's permission, if the thing involved is of petty worth, as, for instance, where he or she buys from a confectioner what children usually purchase, or buys a bird from someone in order to set it free.[3]

The Jafari and Shafii schools state that a transaction by a child whether discerning or not, is altogether illegal, irrespective of whether he or she acts as an agent or for himself or herself, irrespective of whether he or she gives or takes delivery, even if the object transacted is trivial and insignificant, and whether it involves a vow or a confession. Al-Shaykh al-Ansari observes, "The basis for invalidating a child's transaction is a narrated consensus (*al-ijma al-mahki*) strengthened by an unusual preponderance (*al-shuhrat al-azimah*). The criterion is to act in accordance with the preponderance."[4]

The Jafari jurists have mentioned in this regard a number of subtle sub-issues which al-Allamah al-Hilli has recorded.[5] Among these are the following:

1. If one owes something to a person, and he or she tells one, "Give what you owe me to my son," when his son is legally incapable, and one does so on the basis of the father's behest, and by chance the child loses it, in such a situation one's liability concerning the debt does not cease and the creditor is still entitled to demand it from one, although it was he who asked one to deliver it to his son. Similarly, the child will not be responsible for the thing he has lost, and one is neither entitled to claim

it from his guardian nor from him on his attaining majority.

As to one's remaining liable for the debt, this is because the debt is not cleared unless it is validly delivered, and it is presumed that neither the creditor nor his authorized representative has taken delivery. As to the delivery taken by the child, its occurrence and non-occurrence are equal, presuming his incapacity for taking and giving delivery. As to the father's permission to deliver to the child, it is exactly like someone telling one: "Throw what you owe me into the sea," and one does as he tells one. Here, one's liability for the debt is not cast off.

The reason for not considering the child liable for the thing delivered to him is that it is the deliverer who has destroyed it by improperly using his discretion and giving it to someone whose possession has no effect, even if it is by the permission and order of the child's guardian.

2. Where one has in one's possession something belonging to a child and his guardian tells one to give it to him or her, and one gives it to the child who destroys it, one will be liable for it because one is not entitled to act negligently regarding the property of someone legally incapable even if his or her guardian permits it.

3. If a child gives one a dinar to see whether it is genuine or counterfeit, or gives one an article for pricing it or selling it or for some other purpose, it is not valid for one, after it has come into one's hands, to return it to him or her; rather one must return it to his or her guardian.

4. If two children buy and sell between themselves and each takes delivery from the other and then both destroy what they have received, their guardians will be liable if they had permitted the transaction, if not, the liability will be borne from the property of each child.

9.5. A CHILD'S INTENTIONAL ACT IS A MISTAKE

If a child kills a person or injures him or severs any part of his or her body, he or she will not be subject to retribution. He or she will be dealt exactly like an insane person, because he or she is not capable of being punished, neither in this world nor in the hereafter. A Tradition states, "A child's intentional act is a mistake." There is no difference of opinion among the schools concerning this. As to the compensation given to the victim, it will be borne by the paternal relatives (*al-aqilah*). Striking a child is only permissible for reforming the child, not as retribution (*qisas*) or punishment In some circumstances where beating a child is permissible, it is only for reforming him or her, not as retribution (*qisas*) or punishment (*tazir*).

9.6. SEVERE MENTAL RETARDATION

Severely mental retardation (*al-safah*) refers to a person who cannot manage and expend his or her property properly, irrespective of whether he or she has all the qualities necessary for its proper management but is negligent and does not apply them, or lacks these qualities. In short, he or she is negligent and extravagant, in that he or she repeatedly performs acts of negligence and extravagance. The acts of extravagance may be such as donation by him or her of all or a major part of his or her wealth, or building a mosque, school or hospital which a person of his or her social and monetary status would not build, so that it is detrimental to his or her own interests and those of his or her dependents, and the people view him or her as having strayed from the practice of rational persons in the management of property.

9.7. DECLARATION OF LEGAL DISABILITY

The schools—with the exception of the Hanafi—concur that the idiot's legal disability (*al-tahjir*) is confined to his or her financial dispositions, and excepting where his or her guardian permits him or her, his or her position in this regard is that of a child and an insane person. He or she is totally free regarding his or her other activities that are not closely or remotely connected with property. This disability is considered to continues until he or she attains mental maturity, in accordance with the following verse, *"And do not give your property to the mentally retarded which God has assigned to you to manage; provide for them and clothe them out of it, and speak to them words of hon-*

est advice. And test the orphans until they reach the age of marrying; then if you find in them mental maturity, deliver to them their property" (4:5-6).[6]

This is the view of the Jafari, Shafii, Maliki and Hanbali schools, as well as that of Abu Yusuf and Muhammad, the two disciples of Imam Abu Hanifah. Imam Abu Hanifah observes that mental maturity is neither a condition for delivering property to its owners nor for the validity of their monetary dispositions. Thus if a person attains puberty in a state of mental maturity and then becomes an idiot, his or her dispositions are valid and it is not valid to consider him or her legally incapable even if his or her age is less than twenty-five years. Similarly, one who attains puberty in a state of severe mental retardation so that his or her childhood and mental retardation are concomitant, he or she will not be considered legally incapable in any manner after attaining maturity at twenty-five years.

9.8. THE JUDGE'S ORDER

Jafari jurists authorities state that the criterion for considering the dispositions of a severely mentally retarded person as void is the appearance of mental retarded, not the order of a judge declaring him or her legally incapable. Thus every disposition of his or hers during the state of impairment is void, irrespective of whether a judge declares him or her incapable or not, and regardless of whether his or her impairment continues from childhood or occurs after puberty. Hence, if a mentally retarded person acquires mental maturity, his or her disability will be removed, returning only on the return of mental retardation and disappearing with its disappearance.[7] This opinion is very close to the one expressed by the Shafii school.

The Hanafi and the Hanbali schools observe that a mentally retarded person will not be considered legally incapable without the judge's declaration. Therefore, the dispositions prior to the declaration of his or her legal disability are valid even if they were improper. After the declaration his or her dispositions are not enforceable even if appropriate.

This opinion cannot be substantiated unless we accept that

the declaration of the judge alters the actual fact. This view is confined to the Hanafis only. As to the Shafii, Maliki and the Hanbali schools, they concur with the Jafari in holding that the judge's order has no bearing, close or remote, on the actual fact, because it is only a means and not an end in itself.

The Malikis say that when a person, man or woman, comes to be characterized with idiocy he or she becomes liable to be declared legally incapable. But if idiocy occurs after a short period, say a year, after his or her attaining puberty, the right to declare his or her legal incapacity lies with his or her father, because the time of its occurrence is close to the period of his or her attaining puberty. But if it occurs after a period exceeding a year after puberty, his disability can be only declared by a judge.[8]

The Malikis also observe that a woman, even if she becomes mentally mature, is not entitled to dispose of her property unless she has married and the marriage has been consummated. After the consummation of marriage, her right to donate is limited to one-third of the property, and for the remainder she requires the permission of the husband until her old age.[9] But all the other schools do not differentiate between the sexes, in accordance with the general import of the Quranic verse (4:6).

9.9. THE CONFESSION, OATH AND VOW OF A MENTALLY RETARDED PERSON

If a mentally retarded person is permitted to dispose of his or her property and he or she does so, the schools concur that it is valid. As to non-financial acts, such as his or her acknowledgment of lineage or his or her taking an oath or a vow to perform, or abstain from, a certain act that does not involve property, these acts are valid even if the guardian has not permitted them. If he or she confesses to having committed theft, it will be accepted only for the purpose of amputation and not for financial liability, that is, his or her confession will have effect vis-a-vis the right of God (*haqq Allah*) and not vis-a-vis the rights of other human beings (*haqq al-nas*).

The Hanafis state that his or her confession will be given

credence in regard to those of his or her assets which have been realized after his or her disability and not from what he or she owned at its advent. Also, his or her will is valid to an extent of one-third in matters of charity and benevolence. The Jafari state that there is no difference between the former and the latter properties. Rather, they say, it is not valid for a mentally retarded person to hire himself or herself for any work even if advantageous without his or her guardian's permission. They also observe that if a person deposits something with a mentally retarded person with the knowledge of his or her impairment and the person personally destroys it, either voluntarily or by mistake, he or she will be liable. But if the deposited thing is not destroyed personally by the impaired person but as a consequence of his or her negligence in preserving it, he or she will not be liable, because in this situation the depositor himself or herself has been negligent and at fault. As to the liability of the mentally retarded where he or she personally destroys the deposit, it has its basis in the dictum, "He who destroys another's property is liable for it."[10]

9.10. THE MARRIAGE AND DIVORCE OF A MENTALLY RETARDED PERSON

The Shafii, Hanbali and Jafari schools say that the idiot's marriage is not valid but his or her divorce (*talaq* or *khul*) is valid. The Hanbalis allow his or her marriage where it is a necessity. The Hanafis observe that his or her marriage, divorce, and freeing a slave are valid, because these three are valid even when performed in jest, and with greater reason in a state of idiocy. But if he or she marries for more than *mahr al-mithl*, the dowry (*mahr*) will be valid only to the extent of *mahr al-mithl*.

9.11. THE PROOF OF MENTAL MATURITY

The schools concur that mental maturity is ascertainable through testing, in accordance with the words of God Almighty. But the modes of testing are not specific, though the jurists mention as examples such methods as handing over to a child the management of his or her property, or relying upon him or her to buy or sell for fulfilling some of his or her needs, and the like. If he or she shows good sense in these activities, he or she will be considered mentally mature.

As per consensus, mental maturity in both the sexes is proved by the testimony of two male witnesses because the testimony of two male witnesses is a principle. The Jafari say that it is also proved in the case of women by the testimony of a man and two women, or that of four women. But in the case of men, it is only proved by the testimony of men.[11]

9.12. THE GUARDIAN

9.12.1. A MINOR'S GUARDIAN

The legal disability of the minor has been discussed, the insane person and the mentally retarded. It is obvious that every legally incapable person needs a guardian or an executor to attend to the things concerning which his or her disability has been declared, and to manage them as his or her representative. Who is this guardian or executor? It is worth pointing out at the outset that the discussion in this chapter is limited to guardianship over property. As to guardianship concerning marriage, it has already been discussed in the related chapter.

The schools concur that the guardian of a minor is his or her father; the mother has no right in this regard except in the opinion of some Shafii jurists. The schools differ concerning the guardianship of others apart from the father. The Hanbali and the Maliki schools state that the right to guardianship after the father is enjoyed by the executor of his will, and if there is no executor, by the judge. The paternal grandfather has no right to guardianship whatsoever, because, according to them, he does not take the father's place in anything. When this is the state of the paternal grandfather, such is the case of the maternal grandfather with greater reason. The Hanafis say that after the father the guardianship will belong to his executor, then to the paternal grandfather, and then to his executor. If none are present it will belong to the judge.

The Shafiis observe that it will lie with the paternal grandfather after the father, and after him with the father's executor, followed by the executor of the paternal grandfather, and then the judge. The Jafari state that the guardianship belongs to the father and the paternal grandfather simultaneously in a manner that each is entitled to act independently of the other, though the act of whoever precedes acquires legality, in view of that which is necessary. If both act simultaneously in a contrary fashion, the act of the paternal grandfather will prevail. If both are absent, the executor of any of them will be the guardian. The grandfather's executor's acts will prevail over those of the father's executor. When there is no father or paternal grandfather nor their executors, the guardianship will be exercised by the judge.

9.12.2. THE GUARDIAN OF AN INSANE PERSON

An insane person is exactly like a minor in this regard, and the views of the schools are similar for both the cases, irrespective of whether the child has attained puberty while continuing to be insane or has attained puberty in a state of mental maturity to become insane later. Only a group of Jafari jurists differ here by differentiating between insanity continuing from minority and that which occurs after puberty and mental maturity. They say that the father and the paternal grandfather have a right to guardianship over the former. As to the latter, the judge will act as his guardian despite the presence of both of them. This view is in consonance with analogical reasoning practiced by the Hanafis, because the guardianship of both the father and the paternal grandfather had ended on the child's attaining puberty and mental maturity, and that which ends does not return. But the Hanafis have acted here against analogical reasoning and have opted for *istihsan*.

The Jafari[12] say that it is in accordance with caution (*ihtiyat*) that the paternal grandfather, the father and the judge act in consonance, that is, the property of an insane person between whose insanity and childhood there is a time gap, will be managed by mutual consultation among the three. Al-Sayyid al-Isfahani remarks, "Caution will not be forsaken if they act by mutual consent."[13]

Here caution is only desirable and not obligatory, because

the proofs establishing the guardianship of the father and the paternal grandfather do not differ in the two situations. Accordingly, the father and the paternal grandfather will always be preferred to the judge, because the applicability or inapplicability of a particular rule revolves around its subject, and the generality of the proofs proving the guardianship of the father and the paternal grandfather enjoy precedence over the generality of the proofs proving the judge's guardianship. Apart from this, the sympathy of the judge or someone else cannot equal that of the father and the grandfather, and what rational person would approve the appointment by the judge of a stranger as a guardian over a legally incapable person whose father or paternal grandfather are present and fulfill all the necessary conditions and qualifications?

9.12.3. THE GUARDIAN OF A MENTALLY RETARDED PERSON

The Jafari, Hanbali and Hanafi schools concur that if a child attains puberty in a state of mental maturity and then becomes mentally impaired his or her guardianship will lie with the judge to the exclusion of the father and paternal grandfather, and, with greater reason, to the exclusion of the executors of their wills. That which was observed concerning an insane person holds true here as well, that no rational person would approve that a judge appoint a stranger as guardian in the presence of the father and the paternal grandfather. Hence, as a measure of caution, it is better that the judge choose the father or the paternal grandfather as the guardian of their child. However, if the mental retardation has continued from childhood and the subject has attained puberty in that state, the opinion of the three above-mentioned schools is similar to their opinion concerning a minor.[14] The Shafiis neither differentiate between the guardianship of a minor, an insane person and a mentally retarded person, nor between idiocy occurring after puberty and one continuing from childhood.

9.13. THE QUALIFICATIONS OF A GUARDIAN

The schools concur that a guardian and an executor require

to be mentally mature adults sharing a common religion. Many jurists have also considered justice as a requirement even if the guardian is the father or the grandfather. There is no doubt that this condition seals the door of guardianship firmly with reinforced concrete and not merely with stones and mud. Apart from this, justice is a means for safeguarding and promoting welfare, not an end in itself. The inclusion of justice as a condition, if it proves anything, proves that justice was not something rare in the society in which those who consider it necessary lived.

There is consensus among the schools that those dispositions of a guardian which are for the good and advantage of the ward are valid, and those which are detrimental are invalid. The schools differ concerning those dispositions which are neither advantageous nor detrimental.

A group of Jafari jurists observe that they are only valid if the guardian is the father or the paternal grandfather, because the condition for their dispositions is the absence of harm, not the presence of an advantage. But where a judge or an executor is involved, their dispositions are valid only when advantageous. Rather, some of them observe that the dispositions of a father are valid even if they are disadvantageous and entail a loss for the child.[15]

Other non-Jafari schools state that there is no difference between the father, the paternal grandfather, the judge and the executor in that the dispositions of all of them are invalid unless they are advantageous and entail benefit. This is also the opinion of a large number of Jafari jurists. On this basis, it is valid for the guardian to trade with the wealth of his ward be he or she a child, an insane person or a person suffering from mental retardation—or to give it to another to trade with it, to buy with it real estate for his ward, and to sell and lend from what belongs to him, provided all this is done for benefit and with good intention, and the surety of benefit in lending is limited to where there is a fear of the property being destroyed.[16]

9.14. PARDON AND COMPROMISE

Some Jafari scholars have said that a child's guardian can

neither demand retaliation, a right to which his or her ward is entitled, because the child may opt for pardon, nor can he pardon, because the child may opt for the execution of the sentence for his or her own satisfaction. Al-Allamah al-Hilli has then opined that a guardian can demand the execution of the sentence, or pardon, or conclude a compromise regarding a part of the child's property, provided it is advantageous.

9.15. DIVORCE AND PRE-EMPTION
A guardian is not entitled to divorce the wife of his ward, irrespective of whether it is with or without any monetary compensation. If there is along with the child a partner in a property and the partner sells his share to a stranger, the guardian of the child is entitled to opt for pre-emption or to forgo it, depending on the child's interest. This is the more correct of the two opinions subscribed to by the Shafiis.

9.16. DEDUCTION OF CLAIMS
It is obligatory upon the guardian to deduct from the property of his or her ward those claims whose payment is compulsory, that is, debts, criminal damages, poor-due, even if they have not been claimed from him or her. As to the maintenance of those relatives whose maintenance is obligatory upon the child, the guardian will not pay it to the person entitled unless it is demanded.

9.17. SPENDING UPON THE WARD
It is obligatory upon the guardian to spend towards his or her ward's welfare and it is not permissible for him or her to act either niggardly or extravagantly. He or she is expected to act moderately, keeping in mind the standard of those similar to the ward. The guardian and the executor are trustees and are not liable unless breach of trust or negligence is proved. Hence, when a child attains puberty and claims breach of trust or negligence on behalf of the guardian, the burden of proof lies on him or her, and the guardian is only liable to take an oath, because he or she is a trustee.

9.18. A GUARDIAN'S SALE TO HIMSELF OR HERSELF

The Shafiis as well as some Jafari jurists observe that it is not valid for a guardian or an executor to sell himself or herself any property belonging to his or her ward or to sell his or her own property to the ward. Al-Allamah al-Hilli himself has considered it permissible, making no distinction between the guardian and a stranger, provided such a deal is advantageous for the ward and no blame is involved. Similarly it is also permissible for a guardian appointed by the judge to sell to the judge an orphan's property whose sale is valid. This also applies to an executor, even if he or she has been appointed by the judge to act as a guardian. As to the judge selling his property to the orphan, Imam Abu Hanifah has prohibited it on the basis that it amounts to the judge's pronouncing a decision concerning himself, and such a judgment is void. Al-Allamah al-Hilli says, "There is nothing objectionable in it," that is, the opinion of Imam Abu Hanifah.

9.19. THE GUARDIAN'S OR EXECUTOR'S AGENT

The guardian and the executor are entitled to appoint others as their agents for those activities which they are not capable of performing personally, as well as for those activities which they are capable of performing personally but do not consider it appropriate on the basis of custom to perform them personally. But where they consider it appropriate, the opinion prohibiting it is preferable.

It is evident here that acting personally or through an agent is a means for securing the ward's advantage and for fulfilling what is obligatory. So wherever this end is achieved, the act is valid, irrespective of whether it is performed by the guardian or his agent. Otherwise, the act is not valid even if performed by the guardian himself.

9.20. THE INSOLVENT PERSON

'*Muflis*', literally, means someone who has neither money nor a job to meet his or her needs. In legal terminology it means someone who has been declared legally incapable by the judge because his liabilities exceed his assets.

The schools concur that an insolvent person may not be prohibited from disposing his or her wealth, regardless of the extent of his or her liabilities, unless he or she has been declared legally incapable by the judge. Hence, if he or she has disposed of all his or her wealth before being declared incapable, his or her dispositions will be considered valid and his or her creditor, or anyone else, is not empowered to stop him or her from doing so, provided these dispositions are not with an intent to elude the creditors, especially where there is no reasonable hope of his or her wealth returning.

A judge will not declare a person insolvent unless the following conditions exist:

1. Where he or she is indebted and the debt is proven in accordance with the *Shariah*.

2. Where his or her assets are less than his or her liabilities. There is consensus among the schools regarding these two conditions.

The schools also concur on the validity of the declaration of disability where the assets are less than the liabilities. They differ where the liabilities are equal to the assets. The Jafari, Hanbali and Shafii schools state that he or she will not be declared legally incapable.[17] The two disciples of Imam Abu Hanifah, Muhammad and Abu Yusuf, observe that he or she will be declared legally incapable. The Hanafis have followed these two in their edict. But Imam Abu Hanifah has basically rejected the idea of considering an insolvent person as legally incapable even if his or her liabilities exceed his or her assets because legal disability entails the waste of his or her capabilities and human qualities. However, Imam Abu Hanifah says that if his or her creditors demand payment, he or she will be imprisoned until he or she sells his or her property and clears his or her debts.

This form of imprisonment is reasonable—as will be pointed out later—where the debtor has some known property.[18] The
Quran says, *"If the debtor is in straitened circumstances, then
let there be postponement until they are eased"* (2:280).
Moreover, there is consensus on the issue among all the legal
schools of the Community: the Shafii, Jafari, Hanbali, Maliki as
well as Muhammad and Abu Yusuf.[19]

3. The debt should be payable presently, not in the future, in
accordance with the opinion of the Jafari, Shafii, Maliki and
Hanbali schools. But if part of it is to be paid presently and part
of it in the future, it will be seen whether the assets suffice for
clearing the present debts; if they do, he will not be declared
legally incapable; if not, he will be declared so. If he is declared
legally incapable for debts presently payable, the debts payable
in the future will remain till the time of their payment
arrives.[20]

4. That the creditors, all or some of them, demand the declaration of his legal disability.

When all these conditions are present, the judge will declare
him legally incapable and stop him from disposing his property
by selling, renting, mortgaging, lending, and so on, being detrimental to the interests of the creditors.

The judge will sell the assets of the insolvent person and distribute the proceeds among his creditors. If they suffice for
repaying all the debts, they will be so applied. In the event of
their falling short, a proportionate distribution will be affected.
On the completion of the distribution, the disability will automatically end, because its purpose was to safeguard the interests of the creditors and this has been achieved.

9.21. EXCEPTIONS

Al-Allamah al-Hilli observes in *al-Tadhkirah*, "From among
the assets of the insolvent person, the house where he resides,
his slave, and the horse which he rides will not be sold."[21] This
is the view held by the Jafari, Imam Abu Hanifah, Imam Ibn
Hanbal, Imam Shafii and Imam Malik state that all of these
will be sold. A day's provision will also be left for him and his

family on the day of distribution, and if he dies before the distribution, the cost of his shroud and burial will be met from his own assets, because funeral expenses have precedence over debts.

In fact, all that which is immediately necessary will be left for him, that is, clothes, a day's provision or more, in accordance with the circumstances, books that are essential for someone like him, the tools of his trade by which he earns his living, the necessary household goods such as mattresses, blankets, pillows, cooking pots, plates, pitchers and all other things which one requires for his immediate needs.

9.22. A PARTICULAR THING AND ITS OWNER

If an owner from among the creditors finds a particular thing which the insolvent person had purchased from him on credit, that thing will belong to him in preference to all other creditors, even if there exists nothing else besides it. This is the opinion of the Jafari, Maliki, Shafii and the Hanbali schools. The Hanafis observe that he is not entitled to it, but will have a joint interest in it with the other creditors.[22]

9.23. WEALTH ACCRUING AFTER INSOLVENCY

If after legal disability any wealth accrues to an insolvent person, will his disability extend to it exactly like the wealth existing at the time of the disability, or not? Will the insolvent person be completely free in his dispositions concerning it?

The Hanbalis say that there is no difference between the wealth acquired after insolvency and the wealth present at the time of it. The Shafiis hold two opinions, and so do the Jafari. Al-Allamah al-Hilli states that that which is more likely is that the disability extends to it as well, because the purpose of the disability is to give those entitled their claims, and this right is not limited to the wealth existing at the time of the declaration. The Hanafis observe that the disability does not extend to it, and his dispositions as well as acknowledgment (of debt) are valid in regard to it.[23] If a crime has been committed against an insolvent person, if it is unintentional and requires the payment of damages, the insolvent person cannot pardon the crime because the right of the creditors extends to it, and if it is intentional and entails analogical reasoning (*qisas*), the insolvent person is entitled either to take analogical reasoning (*qisas*) or to opt for damages, and the creditors are not entitled to force him to take damages and forsake analogical reasoning.[24]

9.24. THE ACKNOWLEDGMENT OF AN INSOLVENT PERSON

If after being declared legally incapable an insolvent person acknowledges being indebted to some person, will his word be accepted and that person included among the creditors at the time of distribution of the property?

The Shafii, the Hanafi and the Hanbali schools observe that his acceptance will not be valid in respect to his property present at the time of declaration of his or her insolvency. The Jafari jurists differ among themselves, with the author of *al-Jawahir* and a large number of other authorities subscribing to the view of the Hanbali, Shafii and Hanafi schools.[25]

9.25. MARRIAGE

The Hanafis say that if an insolvent person marries after his being declared legally incapable, his marriage is valid and his wife is entitled to be included among the creditors to the extent of *mahr al-mithl*, and that which exceeds it remains a claim against him. The Shafii and the Jafari schools observe that the marriage is valid but the entire dowry will be considered a claim against him and the wife will not be entitled to anything along with the creditors.

9.26. IMPRISONMENT

The Jafari say that it is not valid to detain a person in financial straits despite the disclosure of his insolvency because the Quranic verse says, *"If the debtor is in straitened circumstances, then let there be postponement until they have eased"* (2:280). If he is found to possess any known asset, the judge will order him to surrender it, and if he refuses to comply, the judge is entitled either to sell it and clear the debts—because the judge is the guardian of the uncompliant—or to imprison the debtor until he clears his debts himself, in accordance with the Tradition: It is legitimate to punish and humiliate (as when the creditor calls his debtor 'unjust', 'a delayer', etc.) a debtor who possesses (financial capability) Imam Abu Hanifah observes that the judge is not entitled to sell his property against his will, but he can imprison him. Imam Shafii and Imam Ibn Hanbal state that the judge is empowered to sell and clear the debts.[26]

9.27. PROHIBITION ON TRAVELING

There is no doubt that if it is permissible to punish a debtor by imprisonment it is also valid to prohibit him or her from traveling provided the necessary conditions exist. These conditions are: The debt be proven as per the *Shariah*; the debtor be capable of repaying it, and he or she procrastinate and keep on postponing payment. Apart from this, the interests of the creditors should be feared to be in jeopardy if he or she travels, such as where the journey is long and dangerous. Hence if the debt is not proved, or is proved but the debtor's circumstances are straitened and he or she is unable to repay, or he or she has an agent or surety, or there is no fear of the creditors' interests being hurt if he or she travels, in all these circumstances it is in no way permissible to prohibit him or her from traveling.

PART THREE
SOCIAL ISSUES

10
MARRIAGE

10.1. THE MARRIAGE CONTRACT
AND ITS CONDITIONS

All the major schools of jurisprudence concur that marriage is performed by the recital of a marriage contract which contains an offer made by the bride or her deputy (*naib*) such as her guardian or agent (*wakil*), and a corresponding acceptance by the groom or his deputy. A mere agreement without the recital of the contract does not amount to marriage.

The schools also agree that a marriage contract is valid when recited by the bride or her deputy by employing the words, *ankahtu* or *zawwajtu* (both meaning, "I gave in marriage") and accepted by the groom or his deputy with the words, '*qabiltu*' ("I have accepted") or '*raditu*' ("I have agreed").

The schools of jurisprudence differ regarding the validity of the contract when not recited in the past tense or recited by using words other than those derived from the roots *al-zawaj* and *al-nikah*, such as, *al-hibah* and *al-bay*. The Hanafis say that a marriage contract is valid if recited by any word conveying the intention of marriage, even if the words belong to the roots *al-tainlik*, *al-hibah*, *al-bay*, *al-atal-ibahah* and *al-ihlal*, provided these words indicate their being used for the purpose of marriage. But the contract will not conclude if the words used are derived from *al-ijarah* (hiring) and *al-iarah* (lending), because these words do not convey the meaning of perpetuity and continuity. They have based their argument on this narration from *Sahih al-Bukhari* and the *Sahih Muslim*. A woman came to the Prophet and said, "Oh Messenger of God, I have come to offer myself to you." On hearing this the Prophet lowered his head and did not reply. Then, one of those present said, "If you do not want her, marry her to me." The Prophet asked him, "Have you anything?" He replied, "By God, I have nothing." Again the Prophet asked him, "Have you any knowledge of the Quran?" He replied regarding the extent of his knowledge of the Quran. Then the Prophet said, "I make her your property in exchange for your knowledge of the Quran" (using the word *mallaktu*).[1]

The Malikis and the Hanbalis say that the contract is valid if recited by using the words *al-nikah* and *al-zawaj* or their derivatives and is also valid when the word used is *al-hibah*, with the condition that the amount payable as dower (*mahr* or *sidaq*) is also mentioned. Words other than these cannot be used. They have based their argument for the use of the word al-hibah on this verse of the Quran,[2] "*... And a believing woman if she gave (wahabat, derived from al-hibah) herself to the Prophet, if the Prophet desired to marry her....*" (33:50). The Shafii scholars consider it obligatory that the words used in the contract should be either the derivatives of the root *al-zawaj* or that of *al-nikah*.

The Jafari say that it is obligatory that the offer be made by using the words *ankahtu* and *zawwajtu* in the past tense. The marriage is not concluded if the word used is not in the past tense and does not belong to the roots *al-zawaj* and *al-nikah*, because these two roots conventionally convey the meaning of marriage and the past tense conveys the meaning of certainty and also because the Quran testifies their use.[3] Apart from this, the absence of consensus invalidates the use of words other than these in such a contract. For acceptance, according to them, the word *qabiltu* or *raditu* can be used.

The Jafari, Shafii and Hanbali schools mention 'immediacy' as a condition for a marriage contract. By immediacy they mean the acceptance of the offer without any delay. The Malikis consider a minor delay inconsequential, such as a delay caused due to the recital of a short sermon or the like of it. The Hanafi school is of the opinion that immediacy is not necessary. Even if a man addresses a letter to a woman conveying his proposal of marriage to her and the woman gathers witnesses and reads out the letter to them and says, "I marry myself to him," the marriage is performed.[4]

All the schools concur that the contract can be recited in any language when it is impossible to recite it in Arabic, but differ as regards the validity of the contract when so recited despite the possibility of its being recited in Arabic. The Hanafi, the Maliki and the Hanbali schools consider this as valid. The Shafii and the Jafari schools consider it as invalid.[5]

The Jafari, Hanbali and Shafii schools consider a contract in writing as invalid. The Hanafi school is of the opinion that a written contract is valid, provided the bride and the groom are not present together at the place of contract. The schools concur that a dumb person can convey his intention to marry by signs in case he is incapable of expressing it in writing. If he can express it in writing, it is better for him to combine both, writing and signs, in conveying his intention.

According to the Hanbali and the Hanafi schools, if a clause is included in the contract giving a choice to the bride and the groom to annul the contract, the contract is valid but the condition is void. The Maliki school is of the opinion that if the marriage is not consummated, this condition as well as the contract are both void. But if the marriage has been consummated, the condition is void, not the contract. The Jafari and the Shafii schools have declared both the contract and the condition as void irrespective of whether the marriage has been consummated or not.[6]

As a matter of course, the offer is made by the bride and is accepted by the groom. The bride says, *'zawwajtuka'* (I have married myself to you) and the groom accepts by saying, *'qabil-*

tu' (I have accepted). The question which now arises is, is the contract valid when the acceptance precedes the offer and the groom addresses the guardian of the bride saying, *'zawwijniha'* (marry her to me) and the guardian replies, *'zawwajtukaha'* (I have married her to you)? The Hanbali school considers it as invalid while the other schools concur on its validity.[7] Al-Allamah al-Hilli, a Jafari scholar, says, "A marriage contract cannot be made contingent on a future event because certainty is one of its conditions. If a condition is included prescribing a certain time or a certain quality, such as, when the offer is made with the condition that the marriage will conclude at the beginning of the forthcoming month and this offer is accepted, the contract is not valid. Imam Shafii is of the same opinion." Abu Zuhrah, a Hanafi scholar, writes, "A marriage should be concluded on the recital of the contract, because marriage is a contract and the consequences of the contract cannot be delayed after its conclusion. Therefore it is not possible to postpone the consequences of a contract till the fulfillment of a future condition." In the book Imam Ahmad Hanbali has been referred to as validating a conditional contract of marriage.

Al-Fiqh alal-madhdhib al-arbaah, quoting Hanafi and Shafii scholars, states that if an illiterate person mispronounces the word *'zawwajtu'* and says instead, *'jawwaztu,'* the contract is valid. Al-Sayyid Abu al-Hasan al-Isfahani, a Jafari scholar, in his *Wasilat al-najat*, gives a similar edict.

10.2. Witnesses

The Shafii, Hanafi and Hanbali schools concur that the presence of witnesses is a necessary condition for a valid contract. The Hanafi school considers as sufficient the presence of two men or a man and two women. However, if all the witnesses are women, the contract is not valid. This school does not consider being just as a condition for the acceptability of the witnesses. The Shafii and Hanbali schools consider as necessary the presence of two male Muslim witnesses possessing the quality of being just. According to the Malikis, the presence of witnesses is not necessary at the time of the contract but their presence is necessary at the time when marriage is to be consummated. Therefore, if the contract is recited without the presence of witnesses, it is valid. However, when the groom intends to consummate the marriage it is incumbent upon him to have two witnesses. If the marriage is consummated without the witnesses, the contract becomes, of necessity, void, and this is considered as amounting to an irrevocable divorce.[8] The Jafari consider the presence of witnesses to be recommended but not obligatory.[9]

10.3. CAPACITY TO ENTER INTO A MARRIAGE CONTRACT

All the schools agree that sanity and adulthood are necessary qualities for both the parties to the contract, unless the contract is concluded by the guardian of any of them. The contract with the guardian shall be discussed later. The schools also agree that there should be no obstacle to marriage between the man and the woman such as consanguinity or any other disabling factor of a permanent or temporary character. We will discuss the legal obstacles to marriage in a separate chapter. The schools also consider the ascertainment of both the parties to the contract as necessary. Therefore, when it is said, "I marry you to one of these two daughters," or "I marry myself to one of these two men," the contract will not be valid.

All the schools except the Hanafi consider free consent as a *sine qua non* without which the contract does not conclude. The Hanafis are of the opinion that the contract is concluded even if coercion is present.[10] Al-Shaykh Murtada al-Ansari, a Jafari scholar, after mentioning free consent as a condition, writes, "That which is commonly held by the Jafari scholars of the latter period is that, when a person coerced consents freely later on, the contract is valid. In the book *al-Hadaiq wa al-riyad* their consensus has been reported on this issue." Al-Sayyid Abu al-Hasan al-Isfahani, an Jafari jurist, writes, "Free consent of both the parties is a necessary condition for a valid contract. If both of them or any of them is coerced, the contract is invalid. But if the party coerced consents later, the reason in favor of the validity of the contract seems strong." [11] According to the above-mentioned criterion, if the man or the woman pleads coercion and then willingly live together like a married couple and show the happiness of a newly married bride and groom, or if the woman takes the dowry (*mahr*) or does any other act proving consent, the claim of coercion will be rejected and no other evidence will be accepted contradicting the consent.

According to the Hanafi, Hanbali, Shafii and Maliki schools of jurisprudence, a contract recited in jest concludes the marriage. Therefore, when a woman says jokingly, "I marry myself to you" and the man accepts it in a similar fashion, the contract is concluded. Divorce and the freeing of a slave also conclude if recited in jest according to the Tradition, "The three whose intentional and jestful recital is considered intentional are: marriage, divorce and freeing of a slave." The Jafari school considers all contracts involving jest as null and void due to the absence of the will to contract. As regards the above-mentioned Tradition, they consider the narrators as unreliable. The Hanafi and the Hanbali schools regard the marriage of an mentally retarded person as valid irrespective of whether the guardian has given permission or not. The permission of the guardian is necessary in the view of the Jafari and the Shafii schools.

According to the Jafari and Hanafi schools, the consent given when the two conditions of sanity and adulthood are present concludes the marriage as per the authority of the Tradition. The consent of sane persons even if detrimental to their interest, is valid. Imam Shafii, in the latter of his two views, considers the marriage as established when the bride being a sane adult acknowledges the marriage and the husband confirms her acknowledgment, because marriage is the right of both the parties. Imam Malik recognizes a difference here. According to him, when the bride and the groom are in a foreign land their acknowledgment establishes the marriage. When they are in their hometown they will have to furnish a proof of their marriage because it is convenient for them to do so. This was the former view of Imam Shafi.[12]

10.3.1. ADULTHOOD

There is consensus among the schools that menses and pregnancy are the proofs of female adulthood. Pregnancy is a proof because a child comes into being as a result of the uniting of the sperm with the ovum. Menses, because, like the production of sperm in the male, is a mark of female puberty. All schools, except the Hanafi, consider the growth of pubic hair as a sign of adulthood, but the Hanafis consider it no different from other hair of the body. According to the Shafii and the Hanbali schools, the adulthood of both the sexes is established on their completing fifteen years. According to the Malikis, it is seventeen years for both the sexes. The Hanafis consider eighteen years for a boy and seventeen years for a girl as the age of maturity.[13] The Jafari have mentioned fifteen years for a boy and nine years for a girl as the age of maturity on the authority of the following Tradition narrated by Ibn Sinan, "When a girl reaches the age of nine her property will be returned to her and it will be rightful for her to handle her own affairs, and the law is applied in her favor or against her. Experience also proves that a girl can conceive at the age of nine and the ability to conceive is equivalent to conception in all aspects."

10.3.2. NOTE

That which the Hanafis have said regarding the age of maturity is the maximum age limit for maturity. The minimum age limit according to them is twelve years and nine years for a boy and a girl respectively; because at this age it is possible for a boy to ejaculate and to impregnate, and for a girl to have orgasm, to menstruate, and to conceive.[14]

10.4. STIPULATION OF CONDITIONS BY THE WIFE

The Hanbali school is of the opinion that if the husband stipulates at the time of marriage that he will not make her leave her home or city, or will not take her along on journey, or that he will not take yet another wife, the condition and the contract are both valid and it is compulsory that they be fulfilled. In the event of their being violated, she can dissolve the marriage. The Hanafi, Shafii and Maliki schools regard the conditions as void and the contract as valid, and the Hanafi and Shafii schools consider it compulsory in such a situation that the wife be given a suitable dowry, not the dowry mentioned.[15]

According to the Hanafi school, when the man puts the condition that the woman would have the right to divorce, such as when he says, "I marry you on the condition that you can divorce yourself," the condition is invalid. But if the woman makes such a condition and says to the man, "I marry myself to you on the condition that I shall have the right to divorce," and the man says in reply, "I accept," the contract and the condition are both valid and the woman can divorce herself whenever she desires.

According to the Jafari school, if at the time of contract, the woman stipulates such conditions like the man shall not take another wife, or shall not divorce her, or shall not prohibit her from leaving home whenever she wants and wherever she wants to go, or that the right to divorce will be hers, or that he shall not inherit from her, or any other such condition which is against the spirit of the contract, the condition will be considered void and the contract will be valid.[16] But if she lays down such conditions as that the man will not make her leave her city, or will keep her in a specific home, or will not take her along on journeys, the contract and the condition are both valid. But if any of these conditions are not met, she does not have the right to dissolve the marriage. However, if in such a situation the woman refuses to accompany him, she still enjoys all the rights of a wife, such as being provided with maintenance and the like of it.[17]

When the wife pleads having included a valid condition in the contract and the husband repudiates the inclusion of such a condition, the wife will have to furnish evidence, because she has pleaded this extra condition. On the wife being unable to furnish the evidence, the husband will take an oath regarding the non-inclusion of the condition because he is the one who negates it.

10.5. CLAIM OF MARRIAGE

If a man claims to be married to a woman and she repudiates the claim, or the woman claims so and the man repudiates it, the burden of proof will lie on the claimant and the party negating the claim will take an oath. The schools concur regarding an acceptable proof that it requires the testimony of two just men. The evidence of women, alone or along with a man, is not acceptable except to the Hanafi school which considers the evidence of a just man and two just women as acceptable. Therefore, the fact of the witnesses being just is necessary, according to the Hanafi school, at the time of establishing the fact of marriage when any of the parties negates or contends it, but not a condition at the time of conclusion of the marriage contract. The Hanafi and Jafari schools consider the testimony of a witness as sufficient without his mentioning any conditions and details of the marriage. But the Hanbali school considers it necessary that the witness describe the conditions of marriage because there is a divergence of opinion regarding the conditions and it is possible for a witness to believe in the validity of a marriage whereas it may have been actually invalid. The Jafari, Hanafi, Shafii and Hanbali schools regard a marriage as proved even if a few people have a knowledge of it and it is not necessary that it be commonly known.

From time to time claims of marriage are brought before Shariah courts and often the claimant brings witnesses to prove their living together and having a common residence in the manner of a husband and wife. The question now is, does this prove marriage or not?

On the face of it, it can be said that marriage is *prima facie* considered as established unless the contrary is proved. This means that the living together of a man and woman apparently establishes marriage, and this conclusion compels the acceptance of the claimant's contention unless he is proved to lie. Apart from this, to decide the contention of the claimant claiming marriage as a lie is very difficult on the basis of the Jafari view which considers the presence of witnesses as not necessary at the time of marriage. But this *prima facie* conclusion in favor of the claimant is contrary to the general rule according to which every event—marriage or something else—whose occurrence is doubtful is assumed not to have occurred unless there is evidence to the contrary. Accordingly, the stand of the respondent, repudiating the claim of marriage, becomes congruent with the general rule. Therefore, the proof of marriage will be demanded from the claimant, and in the event of his failure to do so the respondent will take an oath and the claim will be dismissed.

This way of settling a claim is the right approach which corresponds with the rules of the *Shariah*, because the Jafari scholars accept the rule that, when there is a conflict between a *prima facie* conclusion and a general rule, the rule will be given precedence and the *prima facie* conclusion will not be given credence without additional proof in its favor and there is no such proof in this case.

When it is known that a marriage contract has been recited, but there is a doubt regarding its having been carried out correctly, the contract will be undoubtedly considered valid. But when there is a doubt as regards the occurrence of the contract itself, it is not possible to substantiate it on the strength of the social intercourse or co-residence of the two.

A question can be raised here: The principle that the act of a Muslim is to be considered as valid on the face of it, compels the acceptance of the claim of the person claiming marriage by giving precedence to lawful over unlawful and to good over evil. We are also commanded as regards every act in which there is a possibility of it being valid or invalid, that we rule out the possibility of its invalidity and give credit to the possibility of its validity.

The reply is that the consideration of the act of the claimant as valid in the present problem does not prove marriage. That which is proved is that the two have not committed any unlawful by social intercourse and sharing a common residence. The absence of any ground to consider their association as illegitimate may be due to marriage or due to a misconception (*shubhah*) on their part about the legitimacy of marriage, such as when both of them imagine it as lawful and later on discover it to be lawful—details of this will come later while discussing doubtful marriage. It is obvious that a general premise does not prove a particular one. For instance, when you say, "There is an animal in the house," it does not prove the presence therein of a horse or a deer. In the same manner, here, when a man has social intercourse with a woman, not knowing the cause, we may say, "She is his wife," but we should say that, "They have not committed an unlawful act," for it is possible that their associating with one another may be the result of marriage or the result of a misconception of marriage.

Another example will further clarify the point. If you hear a passer-by say something without knowing whether that utterance is a curse or a greeting, it is not lawful for you to consider it a curse. Also, in such a situation it is not binding on you to return the greeting, because you are not sure of the greeting. But if you are certain that he greeted you and doubt whether it was meant as a greeting or intended to ridicule, it is binding upon you to return the greeting, considering it to be a genuine greeting and by giving precedence to good over evil. Our problem is also like this. Even if living together be considered valid, it does not prove the presence of a contract. But if we are sure about the occurrence of a contract and doubt only its validity, we will consider the contract as valid without any hesitation.

In any case, social intercourse by itself does not prove anything, but it supplements and strengthens any other proof available. The decision in such a situation depends upon the view, satisfaction and assessment of the judge, on the condition that he does not consider their living together as an independent proof in itself for basing his judgment.[18]

The above-mentioned conclusion was as regards the establishment of marriage. But as regards children, the rule of considering the act of a Muslim as valid compels the regarding of the children as legitimate at all times, because the living together of the parents is either the result of marriage or the result of a false impression of marriage, and the children born due to such false impression are equal in status to children born of marriage for all legal purposes. Therefore, if a woman has claimed a man as her lawful husband and also of having a child by him, while the man refutes marriage but acknowledges the child as his, his claim will be accepted because it is possible that the child was born due to a false impression of marriage.

To conclude, it needs to be mentioned that this problem is based on the supposition that witnesses are not required for concluding a marriage contract as is the Jafari view. But according to the other schools, it is for the party claiming marriage that it mention the name of the witnesses, and if the party pleads its inability to present the witnesses due to their death or absence, it is possible that the above mentioned criterion be applied.

It is also necessary to point out that the living together does not prove marriage when there is contention and disagreement to that effect. When there is no such disagreement, we settle the claim of inheritance and its like by giving credit to the possibility of marriage, and on this issue there is a consensus among the schools.

10.6. THE PROHIBITED DEGREES OF FEMALE RELATIONS

One of the conditions of a valid marriage contract is that the woman be free from all legal obstacles, which means that she be competent to contract marriage. The restrictions are of two kinds: the prohibition due to consanguinity and those due to other causal factors (*al-muharramat*). The first include seven categories which permanently prohibit marriage. Of the second, ten categories prohibit marriage permanently and others only temporarily.

The schools concur that the female relatives with whom marriage is prohibited are of seven kinds:

1. Mother, which includes paternal and maternal

grandmothers.

2. Daughters, which includes granddaughters how lowsoever.

3. Sisters, both full and half.

4. Paternal aunts, which includes fathers' and grandfathers' paternal aunts.

5. Maternal aunts, which includes fathers' and grandfathers' maternal aunts.

6. Brother's daughters howsoever low.

7. Sister's daughters howsoever low.

The above prohibition has its origin in the following verse of the Quran, *"Forbidden to you are your mothers and your daughters and your sisters and your paternal aunts and your maternal aunts and brother's daughters and sister's daughters...."* (4:23).

These were the prohibited degrees of relations as a result of consanguinity (al-nasab). Those which are the result of causal factors are as follows:

10.6.1. AFFINITY

Affinity (*al-musabanah*) is the relationship between a man and a woman which forbids marriage between them; it includes the following:

1. The schools agree that the father's wife is forbidden for the son and the grandson howsoever high, by the sole conclusion of the marriage contract irrespective of the establishment of sexual contact. The origin of this concurrence is this verse of the Quran, *"And marry not women whom your fathers married ..."* (4:22).

2. The schools concur that the son's wife is forbidden for the father and grandfather, howsoever high, merely by the conclusion of the contract. This view is based on the following verse of the Quran, *"... And the wives of your sons who are of your own loins...."* (4:23.)

3. The schools concur that the wife's mother and her grandmother howsoever high, are forbidden on the mere conclusion of the contract though sexual contact may not have been established as per this verse of the Quran, *"... And the mothers of your wives...."* (4:23).

4. The schools agree that marriage with the wife's daughter is not forbidden merely on the conclusion of the contract, and they consider it lawful for a man, if he divorces that wife before sexual intercourse, or before looking at her or touching her with a sexual intent, to marry her daughter on the authority of this verse of the Quran, "... *And your step-daughters who are in your guardianship, (born) of your wives to whom you have gone in....*" (4:23).

The condition explains the general situation. The schools concur that the daughter is forbidden when a person marries her mother and establishes sexual contact with her. But the schools differ as regards the daughter being forbidden when the marriage has been concluded and sexual contact has not been established, but when he has looked at her or touched her with a sexual intent.

The Jafari, Shafii and Hanbali schools are of the view that the daughter would be forbidden only on sexual intercourse and looking and touching with or without sexual intent does not have any effect. The Hanafi and Maliki schools consider both, looking and touching with sexual intent, as sufficient causes for prohibition and are like sexual intercourse in all aspects.[19]

There is a consensus among the schools that the establishment of sexual contact due to a mistake or a false impression is like marriage itself in establishing affinity and creating its related prohibition. The meaning of 'sexual contact' due to mistake' is occurrence of sexual contact between a man and a woman under the false impression that they are lawfully wedded followed by the discovery that they are not lawfully married and that the contact was a result of a mistake of fact. As a consequence of this latter knowledge, the two will separate immediately and the woman will observe an obligatory waiting period and a reasonable dowry will become obligatory on the man. Affinity would be established as a result, but the two will not inherit from each other and the woman will not have the privilege of alimony (*nafaqah*).

10.6.2. CONSANGUINITY BETWEEN WIVES

The schools concur that combining two sisters in marriage at the same time is forbidden according to this verse of the Quran, "... *And that you should have two sisters together....*" (4:23) The Hanafi, Hanbali, Shafii and Maliki schools agree that a man cannot combine in marriage neither a woman and her paternal aunt nor a woman and her maternal aunt, because they have a general rule, that it is not lawful to marry two women of whom if one were to be a male it would be unlawful for him to marry the other. Therefore, if we suppose the paternal aunt a male, she would become a paternal uncle and it is not lawful for an uncle to marry his niece, and if we suppose the niece a male, she would become a nephew and it is not lawful for a nephew to marry his aunt. The same rule applies to a maternal aunt and her sister's daughter. Among the Jafari jurists there is a divergence of opinion. Some of them concur with the view of the other Hanafi, Hanbali, Shafii and Maliki schools, but most of them are of the opinion that if the niece is the first to be married, it is lawful for him to marry her paternal or maternal aunt even if the niece does not grant permission for this marriage. But if the paternal or the maternal aunt has been first married, the marriage with her niece is lawful only by her permission. The proponents of the above view have based their argument on the following verse of the Quran, "... *And lawful to you are (all women) besides those....*" (4:24).

In this verse, after mentioning those women with whom marriage is forbidden, the rest have been permitted, and this permission extends to combining the aunt and the niece together in marriage. Had it been unlawful the Quran would have explicitly mentioned it as it expressly mentions the prohibition regarding combining two sisters in marriage. As regards the general rule which supposes one of the two women to be a male, it is *istihsan*, which is considered unreliable by the Jafari. Apart from this, Imam Abu Hanifah has considered it lawful for a man to marry a woman and her father's wife despite of the fact that if any of these two were supposed a male, his marriage with the other would not be lawful. Obviously, it is not lawful for a man to marry his daughter or step-daughter, in the same way as it is not lawful for him to marry his mother or his father's wife.[20]

10.6.3. FORNICATION

It comprises the following issues:

10.6.3.1. DAUGHTER BORN OF FORNICATION

The Shafii and Maliki schools consider a man's marrying his daughter born of fornication as lawful and so also marrying his sister, his son's daughter, his daughter's daughter, his brother's daughter, and his sister's daughter, because she is legally non-related to him and because the law of inheritance does not apply between them, nor the law of maintenance.[21]

The Hanafi, Jafari and Hanbali schools regard marriage with a daughter by fornication as unlawful as one with a lawful daughter, because, they say, the daughter by fornication is born of his seed and is therefore considered his daughter in the literal sense and by the society in general. Her legal disability to inherit does not negate the fact of her being his daughter. It only negates such legal effects as inheritance and maintenance.

10.6.3.2. FORNICATION BY MISTAKE

The Jafari have observed that he who commits fornication with a woman or establishes sexual contact with her by mistake, while that woman is either married or is observing the waiting period as a result of a revocable divorce, she would become unlawful for him permanently, i.e. it is forbidden for him to marry her even if she separates from her husband as a result of an irrevocable divorce or death. But if he establishes sexual contact with a woman while she is unmarried or is undergoing the waiting period period as a result of the death of her husband or as a result of an irrevocable divorce, she would not be forbidden for him. According to the Hanafi, Hanbali, Shafii and Maliki schools, fornication or adultery is no obstacle to marriage between the two, regardless of whether the woman is married or unmarried.

10.6.3.3. FORNICATION AND ADULTERY

According to the Hanafi and the Hanbali schools fornication and adultery establish affinity. Therefore, he who establishes illegitimate sexual contact with a woman, the mother and daughter of that woman will become unlawful for him, and that woman will be unlawful for his father and his son. These schools do not make any difference between the establishment of such illegitimate contact before marriage or after it. Therefore, when a person establishes sexual contact with his wife's mother or a son with his father's wife, the wife will become unlawful for her lawful husband permanently; rather, according to the Hanafis,[22] "If a person intends to wake up his wife for intercourse and his hand reaches her daughter and he caresses her with sexual emotion while she, thinking it to be her mother, entertains it, her mother will become unlawful for him permanently. The same will apply to a woman who intends to wake up her husband and (mistakenly) caresses his son from another wife." The Shafii school is of the opinion that fornication does not establish affinity in the light of this Tradition, "An unlawful act does not illegitimate a lawful one."

The Malikis have two views on this question. One of them favors the Shafii view, the other, the Hanafi view. The Jafari consider fornication as capable of creating the prohibition pertaining to affinity. Thus he who fornicates with a woman, makes her unlawful for his father and his son. But as regards adultery after marriage, they observe that it does not illegitimate the lawful conjugal ties. Thus he who commits adultery with his wife's mother or his wife's daughter, his marriage with her stays as it is. The same applies to a father who commits adultery with his son's wife or a son with his father's wife; in both the cases the wife would not be considered unlawful for her lawful husband.

10.6.4. NUMBER OF WIVES

The legal schools concur that it is lawful for a man to have four wives at a time, but not a fifth as per the verse, "... *Then marry such women as seem good to you, two and three and four....*" (4:3) When any one of those wives is released from the bonds of marriage, either due to her death or divorce, it becomes lawful for him to marry another. The Jafari and Shafii schools say that when a man gives one of his wives a revocable divorce, it is not lawful for him to marry another until the expiry of the waiting period period. But if it be an irrevocable divorce it is lawful for him to do so. Also, it is lawful that he marry his irrevocably divorced wife's sister during his wife's waiting period because an irrevocable divorce prohibits marriage and breaks the marital bond.

According to the other schools, it is not lawful for him to marry a fifth wife or the sister of his divorced wife until the expiry of the waiting period period irrespective of whether the divorce is a revocable or an irrevocable one.

10.6.5. OATH OF CONDEMNATION

When a man accuses his wife of adultery or denies the paternity of her child and she denies the charge and he has no proof to offer, it is lawful for him to pronounce the oath of condemnation (*lian*) against her. The method of taking the oath of condemnation is that, first the man swears by God four times that he is indeed speaking the truth in accusing her, and the fifth time that the curse of God fall on him should he be lying. Then the woman will swear four times by God that he is lying, and the fifth time that the wrath of God be on her if he be speaking the truth. If the man refuses to pronounce the oath of condemnation, he is punished with the punishment for *qadhf*. But if he takes the oath of condemnation and the woman refuses to pronounce the oath of condemnation, she is liable to the punishment for adultery. If both of them pronounce the oath of condemnation against each other, none is liable to punishment and the two will separate and the child whose paternity he had denied would not be given to him.

The source of the above discussion are these verses of the Quran, *"If a man accuses his wife but has no witnesses except himself, he shall swear four times by God that his charge is true, calling down upon himself the curse of God if he is dying. But if his wife swears four times by God that his charge is false*

*and calls down His curse upon herself if it be true, she shall
receive no punishment"* (24:6-9).

There is consensus among the schools that it is obligatory
for the two to separate after the oath of condemnation. But
they differ as to whether such a wife is permanently unlawful
for her husband so as to make it unlawful for him to remarry
her later, even if he denies his own charge, or if she is unlawful
only temporarily so as to permit him to marry her after with-
drawing his own accusation. The Shafii, Jafari, Hanbali and
Maliki schools forbid her permanently for him even if he denies
his own accusation. The Hanafi school considers separation
due to the oath of condemnation like divorce. It would not
make her unlawful permanently because the prohibition arises
from the oath of condemnation and is removed on the with-
drawal of his accusation.[23]

10.6.6. NUMBER OF DIVORCES

The schools concur that if a man divorces his wife for the
third time having resumed conjugal relations twice earlier, she
will become unlawful for him and will not become lawful for
him again unless she marries another husband. This requires
that she observe the waiting period after her third divorce and
after the completion of this period consummate a permanent
marriage with another man. Then if she separates from the
second husband, due to his death or as a result of divorce, and
completes the waiting period, it becomes lawful for the first to
remarry again. After this, if he again repeats the same
sequence and divorces her three times, she becomes unlawful
for him until she consummates marriage with another man.
Similarly, she becomes unlawful for him after every third
divorce and becomes lawful by marrying another, even if she be
divorced a hundred times. Accordingly, every third divorce is
considered a temporary not a permanent obstacle to marriage.

But the Jafari observe that if a woman is divorced nine
times in the waiting period, she becomes unlawful permanently. By waiting period they mean that the husband first divorces
his wife, then resumes conjugal and sexual relations; then he

divorces her again during another period when she is not having menses, then again resumes conjugal and sexual relations;
then divorces her in yet another period when she is free from
menses. Now she will not be lawful for him until she consummates a permanent marriage with another man. Now, if this
first husband marries her again after her separating from that
second husband and divorces her three times in the *talaq al-
iddah* form, she becomes lawful again by consummating marriage with another. If he then marries her (for the third time)
and divorces her during the waiting period, the divorces completed, she will become unlawful for him permanently. But
when the divorce is not a *talaq al-iddah*, such as when he
returns to her and then divorces her without establishing sexual relations or marries her by another fresh contract after her
completing the waiting period, she will not become unlawful
for him even if she is divorced a hundred times.

10.6.7. DIFFERENCE OF RELIGION

The schools agree that it is not lawful for a male Muslim
nor for a female Muslim to marry those who do not possess
either a revealed nor a quasi-revealed scripture, or those who
worship idols, fire or the sun, the stars and other forms, or
non-believers who do not believe in God. The Hanafi, Hanbali,
Shafii and Maliki schools concur that marriage is not lawful
with those who possess a quasi-scripture, such as the
Zoroastrians. By 'quasi-scripture' is meant a scripture which is
said to have originally existed, as in the case of the
Zoroastrians, but was changed, causing it to be lifted from
them.

According to the Hanafi, Hanbali, Shafii and Maliki
schools, it is lawful for a Muslim man to marry a woman
belonging to the People of the Book (*ahl al-kitab*), which
implies Christians and Jews. But it is not lawful for a Muslim
woman to marry a man belonging to the People of the Book.
The Jafari scholars agree with the other Hanafi, Hanbali,
Shafii and Maliki schools that a Muslim woman cannot marry
a man belonging to the People of the Book, but differ among

themselves regarding the marriage of a Muslim man with a female belonging to the People of the Book. Some of them hold that intermarriage, either permanent or temporary, is not lawful. They base their argument on these verses of the Quran, "... *And hold not to the ties of marriage of unbelieving women....*" (60:10). "... *And do not marry the idolatresses until they believe....*" (2:221). Here they interpret polytheism as infidelity to the One God (*kufr*) and not having faith in Islam.

According to the Quran the People of the Book are not polytheists (*mushrikun*), as this verse shows, "*The unbelievers among the People of the Book and the pagans did not break off (from the rest of their communities) until the Proof came unto them*" (98:1). Others are of the opinion that such a marriage, both temporary and permanent, is lawful , and as a proof they quote the following verse of the Quran, "... *And the chaste from among the believing women and the chaste from among those who have been given the Book before you (are lawful to you)....*" (5:5)

This verse, according to them, explicitly permits marriage with women of the People of the Book. The third group, seeking to reconcile the texts in favor and against such intermarriage, only permits temporary not permanent marriage. They take those texts which forbid such marriage to imply permanent marriage, and those which permit it are taken to imply temporary marriage. On the whole most of the contemporary Jafari scholars consider permanent marriage with a woman belonging to the People of the Book as lawful and the Jafari *Shariah* courts in Lebanon marry a Muslim male to a female belonging to the People of the Book. They register such a marriage with all the legal effects proceeding therefrom.

All schools, except the Maliki, recognize the marriages of all non-Muslims as valid if performed according to their tenets. The Muslims confer upon such a marriage all the legal effects of a valid marriage without differentiating between the People of the Book and others—even if they permit marriage within prohibitive limits of consanguinity. The Malikis consider such a marriage as invalid because, they explain, it would be invalid if performed by a Muslim. Therefore, the same is true of non-Muslims. Apart from this, the Jafari have recorded these Traditions which confirm their stance, "For one who follows the religion of a community, its rules would be binding upon him.." "And require them to follow that which they consider binding upon themselves."24

In the Jafari work, *al-Jawahir*, there is a useful discussion which is relevant here. Its summary is as follows: If two non-Muslims litigate before a Muslim judge, should he give his judgment according to the laws of their religion or according to the Islamic law? The answer is: If the litigants are non-Muslims under the protection of an Islamic state (*dhimmi*), the judge has a discretion to either judge according to the Islamic law or to dismiss the case without any hearing. The following verse of the Quran gives this discretion, "*... Judge between them or turn aside from them, and if you turn aside from them, they shall not harm you in any way; and if you judge, judge between them with fairness....*" (5:42).

It was asked of Imam Jafar Sadiq regarding two men of the People of the Book between whom there was a dispute and they took the case before their own judge. When this judge judged between them, the one against whom the judgment was given refused to comply and asked that the issue be settled before the Muslim judge. He replied, "The judgment shall be according to the law of Islam."

If the litigants are those who are at war with the Islamic state (*harbi*), the judge is not obliged to settle their dispute and to protect some of them against others, as he is in the case of non-Muslims under the protection of the Islamic state. If one of the litigants is a non-Muslim or a citizen of a country at war with an Islamic state and the other a Muslim, the judge is obliged to accept the suit and to judge between them according to the Islamic law, in accordance with the Divine command, "*Pronounce judgment between them in accordance with Gods revelations and do not be led by their desires. Take heed lest they should turn you away from a part of that which God has revealed to you....*" (5:49). Moreover, if a non-Muslim woman sues her husband, the judgment will be given according to the Islamic law.

The above discussion makes it clear that Muslims should recognize as valid all those transactions of non-Muslims which are in conformity with their religion, as long as they do not refer it to Muslims for a decision. But if they seek a decision from Muslims, it is obligatory for them to decide, at all times, according to the Islamic law. As is understandable from the verses of the Quran and the traditions, it is also obligatory to judge between them in accordance with the norms of justice and fairness.

10.6.8. FOSTERAGE

All the schools concur regarding the veracity of the Tradition, "That which becomes unlawful due to consanguinity becomes unlawful due to fosterage (*al-ridd*)." According to this Tradition fosterage includes the same limits of relationship prohibitive to marriage as consanguinity. Thus any woman who as a result of breast-feeding becomes a foster-mother or a foster-daughter or a sister or an aunt (both maternal and paternal) or a niece, marriage with her is unlawful according to all the schools. But the schools differ regarding the number of breast-feedings which cause the prohibition and the conditions applicable to the foster-mother and the foster-child.

10.6.8.1. NURSING WOMEN

The Jafari say that it is necessary that the woman's milk be the result of lawful sexual relations, and if it secretes without marriage or as a result of a pregnancy due to adultery, the prohibition does not come into effect. It is not necessary that the woman remain conjugally bound to the person who is the cause of her turning lactiferous. Even if he divorces her or dies while she is pregnant or lactiferous, the prohibition comes into effect if she breast-feeds a child, even though she marries another and has intercourse with him. The Hanafi, Shafii and Maliki schools are of the opinion that there is no difference between the woman being a virgin or a widow and between her being married or unmarried as long as she has milk with

which she nurses the child. According to the Hanbali school
the legal effects of fosterage will not follow unless the milk is
the result of a pregnancy, and they do not set a condition that
the pregnancy be due to lawful intercourse.[25]

10.6.8.2. BREAST-FEEDING

The Jafari consider it necessary that the child should have
sucked milk from the breast, so if it is dropped in his mouth or
he drinks it in a manner other than direct sucking, the prohibitive relationship would not be established. The other Hanafi,
Hanbali, Shafii, and Maliki schools consider it sufficient that
the milk reach the child's stomach, whatever the manner.[26]
According to *al-Fiqh alal-madhahib al-arbaah*, the Hanbalis
consider it sufficient that the milk reach the child's stomach,
even if it be through his or her nose.

10.6.8.3. TIME TO ESTABLISH PROHIBITIVE
RELATIONSHIP

According to the Jafari, the prohibitive relationship is not
realized unless the child is suckled one day and one night in a
manner that his exclusive diet during this period be the milk
of that woman without any other food, or is breast-fed fully fifteen times uninterrupted by breast-feeding by another woman.
In the book *al-Masalik* the giving of food has been considered
without effect. The reason given for the above-mentioned quantity is that it leads to the growth of flesh and hardens the
bones. The Shafii and the Hanbali schools regard five breast-
feedings as the minimum necessary. The Hanafi and the
Maliki schools consider that the prohibitive relationship is
established simply by being breastfed irrespective of the quantity fed, be it more or less or even a drop.[27]

10.6.8.4. TIME LIMIT

The Jafari, Shafii, Maliki, and Hanbali schools have mentioned the period of breast-feeding to be up to two years of the
age of the child. The Hanafi school considers it to be two and a
half years.

10.6.8.5. STATE OF WOMAN BREAST-FEEDING

According to the Hanafi, Maliki, and Hanbali schools, it is not necessary that the foster-mother be alive at the time of feeding. Therefore, if she dies and the child crawls up to her and sucks from her breast, it is sufficient to establish the prohibitive relationship. But the Malikis have gone further and observed that even if there is a doubt as to that which the child has sucked, whether it is milk or not, the prohibitive relationship would be established.[28] The Jafari and Shafii schools consider it necessary that the woman be alive at the time of breast-feeding and if she dies before completion of the minimum feedings, the prohibitive relationship would not be established.

The schools concur that the husband of that woman, will become the foster-father of the breast-fed child, and between the two all those things which are unlawful between fathers and sons will be unlawful. His mother will become a grandmother for the breast-fed child, and his sister the child's aunt in the same manner as the woman who breast-feeds the child becomes his mother and her mother his grandmother and her sister his aunt.

10.6.9. THE WAITING PERIOD

There is consensus among the schools that marriage with a woman undergoing waiting period[29] is not lawful and she is like a married woman in all aspects, irrespective of whether she is undergoing waiting period due to the death of her husband or as a result of divorce, revocable or irrevocable, in accordance with the following verses of the Quran, "*And the divorced women should keep themselves in waiting for three menstrual courses....*" (2:228). "*And as for those of you who die and leave wives behind, they (the wives) should keep themselves in waiting for four months and ten days....*" (2:234). The meaning of *al-tarabbus* is to be patient and to wait.

The schools differ regarding one who marries a woman during her waiting period, as to whether she will become unlawful for him. According to the Maliki school she becomes unlawful for him permanently if intercourse takes place, otherwise not. According to the Hanafi and the Shafii schools the two should separate, there being no impediment to remarriage on completion of the waiting period.[30]

It is mentioned in the seventh part of *al-Mughni*, a book of the Hanbalis, "If a person consummates marriage with a woman during her waiting period and both know it and know that marriage is unlawful during waiting period, both of them would be considered fornicators and liable to punishment." In the sixth part of the same book it is stated, "If a woman fornicates, marriage with her will not be lawful for one who knows it unless these two conditions are fulfilled: completion of the waiting period and penitence for fornicating... If these two conditions are fulfilled, there is no obstacle to her marriage with the fornicator or someone else." This shows that according to the Hanbalis, marriage during the waiting period does not result in permanent prohibition to marriage.

According to the Jafari, marriage with a woman during the waiting period, after a revocable or an irrevocable divorce, is not lawful, and if one marries her with the knowledge of the waiting period and the related prohibition, the contract is void and she would become unlawful for him permanently, irrespective of sexual contact. But if he has no knowledge of the waiting period and of such marriage being unlawful, she would not become unlawful permanently unless he has had intercourse with her. If he has not had intercourse, only the contract would become void, and he may marry her after the completion of the waiting period.[31]

10.6.10. THE SACRED STATE

The Jafari, Shafii, Maliki and Hanbali schools say that a pilgrim for the longer or shorter pilgrimage, when in the sacred state, man or woman, cannot marry nor conclude marriage on behalf of another acting as a guardian or an agent. The marriage, if performed, is void in accordance with the Tradition, "A pilgrim may not propose, nor marry, nor conclude marriage for another."

The Hanafi school considers the sacred state as no hindrance to marriage. The Jafari hold that if a marriage is performed without the knowledge of the prohibition during the sacred state, it will make the woman temporarily unlawful. When they are relieved of the sacred state—or he, when the woman had not been in the sacred state at all—it is lawful for him to marry her. But if concluded with the knowledge of the prohibition, the two should separate, and she would become permanently unlawful to him. The other schools hold that she would become unlawful only temporarily.[32]

10.7. MATRIMONIAL GUARDIANSHIP

Guardianship in marriage implies the legal authority granted to a competent guardian to be exercised over one under a legal disability for his or her advantage. This discussion comprises the following issues:

10.7.1. GUARDIANSHIP OF A PREVIOUSLY MARRIED AND SANE WOMAN

The Shafii, Maliki and Hanbali schools are of the opinion that the guardian has the sole authority with respect to the marriage of his sane and major female ward if she is a virgin. But if she is a person who has been married previously (*thayyib*), his authority is contingent on her consent. Neither can he exercise his authority without her consent, nor can she contract marriage without his permission. It is obligatory that the guardian take the responsibility of concluding the contract, which would not conclude if the woman recites it, although it is essential that she consent.

The Hanafis regard a sane, grown-up female as competent to choose her husband and to contract marriage, irrespective of her being a virgin or a non-virgin. No one has any authority over her, nor any right to object, provided she chooses one her equal and does not stipulate less than a proper dower (*mahr al-mithl*) for the marriage. If she marries someone who is not her equal, the guardian has the right to object and demand the annulment of the contract by the judge, and if she marries her equal but for less than the proper dower, the guardian has the right to demand annulment if the husband does not agree to a proper dower.[33]

Most of the Jafari scholars are of the view that a sane girl of full age, on maturing, is fully competent to decide her contractual as well as non-contractual affairs and this includes marriage, regardless of her being a virgin or not. Therefore, it is valid for her to contract for herself or on behalf of others, directly or by appointing a deputy, by making an offer or giving her acceptance, and irrespective of her having or not having a father, a grandfather, or other relatives. It is of no consequence whether the father agrees or not. The social status of the girl, higher or lower, and whether she marries a respectable or an abject person, is of no consequence. No one has a right of objection in this regard. Thus, she is in all respects on a par with a male, without any difference whatsoever. The scholars support this argument by quoting the following verse of the Quran, "... *Then do not prevent them from marrying their husbands....*" (2:232).

The following Tradition of the Prophet narrated by Ibn al-Abbas also supports their view, "One who is without a mate (*aym*) has more authority over himself or herself than his or her guardian." *Aym* is one who is without a mate, man or woman,; a virgin or not. The scholars have also put forth a rational argument and observed that reason dictates that every human being has total liberty regarding his own affairs and no other person, regardless of his being a near or distant relative, has any authority over him. Ibn al-Qayyim has well observed when he says, "How can it be legitimate for a father to marry his daughter without her consent to anyone of his choice, while she disapproves such a marriage and regards him as the most detestable person in the world, and yet he should forcefully marry her and hand her over as a captive to him!..."

10.7.2. Guardianship in Cases of Minority, Insanity and Idiocy

The legal schools concur that the guardian is authorized to

contract marriage on behalf of his minor or insane ward (male or female). But the Shafii and Hanbali schools have limited this authority to the case of a minor virgin or non-virgin. They do not recognize any such authority for the guardian.[34] The Jafari and Shafii schools consider only the father and the paternal grandfather as competent to contract marriage on behalf of a minor ward. The Malikis and Hanbalis further limit it to the father. The Hanafi school extends it to other relatives, even if it be a brother or an uncle. The Hanafi, Jafari, and Shafii schools regard a contract of marriage with a mentally retarded person as invalid without the consent of his guardian. The Maliki and Hanbali schools consider it valid, and the consent of the guardian is not required.[35]

10.7.3. *THE ORDER OF PRIORITY IN GUARDIANSHIP*

The Hanafis give priority to the son as regards guardianship over his mother, even if he be an illegitimate one. After the son, his son is given the right to guardianship and then follow: the father, the paternal grandfather, the full brother, the half-brother (paternal), the full brother's son, the half-brother's son, the paternal uncle, the paternal uncle's son, and so on. From this it is clear that the executor of the ward's father's will does not have matrimonial guardianship even if he has been explicitly given this authority. The Malikis give priority to the father and after him the guardianship goes to the executor of his will. Then comes the turn of the son—even if he be an illegitimate one. Thereafter come the brother, the brother's son, the paternal grandfather, the paternal uncle... and so on. On this order being exhausted the guardianship will finally lie with the judge.

The Shafii scholars give the father priority in exercising guardianship. After him the paternal grandfather, the full brother, the half-brother (paternal), the brother's son, the paternal uncle, the paternal uncle's son, and so on, will exercise guardianship in the descending order until it finally reaches the judge. The Hanbalis regard the father, and after him the executor of his will, as those competent to exercise guardian-

ship. After these two, the order follows the pattern of inheritance till it finally reaches the judge.

According to the Jafari, only the father and the paternal
grandfather—and on some occasion, the judge—are those
authorized to exercise guardianship with respect to marriage.
Both the father and the grandfather are independent in the
exercise of their guardianship over a minor (girl or boy) or over
an adult whose insanity or mental retardation precedes his
adulthood, that is, when he or she has been insane or mentally
retarded when a minor and this state has continued into adulthood. But if insanity or mental retardation has resulted after
maturity, the father and the grandfather have no authority for
contracting marriage on behalf of such an adult. In this case
the judge will exercise his guardianship despite the presence of
the father and the grandfather. When the father chooses one
mate and the grandfather another, the latter's choice shall prevail.

The marriage contracted by the guardian—be it the father,
the grandfather or the judge—comes into effect if it is not
against the interests of the ward. If it is, the ward has the
option of dissolving the marriage on attaining maturity.

The Hanafis have observed that when the father or the
grandfather of a minor girl marries her to a person who is not
her equal or for less than a proper dowry, the marriage will be
valid unless it is evident that there has been a misuse of
authority. But if such a marriage is concluded on behalf of a
minor girl by her guardian who is neither her father nor her
grandfather, the marriage will be considered void *ab initio*.

The Hanbali and the Maliki schools have said that the
father may give his daughter in marriage for less than a proper dowry. The Shafii school says that he may not, and if he
does so, the daughter has the right to claim the proper dowry.

The Jafari have said that if the guardian gives his minor
female ward in marriage for less than proper dowry or contracts marriage on behalf of his minor male ward for more
than such dowry, the contract and the dowry will both be valid
on there being a good reason for doing so. In the absence of

such a reason, only the contract will be valid and the validity of the dowry will depend upon the ward's agreeing to it after maturity. If the ward does not agree the dowry will be reduced to the proper dowry.

There is consensus among the schools that a just ruler can contract marriage on behalf of an insane person, male or female, if he or she has no guardian from among their relatives. This consensus is based on the following Tradition, "The ruler is the guardian of one who has no guardian."

The Jafari and Shafii schools do not consider the judge competent to exercise guardianship over a minor girl. The Hanafi school gives this authority to the judge, but does not consider the contract so concluded as binding. Therefore, the girl can set it aside on maturity.

Thus the position of the Hanafis is in fact similar to that of the Jafari and Shafii schools because the judge becomes redundant in this matter. According to the Maliki school, the judge is competent to contract marriage on behalf of a minor or a lunatic (male or female) with their equals on their not having any relative to act as guardian. The judge is also given competence to conclude marriage on behalf of a sane grown-up girl, with her consent.

The schools concur that it is necessary for a guardian to be be an adult Muslim male. As to the condition of being just, it is required in the judge who is acting as guardian, not for a relative acting as such, except by the Hanbali school which considers being just as necessary for every guardian regardless of his being a relative or a judge.

10.8. EQUALITY

The meaning of equality (*al-kafaah*), according to those who consider it as consequential in marriage, is that the man be an 'equal' to the woman in certain things. Moreover, they require equality of men only, because it is not something disapproved for a man to marry a woman lower in status as against a woman doing the same.

The Hanafi, Shafii and Hanbali schools concur in requiring

equality in religion (Islam), freedom (i.e. in his not being a slave), profession and lineage. These schools differ regarding equality in prosperity and wealth. The Hanafi and the Hanbali schools recognize it, while the Shafii school does not.

The Jafari and Maliki schools do not accept the notion of equality except in religion, in accordance with the following Tradition, "When someone, whose faith and conduct is acceptable to you, comes to you with a proposal, then marry him. If you do not, it will result in corruption upon the earth and great discord." In any case, the condition of equality in marriage does not harmonize with the following verse of the Quran, *"...Surely the most honorable amongst you in God's sight is the most pious among you..."* (49:13).

Also, it is opposed to the practice (*Sunnah*) of the Prophet, who ordered Fatimah bint Qays to marry Zayd ibn Usamah and ordered Banu Bayadah to marry Abu Hind, who was a cupper. That is why we see a group of eminent scholars, such as Sufyan al-Thawri, al-Hasan al-Basri, al-Karkhi among the Hanafis and Abu Bakr al-Jassas and the followers of these two among the scholars of Iraq[36] disregarding equality as a condition in marriage.

10.9. DEFECTS

Is it possible for one of the spouses to dissolve the marriage on finding a certain defect in the other? The schools have differed regarding the defects which justify the dissolution of the marriage and also regarding the rules that apply in these circumstances.

10.9.1. IMPOTENCY

Impotency is a disease which renders a man incapable of sexual intercourse. All the major schools give the wife the right to dissolve the marriage in such a situation. But in a situation where the husband's inability is limited to his wife and he is capable of intercourse with another, the schools have different views regarding the wife's right of dissolving the marriage.

The Jafari have said that the wife's right to dissolve the

marriage is not ascertained unless the husband is incapable of having intercourse with any women whatsoever. Therefore, on his inability being limited to this wife and not others, the right of dissolving the marriage does not accrue[37] because the source of this right is a rule which gives the power of dissolving marriage to the wife of an impotent man. One who is capable of having intercourse with other women is not considered impotent in the true sense of the word. This is so because impotence is a physical defect which renders a man incapable of intercourse. In a case where a person is incapable of intercourse with his wife and not others, then the reason is necessarily an external cause apart from an innate physical defect. The reason could be shyness or fear or a quality of the wife which makes her detestable or something else. It has also been observed that there are such criminals whose dislike of legitimate sexual relations has reached such a degree that they are unable to perform it. On the contrary, their inclination towards the unlawful is such that it gives them the required strength and the pleasure of performing it.

According to the Shafii, Hanbali and Hanafi schools, a person's inability to copulate with his wife gives her the right to dissolve the marriage despite his being capable of it with other women, because in such a case he will be considered impotent with respect to her. Besides, they point out, of what benefit is it to the wife if he is capable of having intercourse with other women!

However, there is consensus among the schools that when a woman pleads the impotence of her husband and he denies the charge, the burden of proof will rest on her to prove that he is impotent. On no proof being offered it will be seen whether she was a a virgin prior to marriage or not. If she had been one, she will be referred to female specialists to determine her present condition, and their opinion will be acted upon. In a case where the wife is not a virgin, the husband will be made to take an oath because it is he who denies the charge made by the wife claiming the presence of a defect sufficient for dissolving the marriage. If he takes the oath, the wife's claim will be

430 Part Three: Social Issues

dismissed. But on his abstaining from taking the oath, the wife will take the oath and then the judge will give him a lunar year's time. When this period also does not yield any benefit for the wife the judge will grant her the option of remaining with him or of dissolving the marriage. If she elects to remain with him, the choice is hers, and if she desires dissolution, she will herself annul the marriage or the judge will act on her request. According to the Jafari, Shafii and Hanbali schools, she does not require a divorce for the separation. The Malikis have said that she will divorce herself by the order of the judge. This observation of the Malikis does in fact mean annulment. The Hanafi school is of the opinion that the judge will order the husband to pronounce the divorce and on his refusal the judge will pronounce the divorce.

The Hanafis, in such a case, regard the payment of the full, proper dowry as necessary. The Jafari consider the payment of half the dowry as sufficient. The Maliki, Shafii and Hanbali schools are of the opinion that she will not be entitled to receive any dowry.

If the husband's impotence is subsequent to the consummation of marriage, the wife will not have the choice of dissolving the marriage. However, if impotence occurs after the contract but before the consummation of marriage, she will have the choice to annulment in the same manner as when impotence precedes the contract.

10.9.2. MUTILATION OF THE MALE ORGAN AND CASTRATION

The state of mutilation of the male organ arises from castration, either by the removal or by the crushing of both testicles. Both the state of mutilation of the male organ and castration, if present before the consummation of marriage gives the wife the immediate right to annul the contract. But if these two defects occur after the consummation of marriage, the right to annul the marriage will not result.

The Hanafis have observed that if the castrated person has the capacity of erection, the right to annul the marriage does not arise, even though ejaculation be absent. The other schools regard ejaculation as a necessary condition regardless of erection, because the inability to ejaculate is a defect similar to impotence.

Al-Shahid al-Thani,[38] has narrated that a castrated person can penetrate and have orgasm, and his condition during the act is more intense than a normal male, although he does not ejaculate. This inability is sufficient for rescinding the contract, because the traditions prove the right of the wife of a castrated person to opt for separation.

The Hanafis have said that when the contract is rescinded as a result of any of these two defects, the wife shall be entitled to full dowry. The other schools have observed that, if the contract is annulled as a consequence of mutilation of the male organ, no dowry need be paid because marriage has not been consummated. But if castration be the cause for rescinding the contract, she will receive her dowry only when consummation has occurred.

The Hanafi school does not recognize any ground on which the husband may annul the contract, even though there may be tens of defects in the wife. On the contrary, the wife has the right of annulling the marriage on the basis of any of the three above-mentioned defects, i.e., impotency, mutilation of the male organ and castration. Therefore, the Hanafis have nothing to say about the forthcoming defects.

10.9.3. INSANITY

The Maliki, Shafii, and Hanbali schools concur that the insanity of one spouse gives the other the right to annul the marriage. But these schools differ regarding the details. The Shafii and Hanbali schools have granted the right of annulment irrespective of whether madness results before or after marriage, and even after consummation. There is no period of waiting before annulment, as required in the case of impotence.

According to the Malikis, if the insanity occurs before marriage, the right to annul the contract results for the sane spouse, on the condition that he or she suffers harm in living with the other. But if the insanity results after marriage, only the wife has the right to annul the marriage after a probationary period of a year granted by the judge. The husband cannot annul the marriage if his wife loses sanity after marriage.

According to the Jafari, the husband will not annul the marriage where the wife has become insane after marriage, because he has the option of divorce. The wife, on the contrary, can annul the marriage on the husband's insanity, regardless of its preceding the marriage or occurring afterwards, and even after consummation.

The Jafari, Hanbali, Shafii and Maliki schools concur that the wife is entitled to receive full dowry if the marriage has been consummated, and nothing if not.

10.9.4. LEPROSY AND LEUCODERMA

According to the Jafari, leprosy and leucoderma are among defects that give the husband, not the wife, the right to annul the marriage on condition that such disease be antecedent to the marriage without the husband's knowledge. The right to annul the marriage does not exist for the wife if her husband suffers from any of these two diseases.

The Shafii, Maliki and Hanbali schools regard these two diseases among the causes that give both the man and the woman an equal right to annul marriage. On one of the spouses suffering from any of these two diseases, the other acquires the right to annul the contract. According to the Shafii and Hanbali schools, the rule that applies in the case of insanity applies here as well.

The Malikis are of the opinion that the wife has the right of annulment equally whether the husband's leprosy antedates the marriage or follows it. As regards the husband's right, he can do so on the wife's being leprous before marriage or at the time of marriage. Regarding leucoderma, both the spouses have the choice of annulment if the disease precedes marriage, and if it occurs after marriage, only the wife can exercise her choice and not the husband. The milder forms of leucoderma, on their appearance after marriage, do not give rise to any right. The judge gives a probationary period of one lunar year for those suffering from these two diseases, for there is a possibility of cure.

10.9.5. OBSTRUCTION IN THE VAGINAL OPENING,, ETC.

Obstruction in the vaginal opening, the presence of a horn-like protrusion inside the vaginal passage, a fleshy obstruction in the vagina or the merging of the anal and vaginal passages' are four defects,[39] which occur only among women, give the husband, according to the Malikis and Hanbalis, the right to annul the marriage contract. According to the Shafiis, only in case of either obstructions in the vaginal opening (al-ratq) or the presence of a horn-like protrusion inside the vagina (al-qarn) the husband has such a right; not when the wife suffers from the merging of the anal and vaginal passages (al-ifda) or a fleshy obstruction in the vagina (al-afal). According to the Jafari, such a legal effect follows only in the case of al-qarn or al-ifda, not in the case of al-ratq or al-afal. They also state that the husband, if he wishes, can annul the marriage contract when he finds blindness or visible lameness in the wife after the conclusion of the contract if he had no knowledge of it before. But either of the defects when found in the husband does not give such a right to the wife.

Any disease, regardless of its being peculiar to one of the sexes or its being common to both of them, that is capable of being diagnosed and cured without leaving behind any deformity or defect, does not give rise to any legal right and its occurrence, like its non-occurrence is legally without any effect. The reason behind this opinion is that, when a disease becomes curable, it becomes similar to any other ordinary disease that may affect any person. The time-honored significance attached by the jurists to the above-mentioned defects is because they could not be treated surgically during the past.

10.9.6. DISPATCH WITHOUT DELAY

According to the Jafari school, the choice of annulling the marriage exists so long as it is exercised immediately. Therefore, if the man or the woman, on knowing the defect, does not initiate the proceedings for annulling the marriage, the contract will become binding. The same rule applies for annulling the marriage in a case of deception.

The author of *al-Jawahir* has said that ignorance regarding the right to annul the marriage, and even immediacy (*fawriyyah*), is a good excuse, considering that this right has been given without imposing any conditions. He has also observed that the annulment of marriage, in all its forms, does not depend on the judge. He has only the power to grant a probationary period in the case of impotence.

10.10. THE OPTION TO INCLUDE CONDITIONS

The difference between *shart al-khayar* and *khayar al-shart* is that in the first the option to annul the marriage be included in the contract. For example, when the bride making the offer says, "I marry myself to you on the condition that I shall have the choice of annulling the marriage within three days," and the groom accepts with a *qabiltu*, or when the bride says, "I marry myself to you," and the groom, while accepting, says, "I accept on the condition that I shall have the choice to annul the marriage within such and such a time;" we see that in both the cases the option to annul the marriage is mentioned in the contract itself, and this, as has been mentioned earlier, results in the contract becoming null and void, according to all the major schools.

But in *khayar al-shart* the option to annul the marriage is not mentioned as a condition per se in the contract. That which is mentioned as a condition in this case, is a particular quality such as the bride's virginity or the groom's possessing a university degree in a manner that if the said condition is not found to exist the other shall have the right to annul the contract. The schools have a difference of opinion in this regard.

The Hanafis have said that if a spouse mentions a negative condition in the contract, such as the absence of blindness or a disease, or a positive condition, such as presence of beauty, virginity, etc., and then the opposite of it comes to light, the contract will be valid. Regarding the condition, it will not apply except when the wife lays down a condition related to *al-*

kafaah; such as a condition regarding lineage, profession or wealth. Here she has the right to annul the contract. But as regards the husband, any similar condition laid down by him will not be considered applicable because quality, as mentioned earlier, is a condition with reference to the husband, not the wife.

The Maliki, Shafii, Jafari and Hanbali schools have said that the condition is valid and if not satisfied results in the spouse making the condition acquiring the option of either upholding or annulling the contract. The following Tradition is cited in support of this view, "Muslims are bound to fulfill the conditions."

Furthermore, they state, the aforesaid conditions are not against the spirit of the contract and do not contradict the Quran or the Prophet's *Sunnah*; neither do they amount to changing lawful into unlawful nor vice versa.

10.10.1. DECEIT

The Jafari have discussed under this heading of deceit (*tadlis*) by the bride to the groom, the deception to the groom by either hiding a defect or by claiming a merit which is absent. In the first case, i.e., her hiding a defect and not mentioning it, the right to annul the contract will not accrue if he has not mentioned the absence of such a condition specifically in some way or another. Imam Jafar Sadiq says about a person who marries in a family and finds his wife to be one-eyed while they have not revealed it to him before, "The contract will not be withdrawn." This is the opinion of all the schools.

As regards the second form of deceit i.e., where she claims a merit which in fact she does not possess if the claimed merit has been mentioned as a condition in the contract, as said earlier, the condition will hold good according to all except the Hanafis. But if the claimed merit has not been mentioned in the contract as a condition—i.e., it has either been mentioned simply as a quality in the contract, or has been mentioned before the contract and the contract has been recited on that basisthen two different situations arise:

10.10.1.1. "FREE FROM DEFECT..."

The merit has been mentioned in the contract as a quality, such as when the bride's attorney says, "I marry this girl to you," or, "I marry this girl who is free from any defect to you." The Jafari state that when it is known that she does not possess the mentioned merit, the husband has the choice to annul the contract.

10.10.1.2. "SHE IS A VIRGIN..."

The merit has neither been mentioned as a condition nor as a quality in the contract, but has been mentioned during the course of the marriage negotiations, such as when she herself or her attorney says that she is a virgin and has no defect, and then the contract is recited on the basis of this statement, so that it is understood that the contract has been recited on the girl's possessing this particular quality. In the legal sources that I have referred to, I have not come across anyone who has discussed this particular aspect except the Jafari, among whom there is a difference of opinion as to whether in such a case the husband has an option of annulment. Some of them, including al-Sayyid Abu al-Hasan al-Isfahani,[40] uphold the husband's option, because, they point out, the negotiations of the contracting parties regarding a particular quality followed by the conclusion of the contract on this basis, makes this quality similar to an implicit condition. Others, who oppose this view, have said that it will have no effect unless the quality is mentioned in the contract or its presence in the contract established in some way or another. Shahid al-Thani holds the same opinion, on the basis that a contract is binding unless there is categorical proof of its invalidity, and such a proof is not present in this case.

To summarize, if the quality has been recognized in the contract in one of the three ways (i.e., as a condition, as a quality mentioned in the contract, or when mentioned during pre-contract negotiations), the husband has the option to annul or retain the contract. If he retains it, he will not have any right. of reducing her dowry, whatever the defect, except when the condition was virginity. According to the Jafari, in this case, the husband may reduce the dowry by an amount equal to the difference between a virgin's dowry and that of a non-virgin.

If he chooses to annul the contract, she will not be entitled to receive any dowry if marriage has not been consummated, according to the Jafari and those of the four schools who permit the option of annulment in case of deceit. On the marriage being annulled after consummation, she will receive the proper dowry not specified in the marriage contract (*mahr al-mithal*), and, according to the Shafii school, the husband paying such dowry will not claim it from the person responsible for the deceit.

The Jafari observe that it depends upon who is responsible for the fraud. If it is the bride, she will not be entitled to any dowry, even after consummation. If someone else, then she will receive her full dowry, and the husband will claim this amount from the deceiver in accordance with the rule, "the deceived will level his claim against the deceiver."

10.10.2. SUPPLEMENTARY ISSUES

10.10.2.1. DEFECT FOUND
If after marriage, one of the spouses finds a defect in the other and claims that the contract was concluded after freedom from such defect was understood, through one of the three above-mentioned modes, the other refuting, the burden of proof will lie with the claimant. If the claimant furnishes the proof, the judge will grant him or her the right to dissolve the marriage. If the claimant is unable to prove his or her claim, the respondent will take an oath and the case will be dismissed by the judge.

10.10.2.2. CLAIM OF VIRGINITY
Where a person marries a woman after it has been understood. through one of the three mentioned ways, that she is a virgin, and then finds her to be otherwise, he will not be entitled to dissolve the marriage, unless it is proved that her loss of virginity preceded the contract. This can be proved, either by

her confession or through evidence, or any such circumstantial evidence as may lead to certain knowledge such as when after the marriage, intercourse takes place within a period during which the chances of her losing her virginity (due to other causes) do not exist.

If the issue stays unsettled and it cannot be proved in any of the said ways, whether she lost her virginity before the marriage or after it, the right to dissolve the marriage will not accrue to the husband, because the presumption is that her loss of virginity did not precede the marriage, and also because the possibility of her having lost it due to an unknown reason—such as riding or jumping also exists.

10.10.2.3. NO MENTION OF VIRGINITY

Al-Sayyid Abu al-Hasan al-Isfahani writes that if a man marries a girl without virginity being mentioned in the negotiations previous to the marriage, without the contract being based on it, and without it being included as a condition or a quality in the contract, but only believing her to be so because of her not having married anyone before him, he will not have the right to dissolve the marriage if it is later proved that she was not a virgin. But he has the right to partly reduce her dowry. This reduction will be proportional to the difference between the dowry of her like if a virgin and if not a virgin.

Accordingly, al-Sayyid al-Isfahani envisages four possible conditions regarding virginity: Where virginity is mentioned in the contract as a condition; where it is mentioned in the contract as a quality; where it is mentioned during settlement of marriage and the contract is based upon it; where he marries her believing her to be a virgin and does not mention it, neither before the contract nor in the contract.

In the first three conditions, the husband has the choice to annul the marriage; in the fourth, he has no such choice, but can reduce a part of the dowry in the above-mentioned manner.

10.11. THE DOWRY

Dowry is one of the pecuniary rights of a wife established

in the Quran and the *Sunnah*, and on which there is consensus among Muslims. There are two kinds of dowry: agreed upon and specified in the marriage contract (*mahr al-musamma*) and not specified in the marriage contract (*mahr al-mithl*).

10.11.1. DOWRY AGREED UPON AND SPECIFIED IN THE MARRIAGE CONTRACT

The dowry agreed by the couple and specified by them in the contract is called *al-mahr al-musamma*. This dowry does not have any upper limit, by consensus of all the schools, in accordance with the following verse of the Quran, "*And if you wish to take a wife in place of another and have given one of them a heap of gold, then take not from it a thing*" (4:20).

The schools differ regarding the lower limit. The Shafii, Hanafi, and Jafari schools observe that everything which is valid as price in a contract of sale is valid as dowry in a marriage contract, though it be a single morsel. The minimum dowry according to the Hanafis is ten dirhams, and a contract concluded for a lesser amount is valid and the minimum—i.e. ten dirhams—shall be payable.

The Malikis have said that the minimum is three dirhams. Therefore, if something less is specified and later the marriage is consummated, the husband will pay her three dirhams. If it has not been consummated, he has a choice between giving her three dirhams or dissolving the contract by paying her half the specified dowry.

10.11.2. CONDITIONS OF DOWRY

It is valid that dowry be specified in terms of currency, jewelry, farmland, cattle, profit, trade commodities and other things of value. It is necessary that the value of the dowry be known, either exactly (e.g. a thousand lira) or approximately (e.g. a particular piece of gold or a particular stock of wheat). If the dowry is totally vague, so that its value is unascertainable in any manner, according to all the schools except the Maliki, the contract is valid and the dowry void. The Malikis observe that the contract is invalid and will be considered void before consummation, but if consummation has occurred it will be valid on the basis of the proper dowry not specified in the marriage contract.

Among the conditions is the being lawful of the dowry and its being valued in terms of a commodity whose transaction is considered legal by the Islamic *Shariah*. Therefore, if it is mentioned in terms of liquor or swine or anything else whose ownership is invalid, according to the Malikis the contract shall be invalid if it has not been consummated, and if consummated, shall be valid and a dowry not specified in the marriage contract shall be payable.

The Shafii, Hanafi, Hanbali and most of the Jafari jurists have said that the contract is valid and she shall be entitled to the proper dowry not specified in the marriage contract. Some Jafari jurists have entitled her to the proper dowry not specified in the marriage contract only if the marriage has been consummated, while others amongst them make no such condition and are in consonance with the Hanafi, Hanbali, Shafii and Maliki schools.

If the dowry is usurped property, such as when she is married for a farm as her dowry and later it is known to belong to the groom's father or someone else, the Malikis have said that if the farm is known to the two and both happen to be sane, the contract shall be invalid if not consummated and if consummated shall be considered valid on the basis of the proper dowry not specified in the marriage contract. The Shafii and Hanbali schools regard the contract as valid and entitle her to the proper dowry not specified in the marriage contract. The Jafari and Hanafi schools are of the opinion that the contract is unconditionally valid but regarding the dowry they observe that if the owner agrees, she shall receive the farm itself. If the owner refuses, she shall be entitled to receive a similar farm or its price because the stipulated dowry in this case is capable of being validly owned though ownership does not materialize, in contrast with liquor or swine which cannot be owned at all.

10.11.3. PROPER DOWRY NOT SPECIFIED IN THE MARRIAGE CONTRACT

The concept of the proper dowry not specified in the marriage contract is relevant in the following cases:

There is consensus among the schools that the dowry is not an essential ingredient (*rukn*) of a marriage contract, as price is in a contract of sale. On the contrary, dowry is only one of the effects of a marriage contract, and even without its stipulation the contract is valid. Thus, the proper dowry not specified in the marriage contract shall be payable on consummation (when the dowry was not specified) and if he divorces her before the consummation of marriage, she shall not be entitled to any dowry, but will receive a gift given by the husband to his wife at the time of divorce (*al-mutah*) in accordance with his status, such as a ring or a dress, etc. If they both agree on this gift, it will suffice. Otherwise it will be fixed by the judge. The issue whether the couple's retiring to seclusion is tantamount to consummation or not, will be discussed later.

The Hanafi and Hanbali schools observe that if the husband or the wife dies before consummation, full, proper dowry not specified in the marriage contract shall be payable as if the marriage had been consummated.[41] According to the Malikis and the Jafari, no dowry is payable if any of the two dies before consummation.[42] The Shafiis have two views: (a) That the dowry shall be payable; (b) no dowry shall be paid.[43]

If the marriage contract is concluded with specification of dowry in terms of a commodity which cannot be owned, e.g. liquor or swine, as mentioned earlier.

All the schools agree that the proper dowry not specified in the marriage contract becomes obligatory as a result of intercourse-by-mistake. Intercourse-by-mistake is intercourse with someone with whom it is not legally permissible, though without the knowledge of it being so. Such as a person marrying a woman without the knowledge of her being his foster sister and coming to know of it later, or his having intercourse with her after both have appointed their deputies for reciting the contract, thinking it to be sufficient for establishing sexual contact. In other words, intercourse by-mistake is intercourse without proper marriage, though the presence of a legal excuse precludes penal action. On this account the Jafari include under this head intercourse by a person who is either insane or intoxicated or in sleep.

The Jafari, Shafii and Hanbali schools have said that one who coerces a woman to fornicate shall have to pay the proper dowry not specified in the marriage contract. But if she had yielded voluntarily she shall not be entitled to anything.

A marriage concluded on the condition that no dowry shall be paid is valid according to all except the Malikis, who say that the contract shall be invalid if not consummated, and valid if consummated due to the obligation to pay the proper dowry not specified in the marriage contract. A large number of Jafari jurists have said that he shall give her something, be it much or little.

According to the Jafari and Hanafi schools, if an invalid marriage contract is recited with a certain dowry and the marriage is consummated, she shall be entitled to receive the dowry stipulated even though it was less than the proper dowry not specified in the marriage contract because of her prior consent. But if the stipulated dowry is more, she shall receive only a proper dowry not specified in the marriage contract, because she is not entitled to receive more than a proper dowry not specified in the marriage contract.

A proper dowry not specified in the marriage contract is computed by the Hanafis by taking into account the dowry of her equals from the paternal, not the maternal side. According to the Malikis, her dowry shall be commensurate with her physical and mental qualities. The Shafiis take the dowry not specified in the marriage contract of the wives of her paternal relatives as reference, i.e. the wife of her brother, that of her paternal uncle, then her sister etc. For the Hanbalis, the judge shall compute the proper dowry not specified in the marriage contract by taking into account the dowry of her female relations, such as the mother or maternal aunt.

The Jafari have said that there is no fixed way of determining a proper dowry not specified in a marriage contract in the Shariah. It is estimated by those who know her status, descent, and all those aspects which influence the increase or decrease of dowry. But this dowry shall not exceed the dowry which is traditional (*mahr al-sunnah*), which is equal to five hundred dirhams.

10.11.4. IMMEDIATE AND DEFERRED PAYMENT OF DOWRY

All the schools concur regarding the validity of deferred payment of dowry, fully or partly, provided that the period be known, either exactly (such as when it is said, "I marry you for a hundred, of which fifty shall be paid immediately and the rest after one year," or in an indeterminate manner (such as when it is said, "The dowry is deferred until death or divorce." The Shafii school disapproves the latter form of deferment. But if the period is so mentioned that it is totally vague, such as when it is stated that the payment of dowry shall be made on the return of a certain traveler, the time clause shall be void.

The Jafari and Hanbali schools have said that if the dowry has been mentioned without specifying whether its payment is immediate or deferred, the entire dowry shall be immediately payable. According to the Hanafis, the local practice shall be observed, that is, the portions to be immediately paid and deferred will follow the local custom. The Hanafis have also said that if the dowry is deferred without mentioning the period of deferment such as when it is said, "Half of it is immediately payable and the rest deferred," the full dowry shall be immediately payable.

The Hanbalis observe that the dowry can be deferred until death or divorce. The Malikis are of the opinion that such a marriage is invalid, it is voidable before consummation, although valid after it on the basis of a proper dowry not specified in the marriage contract. The Shafiis state that if the period is known not exactly but in an indeterminate manner (such as until death or divorce) the dowry stipulated shall become invalid and the proper dowry not specified in the marriage contract will be payable.[44]

The Hanafi and Hanbali schools have said that if the bride's father apportions for himself, as a condition, a part of her dowry, the dowry is valid and the condition shall have to be complied with. The Shafiis say that the dowry stipulated shall become invalid and dowry not specified in the marriage contract shall be payable. According to the Malikis, if this condition is included at the time of marriage, the bride shall receive the entire dowry, including her father's share; and if the condition is laid after the marriage, the bride's father shall receive his share.[45] The Jafari observe that if her dowry has been specified with a fixed portion of it mentioned for her father, she shall get her full stipulated dowry and her father will not get his share.

10.11.5. THE WIFE'S RIGHT TO REFUSE HER CONJUGAL SOCIETY

There is consensus among the schools that the wife, simply after the recital of the contract, has the right to demand her full specified dowry immediately and to refuse her conjugal society until the dowry is paid. But, if she surrenders once willingly without demanding the dowry, she loses her right of refusal. All concur on this issue except Imam Abu Hanifah. He observes that she has the right to refuse even after surrender. Imam Abu Hanifah's disciples, Muhammad and Abu Yusuf, oppose his view.

The wife is entitled to receive maintenance if she refuses her conjugal society until the payment of dowry; because her refusal in such a case is legally valid. But if she refuses to fulfill her conjugal duties after receiving dowry or after voluntary surrender, she shall not be entitled to maintenance except according to Imam Abu Hanifah. If the wife be a minor unfit for marital relations and the husband a major, it is up to her *wali* to demand the dowry; it is not necessary that he wait until her maturity. Similarly, if the wife be a major and the husband a minor, the wife has the right to demand the dowry from his wall, and it is not necessary for her to wait until his maturity. The Jafari and Shafii schools state that if a dispute arises between the couple, with the wife refusing to surrender until payment of dowry and the husband refusing payment until her surrender, the husband shall be compelled to deposit the dowry with a trustee and the wife will be asked to surrender. Then if she surrenders, she shall receive her dowry and be entitled to maintenance. But if she refuses, she shall not receive the dowry and will not be entitled to any maintenance. If the husband refuses to deposit the dowry, he will be ordered to pay her maintenance on her demanding it.

The Hanafi and Maliki schools state that the payment of dowry has precedence over the woman's surrender, and the man may not say, "I will not pay the dowry until she surrenders." If he insists on this, he shall be ordered to pay her maintenance, and if she, after receiving the dowry, refuses her conjugal society, the husband is not entitled to claim the return of dowry. According to the Hanbali school, the husband shall be first compelled to pay the dowry. This opinion concurs with the Hanafi view except that according to the Hanbalis, if she refuses her conjugal society after receiving the dowry, he has the right to demand the return of the dowry.[46]

10.11.6. INABILITY OF THE HUSBAND TO PAY THE DOWRY

The Jafari and Hanafi schools observe that if the husband is unable to pay the dowry, the wife is not entitled to dissolve the marriage, and the judge, too, cannot pronounce her divorce. But she has the right to deny her conjugal society. The Malikis state that if his inability is proved before the consummation of marriage, the judge will grant him time according to his own discretion. If, after the expiry of such period his inability continues, the judge will pronounce divorce, or the wife will divorce herself and the judge shall endorse its validity. But if he has consummated the marriage, she can in no way dissolve it. The Shafii school is of the opinion that if his inability is proved while the marriage has not been consummated, she can dissolve it. But if it has been, she cannot dissolve it. The Hanbalis state that she may dissolve the marriage even after its consummation, provided she had no knowledge of his inability before the marriage. Therefore, if she had the knowledge, the question of dissolving the marriage does not arise. Even when the marriage is dissolvable, only the judge has the authority to do so.

10.11.7. THE FATHER AND HIS DAUGHTER-IN-LAW'S DOWRY

The Shafii, Maliki and Hanbali schools hold that if a father concludes the marriage of his pauper son, he shall be liable for payment of dowry even if the son be a major and the father acts as his guardian for the marriage as his son's deputy. If the father dies before dowry is paid, which was obligatory upon him, it shall be paid out of his legacy. The Hanafi school observes that the payment of dowry is not obligatory upon the father, regardless of whether the son is a well-to-do person or a pauper, a major or a minor.[47] The Jafari state that if the minor son possesses property and his father gets him married, the dowry shall be paid from the son's assets and the father shall not be liable at all. But if the minor has no property at the time of marriage, the father shall be liable to pay the dowry. The husband (son) shall not be liable even if he becomes a man of means later. Also, the father is not required to pay the dowry of his major son's wife unless he guarantees it on the conclusion of the contract.

10.11.8. CONSUMMATION AND DOWRY

Sex relations with a woman fall within these three categories:

Fornication (*zina*) to which she surrenders with the knowledge of its being forbidden. In this instance, she will not get any dowry; rather shall be liable to penal action.

As a result of a misunderstanding on her behalf of its being legal, followed by later knowledge that it was forbidden. Here, her act has no penal consequences and she is entitled to receive a proper dowry not specified in the marriage contract, irrespective of the man's knowledge of the act being forbidden.

As a result of a valid marriage. In this case she is entitled to receive the specified dowry if it has been validly stipulated, and the proper dowry not specified in the marriage contract if no dowry was specified in the contract or was specified in an invalid form (e.g. in terms of liquor or swine).

If one of the spouses dies before consummation, then, according to the Hanafi, Hanbali, Maliki and Shafii schools, she is entitled to receive the entire specified dowry).

The Jafari jurists differ. Some of them, in consonance with the Hanafi, Hanbali, Maliki and Shafii schools entitle her to the entire specified dowry, while others (including al-Sayyid Abu al-Hasan al-Isfahani)[48] to half the specified dowry on a par with a divorcee.

10.11.9. WIFE'S CRIME AGAINST HUSBAND

The Shafii, Maliki and Hanbali schools have observed that if a wife kills her husband before the consummation of marriage she shall not be entitled to any dowry. According to the Hanafi and Jafari schools, she shall not be deprived of her right to dowry, although she loses her right to inherit from him.

10.11.10. VALID SECLUSION

According to the Shafii school and the majority of Jafari jurists, the mere enjoyment of privacy or retirement (al-khalwah) by the couple has no effect on dowry nor any other consequence. Only the consummation of marriage is consequential in this regard. The Hanafi and Hanbali schools have observed that valid seclusion confirms dowry, establishes descent, and requires observance of waiting period in case of divorce, even though such seclusion does not result in consummation. The Hanbalis also consider gazing and touching with a sexual intent and kissing on a par with consummation and therefore sufficient for confirming dowry. By 'valid seclusion' is meant the seclusion of the couple in a place where they are secure from observation by others and where there is no impediment to intercourse. The Malikis state that if the period of seclusion is prolonged, dowry is established even without consummation. Some of them have fixed the period of 'prolonged seclusion' at one complete year.[49]

10.11.11. HALF THE DOWRY

There is consensus among the schools that if the dowry is specified at the time of the contract and then the husband pronounces divorce without consummation, or seclusion for those who consider the latter to be consequential, half the dowry shall be payable. But if the contract is recited without specifying dowry, she shall get nothing except a gift (*al-mutah*), as mentioned earlier, in accordance with the following verse, "*There is no blame on you if you divorce women when you have not touched them or appointed for them a portion; yet make provision for them, the wealthy man according to his means and the needy man according to his means, a provision according to honorable usage; (this is) a duty on the good-doers. And if you divorce them before you have touched them and you have appointed for them a portion, then (pay them) half of what you have appointed....*" (2:236-37). Therefore, if the husband, not having paid anything to the wife whose dowry has been specified, divorces her before consummating the marriage, he shall pay her half the dowry. But if he has paid the entire dowry, half of it shall be returned if it still exists, and the equivalent of it in cash or kind if it has perished.

If the husband and wife do not specify dowry in the contract but later agree upon it and then the husband divorces her before consummation, in this case, shall she be entitled to receive half of the dowry agreed upon as if the dowry had been specified in the contract, or shall she get nothing except the gift, as if they had not agreed upon dowry later? The Shafii, Jafari[50] and Maliki schools are of the opinion that she is entitled to half the dowry agreed upon, and according to the Hanbali book,[51] she is entitled to half the dowry agreed upon after the contract, but not the gift.

This discussion was related to the right to full dowry and the right to half dowry. Instances of annulment of the right to full dowry can be found in our above discussion on 'defects'.

10.11.12. DISAGREEMENT BETWEEN THE SPOUSES

The spouses may at times differ regarding the consummation of marriage and sometimes regarding the specification of dowry, its value, its receipt by the wife, or as to whether that which was received was given as a present or as dowry. Here we have the following issues:

Where the husband and wife differ regarding the consummation, the Hanafi school has two opinions, the more preferable of which is that if the wife claims the occurrence of consummation or seclusion, which the husband refutes, the wife's word shall be accepted and the burden of proof will rest on the husband, because it is she who actually contests the reduction of half her dowry.[52]

The Malikis say that if the wife visits the husband at his home and then claims consummation while he denies it, her word shall be accepted on oath. If the husband visits her at her place and then she claims consummation while he denies it, his word shall be accepted on oath. And similarly, if they both go to see someone else at his place and she then claims consummation while he denies it, his word shall be accepted. According to the Shafiis, in case of dispute regarding consummation, the husband's word shall be accepted.[53]

The Jafari observe that if the spouses differ regarding consummation and the wife denies its taking place in order to preserve her right to deny him her conjugal society until payment of her dowry, agreed to be paid promptly, and he claims consummation in order to establish his claim that her refusal is without legal justification, or if he denies consummation seeking to reduce his liability to half the dowry and she claims consummation to have occurred, seeking to establish her right to full dowry and maintenance during the waiting period, in both these instances the word of the party denying consummation shall be accepted irrespective of whether it is the husband or the wife; and, as said earlier, seclusion has no effect.

This may lead a question to arise in one's mind: how do the Jafari jurists accept in this case the word of the party denying consummation, while, as mentioned earlier, they accept the word of even an impotent man claiming consummation?

The answer is that the issue here is the act of consummation, which is an occurrence and an event claimed to have happened. The presumption is that an event claimed to have happened has not occurred, and therefore the burden of proof rests on the party claiming its occurrence. That which was in dispute in the issue regarding impotence is the presence of this defect, which justifies dissolution of marriage. Therefore, the wife's denial of consummation implies that she is claiming the presence of that defect, and thereby becoming the claimant. The husband's statement that consummation has occurred implies that he refutes the claim of the presence of the said defect, thereby challenging the claim.

If they differ regarding the fact of stipulation of dowry, with one of them claiming that valid dowry was stipulated prior to the contract, while the other refutes it, saying that the contract was recited without dowry stipulation, the Jafari and Hanafi schools observe that the burden of proof rests on the party claiming stipulation and the party refuting it shall take an oath. But if the wife claims that the dowry has been specified and the husband refutes it, and takes an oath after her failure to prove the stipulation, she shall receive the proper dowry not specified in the marriage contract if the marriage has been consummated, on condition that the proper dowry not specified in the marriage contract does not exceed the amount she claims as having been specified. Thus, if she claims that the contract was concluded with a dowry of ten units while he denies it and the dowry happens to be twenty units, she shall receive only ten, in view of her own admission that she is not entitled to more.

The Shafiis are of the opinion that both the parties are claimants, i.e. each one of them is a claimant as well as a refuter. Therefore, if one of them furnishes proof while the other fails to do so, the judgment shall be given in favor of the party furnishing proof, and if both furnish proof or both fail to do so, they shall both take oath and the proper dowry not specified in the marriage contract shall be confirmed.

If both agree that dowry has been specified, but disagree regarding its amount, here the Hanafi and the Hanbali schools are of the opinion that the word of the party claiming an amount equal to the proper dowry not specified in the marriage contract shall be accepted. Therefore, if she claims a proper dowry not specified in the marriage contract or something else, her claim shall be accepted. If the husband's claim amounts to the proper dowry not specified in the marriage contract or more, his word shall be accepted.[54]

The Shafiis state that both are claimants, and if both are unable to furnish proof, the proper dowry not specified in the marriage contract shall be confirmed after their oath. According to the Jafari and Maliki schools, the wife is the claimant and the burden of proof shall rest on her. The husband challenging the claim shall take an oath.

Where the spouses disagree regarding the actual payment of the dowry, with the wife denying that she received it and the husband claiming to have paid it, the Jafari, Shafii and Hanbali schools have observed that the wife's word shall be accepted because she challenges the husband's claim who shall have to furnish proof. The Hanafi and Maliki schools observe that the wife's word shall be accepted if the dispute arises before consummation and the husband's word if consummation has occurred.

When both admit that she has received something and the wife claims that it was a present, while the husband claims it to have been the dowry, the Jafari and the Hanafi schools observe that the husband's word shall be accepted because he knows his own intention. Therefore, he shall take an oath and it is for the wife to furnish proof that it was a present.[55]

Such is the case when there is no circumstantial evidence such as local custom or a particular circumstance of the husband showing that it was a present, such as when it is something eatable or a gift of dress, or what the Lebanese call *al-alamah* (mark or token) and the Egyptians *al-shabakah* (net), which is a ring or something similar given as a gift to the fiancee by the fiancee so that she may decline other proposals. Therefore, if the thing is something of this kind, the word of the wife shall be accepted.

If the fiancee changes her mind about the marriage after having accepted the ring but before the contract, she is liable to return the ring on his demanding it. If the fiancee changes his mind, the custom gives him no right to claim it back. But the rules of the Shariah do not recognize any difference between his or her changing his or her mind and therefore she is liable to return the gift as long as it is with her and she has not sold it or gifted it or changed its form.

The Jafari and Hanafi schools concur that dowry is the sole property of the wife and one of her rights. She can use it according to her own will, bequeathing it or buying her dowry with it, or saving it for her own use at her pleasure, and no one has the right to question or oppose her. The responsibility of furnishing their home lies solely on the husband and she is in no way responsible for anything, because maintenance, in all its different forms, is required only of the husband.

The Malikis observe that it is incumbent upon the wife to buy from the dowry she has received all those things which women of her status buy as their dowry, and if she has not received any dowry then it is not obligatory for her to bring dowry except in the two cases: (1) if the local custom considers it compulsory for the wife to bring dowry even though she has not received anything; (2) if the husband sets the condition that she furnish their home with her own means.

If the husband and wife dispute regarding the ownership of any household item, it will be seen whether the item is used only by men or women or by both. Thus three different situations arise:

Where the item is used by men only, such as his clothes, his books, his measuring instruments if he is an engineer or his medical apparatus if a doctor. The ownership of this kind of items shall be determined by accepting the word of the husband under oath, except when the wife furnishes proof that she is the owner. This is the opinion of the Jafari and Hanafi schools.

Where the item is used only by women, such as her clothes, jewelry, sewing machine, cosmetics, etc., the ownership of

these shall be determined by accepting her word under oath,
except when the husband furnishes proof to the contrary.

Where the item is used by both of them, such as carpets,
curtains, etc., it shall be given to the party furnishing proof of
its ownership. But if both are unable to furnish proof, each of
them shall testify under oath that the said item belongs to
him/her; then the items will be equally divided between them.
If one of the parties takes an oath while the other abstains, the
party taking oath shall be given the item. This is the opinion of
the Jafari. Imam Abu Hanifah and his pupil Muhammad are of
the view that the husband's word shall be accepted regarding
items of common use.

The Shafiis say that if the husband and wife dispute
regarding the ownership of household goods, these shall be
divided between them irrespective of their being of individual
or common use.[56]

10.12. LINEAGE

10.12.1. INTRODUCTION

Every man is free within the limits of law and morality to
say whatever he wants, and no one is entitled to stop him from
doing so but it is also not incumbent upon anyone to heed his
statements or to consider them with respect. This is true irrespective of the speaker's station, whether high or low, venera-
ble or otherwise, when his speech pertains to something outside the area of his specialty. Therefore, if an authority on law
gives an opinion on a question of medicine or agriculture, it is
not correct for a plaintiff to cite that opinion in support of his
case, nor is it correct for a judge to base his judgment upon it.

Similarly, in the case of apostles, prophets, imams and
authorities on law, it is not obligatory upon anyone to believe
their statements about issues concerning physical nature, such
as the creation of the earth and the heavens, the distances
between them, their origin and end, the elements of which they
are composed and the forces therein. Sacred personalities at
times explained a certain phenomenon in their capacity as a
sacred authority. At other times they spoke about things in

their personal capacity, like all other human beings who say what they conjecture or hear from others. Therefore, when they speak in their religious capacity, it is obligatory upon us to listen to them and to obey them, as long as their religious decree does not exceed the limits of their specialty. But when they speak in their personal capacity, it is not obligatory to follow them, because, here, their word is not regarding religion or things related to it.

Thus a legislating authority, religious or secular, should limit itself to framing and expounding laws and regulations, with the aim of encouraging some acts and discouraging others, and explaining their causes and effects, approving one contract as binding together with its terms and conditions and invalidating another as not binding, and issues of this kind which safeguard the social order and ensure the common good.

But as regards natural phenomena-such as the minimum or the maximum period of pregnancy it is not within the domain of a lawgiver to either affirm or deny them or to make amendments. This is because the realities of nature and their causes are not alterable. They do not change due to the change of conditions and passage of time, in contrast with social laws, which are laid down, abrogated and modified by the lawgiver's will.

It is obvious that a lawgiver does make external realities of nature the subject of his laws, for instance, when he lays down that a child in the womb has the right to inherit from the father, that the birth of a child leads to an increase in the statutory allowance of the mother, or that when the wheat produce exceeds the consumption of farmers, the surplus should be taken into government custody, etc. But the explanation of natural phenomena relating to the subject of laws is the task of specialists. If there is anything in the statements of legal authorities explaining or defining such phenomena, it is nothing but an attestation of what specialists have reported. Therefore, when a judge refers an issue for specialist opinion and the fact is known showing the error of its description by jurists, it is not obligatory that their observations be followed, because we know with certainty that the jurists have spoken regarding a phenomenon which pre-existed legislation; the intent of their remarks was to explain this pre-existing fact. Thus, when the opposite is proved, to follow their word would be equivalent to acting against their purpose and intention. The jurists themselves name this kind of mistake "mistake in application." It is similar to the mistake of a person who asks for a cup while pointing towards a stone resembling it.

After this introduction, we move on to our actual subject. As the child is the subject of many Islamic laws such as its right to inherit from the father; the illegitimacy of its marriage with its sibling, the father's right to act as a guardian of its person and property until maturity; the obligations of its maintenance, and such other legal and moral rights the jurists are forced to determine the minimum and the maximum period of gestation. It is obvious that this issue pertains to the specialty of doctors of medicine not of law, and, therefore, it is not necessary that the word of jurists be acted upon if it contradicts actual fact and reality, because, in such circumstances, the logic of reality is stronger than their logic, and its proof prevails over their evidence. When the opinions of natural philosophers and physical scientists collapse before reality, it is more in order that the observations of those who are in no way connected with a particular field of specialization should collapse before facts. We mention here the views of different schools of Islamic law regarding the minimum and maximum period of gestation, on the assumption that one is not obliged to follow these views when they are not in consonance with facts.

10.12.2. THE MINIMUM PERIOD OF GESTATION

The opinion of all the major legal schools of Islam is that the minimum gestation period is six months, because the 15th verse of the *Surat al-Ahqaf* expressly states that the gestation period (*muddat al-haml*) along with the period of suckling (*ridaah*) is thirty months. The 14th verse of the *Surat Luqman* states that the period of suckling is to be two complete years. When two years are substracted from thirty months, the remainder is six months, which is the minimum period of gestation. Modern medicine supports this view and the French legislature has also adopted it.

The following rules are derived from the above observations:

When within six months of her marriage a woman gives birth to a child, the child will not be attributed to her husband. Al-Shaykh al-Mufid and al-Shaykh al-Tusi—both Jafaris—and al-Shaykh Muhyi Din Abd al-Hamid of the Hanafi school have said that the choice of denying or accepting the child's parentage lies with the husband. If he accepts the child as his, the child shall be considered his legitimate offspring, and shall enjoy all the rights of a legitimate child. Similarly, the father shall have all those powers over it as over the other legitimate children.[57]

When the couple differs regarding the period of their conjugal relationship (she claiming that it is six months or more, and he denying it, claiming the period to be shorter than six months and denying the child to be his), Imam Abu Hanifah is of the opinion that the wife's word shall be considered true and acted upon without her taking an oath.[58]

The Jafari have said that if circumstantial evidence favors his or her contention it will be acted upon, and if no such evidence exists, the judge shall accept the wife's word after her taking an oath that sex relations with the husband had existed for six months. Then the child shall be attributed to the husband.[59]

When a husband divorces his wife after intercourse and she, after observing the waiting period, marries another and gives birth to a child within six months of her second marriage, if six months or more but not exceeding the maximum period of gestation have elapsed since her intercourse with the first husband, the child shall be attributed to the former husband. But if more than six months have elapsed after her second marriage, the child be attributed to the second husband.

When a woman contracts a second marriage after divorce and then gives birth to a child within six months of intercourse with the second husband, if more than the maximum period of gestation has elapsed since intercourse with the former husband, the child shall not be attributed to either of them. For example, if eight months after divorce a woman marries another person and after living with him for five months gives birth to a child, supposing the maximum period of gestation to be a year, it is not possible to attribute the child to the former husband, because more than a year has elapsed since they had intercourse. It is neither possible to attribute the child to her present husband because six months have not yet passed since their marriage.

10.12.3. THE MAXIMUM PERIOD OF GESTATION

Imam Abu Hanifah has said that the maximum gestation period is two years on account of a Tradition narrated by Aishah that a woman does not carry a child in her womb for more than two years. Imam Malik, Imam Shafii and Imam Ibn Hanbal state the period to be four years, on the basis that the wife of Ajlan carried her child for four years before delivery. In fact all women of Banu Ajlan have a gestation period of four years, which indicates God's power over His creation. [60]

Abbad ibn Awam puts the maximum period of gestation at five years, al-Zuhari at seven years, and according to Abu Ubayd there is no maximum period of gestation.[61]

It follows from these conflicting opinions, that if a person divorces his wife or dies and she, without marrying again after him, bears a child, the child shall be attributed to him if born after: two years, according to Imam Abu Hanifah; four years, according to Shafiis, Malikis and Hanbalis; five years, according to Ibn Awwam; seven years according to al-Zuhari; and twenty years according to Abu Ubayd.

Legislation in Egypt relieves us from a critical examination of these varied opinions. The Egyptian Shariah courts followed the Hanafi code until the passing of Act 25 of 1929. Section 15 of this Act categorically mentions that the maximum period of gestation is one year.[62]

There is a difference of opinion among Jafari scholars

regarding the maximum period of gestation. Most of them have stated it to be nine months, some of them ten months, and some others a year. Thus there is a consensus that the period does not exceed a year, even by an hour. Therefore, if a woman, divorced or widowed, gives birth to a child after one year, the child shall not be attributed to the husband, because Imam Jafar Sadiq said, "If a man divorces his wife and she claims to be pregnant, and then gives birth to a child after more than a year has passed, even though by an hour, her claim shall not be accepted."[63]

10.12.4. *MISTAKE OF CONTRACT, MISTAKE OF ACT*

Shubhah—that is a mistake which leads a man to have intercourse with a woman unlawful to him, as a result of his ignorance of her being such—is of two kinds: *shubhat aqd* (mistake of contract) and *shubhat fil* (mistake of act).

'Mistake of contract' occurs where a man and woman concludes a marriage contract in a manner in which legal contracts of marriage are concluded and later it is known that the contract was invalid due to the presence of a cause sufficient to invalidate the contract.

Mistake of act' occurs where a man and woman copulate without there being between them any contract, valid or invalid, and they do so either without conscious attention or thinking that they are permissible to each other, and later the opposite is discovered.

Sexual intercourse by a lunatic, or an intoxicated person, or a person in sleep, or a man under the false impression that the woman is his wife, comes under this category. Imam Abu Hanifah has extended the meaning of this form of 'mistake' to its utmost limits where he has observed that where a man hires a woman for some work and then fornicates with her, or hires her for fornication and does so, the two will not be penalized for fornication, because of his ignorance that his hiring her does not include this act.[64]

Accordingly, if she is working in a business establishment or a factory and the proprietor of such establishment copulates

with her believing this to be one of the benefits which accrue to
him as a result of his hiring her, this act will not be termed fornication, but will be considered 'a mistake' and shall be a valid
excuse for the proprietor in Imam Abu Hanifah's opinion.

It follows from the above discussion that a child born as a
result of 'intercourse by mistake' is a legitimate offspring and
is equal in all respects to a child born out of a valid wedlock,
irrespective of whether the mistake is a 'mistake of contract' or
a 'mistake of act'. Therefore, he who has intercourse with a
woman while in a state of intoxication, or in sleep, or in a state
of lunacy or under coercion, or before reaching the age of maturity, or under an impression that she is his wife, with the opposite being discovered later in all such cases if she gives birth to
a child, it shall be attributed to him.

The Jafari have said that in all such cases of mistake, the
legality of lineage is established and if the man refuses to recognize the child as his, his refusal shall not be accepted and
the child will be, of necessity, attributed to him.[65]

Muhammad Muhyi al-Din observes that lineage is not
established in any form of 'copulation by mistake' unless the
person acting mistakenly claims the child to be his and
acknowledges it, because he knows himself better. But this
view is incorrect when applied to a lunatic, to one in sleep, or
to an intoxicated person, because they do not act with conscious intent. It is also inapplicable in the case of mistake of
contract because there is no difference between a valid contract
and an invalid contract except that the couple shall separate
when the invalidity of the contract becomes known, and there
is a consensus among the major schools that whenever a mistake, in any one of its different forms, is proved, it is obligatory
for the woman to observe waiting period, as observed by a
divorcee; she is also entitled to receive the full dowry.
Therefore, the rules which apply to a wife will apply to her as
regards waiting period, dowry and child's lineage.[66]

The mistake may be from the side of the man as well as the
woman, so that both are ignorant and inattentive. It may be
from only one side, such as when the woman knows that she

has a lawful husband but hides it from the man, or when he is aware while she is a lunatic or in a state of intoxication. When the mistake is from both sides the child shall be attributed to both of them, and if the mistake is from only one side the child shall be attributed to the parent acting under mistake and not to the parent who was aware.

If a person copulates with a woman and then claims ignorance regarding its being *haram*, his word shall be accepted without proof and oath.[67]

In any case, the legal principles, according to all major schools, do not permit any ruling ascribing illegitimate birth to a child born of a father when there is a possibility of ascribing its birth to a mistake. Therefore, if a judge has evidence before him to suggest 99% probability of the child's illegitimate birth and only 1% probability suggesting it is 'a child by mistake', it is incumbent upon him to accept the latter evidence and disregard the former, giving preference to lawful over unlawful and legitimacy over illegitimacy, in consonance with the Divine injunctions: *"And speak good to the people"* (2:83). *"Eschew much suspicion, for surely some suspicion is a sin"* (49:12).

Commentators of the Holy Quran have narrated that one day when the Prophet was delivering a sermon, a man who was taunted by people regarding his lineage, stood up and asked, "O Prophet, who is my father?" The Prophet replied, "Your father is Hudhayfah ibn Qays." Another person asked him, "O Prophet, where is my father?" The Prophet replied, "Your father is in hell." Here verse 101 of the *Surat al-Maidah* was revealed, *"O believers, question not concerning things which, if they were revealed to you, would vex you...."*[68] Traditions of the Prophet recorded by jurists in all major schools state, "Penal consequences are repelled by doubts." And, "Leave that which puts you into doubt for that which does not."[69] Imam Jafar Sadiq said, "Reject the evidence of your ear and eye regarding your brother."[70]

The above-mentioned verses of the Quran and the Traditions quoted, as well as many other verses and Traditions of the kind, make it incumbent upon every person to abstain from testifying and judging anyone as an illegitimate offspring unless there exists certainty that he is not in reality a child of mistake in any of its forms.

10.12.5. CHILD BORN OF TEMPORARY MARRIAGE

There is a consensus amongst the major schools that temporary marriage was lawful by the order of the Prophet and that Muslims performed temporary marriage during his time. But they differ regarding its revocation. The Hanafi, Hanbali, Shafii and Maliki say that *mutah* was revoked and made unlawful after being lawful earlier. The Jafari state that revocation has not been proved: it was lawful and shall remain so until the Day of Judgment. The Jafari cite the Quran as evidence, "...*Give them their dowry for the mutah you have had with them as a duty....*" (4:24) and that which Muslim has narrated in his *al-Sahih* as a proof, "The Companions of the Prophet performed temporary marriage during his lifetime and during the reigns of Abu Bakr and Umar."[71] The temporary form of marriage is a marriage for a fixed period of time and according to the Jafari it is similar to the permanent marriage as regards the recital of a contract proving express intention of marriage. Consequently, any form of sexual contact between a man and a woman without a contract will not be considered temporary marriage even if it is by mutual consent and inclination. When the contract is recited it becomes binding and its observance becomes obligatory.

It is compulsory that dowry be mentioned in the contract of *mutah*. This dowry is similar to the dowry of a permanent wife, there being no prescribed minimum or maximum limit, and half of it subsides when the stipulated period is gifted or expires without consummation, in consonance with the rule applied in the dowry of a permanent wife divorced before consummation.

It is incumbent upon the woman with whom temporary marriage has been contracted to undergo the waiting period after the completion of the stipulated time, with the difference that a divorcee observes an waiting period of three months or three menstrual cycles, while in temporary marriage she observes an waiting period of two menstrual cycles or forty-five days. But as to the waiting period observed on the death of the husband, the wife in a temporary marriage observes it for four months and ten days, which is the same as observed by a permanent wife, irrespective of consummation.

The child born of this form of marriage is legitimate and enjoys all the rights of a legitimate child without the exception of a single legal or moral right.

It is compulsory that the temporary marriage be contracted for a fixed period of time and it is necessary that this stipulated time be mentioned in the contract. The wife in *mutah* does not inherit from her husband and her maintenance is also not obligatory upon him, in contrast with the permanent wife, who both inherits and is entitled to maintenance. But a wife in mutah can stipulate at the time of the contract that she shall inherit and be entitled to maintenance, and if the contract is concluded on these terms, the wife in temporary marriage becomes similar to a permanent wife.[72]

In spite of their belief in the validity of temporary marriage, the Jafari of Syria, Iraq and Lebanon do not practice it, and the Jafari *Shariah* Courts in Lebanon, since their inception, have neither applied this form of marriage nor authorized it.

10.12.6. THE ILLEGITIMATE CHILD

One who studies the verses of the Quran, the Traditions of the Prophet, and the statements of Muslim jurists, finds that Islam leaves no room for anyone to accuse others of fornication. Islam has framed the related rules of furnishing proof and giving judgment in a manner that makes this task difficult or even impossible. Whereas Islam considers two just witnesses sufficient for proving homicide, in the case of fornication it requires four just witnesses to testify that they have witnessed the act of penetration itself. It is not sufficient for them to say that so and so fornicated with so and so, or that they saw the two naked people hugging each other in a bed under a single cover. If three witnesses bear witness while the fourth abstains, each of the three shall be liable to a punishment of eighty lashes. Similarly a person who accuses a man or a woman of fornication shall be liable to eighty lashes.[73] The purpose behind all this is to cover the deeds of people, to protect their honor, to protect the family from the fear of ruined descent and the children from homelessness.

Fornication is the committing of the act by a mature and sane person with the knowledge of its being unlawful. Therefore fornication cannot be committed by a person who has not attained maturity or is insane or is ignorant or has been coerced or is in a state of intoxication. The act committed by these people will be considered 'intercourse by mistake', and we have discussed earlier the rules which apply to it. From the above discussion, it becomes clear that the Islamic Law gives a very restricted interpretation to fornication. Firstly, by limiting its application to an act committed with knowledge and intention, wherein there is no scope for attributing it to a mistake or fault in any manner. Secondly, it has restricted the manner of proving it in court by requiring four just witnesses who have seen it with their own eyes, whereas, generally, such an act is not observable. It is possible for a single witness to have seen it, while it is almost impossible for three or four persons to do so. All this clearly indicates that Islam has firmly closed the door in the face of those who seek to raise this thorny issue, because God does not like the spread of indecency among His creatures.

There is a consensus among jurists of all the legal schools that when fornication is proved in its above-mentioned meaning and manner, the child born of it shall not inherit from the father because no legal lineal bond is established between them. But the jurists have landed themselves in a legal difficulty by issuing the edict that an illegitimate issue cannot inherit, and are puzzled in finding a way out of this difficulty: If an illegitimate child is not attributable legally to its male 'parent', then, accordingly, in such a situation, it cannot be impermissible for a man to marry his illegitimate daughter and for an illegitimate son to marry his sister or paternal aunt as long as he is considered a stranger to the male 'parent'. Therefore, an illegitimate son is either a legally recognized issue and thereby entitled to everything to which legally recognized children are entitled, including the right of inheritance and maintenance, or he is not a legally recognized issue and thereby entitled to all those things which are established as regards those who are legally unrelated, including the marriage with a daughter or a sister.

To differentiate between the effects of a single undivided cause is to claim something without requisite proof it amounts to inclining towards something without any reason for doing so. Therefore, we see the jurists differ on this question after having concurred earlier (i.e. in excluding him from inheritance). Imam Malik and Imam Shafi have said that it is permissible (in such a case) for the person to marry his daughter, his sister, his son's daughter, his daughter's daughter, his brother's daughter and his sister's daughter when these relations have been established as a result of fornication, because they are 'strangers' to him and no legal lineal bond exists between them.[74] But this manner of solving the problem reminds one of the saying: "The cure is worse than the disease."

Jafari jurists, Imam Abu Hanifah and Imam Ibn Hanbal, have observed that we ought to differentiate between the two situations. We must disqualify the child from inheriting, while at the same time prohibiting matrimonial relationship between the child or its father within the prohibited degrees of relationship. Apart from marriage, to touch and to look at each other is also forbidden for both of them. Therefore, a father cannot look at or touch his illegitimate daughter despite her inability to inherit from him and his of inheriting from her.[75]

They argue that the establishment of matrimonial relationship is forbidden by pointing out that an illegitimate child is after all an offspring, both literally and by general acceptance. Consequently, whatever is forbidden between fathers and children is also forbidden for the illegitimate child and its father.

Their argument about the child's disqualification from inheriting is based upon the fact that the child is not acknowledged by the Shariah as its father's offspring and this is expressly stated by the verses of the Quran and Traditions.

10.12.7. AN ABANDONED CHILD

An abandoned child (*laqit*) is one found by a person in a state in which it is incapable of fending for itself, whom he or she takes and brings it up along with the rest of his or her family. All the legal schools concur that the abandoned child and its guardian do not inherit from each other because the act of giving shelter to an abandoned child is purely an act of kindness done in the spirit of cooperating in the performance of good and righteous deeds. It resembles the gifting of a fortune to someone making him prosperous after earlier indigence and distress with the hope of acquiring God's grace. As this act of kindness is no cause for inheritance, similarly the giving of shelter to an abandoned child.

10.12.8. ADOPTION

Adoption (*al-tabanni*) is the taking by a person of a child of known parentage and attributing it to himself. The Islamic Shariah does not consider adoption as a cause of inheritance, for it does not change the actual fact from what it is; the lineage of the child is both known and established, and lineage can neither be abrogated nor eliminated. This has been clearly mentioned in this verse of the Quran, "*...Neither has He made your adopted sons your sons (in fact). That is your own saying, the words of your mouths; but God speaks the truth, and guides on the way. Call them after their true fathers; that is more equitable in the sight of God....*" (33:4-5).

The exegetes have mentioned an interesting episode in relation to the revelation of this verse. Zayd ibn Harithah was made captive during the Age of Ignorance and the Prophet bought him. After the advent of Islam, Harithah came to Makkah and asked the Prophet to sell his son to him or to free him. The Prophet said, "He is free; he can go wherever he wants." But Zayd refused to leave the Prophet. His father, Harithah, became angry and said, "O people of Quraysh, bear witness that Zayd is not my son." The Prophet then said: "O people of Quraysh, bear witness that Zayd is my son."[76]

The jurists have mentioned many other subsidiary issues under this heading, and of these are some which are neither acceptable to human reason nor in harmony with the *Shariah*. One of them is the one quoted by the author of from Imam Abu Hanifah,[77] who holds: If a man marries a woman in a gathering and then divorces her in the same gathering before leaving it, or marries her while he is in the East and she in the West, either way if she gives birth to a child six months after the marriage, the child shall be attributed to the husband.

Other opinions are such as whose validity seems questionable from the viewpoint of medical science. The author of *al-Mughni,* in the same volume and on the same page, says, "If the husband is a child of ten years and his wife becomes pregnant, the child shall be attributed to him." Similar is the one quoted by the Jafari author of *al-Masalik,*[78] "If penetration occurs without discharge taking place, the child shall be attributed to the husband."

10.12.9. ARTIFICIAL INSEMINATION:
A hot debate is going on in the West regarding the answer to this question: If a barren husband agrees with his wife that she be artificially inseminated with a stranger's sperm, is this legally permissible?

10.12.9.1. ARTIFICIAL INSEMINATION IS PROHIBITED
Regarding the first question, there is no doubt that such insemination is prohibited due to following reasons: (1) Our knowledge of the *Shariah*, and its warning and emphasis concerning sexual matters, tell us that permissibility of anything in this regard rests upon permission of the *Shariah*. Therefore, the mere possibility of its being impermissible is sufficient for making restraint and caution obligatory. (2) The Quran says, *"And say to the believing women that they cast down their looks and guard their private parts...."* (24:31).

God has commanded women that they 'safeguard' their

organs of reproduction, but He has not mentioned from what they are supposed to be safeguarded. Neither has He specified that they safeguard them from intercourse or some other thing. The jurisprudents as well as linguists of the Arabic language concur that any proposition devoid of any particular specification implies the generality of inclusion. Similarly the inclusion of a specification in a proposition limits the proposition to that extent. For example, if it is said, "Safeguard your wealth from thieves," it denotes that wealth must be protected only from being robbed. But if it is said, "Safeguard your wealth," without specifying any specific thing, it implies that wealth is to be protected from being robbed, from damage, from waste, etc. Accordingly, the verse of the Quran connotes that the organs of reproduction be safeguarded from everything including insemination. This verse is reinforced by another verses of the Quran, *"And who guard their private parts. Save from their wives or those whom their right hands own, for then they surely are not blameworthy. But whoever seeks to go beyond that, those are the transgressors"* (23:5-7).

Any act contrary to the guarding of the parts in this verse amounts to transgression of the lawful limits, except that which occurs through marriage or ownership. Though the verses speak specifically of men, it does not hinder their application to women, because there is consensus that there is no difference between men and women in rules of this kind.

Some may say that the phrase does not prove that this kind of insemination is unlawful. It only indicates the impermissibility of (extra-marital) sexual relations, and this is the meaning that comes to mind and is understood from the verse. In other words, this verse may imply a wider meaning which includes artificial insemination or something else; but that which is apparent from its words is fornication, and it is a known fact that it is the generally understood meanings of dicta that are accepted for deriving the rules of the *Shariah*, not their literal meaning.

The answer is that this apparent meaning of the verse is not inherent in it; rather, this meaning has come to be associated with the verse because of its frequent usage in that context (i.e. to mean fornication). This is similar to the use of the word 'water' in Baghdad to mean the water of the Tigris and in Cairo to mean the water of the Nile, but this apparent meaning is of no consequence at all, for it fades on a little amount of reflection. No one can claim that the word 'water' in Baghdad was coined to mean only the water of the Tigris and in Cairo to mean only that of the Nile. Moreover, if artificial insemination were considered permissible on this ground, so would be the licking of dogs. because both these notions are far removed from the meaning which immediately comes to mind.

10.12.9.2. THE OFFSPRING BY ARTIFICIAL INSEMINATION

Now a child is born as a result of artificial insemination; shall it be a legitimate child, and to whom shall it be attributed? The answer is: As regards the sterile husband, the child cannot be attributed to him under any circumstances, and adoption is not valid in Islam, *"And He has not made those whom you call your sons, your sons"* (33:4).

As to the woman who bears it, some legal schools attribute the child to her, because an illegitimate child inherits from its mother and from its relatives through her and they inherit from it.[79] Therefore, if an illegitimate child can be attributed to its mother, a child born by artificial insemination is better entitled to be similarly attributed.

The Jafari, who do not attribute an illegitimate child to the fornicator or the fornicatress, observe: that the child born by artificial insemination does not inherit from its father or mother, and neither do they inherit from it. Sayyid Muhsin al-Hakim al-Tabataba'i has differentiated between an illegitimate child and a child born by insemination. He observes: A child born by insemination shall be attributed to its mother, because there is no valid reason to negate its status, and the grounds which prohibit an illegitimate child from attribution to its mother do not apply here. But as regards the man whose sperm is inseminated, al-Sayyid al-Hakim says, "The child shall not be attributed to him, because in order for a child to be attributed to a person it requires that he should have had

intercourse irrespective of whether he performs it, or is unable
to perform it but has his sperm reach her reproductive organ
during his effort." Apart from these cases, a child shall not be
attributed to the person of whose sperm it was conceived, even
if he is the husband.[80]

Whatever the case, artificial insemination is forbidden and
no Muslim may pronounce it permissible. But the impermissibility of artificial insemination does not necessarily imply that
the child born of it is an illegitimate issue, for at times intercourse may be prohibited but the child born of it is considered
legitimate as in the case of the person who has intercourse
with his wife during her menses or during the fast of
Ramadan, in both of which cases it is a prohibited act; but nevertheless the lineal bond between the child and the parents
shall be established. Accordingly, if a person has artificial
insemination performed despite its impermissibility, the child
born shall not be attributable to the husband because it was
not born of his sperm, nor shall it be attributable to the man
whose sperm was inseminated, because he has not had sexual
intercourse, neither by marriage nor by mistake. But the child
shall be attributed to its mother because it is her actual offspring and her legal child, and every actual offspring is a legally recognized issue unless the opposite is proved.

10.13. CUSTODY

Custody (*hidanah*) has no connection with guardianship
over the ward with respect to marriage; it is limited to the care
of a child for its upbringing and protection for a period of time
during which it requires the care of women. Custody is the
right of the mother by consensus, though there is a difference
of opinion regarding: the period after which it expires, the person who is entitled to custody after the mother, the qualification for a woman to act as a custodian, her right to receive a
fee for it, and other aspects which we shall discuss subsequently.

10.13.1. THE RIGHT TO ACT AS A CUSTODIAN

If it is not possible for a mother to act as the custodian of her child, to whom will this right belong? The Hanafis observe that it is transferred from the mother to the mother's mother, then to the father's mother, then to the full sisters, then to the uterine sisters, then to the paternal sisters, then to the full sister's daughter, and so on until it reaches the maternal and paternal aunts. The Malikis say that the right is transferred from the mother to her mother, howsoever high; then to the full maternal aunt; then the uterine maternal aunt, then the mother's maternal aunt, then the mother's paternal aunt, then the father's paternal aunt, then his (father's) mother's mother, then his father's mother and so on. The Shafiis say that the mother, then the mother's mother, how high so ever, on condition that she inherits; then the father, then his mother, how soever high high, on condition that she inherits; then the nearest among the female relatives, and then the nearest among the male relatives. According to the Hanbalis, the mother is followed by her mother, then her mother's mother, then the father, followed by his mothers; then the grandfather followed by his mothers; then the full sister; then the uterine sister; then the paternal sister; then the full maternal aunt; then the uterine maternal aunt, and so on.

The Jafari observe that the mother, and then the father, and if the father dies or becomes insane after he has taken the child's custody, the right to custody will revert to the mother on her being alive, because she is better entitled than others including the paternal grandfathereven if she has married a stranger. If the parents are not there, the custody of the child will lie with the paternal grandfather, and if he isn't there nor has an executor, the child's custody will lie with its relatives in order of inheritance, the nearer taking precedence over the remote. If there is more than one relative of the same class, such as the maternal and paternal grandmothers or maternal and paternal aunts, the matter will be decided by drawing lots in the event of contention and dispute. The person in whose name the lot is drawn becomes entitled to act as the custodian till his death or till he forgoes his right.[81] This is also the view of the Hanbalis.[82]

10.13.2. THE QUALIFICATIONS FOR CUSTODY

The scholars concur regarding the qualifications required for a female custodian, which are: her being sane, chaste and trustworthy, her not being an adulteress, a dancer, an imbiber of wine, or oblivious to child care. The purpose of these requirements is to ensure the proper care of the child from the viewpoint of physical and mental health. These conditions also apply if the custodian is a man.

The schools differ as to whether being Muslim is a condition for custodianship. The Jafari and the Shafii schools say that a non-Muslim has no right to the custody of a Muslim. The other schools do not consider Islam as a requirement for a custodian, except that the Hanafis say that the apostasy of a custodian, male or female, terminates his/her right to custody.

The Jafari state that it is compulsory that the female custodian be free from any contagious disease. The Hanbali school says that it is compulsory that she should not suffer from leprosy and leucoderma, and that which is important is that the child should not face any harm. The Hanafi, Hanbali, Shafii, Maliki schools have said that if the mother is divorced and marries a person who is unrelated to the child, her right to custody shall terminate. But if the husband is of the child's kin, the right to custody remains with the mother. The Jafari observe that the right to custody terminates with her marriage irrespective of whether the husband is related to the child or not. The Hanafi, Shafii, Jafari and Hanbali schools have said that if the mother is divorced by the second husband, the disability is removed and her right to custody reverts after its earlier termination due to her marriage. According to the Maliki school, her right to custody does not revert.

10.13.3. THE PERIOD OF CUSTODY

The Hanafis say that the period of custody for a boy is seven years, and for a girl nine years. The Shafii school observes that there is no definite period of custody; the child shall remain with its mother until it is able to choose between the two parents; and when it has reached the discriminating age it will choose between the two. If a boy chooses to stay with his mother, he will stay with her during the night and spend the day with his father, so that the father can arrange for his instruction. If a girl chooses to stay with her mother, she will continue to stay with her during the day as well as in the night. If the child chooses both the parents together, lots will be drawn between them, and if the child keeps quiet and does not choose any one of them, the custody shall lie with the mother. The Malikis consider the period of custody for a boy to be from birth until puberty and for a girl until her marriage. According to the Hanbali school, it is seven years irrespective of the child's sex, and, after that, the child can choose to live with one of the parents. The Jafari have said: The period of custody for a boy is two years, and for a girl seven years. After this, the custody shall lie with the father until the girl reaches the age of nine, and the boy the age of fifteen; thereafter they can choose to live with one of the parents.[83]

10.13.4. FEE FOR CUSTODY

The Shafii and the Hanbali schools state that a female custodian has the right to claim a fee for her services irrespective of whether she is the mother or someone else. The Shafiis clarify that this fee shall be paid from the child assets if any; otherwise it is incumbent upon the father, or upon whoever is responsible for the child's maintenance. The Malikis and Jafari observe that the female custodian is not entitled to any fee for her services. But the Jafari add that she is entitled to be paid for breast-feeding. Therefore, if the child has any assets she shall be paid out of that. Otherwise, the father shall pay it if he is capable of doing so.[84]

The Hanafi school has said that the payment of fee for custody is obligatory if: there does not exist any marital relationship between the female custodian and the child's father; if she is not in the course of observing the waiting period of a revocable divorce given by the child's father; if she is observing the waiting period of an irrevocable divorce of an invalid marriage, in which case she is entitled to receive maintenance from the child's father. If the child has any property, the payment shall be made from it; otherwise the payment shall be made by the one responsible for the child's maintenance.[85]

10.13.5. TRAVELING WITH A CHILD

In case the mother takes the child under her custody, and the father intends to travel with his child to settle down in another town, the Jafaris and the Hanafis say that he cannot do so. The Shafii, the Maliki and the Hanbali schools observe that he can do so. But if it is the mother who intends to travel with the child, the Hanafi school gives her the right to do so if the two following conditions are met: (1) That she be migrating to her own town; (2) that the marriage contract should have been recited in the town to which she is migrating. If any of these two conditions is not met, she is forbidden to travel except to a place so near that it is possible to return before it gets dark. The Shafii and Maliki schools, and Imam Ahmad in one of the two traditions narrated from him, observe: The father has greater right over the child irrespective of whether he is moving or she.[86] The Jafari state that a divorced mother is not permitted to travel with the child under her custody to a far-off place without the consent of the child's father. The father, too, is not permitted to travel with the child to any town which is not the mother's hometown while the child is in her custody.

10.13.6. VOLUNTARY BREAST-FEEDING AND CUSTODY

The difference between custody and breast-feeding is that by 'custody' is meant only the upbringing and care of the child; it excludes breast-feeding, which involves the infant's nourishment. Because of this difference, it is valid for a mother to forgo her right to breast-feed while her right to custody remains intact. The Jafari and the Hanafi schools concur that if a woman volunteers to breast-feed a child gratuitously while the mother refuses to breast-feed without recompense, the woman volunteering shall be given precedence over the mother, whose right to suckle her child is lost. But her right to the custody of her child shall remain as it is, and the child shall be under her care while the nurse comes to feed it or it is taken to the nurse to be fed. If a woman volunteers to act as a child's custodian, the child shall not be separated from the mother according to the Jafari and the other schools which do not require compensation for a custodian's services.

But the Hanafis, who consider the payment of compensation for custody as obligatory, observe: Where the mother refuses to act as a custodian unless she is paid and another woman volunteers to act as a custodian, the mother is better entitled to custody if the compensation is to be paid by the father, or if the woman is an outsider and there are no women custodians among the child's relatives. But if the woman volunteering is related to the child and the compensation lies upon an indigent father, or is to be paid from the child's property, the other woman shall be preferred, because, in such a situation, the child is saved from payment of fee out of its assets by the woman volunteering. Therefore, she shall be given preference over the mother in the child's interest.[87]

10.13.7. SURRENDERING OF THE RIGHT TO CUSTODY

Is the right to custody specifically the right of a female custodian that terminates on her surrendering it—similar to the right of pre-emption which can be surrendered—or is it a right of the child that binds the female custodian precluding her right to surrender it, as in the case of a mother's right which cannot be surrendered?[88]

The Jafari, the Shafii and the Hanbali schools observe that custody is the specific right of a female custodian, and she can surrender it whenever she pleases and she shall not be compelled to act as a custodian on her refusing to do so. There is a tradition from Imam Malik regarding this, and the author of *al-Jawahir* has argued on its authority that the jurists have not concurred that a female custodian can be compelled to act as a custodian, and the *Shariah* does not expressly mention such compulsion; on the contrary, the texts of the *Shariah* apparently consider custody similar to breast-feeding, and, consequently, she has the right to surrender her custody at will.

The same principle applies where a child's mother seeks a divorce from her husband by surrendering in his favor her right to custody of the child, or when the husband surrenders to her his right to take away the child after the expiry of her period of custody. This form of divorce is valid and neither of the two can refrain from discharging their agreement after it is concluded, except by mutual consent. Similarly, if the two compromise and she surrenders her right to custody or he surrenders his right to take away the child, the compromise is binding and its fulfillment is obligatory.

Ibn Abidin has reported a difference of opinion amongst the Hanafis on this issue. He has pointed out that it is better that custody be considered as a right of the child, so that the mother does not have the right to surrender her responsibility to act as a custodian, to make compromise over it, or to exchange it for securing a divorce.

The Hanafi, Hanbali, Shafii and Maliki *Shariah* courts in Lebanon consider a divorce of this kind as valid, but consider as invalid the condition that she would surrender her right to custody; any compromise which includes the surrendering of her right to custody is considered void *ab initio*. But the Jafari *Shariah* courts consider the divorce, the condition, and the compromise as valid.

10.14. THE RIGHT TO MAINTENANCE

There is consensus among all Muslims that marriage is one of the causes that make maintenance obligatory. A similar consensus exists regarding kinship (*al-qarabah*). The Holy Quran has explicitly mentioned the wife's maintenance in the following verse, "...*And on the child's father (the husband) is their food and clothing....*" (2:233).

There is also a Tradition which says, "The right of a woman

over her husband is that he feed her, clothe her, and if she acts out of ignorance, to forgive her." The Quran has referred to the maintenance of relatives. The Prophet has said, "You and your property are for your father." Our discussion comprises two issues: first, the maintenance of a wife and her maintenance during the waiting period period; second, the maintenance of relatives.

10.14.1. THE MAINTENANCE OF A WIFE AND A DIVORCEE DURING THE WAITING PERIOD

The legal schools concur that the wife's maintenance is obligatory if the requisite conditions, to be mentioned subsequently, are fulfilled, and that the maintenance of a divorcee is obligatory during the waiting period of a revocable divorce. The schools also concur that a woman observing the waiting period following her husband's death is not entitled to maintenance, whether she is pregnant or not, except that the Shafii and the Maliki schools state that if the husband dies, she is entitled to maintenance only to the extent of housing.

The Shafiis have said that if he separates from her while she is pregnant and then dies, her maintenance shall not cease. The Hanafis observe that if she is a revocable divorcee and the husband dies during the waiting period, her waiting period of divorce shall change into a waiting period of death, and her maintenance shall cease, except where she had been asked by the court to borrow her maintenance and she had actually done so. In this case, the maintenance shall not cease.

There is consensus that a woman observing the waiting period as a result of 'intercourse by mistake' is not entitled to maintenance. The schools differ regarding the maintenance of a divorcee during the waiting period of an irrevocable divorce. The Hanafis observe that she is entitled to maintenance even if she has been divorced three times, whether she is pregnant or not, on condition that she does not leave the house provided by the divorce (husband) for her to spend the waiting period. According to the Hanafi school, the rules which apply to a woman in a waiting period following the dissolution of a valid contract are the same as those which apply to a divorcee in an irrevocable divorce.

According to the Maliki school, if the divorcee is not pregnant, she shall not be entitled to any maintenance except residence, and if she is pregnant she is entitled to her full maintenance. It shall not subside even if she leaves the house provided for spending the waiting period, because the maintenance is intended for the child in the womb and not for the divorcee.

The Shafii, Jafari and Hanbali schools state that if she is not pregnant she is not entitled to maintenance, and if pregnant, she is entitled to it. But the Shafiis add that if she leaves the house of her waiting period without any necessity, her maintenance shall cease.

The Jafari do not consider the dissolution of a valid contract similar to an irrevocable divorce. They observe that a divorcee undergoing the waiting period of a dissolved contract is not entitled to any maintenance whether she is pregnant or not.

10.14.2. A DISOBEDIENT WIFE

The schools concur that a disobedient wife (*al-nashizah*) is not entitled to maintenance. But they differ regarding the extent of disobedience which causes the maintenance to subside. According to the Hanafis, when a wife confines herself to her husband's house and does not leave it except with his permission, she shall be regarded as 'obedient', even if she denies him her sexual company without any valid reason. Therefore, though such an act is unlawful for her, it shall not cause her maintenance to cease. Thus, the cause which entitles her to maintenance, according to the Hanafis, is her confining herself to her husband's home, and her denial of her sexual company has no effect at all. This view of the Hanafi school is contrary to the view of all the other schools who concur that if a wife does not allow her husband free access to her person without any legal and reasonable excuse, she shall be considered 'disobedient' and shall not be entitled to any maintenance. The Shafiis further add that her allowing him free access is not enough unless she comes forth and says expressly to him, "I surrender myself to you."

In fact, the criterion for ascertaining 'obedience' and 'submission' is the general custom, and there is no doubt that the people consider a wife obedient if she does not deny him access when he demands it, and they do not consider it necessary that she offer herself to him morning and evening. Whatever be the case, we have here the following questions concerning 'obedience' and 'disobedience'.

If the wife is a minor, unfit for intercourse, and the husband a major capable of it, shall maintenance be obligatory? The Hanafis say: There are three types of female minors:

A minor wife who is neither of any use for service nor for sociability, shall not be entitled to maintenance.

A minor wife with whom intercourse is possible enjoys the rights of a major wife.

A minor wife who is of use for service or for sociability alone, but not for intercourse, shall not be entitled to maintenance. The remaining schools state that a minor wife is not entitled to maintenance even if the husband is a major.

If the wife is a major capable of intercourse while the husband is a minor and incapable of it, the Hanafi, Shafii and Hanbali schools observe that her maintenance is obligatory because the hindrance is from his side, not her.

The Malikis and some scholars of the Jafari have said that maintenance is not obligatory because the sole granting of access from her side has no effect while there exists a natural disability in the husband, and a minor husband is free of obligations (*ghayr mukallaf*), and as to the duty of his guardian, there is no proof (that he is responsible for his ward's wife's maintenance).

If the wife is sick or suffers from *al-ratq* or *al-qarn*,[89] her maintenance does not cease according to the Jafari, the Hanbali and the Hanafi schools,[90] and it does according to the Maliki school if she is suffering from a serious disease or if the husband himself is similarly ill according to all the schools. The maintenance of a wife belonging to the People of the Book (*ahl al-kitab*) is obligatory, and there is no difference between her and a Muslim wife from the viewpoint of maintenance.

If a wife leaves her husband's home without his permission or refuses to reside in a house which fits her status, she shall be considered 'disobedient' and shall not be entitled to maintenance according to all the schools. The Shafii and Hanbali schools further add that if she goes out with his permission for his need she shall be entitled to maintenance, and if she goes out not for his need, her maintenance shall cease even if he had granted her permission to do so.

If she goes out for performing the obligatory pilgrimage, her maintenance shall cease according to the Shafii and Hanafi schools, but according to the Jafari and Hanbalis, it shall not.

If the wife is obedient to her husband in granting him access and resides with him wherever he wants, but uses harsh language while talking to him, frowns at him and opposes him in many matters, as is the case with many women, shall this be a cause for the maintenance to cease or not?

Research has not turned up any views of the schools on this question, but it appears that if the wife has a hot-tempered disposition by nature and this is her way of behavior with everyone including her parents, she shall not be considered disobedient. But if she is not so by nature and is well-disposed towards everyone except her husband, she should be considered disobedient and not entitled to maintenance.

If the wife refuses to obey her husband unless she is paid her dowry, agreed to be paid immediately, shall she be considered disobedient? The schools have divided the question as mentioned in the chapter on *mahr* between her refusing him before granting him access to her person and her refusal after granting him access willingly before taking the dowry.

In the first case, her refusal is due to a legally valid excuse and therefore she shall not be considered disobedient. In the second case, her refusal is without any valid excuse and, therefore, she shall be considered disobedient.

Research has not shown any opinion by the Hanbalis that if

a wife imprisons her husband, demanding her maintenance or *mahr*, her maintenance shall cease if he is indigent and unable to meet her monetary rights, and if he has the means to pay but delays doing so it shall not.[91]

This opinion is both good and firm because if she has imprisoned him while he is an indigent man unable to pay, she is oppressing him. If she has imprisoned a husband who has the means to pay her but delays doing it, he is oppressing her. A verse of the Quran says, "*And if the debtor is in straitness, let there be postponement till the time of ease....*" (2:280). There is a Tradition which says that it is permissible to punish and dishonor a person who possesses but does not pay his or her liabilities.

If a wife is divorced while she is disobedient, she will not be entitled to maintenance. If she is undergoing the waiting period of a revocable divorce and turns disobedient during this period, her maintenance shall cease, but on her reverting to obedience, it shall resume from the date of his knowledge of her becoming obedient.

If the wife remains at her father's home after the recital of the marriage contract for a period of time and then claims maintenance for that period, shall she be entitled to it? The Hanafis observe that she is entitled to maintenance even if she has not shifted to her husband's home, either because the husband has not asked her to do so or has but she has refused to come until she is given her dowry.[92] According to the Maliki and Shafii schools, she is entitled to maintenance if the marriage has been consummated or she has offered herself to him. The Hanbali school states that if she does not offer herself, she is not entitled to maintenance even if she remains in such a state for years. The Jafari consider her entitled to maintenance from the date of the consummation of marriage—even if such consummation should occur while she is with her family and from the date of her asking him to take her along with him.

From the above-mentioned views, it follows that all the schools entitle the wife to maintenance if she has offered herself and showed her readiness to comply, and also if the marriage has been consummated, except that the Hanafis do not end with consummation but consider her willingness to confine herself also necessary. Apart from this, it has been pointed in the answer to the eighth question of this section that the wife has the right to refuse obedience until she is paid her prompt dowry, and her doing so is legally valid and does not cause her maintenance to cease.

The Maliki, Shafii and Hanbali schools state that an absent husband is similar to a husband present in regard to the rules of maintenance. Therefore, if an absent husband has any known assets, the judge shall order her maintenance to be paid from them, and if he does not possess such property, the judge shall pass an order of maintenance against him and the wife will borrow against his name. This is the procedure followed in Egypt.[93]

In *al-Ahwal al-shakhsiyyah*[94] of Muhammad Muhyi Din Abd al-Hamid it is stated that the Hanafi school presumes that the absent husband has left in his property a share for his wife, and if he has not left any property, the judge shall consider him liable to pay the maintenance and will order the wife to borrow against his name. If she complains of not having found a person ready to lend her in her husband's name, the judge shall order the person on whom her maintenance is obligatory to lend her on the supposition that she has no husband, and if this person refuses to lend her maintenance, the judge will imprison him.

The Jafari observe that if the husband disappears after her surrendering herself to him, her maintenance is obligatory upon him on the supposition that her obedience still persists from the time he left her; and if he disappears before consummation, she shall appear before the court and declare her obedience and willingness to live with him. The judge will then order the husband to present himself to inform him of her willingness. If the husband presents himself, or sends for her, or sends her her maintenance, it suffices. But if he does not fulfill any of these alternatives, the judge shall allow a period of time sufficient for the issuance of a notification and the reception of his reply or for his sending of her maintenance; he will not issue any order during this period. After the expiry of this period he shall issue orders. If, for instance, such a period is two months, he shall order the payment of maintenance beginning from the date of expiry of the two months. Or if the wife informs the husband of her state without the mediation of the judge and proves it, it shall also suffice. Then she shall be entitled to maintenance from that date.

If the wife pleads before a judge to pass an order against the husband for the payment of her maintenance without mentioning the date from which she is entitled to receive it, the judge shall order payment from the date of her demanding maintenance, after ascertaining that the conditions have been fulfilled. If the wife mentions a date which is prior to the date of demand, shall the judge order payment of her maintenance for the period prior to the date of demand?

The Hanafis have said that past maintenance may not be demanded from the husband; it is annulled by the passage of time except when the period is less than a month or if the judge has ordered its payment, because maintenance ordered to be paid by court remains a debt for the husband irrespective of the passage of time.

The Malikis observe that if the wife demands her past maintenance, and the husband possessed the means to pay her during that time, she has the right to such a claim against him even if it had not been ordered by the court. But if the husband was indigent and unable to pay during that period, she cannot claim her maintenance from him, because, according to this school, indigence annuls maintenance. If his indigence is subsequent to his affluence, the maintenance for the period of indigence shall be void and he shall be liable for the payment of the maintenance pertaining to his period of affluence.

The Jafari, Shafii and Hanbali schools state that the wife's maintenance remains his liability, if the conditions entitling the wife to maintenance are fulfilled, no matter how much time has passed and irrespective of whether he was affluent or indigent during that time and regardless of whether the judge had ordered such payment or not.

10.14.3. DETERMINATION OF MAINTENANCE

The schools concur that a wife's maintenance is obligatory in all its three forms: food, clothing and housing. They also concur that maintenance will be determined in accordance with the financial status of the two if both are of equal status. Here, by the financial status of the wife is meant the financial status of her family and its standard of living.

But when one of them is well-off and the other indigent, the schools differ whether maintenance should be in accordance with the husband's financial status (commensurable with his means if he is well-off and the wife indigent, and commensurable with his indigence if he is indigent and she is well-off), or whether the financial status of both should be considered and a median maintenance be fixed for her. The Maliki and Hanbali schools state that if the couple differ in financial status, a median course will be followed. The Shafii school observes that maintenance will be determined in accordance with the financial status of the husband, and the status of the wife will not be considered; this is regarding food and clothing. But as regards housing, it should be according to her status, not his.[95]

The Hanafis have two views. According to the first, the status of both will be considered, and according to the second only the status of the husband. Most Jafari jurists observe that maintenance will be fixed in accordance with her requirements of food, clothing, housing, servants and cosmetics used by women of her standing among her townspeople. Some Jafari jurists consider the husband's not the wife's financial status as the criterion for fixing maintenance.

Whatever the case, it is necessary that the financial condition of the husband be taken into consideration as the Quran has expressly stated, *"Lodge them where you are lodging, according to your means....Let the man of plenty expend out of*

*his plenty.... As for him who has his means of subsistence strait-
ened, let him expend of what God has given him. God does not
burden anyone except to the extent of what He has granted
him...."* (65:6-7). Under Egyptian law,[96] the wife's maintenance,
to be paid by the husband, is fixed in accordance with his
financial condition, irrespective of the condition of the wife.

Here it becomes clear that providing a servant and expenses of tobacco, cosmetics, tailoring, etc., requires that two things
be taken into consideration: the husband's condition and the
custom prevailing among her likes. Therefore, if she demands
more than that the husband is not obliged to comply, irrespective of his financial condition; and if she demands what her
likes generally require, it is compulsory that the husband meet
her demands if he is well-off, but not if his means are straitened. Here, the following questions are also pertinent:

10.14.3.1. MEDICAL EXPENSES

If the wife needs medicines or surgery, will the husband be
compelled to pay her medical and surgical expenses? The
answer to this question leads us to another one: Is medical
care part of maintenance or something apart from it? When we
refer to the canonical sources, we find that the Quran makes
the wife's food and clothing obligatory. The Traditions say that
it is for the husband to satiate her hunger and to clothe her.
There is no mention of medicine and medical treatment in the
Quran and the Traditions. The jurists have limited maintenance to the providing of food, clothing and housing, and have
not touched the matter of medical care. On the contrary, some
of them have explicitly said that it is not obligatory for the
husband. In *al-Fiqh alal-madhahib al-arbaah* it has been narrated from the Hanafis that medicines and fruits are not obligatory on the husband during the period of dispute between the
couple. In the Jafari work *al-Jawahir*,[97] it is stated that the
wife is not entitled to claim from the husband medicine during
illness, or the expenses of cupping and bathing except during
winter. Sayyid Abu al-Hasan observes that if the medicines are
of common use and needed for common ailments, such medi-

cines are included in maintenance and are obligatory upon the husband. If the medicines are for difficult cures and uncommon ailments, which require expensive treatment, they are not included in maintenance and it is not the husband's duty to provide them.

This was a summary of the opinions of the jurists which I have come across. It is also said that the treatment of simple diseases, such as malaria and ophthalmia, is included in maintenance, as observed by the author of *al-Wasilah*. But regarding surgery, which requires large sums of money, if the husband is poor and the wife is financially well-off, she will bear the expenditure; and if he is a man of means while she is poor, he will meet the expenses—for of all people the husband, being her life partner, is most entitled to be kind to her. If both of them are indigent, they will share in meeting the expenses.

In any case, it is certain that the Shariah has not explicitly defined the limits of maintenance, but has only made it obligatory on the husband, leaving it to be determined in accordance with usage (*urf*). Therefore, we should refer to usage and not make anything obligatory for the husband except after ascertaining that it is considered part of maintenance by usage. And there is no doubt that usage disapproves the conduct of a husband who while possessing the means neglects his wife who needs medical attention, exactly as it considers a father blameworthy if he neglects his ailing children while having the means to buy medicines and pay the doctor's fee.

10.14.3.2. EXPENSES OF CHILDBIRTH

The essential expenses of childbirth and the obstetrician's fee will be paid by the husband when called upon by need.

10.14.3.3. ADJUSTMENT OF MAINTENANCE

If a judge determines a certain sum of money, or the spouses mutually settle it in lieu of maintenance, it is valid to adjust it by increasing or decreasing it in accordance with changes in prices or changes in the financial condition of the husband.

10.14.3.4. THE WIFE'S HOUSING

The Jafari, Hanafi and Hanbali schools state that it is necessary that the house provided to the wife befit the couple's status, and that the husband's family and children not reside in it except by her consent. The Malikis observe that if the wife is of a humble status, she may not refuse to stay with the husband's relatives, and if of a high social status she can refuse to stay with them except if it had been mentioned as a condition in the contract. If so, it is obligatory for her to reside with his family on being provided a room where she can enjoy privacy whenever she desires and does not suffer from mistreatment by his family. According to the Shafii school, it is obligatory that the housing suit her and not his status, even if he is poor.

The truth is that it is necessary to consider the condition of the husband in everything concerning maintenance, without there being any difference between food, clothing and housing in this regard, because the Quran says, *"Lodge them where you are lodging according to your means,"* (65:6) on condition that she have an independent home and does not suffer by staying in it.

10.14.3.5. A WORKING WIFE

The Hanafis are explicit that a woman if she works and does not stay at home is not entitled to maintenance if the husband demands her to stay at home and she does not concede to his demand. This view is in concurrence with what the other schools hold regarding the impermissibility of her leaving her home without his permission. The Shafii and Hanbali schools further state, as mentioned earlier, that if she leaves home with his permission for meeting her own requirements, her maintenance ceases.

But a correct view would be to differentiate between a husband who knows at the time of marriage that she is employed and her employment prevents her staying at home, and a husband who is ignorant about her employment at the time of marriage. Therefore, if he knew and remained silent and did not include a condition that she leave her job, he has no right in this case to ask her to forgo her job; and if he demands and she refuses to comply, her maintenance shall not cease, because he has concluded the contract with the knowledge that she works. And many men marry working women with an intention of exploiting them, and when they are unable to do so they ask the wives to stop working with the purpose of harming them financially.

But if the husband does not know that she works at the time of marriage, he can demand that she stop working, and if she does not comply, she shall not be entitled to maintenance.

10.14.3.6. SURETY FOR MAINTENANCE

Is the wife entitled to claim from her husband a surety to secure her future maintenance if the husband intends to travel alone without leaving anything for her? The Hanafi, Maliki and Hanbali schools observe that she is entitled to do so, and he is bound to arrange a surety for maintenance, and on his refusal she can ask that he be prevented from making the journey. The Maliki further add that she is entitled to claim from him advance payment of maintenance if he intends to go for a usual journey, and if the wife accuses him of planning to go for an unusual journey she has the right to claim immediate payment of maintenance for the period of a usual journey and to provide her a surety for the period which exceeds the period of a usual journey.

The Jafari and Shafii schools state that she is not entitled to claim a surety for her future maintenance because its payment hasn't become due, and in the future the possibility of its ceasing due to her disobedience or divorce or death is always present.

My opinion is that she has the right to claim a surety because the cause on whose basis a surety is demanded is present, and this is her present obedience. Therefore, Shaykh Ahmad Kashif al-Ghita has observed the opinion that she can claim a surety if not opposed by consensus, so that her future maintenance is insured like her past and present maintenance.[98]

As the matter leads to consensus, it lacks strength from the Jafari viewpoint, because, according to their principles of jurisprudence, every consensus reached after the period of the Imams faces the possibility of being refuted. Thus if there is a possibility that the consensus of the concurring jurists is based on their belief that future maintenance does not become payable presently because it is not correct to provide surety for something which has not become payable, the argument on the basis of consensus fails due to the presence of this possibility. Now it should be seen whether the rule that everything which has not yet become payable does not require a surety on which the jurists have based their argument is correct and whether it can be applied here or not. Here, as already explained, the cause (the wife's obedience) is present, which is sufficient to justify surety. Accordingly, the wife is entitled to claim a surety for her maintenance if the husband intends to travel, especially when he cannot be relied upon and is known to be irresponsible.

10.14.3.7. DISPUTE BETWEEN SPOUSES

If after the husband accepts the wife's right to maintenance, the two differ about the actual payment of maintenance (she denying that he has paid, and he claiming to have paid it), the Hanafi, Shafii and Hanbali schools observe that the wife's word shall be accepted because she is the refuter and the burden of proof is not on her.

The Jafari and Maliki schools state that if the husband resides with her in the same house, his word will be accepted, otherwise her word. If the husband concedes that he has not paid maintenance on the excuse that she is not entitled to it due to her not surrendering herself to him, his word will be accepted according to all the schools. The consensus on this issue is a corollary to the consensus of the schools on the issue that dowry becomes payable on the conclusion of the contract and becomes fully payable on consummation; but maintenance does not become payable solely on the conclusion of the contract, it is necessary for her to surrender herself to the husband. It is the practice of the *Shariah* courts of Lebanon, in all major schools, when the spouses differ regarding disobedience (he claiming that she is disobedient and she charging him with disobedience), to order the husband to provide a suitable house and to order the wife to reside in it. If the husband refuses to provide a house, he will be considered disobedient; and if he provides a house which fulfills all the conditions and she refuses to reside in it and to obey him, she will be considered disobedient.

10.14.3.8. THE WIFE'S CLAIM OF EXPULSION
If the wife leaves her husband's home claiming that she has been expelled, and he denies this, the burden of proof will rest on her and he will be made to take an oath, because it is not valid for her to leave home without an acceptable excuse, and as she claims the presence of such an excuse, she is burdened with proving it.

10.14.3.9. LOSS OF MAINTENANCE
When the husband provides his wife with maintenance for the future, and then it is stolen or destroyed while in her possession, it is not obligatory upon the husband to replenish it, irrespective of whether such loss occurs due to an unavoidable cause or on account of her negligence.

10.14.3.10. HUSBAND'S DEBT CLAIM AGAINST WIFE
If a wife owes a debt to her husband, can he adjust this debt against her present or future maintenance? The Jafari jurists have dealt with this issue. They observe that if she is financially well-off and yet refuses to repay the debt, it is permissible for him to adjust it from her day-to-day maintenance, which means that he consider her debt to him as her maintenance for each day, separately. But if she is financially straitened, he cannot do so; because any payment towards debt should be from what exceeds her daily expenditures.

10.14.3.11. MAINTENANCE OF RELATIVES
Who are the relatives entitled to maintenance and who

amongst them is liable to provide maintenance? What are the conditions which make such maintenance obligatory?

10.14.3.12. DEFINITION OF A RELATIVE'S MAINTENANCE

According to the Hanafis, the criterion for the responsibility of the relative to provide maintenance of another is the prohibited degree of marriage, so that if one of them is supposed a male and the other a female, marriage between them would be considered unlawful.

Therefore, this responsibility includes fathers—howsoever high—and sons—howsoever low—and also includes brothers, sisters, uncles and aunts, both paternal and maternal, because marriage between any two of them is prohibited.

The nearest relative shall be liable to provide maintenance, and affinity here has nothing to do with the title to inheritance. Therefore, if there is someone in the two classes of lineal ascendants and descendants, maintenance will be obligatory on him, even if he is not entitled to inherit (from the person he is liable to maintain). One not belonging to these two classes will not be liable to provide maintenance, although he should be entitled to inherit. For example, if a person has a daughter's son and a brother, his maintenance will be obligatory upon the former and not the latter, though the latter alone be entitled to the entire legacy to the exclusion of the former.[99]

Similarly, between two relatives of the same class, the nearer one will be responsible, even if he is not entitled to any share in the legacy. Therefore, if a child has a paternal great grandfather and a maternal grandfather, his maintenance will be obligatory upon the latter not the former, though the former should be an heir to the exclusion of the other. The secret here is that the maternal grandfather is nearer though he does not inherit, while the paternal great grandfather is comparatively distant, though he is an heir. The Hanafis also state that the well-to-do son is responsible for the maintenance of his indigent father's wife, and he is also liable to get his indigent father married if he needs a wife.

The Malikis observe that maintenance is obligatory only on

parents and children, not on other relatives. Thus, a grandson is not responsible to maintain his paternal or maternal grandfathers or grandmothers, and, reciprocally, a grandfather is not liable to maintain his grandsons and granddaughters. On the whole, the responsibility for maintenance is limited to parents and children, to the exclusion of grandparents and grandchildren. They also state that it is obligatory upon a well-to-do son to maintain the state of his indigent parents, even if they do not need him; but it is not obligatory for a father to maintain his son's servant. A son is also liable to maintain his father's wife and her servant and have his father married to one or more wives, if one wife does not suffice.

The Hanbalis state that it is obligatory that fathers, how soever high, provide and receive maintenance. Similarly, it is obligatory that sons, howsoever low, provide and receive maintenance, irrespective of their title to inheritance. Maintenance of relatives not belonging to the two classes is also obligatory if the person liable to provide maintenance inherits from the person being maintained either by *fard* or by *taslb*;[100] but if excluded from inheritance, he will not be responsible for maintenance. Thus, if a person has an indigent son and a well-to-do brother, neither may be compelled to maintain him, because the son's indigence relieves him of the responsibility, and the brother by being excluded from inheritance due to the son's presence.

They also state that it is obligatory on the son to arrange for his father's marriage and to maintain his wife, in the same way as it is obligatory on the father to have his son married if he is in need of marriage.

According to the Jafari and Shafii schools, it is obligatory for sons to maintain their fathers and mothers, howsoever high, and it is obligatory for fathers to maintain sons and daughters, howsoever low. The obligation of maintenance does not transcend these two main lineal classes to include others, such as brothers and paternal and maternal uncles.

But the Shafiis are of the view that a well-to-do father is liable to have his indigent son married if in need of marriage;

and a son is likewise bound to arrange for his indigent father's marriage if in need of marriage. Moreover, the liability for a person's maintenance includes the maintenance of his wife.[101]

Most Jafari jurists state that it is not obligatory to arrange for the marriage of a person whose maintenance is obligatory, irrespective of whether he is father or son. Similarly, it is not obligatory for a son to maintain his father's wife if she is not his mother, or for a father to maintain his son's wife, because the canonical proofs which make maintenance obligatory include neither the father's wife nor the son's, and an obligation is assumed to be non-existent until proved.

10.14.3.13. CONDITIONS FOR THE OBLIGATIONS OF MAINTENANCE

The following conditions are necessary[102] for making the maintenance of one relative obligatory upon another.

The person to be maintained must be in need of maintenance. Therefore, maintaining a person who is not needy is not obligatory. The schools differ regarding a person who is needy and can earn his livelihood but does not do so, as to whether it is obligatory to maintain him or not.

The Hanafi and Shafii schools state that the inability to earn is not a necessary condition for the obligatory of the maintenance of fathers and grandfathers. Therefore, their maintenance is obligatory on sons even if they have the ability to work but neglect to do so. Regarding other relatives who are able to make a living for themselves, their maintenance is not obligatory; rather, they will be compelled to make a living, and a one who neglects to work or is sluggish commits only a crime against himself. But the Shafiis say regarding a daughter that her maintenance is obligatory on the father until she is married.

The Jafari, Maliki and Hanbal schools state that if one who was earlier making his livelihood by engaging in a trade that suited his condition and status later neglects to do so, his maintenance is not obligatory upon anyone, irrespective of whether it is the father or the mother or the son. The Malikis agree with the Shafiis' position regarding a daughter and the reason for this is that formerly women were considered generally incapable of earning their own livelihood.

That the maintainer be well-off, according to all the schools, except the Hanafis who say that being well-to-do of the maintainer is a condition only for the maintenance of those who are neither ascendants nor descendants, but financial capacity is not a condition in the maintenance of the scion by one of the parents or the maintenance of the parents by the scion. The only condition here is the presence of the actual ability to maintain or the presence of the ability to earn. Therefore, a father who is capable of work will be ordered to maintain his child, and similarly a son with respect to his father, except where one of them is indigent and incapable of making an earning, such as due to blindness, etc.

The schools differ regarding the degree of financial ease necessary to cause the liability for providing maintenance to a relative. According to the Shafii school, it is the surplus over the daily expenditure of his own, his wife's and his children's. The Malikis add to this the expenditure incurred upon servants and domestic animals. According to the Jafari and the Hanbali schools, it is the surplus over the daily expenditure of oneself and one's wife, as the maintenance of descendants and ascendants belongs to the same category.

Hanafi jurists differ in defining the state of financial ease. According to some of them, it is possession of an amount of wealth which gives rise to the incidence of poor-due (*nisab*); according to others, it should be enough to prohibit his taking of poor-due. The third opinion differentiates between the farmer and the worker allowing the farmer his and his family's expenditure for a period of one month and the worker a day's expenditure as deduction.

According to the Hanbalis, their belonging to the same religion is necessary. Thus, if one of them is a Muslim and the other a non-Muslim, maintenance will not be obligatory.[103] The Maliki, Shafii and Jafari schools state that their belonging to the same religion is not necessary. Therefore, a Muslim can maintain a relative who is not a Muslim, as is the case when maintenance is provided by a Muslim husband to his wife belonging to the People of the Book. The Hanafis observe that belonging to the same religion is not required between ascendants and descendants, but necessary between other relatives. Therefore, a Muslim will not maintain his non-Muslim brother and vice versa.[104]

10.14.3.14. DETERMINATION OF RELATIVE'S MAINTENANCE

It is necessary that maintenance paid to a relative be sufficient to cover his/her essential needs, such as food, clothing and housing, because maintenance has been made obligatory to protect life and to provide its needs. Thus it is to be determined in accordance with the needs.[105]

10.14.3.15. DISPUTE BETWEEN RELATIVES

The Malikis state that maintenance of parents will not be obligatory on a son unless their condition of need is proved by the testimony of two just male witnesses; the testimony of a just male witness along with two female witnesses or the testimony of a just male witness along with an oath will not suffice. The Shafiis state that the father's word will be accepted without an oath if he claims to be in need. The Hanafis state that need is presumed unless there is proof to the contrary. Therefore, if the person claiming maintenance pleads indigence, his word will be accepted on oath and the person from whom maintenance is claimed is burdened to disprove the claim of the claimant. And if the person from whom maintenance is claimed pleads indigence, his word will be accepted on oath and the claimant will be burdened with proving the former's financial capacity. If the presence of financial capacity was established in the past and incapacity is subsequently claimed, the former state will be presumed to exist until the opposite is proved. The Jafari concur with the Hanafi position on this issue, because it is in accordance with the principles of the *Shariah*, except where the person claiming indigence owns known assets. If he does, his plea will be rejected and the word of the person claiming his financial capacity will be accepted.

10.14.3.16. PAYMENT OF PAST MAINTENANCE

The schools concur that the past maintenance of relatives will not be payable if the judge had not determined it; the spirit of mutual assistance and fulfillment of need being the reason behind it, it cannot be made good for past time. The schools differ where the judge determines it and orders its payment, as to whether outstanding maintenance must be paid after the judge's order or whether it is annulled with the passage of time as if he had not ordered its payment at all. The Malikis state that if a judge orders the payment of maintenance to a relative and then it remains unpaid, it will not be annulled. The Jafari, Hanafi and some Shafii jurists observe that if the judge orders maintenance to be borrowed and the relative entitled to receive maintenance does so, it is obligatory for the maintainer to clear this debt. But if the judge does not order the borrowing of maintenance, or orders but it is not borrowed, that maintenance will be void. The Hanafis require the payment of past maintenance after the judge's order if it accrues for a period of less than one month; so if the judge orders payment and a month passes since its becoming due, the relative will be entitled to claim the maintenance of the current month only, not of the month past.

It should be noted that if a relative entitled to maintenance receives the maintenance of a day or more through litigation, through gift, the poor-due or some other manner, the maintenance due to him will be deducted to the extent of what he received through these means, even if the judge has ordered the payment of maintenance.

10.14.3.17. THE ORDER OF RELATIVES ON WHOM MAINTENANCE IS OBLIGATORY

The Hanafis observe that if there is only one person responsible for maintenance, he will pay it. If two or more belonging to the same category and capacity are responsible—such as two sons or two daughters—they will share equally in providing maintenance, even if they differ in wealth, after their financial capacity has been proved.[104] But where they are of different categories of relationship or of varying capacities, there is confusion in the views of Hanafi jurists in providing the order of those responsible for maintenance.[106]

The Shafiis state that if a person in need has a father and a grandfather who are both well-off, his maintenance will be provided solely by the father. If he has a mother and a grandmother, the maintenance will be solely provided by the mother. If both the parents are there, the father will provide the maintenance. If he has a grandfather and a mother, the grandfather will provide the maintenance. If he has a paternal grandmother and a maternal grandmother, according to one opinion, both are equally responsible, according to another opinion, the paternal grandmother will be solely liable.[107]

The Hanbalis state that if a child does not have a father, his maintenance will be on his heirs; and if he has two heirs, they will contribute in proportion to the share of each in the estate. If there are three or more heirs, they will contribute in proportion to their share in the estate. Thus if he has a mother and a grandfather, the mother will contribute one-third of maintenance and the grandfather the remainder, as they inherit in the same proportion.[108]

The Jafari state that the child's maintenance is obligatory on the father. If the father is dead or indigent, its maintenance will lie upon the paternal grandfather; and if the grandfather is dead or indigent, the mother will be liable for maintenance. After her, her father and mother along with the child's paternal grandmother will share equally in the maintenance of the grandchild if they are financially- capable. But if only some of them are well-off, the maintenance will lie only on those who are such. If an indigent person has father and a son, or father and a daughter, they will contribute to his maintenance equally. Similarly, if he has many children, it will be shouldered equally by them without any distinction between sons and daughters. On the whole, the Jafari consider the nearness of relationship as criterion while determining the order of relatives who are liable to provide maintenance on their belonging to the same class, they are compelled to contribute equally without any distinction between males and females or between ascendants and descendants, except that the father and the paternal grandfather are given priority over the mother.

11
DIVORCE

11.1. THE DIVORCER

A divorcer should possess the following characteristics:

11.1.1. ADULTHOOD

Divorce by a child is not valid, even if of a discerning age (*mumayyiz*), according to all the schools except the Hanbalis, which observes that divorce by a discerning child is valid even if his age is below ten years.

11.1.2. SANITY

Divorce by an insane person is not valid, irrespective of the insanity being permanent or recurring, when the divorce is pronounced during the state of insanity. Divorce by an unconscious person and one in a state of delirium due to high fever is also not valid.

The schools differ regarding the state of intoxication. The Jafari observe that such a divorce is not valid under any circumstance. The Hanafi, Hanbali, Maliki and Shafii schools[1] remark that the divorce is valid if the divorcer has voluntarily consumed an unlawful intoxicant. But if he drinks something permissible and is stupefied, or is coerced to drink, a divorce does not materialize. Divorce by a person in a fit of anger is valid if the intention to divorce exists. But if he loses his senses completely, the rule which applies to an insane person will apply to him.

11.1.3. FREE VOLITION

All the schools except the Hanafi concur that divorce by a person under duress does not take place in view of the Tradition, "My Community have been exculpated of genuine mistakes, forgetfulness, and that which they are coerced to do." The Hanafis say that divorce by a person under duress is valid. The practice of the Egyptian courts has been not to recognize the divorce by a person under duress or intoxication.

11.1.4. INTENTION

According to the Jafari, divorce pronounced unintentionally or by mistake or in jest is not valid. Abu Zuhrah says, "The Hanafi school considers divorce by all persons except minors, lunatics and idiots as valid."[2] Thus, divorce pronounced by a person in jest, or under the influence of an intoxicant by an unlawful intoxicant, or under duress, is valid. It is the accepted view of the Hanafi school that a divorce by mistake or in a state of forgetfulness is valid. Imam Malik and Imam Shafi concur with Abu Hanifah and his followers regarding a divorce pronounced in jest, while Ahmad Hanbal differs and regards such a divorce as invalid." Ibn Rushd states, "Imam Shafi and Imam Abu Hanifah have said, 'Intention is not required in divorce.'"[3] The Jafari, on the other hand, consider intention to divorce as essential for a divorce to take place. The author of *al-Jawahir* says, "If a man pronounces divorce and subsequently denies his intention, his word shall be accepted as long as the divorcee is undergoing her waiting period, because the fact of his intention cannot be known except from him."

11.2. DIVORCE BY THE GUARDIAN

The Jafari, Hanafi and Shafii schools state that a father

may not divorce on behalf of his minor son based on a Tradition. The Malikis state that a father may divorce his minor son's wife in the *khul* form of divorce. Two opinions are ascribed to Imam Ahmad Hanbal. The Jafari, on the other hand, observe that when a child of an unsound mind matures, his father or paternal grandfather may pronounce divorce on his behalf if it is beneficial for him or her. If the father and the paternal grandfather do not exist, the judge may pronounce the divorce on his or her behalf. As mentioned earlier, the Jafari allow the wife of a lunatic to annul the marriage. The Hanafis state that if a lunatic's wife suffers harm by living with him, the wife may raise the issue before a judge and demand separation. The judge is empowered to pronounce divorce to rescue her from the harm, and the husband's father has no say in this affair. All the schools concur that divorce by a stupid husband (*safh*) and his agreeing to *khul* are both valid.[4]

11.3. THE DIVORCEE

There is consensus that the divorcee is the wife. For the validity of the divorce of a wife with whom intercourse has occurred, the Jafari require that she should not have undergone menopause nor she should be pregnant, that she be free from menses at the time of divorce, and that intercourse should not have occurred during the waiting period. Thus, if she is divorced during her menses or *nifas*,[5] or the man divorcing her has intercourse during the waiting period, the divorce will be invalid.

Al-Razi, in his exegesis of the first verse of *Surah al-Talaq* has said, "The waiting period refers to the time of purity from menses, by consensus of all Muslims." A group of exegetes have observed that divorce at the end of the time of waiting period means that the wife may be divorced only at a time when she is not in her monthly period and where intercourse has not occurred during this time.

In brief, it is compulsory that divorce occur during the period when she is not having her monthly period, otherwise it will

not be according to the *Sunnah*. Divorce according to the sunnah is conceivable only in the case of an adult wife with whom
marriage has been consummated, and one who is neither pregnant nor menopausal." There is no *Sunnah* concerning the
divorce of a minor wife, a wife who has not been copulated with,
or a wife in menopause or pregnancy. This is exactly what the
Jafari hold.

In *al-Mughni*,[6] the author states, "The meaning of a *Sunnah*
divorce (*talaq al-sunnah*) is a divorce in consonance with the
Command of God and His Prophet. It is divorce given during
the time when she is not having her monthly period in which
intercourse with her has not occurred." He continues, "A divorce
contrary to the *Sunnah* (*talaq al-bidah*) is a divorce given while
a woman is having her monthly period or during the time when
she is not having her monthly period in which intercourse has
occurred. But if a man pronounces such a divorce, he sins,
although the divorce is valid according to the view generally
held by the scholars. Ibn al-Mundhir and Ibn Abd al-Birr have
said that none oppose the validity of this form of divorce except
the heretics (*ahl al-bidah wa al-dalalah*).

The major schools concur that Islam has prohibited the
divorcing of an adult, non-pregnant wife with whom marriage
has been consummated, who is either having her monthly period or has had intercourse when she was not having her monthly period. But the Shafii, Hanbali, Hanafi and Maliki schools
add that the *Shariah*'s prohibition makes the divorce unlawful
but not invalid, and one who pronounces divorce in the absence
of these conditions sins and is liable to punishment, but the
divorce will be valid. The Jafari state that the *Shariah*'s prohibition is for invalidating such a divorce, not for making it
unlawful, for the mere pronouncing of divorce is not unlawful
and the sole purpose is to nullify the divorce as if it had not
taken place at all, exactly like the prohibition of sale of liquor
and swine, where the mere recital of the contract of sale is not
unlawful but the transfer of ownership fails to take effect.

The Jafari permit the divorce of the following five classes of wives, regardless of their state of menstruation or purity:

A wife whose marriage has not been consummated, regardless of whether she was a virgin or not and irrespective of his having enjoyed privacy with her.

A menopausal wife. Menopause is taken to set in at fifty for ordinary woman and at sixty for Qurayshi women.

A wife who is pregnant.

A wife whose husband has been away from her for a whole month and the divorce is given during his absence from her, since it is not possible for him to determine her condition (whether she is in her menses or not). A prisoner husband is similar to a husband who has been away.

The Jafari state that the divorce of a wife who has reached the age of menstruation but does not have menses due to some defect or disease or childbirth, is not valid unless the husband abstains from intercourse with her for three months. Such a woman is called *al-mustarabah* (a term derived from doubt).

11.4. THE PRONOUNCEMENT OF DIVORCE

The Jafari observe that divorce requires the pronouncement of a specific formula without which it does not take place. This formula is "you are divorced" or "so and so is divorced" or "she is divorced." Thus unless the husband uses the Arabic words only, it will have no effect even if he intends a divorce because the form of divorce is absent despite the presence of its root. It is necessary that the formula be properly recited without any error in pronunciation and that it be unconditional. Even a condition of certain occurrence such as, 'at sunrise', etc. is not adequate.

If the husband gives the wife the option of divorcing herself and she does so, divorce will not take place according to Jafari scholars. Similarly, divorce will not take place if husband is questioned, "Have you divorced your wife," and he answers affirmatively with the intention of effecting a divorce. If the husband says, "You are divorced three times," or repeats the words, "You are divorced," three times, only a single divorce takes place if the other conditions are fulfilled. Divorce does not take place through writing or by gesticulation, unless the divorcer is incapable of speech. It is necessary that the divorce be recited in Arabic when possible. It is better for a non-Arab and a dumb person to appoint an attorney, if possible, to recite the divorce on his behalf. Similarly, according to the Jafari, divorce will not take place by an oath, a vow, a pledge or any other thing except by the word divorce (*talaq*), on fulfillment of all the limitations and conditions.

The author of *al-Jawahir*, citing a statement from *al-Kafi*, says, "There can be no divorce except (in the form) as narrated by Bukayr ibn Ayan, and it is this, 'The husband says to his wife (while she is free from menses and has not had intercourse during the time when she is free from menses), "You are divorced)" and his pronouncement is witnessed by two just witnesses'. Every other form except this one is void.'" Then the author of *al-Jawahir* quotes *al-Intisar* to the effect that the Jafari have consensus on this issue.

Consequently, the Jafari have restricted the scope of divorce to its extreme limits and impose severe conditions regarding the divorcer, the divorcee, the formula of divorce, and the witnesses to divorce. All this is because marriage is a bond of love and mercy, a covenant with God. The Quran says, "*How can you take it back after one of you have gone into the other and they (the wives) have taken a strong pledge from you?*" (4:21). "*And one of His Signs is that He created mates for you from yourselves that you may find tranquility in them and He ordained between you love and compassion*" (30:21). "*And hold not to the ties of marriage of unbelieving women*" (60:10).

Therefore, it is not permissible in any manner that one break this bond of love and compassion, this pledge and covenant, except with a knowledge that leaves no doubt that the *Shariah* has surely dissolved the marriage and his broken the tie which it had earlier established and confirmed.

The Hanafi, Hanbali, Shafii and Maliki schools allow divorce in any manner in which there is an indication of it either by oral word or in writing, explicitly or implicitly such as when the husband says: "You are unlawful to me," or "You are separated," or "Go, get married," or "You are free to go wherever you want," or "Join your family," and so on. Similarly, these schools allow an unconditional as well as a conditional divorce such as when the husband says, "If you leave the house, you are divorced," or, "If you speak to your father you are divorced," or "If I do this, you are divorced," or "Any woman I marry, she is divorced." In the latter case the divorce takes place as soon as the contract of marriage is concluded. The Hanafi, Hanbali, Maliki and Shafii schools permit a divorce in which the wife or someone else has been authorized to initiate it and a triple divorce by the use of a single pronouncement. The presence of witnesses is not a condition for the validity of divorce.[7]

The Egyptian government follows the Jafari view in most aspects of divorce. Apart from this, the Hanafi, Hanbali, Maliki and Shafii schools do not consider the presence of witnesses a condition for the validity of divorce whereas the Jafari consider it an essential condition.

11.5. DIVORCE AND WITNESSES

In *al-Ahwal al-shakhsiyyah*,[8] Shaykh Abu Zuhrah has observed, "The Jafari jurists state that a divorce does not occur if not witnessed by two just witnesses in accordance with the verse, '*Then when they (the wives) have reached their waiting period, retain them honorably or part from them honorably. And have two just men from among yourselves bear witness and give testimony for God's sake. By this then is admonished he who believes in God and the Last Day. And whoever is careful of (his/her duty to) God, He will provide for him an outlet and give him sustenance fro whence he never reckoned...'*" (65:2-3).

According to the Jafari, unless two just witnesses do not hear the pronouncement of divorce, the divorce will not take place. Further, the witnessing of the pronouncement by one of them by listening and of the other by testifying to their admission of having concluded the divorce is not sufficient. The testimony of a group of people will also not suffice, even if it is large enough to make the divorce a known public fact. The testimony of women, with or without the testimony of men, is not sufficient. Similarly, if the husband pronounces the divorce and then brings in the witnesses, it will have no effect.

Two just witnesses are essential, in this view, to a divorce being valid based on the verse, *"Then when they (the wives) have ended their waiting period, retain them honorably or part from them honorably and have two just men from among yourselves bear witness and give testimony for God's sake. By this then is admonished he who believes in God and the Last Day.* "And whoever is careful of (his duty to) God, He will provide for him an outlet and give him sustenance from whence he never reckoned...."* (65:2-3). The command about the witnesses in the Quran follows the mention of divorce and the validity of revoking it. Therefore, it is appropriate that the calling in of witnesses should be related to divorce. Moreover, the reason given for calling in the witnesses that God seeks thereby to admonish those who believe in God and the Last Day, confirms this interpretation because the presence of just witnesses is not without the good advice which they would offer to the couple. This could cause them to change their minds to divorce. Divorce is the most hated of lawful things in the eyes of God.

It is not permissible, in this view, to break the pledge of marriage except with knowledge that leaves no doubt that the Shariah has surely dissolved the marriage and has broken the tie which it had earlier established and confirmed.

11.6. HUSBAND AND WIFE FROM DIFFERENT SCHOOLS OF LAW

If a husband who follows the Hanafi, Hanbali, Shafii or Maliki school divorces his wife who follows the Jafari school, either through a conditional divorce contingent upon something, or during a time when she is free from her monthly period in which sexual intercourse has occurred, or during menses or without two just witnesses being present or by an oath of divorce, or by saying, "Go wherever you want," or in any other form which is valid in accordance with their school of law and invalid according to Jafari law, is such a divorce considered valid by the Jafari, so that the woman may remarry after completing her waiting period?

The answer is that there is consensus among the Jafari jurists that every sect is bound by its own precepts, and that the transactions of its followers, as well as their affairs pertaining to inheritance, marriage and divorce, are valid if performed according to rules of their *Shariah*. Consequently, if a husband from the Jafari school divorces his wife who follows the Hanafi, Hanbali, Shafii or Maliki school according to the principles of her school and not his, the divorce is invalid.

11.7. REVOCABLE AND IRREVOCABLE DIVORCE

A divorce is either revocable or irrevocable. The schools concur that a revocable divorce is one in which the husband is empowered to revoke the divorce during the waiting period, irrespective of the divorcee's consent. One of the conditions of a revocable divorce is that the marriage should have been consummated, because a wife divorced before consummation does not have to observe the waiting period in accordance with verse, *"O believers! When you marry the believing women and then divorce them before you touch them, you are not entitled to reckon for them a waiting period...."* (33:49) Among the other conditions of a revocable divorce are that the divorce should not have been given on the payment of a consideration and that it should not be one which completes three divorces.

The divorcee in a revocable divorce enjoys the rights of a wife and the divorcer has all the rights of a husband. Therefore, both will inherit from each other in the event of death of one of them during the waiting period. The deferred dowry payable on the occurrence of any of the two events, death or divorce, will become payable only after the expiry of the waiting period if the husband does not revoke the divorce during that period. On the whole, revocable divorce does not give rise to a new situation except its being accountable for ascertaining whether the number of divorces has reached three.

In an irrevocable divorce, the divorcer may not return to the divorced wife who belongs to one of the following categories:

A wife divorced before consummation, by consensus of all the schools.

A wife who has been divorced thrice. There is consensus here as well.

A divorcee through *khul*. Some jurists consider this form of divorce void and say that it is not a divorce at all.

A menopausal divorcee, in the Jafari school, which observes that she has no waiting period and the rules applicable to a divorcee before consummation apply to her as well. According to it, in verse 4 of *Surat al-Talaq*, "If you are in doubt concerning those of your wives who have ceased menstruating, know that their waiting period is three months, and (the same is the waiting period of those who have not yet menstruate." The phrase does not imply women who are known to have reached menopause but those whose menses have stopped and it is not known whether the reason is disease or age. Consequently, their waiting period is three months. There is no question of doubt regarding those whose menopause is certain. The doubt arises in cases of uncertainty, as indicated by the words, "*...if you are in doubt...*" of the verse, because it is not the Lawgiver's wont when explaining a law to say, "*If you are in doubt regarding the law regarding something, the law is that....*" This confirms that the doubt mentioned in the verse relates to the fact of menopause, in which case she is to observe a waiting period of three months. The other phrase refers to women who despite attaining the age of menses do not have them due to some congenital or contingent factor.

The Hanafis say that valid seclusion with the wife, even without consummation, requires the observance of the waiting period. But the divorcer is not entitled to return to her during the waiting period because here the divorce is irrevocable. The Hanbalis state that seclusion is similar to consummation in all respects so far as the necessity of the waiting period and the right of revocation is concerned. As mentioned earlier, seclusion has no effect according to the Jafari and Shafii schools.

The Hanafis observe that if a husband says to his wife, "You are divorced irrevocably," or "divorced firmly (with a divorce as firm) as a mountain," and similar strong words, the divorce will be irrevocable and the divorcer will not be entitled to return during the waiting period. Similarly, a divorce pronounced by using words which connote a break of relationship (such as, "She is separated," "cut off," "disassociated").

11.8. THE TRIPLE DIVORCEE

The schools concur that a husband who divorces his wife three times cannot remarry her unless she marries another man through a valid marriage contract and this next man consummates the marriage in accordance with the Quran, "*So if he divorces her, she shall not be lawful to him afterwards, until she marries another husband....*" (2:230)

The Jafari and Maliki schools consider it necessary that 'another husband' who marries her (*muhallil*) be an adult. The Hanafi, Shafii and Hanbali schools consider his capacity for intercourse as sufficient, even if he is not an adult. The Jafari and Hanbali schools state that if in a marriage contract the man causing the woman to become permissible for her former husband to remarry is included as a condition (such as when the husband-to-be says, "I am marrying you to make you lawful for your divorcer," the condition is void and the contract valid. But the Hanafis add that if the woman fears that her husband-to-be (*muhallil*) may not divorce her after the contract, it is permissible for her to say, "I marry you on the condition that the power to divorce be in my hands," and for the husband-to-be to say, "I accept this condition." Then the contract will be valid and she will be entitled to divorce herself whenever she desires. But if the husband-to-be says to her: "I marry you on the condition that your affair (of divorce) be in your own hands," the contract is valid and the condition void. The Maliki, the Shafii and the Hanbali schools state: The contract is void from the beginning if the husband-to-be includes a condition allowing for his wife-to-be to become permissible for her former husband to remarry. The Maliki and Hanbali schools further add: Even if marrying her so she can then remarry her former husband (*tahlil*) is intended and not expressed the contract is void.

The Malikis and some Jafari jurists consider it necessary

that the husband-to-be have intercourse with her in a lawful manner (such as when she is not menstruating or having bleeding following childbirth, and while both are not fasting a Ramadan fast). But most Jafari jurists give no credence to this condition and regard mere intercourse, even if unlawful, to be sufficient for a marriage to have occurred which then makes the wife lawful for her former husband who divorced her three times in an irrevocable divorce.

Whatever be the case, when a divorcee marries another husband and is separated from him, either due to his death or by divorce, and completes the waiting period, it becomes permissible for the first husband to contract a new marriage with her. Then, if he again divorces her thrice, she will become unlawful for him until she marries another. This is how she will become unlawful for him after every third divorce and will again become lawful by marrying another man, even if she is divorced a hundred times.

But the Jafari state that if a wife is divorced nine times in irrevocable divorce (*talaq al-iddah*), and is married twice (i.e. marrying a man so that the woman becomes permissible for her former husband to remarry after an irrevocable divorce), she will become permanently unlawful. The meaning of irrevocable divorce (*talaq al-iddah*), according to the Jafari, is a divorce in which the husband after divorcing returns to her during the waiting period and has intercourse with her, and then divorces her again when she is not having her menstrual cycle, then returns to her and has intercourse, then divorces her for a third time and remarries her, after a temporary husband marries her in order to make her lawful to her former husband, by concluding a fresh contract, and divorces her three times in the same manner, with another temporary husband doing the second marriage to again make her lawful to the first husband, and remarries her again. Now if he divorces her three times again, the ninth irrevocable divorce completed, she will become unlawful for him permanently. But if the divorce is not an irrevocable divorce such as when he divorces her, then returns to her and then divorces her again before having intercourse, she will not become unlawful forever, and will become lawful although a muhallil, even if the number of divorces is countless.

11.9. UNCERTAINTY IN THE NUMBER OF DIVORCES

The schools (except the Maliki) concur that he who has doubt regarding the number of divorces (whether a single divorce has taken place or more) will base his count on the lower number. The Malikis observe that the aspect of divorce shall preponderate and the count will be based on the higher number.

11.10. DIVORCEE'S CLAIM OF HAVING MARRIED SOMEONE IN ORDER FOR THE FORMER HUSBAND TO BECOME LAWFUL TO HER

The Jafari, Shafii and Hanafi schools state that if the husband divorces his wife three times and he or she knows nothing about the other for some time and thereafter she claims having married a second husband and separated from him and having completed the waiting period, her word will be accepted without an oath if this period is sufficient for her undergoing all this, and her first husband is entitled to marry her if he is satisfied regarding her honesty, and it is not necessary for him to inquire further.[9]

11.11. DIVORCE BY A WIFE WHO PAYS HER HUSBAND TO DIVORCE HER

Known in Arabic as *al-khul*, this is a form of divorce in which the wife releases herself (from the marriage tie) by paying consideration to the husband. Here we have the following issues.

11.11.1. THE CONDITION OF THE WIFE'S DETESTATION

When they both agree to this kind of divorce and the wife pays her husband the consideration to divorce her, though they are well settled and their conduct towards each other is agreeable, is their mutual agreement to this kind of divorce valid? The Hanafi, Hanbali, Shafii and Maliki schools state that this type of divorce is valid and the rules applicable to it and their effects will follow but it is not recommended.[10]

According to the Jafari, such a divorce is not valid and the divorcer will not own the consideration. But the divorce (so pronounced) will be valid and revocable if all the conditions for revocability are present according to the Quranic verse, *"Then if you fear that they cannot maintain the limits set by God, there is no blame on the two for what she gives to release herself..."* (2:229). wherein the verse has made the validity of consideration contingent upon the fear of sinning if the marital relationship were to continue.

11.11.2. MUTUAL AGREEMENT TO DIVORCE BY A WIFE FOR A CONSIDERATION GREATER THAN DOWRY

The schools concur that the consideration should have material value and that its value may be equal to, lesser, or greater than the dowry given to her by her husband.

11.11.3. CONDITIONS FOR A WIFE'S DIVORCE FOR A CONSIDERATION

According to the Hanafi, Hanbali, Shafii and Maliki schools, it is also valid to conclude a 'divorce for consideration' agreement with anyone apart from one's wife. Therefore, if a stranger asks the husband to divorce his wife for a sum which he undertakes to pay, and the husband divorces her, the divorce is valid even if the wife is unaware of it and on coming to know does not consent. The stranger will have to pay the ransom to the divorcer.[11] The Jafari observe that such a 'divorce for consideration' is invalid and it is not binding upon the stranger to pay anything. But it is valid for a stranger to act as a guarantor of the consideration by the wife's permission and ask the husband, after the wife's permission, to divorce her for such a consideration guaranteed by him. Thus, if the husband divorces her on this condition, it is binding on the guarantor to pay him that amount and then claim it from the divorcee.

All that which is validly payable as dowry is also valid as consideration in 'divorce by consideration', by consensus of all the major schools. It is also not necessary that the amount of consideration be known in detail beforehand if it can be known eventually (such as when she says, "Grant me a 'divorce for a consideration' for that which is 'at home', or 'in the locker', or 'my share of inheritance from my father', or 'the fruits of my garden').

If this kind of divorce is given in return for that which cannot be owned, such as liquor or swine, the Hanafi, the Maliki and the Hanbali schools observe that if both knew that such ownership is unlawful, the divorce is valid and the divorcer is not entitled to anything, making it a 'divorce without consideration'. The Shafiis say that the divorce is valid and she is entitled to her dowry.[12] Most Jafari jurists state that the 'divorce for a consideration' (*khul*) shall be void and the divorce will be considered revocable if it is an instance of revocable divorce; otherwise, it will be irrevocable. In all the cases, the divorcer shall not be entitled to anything.

If the husband grants her 'divorce for a consideration' that he believes to be lawful and it later turns out to be unlawful such as when she says, "Grant me a divorce for this jar of vinegar," which turns out to be wine, the Jafari and the Hanbali schools observe that he shall claim from her a similar quantity of vinegar. The Hanafis state that she shall claim from her the stipulated amount. According to the Shafii school, he shall claim from her dowry.

If she seeks 'divorce for a consideration', she considers to be her property and it turns out to be someone else's, the Hanafi school and most Jafari jurists observe that if the owner allows it, the 'divorce for consideration' will be valid and the husband will take it, but if he disallows, the husband is entitled to a similar consideration either in cash or kind. The Shafii school states: The husband is entitled to her dowry (*mahr al-mithl*). This is in accordance with the Shafii principle that when a consideration becomes invalid, it becomes void and her dowry (*mahr al-mithl*) becomes payable. According to the Malikis, the divorce becomes irrevocable, the consideration becomes void, and the divorcer gets nothing even if the owner permits.[13]

If the wife seeks 'divorce for a consideration' by undertaking to nurse and maintain his child for a certain period, the divorce will be valid and she will be bound to nurse and maintain the child, as per consensus. The Hanafi, Maliki and Hanbali schools further clarify that it is valid for a pregnant wife to seek 'divorce for a consideration' from her husband in return for maintaining the child in her womb, on the same grounds on which it is valid for her to seek 'divorce for a consideration' by undertaking the maintenance of a born child.

Research has not uncovered any Jafari or Shafii sources which have dealt with this issue, although the principles of the Shariah do not prohibit it, because the cause, which is the child in the womb, is present, and the wife's pledge is a condition by which she binds herself to the effect that in the event of the child being born alive she will be responsible for its nursing and maintenance for a specific period, and Muslims are bound by the conditions they lay down, provided this does not result in something lawful becoming unlawful or vice versa. Hence this condition is valid in itself, for it does not suggest anything legally void; therefore, its fulfillment is compulsory because it is part of a binding contract. The uncertainty concerning the child being born alive or dead, and its dying after birth before the stipulated period, is overlooked in this kind of divorce.

The furthest one can go in asserting its impermissibility and invalidity is by likening a pledge to maintain with a discharge from maintenance. Therefore, when a discharge from maintenance is invalid because it is an annulment of something not binding, similarly a pledge to maintain is not valid because it is not presently obligatory. But there is a great difference between a pledge and a discharge, because it is necessary that a discharge be from something present and actual, while a pledge need not be so. Apart from this, we have already discussed in the chapter on marriage regarding 'divorce for a consideration' in return for foregoing the right to custody of a child by the father or the mother.

11.11.4. A RELATED ISSUE

If a husband grants a 'divorce for a consideration to his wife in return for her maintaining the child, she is entitled to claim the child's maintenance from its father on her not being able to maintain it, and he will be compelled to pay the maintenance. But he can reclaim this maintenance from the mother if she comes to possess the means. If the child dies during the stipulated period, the divorcer is entitled to claim a compensation for the remaining period in accordance with the words of the verse 2:229. It is better for a woman to undertake the nursing and maintenance of the child for a certain period so long as it is alive. Then the divorcer will not have the right to a claim against her if the child dies.

11.11.5. CONDITIONS FOR A WIFE SEEKING DIVORCE FOR A CONSIDERATION

There is consensus among the schools that a wife seeking divorce for a consideration should be a sane adult. They also concur that such a divorce of a stupid (*safh*) wife is not valid without the permission of her guardian. The schools differ regarding the validity of this kind of divorce where the guardian has granted her the permission to seek it. The Hanafis observe that if the guardian undertakes to pay the consideration from his own personal assets, the divorce is valid. Otherwise, the consideration is void, while the divorce takes place, according to the more authentic of two Traditions.[14]

The Jafari and Maliki schools state that with the guardian's permission to her to pay the consideration, the divorce is valid by payment from her wealth, not his.[15] The Shafii and Hanbali schools consider the 'divorce for a consideration' of a stupid wife as invalid irrespective of the guardian's permission. The Shafii school allows one exception to the above opinion, wherein the guardian fears the husband's squandering her wealth and grants her permission to seek a 'divorce for a consideration' from him for the protection of her property. The Shafiis then add that such a divorce is invalid and the divorce is revocable.

The Hanbalis say that neither will the divorce take place nor the consideration given when the husband intends a divorce through 'divorce for a consideration' or if the 'divorce for a consideration' takes place in the words of a divorce.

If a woman seeks a 'divorce for consideration' during her last illness, it is considered valid by all schools. But they differ where she pays as consideration more than a third of her wealth or more than the husband's share to be inherited from her on assumption of her death during the waiting period. As said above, they inherit from each other in this situation. The Jafari and the Shafii schools state: If she seeks 'divorce for a consideration' for her dowry, it is valid and the consideration is payable from her undivided legacy. But if it exceeds her dowry, the excess will be deducted from one-third of her legacy. The Hanafis observe that such a 'divorce for a consideration' is valid and the divorcer is entitled to the consideration if it does not exceed either one-third of her wealth or his share of inheritance from her were she to die during the waiting period. This means that he will take the least of the three amounts: the consideration agreed upon for the divorce, his share of inheritance from her, or a third of her legacy. Therefore, if the consideration for the divorce is five, his share of inheritance four, and a third of her legacy three, he shall be entitled to three.

According to the Hanbali school, if she seeks 'divorce for a consideration' in return for a consideration equaling his share of inheritance from her or something lesser, the consideration and the divorce are valid. But if she seeks divorce for a higher consideration, only the excess will be void.[16]

The Jafari moreover require the wife seeking 'divorce for a consideration to fulfill all the requirements in a divorcee (such as her purity from menses, non-occurrence of intercourse when she is not having her menstrual cycle, if her marriage has been consummated, her being neither menopausal nor pregnant, her not being a minor below the age of nine). Similarly, they require the presence of two just witnesses for the 'divorce for a consideration' to be valid. But the other schools validate such a divorce irrespective of the state of the wife seeking it, exactly like any other divorce.

11.11.6. CONDITIONS FOR A HUSBAND GRANTING DIVORCE FOR A CONSIDERATION

Excepting the Hanbali, all the other schools concur that a husband granting divorce for a consideration is required to be a sane adult. The Hanbalis state that 'divorce for a consideration' (*khul*) granted by a discerning minor is valid, as is a divorce given by him. As mentioned at the beginning of this chapter on divorce, the Hanafis permit a divorce pronounced in jest, under duress, or in a state of intoxication, and the Shafii and the Maliki schools concur with them concerning divorce pronounced in jest. A 'divorce for a consideration' granted in a state of rage is valid if the rage does not eliminate the element of intention.

There is consensus among the schools concerning the validity of a divorce for a consideration granted by a stupid (*safh*) husband. But the consideration will be given to his guardian, and its being given to him is not valid. Regarding a 'divorce for a consideration' granted by a sick husband on his death bed, it is undoubtedly valid, because when his divorcing without receiving any consideration is valid, a divorce along with consideration would be more so.

11.11.7. THE PRONOUNCEMENT OF DIVORCE FOR A CONSIDERATION

The Hanafi, Hanbali, Shafii and Maliki schools permit the use of explicit words such as derivatives of *al-khul* and *al-faskh* (dissolution) in the pronouncement, as well as implicit words such as "*ba-ratuki*," "I relinquish you" and "*abantuki*," "I separate myself from you." The Hanafis have said: The use of the words *al-bay* (to sell) and *al-shira* (to purchase) is valid, for instance, when the husband says to the wife, "I sell you to yourself for so much," and the wife replies, "I purchase," or when he says, "Buy your divorce for so much," and she replies, "I accept."

Similarly the Shafii school accepts the validity of a 'divorce for a consideration' pronounced with the word *al-bay*.

The Hanafis allow a conditional 'divorce for a consideration' by exercise of an option and the 'divorce for a consideration' in which the pronouncement and the payment of consideration is separated by an extended time interval such as, where a husband is away from his wife and it reaches him that she has said, "I seek a 'divorce for a consideration' for so much," and he accepts it. Similarly the Malikis also do not consider the time factor an impediment.

'Divorce for a consideration' is valid according to the Hanbali school even without an intention if the word used is explicit such as *al-khul, al-faskh* and *al-mufddat*, but it requires that the pronouncement and payment take place simultaneously and unconditionally. The Jafaris have said that this type of divorce does not take place by using implicit words or even explicit words other than *al-khul* and *al-talaq*. If desired, they can be used together or singly. Thus, the wife may say, "I pay you this much for divorcing me," and he will reply, "I grant you *khul* for it, and therefore you are divorced." This form of pronouncement is the safest and most suitable in the view of all Jafari jurists. It also suffices if he says, "You are divorced in return for it," or "I grant you *khul* in return for it." The Jafari require that *khul* should be unconditional, exactly as in any other kind of divorce and consider necessary the absence of any time gap between its pronouncement and the payment of consideration.

11.12. THE WAITING PERIOD

There is consensus among Muslims about the general necessity of the waiting period. Its basis is the Quran and the *Sunnah*. As to the Quran, we have the following verse, *"Women who are divorced shall wait, keeping themselves apart three (monthly) courses...."* (2:228) As to the *Sunnah*, there is the Prophet's Tradition commanding Fatimah bint Qays, "Observe the waiting period in the house of Ibn Umm Maktum."

They differ, however, regarding the waiting period of a wife separated from her husband due to divorce or annulment of marriage, the waiting period of a widow, the waiting period of a woman where intercourse took place by mistake, the relief of an adulteress from menses, and the waiting period of a wife whose husband has disappeared.

11.12.1. DIVORCEE'S WAITING PERIOD

The major schools concur that a woman divorced before consummation and before the occurrence of valid seclusion does not need to have a waiting period. The Hanafi, the Maliki and the Hanbali schools state that if the husband secludes with her without consummating the marriage and then divorces her, she will have to observe the waiting period exactly as if consummation had occurred. The Jafari and the Shafiis observe that seclusion has no effect. As mentioned earlier in relation to the distinction between revocable and irrevocable divorce, the Jafari do not require a menopausal wife with whom coitus has taken place to observe the waiting period. The reasons given by the Jafari for this opinion were also mentioned earlier.

The waiting period for every kind of separation between husband and wife, except the one by death, is the waiting period of divorce, irrespective of its being due to 'divorce for a consideration', oath of condemnation, annulment due to a defect, dissolution arising from breast-feeding, or as a result of difference of religion.[17] Moreover, the schools concur that the waiting period is obligatory on a wife divorced after consummation and that the waiting period will be one of the following kinds:

The major schools concur that a pregnant divorcee will observe the waiting period until childbirth, in accordance with the verse, "*And as for pregnant women, their term shall end with delivery*" (65:4). If she is pregnant with more than one child, her waiting period will not terminate until she gives birth to the last of them, as per consensus. The schools differ concerning a miscarriage if the fetus is not completely formed. The Hanafi, Shafii and Hanbali schools observe her waiting period will not terminate by the fetus' detachment from the womb. The

Jafari and Maliki schools state that it will even if it is a lump of flesh, so far as it is a fetus.

The maximum period of gestation is two years according to the Hanafis, four years according to the Shafiis and Hanbalis, and five years according to the Malikis, as mentioned in *al-Fiqh alal-madhahib al-arbaah*. In *al-Mughni*, it is narrated from Imam Malik to be four years. A pregnant woman cannot menstruate according to the Hanafi and Hanbali schools. The Jafari, Shafii and Maliki schools allow the possibility of its occurrence.

She will observe a waiting period of three lunar months if she is an adult divorcee who has not yet menstruated or a divorcee who has reached the age of menopause.[18] This age is seventy years according to the Malikis, fifty years according to the Hanbalis, fifty-five years according to the Hanafis, sixty-two years according to the Shafiis, and according to the Jafari fifty for ordinary women and sixty for those of Qurayshi descent.

A divorcee who has had a monthly period and is neither pregnant nor menopausal has a waiting period of three 'times free from the menstrual cycle' as per consensus. The Jafari, the Maliki and the Shafii schools have interpreted the word '*qara*' to mean 'free from menstrual cycle'. Thus, if she is divorced at the last moment of her present period of time free from the menstrual cycle, it will be counted as a part of the waiting period, which will be completed after two more of such terms of purity. The Hanafis and Hanbalis interpret the term to mean menstruation. Thus, it is necessary that there be three monthly menstruation cycles after the divorce, and the monthly period during which she is divorced is disregarded.[19]

If a divorcee undergoing this kind of waiting period claims having completed the period, her word will be accepted if the period is sufficient for the completion of the waiting period. According to the Jafari, the minimum period required for accepting such a claim is twenty-six days and two 'moments', by supposing that she is divorced at the last moment of her first period of time free from menses, followed by three days of menses (which is the minimum period) followed by a ten-day period free from menses (which is the minimum period of purity according to the Jafari) followed again by three days of menses, then a second ten-day free from menses followed by menses. The waiting period comes to an end with the sole recommencement of menses, and the first moment of the third monthly is to make certain the completion of the third period of time free from menses. Bleeding following childbirth is similar to menses, in the opinion of the Jafari. Accordingly, it is possible for a waiting period to be completed in twenty-three days, if the wife is divorced immediately after childbirth but before the commencement of the bleeding following childbirth (*nifas*) in which case the waiting period is twenty-three days, considering the moment of the beginning of bleeding following childbirth followed by ten days of the first period of time free from menses, followed by three day, of menses which is the minimum period for it followed by a second ten-day period of time free from menses.

The minimum period for accepting such a claim by a divorcee is thirty-nine days according to the Hanafi school, by supposing his divorcing her at the end of her purity, and supposing again the minimum three-day period of menstruation, followed by a fifteen-day period free from menses which is the minimum in the opinion of the Hanafis. Thus, three menses, covering nine days, separated by two periods of freedom from menses, making up thirty days, make up a total of thirty-nine.

11.12.2. MAXIMUM WAITING PERIOD

As mentioned earlier, a mature divorcee who has not yet menstruated will observe a three-month waiting period, as per consensus. But if she menstruates and then ceases to do so, as a result of her nursing a child or due to some disease, the Hanbali and the Maliki schools observe that she will observe the waiting period for one complete year. In the later of his two opinions, Imam Shafi and Imam Hanifah[20] has said that her waiting period will continue until she menstruates or reaches menopause. After this she will observe a waiting period of three months.[21]

The Jafari observe that if menstruation ceases due to some accidental cause the divorcee will observe a waiting period of three months, similar to a divorcee who has never menstruated. If menses resume after the divorce, she will observe the waiting period for the shorter of the two terms, i.e. three months or three *quru*. This means that if three *quru* are completed before three months, the waiting period will be over on their completion, and if three months are completed before three *quru*, then again the waiting period will terminate. If she menstruates even a moment before the completion of three months, she will have to wait for nine months, and it will not benefit her if she is later free from menses for a period of three months. After the completion of nine months, if she gives birth before the completion of a year, her waiting period will terminate, and similarly if she menstruates and completes the periods free from menses. But if she neither gives birth nor completes the periods of being free from menses before the end of the year, she will observe an additional waiting period of three months after completing the nine months. This adds up to a year, which is the maximum waiting period according to the Jafari.[22]

11.12.3. THE WIDOW'S WAITING PERIOD

There is consensus among the schools that the waiting period of a widow who is not pregnant is four months and ten days, irrespective of her being a major or a minor, her being menopausal or otherwise, and regardless of the consummation of her marriage, in accordance with the verse, *"And those among you who die and leave behind wives, (these wives) should keep themselves in waiting for four months and ten days "* (2:234). This is the case when she is sure of not being pregnant. But if she has a doubt she is bound to wait until delivery or attainment of certainty that she is not pregnant. This is the opinion of many jurists belonging to different schools.

The Hanafi, Hanbali, Shafii and Maliki schools state that the waiting period of a pregnant widow will terminate on delivery, even if it occurs a moment after the husband's death. This permits her to remarry immediately after giving birth, even if the husband has not yet been buried, as per the verse, *"And as for pregnant women, their term shall end with delivery"* (65:4).

The Jafari state her waiting period will be whichsoever is longer of the two terms, i.e. delivery or four months and ten days. Thus if four months and ten days pass without her giving birth, her waiting period will continue until childbirth; and if she delivers before the completion of four months and ten days, her waiting period will be four months and ten days. The Jafari argue that it is necessary to combine the verse 2:234 with verse 65:4. The former verse has fixed the waiting period at four months and ten days, and it includes both a pregnant and a non-pregnant wife. The latter verse has stipulated the waiting period of a pregnant wife to last until childbirth, and it includes both a divorcee and a widow. Thus an incompatibility emerges between the apparent import of the two verses regarding a pregnant widow who delivers before the completion of four months and ten days. In accordance with the latter verse her waiting period terminates on delivery, and in accordance with the former the waiting period will not terminate until four months and ten days have been completed. An incompatibility also appears if she does not deliver after the completion of four months and ten days; according to the former verse her waiting period terminates when four months and ten days are over, and in accordance with the latter the waiting period will not terminate because she has not yet delivered. The word of the Quran is unequivocal, and it is necessary that parts of it harmonize with one another. Now, if we join the two verses like this, the meaning will be that the waiting period of a widow who is not pregnant, or is pregnant but delivers within four months and ten days, is four months and ten days; and that of a widow who delivers after four months and ten days is until the time of her delivery.

Therefore it is not possible to apply both the verses except by stipulating the longer of the two terms as waiting period. The schools, excepting the Hanafi, concur that *al-hidad* is obligatory on the widow, irrespective of her being major or minor, Muslim or non-Muslim. The Hanafis do not consider it obligatory for a non-Muslim and a minor widow because they are not responsible for religious duties.

The meaning of *al-hidad* is that the woman mourning her husband's death refrain from every adornment that makes her attractive. Its determination depends on prevailing customs and usage. The Jafari observe that the waiting period of divorce will commence on the recital of the divorce, irrespective of the husband's presence or absence. The waiting period of a widow commences on the news of his death reaching her, if he is away. But if the husband is present and she comes to know of his death after some time, her waiting period will commence from the time of his death, as per the predominant opinion among Jafari jurists.

The schools concur that if the husband of a revocable divorcee dies while she is undergoing waiting period, she is bound to start anew with a widow's waiting period from the time of his death, irrespective of the divorce taking place during the husband's mortal illness or health, because the marital bond between her and the husband has not yet broken. But if the divorce is irrevocable, it will depend. If he divorces her while healthy, she will complete the waiting period of divorce and will not have to observe any waiting period due to the husband's death, as per consensus, even if the divorce was without her consent. Similar is the case if he divorces her during his mortal illness on her demand. But what if he divorces her during his mortal illness without her demanding it, and then dies before the termination of her waiting period? Shall she start the widow's waiting period, like a revocable divorcee, or shall she continue to observe the waiting period of divorce? The Jafari, Maliki and Shafii schools state that she shall continue to observe the waiting period of divorce without changing over to the waiting period of widowhood. According to the Hanafi and the Hanbali schools, she shall change over to the waiting period of widowhood.

In short, a revocable divorcee will start observing the waiting period of widowhood if the divorcer dies before the termination of her waiting period of divorce, and an irrevocable divorcee will continue to observe the waiting period of divorce, as per the concurrence of all the schools except the Hanafi and the Hanbali, who exclude an irrevocable divorcee if the divorce takes place during the divorcer's mortal illness without her consent.

11.12.4. WAITING PERIOD FOR INTERCOURSE BY MISTAKE

According to the Jafari, the waiting period of 'intercourse by mistake' is similar to the waiting period of a divorcee. Therefore, if the woman is pregnant, she will observe waiting period until childbirth; if she has menstruated, her waiting period will be three *quru*, otherwise three months. An 'intercourse by mistake' is, according to the Jafari, one in which the man involved is not liable to penal consequences, irrespective of the woman being one with whom marriage is unlawful (such as wife's sister or a married woman) or lawful (such as any unmarried woman outside the prohibited degrees of marriage). The view held by the Hanbalis is nearly similar to this view, where they observe that every form of sex relations necessitate the observance of waiting period. They do not differ from the Jafari except in some details, as indicated below on the discussion of the waiting period of a fornicatress.

The Hanafis state that the waiting period is obligatory both as a result of intercourse by mistake or an invalid marriage. Waiting period is not obligatory if the marriage is void. An example of the 'mistake' is a man's having relations with a sleeping woman thinking her to be his wife. An invalid marriage is one with a woman with whom marriage is lawful but in which some essential conditions remain unfulfilled such as where a contract has been recited without the presence of witnesses. A void marriage is a contract with a woman belonging to the prohibited degrees of relatives (e.g. sister or aunt). The waiting period for intercourse by mistake according to them is three menstruations if she menstruates, or three months if she is not pregnant. If she is pregnant, the waiting period will continue until childbirth.

The Malikis state: that she will release herself after three *quru*; if she does not menstruate, by three months, if pregnant, on childbirth. Whatever be the case, if a man who has had intercourse by mistake dies, the woman will not observe the waiting period of widowhood, because her waiting period is due to intercourse, not marriage.

11.12.5. THE WAITING PERIOD OF A FORNICATRESS

The Hanafi and the Shafii schools, as well as the majority of Jafari jurists, remark that the waiting period is not required for fornication, because the relations have no sanctity. Thus, marriage and intercourse with a fornicatress is lawful without there being a need for a waiting period, even if she is pregnant. But the Hanafis permit marriage with a woman pregnant through fornication without allowing intercourse with her before her delivery.

The Malikis state that fornication is similar to intercourse by mistake. Thus she will release herself in a period equal to the period of waiting period except when she is to undergo the punishment, in which case she will release herself after a single menstruation. The Hanbalis observe that waiting period is as obligatory on a fornicatress as on a divorcee.[23]

11.12.6. THE WAITING PERIOD OF A FEMALE PERSON OF THE BOOK

The schools concur that a non-Muslim female adherent of a religion having a scripture wife of a Muslim will be governed by the laws applicable to a Muslim wife concerning the necessity of waiting period, and *al-hidad* in an waiting period of widowhood. But if she is a wife of a non-Muslim 'Person of the Book', the Jafari, Shafii, Maliki and Hanbali schools consider the waiting period obligatory upon her. But the Shafii, Maliki and Hanbali schools do not consider *al-hidad* obligatory for her while observing the waiting period of widowhood.[24] The Hanafis state that a non-Muslim woman married to a non-Muslim does not have a waiting period.[25]

11.12.7. WIFE OF A MISSING HUSBAND

A missing person can be in one of these two situations: First, where his absence is continuous but his whereabouts are known and news about him is received. Here, according to consensus, his wife is not entitled to remarry. The second situation arises where there is no more any news of him and his whereabouts. The founders of the various schools of the Divine Law differ regarding the law applicable to his wife.

Imam Abu Hanifah and Imam Shafi, in the more reliable of their two opinions, state that if the first husband returns after she marries another, the second marriage shall become void and she will become the first's wife. Imam Malik observes that if the first husband returns before the consummation of the second marriage, she will belong to the first husband, but if he returns after consummation she will remain the second's wife. It will be obligatory, however, for the second husband to pay her dowry to the first. According to Imam Ahmad Hanbal, if the second husband has not consummated the marriage she belongs to the first; but if he has, the choice lies with the first husband: he may either reclaim her from the second husband and give him the dowry or allow her to remain with him by taking the dowry.[26]

The Jafari state that the case of a missing person who is not known to be living or dead will be studied. If he has any assets by which the wife can be maintained, or has a guardian willing to maintain her, or someone volunteering to do it, it is obligatory for her to patiently wait for him; it is not permissible for her to marry in any circumstance until she learns of his death or his divorcing her. But if the missing husband has neither any property nor someone willing to maintain her, if the wife bears it patiently, well and good; but if she wants to remarry, she will raise the issue before the judge. The judge will order a four-year waiting period for her from the time the issue was brought to him, and then start a search for the husband during that time. If nothing is known, and the missing husband has a guardian or an attorney in charge of his affairs, the judge will order him to divorce her. But if the husband has neither a guardian nor an attorney, or has, but has prohibited him from divorcing, and it is not possible to compel him, the judge will himself pronounce the divorce by using the authority granted to him by the *Shariah*. After this divorce the wife will observe an waiting period of four months and ten days after which she may remarry.

The method of search is that the judge will question about his presence and seek information from those coming from the place where there is a possibility of his being present. The best way of it is to depute a reliable person from among the people of the place where the search is being conducted to supervise the search on his behalf and report to him the result. A search of an ordinary extent is sufficient, and it is neither necessary that his whereabouts be inquired in every place which can possibly be reached, nor that the inquiry be conducted continually. When the search is completed in a period of less than four years in a manner that it becomes certain that further inquiry is fruitless, the search is no longer obligatory. Yet it is necessary that the wife wait for four years; this is in compliance with an explicit tradition and the demand of precaution in marital ties, as well as the possibility of the husband returning during these four years.

After the completion of this period the divorce will take place and one will observe a waiting period of four months and ten days without hidad. She is entitled to maintenance during this period, and the spouses inherit from each other as long as she is in waiting period. If the husband comes back during the waiting period), he may return to her if he wants or let her remain as she is. But if he comes back after the completion of the waiting period but before her marrying another, the preferable opinion is that he has no right over her; and more so if he finds her married.[27]

11.12.8. THE RULES GOVERNING THE WAITING PERIOD

We said in the chapter on maintenance that there is consensus regarding a revocable divorcee's right to maintenance during her waiting period. We also said that there is a difference of opinion regarding an irrevocable divorcee during her waiting period. Here we shall discuss the following issues:

11.13. INHERITANCE BETWEEN A DIVORCER AND A DIVORCEE

There is consensus that when a husband revocably divorces his wife, their right of inheriting from each other does not disappear as long as she is in waiting period, irrespective of the divorce being given in mortal illness or in condition of health. The right to mutual inheritance is annulled on the completion of the waiting period. There is a consensus again regarding the absence of mutual inheritance if the husband divorces his wife irrevocably in health.

11.14. DIVORCE BY A SICK PERSON

The schools differ when a sick person divorces his wife irrevocably and then dies in the same sickness. The Hanafis entitle her to inherit as long as she is in waiting period, provided the husband is considered attempting to bar her from inheriting from him and the divorce takes place without her consent. In the absence of any of these two conditions she will not be entitled to inherit. The Hanbalis state that she will inherit from him as long as she does not remarry, even if her waiting period terminates. The Malikis state that she inherits from him even after her remarriage. Three opinions of Imam Shafii have been reported, and one of them is that she will not inherit even if he dies while she is observing waiting period. It is notable that apart from the Jafari the other schools speak of a divorce by a sick person only when it is irrevocable. But the Jafari have observed that if he divorces her while sick, she will inherit him irrespective of the divorce being revocable or irrevocable, on the realization of the following four conditions.

That the husband's death occurs before the completion of one year from the date of divorce. Thus, if he dies one year after the divorce, even if by an hour, she will not inherit from him.

That she does not remarry before his death. If she does and he dies within a year (of the divorce), she will not inherit.

That he does not recover from the illness in which he divorced her. Thus, if he recovers and then dies within a year, she will not be entitled to inherit.

That the divorce does not take place on her demand.

11.15. WAITING PERIOD AND LOCATION

The schools concur that a revocable divorcee will observe the waiting period at the husband's home. Therefore, it is not permissible for him to expel her. Similarly, it is not permissible for her to leave it. The schools differ regarding an irrevocable divorcee. The Hanafi, Hanbali, Shafii and Maliki schools are of the opinion that she will observe the waiting period like a revocable divorcee, without there being any difference, in accordance with the verse, *"Do not expel them from their homes, and neither should they themselves go forth, unless they commit an obvious indecency"* (65:1).

The Jafari state that irrevocable divorcee is free to decide about her own affairs and may observe waiting period wherever she wants, because the marital bond between her and the husband has snapped. Neither do they inherit from each other, nor is she entitled to maintenance, unless pregnant. Accordingly, the husband is not entitled to confine her. As to the above verse, they say that it relates specifically to revocable divorcees.

11.16. MARRIAGE WITH A DIVORCEE'S SISTER DURING THE WAITING PERIOD

If a person marries a woman, it is unlawful for him to marry her sister. However, if she dies or is divorced and her period of waiting terminates, it becomes lawful for him to marry her sister. But is it lawful for him to marry her sister before her'waiting period comes to an end? The schools concur that it is unlawful to marry the sister of a divorcee in the waiting period if the divorce is revocable, and differ where the divorce is irrevocable. The Hanafi and Hanbali schools observe that neither marriage with her sister permissible nor the marrying of a fifth wife (if he had four, one of whom he has divorced) until the completion of her waiting period, irrespective of the divorce being revocable or irrevocable. The Jafari, Maliki and Shafii schools state that it is permissible to marry the sister of a divorcee and a fifth wife before the completion of waiting period if the divorce is irrevocable.

11.17. CAN A DIVORCEE IN THE WAITING PERIOD BE REDIVORCED?

The Hanafi, Hanbali, Shafii and Maliki schools state that in revocable divorce, he is entitled to divorce her again while she is observing the waiting period without returning to her, but not if the divorce is irrevocable.[28] The Jafari observe that divorce of a divorcee, revocable or irrevocable, does not take place unless he returns to her, because it is meaningless to divorce a divorcee.

11.18. RETURN TO THE DIVORCEE

Al-rajah in the terminology of jurists is restoration of the divorcee and her marital status. It is valid by consensus and does not require a guardian, or dowry, or the divorcee's consent, or any action on her part, in accordance with the verses, *"Their husbands are better entitled to restore them"* (2:228). *"So when they have reached their prescribed term, retain them honorably or separate from them honorably...."* (65:2).

The schools concur that it is necessary that the divorcee being restored be in the waiting period of a revocable divorce. Thus there is no return to the divorcee for an irrevocable divorcee of an unconsummated marriage, because there is no waiting period for her, for a triple divorcee, because she requires a temporary husband and for the divorcee of a 'divorce for a consideration', because the marital bond between the two has been dissolved.

There is consensus among the schools that the return is effected by oral word and they consider it necessary that the pronouncement be complete and unconditional. Thus if the return to a divorcee is made contingent upon something such as when he says: "I return to you if you so desire," it will not be valid.[29] Accordingly, if neither an act nor a satisfactory declaration proving 'return to a divorcee' takes place on his part after the unsatisfactory pronouncement and the waiting period of expires eventually, the divorcee will become a stranger for him.

The schools differ regarding the possibility of 'return to a divorcee' being effected by an act, such as sexual intercourse or its preliminaries, without any pronouncement preceding it. The Shafiis observe that it is necessary that a 'return to a divorcee' be either by spoken word or in writing. Thus it is not valid by intercourse even if he intends to 'return to a divorcee' through it, and such intercourse with her during is unlawful, making him liable for *mahr al-mithl* because it is an 'intercourse by mistake'.

The Malikis state that 'the return to a divorcee' is valid by an act if it is with the intention of returning. Thus, if he has intercourse without this intention, the divorcee will not return to him. But such intercourse does not make him liable to any penal consequences nor dowry, and if she becomes pregnant consequently, the child will be attributed to him and if she does not become pregnant, she will release herself after a single menstrual course. The Hanbalis are of the opinion that 'return to a divorcee' is valid by an act only if he has intercourse. Thus, when he has intercourse, she will be considered restored even if he does not intend it. Any act apart from intercourse, such as caressing and kissing, etc., does not result in 'returning'. According to the Hanafis, 'returning to a divorcee' is effected by intercourse, as well as caressing, kissing, etc., by the divorcer and the divorcee, provided it is with a sexual intent. Also, 'returning to a divorcee' by an act of one in sleep, or by an act performed absent-mindedly or under coercion, or in a state of insanity (as when the husband divorces his wife, turns insane, and has intercourse with her before the termination of her waiting period is valid.[30] The Jafari state that return to a divorcee' is effected through intercourse, kissing and caressing, with and without a sexual intent, as well as by any other act which is not permissible except between a married couple. It is not necessary that the 'return' be preceded by an oral pronouncement, because the divorcee is a wife as long as she is observing the waiting period, and all it requires is an intention of 'returning'. The author of *al-Jawahir* goes a step further, observing, "Perhaps the unconditional nature of the canonical texts and the edicts requires that a 'return' take place by an act even if he does not intend to restore her by it." Sayyid Abu al-Hasan, "It is highly probable that it (the act) be considered 'returning' even if the intent is absent." The Jafari attach no significance to an act of a person in sleep or something done absent-mindedly, or under a false impression (such as his having intercourse under the impression that she is not his divorcee).

11.19. RETURNING TO A DIVORCEE AND WITNESSES

The Jafari, Hanafi and Maliki schools state that 'returning to a divorcee' (*rajah*) does not require witnessing although it is desirable. A Tradition narrated from Imam Ahmad Hanbal conveys the same, and so does the more reliable opinion of Imam Shafi. Accordingly, it is possible to claim a consensus of all the schools regarding the non-necessity of witnesses in 'returning to a divorcee'.

11.20. RETURNING TO A DIVORCEE OF AN IRREVOCABLE DIVORCE

The restoration of an irrevocable divorcee during the waiting period is possible only in the case of a divorcee who has been

granted 'divorce for a consideration', provided that the marriage
has been consummated and the divorce is not one which completes three divorces. The Hanafi, Hanbali, Shafii and Maliki
schools concur that the law applicable here is the one which
applies to a stranger and requires a new marriage contract,
along with dowry, her consent and the permission of the
guardian (if necessary), with the exception that she is not
required to complete the waiting period.[31] The Jafari observe
that a divorcee of 'divorce for a consideration' is entitled to
reclaim what she has paid as a consideration as long as she is
in the waiting period provided the husband is aware of her
reclaiming the consideration and has not married her sister or
a fourth wife. Thus, when he is aware of it and there is no
impediment, he is entitled to recant the divorce. By his recant-
ing she becomes his lawful wife and there is no need for a new
contract or dowry. If he becomes aware of her reclaiming the
consideration but does not recant the divorce, the divorce which
was irrevocable becomes revocable and all the rules applicable
to it and its consequences will follow, and the divorcer will be
compelled to restore what the divorcee had given him for divorcing her.

11.21. DISAGREEMENT DURING THE WAITING PERIOD

If there is a disagreement between the divorcer and a revocable divorcee, such as when he claims, "I have returned to her,"
and she denies it, the divorcer will be considered to have made
the return if it takes place during the waiting period, and similarly if he denies having divorced her at all, because his saying
this guarantees his connection with the wife.

The burden of proof rests on the divorcer to prove 'return to
a divorcee' if the two differ regarding it after the expiry of the
waiting period. On his failing to do so, she will take an oath that
he has not returned to her, if he claims having returned to her
by an act (such as sexual intercourse, etc.). If the divorcer
claims 'return' by oral word and not by an act, she will take an
oath that she knows nothing about it. According to Imam Abu

Hanifah, her word will be accepted without an oath.[32]

If they differ regarding the expiry of the waiting period such as when she claims its expiry by menstruation in a period sufficient for creating the possibility of her claim being veracious, her word will be accepted, as per consensus, although the Jafari, the Shafii and the Hanbali schools also require her to take an oath. The author of *al-Mughni*[33] has narrated from Imam Shafii and al-Khiraqi, "In all cases where we said that her word will be accepted, she will have to take an oath if the husband denies her claim."

If she claims the expiry of the waiting period by the completion of three months, the author of *al-Mughni*, a Hanbali, and the author of *al-Sharai*, a Jafari, observe that the husband's word will be accepted. Both argue that the difference is in reality regarding the time of divorce and not the waiting period and divorce being his act, his word will be accepted. But the author of *al-Jawahir* observes that the acceptance of the divorcer's word is in accordance with the principle of presumption regarding the continuation of the waiting period unless the opposite is proved and the presumption that any new situation is a latter development, but it contradicts the literal import of the canonical texts and the prevalent opinion among the jurists, which place the affair of the waiting period in the woman's hand. He further adds that the sole possibility of her veracity in a matter concerning the waiting period is sufficient for its acceptance. This preference in accepting her word is in accordance with the Tradition that God has placed three things in the hands of women: menstruation, freedom from menses, and pregnancy. In another Tradition, menstruation and the waiting period are mentioned instead of the above three.

11.22. THE ACCEPTANCE OF A CLAIM WITHOUT PROOF

We have referred above to the acceptance of the woman's word in matters concerning the waiting period. Here it is appropriate to explain an important rule of the *Shariah* closely related to our present discussion that has often been referred to in the works of the jurists, especially those of the Jafari and the Hanafi schools. However, these jurists have discussed it as a side issue, in the context of other related issues.[34]

It is a known fact that both in the ancient and modern systems of law the burden of proof lies on the claimant and the defendant is burdened with an oath. The rule under discussion is just the opposite of it. According to it, it is binding to accept the claimant's word where it concerns his intention and cannot be known except from him, and which cannot possibly be witnessed. Examples of it abound in law, both in matters related to worship and transactions. Some of them are the following:

1. If something is entrusted to a person and he claims having returned it, or claims its destruction without any negligence or misuse on his part, his word will be accepted on oath despite his being the claimant.

2. When a marriage contract is concluded between two minors by an official third party, if one of them, on maturing, agrees and gives his/her consent to the contract and then dies before the other's majority, a part of his/her estate, equal to the minor's share will be set apart, and on his/her majority and agreement to the contract, he/she would also be required to take an oath that his/her consent is not motivated by greed for the legacy. On his/her taking the oath, he/she will take his/her share of the deceased's estate. This is so because the intention of a person can be known only from him.

3. If a person pronounces the divorce of his wife and then claims that he did not intend it, his claim will be accepted as long as she is undergoing the waiting period.

4. The claim of a person to have paid the poor-due or the twenty percent tax will be accepted .

5. The claim of a woman concerning her state of menstruation, freedom from menstruation, pregnancy and waiting period will be accepted.

6. The claim of indigence and need.

7. The claim by a woman that she is free of all impediments to marriage.

8. The claim of a youth that he has attained puberty.

9. The husband's claim that he has had intercourse with his wife, after she claims that he is impotent and the judge grants him a year's time. Details of it were mentioned while discussing impotence (in the chapter on marriage).

10. The claim of a working partner in a *mudarabah* partnership (where one partner contributes capital while the other contributes his skill, labor and know-how) that he has purchased a particular commodity for himself, which the partner contributing capital denies. Here the purchaser's word is accepted because he knows his intention better. There are other such examples.

Shaykh Abd al-Karim has mentioned three proofs. The first proof is confirmed consensus, both in theory and practice. I have seen jurists invoking this principle in all instances of its application, issuing edicts on its basis in different branches of law, considering it as one of the most incontrovertible of principles. All this points towards a definite proof and a consensus regarding its being a general premise referred to in instances of doubt. The jurists invoke this principle as a cause while accepting the word of an insolvent person, because if his word is not accepted, it will result in a sentence of perpetual imprisonment due to his inability to prove it.

The second proof is that which has been explicitly reported in some traditions. A certain narrator says, "I asked al-Rida, 'What is to be done if a man marries a woman and then a doubt arises in his mind that she has a husband?' Al-Rida replied, 'He is not required to do anything; don't you see that if he asks her for a proof, she will not be able to find anyone who can bear witness that she has no husband?'"

Thus, the impossibility of producing witnesses is common to all these instances where another person's testimony is not possible due to the act being a private fact between the person and his Lord, which cannot be known except from the person himself. This is in addition to what has been narrated in the Tradition regarding the acceptability of women's claim concerning menses, purity, waiting period and pregnancy.

The third proof is that in the event of not accepting the claimant's word in matters that cannot be known except from him, the dispute would of necessity remain unresolved and there would be no means in the *Shariah* for deciding disputes, and this is contradictory to the basic principle that says that there is a solution for everything in the *Shariah*. Therefore, in such circumstances the claimant's claim will be accepted after his taking an oath, because apart from this there is no other way to settle the dispute.

As to the need for an oath, it is in line with the consensus that in every claim in which the claimant's word is given precedence, he is bound to take an oath, because disputes are solved either by evidence or oath, and when it is not possible to produce a proof, the claimant's oath is the only alternative. Here it is not possible to burden the defendant with an oath, because among the requirements of an oath is certain knowledge of the fact for which the oath is being taken, and there is no way a defendant can have knowledge of the claimant's intention. It is necessary to point out that the need to make such a claimant take an oath arises in the case of a dispute that cannot be settled except by his oath. But if there is no such dispute, his word will be accepted without an oath (e.g. his claim of having paid the poor-due and twenty per cent tax, or his claim of their not being obligatory upon him because he does not fulfill the conditions for their incidence).

Also necessary for accepting the claim of such a claimant is the absence of circumstantial evidence refuting the veracity of his claim. Thus if an act of his proves his intention such as when he buys or sells and then claims that it was unintentional it would result in his proving his own falsity because the apparent circumstances establish his intention. As to the acceptance of a claimant that he did not intend divorce, it is limited, as mentioned earlier, to a revocable divorce as long as the divorcee is undergoing the waiting period and this claim of his is considered his reclaiming her. Hence his word will not be given credence and his claim will not be heard if the divorce is irrevocable or if he makes the claim after the completion of the waiting period.

11.23. COURT DIVORCE

Is a judge entitled to divorce someone's wife against his will? Imam Abu Hanifah says that a judge is not entitled to divorce someone's wife, whatever the cause, except when the husband is insane, *khasi* or *anin*,[35] as mentioned earlier in the section on defects. Thus failure to provide maintenance, intermittent absence, life imprisonment, etc. do not validate a woman's divorce without the husband's consent because divorce is the husband's prerogative. Imam Malik, Imam Shafii and Imam Ibn Hanbal allow a woman to demand separation before a judge on certain grounds, of which some are the following:

1. Non-provision of maintenance: These three jurists concur that when the incapability of a husband to provide essential maintenance is proved, it is valid for his wife to demand separation. But if his inability is not proved and he refuses to provide maintenance, Imam Shafii observes that the two may not be separated. Imam Malik and Imam Ahmad Hanbal remark that separation may take place, because the failure to provide her maintenance is similar to insolvency. The law in Egypt explicitly validates the right to claim separation on the failure to provide maintenance.

2. Causing harm to the wife with word or deed: Abu Zuhrah,[36] says that it is stated in Egyptian law, Act 25 of 1929, that if a wife pleads harm being caused to her by the husband, so that the like of her cannot continue living with him, the judge will divorce her irrevocably on her proving her claim and after the judge's failing to reform the husband. If the wife fails to prove her claim but repeats her complaint, the judge will appoint two just arbitrators related to the couple to find out the reasons for the dispute and to make an effort to resolve it. On their failing to do so, they will identify the party at fault, and if it is the husband or both of them, they will cause their separa-

tion through an irrevocable divorce on the judge's order. This law is based on the opinion of Imam Malik and Imam Ahmad Hanbal. The Hanafi, Hanbali, Shafii and Maliki *Shariah* courts in Lebanon rule separation if a dispute arises between them and two arbitrators specify the necessity of separation.

3. On harm being caused to a wife by the husband's absence, according to Imam Malik and Imam Ahmad Hanbal, even if he leaves behind what she requires as maintenance for the period of his absence. The minimum period after which a wife can claim separation is six months according to Ahmad Hanbal, and three years according to Imam Malik, though a period of one year has also been narrated from the latter. The Egyptian law specifies a year. Whatever the case, she will not be divorced unless he refuses both to come to her or to take her to the place of his residence. Moreover, Imam Malik does not differentiate between a husband having an excuse for his absence and one who has none with regard to the application of this rule. Thus both the situations necessitate separation. But the Hanbalis state that separation is not valid unless his absence is without an excuse.[37]

4. On harm being caused to a wife as a result of the husband's imprisonment. Ibn Taymiyyah, a Hanbali, has explicitly mentioned it and it has also been incorporated in Egyptian law that if a person is imprisoned for a period of three years or more, his wife is entitled to demand separation pleading damage after a year of his imprisonment, and the judge will order her divorce. Most Jafari jurists do not empower the judge to effect a divorce, regardless of the circumstances, except in the case of the wife of a missing husband, after the fulfillment of the conditions mentioned earlier. This stand of the Jafari is in consonance with the literal meaning of the tradition. But a group of grand legal authorities (*al-maraji al-kibar*) have permitted divorce by a judge, with a difference of opinion regarding its conditions and limitations. We cite their observations here.

Sayyid Kazim al-Yazdi, in the appendices to *al-Urwah* (*bab al-iddah*), has said that the validity of a wife's divorce by a judge is not remote if it comes to his knowledge that the husband is imprisoned in a place from where he will never return, and similarly where the husband though present is indigent and incapable of providing maintenance, along with the wife's refusal to bear it patiently.

Sayyid Abu al-Hasan al-Isfahani, in the *bab al-zawaj* of *al-Wasilah* (under the caption, *al-qawl fi al-kufr*), writes that if a husband refuses to provide maintenance while possessing the means to do so and the wife raises the issue before a judge, the judge will order him to provide her maintenance or to divorce her. On his refusing to do either, and it not being possible to maintain her from his wealth or to compel him to divorce, the obvious thing which comes to the mind is that the judge will divorce her, if she so desires.[38] Sayyid Muhsin al-Hakim has given a similar edict in *Minhaj al-salihin* (*bab al-nafaqat*).

The author of *al-Mukhtalif* has narrated from Ibn Junayd that the wife has the option to dissolve marriage on the husband's inability to provide maintenance. The author of *al-Masalik*,[39] while discussing the divorce of a missing person's wife, observes as per an opinion, the wife is entitled to break off marriage on the basis of non-provision of maintenance due to pennilessness. The author of *Rawdat al-jannat*,[40] in the biographical account of Ibn Aqa Muhammad Baqir al-Behbahani, one of the great scholars, says that he wrote a treatise (*risalah*) on the rules of marriage concerning indigence, entitled *Muzhir al-mukhtar*. In it, he has upheld the validity of wife's annulling marriage in event of husband's refusing, despite his presence, to maintain or divorce her, even if his refusal is a result of poverty and indigence.

The Jafari say that if a husband fails to provide his wife clothes to cover her body (*awrah*) and food to fill her stomach, the judge is entitled to separate them." This bestows upon the Jafari jurist the authority to grant divorce on the fulfillment of the requisite conditions and no one may object to him for it as long as his act is in accordance with the principles of Islam and those of the legal schools.

There is no doubt that the scholars who have refrained from

granting divorces have done so on account of caution and the fear lest this power should be misused by persons devoid of the necessary learning and commitment to the faith, resulting in divorces being granted without the fulfillment of the conditions of the *Shariah*. This is the sole reason which has caused me to refrain despite the knowledge that if I do so I would be justified before God. I consider that a sensible solution to this problem and one which would prevent every unfit person from exercising this authority is the appointment by the *maraji* of reliable representatives in Iraq or Iran bound by certain conditions and limitations within which they may affect a divorce was done by Sayyid Abu al-Hasan al-Isfahani.

11.24. USING THE PHRASE "YOU ARE TO ME LIKE THE BACK OF MY MOTHER"

'*Zihar*' means a husband telling his wife, "You are to me like the back of my mother." The schools concur that if a husband utters these words to his wife, it is not permissible for him to have sex with her unless he atones by freeing a slave. If he is unable to do so, he should fast for two successive months. If even this is not possible, he is required to feed sixty poor persons. The schools also concur in considering a husband who has intercourse before the atonement a sinner, and the Jafari also require him to make a double atonement.

The Jafari consider the expression 'You are as my mother's back," (*zihar*) valid if it takes place before two just male witnesses hearing the husband's pronouncement to the wife in a when she is not having her monthly period in which they have not had intercourse, exactly as in the case of divorce. Similarly, researchers among them also require her marriage to have been consummated, otherwise there is no reason to use the expression 'You are as my mother's back".

The reason for opening a separate chapter for the expression "You are as my mother's back," in Islamic law are the opening verses of the *Surat al-Mujadilah*. The exegetes describe that Aws ibn Samit, one of the Prophet's Companions, had a wife with a shapely body. Once he saw her prostrating in prayer.

When she had finished, he desired her. She declined. On this he became angry and said, "You are to me like the back of my mother." Later he repented having said so. Using this expression was a form of divorce amongst the pagan Arabs, and so he said to her, "I presume that you have become forbidden for me." She replied, "Don't say so, but go to the Prophet and ask him." He told her that he felt ashamed to question the Prophet about such a matter. She asked him to permit her to question the Prophet (ﷺ) which he did. When she went to the Prophet (ﷺ), Ayishah was washing his head. She said, "O Messenger of God! My husband Aws married me when I was a young girl with wealth and had a family. Now, when he has eaten up my wealth and destroyed my youth, and when my family has scattered and I have become old, he has pronounced 'You are as my mother's back,' (*zihar*), repenting subsequently. Is there a way for our coming together, by which you could restore our relationship?"

The Prophet (ﷺ) replied, "I see that you have become unlawful for him." She said, "O Prophet of God! By Him Who has given you the Book, my husband did not divorce me. He is the father of my child and the most beloved of all people to me." The Prophet (ﷺ) replied, "I have not been commanded regarding your affair." The woman kept coming back to the Prophet (ﷺ) and once when the Prophet (ﷺ) turned her back she cried out and said, "I complain to God regarding my indigence, my need and my plight! O God, send upon Thy Prophet that which would end my suffering." She then returned to the Prophet and implored his mercy saying, "May I be your ransom, O Prophet of God, look into my affair." Aishah then said to her, "Curtail your speech and your quarrel. Don't you see the face of the Messenger of God?" Whenever the Prophet (ﷺ) received revelation a form of trance would overtake him.

The Prophet (ﷺ) then turned towards her and said, "Call your husband." When he came, the Prophet (ﷺ) recited to him the verses, "*God has heard the speech of her who disputes with you concerning her husband and complains to God. And God hears your colloquy. Surely God is the Hearer, the Seer. Those among you who pronounce zihar to their wives, they (the wives) are not their mothers. Their mothers are only those who gave them birth, and they indeed utter an ill word and a lie, and indeed God is Pardoning, Forgiving And those who pronounce 'You are as my mother's back' to their wives and then recant their words, should free a slave before they touch each other. Unto this you are exhorted and God is aware of your actions. And he who does not possess the means, should fast for two successive months before they touch each other. And he who is unable to do so, should feed sixty needy ones. This, that you may put trust in God and His Apostle. These are the limits set by God; and for unbelievers is a painful chastisement*" (58:1-4).

After reciting these verses the Prophet (ﷺ) said to the husband, "Can you afford to free a slave?" The husband replied, "That will take up all my means." The Prophet (ﷺ) then asked him, "Are you capable of fasting for two successive months?" He replied: "By God, if I do not eat three times a day my eyesight becomes dim and I fear that my eyes may go blind." Then the Prophet asked him, "Can you afford to feed sixty needy persons?" He replied, "Only if you aid me, O Messenger of God" The Prophet (ﷺ) said, "Surely I will aid you with fifteen *sa* (a cubic measure) and pray for blessings upon you." Aws, taking what the Prophet (ﷺ) had ordered for him, fed the needy and ate along with them and thus his affair with his wife was settled.

11.25. Taking an Oath to Refrain from Sex with One's Wife

Al-ila is an oath taken by a husband in God's name to refrain from having sex with his wife. The Quranic basis of this concept is, "*Those who forswear their wives (by pronouncing* ila*) must wait for four months then if they change their mind, lo! God is Forgiving, Merciful. And if they decide upon divorce, then God is surely Hearing, Knowing*" (2:226-227).

The Jafari require that marriage should have been consummated in order for this to be valid, otherwise it will not take place. The schools concur that 'taking an oath to refrain from sex with one's wife' takes place where the husband swears not to have sex with his wife for the rest of her life or for a period exceeding four months.[41] The schools differ if the period is four months. The Hanafis assert that it takes place and the other schools maintain that it does not.

There is consensus that if the husband has sex within four months, he must atone (for breaking his oath), but the hindrance to the continuation of marital relations will be removed. The schools differ where four months pass without sex. The Hanafis observe: She will divorce herself irrevocably without raising the issue before the judge, or the husband will divorce her.[42]

The Maliki, Shafii and Hanbali schools state that if more than four months pass without his having sex, the wife will raise the issue before the judge so that he may order the husband to resume sexual relations. If the husband declines, the judge will order him to divorce her. If the husband declines again, the judge will pronounce her divorce, and in all situations the divorce will be revocable.[43]

The Jafari state that if more than four months pass without sex, and the wife is patient and willing, it is up to her and no one is entitled to object. But if she loses patience, she may raise the issue before the judge, who, on the completion of four months[44] will compel the husband to resume conjugal relations, or to divorce her. If he refrains from doing either, the judge will press him and imprison him until he agrees to do either of the two things, and the judge is not entitled to pronounce divorce forcibly on behalf of the husband.

All the schools concur that the atonement for an oath is that the person taking the oath should perform one of these alternatives: feed ten needy persons, provide clothing to ten needy persons, free a slave. If he has no means for performing any of these, he should fast for three days.

Furthermore, according to the Jafari, only those oaths which are sworn in the name of the sacred Essence of God will be binding. The oath of a child and a wife is not binding if the father and the husband prohibit it, except when the oath is taken for performing something that is obligatory or for refraining from something that is lawful. Similarly, an oath will not be binding upon anyone if it is taken to perform an act refraining from which is better than performing it, or is taken to refrain from an act whose performance is better than refraining from it, except, of course, the oath of *ila* which is binding despite the fact that it is better to refrain from it.

PART FOUR
NOTES

NOTES

PART I: INDIVIDUAL ISSUES
1 PRESCRIBED PURITY

1 Ibn Qudamah, *al-Mughni*, vol. 1, p. 19.

2 Ibn Qudamah, *al-Mughni*, vol. 1, p. 22, 3rd edition; Ibn Abidin, vol. 1, p. 140. The people stood in need of this and similar issues, which have been discussed in voluminous works of jurisprudence, because water was more scarce and expensive in those days than oil is today.

3 Ibn Rushd, *Bidayat al-mujtahid wa nihayat al-muqasid*, p. 32, 1354 AH, edition and *Majma al-anhur*, p. 37, Istanbul.

4 Ibn Qudamah, *al-Mughni*, vol. 1, p. 12.

5 The Hanbalis observe that *al-mal-kathir* does not become impure (*najis*) on contact, provided the impurity (*najasah*) is not urine or excrement. On contact with the two it will become impure (*najis*), irrespective of whether its qualities have changed or not, unless it happens to be like those puddles visible on the way to Makkah (Ibn Qudamah, *al-Mughni*, vol. 1). Apart from these, there are other definitions of a large amount of water (*al-mal-kathir*) which have been omitted. Among them are those which state that a large (*kathir*) amount is forty *qullah*s, 2 pails (*dalw*), and 40 pails.

6 Ibn Abidin, *Hashiyah*, vol. 1, p. 130, printed by al-Maymaniyya.

7 Ibn Abidin, *Hashiyah*, vol. 1, p. 131.

8 an-Nawawi, *Sharh al-muhadhdhab*, vol. 1, p. 136.

9 Ibn Abidin, *Hashiyah*, vol. 1, p. 131.

10 Ibn Abidin, *Hashiyah*, vol. 1, p. 156.

11 Ibn Qudamah, *al-Mughni*, vol. 1, p. 47, 3rd edition.

12 *al-Fiqh alal-madhahib al-arbaah*, vol. 1, *baith qada al-hajahi*.

13 *al-Fiqh alal-madhahib al-arbaah*, vol. 1, *madhath izalat al-najasah*.

14 Ibn Abidin, *Hashiyah*, vol. 1, p. 119.

15 Ibn Abidin, *Hashiyah*, vol. 1, p. 215.

16 al-Shirani, *al-Mizan, mabhath asbab al-hadath*.

17 Ibn Rushd, *al-Bidayali wa-nihayah, mabath nawaqid*.

18 Allamah Hilli, *al-Tadhkirah*.

19 Ibn Abidin, *Hashiyah*, vol. 1, p. 76.

20 Ibn Qudamah, *al-Mughni*, vol. 1, *fasl mash al-raas* and Allamah Hilli, *al-Tadhkirah*.

21 Ibn Abidin, *Hashiyah*, vol. 1, p. 128 and *Sharh al-muhadhdhab*, vol. 1, p. 251.

22 Rida al-Hamadani, *Misbah al-faqih*.

23 Allamah Hilli, *al-Tadhkirah*.

24 Ibn Qudamah, *al-Mughni*, p. 207.

25 Al-Sayyid Sahif, *Fiqh as-sunnah*, 1957, p. 155.

26 *al-Fiqh alal-madhahib al-arbaah*, vol. 1, *mabhath al-istihadah*.

27 The Hanafis say, "A martyr is someone who is killed unjustly, irrespective of whether it is in war or by a robber." The requirement that they lay down for not giving him or her the bath ablution is that he or she should not be in a state of major impurity at the time of death.

28 *al-Fiqh alal-madhahib al-arbaah, mabath al-haqq bil-salat alal-mayyit*.

29 The Shafiis and Malikis permit prescribed prayer to be offered over a dead body while it is placed on the back or a beast of burden or held on the hands or shoulders of people.

30 The description that the dead body's head would point towards the West and his feet towards the East applies to Lebanon.

31 *al-Wajiz*.

32 Ibn Rushd, *al-Bidayah wa l-nihayah*, vol. 1, p. 63, 1935 edition; Ibn Qudamah, *al-Mughni*, vol. 1, 234, 3rd edition.

33 Ibn Rushd, al-*Bidayah wa al-nihayah*, vol. 1, p. 66.

34 *al-Fiqh alal-madhahib al-'arbaah, mabath arkan al-tayam-mun.*

2 PRESCRIBED PRAYER

1 Shaykh al-Kabir, *Kashf al-ghita*, 1317 edition p. 79.

2 The Hanafis use two terms, *'fard'* and *'wajib'*, for something whose performance is prescribed and whose omission is impermissible. Hence they divide obligation into two kinds: *fard* and *wajib*. *'Fard'* (strongly recommended practice) is a duty for which there is definite proof, such as Quranic text (*mutawatir sunnah*), and consensus (*ijma*). *'Wajib'* is a duty for which there is a non-definite (*zanni*) proof, such as analogy (*qiyas*) and isolated Tradition (*khabar al-wahid*). That whose performance is preferable to its omission is also of two kinds *'masnun'* and *'mandub'*. *'Masnun'* is an act which the Prophet and the rightly-guided caliphs performed regularly, and *'mandub'* is an act ordered by the Prophet ( ) though not performed regularly by him. That which is obligatory (*wajib*) to avoid and whose performance is not permissible is *'muharram'* if it is established by a definite proof. If based on a *zanni* proof, it is *'makruh'*, whose performance is disapproved.

3 According to the Hanafis, the *watr* prayer (*salat al-watr*) consists of three cycles (*rakah*) with a single salutation (*salam*). Its time extends from the disappearance of twilight after sunset to dawn. The Hanbalis and Shafiis say that at minimum it is one cycle and at maximum eleven cycles, and its time is after the night (*isha*) prayer. The Malikis observe that it has only one cycle.

4 There are among jurisprudents of the Hanafi, Hanbali, Maliki and Shafii school those who agree with the Jafaris on performing the two prescribed prayers together even when one is not traveling. Shaykh Ahmad al-Siddiq al-Ghumari has written a book on this topic, *Izalat al-khatar amman jamaa bayn al-sala-tayn fi al-hadar.*

5 There is no difference regarding the definition of sunset between the Jafaris and the Hanafi, Hanbali, Maliki and Shafii schools. But the Jafaris say that the setting of the sun is not ascertained simply by the vanishing of the sun from sight, but on the vanishing of the reddish afterglow from the eastern horizon, for the East overlooks the

West and the eastern afterglow, which is a reflection of sun's light, pales away as the sun recedes. That which is rumored regarding Jafaris that they do not break their fast during Ramadan until the stars become visible, has no basis. In fact they denounce this opinion in their books on jurisprudence with the argument that the stars may be visible before sunset, at the time of sunset or after it, and declare that "one who delays the evening (*maghrib*) prayer until the stars appear is an accursed person (*malun ibn malun*)." They have said this in condemnation of the Khattabiyyah, the followers of Abu al-Khattab, who held this belief. They are now one of the extinct groups. Jafar Sadiq was told that the people of Iraq delay the evening prayer until the stars become visible. He answered, "That is on account of Abu al-Khattab, enemy of Allah."

6 The command to face Masjid al-Haram has come in 2:144 "...*so turn your face towards al-Masjid al-Haram*," and the leave to turn in any direction in verse 2:115 "*To God belongs the East and the West; whethersoever you turn there is the Presence of God*." Some scholars have held that the former verse abrogates the latter. Others disagree and point out that there is no abrogation involved here, nor is it a case of one being particular and the other general. The way to reconcile the two verses, they point out, is that the former verse applies to those who know the direction of the *qiblah* and commands them to turn towards it. The latter verse specifically applies to one who is at a loss regarding its direction and orders him to perform prescribed prayer in any direction he wants. This opinion seems to be more credible.

7 Ibn Abi Layla holds an uncommon opinion that prohibits one from baring oneself even for the bath for the reason that water is inhabited by living beings. *al-Majmu shahr al-muhadhdhab*, ii, 197.

8 24:31 mentions those before whom women can expose their adornment and among them are Muslim women. Thus the verse prohibits a Muslim woman from exposing herself before a non-Muslim woman. The Shafiis Malikis and Hanafis construe this prohibition as implying *tahrim*.

Most Jafaris and the Hanbalis say that there is no difference between Muslim and non-Muslim women. But according to the Jafaris it is disapproved for a Muslim woman to expose herself before a non-Muslim woman, because she may describe what she observes to her husband.

9 *al-Fiqh alal-madhahib al-arbaah*, vol. 1, *mabhath satr al-arwah*.

10 Shaykh Jafar, *Kasf al-ghita*.

11 Ibn Abidin, *Hashiyah*, vol. 1, p. 284.

12 Allamah al-Hilli, *al-Tadhkirah*, vol. 2., beginning of *bab al-zawaj*.

13 *al-Jawahir* at the beginning of *bab al-zawaj*.

14 al-Nawawi, *Sharh al-muhadhdhab*, iii, 179.

15 The Jafaris observe that it is recommended for a woman to recite the call to the prescribed prayer for her prescribed prayer, though not as a call to prayer. Similarly, it is recommended for women while holding their own congregation that one of them recite the call to prescribed prayer and the declaration to perform the prescribed prayer in a manner that men do not hear it. The Hanafi, Hanbali, Maliki and Shafii schools consider the declaration to perform the prescribed prayer as recommended and the call to prescribed prayer as disapproved for women.

16 Ibn Rushd, *Bidayat al-mujtahid*, 1935 edition, vol. 1, p. 103, says, "Others have said, 'The phrase "*al-salatu khayrun min al-nawm*"' should not be recited because it is not a *masnun* part of the call to prescribed prayer,' and this is the opinion of al-Shafii. The cause for the disagreement is the question whether it was said (as part of the call to prescribed prayer during the time of the Prophet or during that of Umar. It is stated in Ibn Qudamah's *al-Mughni* (3rd edition) vol. 1, p. 108, "*Ishaq* has said that this thing has been innovated by the people and Abu Isa has said, 'This *tathwib* is something that the learned (*ahl al-ilm*) have regarded with distaste. It is that on hearing which Ibn Umar left the mosque.'"

17 *Bidayat al-mujtahid*, vol. 1, p. 122 and al-Shirani, *Mizan, bab sifat al-salat*.

18 al-Nawawi, *Sharh al-muhadhdhab*, vol. 3, p. 361.

19 *Bidayat al-mujtahid*, vol. 1, p. 125.

20 *Bidayat al-mujtahid*, vol. 1, p. 126.

21 *Majma al-anhur*, vol. 1, *bab sujud al-sahw*.

22 Shahid al-Thani, *Lumah*, vol. 1, *bab al-salat, fasl* 6, observes,

"The obligatory acts of *salat al-jumuah* during the absence of the Mahdi is obvious in the opinion of most religious scholars... and if there had been no claim of *ijma* regarding its not being obligatory, the opinion that it is obligatory *ayni* would have been extremely strong. Therefore, the least that can be said is that there is an option between it (*salat al-jumuah*) and the noon prescribed prayer with the Friday prescribed prayer enjoying preference."

23 According to the Hanafi, Hanbali, Maliki and Shafii schools, the *dua al-iftilah* or *dua al-istiftah* is *subanaka allahum wa bihamdik wa tabarak ismaka wa tala jaddaka wa. la ilaha ghayrika.*

24 al-Nawawi, *Sharh al-muhadhdhab*, vol. 3, p. 365.

25 Provided he returns within one day and one night, because in this case the journey has taken up all his day. Some others among them say, that one should perform the shortened prescribed prayer if he or she intends to return within ten days.

26 *al-Fiqh alal-madhahib al-arbaah*, vol. 4, *mabath shurut al-qasr.*

27 al-Ghazzali, *al-Wajiz, salat al-musafirin.*

28 This is a summary from *al-Fiqh alal-madhahib al-arbaah.*

3 PRESCRIBED FASTING

1 Approximately 800 grams of wheat or something similar to it.

2 The Hanafis observe that if he testifies before a judge who rejects his testimony, it is obligatory upon him to make up for the fasts missed without liability to atonement (*kaffarah*) (*al-Fiqh alal-madhahib al-arbaah*).

3 In 1939 the Festival of Sacrifice (*id al-adha*) was observed on Monday in Egypt, on Tuesday in Saudi Arabia, and on Wednesday in Bombay.

4 Refer to the discussion on this issue in the first volume of *Fiqh al-Jafar al-Sadiq*, the section on the proof of the new moon at the end of *bab al-sawm.*

4 PRESCRIBED PILGRIMAGE

1 *Ihram* is the state of pilgrim sanctity which the pilgrim assumes on reaching the place of the appointed time (*miqat*).

2 *Miqat* (pl. *mawaqit*) refers to a number of stations outside Makkah from where the pilgrims intending the longer or shorter pilgrimage assume the sacred state. They are: 1). Dhu al-Hulayfah (specifically Masjid al-Shajarah); 2) Yalamlam; 3) Qarn al-Manazil; 4) al-Juhfah; 5) three points situated in the valley of al-Aqiq: al-Maslakh, al-Ghamrah and Dhat al-Irq. Those pilgrims whose houses are nearer to Makkah than to any other of the above places of the appointed time (*mawaqit*) assume the sacred state (*ihram*) from their houses.

3 The *talbiyah* is obligatory according to the Jafari, Hanafi and Maliki schools and recommended according to the Hanbali. Its time is the moment of beginning of the sacred state.

4 The area roughly within a radius of six miles, with the Holy Kabah at the center is called the sacred and inviolable territory of the sanctuary of the Kabah (*haram*).

5 According to the Jafari school, *hajj al-tamattu* is obligatory for non-Makkans, and Makkans may choose between *hajj al-qiran* and *hajj al-ifrad*. According to the Hanafi, Hanbali, Shafii and Maliki schools, there is no difference between a Makkan and a non-Makkan with regard to choice of any particular kind of pilgrimage, except that according to the Hanafi school *hajj al-tamattu* and *hajj al-qiran* are disapproved (*makruh*) for the Makkans.

6 The circumambulation (*tawaf*) of the first entry or the arrival (called *tawaf al-qudum*) is recommended (*mustahabb*) from the viewpoint of all except the Maliki school, which regards it as obligatory.

7 According to the Jafari school, one is free to choose between *halq* and *taqsir* if on *umrah al-mufradah*. But a pilgrim on *hajj al-tamattu* is required to perform *taqsir*. Also according to the Jafari, it is obligatory for one on *umrah al-mufradah* to perform, after the *halq* or *taqsir*, a second circumambulation (*tawaf*), the *tawaf al-nisa*, before which sexual intimacy is not permissible to the pilgrim. According to the Hanafi, Hanbali, Shafii and Maliki schools, one is free to choose between *halq* and *taqsir* in both. They do not require the pilgrim of the longer or shorter pilgrimage to perform *tawaf al-nisa* and according to

the Maliki school *halq* or *taqsir* is not obligatory on one performing *umrah al-mufradah.*

8 According to the Jafari school, the pilgrim on *hajj al-tamattu* and its conjugate *umrah* (*mutamatti*) acquires relief (*tahlil*) from the sacred dress (*ihram*) after *taqsir*, even when he brings along with him the sacrificial animal (*hady*). But according to the other schools, the *mutamatti* who assumes *ihram* for *umrah* from the *miqat* obtains *tahlil* on *halq* or *taqsir* when not accompanied by the sacrifice (*hady*); but if he has brought the sacrifice along with him, he remains in the state of *ihram*. However, according to them, the pilgrim of *umrah al-mufradah* obtains *tahlil* regardless of whether the sacrifice accompanies him or not. The author of *al-Mughni*, after making the above statement, says, "I have not come across a contrary opinion on this matter."

9 According to the Jafari school, the halt in Arafat is obligatory for the entire period of time. But according to the other schools, a moment of halt is sufficient. All the legal schools are in agreement that offering the noon (*zuhr*) and afternoon (*asr*) prescribed prayers immediately after one another is recommended (*mustahabb*), because the Prophet had done so.

10 *Fath al-bari; al-Mughni; al-Tadhkirah.*

11 *al-Tadhkirah.*

12 *al-Fiqh alal-madhahib al-arbaah.*

13 Although the times have tended to support this opinion, and even though the Traditions in favor of dispatching without delay (*al-fawr*) of the duty of the prescribed pilgrimage are open to criticism and controversy, but it leads towards negligence, and gradually towards abandonment of this sacred rite. Accordingly, the stress on dispatching without delay is preferable, being more conducive from the viewpoint of the necessity to preserve the vitality of the Islamic faith.

14 *Fath al-qadir*, vol. II, *bab al-hajj.*

15 *Kifayat al-akhbar, al-Mughni, al-urwat al-wuthaqa.*

16 The Jafari, Shafii, and Maliki schools permit hiring another person to perform the prescribed pilgrimage for a fee. The Hanafi and Hanbali schools do not consider it permissible. Nothing more than the expenses of journey, food and lodging may be given to the hired, they say.

17 *al-Mughni; al-Tadhkirah.*

18 *al-Fiqh alal-madhahib al-arbaah.*

19 One who has not performed the prescribed pilgrimage before is called *sarurah*. According to the Shafii and Hanbali schools, if one who has not performed the prescribed pilgrimage before, undertakes it on behalf of another, the prescribed pilgrimage performed is considered his or her own. But according to the Maliki, Hanafi and Jafari schools, the prescribed pilgrimage performed depends on his or her intention (*niyyah*).

20 The minimum distance required for the shortened prescribed prayer (*qasr*) at noon (*zuhr*), afternoon (*asr*) and night (*isha*) prayers is eight parasangs (approximately 44 kms. or 27.5 miles).

21 *al-Jawahir.*

22 *al-Tadhkirah; al-Fiqh alal-madhahib al-arbaah.*

23 Karrarah, *al-Din wal-hajj ala al-madhdhib al-arbaah.*

24 *Fiqh as-sunnah*, vol. V; *al-Fiqh alal-madhahib al-arbaah; al-Jawahir; al-Mughni.* The Quran, 2:196. According to *al-Mughni*, Imam Ahmad ibn Hanbal did not consider the *umrah* as being obligatory for Makkans for the reason that the most important act of the *umrah* is circumambulation of the Kabah (*tawaf*) which they do and it suffices them.

25 In the book *al-Fiqh alal-madhahib al-arbaah*, it is the author's intention to give the text followed by a commentary and notes. In the text he states the points of consensus of the Hanafi, Hanbali, Maliki and Shafii schools, the different position of each is given in the commentary. What we have quoted here has been taken from the text, not from the commentary.

26 According to *al-Din wa al-hajj alal-madhahib al-arbaah* by Karrarah, one of the things which distinguishes the visit from the prescribed pilgrimage is that the sacred state is not assumed from any of the places specified for the prescribed pilgrimage. From the Jafari viewpoint, there is no difference between the place specified for one performing the visit and the place for one on prescribed pilgrimage with regard to the sacred state.

27 The Jafari author of *al-Madarik* says, "The better known and sounder of opinions is that the obligation of the visit is independent of the obligation of the prescribed pilgrimage." The author of *al-Jawahir*

states, "The statements of jurists are not free of confusion... the one which appears sounder is that those who live far away from Makkah are relieved of the obligation of *umrah al-mufradah*, and that which is obligatory upon them is *umrat al-tamattu*, whose *wujub* is related to that of the prescribed pilgrimage.

28 According to *al-Jawahir, al-Madarik, al-Hadaiq* and other Jafari works on jurisprudence, it is not permissible for one already in the sacred state to assume it for another purpose, until he or she completes all the acts of the visit or the pilgrimage for which he or she had assumed the sacred state.

29 Ibn Aqil is alone among Jafari jurists in agreeing with the Hanafi, Hanbali, Shafii and Maliki jurists in that the acts of both the prescribed pilgrimage and the visit may be performed with a single *ihram* in *hajj al-qiran*.

30 Dhu al-Hulayfah, today called Bir Ali or Abyar Ali, is at a distance of about 486 kms. from Makkah to the north and twelve kms. from Madinah.

31 Al-Juhfah lies a distance of about 156 kms. from Makkah to the northwest.

32 There are three points in the valley of al-Aqiq, ninety-four kms. from Makkah in the northeast, from where the sacred state is assumed—al-Maslakh, al-Ghamrah, and Dhat al-Irq. According to the Jafari jurists, it is permissible to assume the sacred state from any of these points, although al-Maslakh is considered best, then al-Ghamrah, and then Dhat al-Irq.

33 Yalamlam is a mountain of the Tahamah range, lying at a distance of eighty-four kms. from Makkah.

34 Qarn al-Manazil, the place at the appointed time for those coming from Taif lies at a distance of ninety-four kms. east of Makkah.

35 *al-Tadhkirah, Fiqh as-sunnah.*

36 *al-Tadhkirah, Fiqh alal-madhahib al-arbaah.*

37 *al-Tadhkirah; Fiqh as-sunnah.*

38 *al-Fiqh alal-madhahib al-arbaah.*

39 *al-Fiqh alal-madhahib al-arbaah*

40 *al-Jawahir.*

41 *Fath al-qadir.*

42 *al-Jawahir; Fiqh as-sunnah.*

43 *al-Urwat al-wuthqa.*

44 *al-Jawahir; al-Muqhni.*

45 According to the Hanafi school, bringing along of the sacrifical animal substitutes for the *talbiyah* as mentioned by Ibn Abidin and the author of *Fath al-qadir.*

46 *Ishar* here means slitting the right side of the camel's hump. *Taqlid* refers to the hanging of an old horseshoe on the neck of the sacrifical animal which is meant to identify the sacrificial animal as such.

47 *al-Tadhkirah.*

48 *al-Tadhkirah; Fiqh as-sunnah.*

49 The *nal* has a sole, but is devoid of the covering on the sides and the back of the foot at the heels. The *khuff* is the common shoe which covers the foot on the sides and the heels.

50 *al-Tadhkirah; al-Bidayah wa al-nihayah.*

51 *al-Jawahir; Fiqh as-sunnah; al-Fiqh alal-madhahib al-arbaah.*

52 After performing *ramy al-jamarat* and *halq*, everything except intercourse and perfume becomes permissible to the pilgrim such as wearing of stitched clothes and other things. This is called *al-hill al-awwal* (or the first relief from the restrictions of the sacred state). After the last circumambulation, all things including intercourse become permissible to him. This second relief, to be explained later, is called *al-hill al-thani.*

53 According to *al-Tadhkirah*, it is necessary during the next prescribed pilgrimage that the 'separation' should take place from the point where the misdemeanour was committed during the first prescribed pilgrimage. The meaning of 'separation' *(tafriq)* is that the two should not be alone together without there being present a third *muhrim*, whose presence acts as a deterrent.

54 *al-Hadaiq; Fiqh as-sunnah.*

55 *al-Hadaiq; Fiqh as-sunnah.*

56 *al-Tadhkirah.*

57 *al-Hadaiq; al-Muqhni.*

58 *al-Jawahir.*

59 According to the Jafari, the atonement for cutting a single nail is giving one mudd (800 grams) of food in charity. If all the nails of fingers and toes are cut in one sitting, the atonement is one sheep, but if

done in several sittings, it is sacrifice of two sheep.

60 *Fiqh as-sunnah; al-Lumah.*

61 *Fiqh as-sunnah.*

621 *al-Lumah.*

63 The author of *al-Tadhkirah* ascribes impermissibility of shadowing oneself while moving to Abu Hanifah, and the author of *Rahmat al-ummah* ascribes to him permissibility.

64 *al-Tadhkirah.*

65 *al-Tadhkirah; al-Fiqh alal-madhahib al-arbaah.*

66 *al-Tadhkirah; Fiqh as-sunnah.*

67 It says in *al-Mughni*, "Those knowledgeable about Madinah do not know of any Thawr, but it is possible that names have changed with time."

68 *al-Mughni; al-Fiqh alal-madhahib al-arbaah; Fiqh as-sunnah.*

69 According to the author of *al-Hadaiq*, the prescribed pilgrimage is invalid if circumambulation is omitted intentionally, but not if omitted by mistake although it is obligatory to perform it after omission.

70 According to Ibn Rushd in *al-Bidayah*, the Hanafi, Hanbali, Shafii, and Maliki schools agree that the pilgrim of *hajj al-tamattu* and its related visit is required to perform the seven fold circumambulation twice. The pilgrim on *hajj al-ifrad* is required to perform the seven fold circumambulation once. They disagree regarding *hajj al-qiran*, in which case according to Imams Shafi, Malik and Ahmad ibn Hanbal, one seven fold circumambulation is required, but two according to Imam Abu Hanifah.

71 *Fiqh as-sunnah*, p. 154, 1955.

72 According to *al-Jawahir, al-Masalik, al-Urwat al-wuthqa* and other works of Jafari jurisprudence, it is not permissible for one in the state of *janabah* or *hayd* to enter or pass through Masjid al-Haram or Masjid al-Rasul (Madinah), to say nothing of ataying therein. However, it is permissible for one in the state of *janabah* or *hayd* to pass, without stopping or halting, through other mosques.

73 *al-Fiqh alal-madhahib al-arbaah*, vol. 1, p. 535, 1939.

74 *al-Jawahir; al-Hadaiq.*

75 *al-Jawahir; Fiqh as-sunnah.*

76 'Ramal' means running without rushing. According to the

Jafari work *al-Lumah*, the fast pace (*ramal*) is recommended (*musta-habb*) in the first three rounds of circumambulation, a position which is exactly the same as that of the Hanafi, Hanbali, Shafii and Maliki schools.

77 The author of *al-Jawahir* makes this remark when comparing those who stipulate such kind of conditions for circumambulation to others with a similar attitude with regard to the making of one's intention known in the prescribed prayers.

78 The *hijr* of Ismail ibn Ibrahim (   ) is the place where his house was built and there he buried his mother.

79 *al-Tadhkirah; al-Jawahir; al-Hadaiq.*

80 *Fiqh as-sunnah.*

81 *al-Tadhkirah.*

82 By *'idtiba'* is meant the style of wearing the cloak (*rida*) whose hanging sides are drawn under the right armpit and then thrown over the left shoulder. In the book *al-Fiqh alal-madhahib al-arbaah*, the *istihbab* of *idtibta* is ascribed to the Hanafi, Shafii and the Hanbali, not to the Maliki schools.

83 Sayyid al-Hakim says, "It is not obligatory to hasten to perform the search after finishing the circumambulation and its prescribed prayer but it is also not permissible to delay voluntarily until the next day." Sayyid al-Khui says, "It is binding on one not to make a consid-erable delay without need in performing the search after the circum-ambulation and its prescribed prayer, and it is not permissible to delay it intentionally until the next day." These verdicts of the two scholars are supported by reliable Traditions.

84 *Harwalah* is a kind of walk which resembles that of a camel when it wants to pick up speed. According to the Jafari, if the one per-forming the search is riding, he should spur it to make the beast walk faster.

85 *al-Tadhkirah; Fiqh as-sunnah.*

86 The author of *al-Mizan* quotes Imam Abu Hanifah to the effect that he does not see any objection in the converse, i.e. performing of the search by starting at Marwah and finishing at Safa.

87 Sayyid al-Hakim in his book on the rituals of the prescribed pil-grimage says that continuity of succession is not required in the *ash-*

wat of the search, and it is permissible to separate or interrupt them even after a single *shawt* and to pick up the count again after the break.

88 *al-Jawahir.*

89 *Kifayat al-akhyar.*

90 al-Shirani, *al-Mizan.*

91 Karrarah, *al-Din wal-hajj.*

92 This agrees with the edicts of al-Hakim and al-Khui. Al-Hakim, however, distinguishes between one who forgets (*nasi*) and one who is ignorant (*,jahil*); he excuses the first not the latter, who is included with the wilful defaulter (*amid*).

93 *al-Mughni.*

94 *al-Hadaiq; Fiqh as-sunnah.*

95 *Fiqh as-sunnah.*

96 Shaykh Abd al-Mutaal al-Saidi says that this order is obligatory in the rites of the visit, but in the rites of the prescribed pilgrimage there is no order of sequence between the circumambulation and the *halq*, or between the the search and the pause at Arafat. See *al-Fiqh al-musawwar ala madhhab al-Shafii.*

97 *al-Mughni.*

98 *al-Tadhkirah.*

99 *Fiqh as-sunnah; al-Tadhkirah.*

100 *al-Fiqh alal-madhahib al-arbaah; Manar al-sabil.*

101 Ibn Rushd, *Bidayah.*

102 This act of the Prophet ( ) makes the grounds for the Jafari for the permissibility of offering the two prayers together, because the Prophet ( ) had said, "Pray in the same way as you see me praying." The fact that something is permitted at one time or a place suggests its permissibility in all places and at all times, unless there is some textual proof (*nass*) to show that it is particular and not general. But there is no textual proof in favor of its being particular (*takhsis*).

103 *al-Jawahir.*

104 *al-Tadhkirah.*

105 *al-Jawahir.*

106 *al-Mughni.*

107 There is disagreement about the *ayyam al-tashriq* as to

whether they comprise of two or three days. As to their naming, it is because during those days the pilgrims used to dry strips of the meat of the sacrificed animals in the sun.

108 Ibn Rushd, *al-Bidayah.*

109 *al-Tadhkirah; al-Bidayah.*

110 Ibn Rushd, *al-Bidayah.*

111 This is in agreement with the edicts of al-Hakim and al-Khui.

112 *al-Mughni.*

113 *al-Mughni.*

114 *al-Tadhkirah.*

115 As mentioned earlier, the Makkan's duty, according to the Jafari, is either *hajj al-qiran, hajj al-ifrad*; but according to the other schools, he can choose one of the three types.

116 *al-Fiqh alal-madhahib al-arbaah.*

117 The distance of Mina from Mecca is one parasang (approx. 4 miles).

118 *al-Tadhkirah.*

119 *al-Mughni; al-Fiqh alal-madhahib al-arbaah; Fiqh as-sunnah.*

120 *al-Jawahir;* Sayyid al-Hakim and Sayyid al-Khui in their books on the rituals of the prescribed pilgrimage.

121 It may be noted that whenever there is an explicit text of the Quran there is also agreement and consensus between the Islamic schools of jurisprudence and no difference between the Hanafi, Hanbali, Maliki and Shafii and the Jafari. The divergence of opinion between them arises either on account of the absence of *nass* (text), or its being synoptic (*mujmal*), or its weakness, or its contrariety with another text, or in its interpretation and application. This is a definite proof of the fact that all of them are derived from a single source.

122 *al-Tadhkirah.*

123 *al-Mughni.*

124 Sayyid al-Hakim says, "The duty to offer the sacrificial animal in charity does not remain if one cannot do it ... and when the poor man would not accept it without money, it is not obligatory."

125 *al-Tadhkirah; al-Mughni; Fiqh as-sunnah.*

126 Al-Zurqani, *Sharh muwatta.*

127 Sayyid al-Hakim, *Manahij al-nasikin.*

128 *Hadhf* means a certain way of tossing in which the pebble is held under the thumb and tossed by the back of the index finger.

129 Sayyid al-Hakim says that it is desirable that the third stoning should be done with one's back toward the *qiblah.* According to *al-Mughni* it should be done facing the Kabah.

130 *al-Tadhkirah; al-Mughni.*

131 Ibn Rushd, *Bidayah; al-Mughni.*

132 *al-Tadhkirah.*

133 *al-Tadhkirah.*

PART II: ECONOMIC ISSUES
5 POOR-DUE
AND TWENTY PERCENT TAX

1 However, sanity and adulthood are not considered essential for liability to poor-due on crops of the field and fruits in the opinion of the Hanafi's.

2 *al-Fiqh alal-madhahib al-arbaah.*

3 The Hanafi's observe that the number of cows between the two limits is exempt from poor-due except when their number is between forty and sixty. After forty, poor-due will be levied on each extra cow at the rate of twenty percent of a *musinnah* (*al-Fiqh alal-madhahib al-arbaah*, bab al-zakat).

4 Allamah Hilli, *al-Tadhkira*h, vol. 1, *bab al-zakat.*

6 ENDOWMENTS

1 The difference between endowment and detention is that in the former the ownership of the founder is completely ended. This prevents the property from being inherited or disposed of in any other manner. In the latter case, the ownership of the detention is preserved, and the detained property may be inherited, sold, etc. This difference was not noticed by Shaykh Abu Zuhrah and he, as will be noticed, has ascribed to the Jafari that which they do not hold.

2 *Sharh al-zarqani, bab al-waqf.* This issue of perpetuity in endowment is intimately linked with the question concerning the

ownership of endowment property, which has been discussed separately in this chapter.

3 *al-Mughni; al-Zarqani* and *al-Madadhdhab.*

4 *al-Jawahir.*

5 Abu Zuhrah, *kitab al-waqf.*

6 Abu Zuhrah has rejected this view (p. 50), on the basis that the concept of the ownership of God is meaningless in this context, for God Almighty owns everything. But it will be noticed that the meaning of God's owning the endowment is not that it becomes a free natural bounty (like air and water); rather, His ownership of it is like His ownership of *khums al-ghanimah*, as mentioned in the Quranic verse, "*And know that whatever you acquire as spoils, a fifth of it is for God...*" (8: 41). *Fath al-qadir*, vol. 5, *bab al-waqf*; Abu Zuhrah, *kitab al-waqf.*

7 Abu Zuhrah, 1959, p. 49.

8 Abu Zuhrah, p. 106.

9 As to those who say that endowment may be created only by using specific words, their argument is based on the presumption of the continuity of the ownership of the property by the owner. That is, the property was the owner's before the execution of the contract. Following it, a person will come to entertain a doubt (due to his failure to make his intent explicit through specific words) regarding the transfer of its ownership from him. Accordingly, the person will presume the existing situation—which is the continuity of the owner's ownership—to continue. It will be noticed that this argument holds where there is doubt as to whether the owner intended the creation of a endowment or not, or where despite the knowledge of his intention of creating a endowment there is doubt as to whether he has executed the contract and created the cause for its existence. But where we have knowledge of both his intention to create a endowment as well as his having fulfilled what is required to prove its existence, there remains no ground for doubt. Now, if a doubt arises, it will be considered a mere fancy and will have no effect, unless the doubt concerns the validity of the form of recital as the cause creating the endowment and its effect from the point of view of the *Shariah.*

10 Ibn Qudamah, *al-Mughni*, vol. 5, *bab al-waqf; Sharh al-zarqani ala mukhtasar Abi Diya*, vol. 7, *bab al-waqf;* Jafari scholars

include Sayyid al-Yazdi in *Mulhaqat al-urwah*; Sayyid Abu al-Hasan al-Isfahani, *Wasilat al-najat*; Sayyid al-Hakim, *Minhaj al-salihin*; al-Shahid al-Awwal and Ibn Idris also hold this view.

11 *al-Mughni*, vol. 5.

12 al-Hisni al-Shafii, *Kifayat al-akhyar*, vol. 1, *bab al-waqf*; Abu Zuhrah, *Kitab al-waqf*, p. 65, 1959 edition.

13 This distinction has been accepted by a group of leading Jafari scholars, such as the author of al-Sharai, al-Shahdayn (al-Shahid al-Awwal and al-Shahid al-Thani), al-Allamah al-Hilli, and others. According to it, a private endowment is a contract (*aqd*) and requires both an offer and an acceptance. There is no legal and logical obstacle in a endowment being bilateral contract (*aqd*) in certain circumstances and a unilateral declaration (*iqa*) in others, although the author of *al-Jawahir* has opposed it.

14 *Sharh al-zarqani ala mukhtasar Abi Diya*, vol. 7, *bab al-waqf*.

15 Shirbini, *al-Iqna*, vol. 2, *bab al-waqf*; *Fath al-qadir*, vol. 5, *kitab al-waqf*.

16 *Ghayat al-muntaha*, vol. 2, *bab al-waqf*.

17 Allamah al-Hilli, *al-Tadhkirah*, vol. 2; *al-Jawahir*, vol. 4; and *Mulhaqat al-urwah, bab al-waqf*. There is no proof based on the Quran, *Sunnah* or *aql* (reason) concerning the invalidity of contingency (*taliq*) in *aqd* and *iqa*, and those who have considered it void have done so on the basis of consensus (*ijma*), But it is obvious that consensus (*ijma*) is authority only when we cannot identify the basis on which it is based. If its basis is known, its authority will disappear, and the basis on which those who take part in the consensus (*mujtamiun*) have relied will itself be weighed to ascertain its authority. In this case those who take part in the consensus (*mujtamiun*) have relied on the assumption that the meaning of *insha* implies its immediate presence, and the meaning of being contingent on a future event is that the insha is not present, and this entails the presence and absence of *insha* at the same time.

This argument stands refuted on the ground that *insha* is present in actuality and is not contingent upon anything; only its effects will take place in the future on the realization of the contingency, exactly like a will, which becomes operational on death, and a vow that is contingent upon the fulfillment of a condition.

18 The schools differ concerning the disability of a mentally retarded person, as to whether it begins at the commencement of mental retardation when the judge has not yet made a declaration of his disability or if it begins after the declaration has been made. We will discuss it in detail in the chapter on wardship (*bab al-hajr*).

19 *al-Fiqh alal-madhahib al-arbaah*, vol. 2, *bab mabhath al-hajr ala al-safih*.

20 By '*Fath al-qadir*' is meant the book which has become popular by this name, although in actuality, it is part of a collection of four books, one of which is *Fath al-qadir*.

21 Abu Zuhrah, *kitab al-waqf*, p. 92 ff.

22 Ibn Dawayan, *Mansar al-sabil*, p. 6, 1st edition.

23 *Fath al-qadir*, vol. 5; *Sharh al-Zarqani*, vol. 7.

24 Sayyid Kazim observes in *al-Mulhaqat* that if a person has a share in a house, he or she can make a endowment of it for a mosque, and those who come for prescribed prayers will take the permission of the other owners. The benefit of an endowment is not clear.

25 Allamah Hilli, *al-Tadhkirah*; al-Shirani, *al-Mizan*; Muhammad Salam Madkur, *al-Waqf*.

26 *al-Lumah al-Dimashqiyyah, bab al-waqf*.

27 *Sharh al-Zarqani al-Abi Diya*.

28 *al-Mughni*; Abu Zuhrah, *al-Shirani, al-Mizan; Mulhaqat al-urwah*.

29 *Nadhir* means one who takes a vow (*nadhr*); *halif* means one who makes an oath (*half*); *musi* means one who makes a will (*wasiyyah*); and *muqirr* means one who makes a confession.

30 Madkur, *al-Waqf*.

31 Abu Zuhrah, *kitab al-waqf*, p. 162.

32 *al-Jawahir* and al-Ansari, *al-Makasib*.

33 *Fath al-qadir; al-Mughni; al-Tadhkirah*.

34 *al-Mughni; al-Tadhkirah*.

35 *Sharh al-Zarqani* and Abu Zuhrah.

36 *al-Tadhkirah*.

37 *al-Jawahir; al-Madadhdhab*.

38 Abu Zuhrah, p. 245, *kitab al-waqf*. In the view of the condition of option (*shart al-khayar*) and the cases of endowment which are limited by a condition, the difference between the following terms com-

monly used by the Jafari jurisprudent are interesting to note. *Shart al-khayar* is involved where the executor of a contract makes an explicit mention of the word *khayar* (option) while executing the contract and thereby reserves for himself or herself the right to use it. For instance, he or she may say, "I sell this article to you and I shall have the option to annul the sale and revoke it within such and such a period." As to *khayar al-shart*, which is more properly an option that results from the non-fulfillment of a condition, the party executing the contract makes no mention of it in the contract. Rather. it is implicit in some condition that he or she lays down such as where the seller says to the customer, "I sell this thing to you on the understanding that you are a scholar," and later on the buyer turns out to be illiterate. The non-fulfillment of the condition gives the seller the option to avoid the sale and revoke it. He or she may either confirm the sale if he or she wishes or revoke it. The difference between the meanings of the two terms is obviously great.

The difference between *al-aqd al-mutlaq* and *mutlaq al-aqd* will become clear when the different forms of the contract are understood. The kind of contract in which no conditions are stipulated is called *al-aqd al-mutlaq*. Another kind is a conditional contract (*al-aqd al-muqayyad*), which may contain either positive or negative conditions. A contract in general, irrespective of inclusion of any positive or negative conditions, is *mutlaq al-aqd*, a term which includes both *al-aqd al-mutlaq* and *al-aqd al-muqayyad*. Accordingly, *al-aqd al-mutlaq* and *al-aqd al-muqayyad* differ from each other, yet are two kinds that fall under *mutlaq al-aqd* (like man and woman with reference to human being).

39 *Fath al-qadir; al-Mahadhdhab.*

40 *al-Zarqani.*

41 *al-Tarqih; Sharh al-Zarqani.*

42 *Fath al-qadir.*

43 *al-Mahadhdhab.*

44 *al-Mulhaqat.*

45 *Fath al-qadir*, vol. 5, p. 61.

46 *Kitab al-waqf*, p. 372.

47 *al-Mulhaqat; al-Tanqih.*

48 *al-Mughni*, vol. 5, *bab al-waqf.*

49 The difference between property purchased from the income of endowment and property purchased from the sale proceeds of a dilapidated endowment is noteworthy. In the former case, the property purchased will take the place of the endowment sold, while the property purchased from the endowments' income will not take the position of an endowment.

50 *al-Makasib.*

51 Mentioned in al-Khwan saris, *Taqrirat.*

52 *Sharh al-Zarqani ala Abi Diya.*

53 *Kitab al-waqf.*

54 *Wasilat al-najat.*

55 *al-Makasib.* ·

56 al-Khwansari, *Taqrirat.*

57 Refer to *al-Akbar* (Egypt) dated July 7, 1964.

7 INHERITANCE

1 The author of *al-Jawahir* says that the preponderant (*mahhur*) opinion among the Jafari jurists is that those related through the mother do not inherit the compensation for involuntary homicide. As to the right to retaliation (*qisas*) it is inherited by all those who inherit the estate excepting the husband and the wife, who, however, will inherit the compensation in lieu of retaliation.

2 Shaykh Ahmad, Kashif al-Ghita, *Safinat al-naqit, bab al-wasaya.*

3 This is the proof (*dalil*) mentioned by Sayyid al-Hakim in *al-Mustamsak, bab kafn al-mayyit.* Shaykh Muhammad Abu Zuhrah, in *al-Mirath inda al-Jafariyyah,* writes that it is obvious in this situation that the right of the creditor relates to the property itself and supersedes all other rights to that property. Through this observation, the shaykh attributes to the Jafari a consensus concerning the preference of the right of the pledger over funeral expenses, while there is a difference of opinion among them on this issue, and neither of the two differing opinions is preponderant to justify the attribution of consensus.

4 There is a difference between the *mazalim* and usurped (*maghsub*) properties. The *mazalim* are those in which unlawful (*haram*) and lawful (*halal*) wealth has been mixed and the owner is unable to

discern due to his ignorance, while the *maghsub* properties have a known owner. The *mazalim* also differ from those properties whose owners are not known (*majhul al-malik*), because in the latter the ignorance is concerning the property itself and its being mixed with other property is not necessary. The rule for the *mazalim* is to give them away as charity (*sadaqah*) on behalf of its real owner when there is no hope of finding him.

5 Sayyid al-Hakim, *Mustamsak al-urwah*, vol. VII, *masalah* 83, says that this—i.e. pro rata distribution—is customary among them, and this is what is required by the principle of not preferring something without a cause for such preference (*tarjih bila murjjih*) as well as the Tradition of the Prophet (   ), "The debt due to God is better entitled to repayment," is understood not to imply a difference between the debts due to God and the debts due to people. Rather it solely explains that it is obligatory to fulfill *haqq Allah* and that neglecting it is not permissible.

6 *Hashiyat al-Bajuri ala sharh Ibn Qasim*, vol. 1, *fasl al-mayyit*; Abu Zuhrah, *al-Mirath inda al-Jafariyyah*, p. 40, 1955.

7 *al-Tanqih fi fiqh al-Hanabilah*, p. 71, *al-matbaat al-salafiyyah*.

8 Abu Zuhrah, *al-Mirath inda al-Jafariyyah*.

9 *al-Jawahir; al-Masalik, bab al-mirath*.

10 *al-Mughni*, 3rd edition, vol. 6, p. 229.

11 The word 'Muslim' includes all those who pray facing towards the Kabah (*ahl al-qiblah*). Hence a Hanafi, Hanbali, Shafii and Maliki inherits from a Jafari and vice versa, in accordance with Quranic *nass*, the *Sunnah*, and *ijma*. Rather, this rule is among the essentials of the faith, exactly like the obligatory acts of prescribed prayer and fasting.

12 *Al-murtadd an fitrah* is a born Muslim who apostatizes. *Al-murtadd an millah* is one born to parents who practice infidelity to the One God who then becomes a Muslim and later deserts his faith, *al-Mughni*, vol. 6.

13 *al-Mughni*, vol. 6.

14 al-Sayyid Abu al-Hasan, *Wasilat al-najat*; Shaykh Ahmad Kashif al-Ghita, *Safinat al-najat, bab al-irth*.

15 *Ghayat al-muntaha*, vol. 2; al-Shirani, *Mizan; al-Jawahir; al-Masalik*.

16 *Sharh aqaid al-Saduq*, p. 63, 1371 AH.

17 Muslims are cautioned to not be quick to judge others and to follow the verse, "*And do not say to anyone who offers you peace: 'You are not a believer'*" (4:94).

18 *Misbah al-faqih*, vol. 1. It is interesting to note two issues here which are dealt with in detail by the Jafari scholar Aqa Rida al-Hamadani. First, if a person appears to follow Islam and pronounces the two testimonies bearing witness to the One God and His Messenger, Muhammad ( ), although it is not known whether or not it is done hypocritically, without faith in it, or pronounced with real faith, there is no difference of opinion in judging him or her a Muslim. But there be knowledge of its falsity and knowledge that he or she has no faith in God and the Prophet ( ), but only presents himself or her-self as a Muslim hypocritically with a certain purpose in view, will that person be considered a Muslim or not? Aqa Rida al-Hamadani argues that this hypocrite is in reality a non-Muslim although he or she presents himself or herself as a Muslim. It is the duty of the reli-gious scholar to leave his or her reality to God Almighty's judgment and there is no doubt that God will deal with him or her as a non-Muslim because it is presumed that he or she is such in reality. However, Muslims will accept his or her appearance and associate with him or her as a Muslim regarding marriage and inheritance because the *Sunnah* so says. The Tradition is, "The life and property of whoever says *la ilaha ill-Allah* is secure." This implies that he or she will be treated as a Muslim, irrespective of any doubt on the part of the Community or its knowledge of his or her verity or falsity. This is also confirmed by the Prophet's treatment of the hypocrites whom he treated in the same manner in which he treated other Muslims although he knew of their hypocrisy.

Second, the secret behind the consensus of Muslims regarding the infidelity to the One God of a person denying an established rule is that this denial as such necessitates the denial of the Prophet's prophethood. It follows from this that a person making such a denial, on becoming aware that his or her rejection amounts to rejecting the prophethood and the messengerhood of the Prophet ( ), will be doubtlessly considered a non-Muslim. But if he or she is not aware of it—either because of ignorance or his or her belief that his or her denial does not necessitate the denial of prophethood—will he or she be considered a non-Muslim. The summary of Aqa Rida Hamadani's argument is that an ignorant person can be viewed from different perspectives. At times his ignorance is the result of his absorption in sin and absence of attention to what is unlawful like a person who has indulged constantly in fornication from the first day to his present old age and this continuity has developed in him the belief that his act is lawful, not unlawful. Such a person is definitely a disbeliever. At times his ignorance is due to his following a person whom it is not valid to follow. Such a person is also a non-Muslim even if he believes that his denial does not lead to denying the Prophet's messengerhood. Third, it may be that none of the two above-mentioned causes are the result of his ignorance. Rather, his ignorance may be the result of his lack of attention to the station of prophethood or that if he is informed about it, he would desist from his denial. Such a person is doubtlessly a Muslim because he resembles one who disputes regarding a certain thing with the Prophet while not recognizing him, but when he comes to recognize that he is the Prophet, he refrains and is penitent. There are other cases mentioned by the author of *Misbah al-faqih* for further reference.

19 This is when he can acquire knowledge of the facts but neglects to do so. But one incapable of acquiring such knowledge is excusable.

20 The author of *al-Jawahir* has narrated from a large number of Jafar jurists that a culprit in an unintentional homicide is prevented from inheriting the compensation, without being prevented from inheriting from the remaining estate.

21 *al-Mughni*, vol. 6; Abu Zuhrah, *Mirath al-Jafariyyah.*

22 Abd al-Muhal al-Said, *al-Mirath fi al-shariah al-lslamiyyah,* 5th ed., p. 14.

23 *Asabiyyah* is of two types, related to *naab* or *abab*, and by *abab* is meant the *wila* of the manumitter and his children.

24 A single daughter and daughters, according to the Jafari, inherit a sharers as well as by 'return'. Similarly, a single sister and sisters. But a son's daughter/daughters take the share of the person through whom they are related, that is the son.

25 These three categories of heirs are natural, because there is no intermediary between the decedent and his/her parents and children.

Therefore, they belong to the first category. Subsequently, after them come the brothers/sisters and the grandparents, because they are related to the decedent through a single intermediary, the parents. Therefore, they belong to the second category. After them is the category of the paternal and maternal uncles/aunts, because they are related to the decedent through two intermediaries, i.e. the grandfather or the grandmother, and the father or the mother. Therefore, they belong to the third category.

26 Shaykh Abu Zuhrah, *al-Mirath* and *al-Jafari*, has dealt with the proofs mentioned by the Jafari refuting *tasib*, but he has not mentioned this argument of theirs.

27 Full or consanguine sister are residuaries with a daughter, and jointly share the estate with her like the full or consanguine brothers.

28 The famous and great Tabii jurist who has been highly eulogized by the Hanafi, Hanbali, Shafii and Maliki religious scholars. He had met ten Companions.

29 *al-Mughni*, vol. 6, p. 211; *Bidayah wa'l-nihayah*, vol. 2, p. 344.

30 *al-Mughni*, vol. 6, p. 206.

31 The paternal grandmother does not exclude a distant maternal grandmother in the opinion of the Shafii and Maliki schools (e.g. the father's mother with the mother's mother's mother), while in the opinion of the Hanafi and the Hanbali schools he is excluded. See al-Saidi, *al-Mirath fi al-shariat al-Islamiyyah.*

32 *Kashf al-haqaiq fi sharh kanz al-daqaiq*, vol. 2, *bab al-faraid fi fiqh al-Hanafiyyah.*

33 *al-Mughni*, 3rd ed., p. 314.

34 The schools differ regarding the signs of life, whether it is the making of sounds or movement (crying or breast-feeding). That which is important is that life be proved in any possible manner. Hence, if it is proved that the child was born unconscious and possessed life, he will doubtlessly inherit.

35 *al-Mughni*, vol. 6, *bab al-faraid.*

36 *al-Mughni*, *bab al-faraid.*

37 *al-Jawahir*, *bab al-mirath.*

38 This is the earlier opinion of Imam Shafi. His later opinion is that a divorcee of a revocable divorce inherits during the waiting period, while a divorcee of an irrevocable divorce does not.

39 *al-Mughni, bab al-faraid.*

40 *Miftah al-karamah*, vol. 28, p. 115.

41 *al-Iqna fi hall alfaz Abi Shuja*, vol. 2, *bab al-faraid.*

42 *al-Masalik*, vol. 2, *bab al-mirath*.

43 The rule that one who is related through another is excluded by the other, is fully accepted by the Jafari, while the Hanafi, Hanbali, Shafii and Maliki schools consider the uterine brothers an exception. Therefore, according to them, they inherit with the mother although they are related through her. The Hanbalis are of the opinion that a paternal grandmother inherits along with the father, i.e. along with her son. See *al-Mughni*, 3rd. ed., vol. 6, p. 211.

44 According to the Hanafi, Hanbali, Shafii and Maliki schools, the mother will receive one-sixth if the decedent has children or son's children, howsoever low. As regards the daughter's children, their presence or absence is of no effect and they do not stop the mother from inheriting more than one-sixth. According to the Jafari, the daughter's children are like one's own children. Hence, the daughter's daughter is considered a child who excludes the mother from inheriting more than one-sixth, exactly like a son.

45 *al-Iqna fi hall alfaz Abi Shuja*, vol. 2.

46 *Kashf al-haqaiq fi sharh kanz al-daqaiq*, vol. 2, and *al-lgna fi hall alfaz Abi Shuja,* vol 2, *bab al-faraid.*

47 *al-Mughni*, vol. 6, p. 180, 3rd ed.

48 *al-Mughni*, 3rd ed., vol. 6, p. 128; al-Saidi, *al-Muath fi al-shariat al-Islamiyyah*, 5th ed., p. 16.

49 *al-Mughni*, vol. 6, *bab al-faraid, kashf al-haqaiq*, vol. 2, p. 356.

50 *al-Mughni*, 3rd ed., vol. 6, p. 172.

51 *al-Mughni*, 3rd ed., vol. 6, p. 170, 172.

52 *al-Mughni*, 3rd ed., vol. 6, p. 169.

53 *al-Mughni*, 3rd ed., vol. 6, *fasl dhawi al-arham; Kashf al-haqaiq*, vol. 2, p. 255.

54 See *al-Jawahir, al-Masalik* and other books on Jafari jurisprudence. The whole text quoted here is from Shaykh Ahmad Kashif al-Ghita, *Safinat al-najat.*

55 Regarding the inheritance of brothers and sisters in the presence of the paternal grandfather, the Hanafi, Hanbali, Shafii and Maliki schools differ among themselves. This is discussed in the part

on grandparents of this section.

56 A *sahih* grandfather, in the terminology of the Hanafi, Hanbali, Shafii and Maliki jurists is one between whom and the decedent no female intervenes (e.g. the father's father), and a *sahih*, grandmother is one between whom and the decedent no *fasid* grandfather intervenes (e.g. the mother's mother). The intervening of a *fasid* grandfather (e.g. the mother's father's mother) makes the grandmother also a *fasid* grandmother.

57 According to the Hanafi, Hanbali, Shafii and Maliki schools, a daughter excludes uterine brothers and sisters from inheritance, although not full or agnate brothers and sisters, despite their opinion that where a sharer and a residuary are present, the distribution will start with the sharer and the remainder will go to the residuary, and a uterine brother or sister is included in sharers while full and agnate brothers or sisters are residuaries. Therefore, it was obligatory here that the daughter not exclude a uterine brother and sister, or if she were to affect such exclusion, to exclude all kinds of brothers and sisters as observed by the Jafari.

58 The Jafari do not give the return to a uterine brother or sister where they jointly inherit with a full or agnate brother or sister; the return goes only to the latter.

59 On the basis that full or agnate brother's sons are regarded as residuaries and the brother's daughters as distant kindred, the Hanafi, Hanbali, Shafii and Maliki schools concur that if the decedent leaves behind a full or agnate brother's son who is accompanied by his own full sister, he takes the whole estate to her exclusion. *al-Bidayah wal-nihayah*, vol. 2, p. 345; *al-Mughni*, vol. 6, p. 229.

60 *al-Iqna fi hall*, vol. 2; *al-Mughni*, vol. 5, *bab al-faraid*.

61 *al-Mughni*, vol. 6, p. 218.

62 They do not inherit only with the paternal uncle's daughters; their presence is similar to their absence in the presence of paternal uncle's sons. Therefore, the Hanafi, Hanbali, Shafii and Maliki schools concur that if a decedent is survived by a full or agnate paternal uncle's son accompanied by the latter's own full sister, he will be entitled to the whole estate to her exclusion.

63 The Hanafi, Hanbali, Shafii and Maliki jurists have extensively discussed about distant kindred, whom they consider a third cate-

gory of heirs after the sharers and the residuaries. They mention different situations and conditions, which cannot be recorded, enumerated and comprehended easily. Hence the instances mentioned here suffice to present a general outline of them. Those interested in details should refer to *al-Mughni*, 3rd ed. vol. 6, and al-Said, *Kitab al-mirath fi al-shariat al-Islamiyyah*.

64 *al-Mughni*.

65 According to the authors of *al-Masalik* and *al-Jawahir*, the preponderant opinion among Jafari jurist is that the decedent's property will not be distributed until after confirming his death, either by *tawatur* or testimony, or by a report supported by indications capable of leading to such knowledge, or by the expiry of a period after which a like person does not generally stay alive.

66 Al-Shiran, vol. 2, *Kitab al-mizan, bab al-irth*.

67 The details of this will be found in the books of principles of jurisprudence of the Jafari (*bab tanbihat al-istishab*); of these is the popular *al-Rasail* of al-Shaykh al-Ansari, *Taqrirat al-Naini* of Sayyid al-Khui, and *Hashiyat al-Rasail* of Shaykh al-Ashtiyani.

68 See *Miftah, al-karamah, al-Masalik*, and *al-Lumah*.

8 WILLS AND BEQUESTS

1 *Fiqh ala 'l-madhahib al-arbaah*, vol. 3, *bab al-wasiyyah*.

2 *Al-Jawahir, bab al-wasiyyah*.

3 *Al-Jawahir*; Abu Zuhrah, *al-Ahwal*.

4 *Fiqh alal-madhahib al-arbaah*.

5 *Fiqh alal-madhahib al-arbaah*; *al-Ahwal*.

6 *Fiqh alal-madhahib al-arbaah*, vol. 3, *bab al-wasiyyah*.

7 *al-Mughni*, vol. 6; *al-Jawahir*, vol. 5, *bab al-wasiyyah*. A *dhimmi* is a person who pays tax to Muslims, while a *harbi*, according to the Jafari, is one who does not pay tax although he may not be at war with them. According to the other schools, *harbi* is one who takes up arms and attacks travelers on public highways (Ibn Rushd, *al-Bidayah wa al-nihayah*, vol. 2, *bab al-harabah*). Al-Shahid al-Thani in his book *al-Masalik, bab al-wasiyyah*, has said that a bequest in favor of anyone who does not fight us due to our religion, irrespective of his being *dhimmi* or *harbi*, is valid, in accordance with the verse (60: 8,9). Here no difference has been made between a *harbi* and others.

8 Among the Jafari religious jurisprudents, Shaykh Ahmad Kashif al-Ghita favors the Maliki view that it is valid to bequeath in favor of a person not in existence. He remarks in *Wasilat al-najat, bab al-wasiyyah* that there is no hindrance in a testator's making the ownership of a bequest conditional to the coming into existence of the legatee. Thus the legatee will not own it unless after his coming into being, as is the rule in *waqf*. But the author has given this view on the condition that there be no consensus opposing it. Allamah al-Hilli, *al-Tadhkirat; al-Fiqh alal-madhahib al-arbaah; al-Uddah fi fiqh al-Hanabilah, bab al-wasiyyah.*

9 The meaning of the word 'property' differs in relation to the owner. Thus, in relation to a person, it means the power and right of disposal over it in any manner the owner desires; in relation to a mosque, it implies the allocation of its income to its use. Consequently, the observation that 'a mosque or something similar has a legal personality capable of holding property and transferring it,' is meaningless.

10 Allamah, *Tadhkirah; al-Fiqh alal-madhahib al-arbaah.*

11 *al-Mughni*, vol. 6, *bab al-wasiyyah.*

12 The Jafari consider it necessary that if the legatee rejects the bequest during the life of the testator and dies later, and after him the testator also dies, the right of accepting the will is transferred to the heirs of the legatee, because, they say that accepting or rejecting a will has no effect during the life of the testator.

13 Abu Zuhrah, *al-Ahwal, bab al-wasiyyah.*

14 It is stated in *al-Sharai, al-Masalik* and *al-Jawahir* that if a testator uses vague words in his will for which the law has no interpretation, his heirs will be referred to determine their meaning. Thus, if he says, "Give him a share from my property," or "a part" or "a portion of it," or "a little of it" or "much of it," or similar terms which do not denote any fixed quantity either lexically, or legally or customarily, the heirs will give anything considered as having value.

15 *al-Mughni.*

16 *al-Bidayah; al-Tadhkirah, bab al-wasiyyah.*

17 Abu Zuhrah.

18 *al-Mughni; al-Tadhkirah; al-Bidayah.*

19 *al-Mughni.*

20 *al-Mughni.*

21 The Hanafi, Hanbali, Maliki and Shafii schools concur on these dispositions being enforceable from a third of the estate, and the Jafari differ among themselves. Most of their earlier religious scholars considered it enforceable from the original estate, while most of the latter jurisprudents from a third.

22 Often Allamah al-Hilli quotes *al-Mughni* verbatim and relies on it to explain the views of the schools. It has become clear as a result of inquiry and research that scientific co-operation between the Hanafi, Hanbali, Maliki, Shafii and Jafaris was much greater in the past than it is today. Allamah al-Hilli quotes in *al-Tadhkirah* the opinions·of the Hanafi, Hanbali, Maliki and Shafii schools. Zayn al-Din al-Amili, known as al-Shahid al-Thani, used to teach jurisprudence in accordance with five schools in Balbaak, Lebanon in 953/1546, apart from teaching in Damascus and at al-Azhar. Similarly, Shaykh Ali ibn Abd al-Ali known as al-Muhaqqiq al-Thani (d. 940/1533) taught in Syria and al-Azhar. If this proves anything, it proves the unity of Islamic jurisprudence and its sources amongst all the schools.

23 *al-Tadhkirah, bab al-wasiyyah.*

24 *al-Mughn*i, vol. 5, *bab al-iqrar.*

25 Sayyid Kazim al-Yazdi, *Mulhaq hashiyat al-makasib.*

26 *al-Fiqh alal-madhahib al-arbaah*; al-Hilli, *al-Tadhkirah.*

27 The Jafari jurisprudents differ as to whether being just (*adalah*) is a condition for an executor (*wasi*). The prevalent (*mashhur*) view among them is that being just is necessary while researchers consider his being trustworthy and reliable as sufficient. There is a third opinion which says that he should not be a known impious (*fasiq*). The second view is correct, keeping in mind the general nature of the proofs, which include just and non-just persons, as well as the exclusion by these proofs of an untrustworthy person because his dispositions do not fulfill the testator's purpose and harm the legally disable beneficiaries.

28 *al-Mughni,* vol. 6, *bab al-wasiyyah.*

29 Sayyid Abu Hasan, *Wasilat al-najat*; *al-Mughni,* vol. 6, *bab al-wasiyyah.*

30 *al-Mughni,* vol. 9, *bab al-shahadah; al-Jawahir, bab al-shahadah.*

9 LEGAL DISABILITY

1 Last illness (*marad al-mawt*) is also one of the causes, considering that it leads the person in last illness to being prohibited from dispositions exceeding one third of his property. This has already been discussed in the chapter on wills under the title, 'Dispensations of a Critically ill-person'.

2 Every moral duty that is a duty vis-a-vis God Almighty is conditional to mental maturity (*aql*) and puberty (*bulugh*), whereas every economic duty vis-a vis people is not conditional to mental maturity and puberty.

3 *al-Tanqih; al-Tadhkirah.*

4 Shaykh al-Ansari, *al-Makasib.*

5 Sayyid al-Isfahani, *Wasilat al-najat.*

6 At first the Quranic verse mentions the property of the legally incapable while relating it to the second person (*kaf al-mukhatab*) and the second time to the third person (*ha al-ghaib*), alluding thereby that everything owned by an individual has two aspects: firstly, his personal authority over it, and secondly, that he apply it in a manner profitable to himself and the society, or, at the worst, in a manner unharmful to the two. *al-Fiqh alal-madhahib al-arbaah*, vol. 2, *bab al-hajr.*

7 *Wasilat al-najat.*

8 *al-Fiqh alal-madhahib al-arbaah*, vol. 2, *bab al-hajr.*

9 al-Zarqani

10 *Wasilat al-najat.*

11 *al-Tadhkirah.*

12 *al-Jawahir.*

13 Isfahani, *Wasilah.*

14 *al-Muqhni; al-Fiqh alal-madhahib al-arbaah*, vol. 2, *bab al-hajr*; Abu Zuhrah and *al-Jawahir*. The author of *al-Jawahir* observes in the *bab al-hajr* that there is consensus among the Jafari that if mental retardation occurs after the attainment of puberty, the guardianship will be exercised by the judge, and if it continues from childhood, the consensus has been narrated that it belongs to the father and the paternal grandfather. But the truth is that there is a difference of opinion in the latter case, and a group of scholars has explicitly mentioned that the guardianship belongs to the two.

15 *Taqrirat al-Naini* in al-Khwansari, *Taqrirat* (1357 AH., vol. 1, p. 324) states that the truth of that the guardianship of the father is a proven fact, even if it entails disadvantage or loss for the child. But the compiler of this work narrates from his teacher, al-Nain, that he retracted this opinion after having been emphatic about it earlier.

16 *al-Tadhkirah, baba al-hajr.*

17 *al-Jawahir, al-Tanqih*; *al-Fiqh alal-madhahib al-arbaah.*

18 Vol. 7, p. 229, *bab al-hajr bi sabab al-daya* in *Fath al-qadir.*

19 *Fath al-qadir*; Ibn Abidin; *al-Fiqh alal-madhahib al-arbaah*; al-Sanhuri, *Masadir al-haqq*, vol. 5.

20 *al-Tadhkirah*; *al-Fiqh alal-madhahib al-arbaah.*

21 *al-Tadhkirah, bab al-taflis.*

22 *al-Tadhkirah* and *Fath al-qadir.*

23 *Fath al-qadir; al-Tadhkirah; Fiqh alal-Tadhkirah; al-Tawahir.*

24 *al-Jawahir.*

25 *al-Jawahir.*

26 *al-Jawahir; al-Tadhkirah.*

10 MARRIAGE

1 There is also another version of this Tradition. According to this version a woman came to the Prophet and said, "Get me married." The Prophet then announced, "Who is ready to marry her?" One of those present stood up and said, "I am." The Prophet then asked him, "What can you give her?" He replied, "I have nothing." The Prophet said, "No." The woman repeated her request and the Prophet repeated the announcement but none stood up except the same man. The woman again repeated her request and the Prophet announced again. Then the Prophet asked him, "Have any knowledge of the Quran?" He replied, "Yes, I do." The Prophet then said, "I marry her to you (*zawwajtukaha*) in exchange for your teaching her what you know well of the Quran." Therefore, the word used was *al-zawaj*, not *al-milk.*

2 Abu Zuhrah, *al-Ahwal al-shakhsiyyah*, p. 36, 1948.

3 See the Quran 28:27; 33:37.

4 *al-Fiqh alal-madhahib al-arbaah*, vol. 4. The discussion regarding conditions of marriage *al-Ahwal al-shakhsiyyah* by Muhammad

Muhyi al-Din Abd al-Hamid.

5 Abu Zuhrah, *al-Ahwal al-shakhisyyah*, p. 27.

6 This is the view of most of the Jafari scholars. But some of them such as Ibn Idris among the early jurists, and Sayyid Abu al-Hasan al-Isfahani among the recent ones, are of the opinion that the contract is valid and the condition is void. Accordingly, the Jafari scholars in both their views are on the whole like the scholars of the other schools. *al-Fiqh alal-madhahib al-arbaah*, vol. 4; *al-Tadhkirah* by Hilli, vol. 2; *al-Masalik*, vol. 2.

7 *al-Tadhkirah* by Hilli, vol. 2.

8 *Bidayat al-mujtahid* by Ibn Rushd; *Maqsad al-nabih* by Ibn Jamaah al-Shafi.

9 Muhammad Yusuf Musa, in his book *al-Ahwal al-shakhsiyyah* (1958) page 74, states that the Jafari consider the presence of witnesses as necessary for marriage. He considers the Jafari and the Hanafi, the Shafii and the Hanbali schools to hold a common view. But there is no source of reference for what he states.

10 *al-Fiqh alal-madhahib al-arbaah*.

11 Sayyid Abu al-Hasan al-Isfahani, a Jafari, *al-Wasilah*.

12 Hilli, *al-Tadhkirah*.

13 Ibn Qudamah, *al-Mughni, bab al-hijr*, vol. 4.

14 Ibn Abidin, 1326 AH, *bab al-hijr*, vol. 5, p. 100.

15 Ibn Qudamah, *al-Mughni*, vol. 6, chapter on marriage.

16 According to the Jafari, an invalid condition in a non-marriage contract results in the contract becoming void. But in a contract of marriage such a condition does not cause the contract nor the dowry to be void unless a choice is given regarding the voiding of the contract or a condition is laid that none of the consequences of the contract will follow, which is against the spirit of the contract. They have argued on the basis of reliable traditions that there is a difference between a marriage contract and other forms of contract. Some of the jurists have said that the secret of this difference is that marriage is not an exchange in the true sense of the word as in the case of other forms of contract. The Jafari scholars have extensive discussions on these conditions the like of which are not found in books of other schools. Those who want further information regarding these conditions may refer to *al-Makasib* of Shaykh Murtada al-Ansari and *Taqrirat al-Naini* of al-

Khwansari, vol. 2, and the third part of *Fiqh al-Imam al-Sadiq* by Javad Mughanniyyah.

17 In *Farq al-zawaj* of Ustadh Ali al-Khafif, it is stated that the Jafari consider these kind of conditions as void. This is a mistake which has been caused as a result of confusing these kind of conditions with those which negate the spirit of the contract.

18 Apart from this, the statements from the jurists in *al-Bulghah*, *al-Sharai* and *al-Jawahir* (Chapter on Marriage) indicate on this point that living together *prima facie* shows the presence of marriage.

19 *Bidayat al-mujtahid*, vol. 2; *al-Fiqh alal-madhahib al-arbaah*, vol. 4, chapter on marriage.

20 *Kitab ikhtilaf Abi Hanifah*; Ibn Abi Layla, chapter on marriage.

21 *al-Mughni*, vol. 6, chapter on marriage.

22 *Multaqa al-anhur*, vol. 1, chapter on marriage.

23 *al-Mughni*, vol. 7; *al-Sharani, al-Mizan*, chapter on *mulaanah*.

24 *al-Jawahir*, chapter on divorce.

25 Muhammad Muhyi al-Din Abd al-Hamid, *al-Ahwal al-shakhsiyyah*.

26 *Bidayat al-mujtahid*; *Hashiyat al-Bajuri, bab al-rida*.

27 *al-Fiqh alal-madhahib al-arbaah*.

28 *al-Fiqh alal-madhahib al-arbaah*.

29 Waiting period is a period of waiting prescribed by the *Shariah* to be observed by a woman on divorce or the death of her husband. The waiting period for divorce is three months (three menstrual cycles), for death, four months and ten days.

30 *Bidayat al-mujtahid*.

31 *al-Masalik*, vol. 2, chapter on divorce.

32 Hilli, *al-Tadhkirah*, vol. 1, chapter on the prescribed pilgrimage; *Bidayat al-mujtahid*, chapter on marriage.

33 Abu Zuhrah, *al-Ahwal*.

34 *al-Mughni*, vol. 6, chapter on marriage.

35 *al-Tadhkirah*, vol. 2; *al-Mughni*, vol. 2, chapter on *hijr*.

36 Ibn Abidin, vol. 2, chapter on marriage.

37 Shahid al-Thani in *al-Masalik* quotes al-Shaykh al-Mufid saying that the criterion regarding the annulment of marriage by a woman is that her husband be incapable of intercourse with her, irrespective of his ability regarding other women. The general notion sup-

ports this view.

38 *Al-ratq* means the presence of obstruction in the vaginal opening making intercourse difficult. *Al-qarn* (lit. horn) means the presence of a horn-like protrusion inside the vaginal passage. *Al-afal* means a fleshy obstruction in it. *Al-ifda* means the condition of merging of anal and vaginal passages.

39 *al-Wasilah*.

40 *al-Wasilah*.

41 *Majma al-anhur; al-Mughni*, chapter on marriage.

42 *al-Mughni, al-Wasilah*.

43 *Maqsad al-nabih*.

44 *al-Fiqh alal-madhahib al-arbaah*.

45 *al-Mughni; Bidayat al-mujtahid*.

46 *Maqsad al-nabih; Majma al-anhur; al-Fiqh ala l-madhahib al-arbaah*.

47 Abu Zuhrah, *al-Ahwal* .

48 Including Sayyid Abu al-Hasan al-Isfahani, *al-Wasilah*; Shaykh Ahmad Kashif al-Ghita, *Safinat al-najat*.

49 *al-Ahwal; Rahmat al-ummah*, al-Dimashqi.

50 The author of *al-Jawahir* has observed about the third problem in this regard. That is, whenever there is an agreement on a thing, that thing shall be the dowry and shall in fact become the property of the wife, either by itself or in the form of a debt, immediately or in a deferred form, and all those rules which apply to dowry specified in the contract, shall apply to it.

51 *al-Mughni*, vol. 6, chapter on marriage.

52 *al-Fiqh alal-madhahib al-arbaah*.

53 *Maqsad al-nabih*.

54 al-Mughni and Ibn Abidin.

55 *al-Jawahir* and Ibn Abidin.

56 *Mulhaqat al-urwah* of Sayyid Kazim, chapter on *qada*; *al-Ahwal* by Abu Zuhrah.

57 The Jafari work *al-Jawahir, bab al-zawaj, ahkam al-awlad* and *al-Ahwal al-shakhsiyyah* of Muhammad Muhyi al-Din, p.476.

58 *al-Durar sharh al-Ghurar*, vol.1, p.307.

59 *al-Wasilat al-kubra* of Sayyid Abu al-Hasan, *bab al-zawaj, fasl al-awlad*.

60 *Al-Mughni* of Ibn Qudamah, 3rd edition, vol. 7, p. 477, and al-*al-Fiqh alal-madhahib al-arbaah*, 1st ed. vol. 4, p. 523, mention the maximum period of gestation according to the Malikis to be five years.

61 *Al-Mughni*, 3rd ed. vol.7, p.477.

62 *Al-Ahwal al-shakhsiyyah*, p.474.

63 See *al-Jawahir, al-Masalik, al-Hadaiq* and other Jafari books.

64 *Al-Mughni*, 3rd. ed. vol. 8, p. 211.

65 *Al-Jawahir, al-Hadaiq* and other Jafaris works.

66 *Al-Mughni*, vol.7, p. 483, vol. 6, p. 534; and the Jafari works *al-Jawahir* and *al-Masalik*.

67 *Al-Mughni*, vol. 8, p.185.

68 See *Majmal-bayan fi tafsir al-Quran*.

69 *Al-Rasail*, al-Shaykh al-Ansari, chapter on al-Baraah.

70 *Ibid.*, chapter on *asl al-sihhah*.

71 *Al-Mughni*, 3rd. ed., vol. 6, p. 644.

72 *Al-Jawahir*.

73 The Jafari work *al-Lumah*, vol. 2, the chapter on *hudud*; the Hanafi, Hanbali, Maliki and Shafii work *al-Mughni*, vol. 8, p. 198 ff.

74 *Al-Mughni*, 3rd. ed., vol.6, p.578.

75 *Al-Mughni*, vol. 6, p. 577, and the Jafari work *al-Masalik*, vol. 1, chapter on marriage, *fasl al-musaharah*.

76 *Majmal-bayan fi tafsir al-Quran*.

77 *Al-Mughni*, vol. 7, p. 439.

78 *Al-Masalik*, vol. 2, *fasl ahkam al-awlad*.

79 *Al-Mirath fi al-shariat al-Islamiyyah* of al-Ustadh Ali Hasb Allah, 2nd. ed. p. 94; Ibn Abidin and Ibn Qudamah in *al-Mughni*, chapter on inheritance, *fasl al-asabat* (male relatives).

80 The letter of al-Sayyid al-Hakim, dated 7th Ramadan 1377, in reply to a question regarding this issue.

81 *Al-Jawahir; al-Masalik, bab al-zawaj; al-hidanah*.

82 *Al-Mughni*, vol. 9, *bab al-hidanah*.

83 The child's right to choose to live with the father or the mother on reaching the age is not in conflict with the [Lebanese] law according to which the age of majority is eighteen years because this age has been considered by the law as a condition for marriage and not for choosing between the parents.

84 *Al-Fiqh alal-madhahib al-arbaah*, vol. 4; *al-Masalik*, vol. 2.

85 *Al-Ahwal al-shakhsiyyah* by Abu Zuhrah.

86 *Rahmat al-ummah fi ikhtilaf al-aimah.*

87 *Al-Ahwal al-shakhsiyyah* by Abu Zuhrah

88 The author of *al-Masalik* has inclined towards the absence of any compensation for custody and the author of *al-Jawahir* has inclined towards its presence. Considering that there is no explicit reference in the *Shariah* about compensation being obligatory, and considering that it is not customary to pay compensation for custody, the opinion expressed by the author of *al-Masalik* appears to be more correct.

89 The Hanafis state that is she falls sick at her husband's home, she is entitled to maintenance and if she falls sick before consummation and it is not possible to shift her to his home, she will not be entitled to maintenance. This opinion of the Hanafis is in accordance with their basic principle that maintenance is a compensation for her confining herself to her husband's home.

90 The Malikis state that the wife's maintenance ceases during the husband's indigence irrespective of consummation. If he becomes well-off later on, she does not have the right to claim maintenance of the period during which he was indigent.

91 By *fard* is meant the specific share of inheritance decreed for an heir by the Quran.

92 Ibn Abidin.

93 *Al-Ahwal*, Abu Zuhrah.

94 *Al-Ahwal*, 1942, p. 269, 272 by Muhammad Muhyi al-Din Abd al-Hamid.

95 Al-Bajuri, 1343 AH, vol. 2, p. 197.

96 Egyptian law act 25, 1929.

97 *Al-Jawahir*, vol. 5.

98 *Safinat al-najat, bab al-daman* by Shaykh Ahmad Kashif al-Ghita.

99 *Al-Durar fi sharh al-ghurar*, vol. 1, *bab al-nafaqat.*

100 *Al-tasib* applies in situations where the total shares of the decreed sharers fall short of the total legacy. Here, the Hanafi, Hanbali, Shafii and Maliki schools assign the balance to be inherited by distant relatives as the nearer relatives have already received their decreed shares and are not entitled to anything in addition to their

decreed shares. For example, if a person dies leaving behind a daughter and an uncle, the decreed share of the daughter being half, the other half will be inherited by the uncle and the daughter will not be entitled to inherit more than her decreed share. The Jafar do not accept this doctrine and in the above example entitle the daughter to inherit the whole heritable interest to the exclusion of the father's uncle. They apply the rule: the nearer in degree excludes the remote.

101 *Maqsad al-bayyinah, bab nafaqat al-aqarib.*

102 Some judges distribute the maintenance of a relative between those on whom his maintenance is obligatory in accordance with the financial capacity of each. Therefore, if an indigent father has two sons, one of them very rich, and the other merely well-off, the first will contribute more than the second to the father's maintenance. The Hanafis give no weight to this difference in financial capacity and consider the two equally liable after their capacity has been proved. The author of *al-Jawahir* also agrees saying that if he has a son who is presently well-off and another son who is in the course of becoming such, the two will contribute equally because the applicable *adillah* are unconditional.

103 *Al-Mughni*, vol. 7.

104 Abu Zuhrah.

105 *Al-Mughni*, vol. 7; *al-Jawahir*, vol. 5.

106 *Al-Ahwal...*

107 *Maqsad al-nabih.*

108 *Al-Mughni*, vol. 7.

11 DIVORCE

1 The Hanafi and the Maliki schools are explicit regarding the validity of a divorce by an intoxicated person. Two opinions have been narrated from a Shafii and Imam Ahmad Hanbal, the preponderant among them is that the divorce does take place.

2 Abu Zuhrarah, pp. 283-286.

3 Ibn Rushd, *Bidayat al-mujtahid*, vol. 2, p. 74.

4 al-Ustadh al-Khafif writes in his book *Farq al-zawaj* (p. 57), "The Jafari accept the validity of a divorce by a *safih* if effected by the permission of his guardian as expressly mentioned in *Sharh Sharai al-Islam.*" There is no mention of this statement in the said book.

Rather, such a statement is not present in any Jafari book and that which is mentioned in *Sharh Sharai al-Islam* is that the *safih* husband is entitled to divorce with out the permission of his guardian. See *al-Jawahir*, vol. 4, *bab al-hijr*.

5 *Nifas* means the vaginal discharge of blood at the time of birth or thereafter for a maximum period of ten days according to the Jafari, forty days according to the Hanbalis and the Hanafis and sixty days according to the Shafii and Malikis.

6 *Al-Mughni*, vol. 7, p. 98, 3rd edition.

7 The author of *Tasis al-nazar* (1st ed., p. 49) has narrated from Imam Malik that he has observed that if a person resolves to divorce his wife, the divorce takes place by mere resolution even if he does not pronounce it.

8 *Al-Jawahir*, vol. 5, *sighat al-talaq*.

9 *Al-Jawahir*, Ibn Abidin; *Maqsad al-nabih*.

10 Al-Ustadh al-Khafif, *Farq al-zawaj* (1958), p. 159.

11 *Al-Mughni*, vol. 7.

12 *Al-Fiqh alal-madhahib al-arbaah*, vol. 4.

13 Abu Zuhrah.

14 *Al-Mughni*, vol. 7.

15 *Al-Jawahir* and *al-Fiqh alal-madhahib al-arbaah*.

16 *Al-Mughni*, vol. 7.

17 The Jafari state that when the husband, a born Muslim, apostatizes, his wife will observe the waiting period of widowhood, and if he apostatizes by returning to his former faith, she will observe a divorcee's waiting period.

18 As mentioned earlier, the Jafari do not consider the waiting period obligatory for a menopausal woman. But they say that if he divorces her and she menstruates once before reaching menopause, she will complete her waiting period after two more months. The Hanafi, Hanbali, Shafii and Maliki schools observe that she will start observing the waiting period anew, for three months, and her menstruation will not be included in the waiting period.

19 *Majma al-anhur*.

20 *Al-Mughni*, vol. 7, *bab al-idad*.

21 *Al-Fiqh alal-madhahib al-arbaah*, vol. 4.

22 The authors of *al-Jawahir* and *al-Masalik* have mentioned the

prevalent opinion in this regard, acting in accordance with the Tradition narrated by Sawdah ibn Kulayb. Both have discussed this issue at length and narrated other views which are not *mashhur* and which most Jafari jurisprudents have deliberately ignored.

23 *Al-Mughni*, vol. 6; *Majma al-anhur*.

24 The following observation has been made in *al-Jawahir* (vol. 5, *bab al-idad*). The waiting period of a non-Muslim woman is exactly like that of a free Muslim woman in regard to both divorce and death. I have not come across any difference of opinion because of the generality of the proofs and an explicit Tradition from Jafari Sadiq from *al-Sarraj*, who asked him, "What is the waiting period of a Christian woman whose husband, a Christian, has died." He replied, "Her waiting period is four months and ten days."

25 Al-Shirani, *Mizan, bab al-idad wa al-istibra*.

26 This is when she does not raise the issue before a judge. But if she suffers as a result of his absence and files a complaint in court demanding separation, both Imams Hanbal and Malik allow her to be divorced in such a situation. Details follow under the section on divorce by a judge.

27 See *al-Jawahir*, appendices to *al-Urwah* of Sayyid Kazim, *al-Wasilah* of Sayyid Abu al-Hasan, and other books on Jafari jurisprudence. But the greater part of our discussion is based on *al-Wasilah*, because it is both comprehensive and lucid.

28 *Al-Mughni*, vol. 7; *al-Fiqh alal-madhahib al-arbaah*.

29 The authors of *al-Jawahir* and *al-Masalik* state that the *mashhur* opinion among the Jafari jurisprudents is that a conditional *rajah* is not valid. The author of *al-Masalik* (vol. 2, *bab al-talaq*) says that the more *mashhur* opinion is that *rajah* will not take place, and even those who consider contingent divorce valid hold this opinion by placing *rajah* alongside *nikah*.

30 *Majma al-anhur, bab al-rajah*.

31 *Bidayat al-mujtahid*, vol. 2.

32 Ibn Abidin

33 *Al-Mughni*, vol. 7, *bab al-rajah*.

34 See *Kitab al-qada* by Shaykh Abd al-Karim Maghniyyah.

35 For the meanings of these terms, see "Marriage According to Major Schools of Islamic Jurisprudence," Part 2.

36 *Al-Ahwal al-shakhsiyya*, p. 358 by Abu Zuhrah.

37 *Al-Ahwal al-shakhsiyya* by Abu Zuhrah; *Farq al-zawaj* by al-Khafif.

38 Isfahani, *al-Wasilah, bab al-zawaj* under *al-qawl fi al-kufr*.

39 *Al-Masalik*.

40 *Rawdat al-jannat*, vol. 4 writing about Aqa Muhammad Baqir al-Behbahani.

41 The secret of stipulating this period is that a wife has a right to sex at least once every four months. It has been said that the difference goes back to the interpretation of the Quran. Here, there are those who say that the verse has not stipulated any period for *ila* and others who consider it necessary that four months pass before the judge may warn the husband either to restore conjugal ties or to divorce her and this obviously requires a period of more than four months, even though by a moment.

42 *Bidayat al-mujtahid*.

43 *Farq al-zawaj*, al-Khafif.

44 Most Jafari jurisprudents state that the judge will allow the husband four months time from the day the matter was brought to his notice, and not from the day of the oath.

GLOSSARY WITH TRANSLITERATION

A

abbadtu (*abbadtu*): "I have perpetually settled..."

ada (*adā*): prescribed prayers performed on time

adha (*adhā*): hurting someone

adhan (*adhān*): call to prescribed prayer

adil (*ādil*): just

afal or *amal* (*afᶜāl* or *ᶜamal*): obligatory acts

afal, al- (*al-afal*): fleshy obstruction in the vaginal passage

ahd (*ᶜahd*): pledge

ahkam al-wadiyyah (*aḥkām al-waḍᶜiyyah*): laws of obligation

ahl al-kitab (*ahl al-kitāb*): People of the Book

ahl al-qiblah (*ahl al-qiblah*): those who pray facing towards the qiblah

ajir (*ajīr*): hired

amal (*ᶜamal*): obligatory act

amid (*ᶜāmid*): wilful defrauder

amm (*ᶜamm*): general

anan, al- (*al-ᶜanan*): impotence

ankahtu (*ankaḥtu*): "I gave in marriage..."

aqd al-mutlaq (*ᶜaqd al-mutlaq*): conditional contract containing neither positive nor negative conditions

aqilah, al- (*al-ᶜāqilah*): paternal relatives

aql (*ᶜaql*): sanity

arkan (*arkān*): pillars

arkan wafaraid (*arkān farā²iḍ*): essentials of the prescribed prayer

Arnah (*ᶜArnah*): one of the boundary points of Arafat

asabah bi nafsiha (*ᶜaṣabah bi nafsihā*): residuary by himself

asabah maa ghayriha (*ᶜasabah maᶜa ghayrihā*): residuary along with another

asabat, al- (*al-ᶜaṣabāt*): residuaries

ashwat (*ashwāṭ*): walking between Safa and Marwah

asr (*ᶜasr*): afternoon prescribed prayer

awl (*ᶜawl*): shares exceed the estate

awlad (*awlād*): children

awlad al-awlad (*awlād al-awlād*) children's children

awqaf (*awqāf*): endowment

awrah (*ᶜawrah*): private parts of the body

591

aydi (*aydī*): hands

ayni (*ᶜaynī*): obligatory individually

ayyam al-bid (*ayyām al-bīḍ*): moonlit days or the 13th, 14th and
   15th of each lunar month.

ayyam al-tashriq (*ayyām al-tashriq*): 11th, 12th, 13th of Dhil Hajjah

azaim al-arbaah, al- (*al-ᶜaẓāᵓim al-arbaᶜah*): four chapters
   of the Quran which contain verses that require a prostration when
   recited.

B

badhl, al- (al-badhl): bequest

baghi (*bāghī*): rebel

baladi (*baladī*): person who starts on the longer pilgrimage from the
   town of the deceased

baligh al-aqil (*bāligh al-ᶜaql*): sane adult

basmillah (*basmillah*): "In the Name of God, the Merciful, the
   Compassionate"

batil (*bāṭil*): invalid, void

bulugh (*bulūgh*): puberty, maturity

D

daif (*ḍāᶜīf*): weak

darar (*ḍarar*): harm

Dhat al-Irq (Dhāt al-ᶜIrq): a station on the way to Makkah where
   the pilgrim assumes the sacred state (*ihrām*)

dhawi al-qubra (*dhawqī al-qubrā*): those who have descended from
   Hashim through their fathers irrespective of whether they are rich
   or poor.

dhawu al-furud (*dhawū al-furūḍ*): sharers in inheritance

dhibh (*dhibḥ*): sacrifice

Dhu al-Hulayfah (Dhū al-Ḥulayfah): a station on the way to
   Makkah where the pilgrim assumes the sacred state (*ihrām*),
   specifically here, Masjid al-Shajarah

Dhu al-Majaz (Dhū al-Majāz): one of the boundaries of Arafat

diyyah (*diyyah*): compensation

dua (*duᶜā*): prayer, supplication

dual-mathur, al- (*al-duᶜā al-maᵓthur*): prayer recommended by
   Tradition

F

fajir (fājir): libertine
fajr (fajr): dawn prescribed prayer
fajr al-sadiq, al- (al-fajr al-ṣādiq): daybreak
fakk al-milk (fakk al-milk): release from ownership
faqir (faqīr): someone who owns less than the minimum even if he is
  physically fit and earning
faraid (farāʾid): prescribed daily prayers
faraid al-wudu (farāʾid al-wuḍūʾ): essentials of shorter ablution
fard (farḍ): obligatory duty, obligatory prescribed prayer
fasiq (fāsiq): transgressor
fawr, al- (al-fawr): dispatch without delay
fidyah (fidyah): substitute
fiqh (fiqh): jurisprudence
furud (furūḍ): duties

G

Ghamrah, al- (Ghamrah, al-): a station on the way to Makkah
  where the pilgrim assumes the sacred state (*ihrām*)
ghanimah (ghanīmah): spoils of war acquired by Muslims
gharimum, al- (al-ghārimun): debtors who have fallen into debt for
  some non-sinful cause
ghayr al-makul wal malbus (ghayr al-maʾkūl waʾl-malbūs): made of
  something which is neither edible nor wearable
ghayr maghsub (ghayr maghṣūb): legitimately owned
ghayr mukallaf (ghayr mukallaf): free of obligation
ghayr mumayyiz (ghayr mumayyiz): under age of discretion
ghusalah (ghusālah): used water when it flows out freely
ghusl (ghusl): bath lustration
ghusl al-hayd (ghusl al-ḥayḍ): bath lustration following
  menstruation
ghusl al-janabah (ghusl al-janābah): bath lustration following sexual
  emission
ghusl al-mustahadah (ghusl al-mustaḥāḍah): bath lustration with
  intermittent discharge of blood
ghusl al-tawbah (ghusl al-tawbah): bath lustration with the
  intention of repentance

H

habastu (ḥabastu): "I have detained..."

habs (*ḥabs*): detention

hadath (*ḥadath*): state of minor impurity, prohibited from performing the prescribed prayer

hadd (*ḥadd*): punishment

hady (*ḥady*): sacrificial animal for offering during the prescribed pilgrimage

haid (*ḥāʾiḍ*): menstruating woman

hajar al-aswad (*ḥajar al-aswad*): the Black Stone

hajj (*ḥajj*): the prescribed pilgrimage

hajj al-ifrad (*ḥajj al-ifrād*): the prescribed pilgrimage for those who live in Makkah with no sacrifice obligatory

hajj al-mustahabb (*ḥajj al-mustaḥabb*): recommended pilgrimage

hajj al-qiran (*ḥajj al-qirān*): the prescribed pilgrimage for those who live in Makkah except to the Hanafi school which disapproves of this type of prescribed pilgrimage for people of Makkah. The sacrifice is obligatory according to the Hanafi, Hanbali, Shafii and Maliki schools. For the Jafari the sacrifice is only obligatory if they bring their animal with them at the time of assuming the sacred state.

hajj al-tamattu (*ḥajj al-tamattuᶜ*): the prescribed pilgrimage of those who live outside of Makkah

hajr (*ḥajr*): legal disability

hakim (*ḥākim*): judge

hakim al-shar (*ḥākim al-sharᶜ*): judge

halif (*ḥālif*): one who swears an oath

halq (*ḥalq*): complete shaving of the head

hamd (*ḥamd*): to praise God

Hanifi (Ḥanifi): Named after Imam Abu Hanafi (699-767 CE), theologian, jurist and traditionist, founder of one of the four major schools of Sunni Law, the Hanifi.

hanak, al- (*al-ḥanak*): where the end of the turban hangs down over the chest

Hanbali (Ḥanbalī): Named after Imam Ahmad Hanbal (241-855 CE), theologian, jurist and traditionist, founder of one of the four major schools of Sunni law. His most notable disciple was Ibn Taymiyya whose thoughts formed the basis for Wahhabism, the Hanbali school.

haqq al-khayar (*ḥaqq al-khayār*): option in a contract of sale

haqq al-nas (*ḥaqq al-nās*): creditors

haqq Allah (*ḥaqq Allāh*): religious duties

haraj (*ḥaraj*): distress

haram (*ḥarām*): sacred area roughly within a radius of six miles with the Kabah at the center

harbi (*ḥarbī*): one who takes up arms against Muslims

harwalah (*harwalah*): running

hayd (*ḥayḍ*): state of menstruation

hibah, al- (*al-hibah*): marriage with the condition that the amount payable as dower is also mentioned

hijamah (*ḥijāmah*): cupping

hijjat al-Islam (*ḥijjat al-Islām*): prescribed pilgrimage

hill al-awwal, al- (*al-ḥill al-awwal*): first relief from the restrictions of the sacred state

hill al-thani, al- (*al-ḥill al-thāni*): second relief from the restrictions of the sacred state

Hiyad, al- (al-Hiyād): boundary of Muḍalifah towards the valley of Muḥassir

hiyazah, al- (*al-ḥiyāzah*): acquisition

hujb (*ḥujb*): exclusion

hujb al-hirman (*ḥujb al-ḥirmān*): exclusion from the actual inheritance itself

hujb al-nuqsan (*ḥujb al-nuqṣān*): prevention from a part of the inheritance

hujjaj (*ḥujjāj*): pilgrims

hunut (*hunut*): seven parts of the dead body to be rubbed with camphor, namely the forehead, the two palms, the knees and heads of the big toes of the feet

I

iarah, al- (*al-iᶜārah*): lending

ibadah (*ᶜibādah*): worship, Islamic duties

ibn al-sabil (*ibn al-sabīl*): traveler cut off from his or her hometown and means

id (*ᶜīd*): festival

id al-adha (*ᶜīd al-aḍḥā*): 10th of Dhil Hijjah

id al-fitr (*ᶜīd al-fiṭr*): end of the month of Ramadan

Idah (Idah): southern boundary of the sacred area of Makkah, 12 kms from Makkah

idayn (*ᶜīdayn*): two festivals

idtiba (*idtibā*): wearing the *riḍā* whose hanging sides are drawn under the right armpit and then thrown over the left shoulder *idtirari* (*idtirārī*): beyond one's control

iflas (*iflās*): insolvency

ifda, al- (*al-ifdā*ʾ): merger of anal and vaginal passages

iftar (*ifṭār*): breaking the prescribed fast at sunset

ihram (*iḥrām*): sacred dress, pilgrim sanctity

ihsar (*iḥṣār*): some hindrance which keeps one from completing
   the rites of the prescribed pilgrimage

ihtidar (*iḥtiḍār*): dying person made to face the *qiblah*

ihtiyat (*iḥtiyāṭ*): caution

ijarah, al- (*al-ijārah*): hiring

ijma (*ijmāᶜ*): consensus

ijma al-mahki (*ijmāᶜ al-maḥki*): narrated consensus

ijtihad (*ijtihād*): strenous endeavor to reason

ikhtiyari (*ikhtiyārī*): choice

ila, al- (*al-ilā*ʾ): oath to refrain from sex with one's wife

imam (*imām*): leader

imsak (*imsāk*): refrain

iqamah (*iqāmah*): declaration to perform the prescribed prayer

Ir (ᶜIr): hill near the place of the appointed time outside Madinah

irtimas (*irtimās*): bath ablution of immersion in water

isha (ᶜ*ishā*ʾ): night prescribed prayer

isra, al- (*al-isrā*ʾ): nocturnal journey

istibahat al-salat (*istibāḥat al-ṣalāṭ*): permissibility of the prescribed
   prayer

istighfar (*istighfār*): seek God's forgiveness

istihbaban (*istiḥbāba*): preferably

istihadah (*istiḥādah*): intermittent bleeding

istihalah (*istiḥālah*): alteration

istilam (*istilām*): greeting the Black Stone by drawing one's hands
   over it

istimna, al- (*al-istimnā*ʾ): masturbation

istinabah (*istinābah*) deputation

istirahah (*istirāhah*): rest

istisqa (*istisqā*ʾ): prayer for rain

istitaah (*istiṭāᶜah*): ability

itikaf (*iᶜtikāf*): retreating to a mosque in the last ten days of
   Ramadan

itlaq (*iṭlāq*): generality, absoluteness

izar (*izār*): loin cloth covering for the whole body

J

jabb, al- (*al-jabb*): state of mutilation of the male organ

Jafari (Ja^cfari): Named after Imam Abu Abd Allah Jafar ibn Muhammad (700-765 CE), religious scholar and the last imam recognized by b oth Twelver and Ismaili Shiites, he is the founder of the major Shiite school of law, the Jafari. He was the teacher of Imam Abu Hanafi

jahil (*jāhil*): one who is ignorant

Jam (Jam^c): another name for Muḍalifah

jamaah (*jamaah*): congregation

jamarat al-aqabah (*jamarat al-^caqabah*): first idol which is stoned in Mina and the idol nearest Muḍalifah

jamarat al-ula (*jamarat al-ūlā*): farthest stone or idol from Makkah and near Masjid al-Khayf

jamarat al-wusta (*jamarat al-wusṭā*): middle stone idol

janabah (*janābah*): state of major impurity following sexual emission

Jaranah, al- (al-Jaranah): eastern boundary of the sacred area of Makkah, 16 kms from Makkah

jayb, al- plural-*juyab, al-* (*al-jayb*, plural-*al-juyab*): veil which covers the chest

jilbab, al- plural-*jalabib, al-* (*al-jilbāb*, plural-*al-jalabib*): garment or shirt

jiryah (*jiryah*): flowing portion of water

Juhfah, al- (al-Juḥfah): a station on the way to Makkah where the pilgrim assumes the sacred state (*ihrām*)

jumhur (*jumhūr*): majority

junub (*junub*): person in state of impurity following sexual emission

junun, al- (*al-junūn*): insanity

K

kafaah, al- (*al-kafāʾah*): equality

kaffan (*kaffan*): hands

kaffarah (*kaffārah*): atonement

kafir (*kāfir*): unbeliever, disbeliever, one who covers over the Truth

karahah (*karāhah*): sin, disapproval

kathir (*kathīr*): large quanity

kathir al-shakk (*kathīr al-shakk*): chronically uncertain person

khabar al-wahid (*khabar al-wāhid*): isolated Tradition

khabath (*khabath*): physical impurities like blood and excrement

khass (*khāṣṣ*): particular Tradition

khayar al-shart (*khayār al-sharṭ*): option to annul marriage not
  mentioned as a condition per se
khilaf al-awla (*khilāf al-awlā*): against preference
khilaf al-ihtiyat (*khilāf al-ihtiyāṭ*): against precaution
khimar, al-, plural, *khumur, al-* (*al-khimār*, plural, *al-khumur*):
  veil covering the head, not the face
khisa, al- (*al-khiṣāʾ*): castration
khuffan (*khuffan*): shoes
khul, al- (*al-khulᶜ*): divorce for consideration initiated by a wife
khums (*khums*): twenty percent tax
kifai (*kifāʾi*): obligatory collectively
kohl (*kohl*): collriyum
kubra (*kubrā*): major flow of intermittent bleeding
kufr (*kufr*): infidelity to the One God
kurr (*kurr*), 1200 Iraqi ritl. A ritl is approximately 330 grams
  water, large amount

L

laqit (*laqīt*): abandoned child
layali al-tashriq (*layālī al-tashrīq*): nights of 11th, 12th, 13th of Dhil
  Hijjah
lian (*liᶜān*): oath of condemnation

M

ma (*māʾ*): water
mal-kathir (*māʾ al-kathīr*): large quantity of water
mal-mudaf (*māʾ al-mudāf*): mixed water
mal-mustamal (*māʾ al-mustᶜamal*): water rung out
mal-mutlaq (*māʾ al-muṭlaq*): pure water
mal-qalil (*māʾ al-qalīl*): small quantity of water
madhy (*madhy*): thin genital discharge emitted while caressing
maful (*mafᶜūl*): object
maghrib (*maghrib*): evening prescribed prayer
maghsub (*maghṣūb*): consuming anything usurped
mahr al-mithal (*mahr al-mithal*): proper dowry
mahr al-musamma (*mahr al-musamma*): dowry specified in the
  marriage contract
mahr al-sunnah (*mahr al-sunnah*): dowry which is traditional
mahram (*maḥram*): person to whom marriage is prohibited because
  of lineage

mahsub (*maḥsūb*): eating something usurped while performing the prescribed fast

majhul al-malik (*majhūl al-mālik*): owners of properties not known

makruh (*makrūh*): disapproved. According to the Hanafi school, it is an act which is prescribed to be avoided based on non-definite proof.

Maliki: Named after the founder, Imam Abu Abd Allah Malik ibn Anas (716-795 CE), of one of the four major Sunni schools of law, the Maliki.

ma mutlaq (*mā° mutlaq*): water, plain, unaltered

mandub (*mandūb*): an act ordered by the Prophet (ﷺ) although not regularly performed by him

marad al-mawt (*maraḍ al-mawt*): final illness resulting in death

mashaqqah (*mashaqqah*): difficulty

Mashar al-Haram (Mashᶜar al-Ḥarām): another name for Mudalifah

mashhur (*mashhūr*): preponderant opinion

Maslakh, al- (al-Maslakh): a station on the way to Makkah where the pilgrim assumes the sacred state (*ihrām*)

masnun (*masnūn*): part of the *Sunnah*. An act which the Prophet and the rightly-guided caliphs performed regularly

masnunah (*masnūnah*): supererogatory prayers

mass al-mayyit (*mass al-mayyit*): touching a corpse requiring bath lustration

mawaqit (*mawāqit*): places outside Makkah from where the pilgrims intending the minor or prescribed pilgrimage assume the sacred dress

mawqif (*mawqif*): permissible place of halting at Arafat

mawquf alayh, al- (*al-mawqūf ᶜalayh*): beneficiary

mawt (*mawt*): death

Mazamayn, al- (al-Maᵓzamayn): boundary of Muḍalifah

miftirat (*miftirat*): things obligatory to refrain from during the fast from dawn to sunset

milayn (*mīlayn*): distance referred to by the Hanifi and Maliki schools which is to be covered running between Safa and Marwah

miqat (*mīqāt*): place of the appointed time where the pilgrim assumes the sacred state

miqat, plural, *mawaqit* (*mīqāt*, plural, *mawāqit*): refers to a number of stations where the pilgrim assumes the sacred state

miqati (*mīqātī*): person who starts on the longer pilgrimage from one of the places of the appointed time

miskin (*miskīn*): a destitute person

mizar (*miʾzar*): loin-cloth

muakkadah (*muʾakkadah*): *Sunnah* which is emphatically
recommended

muallafatu qulubuhum, al- (*muʾallafatu qulūbuhum*): those whose
hearts are to be conciliated

muatat, al- (*al-muʿāṭāṭ*): creation of endowment without the
declaration

mubtilat (*mubṭilāt*): causes rendering the prescribed prayer invalid

mudaf (*muḍāf*): mixed water

mudd (*mudd*): one mudd is a measure of 800 grams used to feed a
needy person in charity

muddat al-haml (*muddat al-ḥaml*): gestation period

mudtarr (*muḍṭarr*): constrained person

muflis (*muflis*): someone who neither has a job nor money to meet
his or her needs

mufti (*mufti*): jurist

muftir (*mufṭir*): an act which breaks the prescribed fast

mudhdhin (*muʿdhdhin*): caller to prescribed prayer

muhallil (*muḥallil*): a new husband before a wife can remarry her
previous husband who gave her a final divorce

muharram (*muḥarram*): an act which is prescribed to avoid and
whose performance is not permissible according to the Hanafi
school; prohibited

mukallaf (*mukallaf*): sane adult

mukhtar (*mukhtar*): unconstrained person

mumayyiz (*mumayyiz*): age of discretion

munjazat (*munjazāt*): dispositions

muqirr (*muqirr*): one who makes a confession

murtadd anfitrah (*murtadd ʿanfiṭrah*): born Muslim who apostasizes

murtadd anmillah (*murtadd ʿanmillah*): one born to parents who
disbelieve who becomes Muslim and then apostasizes

musa bihi (*mūṣā bihi*): bequeathed property

musa lahu (*mūṣā lahu*): legatee

musabanah, al- (*al-musābanah*): affinity

musalli (*muṣallī*): person performing the prescribed prayer

musha (*mushaʾ*): inseparate share of property

mushrikun (*mushrikūn*): polytheists

musi (*mūṣī*): one who makes a will, testator

mustahabb (mustaḥabb): recommended

mustahabb salat (mustaḥabb ṣalāt): recommended prescribed prayers

mustahadah (mustaḥāḍah): a woman in the state of pseudo menstruation

mustajir (mustaʾjir): hirer

mustamal (mustᶜamal): used water when the water is rung out

mustati (mustaṭiᶜ): pilgrim of the prescribed pilgrimage

mutahhir (muṭahhir): purifier

mutamatti (mutamattiᶜ): pilgrim on the prescribed pilgrimage

mutamir (muᶜtamir): pilgrim performing the minor pilgrimage in conjunction with the prescribed pilgrimage

mutarr (muᶜtarr): one who comes to a person for charity

mutawwali (mutawwalī): trustee

mutlaq (muṭlaq): pure water

mutlaq al-aqd (muṭlaq al-ᶜaqd): on conditions stipulated

muwalat (muwalāt): continuity

N

nabidh al-tamr (nabīdh al-tamr): date wine

nadhir (nādhir): one who makes a vow

nadhr (nadhr): vow

nafaqah (nafaqah): alimony

nafilah (nāfilah): supererogatory prayers

nafl (nafl): supererogatory

naib (nāʾib): deputy

najasah (najāsah): impurity

najis (najis): impure

nalan (naᶜlan): sandals

nasab (nasab): consanguinity

nashizah, al- (al-nashizah): disobedient wife

nasi (nāsī): one who forgets

nawafil (nawāfil): supererogatory prayer

nifas (nifās): bleeding following childbirth

nikah, al- (al-nikāḥ): marriage

Nimrah (Nimrah): one of the boundaries of Arafat

nisab (niṣāb): minimun

niyyah (niyyah): declaration of intention

niyyat al-iqtida (niyyat al-iqtidāʾ): intention of following the leader

niyyat al-qurbah (niyyat al-qurbah): intention to seek God's good pleasure

Q

qabiltu (*qabilut*): "I have accepted..."

qada (*qaḍāʾ*): missed prescribed prayer or fast

qadi (*qāḍī*): judge

qadir al-ajiz (*qādir al-ᶜājiz*): physically incapacitated

qalil (*qalīl*): small quantity water

qamis (*qamīs*): covering for the body from the shoulders to the shanks

qani (*qāniᶜ*): poor person who is content with what you give him and does not show his or her displeasure

qarabah, al- (*al-qarābah*): blood relationship

Qarn al-Manazil (Qarn al-Manazil): a station on the way to Makkah where the pilgrim assumes the sacred state (*ihrām*)

qarn, al- (*al-qarn*): presence of a horn-like protrusion

qasr (*qaṣr*): shortening of prescribed prayer

qatl al-khata (*qatl al-khatāʾ*): unintentional homicide

qatl al-tasbib (*qatl al-tasbīb*): accused or indirect cause of homicide

qiblah (*qiblah*): orientation towards the Kabah for prescribed prayer

qiraah (*qirāʾah*): recitation while standing in the prescribed prayer

qisas (*qiṣāṣ*): right of retribution

qiyam (*qiyām*): standing upright in the prescribed prayer

qiyas (*qiyās*): analogy

qullah (*qullah*): bucket of water

qunut (*qunūt*): raising the hands, palms up, during the prescribed prayer and offering a supplication

qurbah (*qurbah*): nearness

qurbatan ill-Allah (*qurbatan ill-Allāh*): nearness of God

R

radd, al- (*al-radd*): the return

rada (*raḍāᶜ*): act of nursing a foster child

radi (*raḍīᶜ*): the woman who nurses a foster child

raditu (*raḍītu*): "I have agreed..."

rahilah, al- (*al-raḥilah*): expenses of the journey to Makkah and back

rakah (*rakᶜah*): cycle of prescribed prayer

ramal (*ramal*): running

ramy al-jamarat (*ramy al-jamarat*): prescribed throwing of stones at the idols while on the prescribed pilgrimage

ratq, al- (*al-ratq*): presence of obstruction in the vaginal opening making intercourse difficult

rawatib (*rawātib*): supererogatory prayers

rida (*ridā*ʾ): cloak

riqab, al- (*al-riqāb*): freeing of slaves with poor-due money

ritl (*riṭl*): approximately 330 grams

rizq (*rizq*): provision

rukn (*rukn*): pillar

ruku (*rukūᶜ*): bending forward in the prescribed prayer

rushd (*rushd*): mental mataurity

ruyah(*ruʾyah*): sighting of the new moon

S

sabbaltu (*sabbaltu*): "I have donated as charity..."

sabil Allah (*sabīl Allāh*): those who have volunteered to fight for the defense of Islam

sadaqah (*ṣadaqah*): charity

safah, al- (*al-safāh*): mental retardation

sahih(*ṣaḥīḥ*): valid

sahw (*sahw*): miskake in the prescribed prayer

said al-tahur, al- (*al-saʾid al-tahur*): wholesome dust

saim (*ṣāʾim*): person performing the prescribed fast

salam (*salām*): the greetings of 'peace'

salat (*ṣalāt*): prescribed prayer

salat al-faitah, al- (*al-ṣalāt al-fāʾitah*): prescribed prayer performed after the lapse of time

salat al-fajr (*ṣalāt al-fajr*): two cycles prayer before the morning prescribed prayer

salat al-idayn (*ṣalāt al-ᶜidayn*): festivals prescribed prayer

salat al-ihtiyat (*ṣalāt al-ihtiyāṭ*): prescribed prayer of caution

salat al-istiqa (*ṣalāt al-istisqāʾ*): prayer for rain

salat al-jamaah (*ṣalāt al-jamāᶜah*): congregational prescribed prayer

salat al-janazah (*ṣalāt al-janāzah*): prescribed prayer for the dead

salat al-kusuf (*ṣalāt al-kusūf*): prayer for an eclipse

salat al-layl (*ṣalāt al-layl*): midnight prayer

salat al-madhurah (*ṣalāt al-madhūrah*): supererogatory prayer to fulfil a vow

salat al-musafir (*ṣalāt al-musāfir*): prescribed prayer of the traveler

salat al-nafilah (*ṣalāt al-nāfilah*): supererogatory prayer *salat al-qada (ṣalāt al-qadāʾ)*: missed prescribed prayer

salat al-tarawih (ṣalāt al-tarāwīḥ): special evening prayer during the
  month of Ramadan

salawat (ṣalawāt): sending greetings to the Prophet (ﷺ)

sawm (ṣawm): prescribed fasting

say (saᶜy): search between Safa and Marwah

Shafi'i: Named after Muhammad Ibn Idris ash-Shafii (767-820 CE),
  theologian, religious scholar, and founder of one of the four major
  schools of Sunni law, the Shafii.

shahadah (shahādah): bearing witness to the Oneness of God and
  prophethood of Muhamamd (ﷺ)

shahadatayn (shahadātayn): two testaments upon the recitation of
  which one becomes a Muslim

Shariah (Sharīᶜah): Divine Law

shart al-khayar (sharṭ al-khayār): executor of a contract makes
  explicit mention of a condition while executing the contract

shawt (shawt): walking between Safa and Marwah

shibh al-amd (shibh al-ᶜamd): quasi-intentional act

shirk (shirk): polytheism

shubhah (shubhah): misconception

shubhat aqd (shubhat ᶜaqd): mistake by contract

shubhat fil (shubhat fiᶜl): mistake of act

shuhrat al-azimah (shuhrat al-ᶜaẓīmah): unusual preponderance

shukr (shukr): gratitude

Shumaysi, al- (al-Shumaysi): western boundary of the sacred area of
  Makkah, 15 kms from Makkah

shurb (shurb): eating and drinking

shurut (shurūṭ): conditions

sighah (sīghah): form of recital, declaration, pronouncement

sughra (sughrā): minor intermittent bleeding

sujud (sujūd): prostration in the prescribed prayer

sujud al-sahw (sujūd al-sahw): prostration for a mistake in the
  prescribed prayer

sulh al-qahri (ṣulh al-qahrī): compulsory compromise

Sunnah (Sunnah): custom of the Prophet

sunnah muakkadah (sunnah muʾakkadah): strongly recommended
  Sunnah

T

taabbud (taᶜabbud): obedience to the Lawgiver

tabanni (*tabannī*): adoption

tabi (*tabīᶜ*): ox or cow in the second year

tadlis (*tadlīs*): deceit, hiding a defect

taharah (*tahārah*): prescribed purity

tahiyyah al-masjid (*tahiyyat al-masjid*): greeting of the mosque

tahjir (*tahjīr*): declaration of legal disability

tahir al-milk (*tahir al-milk*): liberation from ownership

tahlil (*tahlīl*): recitation of "There is no god but God"; relief from the
  sacred state

Taht al-Arak (Taht al-Arāk): area outside Arafat

takattuf (*takattuf*): folding one's arms during the prescribed prayer

takbir (*takbīr*): recitation of "*Allahu akbar*," God is Greater:

takbirat al-ihram (*takbīrat al-ihrām*): the first recitation of "*Allah
  akbar*" which begins the sacred state of the prescribed prayer and
  which prohibits anything but the prescribed prayer

takfin (*takfīn*): shroud

talaq al-iddah (*talāq al-ᶜiddah*): irrevocable divorce

talbiyah (*talbiyah*): recitation of "Here I am, my Lord." It is
  obligatory to be recited at the time of putting on the sacred dress
  in assuming the sacred state according ot the Jafari, Hanafi and
  Maliki schools and recommended by the Hanbali.

Tanin, al- (al-Tanim): northern boundary of the sacred area of
  Makkah

tanjiz (*tanjīz*): unconditionally operational

taqarrub (*taqarrub*): nearness to God

taqlid (*taqlīd*): following the dictates of an expert

taqsir (*taqsīr*): shortening of the hair of the head

tarakhi (*tarākhi*): delay

tarikah, al- (*al-tarīkah*): an estate

tarjih bila murajjih (*tarjīh bilā murajjih*): preferring something
  without a cause for such preference

tarik al-salat (*tārik al-salāt*): person who does not perform the
  prescribed prayer due to laziness or neglect

tartib (*tartīb*): bath lustration of sequence

tarwiyah (*tarwiyah*): 8th of Dhil Hijjah

tasbih (*tasbīh*): praise; recitation of "Glory be to God" *subhān Allāh*

tashahhud (*tashahhud*): sitting back on knees and bearing witness

tashriq (*tashrīq*): 11th, 12th, and 13th of Dhil Hijjah

tasib (*taᶜsīb*): sharing of inheritance by the residuaries along with
  the closely related sharers

tasmiyah (tasmiyah): recitation of "In the Name of God, the Merciful, the Compassionate"

tawaf (ṭawāf): circumambulation around the Kabah

tawaf al-ifadah (ṭawāf al-ifādah): circumambulation of the prescribed pilgrimage pouring forth into Makkah from Mina

tawaf al-nisa (ṭawāf al-nisā²): circumambulation of women, obligatory according to the Jafari school following the prescribed pilgrimage before one's spouse becomes lawful

tawaf al-qudum (ṭawāf al-qudūm): circumambulation performed by persons coming from outside of the sacred area upon the first entry into the Kabah area

tawaf al-tahiyah (ṭawāf al-ṭahīyah): circumambulation following the greeting of the mosque

tawaf al-wada (ṭawāf al-wadā): circumambulation for farewell

tawaf al-ziyarah (ṭawāf al-ziyarah): circumambulation of Kabah as part of the prescribed pilgrimage following Mina

tayammum (tayammum): dry ablution

tayyib(tayyib): pure

thawab (thawāb): spiritual reward

turab (turāb): earth

U

ulama (ᶜulamā²): religious scholars

ummah: community

ummrah: minor pilgrimage

umrah (ᶜumrah): literally means visit but in the Divine Law it means specifically a visit to the Kabah in what is called in English the minor pilgrimage

umrah al-mufradah (ᶜumrah al-mufradah): minor pilgrimage performed independently of the prescribed pilgrimage

umrah al-mufradah al-mustaqillah an al-hajj (ᶜumrah al-mufradah al-musṭaqillah 'an al-ḥajj): minor pilgrimage performed independently of the longer pilgrimage

umrah al-mundammah ila al-hajj (ᶜumrah al-munḍammah ilā al-ḥajj): shorter pilgrimage performed in conjunction with the prescribed pilgrimage

umrah al-tamattu (ᶜumrah al-tamattuᶜ): minor pilgrimage occurs in the same year as the prescribed pilgrimage

uyub, al- (al-ᶜuyūb): defects

W

wadhy (*wadhy*): dense genital discharge emitted following urination

wajh (*wajh*): face

wajib (*wājib*): obligatory, prescribed

wajib aini (*wājib ᶜainī*): duty obligatory individually unless another performs it

wajib kifai (*wājib kifāʾī*): duty collectively obligatory and no longer obligatory individually when another performs it

wakil (*wakīl*): agent

walad (*walad*): child

walad al-walad (*walad al-walad*): grandchild

wali (*wālī*): legal guardian

waqaftu (*waqaftu*): "I have made an endowment..."

waqf ala-salat (*waqf ᶜalā 'l-ṣalāt*): endowment for prescribed prayers

waqif (*wāqif*): doner of an endowment

wasat al-masafah (*wasaṭ al-masāfah*): intervening distance

wasiyyah (*waṣiyyah*): will

wathaqah (*wathāqah*): trustworthiness

watirah (*watīrah*): a single cycle prayer

wudu (*wuḍū*): shorter ablution

wuquf (*wuqūf*): halt at Arafat or al-Mashar al-Haram (Muḍalifah)

wusta (*wusṭā*): medium flow of intermittent bleeding

Y

yadayn (*yadayn*): hands

Yalamlam (Yalamlam): a station on the way to Makkah where the pilgrim assumes the sacred state (*ihrām*)

yamin (*yamīn*): oath

yawm al-nahr (*yawm al-naḥr*): day of sacrifice

yawm al-shakk (*yawm al-shakk*): uncertain day

Z

zad, al- (*al-zād*): expenses for transport, food, lodging, passport fees, etc.

zahir al-zinah (*ẓāhir al-zīnah*): outward adornment

zakat (*zakāt*): alms

zakat al-fitr (*zakāt al-fiṭr*): poor-due marking the end of Ramadan

zann (*ẓann*): probability

zanni (*ẓannī*): non-definite proof

zawaj (*zawāj*): marriage

zawwajtu (zawwajtu): "I gave in marriage..."

zawwajtuka (zawwajtuka): "I married you (masc.)..."

zihar (ẓihār): a husband saying to his wife that she is like his mother's back, i.e., forbidden to him

zina (zinā): fornication

zuhr (ẓuhr): noon prescribed prayer

zuqaq al-attarin (zuqāq al-ᶜaṭṭārīn): the alley of the pharmacists, a point of reference for the running between Safa and Marwah

AUTHORS CONSULTED

Abd al-Karim Maghniyyah
Abd al-Muhaal al-Saidi
Abd Allah al-Mamqani
Abu Yusuf
Ahmad al-Siddiq al-Ghumari
Allamah Hilli
Aqa Rida al-Hamadani
Dimashqi, al-
Ghazzali, al-
Ghuryah, al-
Hisni al-Shafii, al-
Ibn Abi Layla
Ibn Abidin
Ibn al-Qayyim
Ibn Aqil
Ibn Babawayh
Ibn Dawayan
Ibn Hajar
Ibn Jamaah al-Shafi
Ibn Qudamah
Ibn Sawayan
Khwansari, al-
Mahmud Shaltut
Muawwad Muhammad Mustafa
Muhamamd Jawad Mughaniyyah
Muhamamd Salam Madkur
Muhammad Abu Zuhrah
Muhammad Hasan
Muhammad Jawad Mughniyyah
Muhammad Muhammad Safan
Muhammad Muhyi al-Din Abd al-Hamid
Muhammad Salam Madkur
Muhammad Yusuf Musa
Muhaqqiq al-Hilli
Murtada al-Ansari
Naini, al-
Nawawi, an
Qurtubi, Muhammad ibn Hamad ibn Rushd, al-
Rida al-Hamadani
Sanhjuri, al-

Sayyid Abu al-Hasan
Sayyid al-Hakim
Sayyid al-Khui
Sayyid al-Shahrudi
Sayyid Kazim al-Yazdi
Sayyid Sabiq, al-
Shahid al-Thani
Shaykh al-Mufid
Shihab al-Din al-Baghdadi
Ustadh al-Khafif
Zurqani, al-

611

salat al-qada, 110
salat al-watr, 91-92
salawat, 50
satr al-awrah, 191
sawm, 63
Sayyid Abu al-Hasan al-Isfahani,
    221, 283, 543-544
Sayyid al-Hakim, 193, 201, 204,
    210, 217
Sayyid al-Isfahani, 269, 271
Sayyid al-Murtada, 6
Sayyid Muhsin al-Hakim, 470,
    543
semen, 14, 19, 21, 31
seminal secretions, 31
sexual emission, 5-6, 16, 30, 33-
    36, 38, 41, 44, 60, 140-141
shahadah, 63
shahadatayn, 50
Sharh al-zarqani ala mukhtasar
    Abi Diya, 261
shart al-khayar, 436
Shaykh Abu Zuhrah, 254, 507
Shaykh Ahmad Kashif al-Ghita,
    489
Shaykh al-Ansari, 277, 284
Shaykh al-Mufid, 36, 294
Shaykh al-Saduq, 6
Shaykh al-Tusi, 96
Shaykh Jafar, 73
shibh al-amd, 295
Shihab al-Din al-Baghdadi, 209
shroud, 43, 45-49, 53, 288, 393
shubhah, 409, 460
shubhat-aqd, 460
shubhat-fil, 460
shukr, 23
shurb, 138
shurut, 155
sighah, 353
silk, 46, 78-79, 177, 191
Station of Abraham, 194

stranger, 52, 62, 71, 74, 76, 159,
    221, 315, 370, 387, 389-390,
    466, 468, 472, 514, 534, 536
subhan Allah, 94, 105-106, 126,
    130, 153
Sufyan al-Thawri, 430
sughra, 38
sujud, 95, 97-100, 129
sujud al-sahw, 97-100, 129
sun, 18, 65-66, 97, 103, 105, 107,
    130, 205, 208, 244, 418
Sunan, 195, 210
Sunan al-tawaf, 195
sunnah muakkadah, 166, 191
Surat al-Ahqaf, 457
Surat al-Ala, 106
Surat al-Fatihah, 50, 90-92, 98,
    190
Surat al-Ghashiyah, 104, 106
Surat al-Iqtarabat, 106
Surat al-Jumuah, 104
Surat al-Mujadilah, 544
Surat al-Munafiqun, 104
Surat al-Qadr, 195
Surat al-Shams, 106
Surat Luqman, 457

T

taabbud, 13
taawwudh, 106, 130
tabi, 235
tabiah, 235
tadlis, 437
taharah, 3, 190
tahiyyat al-masjid, 188, 204
tahlil, 151, 190, 195, 211, 511
tahrir al-milk, 275
Taht al-Arak, 206
tahur, 4
takattuf, 91, 94
takbir, 50, 60, 151, 153, 190, 195,

vinegar, 8, 17, 515
vomit, 15-16

W

wa al-dalalah, 504
wadhy, 16
wahabat, 400
wajh, 57-58, 61-62
wajib, 42, 63, 263
wajib aini, 42
wajib al-salat, 263
wajib kifai, 42
wajibat, 173
wakil, 399
walad, 269, 305, 314
walad al-mulaanah, 314
walad al-walad, 269
walad al-zina, 314
wali, 143, 155, 446
waqaftu, 255-256
waqf, 251
waqif, 251-253, 255
wasat al-masafah, 199
washing of hands, 25-26
washing the face, 25, 54
Wasilat al-najat, 221, 402
wasiyyah, 264
wholesome dust, 7, 54, 56, 61
wilayah, 269
wiping the head, 25, 28
Wisayah, 370
worship, 3, 29, 33, 35, 83, 112,
    133, 160-161, 223, 276, 293,
    362, 418, 538
wudu, 3
wuquf, 152, 204, 251
wusta, 38

Y

yadayn, 57-58
Yalamlam, 170-171

yamin, 216
yawm al-nahr, 166, 212
yawm al-shakk, 145

Z

zahir al-zinah, 71
zakat, 63, 160, 215, 231, 244
zakat al-abdan, 244
zakat al-fitr, 215, 244
zakat/khums, 63
zann, 67
zawwajtu, 399-400, 402
zawwajtuka, 401
zawwajtukaha, 402
zawwijniha, 402
Zayd ibn Harithah, 467
Zayd ibn Usamah, 430
zihar, 143, 544-545
zina, 448
zuhr, 64
Zuqaq al-Attarin, 199